Planning for Innovation

through Dissemination and
Utilization of Knowledge

206

Planning for Innovation

through Dissemination and Utilization of Knowledge

Ronald G. Havelock

In Collaboration With

ALAN GUSKIN

MARK FROHMAN
MARY HAVELOCK
MARJORIE HILL
JANET HUBER

Center for Research on Utilization of Scientific Knowledge
Institute for Social Research
The University of Michigan
Ann Arbor, Michigan

Second Printing
January, 1971

TABLE OF CONTENTS

ACKNOWLEDGEMENTS

Special thanks are due to several individuals who made significant contributions to the evolution and final production of this report. Ronald Lippitt made valuable editorial comments and provided persistent encouragement. The early drafts of the report were also thoroughly reviewed by Kenneth Benne, Henry Brickell, Floyd Mann, Herbert Menzel, Everett Rogers, and Sam Sieber. Many of their comments have been incorporated in this final version. The project was supported by an able staff of readers who compiled over 500 abstracts used as background for writing: Susan Chacin, Lynne Hirschfeld, Jeanne Hurley, Stuart Lawrence, Craig McEwen, Alicia Nelson, and Nancy Tucker all made major contributions to this task.

Special credit should also be given to Iraj Mahdavi for his work on setting up coding procedures for titles and abstracts, for his editorial assistance on Chapters Six and Eight, and for his strong moral support of the director at times of difficulty. Finally very special thanks are due to Rita Wiegers for final typing of the entire manuscript and the drafting of most of the figures. Her patient understanding and titanic efforts have added immeasurably to the final product.

The research reported herein was performed pursuant to a Contract No. OEC-3-7-070028-2143 with the Office of Education, U.S. Department of Health, Education, and Welfare. Contractors undertaking such projects under Government sponsorship are encouraged to express freely their professional judgment in the conduct of the project. Points of view or opinions stated do not, therefore, necessarily represent official Office of Education position or policy.

SUMMARY

This report provides a framework for understanding the processes of innovation, dissemination, and knowledge utilization, and it reviews the relevant literature in education and other fields of practice within this framework. Dissemination and utilization (D&U) is viewed as a transfer of messages by various media between resource systems and users. Major sections analyze characteristics of individuals and organizations which inhibit or facilitate this transfer. The process is interpreted at four levels; the individual, the interpersonal, the organization, and the social system. Additional chapters deal specifically with specialized "linking" roles between resource and user, types of messages, types of media, and phase models of the process.

Major conclusions from the review are as follows. The principle models of D&U employed by most authors can be grouped under three perspectives identified as (1) "Research, Development, and Diffusion", (2) "Social Interaction", and (3) "Problem Solving". Each of these three viewpoints contributes significantly to our understanding of the total D&U process. They can be brought together in a "linkage model" which incorporates important features of all three. Linkage is seen as a series of two-way interaction processes which connect user systems with various resource systems including basic and applied research, development, and practice. Senders and receivers can achieve successful linkage only if they exchange messages in two-way interaction and continuously make the effort to simulate each other's problem solving behavior. Hence, the resource systems must appreciate the user's internal needs and problem solving patterns, and the user, in turn, must be able to appreciate the invention, solution formulation and evaluation processes of the resource systems. This type of collaborative interaction will not only make solutions more relevant and effective but will build relationships of trust, mutual perceptions by user and resource persons that the other is truly concerned, will listen, and will be able to provide useful information. These trust relations over time can become channels for the rapid, effective, and efficient transfer of information.

Effective knowledge utilization also requires a degree of division of labor, coordination and collaboration throughout the social system. The role of government should be to monitor the "natural" knowledge flow system and develop means to support, facilitate, and coordinate linkage activities so that the total system can function more effectively.

Summary, continued

Seven factors which help in explaining D&U phenomena are:

1. <u>Linkage</u>: The number, variety, and mutuality of Resource System--User System Contacts, degree of interrelatedness, collaborative relationships.

2. <u>Structure</u>: The degree of Systematic Organization and Coordination:
   a) of the resource system
   b) of the user system
   c) of the dissemination-utilization strategy

3. <u>Openness</u>: The belief that change is desirable and possible. Willingness and readiness to accept outside help. Willingness and readiness to listen to needs of others and to give help. Social climate favorable to change.

4. <u>Capacity</u>: The capability to retrieve and marshall diverse resources.
   Highly correlated with this capacity factor are: wealth, power, size, centrality, intelligence, education, experience, cosmopoliteness, mobility and the number and diversity of existing linkages.

5. <u>Reward</u>: The frequency, immediacy, amount, mutuality of, planning and structuring of positive reinforcements.

6. <u>Proximity</u>: Nearness in time, place, and context. Familiarity, similarity, recency.

7. <u>Synergy</u>: The number, variety, frequency, and persistance of forces that can be mobilized to produce a knowledge utilization effect.

The report concludes with implications and recommendations for needed research and development on the process of D&U, itself, and lays down some suggested guidelines for practitioners and government policy makers.

CHAPTER ONE

INTRODUCTION

CHAPTER ONE*

INTRODUCTION

I. AN EMERGING DISCIPLINE

There is a new field of knowledge emerging in the 1960's which might be described as the "science of knowledge utilization". It is probably misleading, however, to describe this emerging discipline as a "science" at this point in time. In reality, knowledge utilization is at best a crude art occupying the undivided attention of only a small scattering of scholars in three or four centers of learning. There are no schools, no curricula, and few courses for training researchers and practitioners in this area, and there is as yet only a dim awareness on the part of the nation as a whole that this field deserves extensive public support.

Nevertheless, there are two social forces in our contemporary society which are lending an urgency to the development of such a "science". The first of these is the knowledge explosion. Due in part to increased public attention and support, and in part to progress in refining and streamlining the methodology of discovery, there has been a very large increase in the output of basic scientific knowledge. This increase has already outstripped the retrieval capacity of the typical scholar, and as a result, traditional modes of knowledge organization and transmission are being constantly modified, streamlined and "automated". Because of the potential significance of these changes for the role of the scholar and for the very shape of our society, there is an urgent need to take stock, to evaluate them systematically and objectively, and to trace their implications.

The second force is the growing expectation on the part of industrial executives, government leaders, and the general public that most, if not all, of our storehouse of scientific knowledge should be useful to man. Such an expectation has long been realized in some specific areas such as agricultural extension and in a few of our largest and most sophisticated industrial establishments, but now the expectation extends to many fields: medicine, social welfare, industry of all types, and education. To meet these demands the federal government is becoming increasingly involved in promoting knowledge utilization, and it needs information for the formulation of new policy in this area. Yet government policy makers now have very little on which to base their planning apart from experience in agriculture, an experience which is viewed critically by some and considered irrelevant by others. Policy makers and planners in the various professional disciplines, inside and outside government, have a clear need for "facts"--guidelines based on the best knowledge currently available concerning how knowledge is most readily communicated and utilized.

To establish a new discipline of knowledge utilization on a firm foundation will require two kinds of development: one could be termed "knowledge building" and the other "institutionalizing". Under "knowledge building", there is first a need for an integration of the many pieces of research, anecdote, case history and theory on utilization now scattered in diverse sources among many fields of research and practice. Secondly, along with this integration should come a more developed, more general, and more useful theory of utilization to replace the fragments of theory borrowed from psychology and sociology which have composed the theoretical base heretofore. Finally, to reach maturity as a science, this field requires a series of coherent and systematic research programs built around evolving, theoretical models.

---
*This Chapter was drafted by Ronald G. Havelock.

To "institutionalize" this new discipline we will need to create organizational bases, university-linked centers, research and teaching faculties and departments focusing on the study of utilization. There is additionally a need to develop training facilities and training programs to build a professional corps of dissemination and utilization consultants and change agents. Thirdly, it will be most important to create and maintain channels which will make the knowledge about utilization highly accessible to users themselves. This field will be under continuous and increasing pressure from persons endeavoring to disseminate, apply or process new knowledge of various kinds in all sorts of settings. The new field should be able to respond to these pressures by providing the best facts and theory about the utilization process currently available. At the same time it must protect itself from being fragmented by catering to the insistent short-run, fire-fighting demands of the everyday world. Finally, it is vital that this emerging discipline be reliably and generously supported by society as a whole.

This listing of needed activities brings us to the purpose of the project on which this report is based. With this project we hope to initiate those activities which appear to be most relevant to the establishment of a new science of knowledge utilization: first, to undertake the above-mentioned integration of existing knowledge in this area; and second, to develop a set of operating principles and plans, derived from the compiled findings, for the guidance of research, practice and public policy, with special reference to the field of education.

II. OBJECTIVES AND PURPOSES

In the broadest terms, this project is part of a continuing effort to understand and improve the process of dissemination and utilization of new knowledge in all fields of practice. In the chapters which follow we will endeavor to make a detailed exploration, analysis, and synthesis of a number of topics which have previously been discussed at length by other scholars in different contexts. The focus and purpose of this effort will be:

1. To assess the current state of knowledge with respect to processes of dissemination and utilization by means of:

   a. a search for and analysis of literature pertaining to such processes as they occur in a number of fields of practice,

   b. the construction of a model for categorization and integration of such literature, based in part on a review of existing models.

2. On the basis of the model and supporting findings, to derive implications for the guidance of researchers, practitioners and policy makers.

III. MAJOR SOURCES ON KNOWLEDGE DISSEMINATION AND UTILIZATION

The most significant integrative effort to date in the general area of dissemination and utilization has been the work of Everett M. Rogers and his associates at Ohio State University and currently at Michigan State University. In particular, Rogers' volume The Diffusion of Innovations (#1824)* is in many respects a model

---

*Numbers in parenthesis together with author's name identify the particular citation in the bibliography.

for the present study. This is especially true with regard to three aspects of Rogers' approach. First, he has undertaken a comprehensive review of the literature (over 500 citations in that volume, and the number has since swollen to over 1,500 with his establishment of a "Diffusion Documents Center" at Michigan State). Second, he has employed an interdisciplinary comparative approach, compiling studies from several different research traditions. Finally, he has attempted to integrate these findings and to evolve a theory based on them.*

However, Rogers' approach has certain limitations, in large part deliberate, which mark off his study from the present effort. First of all, he has formulated and presented findings primarily in terms of research problems directed towards interested social scientists rather than practitioners or policy makers. Second, he has tried to restrict his review to empirical research findings, although much of what is now known and much of the information upon which current practice is based is in the form of anecdotes, untested theories, or case studies. Thirdly, and most importantly, he has limited his content area to "diffusion", generally meaning the diffusion of products or specific practices. In so doing, he has excluded two major blocks of research which are considered highly germane to this review. The first is the very extensive set of general and experimental research findings in social psychology having to do with influence processes, attitude change, group behavior and organizational behavior. The second set of studies which tends to be excluded is that dealing with major personal and social change where a particular "innovation" is not clearly identifiable. Thus, we do not find in Rogers' bibliographies many of the major efforts to apply social science findings to organizations, work groups, classrooms, and so forth. Yet, as Lippitt (#3873) has pointed out, generalizations derived from utilization attempts for physical and biological innovations may not be appropriate for social science utilizations.

Although this review will endeavor to consider these areas, there are some respects in which the Rogers' effort goes further. In particular, by limiting his definition of diffusion research, Rogers has been able to come much closer to exhaustive coverage than will be possible here.

Also in the category of major source materials for this study are three collections of papers. Although none of these collections is aimed directly at the issue of knowledge utilization, they all overlap heavily with this concern. Bennis, Benne and Chin (#1344) define change broadly to include intersystem linkage problems and influence processes as major aspects. This volume gives valuable leads into the social-psychological and sociological literature pertaining to utilization that are not found in Rogers. The integrating chapters are also useful source material, but fall short of the kind of integration offered by Rogers and proposed here as necessary.

Miles (#1046) has also compiled a very useful reference volume. A number of studies are included which define innovation broadly enough to encompass organizational change. Of special note is Miles' discussion of "temporary systems" in which he includes such phenomena as conferences, collaborative action-research

---

*A similar effort has been undertaken by Katz, Levin, and Hamilton (#0297) but on a somewhat smaller scale.

projects, and other mechanisms typically used for dissemination and utilization purposes. Another significant paper by Brickell poses valuable distinctions among the conditions optimal for design, evaluation and dissemination of innovations. As a whole, however, Miles' volume is not intended to be either comparative or comprehensive even within the field of education and does not serve as a handy reference either to the policy maker or to the practitioner.

A third important set of papers has been produced as part of the Cooperative Project for Educational Development (Watson, ed., #6194, #6195). These papers provide a broad theoretical background on the problem of knowledge dissemination and utilization in general, with special emphasis on education. Taken together they contain a great wealth of fresh insights while ranging across nearly every area which is relevant to educational change. They are authored by some of the leading scholars in the field, e.g., Benne, Lippitt, Miles, Thelen and Watson.

Finally, mention should be given to some of the sources which have been most helpful in developing a model for integrating the findings. Some current models have been developed to apply generally across fields, while others are specifically concerned with education. Of the general models, mention has already been made of Rogers who has carefully laid out a five-step theory of adoption and has categorized adopter types. Lippitt, Watson and Westley (#1343) have provided a very useful framework for viewing the change process, particularly the interface between those who plan and initiate change and those toward whom the change is directed. This work is highly relevant because the roles involved are very nearly equivalent to the disseminator and the user in utilization. A seven-phase model for introducing change is offered. Another general model which tries to consider all the factors relevant to the problem of knowledge utilization is offered by Havelock and Benne in An Exploratory Study of Knowledge Utilization (#3872). This paper, one of the previously mentioned COPED set, is a summary of a much larger and more detailed report on the utilization of scientific knowledge in a number of fields of practice. That report, based on a seminar held at The University of Michigan in the spring of 1963, undertook to examine the current state of the art with respect to utilization, using expert informants from seven applied areas: the Research and Development (R&D) operations of a large corporation, agricultural extension, business management, economics, medicine, public health and social action. The seminar project was a logical predecessor to the present project in suggesting the scope of the coverage needed and the kinds of problems likely to be most salient and most relevant to the practitioner.

Special attention will also be given to the conceptual paradigm of factors related to educational change developed by Clark and Guba. These authors (#6003) analyze educational change in terms of four primary stages: *research, development, diffusion* and *adoption*. Although the context of their discussion is the field of education, their classification is very appropriate for analysis of dissemination and utilization in any field and for cross-field comparisons. Models of this kind must be tested against available knowledge in various fields before their validity and utility can be accurately assessed. The present study will consider and, where possible, incorporate these conceptual models and will attempt to assess their relative merits and applicability to specific situations.

IV. A BRIEF HISTORY OF THE PROJECT: PLANS AND ACTUALITIES

The development of a model (or models) and the review of the literature, the two major project objectives, were seen as interdependent. The development of a model was to some degree a task of *definition*, a marking out of the boundaries and the major variables that ought to be included within the topic "Dissemination-Utilization". Hence, the model was needed to provide categories and key words for a literature search, for without the model we would not have had a clear idea of what we should be looking for. At the same time, however, we did not want to limit the search to an arbitrary set of categories; we wanted the literature to speak for itself. We knew that some categories and concepts would only emerge from the reading. The definitions and analyses of previous researchers and theorists had to be accounted for and included, if possible, in our own "new" formulation. Thus on the one hand, we could not proceed with a search without a model, and on the other, we could not proceed with a model (an adequate comprehensive model, at any rate) without first searching the literature.

This paradox between a structural approach and an open approach was resolved through what might be called a "dialogue" between the two processes. We began with a rudimentary model and expanded and polished this model after reviewing some of the basic sources discussed in the previous section. After a few months, a more detailed and refined model emerged; this model served as a "guide" for the major search activity which uncovered over 4,000 titles which appeared to be either relevant or partially relevant.* Still further reading and reanalysis provided an even more detailed model which emerged as the first draft of a "Chapter Outline" for this report. This chapter outline served as a guide for the selection of readings to be analyzed and reviewed in each chapter. The detailed readings in turn often forced further modifications in the model as the first draft of the report came into being.

This first draft was discussed and criticized by a panel of scholars and researchers in February, 1968.** Their taped comments were later used as the basic of further revisions.

It should be stressed, however, that this was not a smooth evolution. Along the way many plans had to be drastically revised or totally discarded after much time and effort had been invested. A review of some of these mistakes and mis-judgments may help the reader to understand the development of the final product and possibly enable him to avoid similar problems.

A.   AN ILL-FATED LIST OF KEY TERMS

One of the earliest documents generated by the project was a list of key terms which were thought to define the subject-matter of the search. This list is reproduced below.

[Insert Table 1.1 here]

This list was developed for use by the bibliographic search staff on the assumption that a general guide of this sort would be sufficient for getting a head-start on the compilation of the bibliography while the model-building process was under way. However, each of the four staff members who tried to use this list concluded independently that it was useless. They found that manifestly relevant materials could not be easily identified by this list, either from their titles or from indices.

*This "guide" is reproduced in the introductory pages of the bibliography.

**Kenneth D. Benne, Boston University
  Henry M. Brickell, University of Indiana
  Ronald Lippitt, University of Michigan
  Floyd C. Mann, University of Michigan

Herbert Menzel, New York University
Everett M. Rogers, Michigan State
  University
Samuel D. Sieber, Columbia Universit

1-5

TABLE 1.1   Key Terms Used in the Initial Comparative Literature Survey (CLS)
             Index Search

(The team of searchers were asked to select only articles which stated or implied
one of the following phrases)

Acceptance		Innovations
Adaptation		New Knowledge
Adoption		New Practices
Application		New Products
Assimilation		Research
Communication		Scientific Information
Diffusion		Scientific Knowledge
Dissemination		Technology
Distribution		
Exchange	of	
Flow		
Reception		
Rejection		
Retrieval		
Transfer		
Transmission		
Utilization		

The staff discovered that to carry on a bibliographic search with any
degree of accuracy and thoroughness they had to have a much clearer and more
detailed knowledge of what was meant by "knowledge dissemination and utilization". For this reason, several long discussion-briefing sessions were held
by the entire staff at which the first tentative model was hammered out and
thoroughly digested by all. This model was then summarized on two sheets
which became the "search guide" for future bibliographic explorations. Thus
in the end it appeared that a successful retrieval effort on a complex topic
required more than key word identifications. *Each searcher needed to internalize
a detailed conceptual paradigm of the topic* before he could conduct a meaningful bibliographic search. This "search guide" formed the
basic conceptual model of the project and subsequently of the report. The
model will be presented in detail in Chapter Two.

B.   THE UNHELPFUL INDEX

Another disappointment in this early phase of the project was the discovery that the subject-matter headings of the typical index could not be used with any degree of efficiency. For example, two members of the search staff assigned to different years of the Psychological Abstracts* found that they could scan through appropriate sections in the body of these ponderous volumes at a much faster rate and with greater assurance of picking up relevant items than they could by relying on the index alone. Apparently, for a broad interdisciplinary topic such as knowledge dissemination-utilization, the specific categories of the traditional index are inadequate.

C.   SORTING 4,000 STUDIES: THE TITLE CODE

Using the search guide, in a few months the staff had identified over 4,000 items which appeared to be relevant on the basis of title, source, and whatever abstracts were available. This accumulation of potential sources presented quite a challenge for meaningful sorting and selection for reading.

A sensible solution seemed to be provided by what became known as the "title code", a list of categories which was generated from three sources: (1) the guide itself; (2) the now emerging chapter outlines; and (3) certain obvious characteristics of each reference (e.g., "year of publication", "type of publication"). This device allowed the staff to classify each title by a small number of numerical codes which could be punched onto IBM cards for machine sorting and tabulation.   Although this procedure was subsequently carried out, and although many of the resulting tabulations proved interesting, they were not much help when it actually came to choosing material to be read and discussed in the report. The detailed thought sequences of the writing process seemed to follow along paths that could not easily be predicted and quantified in advance. Hence, those members of the staff who undertook the writing of given chapters found themselves sifting through titles again and again to find the right piece for the right place.

D.   THE CLASSIFICATION CODE AND THE "FLOW CODE"

In the beginning, the project directors had high hopes of being able to quantify what they read so that through machine analysis they could compare the results of numerous studies for the same variable (e.g., "insideness" of the sender of an innovation). It was known that Rogers had developed a code of this type for analyzing diffusion studies, and it was hoped that a similar scheme could handle the somewhat broader range of materials included in this review. Of special interest and concern was the development of a *"flow code"*, a specification of the flow of knowledge depicted in each bibliographic reference. In this "flow code", an attempt was made to classify each reference in such a way that "sender", "receiver", "channel", and "effect" could be identified for each knowledge transfer "event" described in the literature. It was hoped that this sort of analysis would eventually allow us to make quantitative comparisons and summaries of utilization phenomena across a wide range of diverse sources and diverse content areas.

---

*For a partial list of major sources searched see introduction to the bibliography.

These efforts to invent new ways of "reading" the literature were
challenging and absorbing but were also, in the end, frustrating. After
weeks of effort it became obvious that anything much beyond a simple classification of studies constituted a major project in itself.* With reluctance,
the more elaborate plans, especially those concerning the projected "flow
code", were trimmed down so that the actual reading process could begin.
The resultant "classification code" was used to classify approximately 500
studies. Once again, however, numerical analysis proved less useful at the
writing stage than had been hoped.

E.   CHAPTER READING AND WRITING "BY THE NUMBERS"

A little over six months from the beginning of the project, the groundwork had been laid for this reading-writing process to begin. A model and
tentative chapter plan had been developed and several thousand potential
sources had been identified and roughly sorted.

A plan was now devised whereby chapter outlining, reading and actual
writing could proceed simultaneously. A chapter "coordinator" was designated
for each chapter. This coordinator was to prepare a detailed outline for
his chapter to present to the entire staff at the beginning of the reading
period for that chapter (usually 2-3 weeks). Each of the six or seven
"readers" would then presumably have a clear idea of what should go in the
chapter. This mental picture approach had previously been successful in the
over-all search process (see again discussion of the "search guide"). The
coordinator could concentrate on the reading of basic materials pertaining to
the chapter and could discuss abstracted materials with the readers while
such material was fresh in their minds.

Once again the operational reality did not live up to the design. Time
estimates were far too short and the coordinator and his readers were usually
out-of-phase. The hoped-for continuous interaction among the staff during
the reading-abstracting-writing processes simply did not take place. The
job of absorbing and integrating the diverse materials to write a chapter
usually was so complex that it went on for weeks after the basic reading
had been done. As a result of this process of reintegration, the original
chapter outline usually bore only a vague relationship to the chapter which
finally emerged.

It is interesting to note here again, however, the continuous tug of
war between our own theory, as represented in the original outlines, and the
"reality" of outside scholarship and research, which were represented in
the readings. The process of achieving synthesis between fact and theory,
and between one theory and another, was always painful.

---

*It is strongly urged that projects of this type be funded and undertaken at the
earliest opportunity. Only through such development activities can we hope to
control the knowledge explosion and improve the integration of scientific knowledge.

F. SOME RETROSPECTIVE LEARNINGS AND INSIGHTS

From the beginning this was an ambitious venture and probably there was always a dim awareness that there would be a discrepancy between promise and delivery. Nevertheless, the history of the project and the pitfalls and shortcomings which have been recited above do leave us with some lessons to ponder.

First of all, in this project we struggled with the problem of information retrieval on a topic that seemed to cut across traditional disciplinary lines, and we found that we had a far more complex and expensive task than we had originally anticipated. In the end, we were not really sure that our search had been exhaustive even with respect to the most important references. When the final chapters were being written we would occasionally be embarrassed by colleagues calling to our attention an article or a book which had utterly escaped our attention. As we ponder our own problem of retrieval, with all the resources at our disposal and all our preparatory conceptualiza- tion, we are impressed by the enormity of the retrieval task for the *practitioner* or the would-be *consumer* of knowledge who tries to retrieve something useful from this so-called knowledge "storehouse" that the scholars and scientists have built.

Another source of our problems was organizational; we tried to make the project a team effort. Organizing and writing a unified document on a complex subject is a task usually best done by a single author or perhaps two close collaborators working together over a period of years. In this project, however, we were faced with a very large integrative task which had to be accomplished in less than a year from the time writing actually began. This necessitated *collective scholarship,* the pooling of several somewhat diverse intellectual backgrounds and approaches. True collaboration was something with which the team struggled continuously; but in the end we were not sure that we had found the best means of achieving it. We would suggest, however, that the time has nearly arrived when a topic like "knowledge utilization" can no longer be handled by individual scholarship. When the number of titles jumps from 4,000 to 40,000, as it will surely do in the next decade, the individual human computer will be taxed beyond its capacity. Experimentation in how to "automate" this process using teams, and perhaps even electronic computers is badly needed.

Related to this problem of collective scholarship is the question of collective or consensual theorizing. We became acutely aware as we argued with one another, that one man's beautiful model may be another man's iron maiden. Our thinking is governed by our own schemas or models; if we are confined within another man's schema, then we are under the control of that other man's thinking, and some of us may not like to feel controlled in this way. It is not always a comfortable arrangement for intellectually restless and creative people. This project began with a model, the Havelock-Benne model of knowledge utilization (#3872). But as Guskin, Hill, Frohman and others became involved in the project, they brought with them their favorite models which did not always necessarily fit with the Havelock-Benne schema. We hoped for synthesis, at least among ourselves, and if possible, with others who have made major contributions. Rogers, Miles, Brickell, Clark and Guba, Lippitt, and their co-workers all had made important theoretical contributions that could not be ignored. We wanted to incorporate these ideas because we believe that scientific knowledge is collective knowledge based on some consensual perception and definition of "facts" and some agreement on how to measure these facts. Social scientists in the past have not tried hard enough to achieve this consensus even on very narrowly defined issues, so that our separate "models" or "theories" too often define separate realities with their own variables, facts, and legitimate ways of measuring the facts. The authors of this study did not want to travel down this same road. We wanted to be original, of course, but at the same time we knew that we needed to be eclectic, catholic, and open to influence from all of the writings in this field. Most of all we needed to push toward a consensus with the Lewins, Morts, and Gubas who have gone before.

V. PLAN OF THE REPORT

This work has been designed to cover every aspect of the topic: "knowledge dissemination and utilization".* For that reason, the chapters have been arranged in a sequence which will lead the reader by steps toward a total picture.

Chapter Two introduces the basic concepts that constitute the core of the model: the knowledge transfer *process* and the knowledge flow *system*. The *process* can best be understood as an interaction or linkage between a potential "user" and a potential "resource", and it can be analyzed into six categories or problem foci by the formula: <u>who</u> says <u>what</u> to <u>whom</u> by <u>what</u> <u>channel</u> to <u>what</u> <u>effect</u> for <u>what</u> <u>purpose</u>.** Figure 1.1 gives a schematic representation of the process, and Table 1.2 provides several examples of how this formula applies to concrete situations.

FIGURE 1.1   Basic Elements of the Process

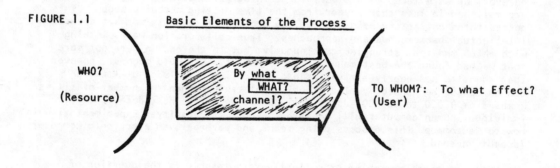

WHO?

(Resource)

By what
WHAT?
channel?

TO WHOM?: To what Effect?
(User)

[Insert Table 1.2 here]

In Chapter Two the elements of this diagram will be explained in detail. Later chapters will take up various components of the formula and will present a complete analysis of each component with supporting references from the literature, where available.

---

*Frequently referred to throughout this report simply as "D&U".

**This same model has been used by several authors as a basic paradigm of the communication process. See, for example, Hovland (#7001) or Smith, et al. (#7002).

TABLE 1.2

Some Examples of Knowledge Transfer Events

WHO?	transfers WHAT?	by what CHANNEL?	to WHOM?	to what EFFECT?
A team of university scientists, educators, and publishers	A new high school science curriculum	Packaging, publication, and setting up training programs	Teachers of high school science across the nation	Nationwide acceptance and adoption in majority of high schools
A social psychologist	Research on detrimental effects of segregated schools	Contributing to a formal brief and presenting testimony	U.S. Supreme Court	Court decision to ban segregated schools as unconstitutional
Sociology professor doing research on small groups	A method for systematic recording and analysis of small group interaction processes	Book reporting small group experiments, personal correspondence, exchange of sample materials	Education professor specializing in teaching behaviors	A new system for the analysis of teacher-student interaction in the classroom
A team of university experts on human relations training, and locally based "inside" change agents	New approaches to collaborative problem-solving on a range of school related issues	Inter-university action research project	All levels of a school system	An internalized capacity for self-renewal and innovation
A pharmaceutical manufacturer	A new antibiotic which has proven effective in laboratory and clinical trials	Published reports and reprints, mailed advertising, and office visits by drug "detail" men	Physicians in private practice in the company's market area	Rapidly increasing frequency of prescriptions for the antibiotic among physicians in the area
Bell Telephone Laboratories	Transistor technology	Coordinated disseminative program using printed literature, manuals, demonstrations, conferences, consultative visits	Electronics manufacturers in several countries	Very rapid adoption of transistor technology and growth of transistor applications
University research centers studying auto safety	Research evidence that seat belt installation and use is a highly effective means of reducing highway fatalities	Research reports, testimony at hearings, promotion by safety groups	Federal officials charged with administration of safety legislation	Federal standards requiring seat belt installation in all new cars
Population planning experts	Tested inexpensive and effective birth-control devices	Local health clinics and specially trained local midwives	Impoverished women with large families	Decreasing birth rate and increasing per-capita income in target area
Agricultural researchers and developers	Hybrid seed corn	Cooperative extension service reports, radio programs, demonstration farms, county agent visits, promotion by seed manufacturers and retailers	Corn producing farms in the United States	Increasing corn yield, increasing farm income
Cancer researchers and epidemiologists	Close association of cigarette smoking and several major diseases	Research reports, investigations, promotion by American Cancer Society	U.S. Congress and various federal regulatory agencies	Movement towards limitations on advertising and sale of cigarettes

In Education

In Other Fields

EXAMPLES

However, the communication process formula, by itself, does not provide the framework for a complete and comprehensive presentation, primarily because it reduces a complex set of interactions among a large number of people and groups down to two elements: a "resource" and a "user". To deal with this complexity, it was necessary to add the concept of "social system" and the concept of *"knowledge flow system"*. It seemed helpful to think of the pattern of the flow of knowledge from its generation to its final utilization as a complex social system in which there are many senders and many receivers all clustered in various types of groups, associations, and organizations, and linked together, sometimes tightly and sometimes tenuously, by various mechanisms such as overlapping memberships, proximity, shared values, and established communication channels. The major entities or sub-systems within this over-all knowledge flow system were identified as "basic research", "applied research and development", "practice", and "the consumer". Figure 1.2 presents the bare outlines, with arrows to suggest not only 2-way communication but also <u>interdependence</u> among the major sub-systems. Within this over-all social system approach we were also able to introduce important subsidiary concepts such as *"institution", "organization",* and *"role"*. In particular, the concepts of "<u>linking</u> institution" and "<u>linking</u> role" are crucial to our understanding of knowledge dissemination and utilization.

FIGURE 1.2 <u>Dissemination and Utilization Viewed as a System</u>

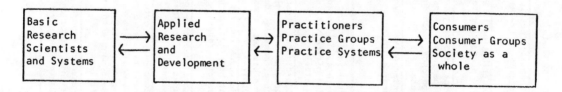

We recognized, however, that "system" and "process" are only two different ways to describe the same phenomena; therefore, we have tried to synthesize these two concepts. In Chapter Two we will try to show that at each linkage point in the knowledge flow system, a knowledge transfer process is taking place. In Figure 1.3, we try to represent this integration graphically. Both the micro-perspective and the macro-perspective illustrated in this diagram are essential to a full understanding of knowledge dissemination and utilization.

[Insert Figure 1.3 here]

In Chapter Three we will take the abstract concept of "knowledge flow system" and apply it to actual knowledge utilization networks which serve various practice fields such as education, medicine, and law. This overview introduces us to some of the problems of utilization in education from a "macro"-perspective.

In Chapter Four we begin our detailed review from a micro-perspective, examining the utilization process *inside the individual*. In this chapter we consider personality factors, cognitive and attitudinal variables, and the various specific characteristics of people which have been found to be related to receptivity to new knowledge.

FIGURE 1.3   <u>System and Process: Two Ways to Look at One Problem</u>

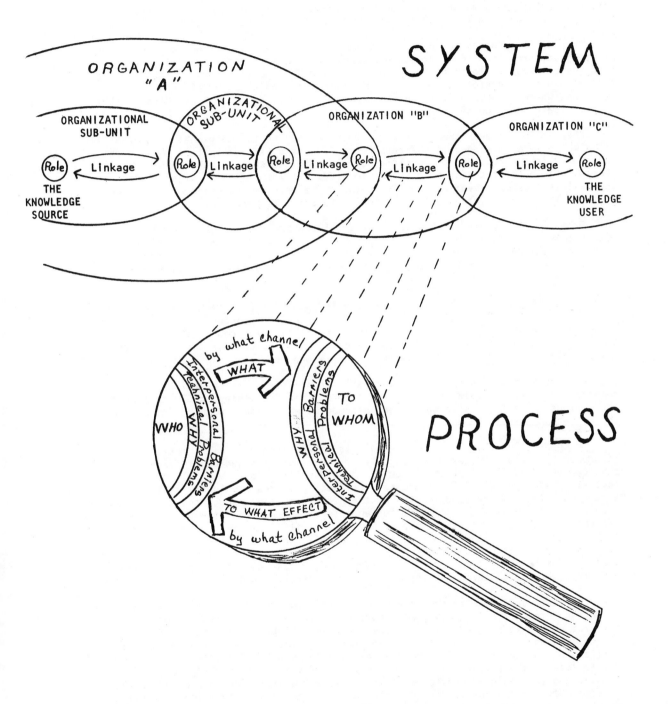

Chapter Five broadens this perspective slightly by considering knowledge transfer as a two-person situation in which information is exchanged between a "sender" and a "receiver", each with his own separate identity and his own set of motives, resistances, values, and understandings. These various differences between sender and receiver constitute potential barriers between them.

Chapter Six expands our perspective even further by introducing considerations of group and organizational structure and process. This chapter summarizes the findings of organizational research and theory, and it applies them to the organization viewed as a generator, processor, disseminator, and consumer of knowledge. Also considered in Chapter Six are *inter*-organizational relationships which inhibit or facilitate the flow of knowledge.

Chapter Seven takes some of the concepts pertaining to individuals and organizations which were developed in Chapters Four, Five, and Six and applies them to the topic of "Linking Roles", the specific positions in the social system where specialists in the transfer process are located. It identifies a number of such specialists located at various points in the social system and performing various distinct functions related to the linking of research to practice.

From this first set of chapters, Three through Seven, we should arrive at a rather complete idea of what is meant by "who" and "to whom". We will have looked at a great variety of senders, sender systems, receivers and receiver systems, and we will have seen how they fit together to form a macro-system for knowledge transmission.

Chapter Eight then takes us into a detailed analysis of "what", the "knowledge which is transmitted" or "the message". This chapter is intended to give the reader a grasp of the complexity and variety of things which could be considered to be "messages" in the knowledge flow system. These include not only scientific research, but also prototypes, methods, products and services, and even needs.

Chapter Nine examines how the message is transmitted. It identifies and compares the various media and the various forms that the message could take, and the various mechanisms, strategies, and procedures which could be used for getting the message across.

In Chapter Ten this question of "how" is viewed from a more theoretical standpoint; in that chapter we will consider the temporal sequence of stages that can be identified in both dissemination and utilization. We will compare several "phase models" of D&U processes. If such patterns are identifiable, then a next question will be to determine whether they are clear enough and consistent enough to provide us with the basis for an integrated theory of the utilization process. In the early part of Chapter Eleven, our final chapter, we will suggest such an integration. Included in this chapter will be an overview and reexamination of a variety of conceptual models of the "change" process, the "dissemination" process, the "innovation" process and "adoption" process as postualated by various authors. We will be searching for ways to synthesize these different points of view.

The final chapter will continue with a brief summary of patterns or themes which run through the literature with some consistency. From these emergent patterns we try to suggest further steps for research, problems which need unravelling and new areas which need exploring, particularly with respect to utilization in education. This chapter also includes a brief section in which we try to look at these conclusions from the point of view of the practitioner of change, and the would-be knowledge linker. We ask what is needed now and in the immediate future to improve dissemination and utilization in education. Finally, we will suggest some specific directions for a national policy for D&U.

VI. QUANTITATIVE OVERVIEW

An analysis of the 4,000 entries of our bibliography provides some rough summary statistics on the domain which is being surveyed in this report. These data are subject to two interpretations: first, they are simply a statement of what was found, a sort of definition of the field we wish to cover; second, they give some clues as to the shape of the domain, i.e., they illustrate some of the gaps and some of the problem areas. The extent to which we can move to solve these problems depends upon the thoroughness and objectivity of the search process itself.

A. FIELDS OF KNOWLEDGE

Table 1.3 indicates the number of utilization-relevant studies which were identified in eleven different subject matter fields. We find that

[Insert Table 1.3 here]

education has the largest contribution, but this finding must be qualified. It is possible that more studies were found in education because a greater effort was made in this field than in any other. Although the research con- tract specified all fields, there was special concern that education receive thorough coverage. Secondly, "number of studies" is a poor index of *quality* of information. For example, articles coming from education were less likely to be quantitative research reports than were those in agriculture.

Some of the "field" categories that appear in this table were not predetermined but emerged gradually from efforts to classify the literature. Hence, for example, we did not originally include "communication" as a field but had to add this category because of the large number of studies which could not be placed elsewhere. On the other hand, some other field categories are probably over-represented because a deliberate effort was made to identify material within them. For example, the number of citations under "mental health" and under "law" probably gives an inflated impression of tne concern for scientific knowledge utilization that is exhibited in those fields. Indicative of the under-emphasis in such fields is the almost total absence of cross-citations to the voluminous literature on diffusion and innovation in agriculture, medicine, and education.

Technology utilization is an area which is probably under-represented for a variety of reasons. First of all this literature tends to be widely scattered, appearing in such diverse forms as technical reports, trade journal articles, newspaper stories, television programs, and conference proceedings. There are few reliable research information channels through which such material is likely to be funnelled. Secondly, in this field, too, there is some tendency toward insularity with a lack of cross-referencing to agriculture's diffusion research tradition. Finally there is probably a considerable amount of information about technology transfer for specific innovations that is viewed as proprietary or secret by the private corporations or government agencies in which it was generated. We have no way of determining how much of this literature there is and, more importantly, how valuable it is. On the latter count we might have reasons to be suspicious simply because it is difficult to maintain scientific rigor and quality without public scrutiny by the scientific community.

TABLE 1.3   Number of Studies by the Field of Knowledge*

FIELD OF KNOWLEDGE	NUMBER OF STUDIES	PERCENT OF TOTAL
1. Education	674	17.1
2. Agriculture	502	12.8
3. Communication	502	12.8
4. Mental Health	278	7.1
5. Basic and Applied Sciences	257	6.6
6. Technology	241	6.1
7. Medicine	212	5.4
8. Law	176	4.5
9. Public Health	170	4.4
10. Administration	163	4.1
11. Social Welfare	88	2.2
General (applicable to all fields)	131	3.3
Others	139	3.6
Inadequate Information for this category	398	10.1
TOTAL	3,931	100

*Based on Comparative Literature Survey (CLS) Title Codes

These same remarks apply also in large measure to the field of advertising and market research, which is subsumed under the heading "communication" in Table 1.3. However, with the rapid growth in recent years of university departments, schools and research centers devoted to "communication", we may be witnessing the birth of a public, and hence a truly scientific, discipline of advertising and marketing.*

Finally with reference to Table 1.3, a comment should be made about the heading, "administration". Included here are the many studies on organizational and managerial change and development which represent the efforts of social scientists to apply their understandings, insights, knowledge, and methodology to help complex organizations improve their functioning. Although the scientific basis for such change efforts is not always clear, the models and the strategies of change developed by social scientists working with organizations have been well described in the literature and provide valuable insight into knowledge transfer and utilization in organizational contexts.

B.   TYPES OF STUDIES IDENTIFIED

Table 1.4 gives us a rough idea of the type of material contained in the bibliography. We can see that the preponderance of studies were "quantitative". This means that some effort was made to collect data, whether in the field or

[Insert Table 1.4 here]

the laboratory or in available records. This does <u>not</u> mean that each of these studies was methodologically sound or that the data presented met any criterion of reliability or validity. In short, the quality of the quantity is a question which is not answered in this table.

Under "theoretical studies" we have included any sort of serious discussion or analysis which did not include data. The actual number of such studies was probably much larger than the 25% indicated here. Such studies were included only if they represented what appeared to be a significant or novel contribution.

We were disappointed to find *so few case studies*. Of the thousands of dissemination and utilization events that take place each year it is unsettling to find so few documented in such a way that others could learn from them. This deficiency in the literature was one of the factors that thwarted our efforts to code, analyze, and compare utilization processes across studies and fields. Each investigator, in effect, has his own special interests or his own special point to make, and few appear to be motivated simply to report what happened in specific utilization events.

On a very selective basis the search also included popular magazine articles and newspaper stories. Usually these were brought to our attention by colleagues who knew of our project. Such items were included only when they seemed to add information not available elsewhere. In a new and emerging

---

*Here again, however, agriculture has led the way. Fifty years ago the U.S. Congress gave a mandate for the inclusion of the study of "marketing" in agricultural research. From this mandate there gradually evolved the field of rural sociology and, more recently, departments of communication in the land grant universities.

TABLE 1.4   Number of Publications by Type of Study*

TYPE OF PUBLICATION	NUMBER OF STUDIES	PERCENT OF TOTAL
Quantitative Studies	1,621	53.3
Theoretical Studies	748	24.6
Case Studies	226	7.4
Popular or Semi-popular Articles	187	6.1
Books and Reviews:** (high relevance)	259	8.5
TOTAL	3,041	100
Others: partially relevant and/or unclassifiable	890	
GRAND TOTAL	3,931	

*Based on CLS Title Codes

**I.e., Reviews of the literature on a topic, not book reviews.

discipline without its own "house organs", these sources are often valuable for casting light on government policy directions as well as highlighting innovations* and innovative behavior. Indeed, in many fields, and especially in technology and medicine, the installation of new ideas is only documented in the popular press and in trade journals. In education, agriculture, and in mental health, social scientists are more likely to be on hand to record and study the innovation process.

It is noteworthy that our team of searchers found as many as 259 studies that merited the designation "books and reviews--high relevance". This strongly suggests that D&U topics have received wide scholarly attention in one form or another. Much of this literature is concentrated in three areas: education (70 items), agricultural innovation (57 items), and change in organizations (40 items). Together these three fields provided 64% of the total publications in this category. However, very few of these works actually make an effort to go deeply into both the dissemination and the utilization process and very few take a field-comparative approach: no previous study takes the total problem of the utilization of scientific knowledge as its specific focus.

C.   NUMBER OF NEW STUDIES PER YEAR

Figure 1.4 shows us the number of studies ordered by year of publication.

[Insert Figure 1.4 here]

Before the project was undertaken, the staff had some doubt about how much material would be available. As the search proceeded, however, doubt gave way to dismay over the very large amount which was identified. We now had to face the realization that the flood of studies would be too great to be adequately summarized in this project. Figure 1.4 reveals another encouraging but frustrating fact: *The output of relevant studies has been increasing at a very rapid rate* over the past decade. At the date which was arbitrarily chosen as a starting date for the search of major indices, 1955, a little over 100 studies appeared, a respectable but easily reviewable number, but by 1964 the figure was nearly five times as great. Truly, there seemed to be a knowledge explosion on the topic of knowledge dissemination-utilization.** One regrettable consequence of this explosion will be the early obsolescence of our bibliography. Within a year at least 1,000 additional studies will appear in the literature. There is therefore a clear need for a continuing effort to compile, screen and synthesize research on these topics and to publish bibliographies on an annual basis. It would seem that a fully staffed clearinghouse will need to be established to coordinate future bibliographic efforts in this area.

---

*A good many of those in this category are new technologies or "gimmicks" in electronic media, automated retrieval, and the like.

**We surmise that the apparent fall-off in 1965 and after shown in the figure is due only to the lag in the identification and indexing of available materials.

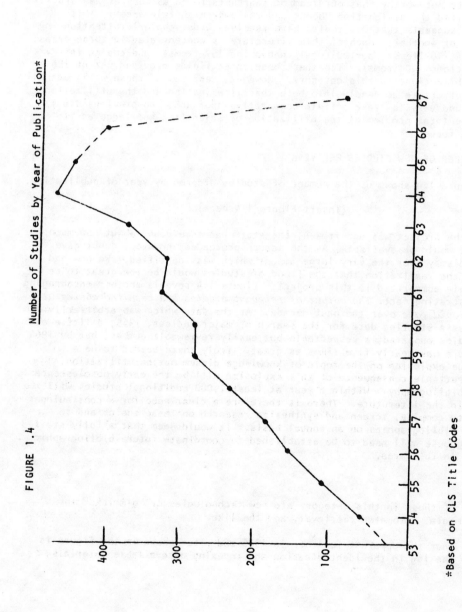

FIGURE 1.4

Number of Studies by Year of Publication*

*Based on CLS Title Codes

**Arbitrary cut-off date for systematic bibliographic searching.

D.   NUMBER OF STUDIES RELEVANT TO EACH ELEMENT OF THE COMMUNICATION PROCESS

We include in this overview section two additional tables to give some idea of how the "search guide" materials, described briefly in the previous section, were utilized in the selection and coding process.   It may be recalled that two concepts governed our thinking as the search went on: "the process" and "the system".   Table 1.5 illustrates how the "process"

[Insert Table 1.5 here]

part of the search guide was used to classify studies. We note that the largest number of studies (36.2%) were those in which the author's primary concern was "to whom" (e.g., Coughenour, L.M., "Who Uses the County Extension Agent").   The "to whom" or receiver of new knowledge may be a person, a group, an organization or even a culture.

We also find that 14.8% of identified studies are concerned primarily with describing or discussing the "who", the initiator or originator of a knowledge transfer event. Here again the sender may be an individual or a larger collectivity. These two categories, "who" and "to whom", together constitute over half of the total number of studies identified (51%). It is appropriate, therefore, that a major portion of this document is devoted to these two elements of the process. Chapters Four and Five, covering senders and receivers as individuals in interaction; Chapter Six, considering them as organized groups in interaction, and Chapter Seven, considering the role of knowledge linkers as a special type of sender and receiver, will collectively provide us with a detailed understanding of "who" and "to whom".

The second most popular category, "how", is taken up in detail in Chapter Nine under the heading, "technology or knowledge flow". Included under this heading are descriptions of various sorts of *media* or mechanisms for the dissemination or transfer of knowledge: television, printed material in various formats, information banks and services, conferences, groups, and individual contacts of various sorts. Also included under "how" are discussions of strategies and tactics for bringing about successful utilization.

A somewhat smaller number of studies are concerned with the "what", the characteristics of the knowledge or findings or innovation being disseminated. However, in this area the search team encountered special difficulty, because they were asked to make a distinction between two kinds of bibliographic entry: they were asked to *include* studies in which characteristics of knowledge or innovations were specifically analyzed from the point of view of D&U but to *exclude* studies which merely described the knowledge content of the innovation. This distinction was often a very fine one in which we may have erred more on the side of exclusiveness. The analysis of the content of messages of various kinds and their impact on utilization is taken up in Chapter Eight.

The remaining two categories, "to what effect" and "why" (or "to what purpose"), are not considered in separate chapters, but they are nevertheless viewed as being of high importance. These two topics are relevant to every chapter. The "effect" or "outcome" is the criterion of success of any utilization effort. It is therefore important as a guidepost in evaluating every aspect of the total process.

1-21

TABLE 1.5   <u>Number of Studies by Primary Process Focus*</u>

Each study was classified on the basis of its primary relevance to one of the elements in the process formula: <u>who</u> says <u>what</u> to <u>whom</u> by <u>what channel</u> to <u>what effect</u> for <u>what purpose</u>.

PROCESS FOCUS	NUMBER OF STUDIES	PERCENT OF TOTAL
1. To whom	1,023	36.2
2. How (what channel)	610	21.6
3. Who	418	14.8
4. What	323	11.4
5. To what effect	269	9.5
6. Why (what purpose)	180	6.4
TOTAL	2,823	100
General or inadequate information for this category	1,108	
GRAND TOTAL	3,931	

*Based on CLS Title Codes

Likewise, the "why" adds a dimension of broad perspective to the total picture and again it applies to all aspects: Why do people <u>want</u> to utilize scientific knowledge or to adopt innovations? Why do people want to change or to influence other people or to bring them new things? Why should people be concerned about learning about the knowledge utilization process? The question of "why" needs to be asked at every stage and at every level of analysis. It needs to be asked of the senders, of the receivers, of the researchers, practitioners, and consumers of knowledge, and it even has to be asked of those who study the process.

E. NUMBER OF STUDIES RELEVANT TO EACH MAJOR ROLE IN THE DISSEMINATION-UTILIZATION CHAIN

Table 1.6 is based on the second part of the search guide, which analyzed dissemination-utilization as a "system" problem. This table shows us the relative frequency of references to different sub-systems as receivers. We note that in a majority of studies the receivers can best be described as having practitioner-type roles. This finding largely reflects an intentional bias in the bibliographic search process. Searchers were asked to concentrate their attention on the flow of knowledge *from research to practice*, i.e., in the direction of being more practical or more useful.* It may be recalled from Figure 1.2 that <u>four</u> major roles or role groupings were distinguished for the purpose of analyzing the overall knowledge flow system, but among these

[Insert Table 1.6 here]

four our greatest concern was for flow *to the practitioner* and *from* basic and applied research (the table enumerates only flow *to*, not flow *from*). Second highest priority was given to studies of flow to the consumer, and this is reflected in the high percentages of studies in these categories (#2 and #3). Here again the distinction between practitioner and consumer was not always easy to draw. If the recipient, himself, was going to use the knowledge or the innovation to provide a service for someone else, then he was listed as a practitioner. For doctors or teachers this was a relatively clear matter, but for some much discussed audiences (e.g., farmers, homemakers, factory workers) it was not.**

Much less emphasis was placed on the flow of knowledge within the research community itself, either among basic or applied researchers or between basic and applied. This lesser emphasis is reflected in the much smaller percentages of studies in these receiver categories. The 329 studies in which researchers were identified as receivers of information are those in which the issue of dissemination or utilization is a salient one. For example, studies on the characteristics of scientists, or on scientific creativity, were generally *excluded*. However, major works on information flow among scientists were *included*.

---

*See bibliography, page iv, for clarification of this emphasis.

**After some dispute among project staff, farmers were counted as "practitioners" since they were providing a service, food production for the community as a whole. Home-makers, on the other hand, were rated as belonging to the "consumer" group even though they could in some respects be seen as the practitioner who <u>serviced</u> the everyday living needs of the family.

TABLE 1.6   Number of Studies by the Category of Receivers of Information*

RECEIVERS OF INFORMATION	NUMBER OF STUDIES	PERCENT OF TOTAL
1. Practitioners	1,535	54.8
2. Community or Society	509	18.1
3. Consumer	430	15.3
4. Applied and/or Basic Researcher	140	5
5. Applied Researcher	115	4.1
6. Basic Researcher	74	2.6
TOTAL	2,803	100
General or inadequate information for this category	1,128	
GRAND TOTAL	3,931	

*Based on CLS Title Codes

We began this Introductory Chapter by explaining how and why this study originated, how it was carried out, and where it encountered difficulties. We have also endeavored to give an overview of the model which guided the selection of literature and which determined the form that is to be followed in succeeding chapters. Finally, we have tried to suggest certain descriptive dimensions of the content of the literature used in the review through a quantitative coding and tabulation of titles in the assembled bibliography. In sum, this first chapter is intended to provide the reader with the *operational background* for the study. The next chapter will be devoted to providing the *conceptual background*.

CHAPTER TWO

BASIC CONCEPTS

Table of Contents

CHAPTER TWO *

BASIC CONCEPTS

We begin this study of dissemination and utilization by considering a typical knowledge user. Dave Robbins is a high school science teacher who is trying to teach physics in a new way this year. Dave is a *practitioner* in a profession with a clearly defined mission. He provides a service to a population of *consumers* called "students". He is both a *receiver* of knowledge (from his culture) and a *disseminator* of knowledge (to his students). These two roles, receiver and disseminator, are both routinely filled by Dave in his day-to-day activities. But from our perspective in this report, we are not so much concerned with these routine aspects of Dave's occupation; rather, we are looking at him now primarily because at this particular point in time Dave may be about to become an *innovator* in the act of innovation. He has decided to change and hopefully to improve his way of doing things by reaching out for something new. In this report we will try to learn as much as we can about Dave's situation. We are going to take a look *inside* Dave to see *why* he was motivated to change, *how* he made his decision, *what* inhibited or facilitated his thinking about the change, and *what* kinds of creative processes were at work within him.

We are also going to look at Dave as a *receiver* of new scientific knowledge. As he fills his role as teacher, we will see Dave taking in the knowledge from the "expert" sources in his environment: the professors, the curriculum specialists, the researchers, the textbook writers. We will try to analyze the various forces in his social environment which impinge on his decision-making process; the experts just mentioned, his fellow science teachers, his principal, his local school board, and his students.

We would also like to look at Dave as a *processor*, translator, and transmitter of this new scientific knowledge to his colleagues and to his students, and we would like to see how these same social forces affect Dave, the *sender*.

A delineation of these intrapersonal and interpersonal forces will go a long way in helping us to understand Dave's act of changing but they will not go the whole way. We will also need to know something about the scientific *knowledge* which is available to Dave: e.g., (1) the knowledge base from which he starts (his college training and experiences since beginning to teach); (2) the kind, quantity, and quality of the new knowledge that he can draw on from the "expert" sources as he is bringing about this change; and (3) his degree of exposure to the proselytizing efforts of various "experts". We know, for example, that Dave is especially fortunate to be a physics teacher, because he can draw on the extensive efforts and products of the Physical Science Study Committee (PSSC), a national project to revise the physics curriculum. This gives Dave some options he might not have had if he were a social science teacher. But we do not know if the PSSC materials are appropriate for Dave, or for the level of the class he teaches, or for the kinds of equipment and classroom space he has at his disposal. Therefore, to understand Dave's situation we also need to know what *media* are available to him either as a receiver or as a sender. What *mechanisms and strategies of receiving and sending* does he know about, does he have access to, does he feel competent and comfortable to handle?

---

*This chapter was drafted by Ronald G. Havelock.

To really understand Dave Robbins' decision we would also have to look at Dave as a member of a particular culture at a particular point in time. If Dave lives in a tightly-knit middle class community which is suspicious of change, he may move very slowly to introduce his new curriculum; but if the Russians have just landed a man on the moon, Dave's neighbors and his school board in this same community may be very eager for Dave to change his physics course so that "our science" will be at least as good as and preferably a whole lot better than the Russians'.

It should be clear at this point that Dave Robbins' attempt to improve his physics course is an extremely complex piece of behavior: it has a chain of "causes" and "conditioning factors" which seems to defy coherent analysis and understanding. Nevertheless, in this report we have set ourselves the task of understanding as much as we can about Dave Robbins and the countless others in education and other fields who seek to improve their world through the dissemination and utilization of new scientific knowledge.

To begin this task of analysis, we will be aided greatly if we have some sort of framework or schema which will order the myriad factors to which we have just alluded into some meaningful whole. The purpose of Chapter Two is to derive such a schema, using the currently popular "systems" model approach. This analytic overview is offered on the assumption that it will help the reader by providing him with what Chin calls a "mind-hold" (Bennis, et al., #1344, p. 201) on a rather complex, diverse and poorly charted domain.

The chapter will be divided into eight sections. The first five will build systematically upon one another as five "levels of discourse" for considering the basic concepts to be used in the report. These five are: (1) the general (abstract, or ideal) level; (2) the intrapsychic level;* (3) the interpersonal level; (4) the social system level; and (5) the intersystem level. The sixth section introduces some ideas about the content of messages (the "what") and the seventh discusses the means by which messages are transmitted (the "how"). Finally in section eight we will review three dominant models, the three most frequently used ways of conceptualizing the process of D&U as a whole.

I.   BASIC CONCEPTS: SYSTEM, MESSAGE, BARRIER

Most of the analysis in this chapter and those that follow can be generalized into combinations and variations of three basic concepts: "system", "message", and "barrier".

A.   SYSTEM

In the abstract a system may be thought of merely as a set of components which act with and upon one another to bring about a state of balance, interdependence, or "wholeness". The components may be of any size or composition and the "state of balance" may be defined in any number of ways; yet if the components are interdependent with respect to this defined type of balance, then they constitute a system in that respect. Chin states this very rudimentary concept of system as follows:

---

*"Intrapsychic" refers merely to processes that go on inside the person. As used here, it is intended to be synonymous with such expressions as "intrapersonal", "mental", and "psychological".

"It is helpful to visualize a system by
drawing a large circle. We place elements, parts,
variables, inside the circle as the components, and
draw lines among the components. The lines may be
thought of as rubber bands or springs, which stretch
or contract as the forces increase or decrease. Outside the circle is the environment, where we place
all other factors which impinge upon the system."

(Bennis, et al., #1344, p. 203)

1. Incomplete or Partially Complete Systems

The degree of balance or interdependence within systems
is entirely *relative*. That is, there is tremendous variance
among systems in the amount of interdependence, and there is
variance among the components within a system on the amount of
interdependence. Hence we can talk about "loosely structured"
systems and "tightly structured" systems; we can also describe
certain system components as only partially or loosely interdependent so that the resultant state of balance is weak or
at least potentially unstable. The system may also include
unpredicatable components which appear and disappear either
at random or as they may be required by the other components.
When these unpredictable components are not present the system
is incomplete, and may not be able to function as a system.
For example, a motor vehicle can "exist" without gasoline or a
driver, but it cannot "function" as a motor vehicle unless these
components are included as part of the system. Virtually all
of the systems which we can observe in the real world are "open"
in this sense. The degree of interdependence existing among
components of a system can be referred to as the *"integrity"*
of the system.

2. Dynamic Systems

We should also distinguish between "static" and "dynamic"
systems. In static systems components simply exist in a more
or less fixed relationship to one another. In contrast, dynamic
system components act upon one another. Figure 2.1 suggests the
distinction between these two types of systems:

FIGURE 2.1   Static and Dynamic Systems

Static System   Dynamic System

2-3

The components of a static system are related to one
another in fixed patterns. Examples would be the pieces of
a pie, the atoms that form a molecule, a jig-saw puzzle, the
pages of a book or the bricks of a building. The components
of a dynamic system, on the other hand, push and shove at one
another, displace each other, or force changes in each other
in a pattern of action and reaction that maintains what might
be called a dynamic equilibrium or balance of forces. As
examples of dynamic systems one could cite the internal structure
of the atom, the solar system (or the system formed by any two
heavenly bodies), any circulation system (air in a building,
water in an engine, blood in the body), or any dialogue or other
form of reciprocal interaction between people. Most systems
in the real world have both static and dynamic properties.

B. MESSAGE

The dynamic property of systems could go under many labels. Chin suggests
terms such as "tension, stress, strain, and conflict" (Bennis, et al., #1344,
p. 204). Lewin typically uses the term "force" (e.g., in #6500, pp. 77-79)
and Katz and Kahn refer to "energy exchange" (#6223, pp. 19-21). However,
when our special concern is knowledge dissemination and utilization, it
may be clarifying to describe this dynamic component of a system as a
"message".

Within a dynamic system there must always be at least two messages, one
which could be called the "action" and another which could be called the
"reaction", the latter being the message which returns the system to its
initial balanced state. When action and reaction messages occur in a routine
and regular cycle, the system may be said to be in a state of "dynamic equilibrium". New messages, however, will upset the equilibrium and force the
closed system to change. Open systems, on the other hand, may need a *continuous*
input of new messages to *maintain* their equilibrium.

C. BARRIER

The static property of a system could also be identified by many labels,
but in the context of knowledge flow the term "barrier"* is probably most
expressive. Its defining property is that it stops messages. It keeps them
inside or it keeps them outside a system; the barrier thereby prevents messages
from upsetting or destroying the system's integrity. Indeed, barriers define
the "inside" and the "outside" of a system. Figure 2.2 may help to clarify
this concept.

[Insert Figure 2.2 here]

Again, however, in the real world, almost all barriers are at least
partially *permeable*. In other words, most barriers allow some messages to
go through. Figure 2.3 illustrates this fact by showing us a closed system

---

*The term "boundary" is more popular among systems theorists, e.g., Chin in Bennis,
#1344; Kuhn, #6434, p. 48ff, but "barrier" has also been used by major theorists,
e.g., Lewin, #6500.

FIGURE 2.2   A Barrier Defines Inside and Outside

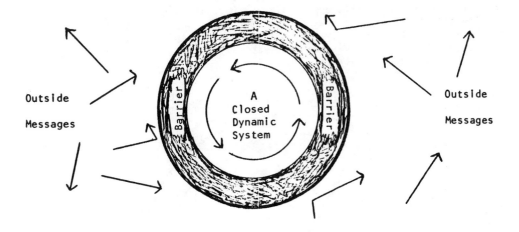

Outside

Messages

Outside

Messages

which has both static and dynamic components. The figure shows us a message, 'a', striking a semi-permeable barrier, 'x', so that a second message 'b' is generated.

The process could be called "filtering", "screening", "decoding", "encoding", "translation", "transfer", or "adaptation". Message 'c', in turn, is the translation of message 'b' and 'a' is the translation of 'c'.

FIGURE 2.3   A Closed System with Static and Dynamic Components

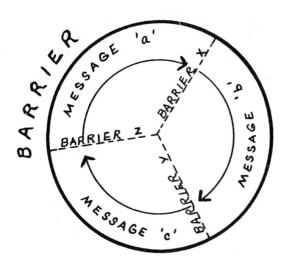

We can now bring together all the ideas discussed so far as we consider once again the kind of systems that are most likely to be found in the empirical world. Virtually all of the systems that can be identified and examined in the real world are likely to be <u>open systems</u> which contain both dynamic and static components which are themselves open subsystems. Figure 2.4 has been drawn to illustrate all these characteristics.

FIGURE 2.4 <u>An Open System with Subsystem Components</u>

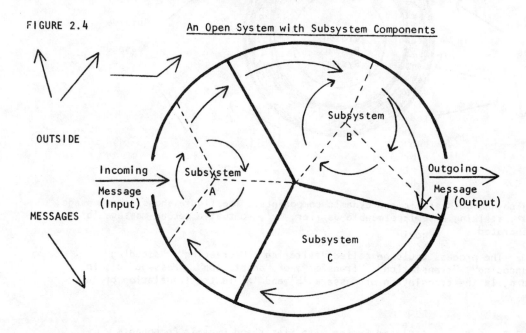

We should note, however, that two new concepts have been introduced in Figure 2.4: *"input"* and *"output"*. "Input" may be defined as messages coming into a system, and "output" as messages leaving a system. Subsystem A receives input from outside which is translated and retranslated until it gets to subsystem B. In B some output occurs in addition to further translation into subsystem C. Finally, subsystem A gets a message from C; this message completes the greater system and at the same time constitutes *feedback* to A. "Feedback" is, therefore, any input message to a system (or subsystem) which is directly and causally related to its own output.*

The entire sequence of messages that binds together subsystems "A", "B", and "C" could be referred to as the *"throughput"* of the greater system which they comprise.

---

*If two systems are in interaction, then the feedback message to one is the output message from the other and vice versa. "Feedback" is, therefore, a relative term depending on who is seen as the originator of the message cycle.

Figure 2.4 may be viewed as a representation of our innovator Dave Robbins. Dave receives *input* from the outside environment in the form of the PSSC (Physical Science Study Committee) curriculum materials. In subsystem A, *Dave, the receiver*, takes in the new knowledge, turns it over in his mind, relates it to previous knowledge and to his own creative processes. In this translated or modified form the new knowledge now passes to *Dave, the sender*, represented by subsystem B.

Dave now has to consider how to retranslate the new knowledge so that his students can understand it. He has to blend and adapt and adjust the PSSC knowledge to his own style of teaching and to his students' styles of learning. After Dave has reprocessed his newly acquired knowledge for sending, he will want to evaluate his "product", asking himself if it is adequate for his needs, or if it has the "right feel" for him. This evaluation process could be represented by subsystem C, i.e., a subsystem which gives internal feedback to "Dave, the receiver", on his own behavior as "Dave, the sender". If system C says "no", then subsystem A has to be reactivated so that more information can be brought in and added in order that Dave may refine or revise his course. If system C says "yes", it is an indication to system A that the job has been done well enough so that additional inputs are not necessary.*

In the remainder of this chapter we will try to apply these concepts to processes of knowledge utilization in the real world as they occur at four levels, *intrapsychic, interpersonal, social system and inter-system*. Figure 2.5 gives us an overview of these four levels.

(Insert Figure 2.5 here)

Figure 2.5a shows us the individual person as an open system. It is very important that we start here with individual man, his needs, and his activity in the service of his needs. Man's search for individual help, for food and health, life, liberty, and the actualization and fulfillment of his own personal system is perhaps the most significant and meaningful level on which we can consider knowledge utilization. This is the process that goes on inside Dave Robbins' head as he thinks about change and as he tries to innovate.

Figure 2.5b shows us <u>two</u> individual systems relating to one another, and hence forming a single two-man system. This is the system which is formed by Dave Robbins and his department chairman, or Dave and his favorite professor back at the university, or Dave and his favorite student, or Dave and a textbook salesman, or Dave and his wife. The individual person lives in an interpersonal environment populated by two-person systems; interpersonal messages are crucial in the fulfillment of intrapersonal needs. We should note here in addition that this model of the interpersonal interaction process is also the traditional model of the communication process.

---

*In this example, we have only considered *internal* feedback to Dave from his own behavior. Dave will also receive *external* feedback from his social environment, i.e., his students, which will come back to him as another type of input message, perhaps entering again at subsystem A. This type of feedback will be considered in more detail in the section on interpersonal linkage.

FIGURE 2.5   Knowledge Dissemination and Utilization: Four Levels of Discourse

a.   Individual Intrapsychic

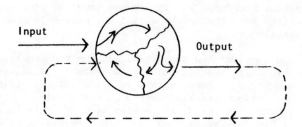

b.   Interpersonal

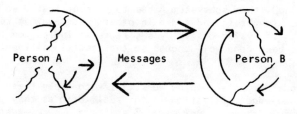

c.   Social System

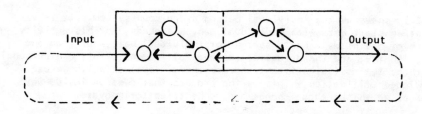

d.   Inter-System

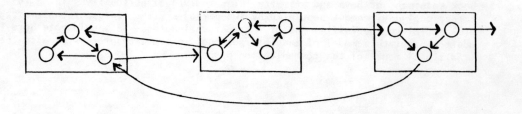

With Figure 2.5c we move from psychological to sociological considerations. The human environment is not only interpersonal, but it is also ubiquitously organizational and institutional. All people live within a complex of overlapping social structures of greater or lesser openness. This is the classroom, or the high school, or the school district system in which Dave Robbins works. The diagram also reminds us that social structures have all the generic properties of open systems and are composed of inter-related dynamic subsystems called "human beings".

Finally, in Figure 2.5d we recognize the fact that social systems can themselves be subsystems within a greater network or "macro-system". The high school in which Dave works, the university in which Dave was trained, and the publishing firm which provides Dave with curriculum materials, are all related to one another in a loosely coordinated "macro-system" of knowledge D&U. Our understanding of the knowledge utilization process will not be complete unless we also include this most encompassing system, the society as a whole and the various knowledge producing and knowledge consuming entities within it.

D. SUPPLEMENTARY CONCEPTS

In the foregoing presentation we have been intentionally parsimonious, restricting the analysis to three essential concepts: system, message, and barrier. However, it will often be convenient to refer to a larger lexicon of terms which are typically employed by scholars in the field of communication and in the related social sciences. Special note should be made of the concepts of *interface, channel, medium, linkage, chain* and *network*.

1. Interface

Although this term is almost totally absent in the psychological and sociological literature, it is a useful one to apply when describing the relationship between two systems or subsystems because it is neutral. It is simply a word for the state of affairs that exists between two systems, whether the two are interrelated or not, whether they are in conflict or not, and whether or not messages are passing between them. Let us suppose for example that Dave's high school seldom makes any contact with the state university: we cannot speak here about a "relationship" between a user system (the high school) and a resource system (the university) because no meaningful relationship exists. However, we can describe the *"interface"* between this user and this resource and we can analyze the various barriers which prevent the development of a relationship at this interface. There is, of course, some overlap of meaning between "interface" and "barrier". If two subsystems are separated by a barrier, then the barrier is the interface. If they are sepearted by a complex of barriers which surround each subsystem (which is the case in our high school-university example), then the two sets of barriers plus the intervening space represent the interface.

2. Channel and Medium

Within our conceptual schema, *channel* can be defined as the point at which a barrier is permeable. If a message passes from system A to system B, then the region between A and B through which the message passes is the channel.* The channel may, in fact, be a third intervening

---

*Note that a channel is therefore a specific type of interface; i.e., the region between A and B is the interface. If a message passes through the region, then by definition the region has become a channel for that type of message.

system, or a series of intervening systems. That is the case in the transmission of messages in the human body; each nerve cell is a specialized intervening system between receptors (the "senses") and effectors (the muscles, the motor apparatus of the human being). Any complete circuit requires the transmission of a message in the form of electrical energy through thousands of these intervening subsystems.

In the context of D&U in the high school the channel might be a popular magazine on educational technology put out by the university, or it might be a curriculum coordinator who retrieves information from the university and other expert sources so that he can consult with Dave Robbins and other teachers and can give them valuable advice on new curricula or other matters that concern them.

"Channel" and *medium* are essentially synonymous. There is no adequate way to distinguish between the two terms, although tradition may prefer one or the other in given contexts.

3. Linkage

Linkage is a term we use to indicate that two systems are connected by messages so as to form a greater system. If the barriers between the two systems are permeable enough so that messages can flow out of each to the other and so that response messages can flow into each from the other (feedback), then a link or a state of linkage has been created between the two. Throughout this report, when we use terms such as "linkage to resources" and "knowledge linker", we will be referring to this sort of relationship between two systems. It should be stressed, however, that a single exchange of messages will not suffice as an adequate definition of linkage. Rather, the term is used here to suggest a regularized pattern of interaction between two systems which in a real sense forms a bond between them. Linkage is exemplified in the firm bond of friendship and frequent mutual visiting between Dave and his favorite professor at the state university. Because they trust each other Dave and his old professor are able to exchange messages on new ideas and on problems which they are having; together they form a system of mutually reinforcing dissemination and utilization. In Chapter Eleven of this report we will suggest how this concept of linkage can be used to bring together much of the theory and research on D&U.

4. Chain

"Chain" simply carries the metaphor of the link one step further: in formulating a model of knowledge utilization we have postulated a "chain of knowledge flow" which includes messages flowing from basic research to the consumer and from the consumer to basic research through various intermediaries. This chain is composed of a series of links between individual systems such as were described in the preceding paragraph.

5. Network

To a certain extent, the term "chain" inadequately represents the real state of affairs with respect to knowledge flow in a complex system (such as a human brain or a society). Rather, there are many chains and many links which cross each other, run parallel to each other and interconnect with one another. To carry our metaphor further, we could reasonably call this "the knowledge flow mesh", but we will conform to standard usage by defining this complex of interweaving relations as a *"network"*.

II. THE INTRAPSYCHIC LEVEL

Knowledge utilization starts with some very elementary psychological assumptions about human behavior and its causes. The key words for this section will therefore be: *"need--pain and pleasure, arousal and satisfaction"*, and *"behavior--search and consumption"*.

A. NEED

Any satisfactory definition or determination of usefulness must begin with man's motivation: his aspirations, his feelings of want, his hunger, his pain. Individual human needs are the basic "why" for knowledge utilization, and they must always stand foremost in our consideration of D&U phenomena. At this juncture, however, we will not give a thorough accounting or analysis of these needs but will merely assume their basic importance and recognize needs as being very significant messages within the human system. They are the dynamic forces which create instability within the person-system and which lead to a cycle of behaviors that ultimately will correct this instability (although such correction or restabilization may be achieved only temporarily or partially). If we observe fluctuations in the need message alone, however, we will perceive over time a cyclical pattern as suggested in the hypothetical oscillating curve of Figure 2.6. This cycle is truly the vital balance for human and animal systems: if either the arousal curve or the satisfaction curve flattens or peaks abruptly, the entire organism is in trouble. The rest of the body depends on an alternating sequence of pain and pleasure messages as outputs from the need subsystems.

We can see this need cycle operating in Dave Robbins throughout the year as he teaches his course in physics. Dave is neither continuously pleased nor continuously dissatisfied with his course, but at periodic intervals his feeling of dissatisfaction grows and subsides.

FIGURE 2.6   The Need Cycle

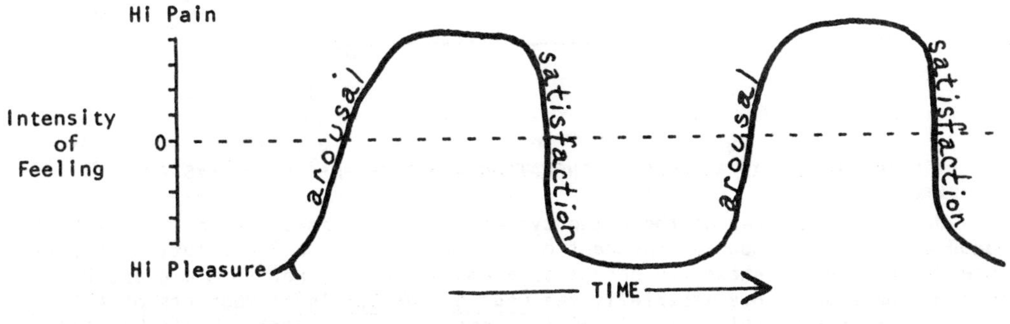

B. BEHAVIOR

Like need, we can think of *behavior* as forming a subsystem within the individual. Also like need, we can think of this behavioral subsystem as following an oscillating pattern moving from low activity to high and back again. Figure 2.7 depicts this hypothetical curve and in addition introduces us to the two classes of behavior that tell much of the story of knowledge utilization: *"search"* and *"consumption"*. The figure is, of course, a drastic over-simplication of all the complex sets of responses which make up human behavior, but it suggests that if we could generalize the responses to any given set of stimuli and if we could come up with one index of "activity", we would find an oscillating pattern roughly along these lines. It suggests also that if the "activity level" could be further analyzed into these two aforementioned broad classes of behavior, we would find that the initial stages could be labelled "search" activities, i.e., activities relating to the struggle by the organism to find problem solutions, whether they be in the form of food, shelter, clothing, comfort, praise, facts, formulae, or scientific knowledge; while the closing stages of the activity could be described as consummatory reponses such as eating, enjoying, accepting, absorbing and learning. This behavior cycle, like the need cycle, is as essential to the maintenance of life as is the beating of the heart itself: if either the search behavior or the consumption behavior fail to take place, again the organism is in trouble.

Again as we look in on Dave we will find him at one time taking tentative steps to seek out new ideas for his course. Later we may see him completely preoccupied with searching and learning about a new curriculum or a new style of teaching. Later still we will see little innovative activity as Dave struggles to catch up with routine chores of grading, lecturing, and counselling, or as he takes time out to relax with his family.

FIGURE 2.7   Behavior as a Cycle

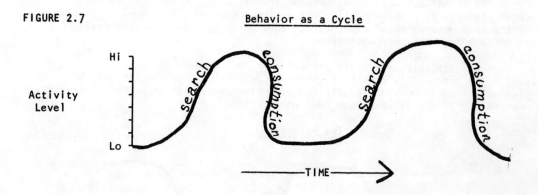

C. THE INDIVIDUAL AS A PROBLEM-GENERATING AND PROBLEM-SOLVING SYSTEM

Of course, neither of these two cycles or systems makes sense in isolation because each is thoroughly dependent on the other. Figure 2.8 illustrates this interdependence: it shows two open subsystems which together form a greater system. We should note especially the message and barrier components of this figure because they point to some of the most important intra-psychic knowledge

2-12

FIGURE 2.8   The Need-Behavior Cycle Inside the Person as a System

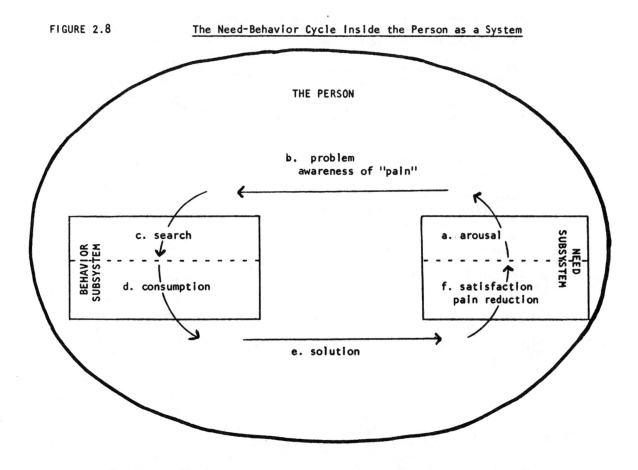

utilization problems. Starting from point "a" in diagram, we see first that
there has to be a translation of "arousal" into a message to be sent outside
the need subsystem (a to b). This resulting message is the expressed *"pain"*
or the stated *"problem"*. This message will provide a more-or-less accurate
representation of the aroused need, depending on the adequacy of the translation process. At various points in later chapters we will refer to this
"articulation of need" as an essential yet problematic aspect of many utilization systems.

     At the next point on the cycle, moving to the left in the figure, we find
another much discussed stumbling block to utilization: generating meaningful
search behaviors from stated or expressed problems (b to c). Then within the
behavior subsystem we find yet another potential barrier as we move from
search to consumption (c to d). Not pictured, but assumed in the figure, are
such additional intervening steps as "finding alternative solutions",
"choosing among alternatives", and "preparing for consumption" (or "utilization").

The act of consumption, itself, will generate a message back to the need system (d to e). If the "solution" is not satisfying (e to f), the cycle will be regenerated with more urgency.*

Even moving from satisfaction to arousal (f to a) may present some difficulties. If the individual has executed a problem-solving cycle and has reached a state of satisfaction, it may be very difficult to regenerate the cycle if the need should occur again. Many authors speak of the importance of shaking people out of such a state of complacency, "unfreezing" them, so that a problem-solving sequence can be generated internally.**

Once again Dave Robbins may help us understand the internal utilization cycle. Dave has been teaching his physics course according to the same pattern for a number of years, and until now he has been pretty satisfied with what he has been doing. Last year, for example, Dave did not make any effort to change. He taught his course pretty much the way he had the year before and the year before that. This year, however, he is dissatisfied with what he is doing, dissatisfied sufficiently to realize that a change is needed (point "a" in Figure 2.8). But dissatisfaction is not enough. Dave must translate his dissatisfaction into a specific thought which in this case was articulated as "I need to improve the content of my course". When Dave can say this to himself he has moved from point "a" to point "b" in the cycle. When he starts to scan his own memory for things he has learned in the past which could be added to his course, he has entered the behavior subsystem and is conducting his own internal "search" activity (point "c"). Once he makes a choice among alternatives derived from his search and follows this choice with a decision to try out that alternative, he is engaging in a consumption activity (point "d") which will lead him to the formulation of a revised physics course (point "e"). Finally he will evaluate this revision to determine whether or not it reduces his original feeling of discomfort with his old course (point "f").

Although all these internal psychological issues are important, the focal issue for the student of dissemination and utilization is the *search process*, for it is through the search process that *new knowledge* is brought to bear on real life problems. There are two types of search processes, one *internal* and one *external*. In the internal search process the individual acts as a self-sufficient closed system. He contains within his own memory all the facts necessary to arrive at a solution. There is, therefore, no need to seek knowledge or resources outside himself. If, for example, our physics teacher, Dave Robbins, were to decide to change his physics course merely by altering his sequence of lectures, he would not require any outside knowledge.

---

*It is recognized that there are many psychological theories of motivation, but for the purposes of this analysis we are offering need-reduction as the primary motivating force behind behavior. Assuming a broad enough interpretation of the concept of "need", and assuming that behavior always has some direction or purpose, if follows that the behavior takes place for the purpose of achieving a satisfactory state or of satisfying some need.

**The resistance of many practitioners to continuing education may stem from a feeling that once they had struggled through to get the professional degree or license they were "through". The fact that scientific knowledge continues to accumulate means that the optimal solutions of yesterday may not be optimal in the world of today, even though the individual still feels satisfied.

In the external search model, on the other hand, memory search alone is inadequate and the user is therefore forced to turn to the outside world for help. Hence there is a necessary interaction with resource systems in the external environment. A message must be formulated and sent out in such a way that (a) it will generate appropriate search activities by *others* and so that (b) these others will be able to generate, in turn, resources which will help the user solve the problem. To initiate a major change in his physics course, Dave will have to go to his curriculum coordinator or perhaps to some professor he knows at the university. He will have to explain what he wants to these outside resource persons, and if he is lucky, he will get them to search for and provide to him information that will be relevant and appropriate to his particular needs. Figure 2.9 compares these two models.

FIGURE 2.9   Intrapsychic Knowledge Utilization

a.   Internal-Closed System Model

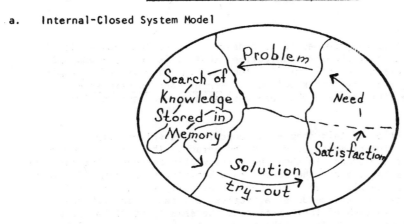

b.   External-Open System Model

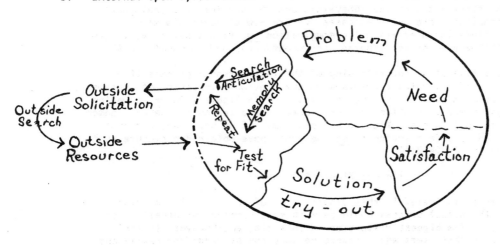

III. THE INTERPERSONAL LEVEL

Figure 2.10 depicts a part of the standard paradigm for the analysis of communicative acts.

FIGURE 2.10   A One-Way Communicative Act

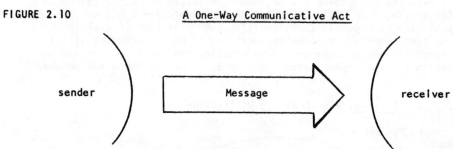

Inadequate though this diagram may be as a description of the real world, it does illustrate a central fact about communication: that it is *an interpersonal process*. A minimum understanding of communication and, in our case, of dissemination-utilization (D&U), requires some knowledge of senders and receivers: who they are, what they are like, and why they are motivated to send and receive messages.

In the previous section of this chapter we concerned ourselves with the barriers to the transmission of messages *within* the person. The barriers *between* persons are in many ways analogous to those barriers within persons. The receiver is analogous to a need subsystem and the sender to a behavior subsystem. The same basic steps which take place within an individual as he satisfies an internal need must also take place when the needs of a receiver are satisfied with the assistance of a sender. In each of these processes the same types of barriers are encountered at each stage. These are the barriers to the proper translation of messages; needs must be articulated and then translated into search questions, search questions into resources, resources into solutions and solutions into consumptions. However, even though the subsystems and the barriers are analogous in the intrapersonal and interpersonal cases, we are now discussing a more complex process, since in interpersonal communication two transmission events are taking place which have to be coordinated, an *output event* and an *input event*.

We can best arrive at an understanding of the interpersonal process if we integrate this pair of communicative acts with our previous discussion of systems and the need-behavior cycle. It may be recalled that in Figure 2.9b we showed an external-open system model in which the individual made a search of the environment outside himself to pull in a solution to his problem. If we had populated that environment with an outside resource person we would have obtained a picture such as that appearing in Figure 2.11.

[Insert Figure 2.11 here]

The subprocesses indicated in this diagram are, of course, only speculative and suggestive. The actual process would be much more complex and usually less clearly delineated. The biggest distortion in this diagram, however, is the impression it may give that users and resource persons can be wedded so neatly and easily and that they can synchronize their separate internal problem-solving

2-16

FIGURE 2.11   A Two-Person Knowledge Utilization System

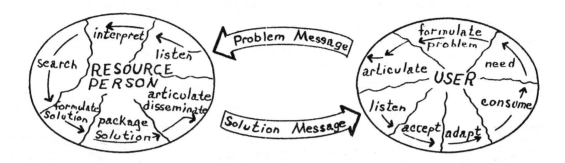

sequences so that together they really form a single system. There are innumerable
barriers which work against such collaboration. Among these, four are worth noting
at this time:

1.   Role Perception and Definition:

     To be able to act as either a "resource person" or a "user",
an individual must be able to perceive himself as filling a
"resource" or "user" role, and he must be able to define his role
in these terms. Many individuals may be unwilling or unable to
think of themselves either as "resource person" or as "user". To
admit to the need for outside resources is sometimes unacceptable
for some, and, conversely, to identify oneself as a "resource" or
"helper" (one who gives service) is unacceptable for others.

2.   Status Discrepancy and Ambiguity:

     A person may also feel that acting in one or the other of
the roles of sender and receiver will endanger his status, particularly
if he notes a status discrepancy between himself and the other person,
or if his status relative to the other person is ambiguous.

3.   Language:

     We may also find that sender and receiver do not speak the
same language, literally or figuratively.   For example, the sender's
words may be excessively technical or loaded with jargon and private
meanings.

4.   Being Out of Phase:

     We may also find that the sender and receiver are simply out
of phase; the sender may be giving a solution before the receiver has
articulated his problem, or the sender may not be prepared to offer
a solution when the receiver is asking for one.

All these examples suggest that the user and the resource person are each enclosed in a very thick shell made up of numerous interpersonal barriers, more or less as suggested in Figure 2.12. Personal identity and self image

FIGURE 2.12   Interpersonal Barriers

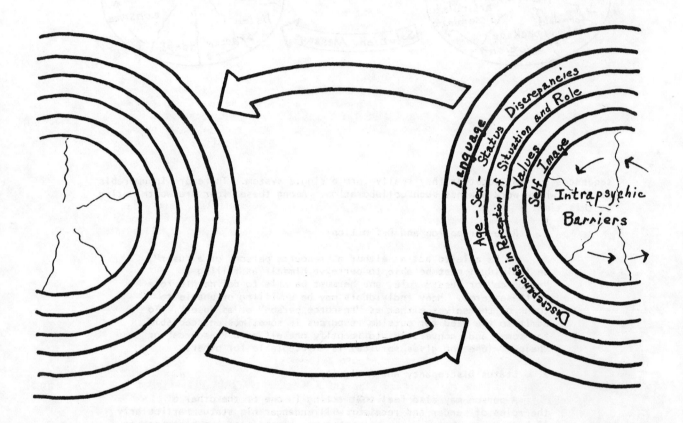

(e.g., not wanting to be seen as in need of outside help) represent one type of barrier. Discrepant values (e.g., on such things as giving "service" and "self help") represent another. Status differences represent yet a third type of barrier, and language, space and time are others. In Chapters Four and Five, we will explore these interpersonal barriers in depth.

Figure 2.12 is distorted, of course, in its suggestion that these two people alone make up a closed system. The resource person, for example, may not have a solution inside himself; rather he may have to reach out to some other resource person or persons in his search efforts. Likewise the "user" may not want the information for himself but may only be passing on a problem message which he received from someone further down the line.* It may also be that the "user" seeks external assistance from *more than one* resource person, or he may be referred to another resource person by the first one to whom he goes for help. Each of these complications represents a separate and additional interpersonal transaction and a separate "open" subsystem with all the barrier problems discussed. Each of these "linkages" can be interpreted or understood by itself as an inter- personal process, but, taken as a whole, a network of such linkages introduces additional problems and an additional perspective that we will discuss in the next section of this chapter.

IV. THE SOCIAL SYSTEM LEVEL

Earlier in this chapter we presented a picture of an "ideal" internal know- ledge utilization process (see again Figure 2.9a). It might be useful to review that discussion now, using an example to introduce many of the complexities which make social organizations necessary for the fulfillment of personal needs in advanced societies.

A. AN IDEAL FLOW OF KNOWLEDGE

Let us consider once more the imaginary case of the self-sufficient man with unlimited internal resources (in terms of capabilities, materials, energy, and time), and let us say that he faces this problem: in his observa- tions in his community he has noticed others who, after a period of illness, were paralyzed, and he feels that this sickness, which he calls "polio", is undesirable. He wants to prevent himself from falling victim to this disease. He studies other patients and concludes that the disease is caused by a virus. He applies this finding to make a vaccine which should immunize him against the virus. He administers the vaccine to himself and thus achieves the goal of reducing the probabilities of his being the next victim of the disease. If this process of diffusion and utilization of knowledge could take place within one individual it might look like Figure 2.13.

[Insert Figure 2.13 here]

We should note that in each step the nature of knowledge is altered to trigger successive activities. A series of abstractions, recalls from memory, and recombinations of memories take place. The individual learns that the cause of polio is a living organism. Abstracting this idea further, he categorizes this organism as a virus. This abstraction activates his memory to supply him with his past experiences with viral-diseases. He remembers that immunization against such diseases is possible. These two abstracted ideas (viral nature of the disease, and immunization possibilities) are then combined to lead the individual to undertake activities to make a vaccine against polio.

In this idealized case, the flow of knowledge was unimpeded by any sort of barrier: the needs were immediately felt; research was immediately undertaken; results of findings were immediately translated into applicable

---
*As when Dave seeks out new material for his course because he senses that his students are bored.

FIGURE 2.13   <u>A Knowledge Utilization Sequence Inside the Self Sufficient</u>
                <u>Man: A Hypothetical Case</u>

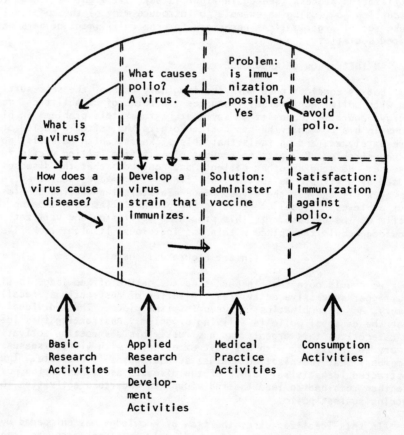

products; and the end result was immediately administered to the system. There were no time-lags, no errors, and no limits on the resources. Messages flowed smoothly and rapidly from one sector to the next. They were always the <u>right</u> messages, and they were always transmitted to the <u>right</u> sector at the <u>right</u> time.

We know, of course, that this "self sufficient" man does not exist in reality, because no one man contains within himself *the capacity to mobilize and coordinate massive, complex, and diverse resources and capabilities.* The existence of these limitations within the self in real life leads the individual to *seek the assistance of others.*

In the previous section we explored some of the severe barrier problems that confront us when we try to match up just two individuals as "resource person" and "user", but in so doing we may have made the problem sound much worse than it is. Fortunately, interpersonal contacts in the real world are regulated and stabilized by long-standing traditions, beliefs, and established social arrangements which we call "institutions".* It is only through such institutions or institutional arrangements that functioning <u>social</u> systems involving two or more individual members can come into being. Therefore, let us now consider an example at the level of the social system.

B. AN EXAMPLE OF AN OPERATIONAL KNOWLEDGE UTILIZATION SOCIAL SYSTEM

A patient, Mr. Jones, goes to a medical clinic and asks for immunization against polio; consequently, the vaccine is administered to him and he obtains the desired polio immunity. This sounds like a very simple process. As shown in Figure 2.14 it consists of an input message to the clinic (request to be vaccinated) and an output message from the clinic (being vaccinated).

FIGURE 2.14   A Knowledge Utilization System: Overview

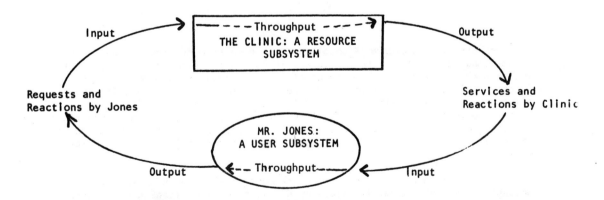

---

*This word has two prominent meanings, one denoting "formal social grouping", "organization", "society", etc., and the other denoting "law", "custom", "folkway", or "formalized norm". These two meanings are not entirely divergent: they have the common thread or theme of *"formal"* or *"formalization"*, whether referring to social groups or social norms. In fact, *"institutions"*, the group kind, are created and held together by *"institutions"*, the norm kind.

Closer inspection reveals an internal social organization within the clinic, a network of individuals who coordinate their separate behaviors to bring about the "output". The chain of activities and events that transpire within the clinic to produce the output could be designated as the "throughput" of this social system.

Let us consider what the throughput of this social system (which we have labelled "the resource subsystem") might look like. A simplified version of this hypothetical clinic might include three roles: an intake clerk, a doctor-director, and a nurse. The clerk receives and records Mr. Jones' request and transmits it to the doctor for a decision. The doctor, in turn, makes a diagnosis of the patient and chooses what action should be taken, recording this choice as a "prescription", which he passes on to the nurse. The nurse fills the prescription by administering the appropriate vaccine and discharging Mr. Jones.

FIGURE 2.15   The Resource Subsystem Component: The Social Organization
                                    of the Clinic

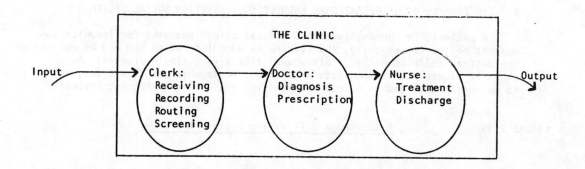

The picture becomes more complicated when we examine some of the assumptions which underly it. Figure 2.16 spells out some of the details of the throughput process, each element of which is subject to error or malfunction. First, it is assumed that the input, Mr. Jones' request for immunization, is received "properly". That is to say, if Mr. Jones' message were to go to the janitor of the clinic, it is very likely that no appropriate response to the message would result. It is important for Mr. Jones to go to the clerk, who functions as the "proper" receiver for that kind of information message.

As a second necessary step the clerk must be able to understand the message correctly; the words spoken by Mr. Jones must be meaningful to her. Without this understanding on her part, the other steps will not be taken.

Thirdly, when the clerk directs Mr. Jones to a doctor, she recalls from memory (her own knowledge, or from the files available to her) the name and office location of a doctor whose specialty is most relevant to the message. The process which takes place here can be described as a recombination of information received and information recalled from memory by the clerk.

2-22

The doctor, after receiving the information about the desire of the patient, refers to his memory to see if there is anything which can be done for the patient. He recalls that indeed there is a product called "Salk vaccine", which has been used against polio. He recombines that information with his information about Mr. Jones' expressed desires and with his own evaluation of Mr. Jones' needs, and orders a nurse to vaccinate Mr. Jones against polio using Salk vaccine.

The nurse, in turn, receives the doctor's prescription, recalls from memory the storage location of the vaccine, retrieves the vaccine, syringe, cotton, alcohol, and her own skills at filling the syringe and innoculation, and synthesizes this knowledge, equipment, and skill in the act of innoculating Mr. Jones.

With this act the clinic system has completed one throughput, but the cycle of activity which joins the clinic and Mr. Jones into one system goes on. *Mr. Jones reacts* and his reactions represent vital additional inputs to the clinic subsystem. To begin with, Mr. Jones or someone acting on his behalf (e.g., an insurance company) must reimburse the clinic for the services rendered. This sort of feedback is prerequisite for the continued existence of the clinic as a system.

FIGURE 2.16   <u>The Resource Subsystem: Details of a Hypothetical Throughput Process</u>

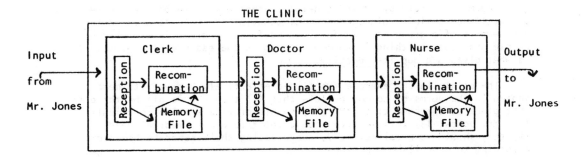

But feedback from Mr. Jones will be in other forms, too. If Mr. Jones suffers no side-effects, and is immunized against polio, this information also is (or should be) relayed to the system as feedback. In this case, the feedback is positive, and its effects are reinforcing to the behavior of the system, i.e., the system learns that "it is okay to continue to prescribe polio vaccine for people."

However, if Mr. Jones suffers side-effects from the vaccine and goes back to the clinic to inform them of these effects, then he is giving negative feedback to the system about the consequences of the system's actions. Such

negative feedback alerts the system to adjust its behavior. If the side-
effects that Mr. Jones suffers are unexpected but normal (e.g., possible
allergy), the feedback he supplies to the clinic will be interpreted by the
doctor as a demand for corrective treatment for allergy reaction. Thus,
feedback from Mr. Jones causes the clinic system to make a temporary change
in its behavior.

But if Mr. Jones' side-effects are unexpected *and abnormal*, the feedback
he supplies will lead the clinic to investigate the causes of such side-effects
and to hospitalize him immediately to prevent severe consequences. In this
situation, the feedback induces the system to make internal rearrangements in
its memory, practice and prescriptions. This type of negative feedback permits
the system literally to learn just as the individual human being learns from
a knowledge of the effects of his own behavior.*

In the discussion of this example we hope that we have already made
some points clear: first, that through a division of labor the organization
can do for the individual what he could not possibly do for himself,** and
second, that an organization can be a true system which, like the individual
person, can learn and adapt to change. Also introduced with the example,
but less obvious from the discussion so far, are four concepts that will be
very important throughout most of the chapters which follow. These concepts
are: norm, role, communication system, and structure. Each of these concepts
is introduced briefly below and will be considered in more detail in Chapter
Six.

C. NORMS

"Norm" is a very broad and general concept which can be used to describe
any attitude, belief, value, or mode of behavior which is held in common by
the members of a group.*** In fact, in so far as a group is a number of
people who have something in common, a norm is the essence of a group. It
is what gives a group its identity.

The clinic in the example functioned effectively because its members
shared in the norms or common beliefs that (1) they should all be there in
that place at the same time; (2) they should provide service to clients
like Mr. Jones; (3) this service should cater to Jones' medical needs; and
(4) they should work collectively, coordinating their separate behaviors
according to established routines.

---

*In describing this sort of organizational learning process, Karl Deutsch (#0903)
uses the term "self-steering" mechanism. Deutsch thus applies Wiener's theory
of cybernetics to the study of organizations. In this discussion we have borrowed
Deutsch's notion and have applied it to knowledge utilization systems.

**Kuhn (#6434), for example, defines "organization" as "any relation of persons
for joint production". Kuhn makes an assumption which we share that the basic
raison d'etre of organizations is their capacity to provide "goods" which the
individual alone cannot provide for himself.

***This definition conforms to common usage among social scientists, e.g., Kolb:
"A standard shared by the members of a social group to which the members are
expected to conform, and conformity to which is enforced by positive and negative
sanctions." (Gould and Kolb, #7038).

All these norms were clearly facilitative as far as solving Mr. Jones' particular problem was concerned, but norms are not always facilitators. They may also function to a large extent as barriers which restrict behavior and allow only a very limited range of messages to pass into the system. If, for example, Mr. Jones had come with a real need for *psychiatric* help, as distinct from medical help, the clinic might have rejected him. Moreover, if he had come in the middle of the night when the clinic was closed he would also have been rejected, in effect. In fact, most norms typically act as barriers restraining or inhibiting outside messages from intruding on a group or on a social system. They form the same type of protective shield around a group that, as was noted earlier, surrounds the individual (see again Figure 2.12). The personal identity of an individual and his identity with the groups to which he belongs are inseparable. Attitudes, values, thought patterns, and even language, itself, are examples of social norms which bind together some people and set them apart from others. They make it easier for communication to take place within a system, and, by the same token, they make it less easy for communication to take place between systems.

D.   ROLES

The rationalization and separation of functions that takes place in a knowledge utilization social system is generally accompanied by a designation and separation of roles. That is, functions, as they become clearly defined, are assigned to separate individuals. Parsons and Shils (#7039), for example, define social systems largely in terms of roles:

> "A social system is a system of the actions of
> individuals, the principal units of which are
> roles and constellations of roles. It is a
> system of differentiated actions, organized into
> a system of differentiated roles".

Roles are, in fact, complex norms representing as they do the normalization and standardization of functions.* They are maintained by shared expectations about the background, training, and characteristics of the role holder, and the manner in which the role is to be acted.

In the example of the clinic, at least four types of roles were exhibited: the "clerk", the "doctor", the "nurse", and the "patient" (Mr. Jones). The patient has to be included as one of the roles in this system even though it is a temporary role, being continuously vacated and refilled.** Mr. Jones is a necessary part of the system because he helps the system to complete its cycle of functioning. Any service-oriented system has this sort of open-role feature.

In studying knowledge dissemination and utilization systems, only certain kinds of roles are going to be of central concern; specifically those roles related to the production, processing, and consumption of new knowledge. We have already noted the consumer role in Mr. Robbins (our teacher), and Mr. Jones (our patient). It is synonymous with such role designations as

---

*For detailed analyses of the role concept as such, see Gross, et al. (#5169) and Kahn, et al. (#3072). Both of these sources combine extensive and advanced theoretical analysis of the concept with supporting empirical research evidence.

**Actually, of course, all roles in a social system are refilled periodically as role holders leave the system, die, or change roles.

"client", "user", "adopter", and "receiver". Sometimes the expression "ultimate consumer" will be used to designate those persons in a complex utilization system who will be the eventual beneficiaries of the disseminated knowledge even though they are not the focus of our immediate concern. Thus, for example, in a program of continuing education for teachers, the teacher is the "user", but the teacher's *students* are the "ultimate consumers".

Heretofore, we have not discriminated among any of the potential *helping and problem solving roles;* collectively they have been identified as the "resource person", but henceforth we will want to make some more detailed distinctions. Three major categories of resource persons will be used throughout this review: *"practitioner", "applied researcher-developer",* and *"basic researcher".*

The term "practitioner" will be used to designate someone who gives direct service to the consumer as a major part of his role. The doctor and the nurse in the example of the clinic fit in this category, as do lawyers, plumbers, teachers, social workers, and a host of others. Practitioners will be defined here as people who apply expert knowledge in the course of their service function. In general, however, practitioners do not create knowledge* and they consume knowledge only for the purpose of processing it so that others can subsequently consume it (i.e., so that clients can be "helped" or "served").

For knowledge creators or generators we have reserved two additional role designations: the *applied researcher-developer* and the *basic researcher.* The former generates knowledge explicitly for use by the practitioner or the consumer. The latter generates knowledge without concern for its possible application. In Figure 2.16 we indicated several sets of specialized activities (functions or processes) that the imaginary self-sufficient man performed in sequence to solve his problems. In advanced societies, however, these are divided up among a number of different individuals who develop special identities around separate functions. Hence, the functions are transformed into roles, and the interconnected network of these roles forms a problem-solving social system.**

---

*It is recognized, however, that practitioners can be extremely creative and are the source of much of our present-day expert knowledge. When practitioners are in the position of being "knowledge creators", "innovators", "inventors", etc., it is sometimes more convenient to consider them as being within the role designation of "applied research and development", which will be discussed subsequently.

**As specialization further increases, these functions are further subdivided and the "roles" become social systems. Hence, the expression "basic research" may designate (a) one set among a number of activities which could be performed by an individual person (as in Figure 2.13); (b) the role or primary occupational identification of a person (as in "basic researcher"); or (c) an organization or social system which performs the set of activities (as in "basic research laboratory"). These three levels specify to some degree three successive stages in the development of a complex social system.

In large part, this report has been organized around an ideal model which posits four interrelated roles: "basic researcher", "applied researcher-developer", "practitioner", and "consumer". (See again Figure 1.2). Sometimes we will refer to these four entities as "roles" and sometimes as "functions". In either case they designate sets of specialized activities performed by individuals or groups of varying sizes and structures.

The ideal model of four distinct roles in the D&U process and in the knowledge flow chain is defensible on at least three grounds, one logical, one practical, and one empirical. First, *logically*, we feel that these four roles delineate a series of activities which form a good paradigm for the total problem arousal-knowledge utilization-problem solving sequence. Second, practically and pragmatically, it is *convenient* to group the great range of possible behaviors relating to a complex process under four general headings. Finally, we think it can be argued that these four designations have some equivalence with the *actual shape* of social organization. That is, people do tend to group themselves around these four sets of activities in their daily lives, and the primary organizational structures within our society reflect this four-part division. For example, basic research tends to be an activity carried on exclusively within university settings, whereas practitioners are grouped into practice organizations such as hospitals, schools, and businesses. Less clear are the organizational identities of applied researchers-developers and of consumers. Nevertheless, clearly identifiable social institutions are emerging which represent these roles also. For example, consumer organizations, unions, "disease" societies, student associations and even political parties are the institutional forms which represent various consumer interests. Applied research and development only began to take insitutional form after World War II, but today we can point to various "research and development" laboratories, professional schools, and research corporations which represent the trend toward a clearer organizational identity for applied research and development, also.*

Finally something must be said for a type of role which is of very special concern in this report, namely the *role of "knowledge linker"*. As basic research, applied research and development (R&D), practice and consumer roles and subsystems become more and more firmly established in institutional molds, there appears to be a greater and greater need for specialized roles which link these systems to one another. In Chapter Seven we will review in detail the various alternatives for such linking roles.

E.   COMMUNICATION AS A SOCIAL SYSTEM

Ennis (#0897) argues cogently that any communication activity, including mass communication, should be viewed as a social system which is differentiated into the roles of "producers (creators), distributors, critics, and audience" (p. 126), each of which can be further subdivided and differentiated in various ways.

---

*In Chapter Eight we provide some background on the history of the R&D concept.

This type of analysis is dependent on a fairly loose definition of the "social system" concept in which literally anyone who attends to a message becomes a part of the message-sender's system. The degree of interaction among audience members is one of the critical variables which must be considered in making such a determination. Other factors which Ennis considers to be important systemic variables include (1) the variety and degree of normative control exerted on the audience by the media, (2) the extent to which shared expressive symbols provide cohesion for the audience, (3) the degree to which the audience can be mobilized by producers and distributors, and (4) the extent to which the producer can be influenced by the audience.

It is becoming increasingly popular to make analyses of information flow as a system, but two such analyses are particularly worth noting. Orr, et al. (#5270) try to show how the various individuals, groups, and media concerned with biomedical information act together as a system. A roughly similar analysis has been made by the Far West Laboratory for Educational Research and Development (#6613) pertaining to educational R&D information. System anslyses such as these are important because they provide ideal models or conceptual frameworks against which the current operational reality can be tested. Orr, et al. (#5270) note five ways in which such system models can be useful:

1. To identify critical operations and activities where limited capacity may disrupt the functioning of whole components or of the entire system;

2. To specify the type of processor required for different services;

3. To determine where innovations may be advantageous and to predict their effects on other parts of the system;

4. To assess mechanisms for coordinating component operations and activities;

5. To provide a holistic perspective for examining the problems of (biomedical) communication.

F. ORGANIZATIONAL STRUCTURES

As a social system develops stable routines and forms for regulating its functioning, it begins to deserve the designation *"organization"*. In this hardening or solidifying process certain structural features of social systems begin to come into prominence. These structures are standardized and routinized patterns of relationships among roles; they may be viewed as separate but overlapping subsystems which perform important functions for the organization as a whole. Since these structures profoundly affect the flow of knowledge into, through, and out of organizations they will be considered in some detail in Chapter Six.

The one structure that concerns us most in this review is what will be designated as the *"knowledge flow structure"*. This is the sequence of organizational roles and mechanisms through which knowledge is processed in an organization from input to output. This was the structure that was described in the example of the clinic (Figure 2.16) and this will be the structure that will usually be under consideration whenever we are discussing organizations in this review.

To understand how the knowledge flow structure works we must take note
of certain other structures within the organization which complement or
support the flow of knowledge. Havelock and Benne have suggested the analogy
between knowledge flow and the nervous system in the human body:

> "But the flow structure, like the nervous system,
> does not and cannot exist by itself. The nervous
> system is supported, supplied, built and rebuilt,
> protected, and to some extent controlled by other
> organs and subsystems within the total body system.
> In the same way, the flow structure of knowledge
> utilization is supported and controlled by many
> groups and individuals in the greater society who
> are not primarily or necessarily information
> carriers. Such groups and individuals, and the
> subsystems of which they are a part, we have
> designated collectively as the "administrative"
> structure of utilization. We have isolated five
> aspects--although there are probably more--of
> this administrative backup to utilization. These
> are (1) education, (2) financial support, (3) legal
> or administrative control, (4) protection, and
> (5) growth or change maintenance."

(Havelock and Benne in Watson, #6194, p. 51)

Havelock and Benne's five administrative support substructures find
parallel in Katz and Kahn's (#6223) delineation of six types of structure
which act as interrelated functional subsystems within the complex organization:

> "As organizations develop the various functions of
> carrying on the work of the system, insuring
> maintenance of the structure, obtaining environmental
> support, adapting to environmental change, and of
> coordinating and controlling activities, they become
> differentiated into appropriate subsystems. Thus the
> (1) technical or productive subsystem grows around
> the major type of work that gets done. The (2)
> maintenance subsystem insures the survival of
> organizational forms through the socialization of
> new members and the use of penalties and rewards in
> rule enforcement. The supportive functions of
> (3) procurement and disposal are directed at trans-
> actions with agencies in the external environment.
> The most critical supportive task of relating to
> the larger society and of legitimizing the part
> played by the organization is carried by the
> (4) institutional subsystem. The anticipation of
> changing forces which may affect the organization
> is carried on by an (5) adaptive subsystem with its
> research and planning activities. Finally cutting
> across all subsystems is the (6) managerial structure
> which adjudicates conflicts within the organization
> and coordinates the activities of the subsystems both
> in relation to one another and to the external world."

(p. 456)

There is direct correspondence between several of the proposed structures
in these two models. From the perspective of D&U, the central and crucial
task of an organization is to ensure the flow of knowledge; therefore the
"knowledge flow system" as used here may be considered to be roughly
analogous to Katz and Kahn's "technical or productive subsystem". In each
case the other subsystems operate to support, control and maintain the
major function of the organizational system, and it is not surprising to
find parallel functions for these subsystems as described in the two models.
For example, Katz and Kahn's "maintenance" is similar in meaning to "education
structure" as used by Havelock and Benne, and "managerial structure" is
equivalent to "legal and administrative control". Finally, there is a direct
correspondence between the concept of "growth or change maintenance structure"
and "adaptive subsystem". In Chapter Six these and other paradigms for
categorizing organizational structure will be discussed and compared.

G.   SOME DISTORTIONS IN THE SOCIAL SYSTEM LEVEL OF ANALYSIS

The social system level of analysis is especially helpful in illuminating
the social nature and the interdependent nature of individual human activities.
It suggests how individuals can work together and coordinate their separate
behaviors as part of a larger functioning organism which has sensing and self-
steering features analogous to those of the individual person. But inherent
in this type of analysis are certain distortions which should be enumerated
before we leave this topic.

   1.   Real Social Systems are Open Systems

        The system approach may give the impression that social
   systems are self-contained, but just as individuals are dependent
   on a larger environment for resources, so too are most social
   systems.   Hence, they are always open systems, thoroughly
   dependent upon and interrelated with a multiple-system environment.

   2.   Social Systems May Not See Themselves as Systems

        The human being, like any living organism, is a true system
   by nature. The brain, the complex neutral connections, the
   internal organs, muscles, skeleton, and skin, form one integrated
   unit, evolved and refined over millions of years. The same cannot
   be said in any respect of organizations. They seem to be analogous
   to individual human systems in some respects but "the organic
   unity of social organizations" is debatable.

        Any social scientist may posit the existence of systems,
   but to a great extent social systems exist only in the minds
   of their members. Hence, there may not be very much validity in
   identifying a system of "medical researchers" or "highway safety
   practitioners" when there is no group of individuals who are able
   or willing to identify themselves by that label. Shared identity
   and self-consciousness of identity may not be the only criteria
   for the existence of a system but they are surely an important ones

In this respect the assertion made by Ennis (#0897) that
communication is a "social system" and the assertion made by
ourselves that any act of dissemination-utilization is a
"social system" may be open to some criticism.*

3.   Systems Serve People as Well as Systems

      Social organizations come into existence and survive for
many reasons and to achieve many purposes but chief among them
should be the fulfillment of <u>individual</u> human needs. It is
difficult to justify the existence of social systems either
as ends in themselves or means to their own maintenance and
aggradizement, yet our depiction of them as "self-steering"
mechanisms seems to convey that impression.

4.   Social Systems are Multi-Purpose

      Related to the above point is another fact about most social
systems which is obscured by a simplistic "system" treatment:
they are almost always multi-functional. Different members of a
system derive different types of benefits and any individual
member is likely to derive a variety of benefits. It is not
possible, for example, to say that the Jones Tire Company produces
only tires. In fact, it produces dividends for stockholders,
wages for employees, a preoccupying pastime for its employers,
profits for its dealers, and on and on. It is impossible to say
that it exists solely for the benefit of one particular group or
that it serves only one particular function.

      This multi-purpose aspect of all social systems is especially
confusing for those of us who are attempting to talk about only
one function, as we are in the case of "dissemination and utilization
of knowledge". Most systems do not exist primarily as D&U systems,
although in this report they will be considered almost exclusively
in terms of this one function.

5.   A Social System-Level Analysis Does Not Adequately Depict
      Inter-System Phenomena

      The formal organization is usually only a part of a greater
picture as far as D&U is concerned. As we saw in the case of the
vaccine (see again Figure 2.14), the clinic, although intricately
complex within itself, was only part of a larger system which
included Mr. Jones. The clinic was dependent for its very survival
upon a continuous stream of inputs which included financial resources, products, and trained personnel as well as information.

---

*Where important societal functions are not filled by self-conscious systems, the
social change agent or leader may set for himself the task of bringing such a
system into being. Nader and Haddon have really achieved this for the field of
highway safety. Nader created a national awareness of a need for a new and
realistic look at the problem while Haddon insisted that the various power
groups involve themselves in a common systemic effort.

The maintenance of this stream of inputs requires the clinic to build and maintain relationships with other organizations such as equipment suppliers, medical and nursing schools, pharmacies and drug houses, insurance companies, hospitals, other clinics, and government agencies. Because these inter-system relations are so vital to the life of the clinic as an organizational entity, the internal structure of the clinic will be largely conditioned by their existence. Hence, it is nearly impossible to understand organizations apart from inter-organizational relationships. This fact suggests an additional danger: if we focus myopically on the organization as the "system", we may underrate the importance of inter-system relationships. With this point in mind let us now turn our attention to the inter-system level of analysis of D&U processes.

V. THE INTER-SYSTEM LEVEL

A major premise of this report is that dissemination and utilization cannot be understood unless we look at society as a whole and include in our analysis all the major systems that are concerned with the generation, production, distribution and consumption of knowledge. This premise necessarily carries us beyond the level of analysis usually encompassed in the study of organizations to a consideration of the relationships among numerous organizations of varying size and complexity.

In the last section we presented four generic roles or functions into which the knowledge flow system could be subdivided, *consumer, practitioner, applied researcher-developer, and basic researcher,* and we suggested that each of these four role types was likely to be represented in the society at large by separate organizational and institutional forms. The implication of this assumption is that knowledge utilization is an inter-organizational and inter-systemic problem. Hence, we need to include another level of analysis beyond that which is usually designated "systemic". Chin has discussed the importance of this level of analysis for those who are concerned with change:

> "In brief, the intersystem model leads us to examine
> the interdependent dynamics of interaction both within
> and between the units. We object to the premature and
> unnecessary assumption that the units always form a
> single system. We can be misled into an utopian
> analysis of conflict, change-agent relations to client,
> and family relations if we neglect system differences.
> But an intersystem model provides a tool for diagnosis
> that retains the virtues of system analysis, adds the
> advantage of clarity, and furthers our diagnosis of the
> influence of various connectives, conjunctive and
> disjunctive, on the two systems. For change-agents,
> the essence of collaborative planning is contained in
> an intersystem model."

(Chin in Bennis, et al. #1344, p. 208)

Even at the inter-system level, however, the same basic concepts of "message", "barrier", and "system" apply. Each of these terms therefore deserves some further elucidation in this new context.

A.   INTER-SYSTEM BARRIERS

Our previous discussion of organizations focused on the development of structural forms which we discussed primarily in terms of *internal* relations, e.g., the routinization of roles, functions, and coordinated activities. But another significant aspect of the process of organization formation is the development of a set of internally shared norms, attitudes, and values which could be called the "culture" of the organization. These shared norms create a distinct identity for the organization within the larger multi-organizational, multi-system, multi-person environment, and they clearly delineate "inside" from "outside" and "us" from "not us".

The nation-state with the accompanying phenomena of nationalism is perhaps the most illustrative example of these group barrier phenomena. It includes a shared feeling of pride in belonging, a common belief that the system stands for something special and important in the world in terms of "form of government", power, prosperity, expertise, righteousness, invulnerability, and defense of certain values such as freedom, equality, humanity and community. Although the most dramatic illustrations of organizational identity occur in nationalism, we find similar phenomena in organizations of all types and sizes, including universities, professions, and research, production and service organizations.

The norms, attitudes and values which preserve organizational unity and identity are especially significant for the D&U process because they tend to restrict, regulate, and block the free flow of knowledge *between* systems, i.e., they represent barriers both to the receiving and the sending of messages.

Inter-system barriers do not differ fundamentally from the interpersonal or intrapersonal barriers discussed earlier. However, at the inter-system level certain types of barriers take on special significance. In particular, *values* are assumed by most members of a system to be features which radically distinguish "us" from "not us". Assumptions about values in many cases dictate what is defined as "knowledge" or "relevant knowledge" or "legitimate knowledge" either to be taken into the system or to be disseminated from it. Thus, for example, all information coming from the Soviet Union may be interpreted by the United States as "lies", "deceit", "propoganda", or pseudo-knowledge not worth paying any attention to, whereas the information which we disseminate may be seen as always "true", "good", solid, legitimate, and genuine information. Any social system can take this position with respect to inter-system knowledge transfer if it believes that the other system does not share its basic values.

The very same phenomenon is often observed in the relations between research and practice organizations and professions. Researchers can dismiss practice information on the basis that practitioners do not understand what it means to collect valid and reliable information. The practitioner like-wise may reject research sources because "they don't care about practical problems and will never provide information that is truly relevant to people's needs." Real or imagined, these value differences probably constitute the major barrier to inter-system knowledge linkage.

There are, of course, many other types of inter-system barriers which will be discussed in detail in Chapter Six. We have already noted some of these in the case of the relations between Mr. Jones and the clinic. We saw, for example, how the norm of a fee-for-service, a very typical organizational barrier, could prevent Mr. Jones from receiving the type of message he wanted. Yet if Mr. Jones were actually a <u>member</u> of the clinic he might well receive the same service for no charge. Perhaps the medical profession's tradition of "professional courtesy" (the agreement among physicians not to charge for service to colleagues) best exemplifies the barrier quality of most types of financial charges.

In-group professional *languages* serve with equal effectiveness to restrict information flow from research to practice. The technical and pseudo-technical language of the research journal either scares off the practitioner or forces him to work extra hard to derive each morsel of meaning. Hence even in the academic world where knowledge is "free" by tradition, it may be very expensive in time and effort for non-members of the academic fraternity. We can imagine the plight of our poor Dave Robbins if he had to sort through recent issues of physics journals to derive "new knowledge" for his high school class.

B.   INTER-SYSTEM MESSAGES

Systems are able to communicate with one another in a variety of ways. Any output of one system is a potential input for another. Sometimes outputs are intended to be inputs to others; sometimes they are not. Hence, a major distinction must be made between inter-system messages which are "official" and those that are "unofficial".

1.   Official Messages Between Systems

The type of information which systems intentionally produce for outside consumption is likely to be highly screened, processed, and packaged in such a way that the producing system itself will profit by it. Hence, General Motors produces motor vehicles, advertising, and self-serving press-releases. It does not give out details on how cars are made, what defects they are likely to have, what difficulties are being encountered in production or management or planning.

In like manner a hospital will not provide its patients or the public with statistics on the number of false diagnoses, unnecessary operations, and medical miscalculations that take place daily within its walls, nor does it typically disclose for public consumption the details of its emergency room and operating room procedures or its differential policies with regard to intensive care.

While such official messages obviously serve to advance the selfish interests of the sending system, they cannot be dismissed merely as propoganda. The fact should not be forgotten that most of General Motors'official messages (e.g., the vehicles which they manufacture and distribute) are useful to people and systems outside General Motors. Likewise most medical services do benefit most patients directly.

2.   Unofficial Messages Between Systems

A large quantity of information travels from one system to another without following official or intended channels; this informal information may be vitally important not only because it is directly useful but also because it is a key factor in the establishment of true linkage between systems. Between governments or large competing corporations such information is transferred through the secret but intentional efforts of spies. It may also be collected through polling or monitoring internal media; and to some degree this is exactly what the practitioner is doing when he reads a research journal.

However, the most ubiquitous unofficial message transmission medium is *informal personal contact*. It is, of course, impossible to transmit either products or complex technical data or prototypes in this manner, but important subsidiary information on such things as defects, errors, and misleading implications or emphases in official messages can be effectively transmitted by word of mouth if the opportunities for such contacts are provided.

C.   INTER-SYSTEM LINKAGE: How is it achieved?

Much of this report will be devoted to inter-system linkage problems and the mechanisms for overcoming them and creating effective linkage. A brief preview of the most common of these mechanisms may be helpful.

1.   Interpersonal Contact

The previous discussion of "unofficial messages" suggests a major avenue to effective linkage, simple human contact. When two people get together at frequent intervals and/or for long periods, communication is inevitable. Organizational secrets are leaked and all sorts of "inside" and confidential information is transmitted. Contrary to what an organization may officialy believe, such leakage is often very functional for the following reason: true information exchange breeds trust which in turn leads to firmer interpersonal relationships; these in turn lead to a firmer institutional linkage, and finally to a more meaningful and effective exchange of official messages between the systems involved.

2.   Specialized Inter-System Media

Sometimes members of one system will make a special effort to communicate outside their own system to others through a publication, a television program or series, or some other medium. For example, Psychology Today is a popular magazine emanating from the psychological profession but aimed at a wider audience. The magazine, Transaction, serves the same purpose for the social sciences. Such specialized media, when they are properly conceived and well-executed, have the advantage of providing an inter-system channel of communication without challenging or disturbing the internal integrity of the sending system.

3.   Inter-System Linking Roles and Linking Organizations

The medium of communication between two systems may be *human* as well as printed or electronic. In Chapter Seven we will review a number of specialized linking roles.   These are carried out by

the consultants, conveyors and special agents who act as facilitators
and transmitters of messages between systems.

4.   Specialized Receiving and Sending Roles within Systems

A variant on the above pattern is the linking role within the
sending or the receiving system. We saw that the clinic to which
Mr. Jones went included a specialized *receiver* role, the clerk, and
a specialized *sender* role, the nurse. Most complex organizations have
such roles and the larger organizations will have elaborated the role
into complex receiving and sending subsystems (e.g., the "sales"
department, the "public relations" department, etc.). Earlier in
this chapter we discussed the "change structure" within an organization, the "adaptive subsystem" which has the task of reaching out
for new innovations and new markets; in effect, of receiving and
processing inputs from a variety of other social systems. This was one
example of a specialized receiving subsystem as a solution to the inter-
system linkage problem.

5.   Overlapping Organizational and Associational Groupings

Fortunately from a linkage point of view, organizations are not
discrete entities with exclusive memberships. Most people belong to
a large number of organizations simultaneously, and these multiple
memberships create a complex social fabric composed of overlapping
organizations and associations. The university research psychologist
may belong to the psychological association which also includes
psychologist-practitioners in mental health, education, and industry.
The educational psychologist may also belong to a school system in
which he shares colleague status with teachers and administrators.
Teachers and administrators may have meaningful contact with the general
public through PTA's and through direct exchange with students in the
classroom. Hence, overlapping organizational arrangements can provide
opportunities for continuous person-to-person contacts that stretch
from basic research to the consumer.

6.   Linkage through the Building of Super-Systems

Overlapping memberships, special roles and special media help
bridge the gap between systems but they do so in hit-or-miss fashion.
The key to truly dependable and successful inter-system linkages is
the creation of genuine and permanent exchange relationships which are
mutually rewarding and reinforcing.

Such inter-system linkages may be bilateral or multilateral.
Typically, numerous systems relate to one another in a knowledge
exchange super-system which is functionally subdivided and at least
loosely coordinated for the common good.

D.   THE INTER-SYSTEM SYSTEM

Complex inter-system linkage will probably only be effective when the
various inter-connecting systems work together as parts of a single self-

regulating unit. Such a super-system would presumably develop and become
structured in a way analogous to organizations.*

Whether separate social organizations typically relate to one another
in a truly systemic fashion may be an open question, however. When we
talk vaguely about how our society "works", it is comforting to think that
it is a "system", a giant organic unity in which the necessary messages
(e.g., goods, services, and information) flow smoothly from organization to
organization and person to person so that those who are in need always are
satisfied, the sick always cared for, the hungry always fed, and the naked
always clothed. To sustain this image of a society which "works" we may
suppress our awareness of obvious symptoms of malfunction such as highway
death statistics or infant mortality rates or we may dismiss them as
"accidents".

This image of society as a benevolent "natural" system is reinforced
by a popular belief in laissez-faire capitalism. In its barest essentials
this theory tells us that independent business organizations will provide
fully for the good of all if we only leave them alone to compete economically
in a free market place. Those who continue to endorse this theory attack
the notion that a centralized super-organizational authority (e.g., government) should make an effort to regulate or control these inter-organizational
relations.

This thesis and antithesis between central control and laissez-faire
is a theme that is very relevant to any consideration of knowledge utilizat
systems. Are they natural or can they be improved by regulation and manipu
lation? In part, a report like the present one should explain what the
"natural" process is like, but in part it should also indicate what could
be changed and how it could be improved.

In order to help us understand this "natural" process and to determine
how the process could be made better, we have found it very useful to formulate an *idealized picture of a knowledge flow system*. It is by no means
certain that such a system truly exists or even could exist in ideal form,
but it is hoped that by comparing the ideal model with contemporary reality,
and perhaps by modifying the model to conform to unalterable aspects of that
reality, we will be in a better position at the end of this work to indicate
the kind of policies that should be pursued by those who have the power to
control and bring about change in the society as a whole. For this reason
we have invented the concept of the *"knowledge dissemination and utilization
macro-system"* which will be presented in Chapter Three.

VI. THE CONTENT OF MESSAGES ("WHAT?")

The reader will already have noted from the earlier definition and discussion
of "messages" that we define this concept very broadly. There is no clear line
between messages construed as "words", "information", "knowledge", "services",
and "products". We have tried to *focus* our concern on the exchange or transfer
of new information, regardless of the form it may take. However, we will not be
able to discuss the transfer of new knowledge to the exclusion of other types of

---

*Galbraith #7136 appears to be describing such a process in the evolution of the
"new industrial state".

messages; those other messages that are redundant and familiar (e.g., money) are sometimes going to be discussed because they remain an essential component of the total process. An innovation, such as a new drug, will only pass freely from developer to consumer if there is a reciprocating message of a more traditional sort.

In Chapter Eight we are going to try to sort out these various types of "old" and "new" messages and weigh the significance of each to an overall understanding of D&U. Here in this "Basic Concepts" chapter, however, we can give some indication of the range of phenomena that we are willing to consider as messages for the purpose of this review.

A.   MESSAGE TYPES

The range of message types is suggested, first of all, by our four-part division of the knowledge flow system: basic research, applied research and development, practice, and consumption. Each of these roles or subsystems generates its own peculiar type of knowledge.

1.   Basic Research Output

Basic research generates "basic" knowledge in the form of *theories*, laws, and classifications which underly the masses of empirical phenomena of our world. But the basic researchers do more than provide these general principles: they also give us the *empirical data* on which these principles are based and the *methods* by which such data are collected.

2.   Applied Research and Development Output

Applied research gives us the same types of information, *theories, data, and methods*, but in a form which is classified to correspond to broad areas of human and social need (e.g., health, welfare, education). From applied research and development we also get *prototypes* of new products and services, working models and "inventions", which the practitioner can adopt and adapt to his own special circumstances.

3.   Practitioner Output

The major message output of practitioners is in the form of products and services, knowledge which has been developed, packaged, and tested. Dave Robbins, the practitioner, delivers to his students a "physics course" which is a kind of *product*, the result of (a) basic research on physics (and on learning), (b) development work by a national group of physics and curriculum experts, (c) further development and packaging by a publisher, and (d) even further screening and adapting by Dave, himself, perhaps with the help of the science curriculum specialist in his school system, his own department head or a fellow teacher.

4.   Consumer Output

As we have construed the concept of "message", however, even the ultimate consumer produces some output which is very significant and very important for the maintenance of the whole chain. In the broadest terms, the consumer produces messages of *satisfaction* and *dissatisfaction*, pleasure and pain, designating as best he can the specific locations in his life space where these sensations are felt. The form of these messages may vary widely. The dissatisfaction and pain messages may

2-38

come as fully articulated requests for problem solutions in a given area; they may come in the form of symbolic acts, e.g., a scream or a grimace or a writhing motion to symbolize pain; fainting to symbolize severe shock or trauma; sit-ins, marches, and riots to symbolize discontent on social issues. Satisfaction and pleasure have their symbolic message forms, also, although perhaps they are fewer in number; money is one way of expressing satisfaction, although, as we point out in Chapter Eight, it does not usually have this meaning. Thanks, gifts, and various signs that things are "OK" or that we now feel relieved or feel good are all important output messages from the consumer. These messages are important because they provide return inputs to the practitioner and to the researcher. They keep these resource persons functioning by reinforcing their output and by providin guidance for their future activities. These guiding messages may be in the form of new problems or continuing problems for which solutions are needed, or they may be in the form of "feedback" on the effects of past solutions.

In providing this broad definition of the word "message" we do not wish to slight important differences that may exist between one form and another and between the knowledge conveyed in one field and that conveyed in another. Chapter Eight will concern itself with these differences: it will examine such important dimensions as "software versus hardware knowledge", "social science versus physical science" and "science-based versus non-science-based knowledge".

Different types of knowledge obviously require different types of diffusion processes and different types of adaptation and adoption activities. On the other hand, there are also some generalities that apply to D&U in all fields. To identify these generalities is a primary task of this work.

VII. THE MECHANISMS OF MESSAGE TRANSMISSION AND TRANSFORMATION ("HOW?")

Thus far in this overview of basic concepts we have devoted little attention to the specific means or mechanisms by which messages pass from one person to another and from one social system to another. In Chapter Nine we will review what is currently known in this area.

We will examine some of the more obvious questions usually associated with transmission, considering the relative merits of written versus oral media, personal versus impersonal channels, and one-way versus two-way message flow. But there are other questions here of a subtler variety with which we will try to cope. We find, for example, that the *processing* of knowledge and the *transmission* of knowledge cannot always be clearly separated; "processing" (e.g., translating, reordering, coding, checking, editing, etc.) is a type of transmission in that it involves the movement of knowledge from one state to another. We also know that choice of channel for transmission is thoroughly dependent upon the type of processing that is done both by the sender and by the receiver. The receiver does not simply receive, in a single passive act; he must also decode, reformulate, select and adapt the information that comes to him. Dave Robbins does not simply adopt a college physics text; he goes through a complex sequence of reception behaviors, he sifts out what is appropriate for his high school students and what is appropriate for his own style of teaching, and he reformulates this information so that it fits into his course plan.

McLuhan has challenged traditional thinking about the flow of knowledge and we are ready to agree with him that "the medium is the message" or at least a pretty important part of the message. Indeed the McLuhan dictum makes more sense when we view the medium as including these various processing and packaging aspects.

The question of "how" can be asked either in terms of the separate sub-strategies of knowledge development, dissemination, adaptation, utilization, etc., or in the broad terms of overall *strategy* of dissemination and utilization. A discussion of the merits of specific media and specific knowledge processing activities will only give us boards, hammer and nails. It will not show us how to build a house. Therefore, we need to consider the various ways in which these materials can be orchestrated, ordered in time and space, to bring about a complete D&U cycle. Chapter Nine will only take us part of the way along this road by suggesting some of the major orientations that could be brought to bear in making a complete strategy.

In Chapter Ten we try to bring these elements together by comparing the theories of a number of different authors, grouping them into three major "models". Then in Chapter Eleven we offer our own model as a summary and synthesis of what we have learned in this journey through the complex and diverse literature on the dissemination and utilization of knowledge.

VIII. MODELS OF DISSEMINATION-UTILIZATION

In the course of our review we have identified three distinct points of view toward D&U represented in the models, theories, and analyses of different authors. We are going to use the word "model" for each of these points of view because each designates a complete conceptual system within which all of the facts pertinent to D&U can be ordered. The three models have been labelled as follows:

A. The Problem Solver Model

B. The Research, Development and Diffusion (R,D&D) Model

C. The Social Interaction Model

In this chapter on basic concepts we have borrowed extensively from all three of these models and have blended them into one overall view. In this closing section, however, it may be helpful to consider them separately out of respect for the theorists and researchers who generated them.

A. THE PROBLEM SOLVER MODEL

To most practitioners and to those who work most closely with them, the need of the client whether stated, implied, or assumed, is only one place to start an analysis of knowledge utilization. This is a viewpoint that is very consonant with our individualistic and humanistic tradition and it finds its expression in such terms as "client-centered therapy" and "student-centered teaching". The writings of Thelen (#3692), Lippitt, et al. (#1343), Benne (#7099), and Miles and Lake (#3871) among others, appear to be modified by this basic value premise.

Even though most of these authors write as outside "change agents", they stress collaboration with the client system and diagnosis of the client system's needs as the two essential ingredients of the change process.

Successive stages in this model generally follow the psychological theory of need reduction through problem-solving similar to the one posed earlier in this chapter in discussions of the D&U process inside the individual person. The process can be depicted as a cycle composed of five stages as in Figure 2.17 beginning with "1a" and concluding with "1b". The fifth stage (application of a solution) leads to a reduction of the original need "1b" if the solution is right. If it is not right then presumably stage "1a" is reinitiated and the cycle is repeated until a solution which is truly need-reducing is discovered.

FIGURE 2.17   <u>The Need Reduction Cycle</u>

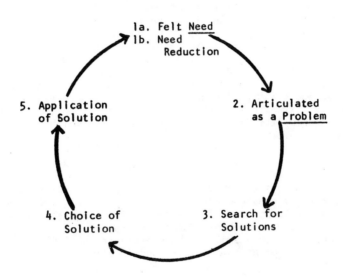

The model is a general one and could apply to a process inside a single person, or inside a group, an organization, a community, or society as a whole.* As viewed by this model, the problem solvers may also be outside specialists ("change agents", "resource persons", etc.) but they will act in a two-way reciprocal and collaborative manner if they are to be effective.

B.   THE R,D&D PROCESS MODEL

Another orientation toward D&U processes is represented by those who start from research and the products of research and delineate a path toward the consumer. This point of view could be caricatured by the statement that "if the knowledge is there, a user will be found for it".

_____
*Lippitt, et al. (#1344) discuss planned change at each of these levels.

Although consumer needs may be implicit in this approach, they do not enter the picture as prime motivators for the generation of new knowledge. Research does not begin as a set of answers to specific human problems. Rather, research starts as a set of facts and theories about the nature of the universe, knowledge which can only be made useful to men through an extensive process of *development*. In development, basic theories and data are used to generate ideas for useful products and services, and these ideas are then turned into prototypes which have to be tested and redesigned and retested before they represent anything that is truly useful to the bulk of humanity.

Once knowledge has passed through this development phase it is ready to be mass produced and diffused to all the members of society for whom it might be useful.

This model has been popular in American culture for at least a generation* and is the basis upon which much of our national investment in basic research has been rationalized. It would appear to be an article of faith in the United States that basic science is useful to man and presumably this is why it is taught in the schools. It is assumed that medical progress is based on progress in the basic biological sciences and that engineering and the marvels of technology have been made possible by great advances in the physical sciences. Usually there is only a dim understanding of how the knowledge gets transformed into something useful, but the firm belief remains that somehow it filters down. The one field which appears to exemplify the transformation process in a very clear way is that of agriculture. Agricultural research, development and dissemination in the United States seems to follow an orderly process which most clearly exemplifies the R,D&D model. There is a transformation of knowledge from basic research to applied research and development which goes on in the agriculture-related departments of the land grant colleges and universities. This R&D process is systematically linked to the Cooperative Extension Service, an elaborate mechanism which diffuses the developed knowledge to the farmer. This system, taken as a whole, thus seems to exemplify the orderly transition of knowledge from the *research* to *development* to *diffusion* and finally to *adoption* by the consumer.

Because this agricultural model appears to be so elegantly mapped out and so successful, it has been used as an exemplar of how knowledge D&U should take place in other fields, including industrial technology, medicine and education. Within the field of education, major spokesmen for this orientation have been Clark and Guba (#6003) and Brickell (#3076).

C.   THE SOCIAL INTERACTION MODEL

A third approach to D&U emphasizes the *diffusion* aspect, the measurement of the movement of messages from person to person and system to system. This approach has probably generated the richest and most extensive body of

---

*Some may want to date this from the Atom bomb development and the subsequent popularization of the belief that scientists are the generators of technological change, Price (#7133), p. 1 and Hall (#1231). More background on the origin of R&D concepts is provided in Chapter Eight.

empirical data on D&U phenomenon. It has given us the theory of the two-
step flow of knowledge and has thoroughly demonstrated the importance of
such factors as opinion leadership, personal contact, and social integration.
It is exemplified in the medical field by the work of Coleman, Katz and
Menzel (Coleman, et al. #6399; Katz, #0295; Menzel and Katz, #3404), in
agriculture by Ryan and Gross (#2621), Lionberger and Coughenour (#0766),
Rogers (#1824) and Sower, et al (#5344), to name only a few, and in education
by Mort (#1191), Carlson (#0585), and Lin, et al. (#3903), again to name only
a few.

The social interaction theorists usually do not view society as a
systemic unity in the way in which this concept has been developed in this
chapter. For example, the viewpoint put forth by Karl Deutsch (#0903) of
a cybernetic system, with each part orchestrated toward a common system
output, is usually not considered. Rather they see the society as a network
of roles and channels of communication with organizational and formal and
informal associations forming barriers and overlapping connections.

D.   SYNTHESIZING THE THREE MODELS

Although the theories of most writers on D&U and related topics seem
to fall distinctly within one or another of these three orientations, there
is no necessary contradiction among them. Indeed, in this presentation we
would like to bring them together as parts of one overall picture. We have
accepted the need-reduction cycle as a necessary starting point at least in
our thinking about D&U. Utilization as a concept does not make much sense
without first thinking about the utilizer and the state within him which
might require some new knowledge from outside. But we also recognize that
in a complex society which wants to satisfy complex needs in an effective
way, an elaborate division of labor is necessary, a division which may find
certain roles far removed from the locus of need. Basic research, we believe,
is a necessary part of the total D&U process, but we know that basic scientists
seldom, if ever, formulate and conduct their research with a consumer in
mind. Moreover, it is by no means certain that they should have anything
in mind apart from the further extension and elaboration of basic scientific
theories. Finally, we know that knowledge does not just "filter down"
and it does not get generated in neat need-reduction cycles. It has to
flow back and forth within a complex network of roles and relationships.

In the next chapter, we will try to lay out this synthesis of the three models
in graphic form when we consider the possibility of macro-systems for the
dissemination and utilization of knowledge in various fields.

CHAPTER THREE

THE MACROSYSTEM OF KNOWLEDGE FLOW

Table of Contents   Page

CHAPTER THREE

THE MACROSYSTEM OF BIOMEDICAL R&D

Paula O. Canceran

CHAPTER THREE*

THE MACROSYSTEM OF KNOWLEDGE FLOW

INTRODUCTION

Let us consider for a moment the phenomenon of a nation at war: the farmers work hard to turn out eggs and butter for the boys at the front; the consumer invests his excess savings in war bonds; the factories work around the clock to turn out guns and tanks; the universities are turned into officer training camps; the economists devote their entire energies and skills to coordinating the economy for the war effort; and all transportation facilities (trains, ships, planes) are turned over to the task of moving men and materials to the front lines. All of these efforts are planned at the national level and coordinated so that the whole society becomes one system with one over-all goal. Virtually all the professions are included in this mobilization of effort, doctors, lawyers, and all levels of scientists.** Virtually all research becomes applied and product oriented to help the war effort in some way. Psychologists turn their efforts to creating tests and training programs to screen and develop manpower for various tasks: physicists develop nuclear devices; chemists create new rocket fuels, and substances to kill plants, insects, and people. Finally the total effort succeeds (or fails), peace comes, and with a great sigh of relief on all sides, this war machine is dismantled. This gigantic system is deliberately taken apart and dismantled so that it almost seems to disappear.

What is the lesson in this for dissemination and utilization? This "war machine" example illustrates the point that a *society as a whole is a system* which can be coordinated to achieve a single goal. That potential is always there, ready to be mobilized when the citizens or their government decide that an extreme emergency exists.

However, when the dust settles and "normalcy" returns, we may be very reluctant to look at our individual selves as parts of a giant system. As students of dissemination and utilization, however, it will be very instructive to take this point of view and to examine the great range of institutions which are involved in the generation, processing, transmission, and consumption of knowledge as parts of a gigantic knowledge flow system.

We can also begin to approach the concept of the knowledge flow macrosystem through the case of the science teacher, Dave Robbins. From the previous chapter we already understand Dave as a human sub-system within a social sub-system and we know in a general way that his attempts at innovation will be conditioned by organizational memberships, barriers, and the quantity and quality of resources available to him internally or externally. But we have not yet spelled out the details of this

_____

*This chapter was drafted by Ronald G. Havelock.

**Dupree (#1265) discusses the mobilization of U.S. science in World War II, citing the "Office of Scientific Research and Development" as the agency which coordinated and controlled the national science effort. It was disbanded at the end of the war.

system in which he is embedded. Who are these "resource persons"? What are the "barriers" and the "channels" which are likely to impinge upon Dave directly or indirectly? We also need to see Dave, the individual teacher, as only one element in a much larger configuration of educational innovation. We cannot clearly understand the single teacher in the single classroom at a single point in time attempting to change the physics curriculum without considering the social context which includes (a) the same teacher over time, (b) other teacher norms toward curriculum innovation in the same school, the same district, different schools and different districts, (c) his local school system's past and present efforts at new curriculum innovation, (d) the system's history of encouragement of innovation in general, (e) the current state of development of the physics curriculum nationally, (f) the current national mood with regard to educational change, and (g) specific efforts to bring about curriculum reform through national action.

Although we may have difficulty in comprehending and synthesizing this vast array of considerations, each is important and each is a part of the equation which will predict whether or not innovation will take place in classroom X with teacher X in school X in school system X in state X at time X. In Chapter Two we provided the conceptual elements for this equation. In Chapter Three we hope to look at education and several other fields of knowledge to see if these elements can be put together sensibly to constitute a true knowledge flow system. This is the grossest level of analysis, the gross anatomy of knowledge utilization, but it is a level of analysis which seems to be very important and relevant to our understanding of the whole.

Several theorists have recently come forward to endorse this macroscopic approach. For example Etzioni makes the following comment:

> "As the input of knowledge becomes a major *guided* societal activity (about three-quarters of the expenditure on R & D in the United States is federal) and as the ratio of this input as compared to other societal inputs increases both in relative expenditure and in socio-political significance, the macrosociological study of the organization of knowledge production and consumption becomes an unavoidable part of studies of societal change and guidance." (#7076)

One author, Machlup (#7041) has gone so far as to treat knowledge as a commodity; he subjects the production and distribution of knowledge to the same sort of quantitative analysis that is undertaken for other economic variables. Machlup demonstrates the exceedingly large and growing role of knowledge production and distribution in the total national economy.

In this chapter we will make four principle points. First we will note that *the university is the primary source*, storage point, and cultural carrier of expert knowledge in all fields, basic and applied.* We will also note, however, that the university does not take any active responsibility for diffusing this knowledge or insuring that it gets used. Our second point, then, will be to suggest that this *responsibility seems to reside in the three sectors of the practice world, the professions, the product organizations,* and *the service organizations.* A third point will be that the *consumer's power to influence his would-be "helpers" in the practice world and the research world is very limited;* this consumer powerlessness is to the detriment of the system as a whole. However, there are some signs that the picture is changing for the better. Finally, as a fourth point, we

---

*This point may be debatable. The university is, of course, not the sole source and storage point of expert knowledge and in some fields it may not even be primary. Perhaps the stress should be placed on the word "carrier" because nearly all training and passing on of expert knowledge does take place in university settings. Universities and their professional schools have largely replaced the apprenticeship system which in former times had this carrier function.

will indicate that there are some *integrating forces*, some organizations and individuals who are working for a greater coordination of the total process from the university laboratory to the classroom and the hospital bed.

Figure 1.2 delineated four different roles or functional subdivisions within the knowledge D & U system. These were "basic research", "applied research and development",* "practice" and "consumption". (Pages 2-25 to 2-27) In Chapter Two these four categories were discussed briefly but without any specific context. In this Chapter these four role concepts will be featured as the underlying pattern of all knowledge D & U macrosystems. Ideally, effective knowledge utilization takes place when sub-systems representing the consumer, the practitioner, the developer, and the researcher are interrelated and coordinated in one system.

Figures 3.1 and 3.2 represent alternative ways of grouping these four subsystems to indicate the relations that exist among them ideally. Figure 3.1 is drawn to indicate complete mutual access among all four sub-systems without distinction. It is a status-free model, indicating no priorities, no prestige or precedence distinctions; hence, it may be the least controversial method for showing interrelationships. However, in this report we will rely much more on the type of representation suggested by Figure 3.2 because the latter is more suggestive both of a sequence of knowledge flow which is most efficient and effective and of one that corresponds more closely to empirical reality.

[Insert Figures 3.1 and 3.2 here]

Figure 3.2 suggests that the research community is connected to the consumer through a *"mainstream"* of channels flowing through development and practice subsystems. It also suggests that *subsidiary channels* do exist connecting all subsystems to one another. However, neither of the above diagrams suggests anything about the *institutional framework* within which these four sub-systems are cast. It is this institutional framework which largely determines what actually happens to knowledge, and for this reason it will be the major preoccupation of Chapter Three. The major components of this framework are (1) the university, (2) the scientific professions, (3) the practice professions, (4) the product organizations, (5) the service organizations, (6) the consumer organizations, (7) the government, and (8) the media. Figure 3.3 suggests a "typical" framework for viewing the interrelations among these institutions regardless of the specific fields under consideration.

Studying the elements of Figure 3.3 from right to left, we start with the

[Insert Figure 3.3 here]

largest and most diffuse sub-system, which represents the *consumer*. Even though the consumer (variously specified as the "client", the "patient", the "student", etc.) is the ultimate receiver and beneficiary of the macrosystem of D&U, his "sub-system" is likely to be the least organized and the least influential among the various components. He does, of course, influence other sub-systems through his purchasing and requesting behavior and, in a democracy, through his elected representatives in a government. Primary imputs <u>to</u> the consumer are in the form of direct services from professionals (e.g., physicians) or service organizations (e.g. hospitals) or in the form of products and product advertising from the product organizations (e.g., General Motors). Some imputs can come to the consumer directly from the

---

*Hereafter, for the sake of simplicity of presentation, the one word "development" will be used to designate "applied research and development".

FIGURE 3.1   Knowledge Flow Macrosystem Roles: An Ideal
              Model with Complete Interconnections

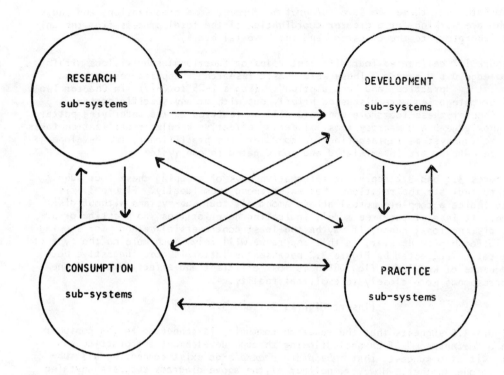

FIGURE 3.2   Knowledge Flow Macrosystem Roles: An Ideal
              Model with Controlled Access and Sequence Suggested

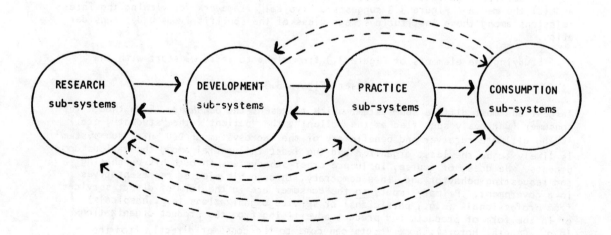

FIGURE 3.3   An Institutional Framework for Viewing D&U Macrosystems

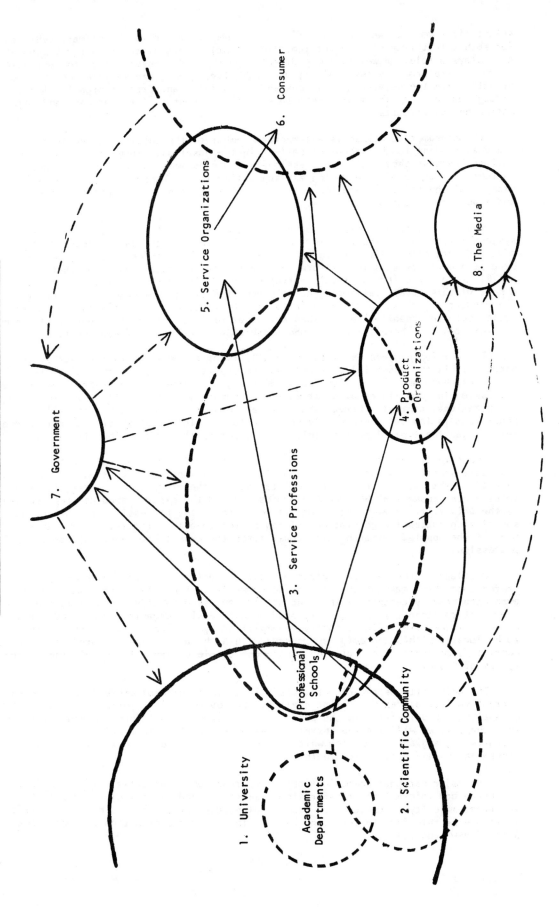

scientific community and the university: formal education is the primary vehicle for such direct transmission but reporting of scientific discovery and development also plays a role. However, these direct inputs to the consumer from the scientific community are probably less salient and less significant than messages which come directly from the service professions and the service and product organizations. Through advertising, the media are also significant sources for awareness and information on new products.

The consumer sometimes is a temporary member of the *service organization*, e.g., as student in the school or patient in the hospital. Such service organizations, because they include professionals and consumers and a complex organizational structure of intervening and supporting roles (as suggested in the clinic example of Chapter Two), are the prime mechanisms of linkage between the consumer and expert resources of all kinds.

The *product organizations* represent another important set of intermediary systems through which the consumer receives the benefits of new knowledge. In advanced technologically-oriented societies the consumer is continuously deluged by a stream of messages in the form of advertising and retailing of products of all kinds to serve (or supposedly serve) his needs in every sector of his being. A *part* of this stream reflects genuinely new scientific knowledge and technology. The product organization may also influence the consumer indirectly through sales to the service organizations as when a teacher or a school system orders a particular textbook or a hospital uses a manufactured drug or piece of equipment.

The *service profession* is an especially important element in the macrosystem because it is the essential link between the expert resources of the university on the one hand and the service and product organizations on the other. The service profession in some fields also serves the consumer directly, outside any intervening organizational context. Direct professional service to the consumer is still the model form in law but decreasingly so in medicine. In education direct professional service was the typical pattern before Plato set up the academy, but it is rare today.

The core of expertise in the service profession is contained within the *professional school*. The school serves at least three important functions in the maintenance of the macrosystem and the maintenance of the profession. First, it maintains a *continuous link* between the profession and the expert resources represented by the university as a whole; second it *replenishes* the profession, recruiting and socializing successive generations of new professionals. Finally, it *generates* much of the applied research which constitutes the expert knowledge base of the profession.

Overlapping the service professions and the university are the *scientific professions* which make up the scientific community. The scientific community is even more heavily centered within the university, sending only its most marginal (or most courageous) members into product and service organizations. The core members of the scientific community, exemplified by the Nobel Prize winners, tend to be located within *academic departments* within the university. Hence these departments in some sense constitute the inner-most circle of expertise within the macrosystem of D & U.

The university as a whole provides a large institutional umbrella under which a great variety of "experts" find shelter. For every field of endeavor without exception, the university is the place that the experts call "home". Hence throughout this chapter, we will see the university as a primary institutional element in the macrosystem, a giant sub-system which plays an important part in any successful dissemination and utilization chain.

The major national communications *media* represent a potential <u>direct channel</u> of influence and information transfer from researchers and experts of various sorts to the great majority of consumers. Commercial product organizations have been swift to recognize this face in investing heavily in mass media promotion to create awareness of new products.

3-6

Finally, hovering over this complex conglomerate of institutional forms, we find the *government,* attempting, at least, to serve and represent the consumer through influencing the other systems in various ways, "coordinating" their efforts so that together they will all function as a system to benefit the consumer. The government is also a special type of consumer of knowledge, often directly transmitted by university experts employed as scientific consultants, economic advisors, defense policy analysts, etc.*

Figure 3.4 shows the same elements in a much more idealized and functionalized form. This figure tries to show us what the macrosystem might look like if it really

[Insert Figure 3.4 here]

were a complete system. It envisages a coordinated transfer and evolution of expert knowledge from research to development to production and practice to consumer; and at the same time it also illustrates the "return flow", i.e. the systematic transformation of need messages from the consumer to the practitioner to the developer to the re-searcher. The four major functions are connected by linkage mechanisms which might be in the form of a) special roles, b) special linking organizations, c) media, or d) exchange activities of one sort or another.

The whole of this functional chain from research to consumer is orchestrated by a governing mechanism which has enough influence on each sub-system to insure that all will work together to serve a common purpose, "the public interest". Conceivably the government could undertake to fulfill each of the ten sub-functions of governance listed in the diagram, but in practice many of these are delegated, left to self-government by the chain sub-systems, or simply left undone.

Determination of the actual number of functions which must be fulfilled by government is, of course, an entirely arbitrary and debatable matter. However, the ten listed in this diagram serve as a useful summary of what we mean by "system governance". Each deserves at least brief mention here.

1. Planning. Someone needs to be looking to the future, defining what would be "ideal" from the perspective of the macrosystem as a whole over a long period of time.**

2. Design. After planning has revealed areas where change seems desirable and where experimental innovation (e.g., in new types of media or linking roles) seems called for, designs and prototypes for such innovations need to be generated.

---

*This crucial role of government as a knowledge consumer is stated in a generali-zation by Etzioni (#7076) as follows: "Information that has been processed might still be wasted as far as the societal unit is concerned if it is not *systematically introduced into the unit's decision-making and implementation overlayer* where the main societal 'consumption' of information takes place."

**At one time national "planning" was a dirty word to the business community, who saw in this concept some sort of socialist encroachment on private enterprise, but in recent years, perhaps with the planned space program as an object lesson, the industrial establishment is looking at it differently. Arjay Miller, Vice Chairman of Ford Motor Company, recently advocated the establishment of a "national goals institute" supported by the federal government. This institute would not make policy decisions but would "point out directions and possibilities and pro-vide a factual basis for enlightened public discussion and decision-making"... "Our concern is not with absolutes, but with choices, with the kind of information that we as a people must have if we are to be able to see clearly the various alternatives open to us and choose rationally among them." (UPI Release reported in Ann Arbor News, December 30, 1968.)

FIGURE 3.4

A Functional Framework for Viewing D&U Macrosystems

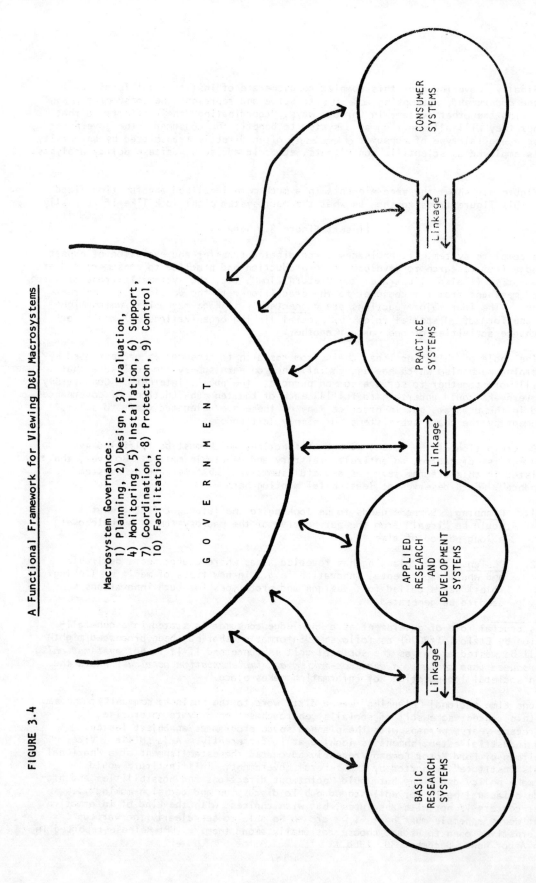

Macrosystem Governance:
1) Planning, 2) Design, 3) Evaluation,
4) Monitoring, 5) Installation, 6) Support,
7) Coordination, 8) Protection, 9) Control,
10) Facilitation.

G O V E R N M E N T

CONSUMER SYSTEMS

PRACTICE SYSTEMS

APPLIED RESEARCH AND DEVELOPMENT SYSTEMS

BASIC RESEARCH SYSTEMS

Linkage

Linkage

Linkage

Any or all of the 10 functions of governance can be *delegated, contracted out,* left to the *self-governance* of each sub-system, or left to the play of "natural" forces.

3. Evaluation. Before rational decisions can be made concerning the mainte-
    nance or change of the macrosystem, the current level of performance in
    each sub-system must be measured and assessed.

4. Monitoring. Evaluation is, in turn, heavily dependent on the collection of
    information on current activities in the various sub-systems. Good govern-
    ment requires an accurate reading of the existing state of affairs.

5. Installation. After planning has dictated the necessity of innovations
    to improve the system and after these innovations are designed and evalu-
    ated, there remains the important task of *installing* such changes so that
    they will fit within the existing system and will not be rejected by
    pre-existing sub-systems.

6. Support. A major function of government is the allocation and distribu-
    tion of financial support for the various D & U sub-systems. Older and
    established sub-systems may be relatively self-supporting, but the newer
    and more marginal sub-systems, especially those concerned with development
    and linkage, tend to be heavily dependent on some sort of government sub-
    sidy. Through its pattern of support, subsidy and taxation government
    can implement policies to coordinate and control the macrosystem. Large
    private foundations may also gain the same policy making power through the
    allocation of grants in areas which they determine are "needed".

7. Coordination. The most difficult and most essential task of governance
    is coordination. This function includes the development of communication
    and reciprocal interaction among all sub-systems (linkage) and the mainte-
    nance of a meaningful division of labor so that each sub-system performs
    a task which is relevant and complementary to the tasks of all the others.

8. Protection. Government also has a primary obligation to protect its members
    and its member sub-systems from unwarranted intrusions or violations
    of their integrity. Safety, security, maintenance of "standards", and pri-
    vacy are all subsumed under this function.

9. Control. To protect some members the government also has to control
    others. To protect the consumer it must regulate the producer; to pro-
    tect the rights of black citizens it must force white-dominated communities
    to desegregate their facilities. Direct compulsion through legal sanctions,
    however, is only one of many ways in which control can be exercised.
    In fact each of the other nine functions listed here could be considered
    a means of controlling the macrosystem.

10. Facilitation. Finally the positive role of government as a helper and
    a mechanism to facilitate communication among D & U sub-systems should
    be emphasized. Through establishing national libraries and information
    centers, through providing funds for curriculum development, national
    conferences, training programs, indeed through delivering the mail and
    providing roads and subsidies for all kinds of transport, the government
    facilitates linkage between sub-systems and *facilitates* action within
    sub-systems.

The best government performs all ten of these functions to a degree, but its
goal should always be to move towards *a macrosystem which runs itself,* self-supporting, self-protecting and self-controlling, while still being coordinated for
the common good.

I. THE RESEARCH WORLD

In complex contemporary society, there are certain sub-systems which specialize in the production, certification, and storage of *general knowledge* pertaining to our world. Usually these special sub-systems take the institutional form of university departments, scientific societies, and research institutes. Collectively they constitute the "research world" and represent a necessary and significant portion of the macrosystem of D & U. The two rather loosely organized institutional forms which dominate the research world are the university and the professional scientific society. The peculiarities of each of these forms are worth noting at least briefly.

A. THE UNIVERSITY

The university has been recognized by several observers as the center of expert knowledge for virtually every field. Benne (#3526, p. 5), for example, writes as follows:

> "The distinctive virtue of the university center is to discover and communicate precise, accurate, sufficiently qualified statements about any number of things and events. The center maintains tentativeness with respect to matters of knowledge where tentativeness is needed and attacks with vigor knowledge claims which incorporate insufficient evidence and intellectual rigor. A university could not be a university without this virtue."

The significance of the modern university for the rest of the D & U macrosystem is clearly accented by Commager (#3526, p. 79) when he says that the university

> "is, next to government itself, the chief servant of society, the chief instrument of social change. It occupies something of a symbolic role of both the church and the state in the Old World, but it fills a role which neither church nor state can effectively fill; it is the source, the inspiration, the power-house, and the clearinghouse of new ideas."

If we can accept these grand statements of the university's *potential* role as more or less valid, we need also to recognize that the problem-solving mission of the university center is only partially realized and actualized by the university, itself. A bastion for new ideas, it is also a prison for new ideas, surrounded by high walls which the academics have built for themselves, the norms and values which maintain the purity of "basic" science and the complete independence of the basic scientist.* Stated another way, the university is very ambivalent about its role as universal expert and problem solver for the practical world. Traditionally and particularly in England and Germany where the university came into being, applied work and "service" have been shunned altogether. In the more practically minded United States, however, the concept of a university as a center for teaching, research, and application came into being with the land grant college legislation beginning in the 1860's. A century later, however, the image of the U.S. university is not clear even to itself (e.g., see Parsons, #7082). A struggle goes on between teaching and research interests which virtually crowds out serious consideration

---

*Znaniecki notes the positive value to society as a whole in the maintenance of the ivory tower and the scholar as the guardian of truth. (#6033)

of the university's role as the problem-solver and expert for the greater society. Meanwhile, the average citizen looking on from the sidelines insistently asks when the professors are going to stop "studying" problems and start "helping" the society by using what they know.

The internal dissension, the blurred image, and the confusion about priorities in the modern university are all related, in part, to the one outstanding fact about the university as an institution: the independence and dominance of the tenured faculty. The university has an "administration" which is a form of government, to be sure, but it is generally recognized that most substantive policy matters within the university, e.g., the curriculum, the methods of instruction, recruitment of students and faculty, and the content and nature of research and service, are determined by individual faculty members, governed loosely by the supposedly shared norms of scholarship, science, and academic professionalism.

If these norms were thoroughly explicit and universally enforced, there would probably be very little attention devoted to knowledge application and utilization by universities. In fact, however, there is only vague consensus and some reluctance to enforce such norms with the result that the university has expanded and diversified its activities enormously. U.S. universities today, even the most prestigious, are hardly recognizable from their 19th century English and German ancestors, including as they do such diverse components as business, nursing, and social work schools, bureaus and institutes of research and service, colleges of continuing education and departments of communication, packaging, hotel management, home economics, and on and on.

However, even with this great diversity and evident concern for training and research in the practical arts, there remains a kind of *implicit hierarchy* within the university. New components, particularly those with an applied emphasis, are accepted only reluctantly and viewed suspiciously by the older, more academic, more "central" departments. But the university changes in spite of itself, first because it has no strong central government to enforce the traditional conception of its mission, and second because outside pressures force these changes upon it. As Commager points out (#7086, p. 78), most of the outside pressure has come from the federal government and mostly from government efforts to mobilize society to fight wars.

In this fulminating growth, mostly unplanned and uncoordinated, some authors are able to detect a meaningful pattern which bodes well both for the university and the society. Clark Kerr (#7087) describes the new university as a "multiversity", the core of expertise and problem solving power for the whole society. Benne tells us how the newer peripheral elements form a bridge between academic scholarship and the rest of society:

"The periphery of the university has its distinctive virtues too. Typically it is closer to the interests, concerns and maintenance and growth requirements of other parts of the society than the center is. Members of the periphery cannot dispense with the category of human and social importance in their work; indeed they must define and redefine this category in their responses to the urgencies and emergencies of the part of society they serve, in making their judgments about teaching and about applied research.

In a real sense they must bring the wider society to the university -- they must mediate between the wider society and the center
of the university." (#7082, pp. 5-6)

Robert Solo is another observer who shares with Benne and Kerr this
conception of the university as the vital central knowledge resource for
the society, but for Solo the potential of the university in this regard
has not been realized. He writes:

"For the academic scientist, it is a physical haven that provides him
with students and pays him for teaching them, that forwards his research proposals, that hires his secretary, and, perhaps, offers him
an alternative career in administration. Can, or should, the university be more than a locale and a facade, a fund raising agency and a
bureaucratic apparatus, that sometimes services and sometimes hinders
the individual achievement of teachers and researchers -- but itself
contributes nothing? A university might be more, and in becoming more
achieve a fusion of the disciplines and a community of spirit that
would stimulate a diversity of individual achievement." (Solo, #6314,
pp. 46-47)

Solo goes on to give us an idea of what could be achieved by coordinated mobilization of university resources:

"It is possible that some universities might find a viable unity in
their diversity, by deliberately organizing themselves as incubators
of change, for a major social problem area. The university might
choose as a common point of emphasis for many of the facets of its
research and teaching, a great and continuing problem such as the
achievement of political, social and economic development in India,
where the basis of policy must be wrought through the creative
initiatives of an unbounded range of skills and competencies. A
contribution in understanding the complex of phenomena related to
these real problems or otherwise in finding a way towards their solution could be made, conceivably, by those expert in every field of
economics, of engineering, of business administration, of sociology,
of anthropology, of education as a science and of education in all
the sciences, of jurisprudence and political science, of geology, of
geophysics, of oceanography, of geography, of the medical and veteri-
nary sciences, of pedagogy, agronomy, animal husbandry, forestry and
all the sciences and technologies related to agriculture, of chemistry,
of electronics and nuclear physics and all the sciences related to industry, and so on. All could relate to the development of a basis for
choice and action in supporting the social and economic development
of India, providing that all are oriented to the realities and particu-
larities of that great, complex and ancient society. This does not mean
that specialists would agree on preferred alternatives or would
produce a policy or a plan. It would mean that out of the focussed
ferment, new alternatives in that policy area might be expected continually to emerge, thereby broadening and deepening the basis for
choice." (Solo, #6314, pp. 47-48)

In fact, however, such coordinated interdisciplinary activity is rarely
initiated by universities. Indeed even the efforts to combat the knowledge
explosion which threatens the very existence of the academic scholarship
system have been undertaken almost exclusively outside the universities by
industry and government (Brownson, #0925). Major national projects using
interdisciplinary teams of university scientists have been undertaken on

3-12

many occasions, but the initiative has usually come from foundations or from the government, and the institutional mechanism has rarely been a university. The atom bomb development was one such project and more recently the Physical Science Study Committee's high school science curriculum was another (Marsh #1016 and #1193).*

In summary, the potential role of the university as the principle societal resource for expert knowledge is clear. Both central and peripheral (basic and applied) sectors of the university community play a critical role in the maintenance of culture and the generation of new ideas. However, the coherent and effective utilization of the university as a resource system has yet to be realized,** owing primarily to the weakness and narrowness of university administration and the dominance of the decentralized norm of faculty self-governance.

B.   THE SCIENTIFIC COMMUNITY

Few topics have been subjected to more intensive sociological enquiry in recent years than the organization and patterning of scientific activity. More than two dozen sociologists and social psychologists have defined their major research interests within this area and at least two university centers (at Johns Hopkins and Stanford) have a major focus on the study of scientific communication. This report is not the place to summarize these efforts. Major reviews of much of the quantitative research have been published by Menzel (#0731) and Paisley (#1240) and at least one substantial collection of readings has appeared (Barber and Hirsch, #5067). Detailed consideration of these studies in this report has not been undertaken because they do not treat the utilization or the application of science in the world of practice as a central issue.

Such studies are relevant, however, in at least two important ways; first, because they provide models for the analysis of communication, models which have applicability to the transfer of knowledge from research to practice; and second, because the scientific community is a significant sub-system within the D&U macrosystem. Whether or not scientists themselves are clearly aware of it, or whether or not they care about it, the fact remains that they do serve as a kind of linking system between the academic cloisters of university research and the application-oriented practice professions and product organizations.

Research on the scientific community has had three major topic foci, each of which has some relevance to an understanding of the macrosystem and its linkage processes. These three are *the scientific communication focus, the scientist-in-organizations focus, and the scientist-in-government-and-national-policy focus.****

---

*In spite of the university administration's incapacity for coordination and planning of major projects, many academics insist that only the university should have decision-making power in such important areas, e.g., Piel (#0434), "Initiative and decision in the deployment of funds for research and education must be restored to the universities." (p. 15)
**In every field with the possible exception of agriculture. Agriculture, however, is a special case, sustained and subsidized by the federal government and the states and assisted by the vast network of the Cooperative Extension Service.
***Storer (#6917) makes a more extended analysis of the liturature on the sociology of science, using seven categories: (1) science as a social institution, (2) scientists as members of concrete groups, (3) scientists as members of a profession, (4) scientists as creative individuals, (5) scientists as members of specific disciplines, (6) science as an influential participant in national decision-making, and (7) science as a communication system. (See his pages 8-9.)

1. Scientific Communication Patterns

In the scientific community the coin of the realm is <u>recognition</u>
from colleagues.* Scientists work for it, and fight hard in competition for
it, sometimes to the exclusion of other considerations, even their own professed values (see, for example Merton, #1268, Reiff, #2804, and Hagstrom,
#6324, Chapter 2).   Among scientists there is a tremendous motivation to
communicate, especially to disseminate one's own ideas in printed form
to the relevant professional audience of other certified scientists in
one's own discipline.

Not suprisingly, therefore, the major function and major activity
of formal scientific associations is the maintenance of journals and other
mechanisms such as conventions which are primarily designed to permit formal
and informal communication of current research activities. Most of the
evidence indicates that the associations perform these functions very well.
In psychology, for example, a field in which communication patterns have been
extensively studied (see Garvey and Griffith, #5150, #6793, #1205, #2107,#6218,
and #6349), there are at least 50 journals** which specialize in research
reports for various sub-fields. These, in turn, are linked together by two
journals of reviews on specific topics, a journal of book reviews, a
journal for theoretical presentations and a journal of abstracts. Any
researcher who prepares a research report following the standard formula
accepted in the field is very likely to deliver it first at a regional associa-
tion· convention or the national convention, a year later publish it, a
year after that find it abstracted and a year after that summarized in a
review. Every professional psychologist who is likely to find the research
directly relevant to his own work has several opportunities to find it and
if he is working in a closely related field is likely to be included in a
preprint exchange circle which will give him the information soon after it
is first presented. Price (#5127) and Price and Beaver (#5125) in describing
these preprint exchange systems as an "invisible college"*** note that
there are subsystems even within these groupings which are identified by
overlapping authorships, a prolific leader or "star", and a common
institutional origin.

Most studies seem to show that the various mechanisms of communication in
a scientific discipline, taken together, make for a tight-knit network;
this network functions effectively at least for communicating <u>among scientists</u>
the information which <u>they</u> think is relevant and necessary.

In a particularly clear analysis of scientific associations and their
functions, Adkinson (#0938) notes that those representing a narrow disciplinary
orientation are supplemented by other associations which take science as a
whole as their scope of concern and still others which represent a broad
scientific discipline, inclusive of many specialities related applied research
and development, and even practitioners. Hence many of these larger
scientific associations (such as the American Psychological Association and
the American Educational Research Association) are able to form significant
bridges between different universities, between different sub-specialties,
between university and non-university researchers, and even between basic
and applied researchers in the same general discipline.

*Storer (#6917) uses the expression "competent responses".

**Eight of which are published by the Association, itself.

***Price derives the term from the original 17th century description of the Royal Society
of London *before* it was formally established as an institution.

Although these positive linking features of scientific communications networks are highly significant, they do not tell the whole story. Scientific associations are also conservative, protective, and exclusive by nature. They are designed to preserve the established order in a specialty and to resist innovative outsiders particularly when they are seen to threaten existing "standards." (See, e.g., Barber, #2807). Moreover, the existing leadership of a specialty is able to sustain these standards through monopolization of review and reference panels and through its control of editorial policy in journals and effective control of research funding policies of government agencies (Crane, #6577).

The same scientists who resist new ideas in their own disciplines (e.g., as described by Barber, #2807) presumably will be even more suspicious of new ideas or incursions which violate the norm of "purity" by being application-oriented. Hence, the formal scientific communication network may be a barrier to effective dissemination and utilization in the broader macrosystemic sense. As Archibald (#7088) notes in her analysis of social science utilization in policy making, because pure science is a relatively closed social system, those who turn away from it by taking on applied interests and activities may suffer the costs of alienation unless they are able to develop applied science social systems of equivalent integrity. Organizations such as the American Educational Research Association represent such an attempt to create application-oriented social systems which have the essential attributes of the basic scientific communities.

It is possible that through the proliferation of associations, each with a slightly different ratio of applied and basic concerns, the gap between basic science and applied R&D can be bridged effectively, but we may have reason to believe that this will not happen automatically. Although all the scientific associations are faced with an explosive growth of research and research reporting, and although traditional demarcations of disciplinary boundaries are changing (Adkinson, #0938), most scientists appear to be *indifferent* to the need for new mechanisms for recording, synthesizing, and retrieving knowledge (Appel and Gurr, #5050).

On the whole, the literature on scientific communication suggests that scientists have built for themselves a system which works reasonably well to convey information from one scientist to another,*but this system may be less effective in forming a linkage between research and practice or even between research-basic and research-applied. Traditionally scientific associations have bound together university-based scientists, affirming and reinforcing the norms and values of the scientific profession. The emergence of broader semi-scientific associations, however, may signify the coming of a more effective pattern of linkage. As these organizations move out of their present marginal status (e.g., Goode, #7078) they may become important linkage sub-systems, but if, in the struggle to gain status and integrity, they become excessively concerned with "purity" and deny access to practitioners and developers, they may not serve this important function.

2. Scientists in Organizations

A second major focus of research on science considers the organizational context of scientific activity and the organizational parameters of scientific *productivity*. Many of these studies shed light on organizational and institutional barriers which will be discussed in Chapter Six. However, such studies are also helpful in showing what is perhaps the most

---

*See for example a recent study of University Physicists by Cole and Cole (#7072). All the major scientists in this field were fully aware of each other's work.

critical interface in the macrosystem: when scientists are employed in
large numbers to carry out research and development projects in industry
or government they are forming a significant *linkage between the scientific community and the world of practice.*

The research evidence suggests that these scientists who choose to
work in organizations are most effective when they maintain a strong
professional orientation (Neff, et al., #6192) and maintain firm connections with colleagues outside the organization (Pelz and Andrews, #6067).

However, maintaining linkage to the scientific community is not the
only correlate of high productivity. Pelz and Andrews (#6067) also have
shown that scientists who are stimulated by diverse sources and contacts
including service in administrative tasks are more productive than those
who remain in narrow specializations. This finding has important implications for the macrosystem because it suggests that the scientist who is
truly bridging the gap between research and practice by working on applied
problems and by becoming partly involved in practical concerns *is actually
the better scientist*, even in the coinage of science, itself, publication
and contribution to knowledge building.

However, the role of scientist in industry and other applied settings
(e.g. medical and business schools) is not an easy one. There is always
a threat of being marginal, alienated from the parent discipline yet not
accepted as a full member in the applied field. There is a trade-off between the need for professional autonomy and the desire to influence
practical policy (Archibald, #7088) and a threat that one could be lost
without gaining the other. Some authors (e.g., Kornhauser, #2953) indicate
that in spite of these tensions the scientist can be made an effective
part of the practice organization. Pelz (#7094) goes so far as to suggest
that the tension between the drive for autonomy and the stimulation from
applied problems is the energy source for the spark of creativity. In
any case the scientist in the applied organizational setting is one of the
critical linking agents in the D&U macrosystem. (See also discussion of
applied researchers and R&D managers as linkers in Chapter Seven.)*

3.   The Relationship of the Scientific Community to the Government and
     to the Nation as a Whole

Science is not a self-supporting activity: it depends very largely on
the good will, the faith, and the enlightenment of the people as a whole
expressed through their government representatives. The people and the
government *assume* that they get something important out of science, and
this is why support for science has grown so substantially since World
War II.**

Up into the mid 1950's, this relationship between government and
science was taken for granted, and the assumption that science was useful

---

*The most extensive analysis of the overlapping, ambiguous, and conflicting rela-
tions between basic and applied science orientations is provided by Archibald
(#7088), especially in Chapter IV, "The Social Structures of Pure and Applied
Science."

**The development of the atomic bomb was probably the crucial event that generated
this mass acceptance of science as a useful enterprise (Hall, #1231), but the faith
of the public and their representatives was based on very little knowledge or real
interest (Withey, #3441).

to society went more or less unchallenged. Increasingly in recent years, however, the place of science in society and the relations between science and government have been subjected to critical inquiry and analysis. Of special note is the work of Don K. Price (#7090, #7091, #0601), Etzioni (#1162, #7076, #0893), Kidd (#7092, last chapter reprinted in Barber, #5067, #1272, #0601) and Dupree (#1265, #7093). Related issues are also aired frequently by scientists in various fields in the pages of <u>Science</u> and in the <u>Bulletin of the Atomic Scientists</u>.

Although some voices (e.g., Lynd, #6098 in 1939) long ago urged an active involvement of scientists in the policy process, the weight of concern among the scientists, themselves, in the early post war years was to maintain the independence of basic research establishments from government interference. Government support was fine but it had to be delivered without strings. Some scientists even argue that this is best for government, e.g., Kistiakowsky (#0284):

> "A serious danger of the present situation is the spread
> of the idea that basic science can be planned in detail
> and that money need be allocated only to specific topics
> to provide the necessary scientific knowledge for the ad-
> vance of technology. Unfortunately, it just does not
> work this way" (p. 13).

He goes on to assert that advances in technology most often stem from disconnected discoveries in pure research, a statement that would not seem to be confirmed by empirical evidence (see e.g., Jewkes et al., #0941).

Closely related to this view that government should keep hands off science is the view that science should keep hands off government, remaining aloof from the political fray and maintaining a stance of "professional objectivity" (e.g., Leiserson, #1146).

A contemporary viewpoint is taken by Greenberg (#7089) and Price*, who document the extensive and increasing involvement of science in politics and policy. Price states the case succinctly:

> "...science can no longer stand apart in complete indepen-
> dence from the flux of political controversy, and thus
> appear as a clearly objective source of truth. For when
> research must be supported by government grants, science
> itself becomes part of the political system." (#7090)

Increasingly government has turned to scientists and now involves them in policy-making not only as consultants but through *contract research* as an arm of government.** As a result, there is a significant de facto overlap between the scientific community and government, even though many scientists are reluctant to accept this fact. From the point of view of D & U this overlap is probably very beneficial because it increases the involvement of the scientific community in the macro-system and makes it more likely that the scientific community will, in the long run, serve the public interest.

---

*The fact that both these men have some background as news reporters is perhaps not entirely coincidental.

**This development is discussed at length by Price, #7060.

In concluding this section on the scientific community we note a perceptible shift toward applied concerns and the evolution of stronger applied research establishments. Storer's summary is worth quoting:

> "...the traditional social system of science must 'move over' to some extent to make room for the growing and more obviously independent part of science that is directly concerned with application of scientific knowledge and research techniques to the problems of the larger society."
> (#6917, p. 166)

II. THE PRACTICE WORLD

The great majority of male members of our culture spend their working hours making and distributing products and providing services for which we are all consumers. Collectively these product and service activities constitute "the practice world", a conglomerate of millions of people in thousands of organizations fulfilling thousands of different functions. The size and chaotic structure of this world makes it rather difficult to describe and to study as a whole so that typically we think in terms of specific practice worlds serving specific consumer needs: medicine, education, agriculture and food production, law, etc. Indeed, in spite of considerable overlap and interrelatedness in structure, these fields do represent distinct social systems and they are usually studied separately.

From the perspective of the D & U macrosystem these practice worlds are the prime utilizers of research knowledge. Although it is the consumer who ultimately benefits from the activities of science, he does so primarily through the manufacturer and the practitioner. It is they who determine what is useful in the scientific warehouse, and it is they who must transform this knowledge into useable forms.

From a somewhat closer view one can see that the practice world in most fields is subdivided into three types of subsystems which we will call *the professions, the product organizations, and the service organizations*. These three subsystems are complementary; no one of them can effectively do the whole job of serving the consumer. Thus for example, our medical needs require a profession of doctors, product organizations to manufacturer and distribute drugs, prosthetics, and other medical supplies, and service organizations such as hospitals and medical centers to provide intensive care. Our educational needs are met similarly by a teaching profession, aided by textbooks, equipment, and facilities provided by various product organizations, in the context of the service organization, which we call the school.

Because each of these three subsystems is an important feature of the D & U macrosystem and because each presents rather distinct problems and issues for dissemination and utilization, they will be discussed in three separate sections below.

A. THE PRACTICE PROFESSIONS

We have already considered science as a "profession" or an overlapping network of professions. The professions *of practice* to which we now turn our attention are similar to the professions of science in some respects, but there are also important differences. The professions of practice represent giant national systems for stabilizing and preserving the norms of service in a given area of human need. They are usually dominated by one inclusive and roughly representative organization, the *professional association*. The association acts in various ways to safeguard and advance the interests of the profession as a whole.

3-18

Communication is one important function of the association but is far less salient than it is as a function in the scientific association. Nevertheless the practice profession plays an even greater role in the D&U process because of its great power and its effective control of consumer access to new knowledge in particular service areas. Therefore, the study and sociological analysis of the professions is highly relevant to any macroscopic study of D&U.

A generation ago Parsons placed major emphasis on professions in his exposition of sociological theory (e.g., see Parsons, #7082). Unfortunately, however, few scholars have followed his lead and there is a paucity of major works in this area. Lynn (#7061) provides an interesting and informative collection of papers on various professions with some integrative analysis by Barber (#7063). Gilb (#7071) offers a more detailed, well-researched, and clearly thought-out analysis of the professions as a whole and gives some special attention to D&U issues. Lazarsfeld, et al. (#7207), provides a series of ponderous review papers which summarize sociological research in various applied professional settings but little of this material focusses on the professions as such.

Barber provides the following definition of professional activity:

"Professional behavior may be defined in terms of four essential attributes: a high degree of generalized and systematic knowledge; primary orientation to the community interest rather than to individual self-interest; a high degree of self-control of behavior through codes of ethics internalized in the process of work socialization and through voluntary associations organized and operated by the work specialists themselves; and a system of rewards (monetary and honorary) that is primarily a set of symbols of work achievement and thus ends in themselves, not means to some end of individual self-interest." (#7063, p. 672)

However, Barber's definition probably represents the ideal more than the reality, as we can judge from the activities of the typical professional association. Prominent among the purposes of such associations are:

1. Preservation and advancement of the special social role represented by the majority of members. This may include active promotion and advertising, recruitment, and various moves to include, exclude, standardize, and regulate.

2. Fellowship and relaxation. This purpose is rarely stated explicitly but has central importance motivationally. The feeling of belonging to a special status in-group may be prerequisite to the fulfillment of other more socially legitimized purposes.

3. Information exchange on a variety of matters of direct personal concern to members. New scientific knowledge and improved services may be far down the list of concerns, however.

4. Service to the community is a legitimizing purpose to outsiders and to members, themselves. On closer examination, however, much of this "service" may be self-serving, being either promotional advertising or furtherance of professional self-interests *in the name of* the common good.

3-19

5.   Maintenance or advancement of prestige and power of mem-
     bers is another important but unsung purpose of associations.
     It may be manifested in efforts to set high fee schedules,
     exclusive rights and privileges, monopolistic control of
     certain kinds of information, prerogative and veto power in
     certain community factions and power to limit and even ex-
     propriate certain consumer freedoms (e.g., the power to
     commit individuals for medical or psychiatric treatment).

6.   Maintenance of independence from encroachment and exploita-
     tion by the bureaucracies of business and government. In
     this respect professional associations and industrial unions
     are very similar.

7.   Enforcement of uniform standards of service and a uniform
     code of ethics among members. This self-regulatory function
     is often highly touted, but just as often half-hearted and
     ineffective in practice.

The significance of these seven purposes for D&U becomes obvious when we
consider their practical effects at three critical points: (1) the interface with the research world; (2) the interface with the consumer; and
(3) the interface between the professions. At these three points the consequences of organized professionalization are potentially both facilitative
and inhibitory.

1.   Interface of the Professions with the Research World

     In Figure 3.5 we try to illustrate the major features of the inter-
face between the research world and the practice professions.

[Insert Figure 3.5 here]

As the figure shows, the key bridging institution between research and
practice is the University-based professional school. The professional
school serves as a bridge in several ways: (1) it provides for profession renewal through continuous recruitment, training and certification
of new members; (2) it provides a home base for specialists and for
applied researchers; (3) it furnishes much of the new knowledge content
for professional journals; and (4) it is likely to provide a large proportion of the formal and informal leadership to the profession.

     Again the ideal role of the university professional school is well-
described by Barber:

     "The university professional school has as one of its basic
     functions the transmission to its students of the generalized
     and systematic knowledge that is the basis of professional
     performance. Not only the substantive knowledge itself, but
     knowledge of how to keep up with continuing advances in pro-
     fessional knowledge is what the university school seeks to
     give its students. Where the body of professional knowledge
     is changing very rapidly, the university professional school
     may take a direct role in promoting the 'adult' education of
     the members of its profession through postprofessional training
     courses, seminars and institutes.

FIGURE 3.5   The Interface of Research and Practice

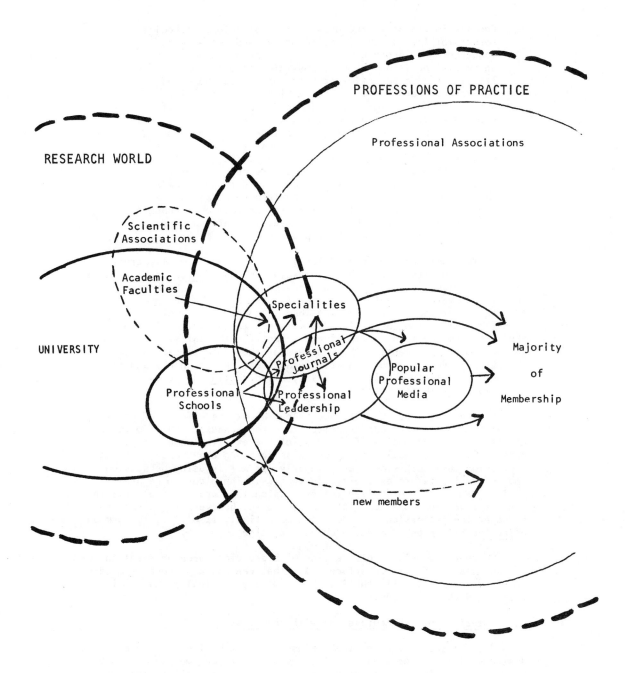

Equally important is the university professional school's
responsibility for the creation of new and better knowledge on which professional practice can be based. Its
university position makes it possible for all members of
its staff to be part-time scholars and researchers and
for some to carry on these activities full time. The
university professional school can borrow resources of
knowledge from other university departments, either by
co-opting full-time teaching and research personnel or
through more informal, part-time cooperation in the university community. The better the university professional
school, the more likely it is to use resources from the
other professional schools in the university and from all
the other departments of basic knowledge insofar as they
are relevant. In sum, the university professional schools
are the leading, though not the sole, innovators and sys-
tematizers of ideas for their professions." (#7063, pp. 674-675)

In practice, however, the professional school is not a wholly creative
force. Many of its members have an exclusively academic career orientation and are so insulated from the service function of the profession
that they have no current conception of consumer needs and problems and
no interest or concern for meeting them. At the same time the professional school (as noted earlier) is marginal to the university, partially
shut off from the main stream of new scientific thought emanating from
the academic departments. The weakness of the professional school as
a linking mechanism is most glaringly apparent in the shabby and poorly
financed efforts to provide university-based continuing education for
the members of the profession.

Most professions are also ambivalent about the efforts of professional schools to "upgrade" service standards because such efforts run
counter to the personal self-interest of the existing membership.
Members of professional schools who wish to bring about change in the
profession must work slowly and gingerly, primarily using persuasion
and informal pressure as their only tactics. The older, more prestigious, and better organized the profession, the more powerful will these
conservative tendencies be. At the same time, however, the older and
stronger the professional school, the more likely it will be to form an
effective bridge between research and practice.

We cannot conclude this section with any clear pronouncement on the
current status of this interface. All that can be said can be summed
up in two comments: (1) the interface is very difficult; and (2) it
deserves much more study.

2.   Interface of the Professions with the Consumer

Much of the concern of the professions as exhibited in the purposes
listed earlier is focussed on relations with the consumer and the community as a whole. Again the consequences are both facilitative and
inhibitory as far as effective linkage is concerned. In spite of strongly
voiced concern for service to the public, much of the activity of the
professions is directed toward building barriers between practitioner
and consumer, setting limits to service, exerting control over the consumer,
limiting the consumer's rights, preventing effective feedback from the
consumer, and making rational choice of service by consumers difficult

3-22

or impossible (Goode, #1678, p. 198). At the same time, much of this activity may benefit the consumer by insuring a roughly standard quality of service or at least an equal chance of getting good service. It may also avoid the most outrageous forms of consumer exploitation.

The consumer-professional interface is usually characterized by a gross status and power differential in favor of the professional. This differential allows unfettered "service" by the professional, but it makes direct feedback from consumers almost impossible (for an extended discussion of this problem see section of Chapter Eight on "user messages"). Three professions, medicine (doctor-patient), mental health (psychiatrist-mental patient), and education (teacher-student) most dramatically illustrate this difficulty. There are some signs that in higher education, at least, the student is doing something to correct this imbalance. (We will return to this issue later as we discuss the consumer.)

The twentieth century has seen a tremendous growth of the professions and the professional associations in numbers and social influence (Gilb, #7071). On the whole the effect has been a stabilization and an improvement of service. However, the professions are to some extent powerful special interests which encroach on the rights of others and create an unfair distribution of wealth and power in our society Until other groups such as consumers can organize to equalize this balance, we cannot be assured that professionalism will adequately live up to its claims as a progressive social mechanism.

3. The Interface between Professions

A number of authors have noted the inhibiting effects of professionalization on interprofessional communication. For example, Lynn comments as follows:

> "...at the same time that they help to bridge the gulf
> between nations (through international associations),
> the professions erect 'No Trespassing' signs between them-
> selves and other professional groups, especially the
> newer ones." (Lynn, #7061, p. 653)

Interprofessional rivalry is particularly acute among marginal professions where a good deal of status ambiguity is present (e.g., see Segal, #3216, for relations between psychiatrist and sociologist, or Zander et al., #7114, for psychiatrists, psychologists, and social workers).

Status ambiguity is not the only reason for interprofessional communicative barriers, however. As Frank points out (#3297), each profession constructs a "virtual world" by means of which it orders and comprehends the environment: the lawyer sees things in terms of relations between people, "obligations" and "rights"; and the doctor sees people in terms of organic functions and malfunctions.

Interprofessional communication is relevant for D&U in two important ways. First, it provides a significant "lateral" route for the passage of new ideas from research to practice, and second, it has a potentially catalytic influence at the consumer interface. Each point deserves some explication.

The "lateral flow" of knowledge will not be given much attention in this review because it has received little attention in the literature, but it may be a most significant means of moving knowledge from research to practice. In a complex multiprofessional society like our own, different types of professionals with entirely different formal training and background will find themselves working side-by-side in service activities. Such co-location and teamwork provides innumerable opportunities for informal transfer of knowledge in both directions. These contacts are likely to be more fruitful than the formal and stylized communication patterns and "teamwork" which is likely to take place between researchers and practitioners in the same field.*

At the practice-consumer interface one of the serious and chronic consequences of professionalization is scarcity. Upgrading a service role to a "profession" usually results in severe restriction on membership and consequent higher service fees, overload for the practitioner and trial and aggravation for the consumer. To fill the gap we have sometimes been able to generate "sub-" professions or "para-" professions; marginal or incomplete professions which take some of the burden off the fully established professional. Effective utilization of these newer marginal professions seems essential if our society has any intention of meeting consumer needs; yet the older more prestigeful professions have viewed their emergence with suspicion and have acted to suppress and circumscribe their activities. The case is stated clearly by Lynn:

> "Because the professionals have been no more willing than
> the general public to face up to the predicament in which
> their triumph has placed them, they have clung to formal
> standards of professional training (e.g., the educationists
> who steadfastly insist that without education courses a
> person could not possibly qualify as a school teacher) and
> have guarded their exclusive rights of performance (e.g.,
> the doctors who are loath to delegate significant authority
> to medical and psychiatric social workers) as if they had
> world enough and time for all their responsibilities."
> (Lynn, #7061, p. 652)

The significant and problematic role of the profession in the contemporary D&U macrosystem is best summarized by Gilb:

> "The modern economic system, with its anonymity and inter-
> dependence, could not function if there were no institu-
> tions to define occupational boundaries, rights, and ob-
> ligations. From a social stand point the problem has
> been how to keep those boundaries, once they are defined,
> from becoming so rigid that they preclude necessary
> adaptation to changing technology, changing social or-
> ganizations, and changing consumer needs and demands."
> (Gilb #7071, p. 82)

---

*In Chapter Seven we will consider various "linking" roles or "change-agent" roles which help bridge the gap between research and practice. The change-agent may function most effectively, however, in bringing about linkage between practice professions.

B.   THE PRODUCT ORGANIZATIONS

The consumer benefits from new scientific knowledge largely through the new products which he is able to buy in the marketplace. For these he is dependent on the *product organizations* which constitute the economic basis of our affluent society. However, the product organization both historically and structurally is isolated from the main stream of scientific knowledge flow. Its connections with the university are tenuous and sporadic, and it rarely attains an internal competence to seek out and effectively utilize scientific sources of information.

However, in the last two decades a few of the largest industrial corporations have endeavored to build a greater internal capacity for knowledge retrieval and utilization through the institution of the "R&D" laboratory and through the active recruitment of university-trained scientists. These scientist recruits to industry form a major bridge for D&U in the product organization and they have been studied extensively by sociologists and organizational psychologists (e.g., see earlier discussion in this chapter on scientists in organizations). Most of this research literature highlights the marginality and difficulty of this role.

The product organizations are usually much more frank about expressing their self-interest than are the professions; they are in business for profit, and to this end they advertise and promote their products to consumers through all possible and legal means.

As long as an open competitive market exists the consumer remains on an equal footing with the manufacturer because he retains the right of <u>choice</u>. He can buy or not buy and, in theory, he can select from a range of offerings the one item which works "best". This sort of product competition would in the long run force the effective utilization of the latest validated knowledge by all product organizations. They would have to stay up-to-date to stay in business because the consumer would always be ready and able to shift to another product as soon as that other product could demonstrate higher performance.

In practice, however, this ideal of the open market is seldom realized. Typically product organizations are able to avoid open competition *on quality* through advertising, packaging, financing and pricing to make true product value comparisons impossible. In his efforts to avoid competition based on quality comparison, the producer is aided by the natural tendencies of the typical consumer who usually takes the path of least effort and seldom bases purchase decisions on sound comparative reasoning.

There are very few sources to which we can turn to gain greater understanding of the important role of the product organization in the total macrosystem of knowledge flow and utilization.* However, the internal flow system within one of the largest corporate giants, American Telephone and Telegraph Company, has been described briefly by Morton (#6840) and analyzed from a D&U perspective by Havelock (#6183) and Havelock and Benne (#3872). This AT&T example is probably not a good model for other fields, but it does suggest that the large profit-making concern is capable of developing coordinated research, development, production, and service capabilities, and of shaping these separate components into a single functioning knowledge flow system.

---

*The literature which does exist in this area will be reviewed in Chapter Six.

C. THE SERVICE ORGANIZATION

A third major mechanism for the transfer of knowledge from research to user is the <u>service</u> organization. We will find service organizations in every field although their significance in the macrosystem varies greatly from one field to another. In medicine, hospitals and clinics play an important role although a large portion of medical services in the United States are still provided by physicians in private practice on an individual basis. Similarly, in law, the courts and penal institutions are important but are treated as a last-resort mechanism; the vast majority of legal services are provided by individual lawyers. In education, of course, private practice has almost completely disappeared; the school, the primary service organization of education, is today virtually the only mechanism through which educational services are provided.

Three purposes of service organizations can be distinguished, each of which has some significance for D&U. First, the service organization may be a convenient home base for the service professional. The law firm or the medical partnership may be little more than this. Second, they may represent an effort to coordinate service and to provide more complex services than can be provided by individual professionals working alone. The major surgical operation in the modern hospital is perhaps the most prototypical example of this function. Third, it may serve as a mechanism for extending and stabilizing the relationship between practitioner and consumer. The mental hospital and the prison may most dramatically represent this purpose in action. However, all three purposes are served at least to some degree by almost all service organizations. The pursuit of each of these purposes will have both positive and negative effects on D&U; these are considered briefly below.

1. <u>The Service Organization as a Convenience to the Professional Prac-titioner</u>

By forming partnerships, professionals are better able to balance their work load and take time off for further training, attending meetings, or for rest and recreation. They can provide 24 hour service, can refer clients to colleagues without losing their business, can pool routine clerical and accounting tasks, share rent and utility costs, etc. For the most part these advantages to the professional are also advantages to the consumer; they make it easier for the professional to do his work and hence they make it easier for him to serve the consumer; the result should be faster service, more reliable service, more frequent and timely service and less expensive service. Moreover, if the practitioner uses his released time to continue his own training by reading, attending professional meetings and enrolling in extension courses, the consumer may derive the additional benefit of improved, more up-to-date, scientifically-based service.

However, the professional partnership may not providing any of these benefits for the consumer. It may be used only to solidify the power of the professional vis-a-vis the client; reduced costs may <u>not</u> be passed on to the consumer; through monopolization of services, the service organization may actually <u>increase</u> fees as it sees fit in its own self interest. The personal accountability of the individual practitioner

can be effectively buried in endless rounds of buck-passing.* Additional
time freed up by the partnership may not be used for professional growth
and renewal of skills, but may be used instead exclusively for financial
aggrandizement and recreation.

Therefore, whether or not a partnership will benefit the consumer
or simply become a further means of exploiting him will depend on other
factors, not the least of which are the values and attitudes of the professionals, themselves. Those who are truly dedicated to service and
to *improved* service will utilize the advantages of partnership in a
service organization to the great benefit of the consumer and of the
total macrosystem of D&U.

2. The Service Organization as Provider of Complex Services

The significance and the value of divided labor has been stressed
throughout our discussion of the knowledge macrosystem. As services
become more scientific and as they help the consumer to solve more and
more of his problems, they necessarily become more complex, and less
and less within the performance capacity of single individuals. Dramatic
examples such as heart transplant surgery and air transport can be used
to demonstrate this point. The usual ingredients which make service organizations prerequisite are (1) the requirement of very expensive and
complex equipment and facilities, (2) the requirement of coordinated
services by several professions, and (3) the requirement of serving large
numbers of consumers simultaneously and rapidly.

If service organizations fill these requirements, then obviously
they facilitate D&U and represent a necessary link between research and
consumer. However, the complexity of services may be more apparent than
real; the compelling logic of the service organization for truly complex
services has sometimes been used as a rationalization for bureaucracy
and inefficiency and for reducing practice accountability to the consumer.
Most readers will have had some personal experience with auto-repair
services provided both by individual mechanics and by large service centers; in the service center the mechanic becomes anonymous, and the
quality and true cost of service almost impossible to measure. Because
of the potential for almost limitless consumer exploitation under such
circumstances, some sort of government surveillance or regulation of complex services would appear to be the only way to prevent abuses.

3. The Service Organization as an Extension and Stabilization of the Practitioner-Consumer Relationship

It is sometimes deemed necessary for practitioners to assume general
control over the consumer so as to provide more effective service. The
extreme of this type of "service" organization is represented by the
custodial hospital for "chronic" mental and physical illness or by the

---

*Indeed avoidance of personal accountability may be a prime motivator for profes-
sionals to pool services. One-to-one accountability with individual clients
forces the practitioner to stay on his toes at all times and to maintain his competence and his client-related skills at a high level. Not surprisingly, many
professional practitioners are eager to escape from such a burden.

prison in which the facade of "service" is usually dropped altogether. Although these examples are extreme, they are useful in pointing out the deficiencies in this general approach to consumer service. The most eloquent statement about the exploitive tendency of service organizations is presented by Erving Goffman in his essay on what he calls "total institutions" (#7135).

The total service concept at first glance seems to have some validity, however. Most certainly individual consumers are sometimes so helpless (in early infancy and in advanced stages of illness and old age, for example) or so dangerous that anything less than total service would be unthinkable; but short of extreme cases the marked disadvantages of total service far outweigh its advantages. First of all, regardless of how it may appear on paper, the total service organization is grossly expensive, inefficient, and wasteful in practice. The range of human needs are so great and so variable that a truly adequate system which does not rely on consumer initiative and consumer choice will not only be expensive but it will fall far short of its objectives.

It should further be noted that the total service organization represents the ultimate in domination of the consumer by the practitioner; hence as Goffman notes, the opportunity for exploitation become infinite. Finally, by assuming greater and greater responsibility for the consumer's needs, the total service organization trains the consumer to be more and more dependent, less competent to make rational choices, less able to give feedback, less able to diagnose his own needs. This "trained incapacity" is perhaps the deadliest consequence of certain types of service organizations from the point of view of D&U and from the perspective of the overall health of the macrosystem.

III. THE CONSUMER

The consumer is the third and most important component of the knowledge-flow macrosystem. It is for the consumer that the system exists. However, much of what can be said about the role of consumer has already been said in the discussion of the practice world; what remains is for us to tie together these various threads by focussing now on the organization of the consumer's world and by examining the interface between the consumer and the various practice systems. Figure 3.6 summarizes the principle types of relationship that occur at this interface.

[Insert Figure 3.6 here]

A.   THE DISORGANIZED CONSUMER

The first fact which Figure 3.6 tries to convey is the relative disorganization of the consumption sub-systems. To a surprising degree consumers in our society act as individuals (or as small family units) in their relations to the practice world. As we have noted, this sometimes puts them at a distinct disadvantage. When the practice world is highly organized and tooled up to do a slick selling job, it may be able to manipulate and exploit the average consumer at will. Most consumers lack the training and the resources to do an effective job of rational retrieval and selection with respect to the sea of products and services that surrounds them. This fact would put them completely at the mercy of forces emanating from the practice world (advertising, promotion, monopolization, etc.) were it not for the *informal structure* of user systems.

FIGURE 3.6   The Interface of Practice and Consumption

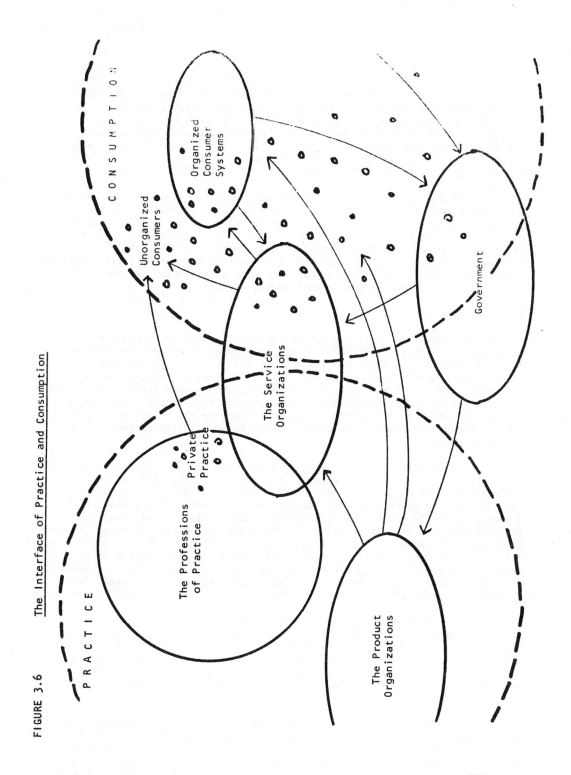

Throughout this review we will have many opportunities to comment on the
informal system of social relations among consumers which substitutes for an
organized rational system of decision-making. Research evidence suggests that
the typical consumer depends heavily on what his next door neighbor does in
making his decisions about the practice world. The focal point of this informal system is the informal "opinion leader", the man who is seen by most
of his neighbors as the norm setter, the one who is safe to follow.

The opinion leader, himself, may or may not be an expert in the art of
consumption and he may or may not be a "progressive" innovator. Hence, while
the informal system serves to protect the average consumer from some forms
of gross exploitation, it does not do so in a very reliable way. Very cau-
tious or conservative opinion leaders can virtually stop the flow of new
knowledge to consumers altogether, while innovative but poorly trained opinion
leaders can lead the average consumer into innovations which are worthless
or dangerous or generally detrimental to his welfare.

B. THE ORGANIZED CONSUMER

Increasingly over the last decade consumers in various categories have
become aware of their relative vulnerability and powerlessness in dealing
with the world of practice, and they have endeavored to organize themselves
for effective defense and counter-influence. Following a pattern not unlike
the trade union and labor union movements of previous generations, the 1960's
saw the rise of the *organized* poor, the *organized* food shopper, and the *organized* student. In the future we may expect to see the emergence of additional unions of tenants, car buyers, patients, legal clients, and perhaps
even prisoners.

The organized consumer movement is probably a very positive force for
improving the D&U macrosystem because until now the consumption component
has been the weakest and least organized. Consumer organizations not only
help to equalize power with the practice organizations but they also provide
the opportunity for scientific investigation and evaluation of practice so
that individual users can be better informed and more discriminating. Furthermore, blocks of consumers are able to enter into *contracted relations* with
service and product organizations to provide products and services at a
specified standard for a specified cost; *accountability* is a built-in feature
of such contractual relations. Individual users are seldom, if ever, able
to enter contracts of this type and certainly not on such favorable terms.

Organized consumers are also in a much better position to act as a pressure group and to lobby with government for regulation of practice and support of research. Sometimes this pressure may be detrimental to the benefit
of the total system (as some may argue concerning anti-fluoridation groups)
but until such a time as consumer power balances out practitioners' power,
such negative influence will be atypical. We have a long way to go before
such power-equalization is achieved.

The consumer is also helped by numerous "public interest" groups even
though such groups are not strictly speaking representative of any one class
of consumers. Most notable among these is "Consumers Union", an independent
non-profit corporation established in the mid-1930's as a mechanism by which
consumers could get objective performance data on various products and services.
It is supported entirely by subscribers to its publication, "Consumers Reports",
with a circulation which has swelled into the millions in recent years. This

increased income has allowed the organization to extend its testing and evaluation program to life insurance and various types of medical services in addition to the familiar product tests. Even so, it has not had the resources to really act as a representative of individual consumers or as a clearinghouse or advisory agency for specific consumers with specific problems. It is not a true "union" in this sense, although the services that it does provide through its publication are unique and valuable. In spite of its relative narrowness of mission it provides a very healthy influence in the D&U macrosystem by setting forth a strictly objective and scientific criterion for judging and selecting products and services.

The consumer spokesman function is also served to some degree by a variety of philanthropic organizations such as the March of Dimes and the American Cancer Society. Such "disease organizations" have been strong forces supporting more effective D&U in the medical arena because they not only provide extensive research support but they also help out particular victims and support public-information, better medical practice and government legislation in their respective areas. In all these ways, these "lay" groups foster a more effective macrosystem of medical care. Similar types of "public interest" groups are found in other fields. For example, the American Civil Liberties Union has been successful in representing the legal interests of various otherwise powerless individuals and minorities, and Ralph Nader has proposed the establishment of a law firm that would represent the interests of consumers exclusively.

C. GOVERNMENT AS SERVANT OF THE PEOPLE AND THE PUBLIC INTEREST

The independent voluntary "public interest" organizations are so small and so relatively powerless that they would have virtually no effect on the macrosystem whatsoever if the society as a whole were unresponsive. Fortunately, however, the United States, like most democratic societies, is sometimes capable of responding to the voices of underprivileged minorities.

At a very gross level government is responsive through the electoral system, but although at the Federal level there is the opportunity for major administrative change every four years, the needs of consumers are rarely expressed in any clear way through this medium. Perhaps the only exception in modern history was the presidential election of 1932 (and the congressional elections of 1930, 32, and 34) which expressed the strong desire of the people for more federal action to change its pro-business economic policies and to engage in extensive regulation and subsidization which favored economically depressed groups. For the most part, however, government is responsive primarily to pressures from groups and individuals who make themselves vocal and articulate on a day-to-day basis, i.e., those who are there at the elbow when critical legislation is about to be enacted and when important policies are about to be promulgated. Unfortunately, at least until recently, unorganized consumers did not have this continuing presence in government; there was no effective consumer lobby.

However, the 1960's brought a change in attitude on the part of many people in government in both the legislation and executive branches. There has been an increasing self-perception of government as the defender and promoter of "the public interest" (most forcefully expressed by John F. Kennedy in successfully insisting on a price roll-back in the steel industry). This has led to the creation of consumer councils and appointed consumer representatives within state and federal governments, and it has also led to several pieces of legislation in long-neglected silent sectors of consumer need such

as care for the aged, auto safety, community mental health, and various programs to aid the poor. An especially significant step in the direction of
a more responsive and responsible government role as monitor and promoter
of the macrosystem of D&U was the proposal by Senator Mondale of Minnesota
for a "Council of Social Advisors". Such a council would supervise the
collection of "Social Accounting" data equivalent to the economic indices
now collected. Mondale's bill (Senate #0843) died in committee in 1967 but
is almost certain to be revived in some form in the near future. Such a
monitoring, if conducted scientifically and if heeded, might herald the beginning of a new era of government responsiveness and effective government action to coordinate and facilitate knowledge D&U macrosystems.

IV. <u>INTEGRATING FORCES</u>

We began this chapter by considering an ideal macrosystem for D&U of five
components (see Figure 3.4), "Basic Research", "Applied R&D", "Practice", "Consumption", and "Government". In successive sections we have analyzed the major
<u>existing</u> system components of knowledge flow in the *scientific, practice* and
consumption domains, and we have emphasized their relative isolation from each
other and the discontinuities and barriers to knowledge flow that are represented
by each. In this final section we would like to consider briefly some of the
more important forces that bring these systems together, that make for continuity
in knowledge flow, and that create effective linkage between research and practice
and practice and consumption.

Four types of integrating forces will be discussed: (1) the communications
media, (2) specialized linking roles, (3) temporary linking systems, and (4) permanent linking systems. The discussion of each will be very brief and presented
only with reference to the macrosystem because each of these integrating forces
receives much more extended treatment elsewhere in this report (notably in Chapters
Seven and Nine).

A. COMMUNICATIONS MEDIA

There is no doubt that communications media of various sorts are important in bridging the gap between components of the macrosystem. Innumerable
journals and magazines "explain" research to practitioners and practice to
consumers in various areas. Such media create <u>awareness</u> of new products,
new scientific discoveries, and new practices long before they are made
available on a mass scale. Hence they prepare practitioners and users for
what to expect in the near and distant future; they alert them to potential
needs, potential dangers, and potential benefits that had never concerned
them before. The mass electronic media, in particular, seem capable of bringing dramatic new developments to the attention of the vast majority of people
within hours and even minutes (as in the case of the assassination of John
F. Kennedy); they can, in crisis situations, bring people together, hold them
together, and sustain them through terrible difficulties.* In more normal
times, however, the mass media are not by themselves an effective vehicle
for conveying significant amounts of information and for effecting behavioral
change.

---

*Note, for example, Harrison Salisbury's account of the key role of the radio
station in sustaining the people through the most terrible days of the seige
of Leningrad. Salisbury, Harrison E. <u>The 900 Days: The Seige of Leningrad,</u>
New York: Harper and Row, 1969.

As we shall note in Chapter Nine, the primary shortcoming of the mass media as an integrating force is their inability to involve the audience directly and actively in the communication process. Without two-way interaction it is very difficult to arouse this type of involvement in the average user. Fortunately, however, all users are not average; some are so cognitively tuned to the medium that they are able to assimilate large quantities of information which they can translate into behavior. If such exceptional media-oriented and innovative individuals have influence in their "home" systems, then through them the media can have an impact beyond mere awareness of new ideas. These possibilities will be discussed in detail in other chapters.

B.   SPECIALIZED LINKING ROLES

As discussed already in Chapter Two and later in more detail in Chapter Seven, it is possible to identify many individuals in various fields who <u>stand between</u> systems of research and practice. Sometimes these "linkers" are merely conveyors of information from one sub-system to another but sometimes they play a more significant role in orchestrating sub-systems so that these components perform more nearly like parts of a macrosystem of D&U. . This seems to be true in the case of the "systems engineer" in the American Telephone and Telegraph Company. Holders of this role are charged with considering the overall objectives of the system and the needs of its various components (basic research, applied research, development, manufacturing, and service), alerting each component to needs and resources of other components. The possibilities for the use of such linking roles are virtually endless, the AT&T model being only one of many variants discussed in Chapter Seven.

C.   TEMPORARY SYSTEMS

It may be possible under certain conditions at certain times to bring together representatives of different sub-systems to discuss barrier problems and to form personal relationships which will eventually lead to more effective inter-system linkage. Quite frequently these temporary inter-system gatherings are initiated and supported by some "third" force such as a philanthropic organization, foundation, or government, itself. Such events have never been studied systematically so that it is difficult to evaluate their general effectiveness as an integrative force for the macrosystem. Presumably, however, they have some catalytic effect: i.e., they create the opportunity for people from different worlds (research, practice, policy, consumption) to initiate long-term personal contacts, and they may lead to the creation of more permanent organizations which represent a continuing linkage. If properly designed, temporary systems can represent significant training experiences in the processes of communication and knowledge utilization for those who participate. It is even possible to simulate the D&U macrosystem by bringing together individuals who represent each component and by having them act out together the process of solving a specific problem or of utilizing a specific piece of research knowledge.

D.   PERMANENT LINKING SYSTEMS

Efforts have been undertaken in various fields to build a complete formal system for D&U, which would come as close as possible to the ideal macrosystem depicted in Figure 3.4. The oldest, most elaborate, and most ambitious such effort is the Cooperative Extension Service which supports U.S. agriculture (for general description, see Sanders et al., #2267). The major components of this system are reproduced in Figure 3.7.

[Insert Figure 3.7 here]

3-33

FIGURE 3.7   Agricultural Extension in the United States: An Example of a Formal Macrosystem for Knowledge Production, Dissemination and Utilization

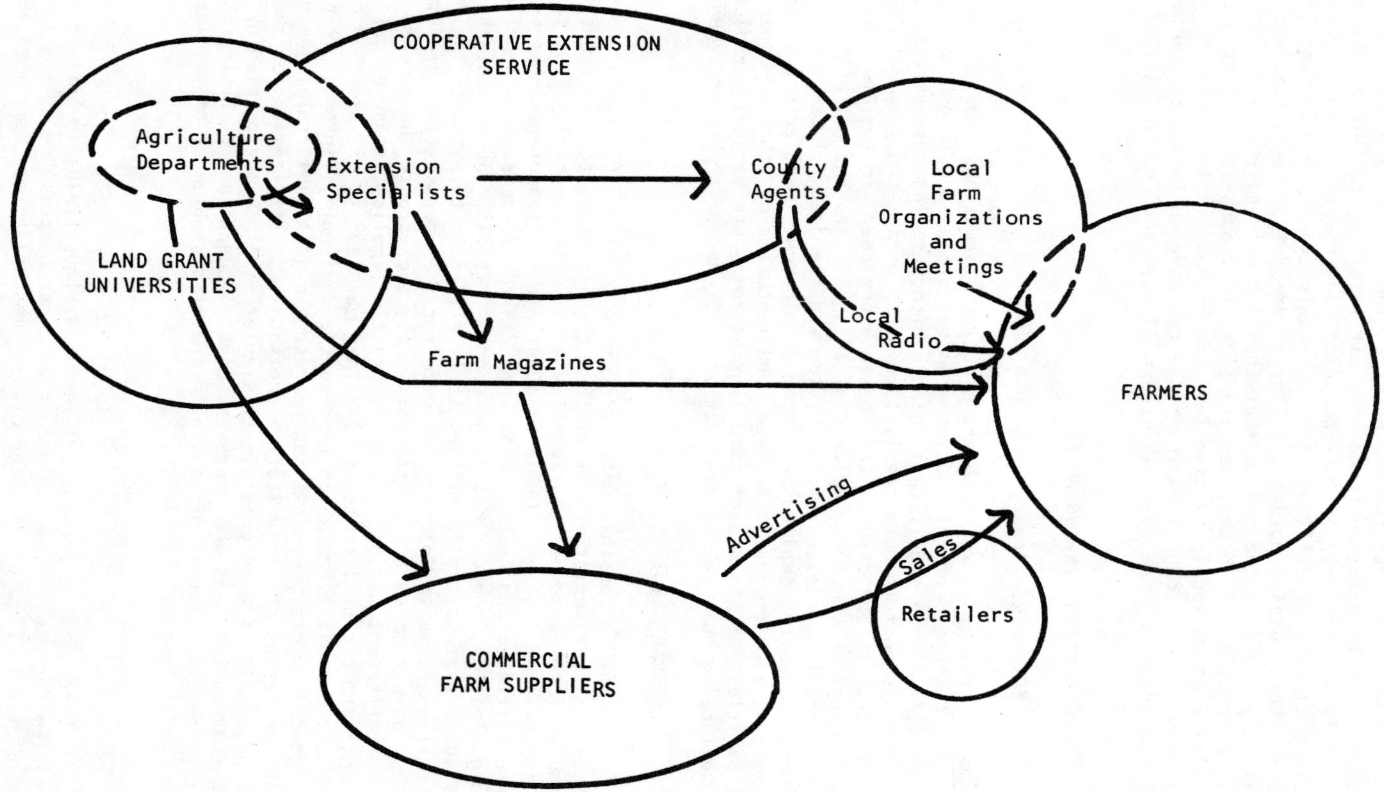

We note first of all that this system provides a very large organizational umbrella and a series of connections which form a chain from researchers in the university to users on the farm. Secondly we note that it employs each of the mechanisms discussed above under headings "A", "B", and "C": it utilizes a number of specialized and generalized media including farm magazines, bulletins, and leaflets on specific products and problems, radio program material, handbooks (for the county agent) and lectures and courses on farm related topics inside and outside the university. We also can find in this system several specialized and thoroughly institutionalized *linking roles* of which only two are depicted in the figure, the extension specialist (university-based expert on a specific area of practical concern to farmer-users) and county agents (locally-based generalists in farm problems). Finally we find considerable use of temporary systems to bring together specialists and users.

A third point to note about the CES is the fact that it is not really complete unto itself. As illustrated in the figure, the CES functions in parallel to a private system of product, information, and service distribution. Close examination would reveal a complementary relationship between these two systems. The CES creates awareness and know-how in the farm community which in turn creates a market for commercially produced innovations. At the same time the presence of an extensive private marketing network relieves the CES from the costly and cumbersome distributive function.

There is much debate about the applicability of the "agricultural model" to other fields, but such a question cannot be answered by any flat statement. There seem to be elements here that should be a part of any macrosystem but we certainly do not know, for example, what combination of roles or sub-systems are going to be optimal for education, or law, or medicine. We do not know from this one case what combinations of institutions and institutional inclusions are optimal, and we do not know what the best balance is between public and private efforts.

The important facts to remember about the CES, however, are that it is a system for D&U, and that it seems to work reasonably well. Education and other fields may do well to borrow from it but to borrow intelligently, remaining fully cognizant of their different objectives and of the advances in information transfer technology that have occurred in the fifty-five years since the inception of the CES. For example the technology transfer system created in the 1960's by the National Aeronautics and Space Administration (NASA) incorporates many exciting new features of information storage, coding, retrieval and selective dissimination that go beyond the CES. This "model" also has many components which other fields will want to copy and adopt. We need to focus on what can be done to simplify, accelerate, and automate many of the transfer processes in the macrosystem.

CONCLUSION: SOME PRESSING NEEDS IN MACROSYSTEM DEVELOPMENT

This brief discussion of the concept and operating reality of the "D&U Macrosystem" brings to light three important facts which we would like to emphasize in closing. There are three outstanding deficiencies in the current state of affairs particularly in education: first, there is a gross underdevelopment of the component we have described as "AR&D" or "Development"; second, there is an inadequate appreciation of "consumption" as a system component; and third, there is very little shared understanding among all components of their mutual relatedness and interdependence. Few of us realize that we are part of a D&U macrosystem and that we would all be able to function more effectively and build a better society if we worked together in a systemic way.

CHAPTER FOUR

THE INDIVIDUAL

Table of Contents   Page

CHAPTER FOUR*

THE INDIVIDUAL

INTRODUCTION

The next three chapters will present individual, interpersonal and organizational factors involved in the dissemination and utilization of scientific knowledge. While each chapter will be presented as a separate unit, they are meant
to be seen as a whole and representative of the effects of all parts of a social
system on the D&U process. There is a problem, however, in this approach.
Because the field of knowledge utilization is in its infancy, few social scientists
not concerned directly with it have attempted to understand how social system
factors relate to the knowledge utilization process. As a result, we have extensive
literature on individual, interpersonal and organizational variables but almost no
application of them to the structures and processes involved in disseminating and
utilizing new knowledge. In these next three chapters we will present these
variables and attempt to relate them to relevant issues in knowledge utilization.

The next two chapters on individual and interpersonal factors will selectively
review the theoretical and field** research literature in social psychology. Such
a review presents formidable problems to the reviewer and the reader. Social
psychology is a field composed of an enormous array of individual experiments
and studies on all the myriad aspects of the individual and groups without any
clear coherent integration, except in small limited areas. Thus, we are forced
to review this literature as a series of relatively discrete areas rather than
an integrated whole.

In this chapter we will present a selected review of those individual variables
that seem most relevant to knowledge utilization.   Where feasible, we will draw
the connections between these variables. At the end of the chapter we will attempt
to integrate in a very general way what we see as some major themes present in
the chapter. We will begin the chapter with a presentation of the ''deeper'', more
enduring, psychological characteristics (sense of competence, personality, values
and needs) and move towards those factors that tend to be more susceptible to
situational and interpersonal influence.

---

*This chapter was drafted by Alan E. Guskin.

**By theoretical literature we mean the non-applied relevant research and theor-
etical studies in the fields of psychology, social psychology and sociology. By
field literature we are referring to studies dealing with attempts to disseminate
and utilize knowledge in action settings. For the most part there is little
overlap in these two areas with the major exception of the public health
literature in smoking

A.   SENSE OF COMPETENCE AND SELF ESTEEM

The manner in which individuals react to their environment and to the way others attempt to influence them is very much dependent on their own feelings of confidence or sense of competence. A sense of competence has been defined by Robert White (#6269) as the "cumulative result of the whole history of transactions with the environment.... In the mature adult the sense of competence may become well organized and differentiated with respect to different spheres of activity. We learn what we can and cannot do, and we may be satisfied to concentrate on the former." (p. 39) This sense of competence is an important motivating force for the individual.

By having confidence in certain of our actions we will tend to take risks, we will tend to explore those aspects of our world related to these actions. White points out that a sense of competence is important for survival because there is a distinct advantage to an individual who explores his environment and manipulates things. The knowledge and skills developed by an individual who has such curosity makes him better able to take advantage of future opportunities.

These feelings of competence would seem to be extremely important in the D&U process. One would expect that individuals who have considerable confidence in their abilities would be more prone to try innovations or to be willing to evaluate new knowledge. In those areas of their competence they will tend to be less likely to reject the new and the strange because of its threat to them.

Closely related to one's feeling of competence is the extent to which he values himself; i.e., the esteem in which he holds himself and his abilities. It can be hypothesized that the more competent an individual is in his own and others' eyes, the greater his sense of self-esteem. One's self-esteem is directly effected by other people's evaluation of him. As White (#6269) states, "through their acts and attitudes (an individual) learns how (others) perceive him and is influenced to perceive himself in the same way" (p. 35). However, he also emphasizes the role that the individual plays in regulating the flow of external sources.

A number of studies have dealt with the role of self-esteem in the acceptance of innovation. Watson (#3690) proposes that self-distrust and a feeling of impotence lead an individual to resist change. Chesler (#2248) refers to a fear of failure which makes teachers more resistant to new practices, and Lippitt, et al. (#1343) propose that a reluctance to admit weakness leads to a lack of acceptance of change.

But self-esteem can be viewed in a different light. While feelings of impotence or failure creates resistance to change when an individual is left by himself, the individual with such low evaluations of himself also tends to be more dependent on others and to seek out others in order to gain approval (Janis, #6270). Such a desire for approval leads the individual to conform with greater intensity to the norms of the groups of which he is a member. As a result, individuals with low self-esteem who are members of a group which makes a decision to accept a new practice will have a strong tendency to accept the innovation. On the other hand, a group which decided to reject a new practice would have considerable influence on such a person and cause him to reject the practice.

Janis (#6270) uses the concept of low self-esteem as a major variable in his proposition of a general factor of "persuasability", i.e., a predisposition to accept the opinion of others.* Michael (#3892) proposes that individuals whose jobs do not enable them to feel competent would tend to be more resistant to change. Unfortunately, this is only half the story because teachers who feel competent may also desire not to accept change from "outsiders" as an attempt to assert their own feelings of competence in determining their work (Chesler and Barakat, #2248).

Carlson (#0585) reports on the distortions that can occur in the adoption of innovations when they threaten a teacher's competence in an established area of self-esteem. When programmed instruction was introduced in a school system, the students, as expected, were able to learn the material at their own rates; the better students moved at a much faster rate than the poorer students. This created a problem for the teachers: one way in which they had gained a feeling of competence was from their ability to teach students as a classroom *group*, but with programmed instruction they could no longer gain this feeling

---

*Besides low self-esteem, Janis cites four other variables as contributing to this general trait:

--men who respond with rich imagery and strong empathic responses to symbolic representations tend to be more persuasable than those whose fantasy responses are relatively constricted;

--men with an "other directed" orientation are predisposed to be more persuasable than those with an "inner directed" orientation;

--men who display social withdrawal tendencies are predisposed to remain relatively uninfluenced by any form of persuasion;

--men who openly display overt hostility toward the people they encounter in their daily life are predisposed to remain relatively uninfluenced by any form of persuasion. (Janis, #6270, p. 60-64).

It should be noted that the research to which Janis refers in developing a general factor of persuasibility showed significant results only for males but not for females; all the subjects were high school and college students.

Besides such individual characteristics, tendency to be persuaded is affected by the cohesiveness of groups in which he is a member, the context within which the group operates and so on. These points will be discussed in the next chapter.

because students were at different stages in their mastery of the content.
In order to be able to continue teaching the students as a group they devised
two methods to equalize the students' pace; first, they began pacing the
faster students by the use of "enrichment materials," and secondly, they
allowed the slower students to take the "programs" home but did not permit
the faster students to do the same. By these ingenious methods the teachers
equalized the pace of all the students and thereby were able to teach the
students as a group. Carlson concludes:

> "Programmed instruction does not give the teachers as much opportunity to
> perform as they apparently desire; it does not give them sufficient
> opportunity to teach. In their eyes, because teaching means performing,
> using programmed instruction is not teaching." (p. 83)

> "It would appear, therefore, that if the logic of programmed instruc-
> tion is to have its way in schools, a new definition of what teaching
> consists of must be instilled in the teachers." (p. 84)

An individual's feeling of competence is a strong motivating force--
whether it be his general feeling of competence as an individual, or as
part of his role as a teacher. The teachers proved this by their novel
approach to programmed instruction. No doubt, many other innovations which
require changes in work habits and thereby require new estimations by the
individual of his competence and performance have been resisted. New practices in areas as complex as education require more than merely re-writing
curricula or providing inservice training for teachers. They also, to some
extent, require a reorientation of the manner by which teachers, supervisors,
and students view themselves.

B.   THE AUTHORITARIAN PERSONALITY

Probably the most widely discussed and researched area of personality
theory is that dealing with the authoritarian or prejudiced personality. This
personality type is said to result from severe discipline in the person's
childhood and is usually manifested in strong prejudice and aggression
towards minority groups (and outsiders generally), a very strong tendency
to accept directives from dictatorial leaders, and a rigid rejection of any
changes emanating from "outside" sources. The major work in this area is The
Authoritarian Personality (Adorno, #6253) which was published in 1950 and represents
research carried out to investigate the psychological roots of Fascism and
anti-semitism in the late 1930's and 1940's. While it has been criticized
from a methodological point of view, its influence has been great. From
1950 to 1956, 230 research projects dealing with authoritarianism were
reported.

Of some importance for our interests is the finding that authoritarian personality types tend to be less tolerant of ambiguity than other individuals. They tend to hold on for a longer time to an original interpretation about which they were certain; when faced with changes in their environment they tend to respond quite slowly; and they tend not to see things that cannot be reconciled with their original interpretation of a situation. While this notion and the research on which it is based has received considerable criticism (see Brown, #6254), it does point out the very important potential relationships between an individual's personality and the manner in which he interprets or evaluates information (i.e., cognitive style).

Delving a little deeper into this relationship between personality and cognitive styles, and separating it from the area of prejudice, Rokeach (#6255) has investigated the extent to which a person has an "open" or "closed mind." "Open-mindedness" is described as a cognitive style in which the information about the nature of the source and the information the source has communicated are evaluated separately. An open minded individual tends to be governed less by irrational forces and is able to resist pressures to change exerted by external sources.

On the other hand, a person with a tendency towards "closed mindedness" has difficulty distinguishing between the source of information and the information itself. Such a person tends to be unduly influenced by internal and external forces. Moreover, there will be a tendency either for him to accept the pressures, rewards, and punishments from the source and to evaluate and act on the new information in the way the source desires, or to reject the source and the information together.

In order to measure open- and closed-mindedness, Rokeach has developed a scale which he calls the dogmatism scale. High dogmatism is equated with closed-mindedness, low dogmatism with open-mindedness.

These concepts of authoritarianism and dogmatism would appear to have a direct bearing on individual attitudes toward new knowledge and practices. For example, one would predict that farmers who are more innovative would score low on a dogmatism scale and would tend to be less influenced by community norms. Jamias (#2265) carried out a study to test these hypotheses and found supporting evidence. Lin, et al. (#3903), in a study of teachers, found that those who scored lower on the dogmatism scale tended to be predisposed to accepting educational innovations. It would also seem to follow from the concepts of authoritarianism and dogmatism that those scoring high on such scales would be prone to accept innovations proposed by dictatorial leaders or leaders whom they respect. Unfortunately the literature doesn't provide us with such examples.

C. VALUES

Another series of concepts that are deeply embedded in an individual's psychological structure are values. Unfortunately, the literature on values is very diffuse; it ranges from laboratory research to theology and seems to elude a clear definition. Generally, values refer to lasting and deep-seated beliefs about the most significant objects in an individual's world: God, nation, family and so on. According to Katz and Stotland (#6280), for example, values are a highly integrated set of attitudes about particular objects in a person's environment.

Values, when seen as a highly integrated and very pervasive and interlocking set of beliefs or attitudes, tend to be important determinants of an
individual's decision to adopt or reject an innovation--provided that the
innovation is seen as conflicting with, or supporting, the values. Generally,
the literature indicates that when innovations run counter to important
values (such as religious beliefs in a supernatural being, Olsen, #2979),
to values regarding the elements being changed (sacredness of cattle,
Niehoff, #3005), or to values about social customs (Moslem women's purda,
Luschinsky, #3378), the innovation will be rejected.

However, even when dealing with such strong and enduring factors as
values, initial resistance to innovation may be avoided. This can be done not
by changing people's values but rather by associating the values with the
desired change. Luschinsky (#3368) showed that when a government educator
working in an Indian village associated cleanliness in childbirth with the
villagers' belief in a spirit, and smallpox vaccinations with a belief in a
goddess, the villagers accepted these new health procedures. However, when
such an association was not made for a change in cleanliness of women in
purda (the custom of seclusion of women), the proposed practice was rejected.

A similar procedure was used in a controlled laboratory experiment by
Carlson (#6256) in an attempt to change a white audience's attitudes which
were in favor of housing segregation. He theorized that such attitudes are
based on the belief that integrated housing would contradict some basic
values. To test these relationships he investigated the nature of these values
and found that while some values of the audience were supported by their
attitudes about integrated housing, others were not. (Four values were isolated: "high real estate values are good," "being broad minded is good,"
"having all people realize their particular potentials is good," "high
international prestige for America is good.") The experimental subjects were
then presented with evidence that integrated housing would further their
values rather than thwarting them. By doing this he was able to show the
subjects that the new attitudes were instrumental for their values while the
old attitudes were not. Following this informational input he found that the
attitudes towards segregation were significantly changed, except in the case
of the extremely prejudiced subjects who showed little or no change.

Therefore, by changing the connection between the individual's attitudes
and values, Carlson was able to change the attitudes. In a sense, the subjects seemed to be evaluating alternative attitudes and chose those which
were more consonant with their values. However, those individuals who were
extremely prejudiced were apparently unable to make such judgments. Their
prejudice seems to prevent this. Also of importance in this experiment was
the fact that the experimenter was of a high status and considered an expert.

It should be noted that while in some situations such associations
can be made, there are many values which do not lend themselves to such manipulation because they directly conflict with the proposed changes. In an attempt
to specify how values can be coped with, Havelock (#6183) has distinguished
six potential strategies.

1. Put emphasis on those values which are shared by the source and
   receiver. In so doing, we must be careful not to assume that
   because a receiver agrees with you he will make the desired
   change. Behavior is determined by other factors as well as
   values. The dope addict may agree on the terrible effects of
   narcotics but he still may be unable to control his use of
   them.

4-6

2. By-pass value issues. The problem here is that if you are unsuccessful you may increase suspiciousness and distrust.

3. Negotiate. Like any interpersonal differences, value issues, once they are known, can be negotiated.

4. Expose value issues. It might be that the mere recognition by the receiver that his values are considered and respected will help create an atmosphere of trust and acceptance.

5. Find key values and appeal to them. This is the same as presented above in the reference to Luschinsky (#3368).

6. Respect value barriers. Values are an important element of our life. "Before we charge headlong over a value barrier, we should ask ourselves how it got there. The reason may still be valid, and as often as not, we should respect the value and respect the barrier it creates." (p. 174)

D. NEEDS

Another psychological characteristic that is pervasive in an individual's psychological structure and which is, generally. poorly defined is the concept of need. Usually, needs refer to an individual's basic desires, drives, motives, and so on. The concept has been used to describe such broad areas as the need for food, the need for consistency in one's image of self, or the individual's need for particular types of courses in order to get a good education. Needs such as hunger and self-consistency can be described as extremely important and deeply embedded in the psychological structure of an individual. On the other hand, the need for particular courses can, for the most part, be described as rather peripheral, unimportant, and rather limited in its effect on other psychological structures.

Relating this to the D&U process, we can hypothesize that when an innovation requires a shift in a need which is highly important and salient to the individual, it tends to be rejected. Conversely, when a desired change requires a shift in needs which are peripheral to the individual, change is more likely (see Newcomb, #6257, and Marmor, et al., #3160).

However, salience of a need can lead to rather quick acceptance if the innovation is directly relevant and effective in fulfilling that need (Coleman, et al., #3893). Similarly, needs which are not being satisfied and are causing considerable tension and frustration will make an individual more prone to change in a direction that reduces the tension. Lippitt, et al. (#1343) refer to this when they say that individuals or systems will be more predisposed to change when they feel "pain."

Thus, when particular needs are seen as important to the individual and relevant to a particular situation, innovations or new knowledge will be accepted only when they fit these needs. A number of field studies support this notion of "fit". Katz, et al. (#0297), in their review of the adoption literature (mainly the agricultural and medical literature), state that material items find more ready acceptance than non-material ones, mainly because of the fewer ramifications in other spheres of personal and social life. Pelligrin (#1043) draws a similar conclusion from his review of the educational adoption literature. In a similar vein, Menzel (#1386) reports that the less pervasive the changes required by a medical innovation, the more likely doctors are to accept it.

4-7

The reason for this necessity for fit, even in times of predispositions to change, is that an individual's personality, needs, attitudes, values, etc., are interdependent with each other. If an innovation is proposed which requires a change in an important need or value, other needs and values must likewise change. Highly salient aspects of an individual's psychological make-up are embedded in many other parts, each interdependent with the other. The overall effect seems to be that an equilibrium has been established. When this equilibrium or balance is upset, a great number of changes must occur to restore it. Hence, there is resistance to such changes.

It is important to emphasize that in order for values, needs, or most psychological characteristics to react in the ways discussed above, they must, at the minimum, be in a mild state of arousal. If there appears to be no need evidenced in response to a particular set of conditions which an observer thinks should produce some reaction, this may not be the result of poor fit but may signify a lack of arousal of the need at that point.

When particular needs or values are not activated or aroused, innovations which to an observer seem to be in conflict with these needs or values may be adopted. Wolff (#0533), and many other observers, have noted these seemingly "peculiar" events. In Malaya, Wolff found that new health practices, if they fitted into the existing cultural norms and traditions, were accepted. The new element was merely added on to all the old ones without any real acceptance of or concern about the ideas that led to the development of the health practice. The outside observers seemed to feel that the ideas behind the new practices (e.g., germ theory) were inconsistent with older practices which were followed almost simultaneously (e.g., certain religious rituals). Wolff states that the inconsistency seen by Westerners is just not felt by Malayans, as long as everything is seen in balance. Another way of stating this is that while these innovations may have aroused certain values in Westerners they do not--for whatever reasons--seem to do so in Malayans.

It seems, then, that the required fit between needs or values and innovations is an important concern when the needs or values are activated. When no such activation occurs, the innovations may merely be added on. An important consideration is the extent to which the individual is aware of the conflict (or lack thereof) between the values inherent in the innovation and his own values. With low activation of his own values, the conflict might not be seen. However, if at a later date the values are aroused and the conflict is perceived, then the issue of fit might be relevant, and the individual may reject a previously "accepted" innovation.

One can easily get the feeling from much of the literature on enduring psychological characteristics that man is a passive animal controlled by a whole series of relatively irrational forces. This is probably not true for most of the people most of the time. When needs, values and other psychological characteristics are not aroused, more rational processes are at work. These processes can be described as an evaluation of the alternatives present in the individual's environment in terms of general cognitive styles. Often the individual does not totally reject information contradictory to these psychological characteristics but desires to become aware of such information in order to properly evaluate his position in terms of all the possible alternatives.

These first four sections have dealt with a selective group of psychological characteristics that are typically referred to as "deep" or highly im-
bedded psychological structures. These characteristics are the result of
the development of the individual over many years, and, as a result, are
difficult to change. Some theorists, namely Freud and his followers, have
stated that these characteristics are formed during the first few years of
an individual's life and are extremely difficult to change after that.
More recently, emphasis is being placed not only on the formation of these
characteristics in the first few years but also on their development and
reinforcement throughout an individual's life.

The remainder of the chapter will deal with less embedded psychological
characteristics and how they effect an individual's tendency to accept or
reject new knowledge or innovations. These characteristics are thought
to be much more likely to change as a result of alterations in an individual's
environment.   Such psychological characteristics are of particular importance to us because they point to areas which have potential for strategic
intervention in inducing change in individuals.

It should be emphasized that the characteristics to be presented in
the rest of this chapter are greatly influenced by the type of psychological
structures presented in the first four sections. Under some circumstances
there will be a direct relationship between an individual's needs, values,
personality and/or esteem and one of the less embedded characteristics.
More often the characteristics to be presented will be influenced by the
general psychological style of the individual which results from the interaction and interdependence of a number of the deeper, more embedded
characteristics.

E.   PAST EXPERIENCE

In all our previous discussions in this chapter we have emphasized how
past experience creates in individuals predispositions to act with certain
types of behaviors. The individual who is an authoritarian personality or
closed minded type developed his rather inflexible tendencies from early
childhood experiences which were reinforced throughout his life. The
development of certain values and needs occurred as a result of continuous
experiences in the individual's life. Similarly, a person's sense of competence or self esteem emerges from his past experiences.

In this section we will discuss more directly how certain types of past
experiences relate to later tendencies to adopt or reject new knowledge,
practices or innovations.   We will be concerned with how experience
with certain types of innovations will predispose individuals to adopt
similar innovations or adopt innovations in general.

A number of authors have referred to the role of past experience in
predisposing an individual to change. Newcomb et al. (#6297) state that the
greater the amount of information an individual has about a particular topic,
the more difficulty there will be in changing his attitude in that area.
Since the individual is aware of the many aspects of the particular topic,
new information will have relatively little effect compared to its effects
on an individual who is more ignorant.

This same finding is reinforced by McGuire (#6261), who reviews research
showing that training to resist influence in a specific area is quite effective; he finds that individuals who are forewarned about an impending persuasive attempt (which he calls attitude "innoculation") will be resistant

4-9

to such influence. McGuire's findings on attitude immunization are derived from research using cultural truisms (statements about which individuals have never, or rarely, heard negative remarks) and may not apply, as he states, to other more controversial situations. However, one implication might be drawn for D&U from his research: namely that individuals who are consistently exposed to innovations which fail or innovations which produce only minimal success may develop a general resistance to the acceptance of innovations. This resistance would result from the building up of defenses under conditions of repeatedly unsuccessful innovative efforts.

But, conversely, does this mean that individuals who have adopted innovations in the past will continue to do so in the future? Most people would probably respond affirmatively to this question, basing their response on the assumption that individuals who adopt a number of innovations do so because of their implicit faith in the products of modern science, and also that newness means "progress" which in turn means greater benefits or satisfaction to themselves.

In an attempt to respond to this we shall first report studies dealing with the relationship between prior use of a specific innovation and the use of new forms of that innovation (e.g., the prior use of one type of contraceptive and the present use of a new type). We will then report studies dealing with broader issues of the relationship between the previous use of innovations and the present or future use of any innovations.

In a study of early Salk vaccine adopters, Clausen, et al. (#6010) found that those individuals who consented to the Salk vaccine trials (in 1954) were more likely to have tried other precautions against polio. Similarly when a birth control program was undertaken in Taiwan (Freedman and Takeshita, #1403), it was found that an action program--which included information, mass media and personal contact--to convince women to use contraceptives resulted in greater adoption among those women who had previously, though unsuccessfully, used contraceptives. In another study (Coleman, et al., #3576) it was found that doctors who had used a certain family of drugs were highly predisposed to use a new drug of the same group.

Some of the possible dynamics at work may be seen in a study of agricultural innovations by Brandner (#2471). He states that "the research strongly suggests that individuals in position to use previously adopted practices to evaluate subsequent innovations will adopt the subsequent innovations much more rapidly than individuals who use other evaluative processes." Another way of saying this is that past experience provides information about the alternatives under consideration and tends to provide greater weight to those alternatives which are similar to those which have been successful or which have shown the possibility of success.

Somewhat related to the above studies is an observational study of the relationship between the Bureau of Indian Affairs and the American Indians (#2262). Leon states that the Bureau has over the years maintained rather extreme paternalistic attitudes toward the Indians. The attitudes and behavior have led to very "destructive environmental experiences" for the Indians: "...this treatment, in turn, is a reaction to the Indian's appearance of being unmotivated and his tendency to do passively what he is told to do. When this cycle is operating, help is given in such a way as to be unacceptable, and if it is accepted, psychological resistance in the client tends to insure failure or at least to militate against success." (p. 727) The prior experience of the Indians has made any new attempts at help by the Bureau very difficult to achieve.

The notion that past experiences with an innovation produces a tendency
to accept new practices or products which are similar seems quite obvious.
Somewhat more questionable is the notion that there exists a general orientation to the adoption of innovations.

Morgan, et al. (#6326), in their study of PRODUCTIVE AMERICANS, presents
what would seem to be support for such a general tendency. In analyzing
the difference between those who use automobile seat belts and those who
do not, he concludes that use is directly related to formal education,
planning to avoid risk in most other areas, a general receptivity to new
products and services, and a generally approving attitude toward modern
science. Hudspeth (#1190) seems to provide some support (though his
subject matter area is more limited) in his finding that faculty members
who use graphics are significantly more likely to have a favorable attitude
toward all educational media than are those faculty members who do not use
graphics in their teaching.

But other evidence does not agree with these findings. Carlson (#0585)
reports that of three educational innovations studied, adoption of one innovation was not necessarily a reliable predictor of adoption of any of several
other innovations. Rogers (#1824), in his extensive review of the adoption
literature, concludes:

> "There is no clear-cut evidence as to whether or not innovation
> behavior (i.e., early adoption)* is completely consistent.
> (It was) found that families who adopted one consumer innovation,
> for example, home air conditioning, were likely to adopt other
> consumer innovations. There is less evidence, however, that a
> farm innovator is also an innovator in political ideology, con-
> sumer behavior, or other areas of life.
>
> (But) in any event, it is doubtful whether an individual who is
> an innovator for one idea is a laggard for another idea." (p. 187)
>
> "Research findings, although somewhat fragmentary at the present
> time (1962), indicate there is considerable shifting of individuals
> in a social system from one adopter category to another over
> time" (usually the direct neighboring category). p. 192**

From these findings, it is probably best to conclude that individuals
are just not very simple; they continue to elude the social scientists'
attempt to place them in neat categories which would provide the base for
clean theoretical statements. A faith in modern science is no doubt the
mark of many highly educated individuals; so too is the tendency to take
risks regarding adoption of innovations. But, individuals also do not
like uncertainty and the unknown. Highly educated, young, risk-oriented,
and progress-oriented individuals may tend to accept innovations which
require little change in their overall behavior or which have some known
risk value attached to them. They probably are not so likely to accept
innovations which lead to some kind of pain or anxiety.

---

*It should be noted that Rogers is referring to early as against late adoption.
We are using the terms adoption of innovation and early adoption synonymously.
Late adopters are those who adopt an innovation when it is really no longer an
innovation for most people.
**Rogers is referring to a continuum of adoption categories: innovators, early
adopters, early majority, late majority, laggards (see #1824, p. 169-171).

F.   FEELINGS OF THREAT AND RESULTANT SUSCEPTIBILITY TO INFLUENCE

One of the most heavily researched psychological characteristics is that which we shall call "feelings of threat". Studies have used many different words to describe this: "fear", "anxiety", "insecurity", "feeings of threat", and so on. Researchers have suggested that, typically, an individual will feel threatened if his self image is questioned unknowingly by another (Hyman and Sheatsley, #2026), if new behavior represents unfamiliar elements (Mitchell and Mudd, #3958), if the desired change threatens the individual's status (Willower, #0637), or if the individual feels relatively secure in his present status position and insecure about the prospect of change (Gallaher, #2613).

All these different types of feelings of threat are based on external sources which tend to be ambiguous and relatively impervious to direct action by the individual. This ambiguity and uncertainty tends to increase anxiety. A possible result of these feelings has been proposed by Schachter (#6260) and Festinger (#0264). They have demonstrated that under conditions of uncertainty and/or anxiety individuals will seek out others in order to compare themselves with these others: this, in turn, enables them to evaluate the status of their own ability, opinions and emotions. This has been referred to by Festinger (#0264) as the social comparison processes. Typically, individuals in such a condition seek out others who are similar to themselves and who seem to be undergoing similar reactions. Schachter (#6260) states that "misery doesn't love just any kind of company, it loves only miserable company". (p. 24)

These results raise some problem for the public health educator. If he attempts to reduce cigarette smoking through an increase in threat, anxiety and the like, he may actually be pushing the listener into the arms of friends who smoke. For, under conditions of high anxiety or ambiguity, individuals will seek out others similar to themselves (i.e., those who smoke) in order to make an "accurate" comparison or evaluation of their actions.

G.   EFFECTS OF FEAR

While fear or anxiety do effect an individual's receptivity to new information, the question arises as to the effects of different degrees of fear on a person's tendency to change his attitudes. Early research by Janis and Feshback (#6262) emphasized that lower levels of fear had a greater effect on attitude change than did higher levels; it was hypothesized that a sort of defensiveness developed to resist high fear influence attempts.

Recent research has found this to be only partially accurate. Rather, Leventhal and others (#3851, #6296) have found that the higher the fear the greater the attitude change. It is quite obvious that both these sets of results which are based on large numbers of research projects cannot be accurate under similar conditions. McGuire (#0390) attempts to resolve the seeming contradiction between these two groups of studies and in the process gives us some insight into how fear and anxiety operate. He says that "at low levels of initial concern, increased fear arousal would enhance attitude change, but, with higher initial concern, further arousal would impede opinion change" (p. 485). Hence, in situations where individuals show some concern

4-12

about an issue, high fear would not be effective. But, in a situation in which an individual showed relatively little concern--or awareness--high fear arousal would have a positive effect on attitude change. What seems to occur, then, is that in situations in which there is a prior arousal of anxiety, high fear is not effective because it may raise the level of anxiety beyond a point that individuals will accept and they might resist as a defense or avoid the issue; or, prior arousal sensitizes the individual to defend himself against influence attempts.

These findings lead to certain interpretations about the effects of anti-smoking advertisements on smokers. What may be occurring when cigarette smokers resist high fear appeals by the American Cancer Society is that their anxiety is so high that they defensively reject the message. The high anxiety would result from their prior sensitivity to the dangers of smoking Thus, while it may be good to initially have high fear appeals, over time a more moderate approach may be most effective. Stated another way, when dealing with issues about which individuals are unaware, one should start off with the "hard sell" and move to a "soft sell" approach.

Considerable field and laboratory research has been generated by the findings that show a correlation between smoking and cancer. Almost immedi-ately following the publication of the United States Public Health Services Report (in 1964), which linked cigarette smoking and cancer, Swinehart and Kirscht (#0457) administered questionnaires to college students. The results showed that "smokers, as compared to non-smokers, become less accurate in recalling the content of the Report, and evaluated the Report less favorably " (p. 519). Many smokers were aware of the link and the possibility of per-sonal harm, but they were able to rationalize their continued smoking by believing that they could quit if they decided to do so. "An intention to quit apparently helped some smokers tolerate the disturbing discrepancy between their beliefs and their behavior " (p. 519).

Working in the same area, Lane (#0333) found that after watching TV programs about the relationship between cancer and smoking, smokers, as compared to the non-smokers, believed less in the smoking-cancer link. It was also found that these smokers who had no intention of quitting had pro-smoking attitudes while those smokers who were going to quit had an anti-smoking reaction.

The findings on fear discussed above are relevant here: those smokers who rejected the link might have been those who were previously concerned about the high fear induced by the Report, and the TV program might have caused too much anxiety which led to a defensive reaction, i.e., they rejected the information. Those who felt they could or were going to quit might not have felt this type of anxiety and, therefore, may not have reacted defensively and rejected the information.

Some supporting evidence for this analysis of the effects of different levels of fear might be found in a study by Brock reported in Jones and Gerard (#6285). He showed that when smokers had a choice of materials to read, articles supporting the cancer-smoking link were chosen as often as they were rejected. However, when they were *forcibly* exposed to pro and con information about cancer, the smokers preferred articles discounting the evidence.

Further evidence for the positive effects of high fear is seen in a study by Insko, et al. (#0318) of non-smoking 7th grade students. They found that high fear-arousing communications from authoritative sources were more effective in producing opinion change about future smoking behavior than were low fear arousing communications.

4-13

An important aspect of all of the above research is that the influence attempt was presented to a large audience (readers of a report, viewers of a television program) and therefore tended to be depersonalized. This raises an interesting question about the defensive reaction of "concerned" individuals under high fear conditions: would they reject the influence attempt if it were highly personalized (in terms of personal harm) about some of their unique problems? An example of this might be seen in the following case. A smoker had experienced a precancerous inflammation which subsided when he stopped smoking and returned when he continued. The physician, attempting to impress upon his patient the seriousness of the inflammation if he continued smoking, showed him slides of each of the subsequent stages of the inflammation with the last slide being cancer of the upper portions of the throat. He impressed upon the patient that he was at stage 1 and that nothing serious would occur if he stopped smoking. If he continued and cancer set in, the only "cure" was exorcizing the tissue, that is, removing part of his face. To say the least, this was an extremely high fear situation and the patient stopped smoking, even though it was difficult, While this high fear produced considerable anxiety, the alternatives personally open to the patient were quite clear: continue smoking and get cancer, stop smoking and be healthy. The most important variable seemed to be the personalized nature of the information.

Fear can also be seen from a very different point of view. An individual can be afraid that if he adopts an innovation it will be harmful to him. In the discussion on the cancer-smoking link, we emphasized the effects of fear on the continued performance of a behavior. Individuals who were smokers were being presented with information which was dissonant with the way they were acting--assuming that they were concerned with their future health. To accept the information being presented (on the cancer-smoking link) and to act upon it, meant giving up a practice. But one can also look at the fear that results from concern about beginning a new practice.

Merrill, et al. (#6002) report that one of the reasons that mothers refused permission for their children to be vaccinated with the Salk vaccine in the early days of its use (pre 1958) was their fear of its negative effects. While some of this fear may have been realistic, much of it was based on misinformation. This question of safety or misinformation and non-acceptance in the use of the Salk vaccine is also reported by Clausen, et al.* (#6010).

As would be expected, other things being equal, a feared object is generally rejected. Of course, other things don't have to be equal. The disseminator can offset fear through programs which emphasize the benefits of the innovation. However, the fear induced by an innovation would require the disseminator to orovide conclusive evidence of his views.

What emerges from this discussion on fear and anxiety is the conclusion that fear is a very complex variable which must be viewed within the framework of the individual's previous and potential behavior, the extent to which the fear directly affects him personally, the nature of the fear itself, its intensity, and the general context within which it occurs. One cannot merely state that fear-inducing communications of a certain level will or will not lead to acceptance or rejection of scientific knowledge, new practices, or innovations.

---

*We will deal with the question of information and rational fears related to safety in a later part of this section.

H.   SELF FULFILLING PROPHECIES

1.   *Self Expectations*

As a result of past experiences an individual develops certain expectancies about his own behavior. He has been reinforced in these expectancies by his own evaluation of his behavior, his estimate of himself in relation to others, and his impressions of others' feelings about himself. Brickman (#6263) reviews a large part of the literature on the effects of expectancies of self and others on actual behavior. These studies, for the most part, dealt with the effects of experimental manipulation on an individual's expectancies. He derived at least two generalizations from the literature on the effects of self-expectancies on an individual's performance:

1.   "People who expect to fail are more likely to fail even when they succeed and want to succeed."

2.   "If they do perform well, they are more likely to discount the evidence of their success."

Why should this be so? Brickman states that this occurs because behaviors that disconfirm expectations lead an individual to feel dissatisfied and uncomfortable. As a consequence the individual desires to live up to his own expectations.

2.   *Effects of Early Experiences*

An example of the importance of expectancies is the effect of the first or early contacts on a relationship. A number of different studies report these effects. One study showed that in social casework interviews, mistakes in the first interview were much more critical than later mistakes (Stark, #1795). Another reported that the resistance to research by clinicians is affected by the lack of understanding and the lack of perceived relevance that grows out of initial meetings with researchers (Poser, et al. #2210). Guskin (5162) reports that administrators who perceived a researcher as not being overly articulate and being lack-luster in the first meeting tended to discount future briefings and reports. And a related finding by Lippitt, et al. (#0791) showed that when initial phases of planned change attempts are exhausting, resistance to such attempts in the future will occur.

In short, early experiences in a relationship lead to relatively lasting effects. Another way of saying this is that expectations developed in early phases of a relationship lead one to develop certain expectations about another individual, and about one's relationship to him. As shown above, these expectations tend to lead to self-fulfilling prophecies. The self-fulfilling prophecy in some situations may operate through what Newcomb (#6257) has called "autistic hostility." Individuals, especially when their early encounters are experienced as unpleasant, tend to withdraw from interactions with the others. As a result of this withdrawal, early impressions are not checked against future interactions. Further, the individual tends to distort the behavior of the other to fit these first impressions. This results in a continuing building up of negative impressions of the other which go unchecked. In time, both partners in the interaction have built up,

on an autistic* basis, hostile reactions to each other which predisposes each not to interact with the other. Thus, early expectations are maintained and future interactions are interpreted so
as to reinforce these expectations.

Complicating and intensifying these notions are the findings
of studies on the relationship between similarity of attitudes and
opinions and the tendency to interact. Newcomb, et al. (#6297)
review many studies that show that the greater the attitudinal
similarity, the greater the interaction and the greater the attraction. Triandis (#1759) shows that individuals with similar cognitive styles tend to understand each other better than those with
dissimilar styles. Guskin (#5162) shows that the dissimilarity
in the style of work of administrators and researchers leads to
problems in understanding the role of the other and thereby a
difficulty in the utilization of research findings by administrators
And Schmuck (#6229) has noted the same phenomenon in the
relations between social psychological researchers and school administrators.

Therefore, first impressions and early experiences in interpersonal interaction greatly affect future relationships through
the development of withdrawal tendencies by individuals who have
difficulties relating to each other. These tendencies are created
by an autistic process of embellishing early images into full blown
impressions of others, which, in turn, lead to the self-fulfilling
prophecy of these impressions. One would expect that such occur-
rences would place great difficulties on the introduction of changes.

Typically, change attempts are initiated by individuals--
change agents, technical advisors, and the like--who are outside
the system to be changed and whose styles of work and cognitive
orientations tend to be different from those who are the recipients
of change. One might suspect that many failures in attempted change
may result from such dissimilarities and that these failures may, in
turn, create expectations of future failures.

This vicious cycle can be broken by interventions which encourage or force continued interactions, thereby preventing the
autistic processes and creating confrontations between the participants. Under such conditions continuous feedback may create
new impressions which might tend to be more veridical. The continuous feedback probably has the effect of creating a common
ground for understanding; it also might create greater attraction
through the continuous interaction.

3. *Others' Expectations*

Changing the focal point from the individual's expectations
for himself and how they affect behavior to how the expectations

---

*Autistic can be defined as follows: without any communication to the other person,
only on the basis of one's own thoughts.

of others affect the individual, Brickman (#6263) concludes from his
literature review that:

1. "People who expect someone else to fail are more likely to
    induce him to fail even when they intend him to succeed.

2. "If the other individual does do well, they are more likely
    to discount the evidence of his success.

3. "If he does succeed, they are likely to be less attracted
    to him." (p. 38)

In other words, not only do individuals maintain their expectations
through their own tendencies but others help them along, even though
they may not consciously desire to do so. One study by Rosenthal and
Jacobsen (#6264) reports that first and second grade students whose
teachers were falsely told they had scored higher on a test which
supposedly measured "sudden intellectual growth" actually gained in I.Q.
points when compared to a control group of students whose teachers
were not so informed. This was true even though the teachers had
trouble recalling which students had "higher" test scores. The teachers
were doing something to reinforce the students even though they themselves may not have been aware of it. The results did show, however,
that the teachers were not spending more time with the "brighter"
students than the others. Rather, the teachers seemed to be communicating something non-verbally which affected the children.

A study by Beez (#7222) points to some of these dynamics. Using
naive tutors and a random selection of tutees from a population of pre-
school children, Beez presented to each tutor a falsified set of test
results for each tutee. The experimenter told the tutors that the
tutees had been given a battery of tests (intelligence, etc.) and that
the summary they received represented the tutees' scores. On the basis
of these purposely falsified results the tutors could be divided into
two groups--one whose tutees had reportedly done very well and one whose
had not. Each tutor then proceeded to teach his tutee ten symbols
in a ten minute period. The results were astounding; the tutees who were
said to have done well on the previous tests learned a great deal
more than did those tutees who were said to have done poorly. An analysis
of the interaction of the tutors and tutees showed that those tutors
who expected their tutees to do well taught the ten symbols quickly with
relatively little explanation of each symbol. On the other hand, the
tutors who expected their tutees not to do well spent a great deal of
time explaining each symbol: As a result, these students learned less.
It is possible that over time such teaching practices could lead the
students to develop expectancies about their own behavior. (It might
also be that the "slower" group would retain more.)

The implications of these studies are quite important. Rosenthal
(#6265) writes:

"some interesting practical questions arise from these considerations. When an experienced physician or psychotherapist tells
the neophyte that his patient has a poor or good prognosis, is
the experienced clinician only assessing or is he actually
'causing' the poor or good prognosis? When the master teacher

4-17

tells his apprentice that a pupil appears to be a slow learner, is this prophecy then self-fulfilled? When the employer tells the employee that a task cannot be accomplished, has the likelihood of its accomplishment thereby been reduced? More subtly, might these phenomena occur even if the supervisors never verbalized their beliefs? The data cited suggested that they may."

4. *Some Applications*

    a. *Cross-Cultural Change Agents*

    Among the phenomena which could be explained by these self-fulfilling prophecies are the many failures of United States technical advisors overseas. In general, United States technical advisors have expectations that their work will be difficult and the living conditions extremely uncomfortable. Implicit in these expectations is an unspoken assumption that the major difficulty in their work results from the inferiority of the "natives" of the host country ("why else would I be here as an advisor"). This inferiority is conceived of mainly in terms of skills, education, and the like, but it also has traces of the American's feeling that Western, and particularly American, civilization is somehow superior to others. Many of these feelings are intensified by the perceived "hardship" conditions under which they live, the fear of "filth" and disease, and the difficulties caused by the adjustment to a new culture.*

    These negative reactions are often communicated to the host country national by the facial expressions of frustration, the loud angry voice, the expressions of hopelessness and so on. The nationals pick this up very quickly; first, because of the extreme sensitivity to foreigners' reactions caused by their feelings of inferiority; second, because of the typically greater concern in many developing societies for the interpersonal reactions of others and the resultant extreme interpersonal sensitivity to the behavior of others; third, the general sensitivity of both communicators and receivers during the early stages of a relationship.

    The combination of negative expectations held by the advisors and the sensitivity of the host country nationals may very often lead the national to feel that the advisor expects him to fail-- and, therefore, he frequently does. Complicating this picture is the fact that advisors often reject, either directly or indirectly, those nationals who tend to be deviants from the societal norms of the host country. Because the advisors expect the nationals to behave in a certain way, those that do not conform these expectations are reacted to unfavorably. For example, in Thailand foreigners tend to have an image of the Thais as passive, always happy, always smiling, etc. While American advisors feel that the passivity and a "happy-go-lucky" attitude is detrimental to the development of the country, they are disturbed by those Thais who do not behave in this manner. The expression used is that these deviants are not "real Thais." (See Guskin, #5163) So, those

---

*Following the previous analysis on anxiety and social comparison we would expect the advisors to seek out others--Americans--who have similar anxieties and fear. These individuals together would reinforce the justification for the cause of the anxiety. Hence, the American overseas enclaves.

Thais who represent the greatest potential for the development of Thailand are often rejected because they are deviants; i.e., the activists are rejected because they are deviants. The activists are rejected in favor of those who are passive, thereby further sealing the failure of the advisor's change program.

While many Peace Corps Volunteers overcame the above problems because of their non-advisor role and their continuous interaction with host nation colleagues as equals, the effect of expectations of the "real" national caused great difficulty. Guskin (#5163) reports the following:

> "Before joining the Peace Corps, the image that the potential PCV develops of his role overseas... is that he will work in rural areas, in isolated, unacculturated places. He pictures himself teaching children through an exotic language, roughing it on a community development project, or introducing new agricultural techniques to people still adhering to a comparatively "pure" tradition much different from the American. A metropolis like Bangkok does not, to him, represent the "real" Thailand or the "real" Thai people. And (the major) university, run by a faculty who are in many ways highly acculturated to western norms and values, hardly represents the monolithic cultural challenge anticipated by the Volunteer. As a result, it is probably generally true that PCVs assigned to the metropolis have been less happy than those assigned upcountry." (p. 99)

> "A good part of our first year at the (university) was, therefore, characterized by confusion as we struggled to learn when to behave in the Thai mode and when in the western. Often we would behave in the Thai mode, only to perceive that our Thai acquaintance wanted to deal on western terms.... At such moments, the simplicity of the "rural image" seemed particularly inviting." (p. 100)

b. *Labeling Children as Mentally Retarded*

Another important implication of the research presented above for the utilization of scientific knowledge is seen in the labeling of children as mentally retarded. This labeling is often made on the basis of psychological tests (e.g.,intelligence tests). What happens is that children labeled as mentally retarded are placed in special classes which theoretically provide them with special attention. More often, these classes tend to fulfill the expectancies of the label-- children are moved along very slowly, are not challenged, etc. In short, on the basis of the utilization of scientific evidence (from tests) children are placed in special classes which were set up following a scientific perspective that emphasizes special treatment for children who have special problems.

Unfortunately, there are two major flaws in this approach. First, because of inadequate knowledge and the lack of expertise of many special class teachers, the children are not taught with specialized techniques but instead are often treated with a lack of concern for their intellectual growth and a type of special care which prevents them from escaping from this type of class. (See Robinson and Robinson, #6266)

Secondly, while the use of such scientific evidence as psychological tests may, in some cases, be very desirable, in this instance they are often erroneously used to label children as "mentally retarded." Many children who are labeled in such a manner come from low income Negro families. Research has overwhelmingly shown that the standard intelligence tests are not suitable for measuring the general intellectual potential of Negro children and particularly of low income Negro children. This has typically been referred to as the cultural bias of intelligence tests (see Pettigrew, #6267).

The important point in the above for an understanding of the utilization of scientific knowledge is that one must be aware of more than isolated pieces of scientifc findings (e.g., that intelligence tests predict future intellectual potential). Because social science research is still in its infancy, no particular finding can be assumed to be "fact;" one must delve deeper into its implications and the new research on the original finding.

The effects of the expectations of teachers and the school on the pupils are very strongly and eloquently stated by Kenneth Clark in The Dark Ghetto: (#6268)

"... once one organizes an educational system where children are placed in tracks or where certain judgments about their ability determine what is done for them or how much they are taught or not taught, the horror is that the results seem to justify the assumptions. The use of intelligence test scores to brand children for life, to determine education based upon tracks and homogeneous groupings of children, impose on our public school system an intolerable and undemocratic social hierarchy, and defeat the initial purposes of public education. They induce and perpetuate the very pathology which they claim to remedy. Children who are treated as if they are uneducable almost invariably become uneducable. This is educational atrophy. It is generally known that if an arm or a leg is bound so that it cannot be used, eventually it becomes unusable. The same is true of intelligence." (p. 128)

I. DISTORTION OF NEW INFORMATION

The effects of personality and other psychological characteristics on an individual's ability to objectively process information has received a great deal of attention. Clinical studies of ego-defense mechanisms point to the prevalence of an individual's use of distortion to maintain internal balance. Using a different theoretical framework, Carl Rogers (#6271) has suggested that a person has a need for consistency in his self-image and a resulting tendency to distort new information in order to maintain it. This particularly applies to distu.bed individuals. Festinger (#0264) has described the phenomenon of selective exposure whereby individuals will avoid information which is contrary to a decision already made and seek out information supportive of that decision. And Sherif and Hovland (#6272) propose that there is a tendency to assimilate information in close proximity to one's views and either to reject information which is relatively distant or distort it even more in the direction of the distant extreme. These and other tendencies of people to distort information are frequently reported in the psychological literature and are quite influential in the thinking of many theorists. Campbell (#6298) reviews ten separate types of distortion which have received some support--including those just mentioned.

4-20

However, more recently Freedman and Sears (#6273) and others have begun to
question one of the key propositions of Festinger's dissonance theory and one of
the most prevalent assumptions of recent research on attitudes and the distortion
of new information--that individuals will avoid information that contradicts their
beliefs and seek out information that supports their beliefs. Citing numerous
studies, they show that there is no empirical support for this notion, and, in
fact, that there may be support for a very different conception. They state,
and show some evidence from their own and others' research, that individuals
will seek out information contrary to their beliefs and will want to hear both
sides of a story when they feel they have received only one point of view. Individuals are not as irrational as many theorists have shown them to be, as well
as not being as fragile in the face of contradictory information; individuals
want to hear both sides even if they will reject one of them. Janis and Smith
(#6274), after reviewing a great deal of the research literature on the effects
of persuasion on attitude change, conclude:

"All the same, this focussed concentration of research should not obscure
the importance, in effective communication, of the cogency, reasonableness
and in the long run, truth of the message." (p. 229-230)

They call for more research on the rational processes involved in the effects of
information appeals on individuals.

It should be noted that Freedman and Sears are not rejecting all theories
of distortion; they are, however, raising the question of the ubiquity of the
concept. Individuals who are dominated by certain ego-defenses, or who need the
distortion to maintain their tenuous hold on their self-image, no doubt will
distort contradictory information. The general applicability of these notions
to individuals not in these states is being brought into question. A similar
question is raised by the literature on fear arousal; individuals who are not
overly defensive or concerned about their smoking or health habits might react by
changing their attitudes under high fear rather than being defensive.

Related to this are a series of research projects on the timing of
information input in an individual's decision-making process. An individual
who has not yet made a decision or who does not feel he has to communicate
information to others, might be receptive to many different kinds of information, whether or not they are contradictory to his desires. For example,
if an individual requires information to fulfill a task he will accept
inputs contradictory to his attitudes. Jones (#6285) shows how segrega-
tionists accept information about desegregation--without attitude change--
when they need this information to finish a task in a laboratory experiment.
Similarly, Zajonc (#6275) and Cohen (#6299) show that individuals who do
not have to transmit information to others will be receptive to contradictory
proposals, while those who have made a decision and have to transmit it to
others will be much less receptive to such information. In other words,
individuals will be receptive to information--whether or not it is contra-
dictory--when they see it as useful for them. If it lacks such utility
(e.g., occurs after they have committed themselves to a decision) they are
less likely to be receptive to contradictory information.

A related line of research, but one which has often been cited as an
indication of man's irrationality, is the set of studies on "perceptual
defense". The early investigations in this area (occurring in the 1940's)
showed rather consistently that strongly disliked or very noxious stimuli
are distorted or not recognized by individuals. This has been described as
a defensive reaction on the part of the person. Later research in this area
showed that such a defensive reaction only occurs when the subject cannot avoid

or escape the shock associated with the words in the training phase of the experiment. On the other hand, when a noxious reaction was associated with the stimulus word and when there was a possibility for an escape from this undesirable condition, the individual was attentive to the noxious stimuli (this is called "perceptual vigilance") and reacted with attempts to cope with the situation.*

These results have important action implications for D&U. Rather than presenting a pessimistic view of the utilization of new knowledge when attitudes and values are contradictory to it, these findings hold out the hope that new information may, at the least, be heard, provided that it is useful for some future actions of the individuals concerned. For example, in the school integration process, the inevitability of integration may lead many segregationist-oriented teachers and school administrators to a rather open stance toward information related to methods of teaching integrated classes, information about Negro students and so on. Thus, teachers desiring to be effective in the classroom may very well be receptive to information which will enable them to be most effective in teaching Negro children (about whom they know very little), no matter what their attitude on school integration. This statement assumes that many southern teachers who have accepted the norms of southern society are not evil people attempting to ruin Negro children, but rather that once they are shown the necessity of integration, by court rulings or otherwise, they will seek out that information which will satisfy what is possibly a deeper value--a sense of competence as a teacher.

J. PROCESSES OF ATTITUDE CHANGE

This example also brings us to another important issue--the processes by which attitudes change. We could say, following Festinger's dissonance theory, (#0264)**that the teachers who are concerned with the development of Negro children (because they are their students) and desire information in order to make themselves more effective in teaching them, will, over time, begin to have more positive attitudes toward Negroes in general. Stated more formally, one who behaves in a positive manner towards an object to which he has a negative attitude, will, over time, change his attitudes to be consonant with his behavior. Similarly, one who has committed himself to a certain position will change his attitudes so that they are consonant with his commitment. A critical variable in this change is choice: one has a choice of whether or not he will make the commitment. If he has a choice, then he must in some way justify his decision; this effort to justify in turn leads to the attitude change. If he has no choice there is no need to justify his decision and, hence, there is no attitude change. (Numerous research studies have been done which bear on these general issues. Also, a number of important critiques have seriously questioned certain methodological and theoretical aspects of this theory, e.g., Freedman and Sears on selective exposure (#6273) cited above, and Chapanis and Chapanis (#6278).

1. Overcoming Resistance

Related to the above analysis on the effects of prior commitments on attitude change is the rather extensive literature on ways of overcoming the effects of resistance. Janis and Smith (#6274) reviewed this literature and have come to a number of conclusions:

_____
*For a good analysis of these points and the literature, see Jones and Gerard (#6285).

**See also Brehm and Cohen (#6277); Cohen (#5108) presents a simpler, more readable presentation.

a. Role Playing: "When exposed to persuasive messages, persons who are required to play a role that entails putting the content of the message in their own words to others will be more influenced than those who are passively exposed" (p. 215): these results can probably be explained by dissonance theory (see above).

b. "Side Attacks:" "Instead of assembling hortatory, polemical, or refutation arguments against widely accepted beliefs, the side attack judiciously selects minor or subsidiary issues on which relatively low resistance can be expected." The side attack approach is a piecemeal one whereby small changes are made over time. The effect of such an approach is much greater when the "audience lacks a well organized, tightly articulated attitude structure regarding the given object. When the attitude structure is not highly integrated (as with emotionally charged stereotypes), audiences must be subtly taught to disassociate the piece from the whole; otherwise the piecemeal effort is likely to be completely lost." (p. 213)

c. Preparatory Communications: By preparing the receiver for the communication, the communicator can influence the impact of events either "to sensitize the audience to the implication of an expected event or to dampen its emotional and cognitive impact." (p. 217) Types of preparation are: avoiding fear by predicting threatening events; avoiding pessimistic expectations by presenting grounds for maintaining optimistic expectations; avoiding possible failure by creating a frame of reference for discounting failures; avoiding effectiveness of counteracting communications by requiring the receiver to make public commitment of his position.

d. Communication Effects in Spite of Resistance: "Even when the audience remains highly suspicious of the source and is strongly motivated to resist being influenced, communications sometimes prove to be surprisingly effective." "... if some degree of exposure can be achieved--as by the use of provocative 'news releases'--even a despised communicator may exert an influence in the limited sphere of inducing acceptance of allegedly factual statements." (p. 211)

These four strategies for overcoming attitudinal resistance are important practices for any dissemination-utilization effort. They give hints at ways of increasing the likelihood of adoption without the necessity for attempting major changes in people's attitudes.

2. Motivational Bases of Attitudes

Any attempt at changing significant attitudes in order to facilitate the adoption of innovations or new knowledge must be prepared to work on a deeper more individual and more motivational level than is suggested by the strategies above. This is due to the fact that important attitudes usually are closely tied into an individual's aspirations, desires, and so on--that is, his motivation. An individual's attitudes provide the instrumental means for the expression of his motives and reaching his desired goals. We referred to this earlier when discussing Carlson's (#6256) attempt to change a white audience's favorable attitude toward housing segregation.

4-23

People's attitudes related to a particular object may have been formed for very different reasons. A teacher may have a very strong positive (or negative) attitude toward his students which was derived from a number of different sources. For example, he might have this attitude because of his desire to rise in the educational hierarchy and he sees that to be recognized as a good teacher may be an important stepping stone; he might have developed this attitude as a defense against his inadequate personal life; he may have this attitude because of his desire to be a competent teacher, to express his own self-image and views, and he therefore uses the performance of his students as an indication of his effectiveness; finally, this attitude may be a function of his desire to understand how students and youth think and behave.

Each of these motivational bases would require different strategies for changing the attitude. D. Katz (#6279) developed a typology of motivational-functional bases of attitudes which is presented in the four examples used above: adjustment-utilitarian function (desire to rise in educational heirarchy), ego defense (defense against inadequate personal life--see earlier discussion), value expression (express own self-image), knowledge (desire to understand).

The motivational approach to attitude change conceptualized by Katz enables us to place a number of concepts previously discussed in this chapter within the context of attitude change.

a. The adjustment-utilitarian function of attitudes refers to the utility of an attitude object in satisfying needs. An individual's positive or negative attitude towards his place of employment might be the result of his need for achievement. In the above examples, the desire of the teacher to rise in the educational heirarchy might be the result of such a need. If one wanted to influence such a person to adopt an innovation he could do it through the arousal of the need for achievement (discussion of possible avenues for promotion) and emphasizing how the acceptance of the innovation might lead to the desired goal.

b. The ego defensive function of attitudes refers to the manner in which attitudes protect the individual against internal conflicts and external dangers. One of the commonly referred to ego-defensive attitudes is that of the highly prejudiced individual, sometimes called the authoritarian personality. Any attempt to change such attitudes would require avoiding arousal conditions (e.g., threats, appeals to hatred, rise in frustrations and use of authoritarian suggestion) and emphasizing the development of self-insight, catharsis or removal of threats. As was emphasized in earlier discussions, ego-defensive attitudes are difficult to change.

c. The value expressive function of attitudes refers to the manner in which attitudes maintain the individual's self identity or enhance a favorable self-image. The effects of attitudes based on this type of motivation were seen in our earlier discussion of the role of a sense of competence in the resistance to effectively utilizing teaching machines. The extent to which a desire to enhance one's self-image affects adoption is seen in our earlier discussion

of how individuals with a low sense of self-esteem are more per-
suasible. While attitudes based on an individual's self-image
are not easy to change, a number of concepts discussed earlier
have considerable effects: if the expectations that others have
of an individual are relatively consistent and maintained over time,
his image of himself might change; if environmental supports are
withdrawn the individual might become more susceptible to changes
in his self-image.

d. The knowledge function of attitudes refers to an individual's
need for understanding and for meaningful cognitive organization.
The knowledge base of an attitude (and therefore the attitude
itself) can be changed by a presentation of more meaningful information or by the ambiguity created by new information or changes
in the environment. In the discussion on distortion (or lack of
it) of information we referred to the tendency of individuals to
seek out two sides of an argument and information that will enable
them to cope with the environment.

3. Attitudes and Behavior

The literature on attitude change often leaves one with a big
question: to what extent do such attitude changes lead to behavioral
changes? A now classic study demonstrated that while motel owners
stated over the telephone that they would not rent rooms to Chinese
individuals, when a Chinese person showed up at the motel the owners
accepted and did give them a room LaPiere, R.(#6300). D. Katz was very
much aware of the difference between what a person says and what he
does. He and Stotland (#6280) proposed that attitudes be divided into
three components--"cognitive," "affective" and "behavioral." Following
this division, one could say that an individual could evaluate (cognitive)
any tendency to move towards an object in a positive manner (affective)
but not have any meaningful tendency to move towards or away from the
object of his attitude (behavioral). In such a case, the individual
may talk and feel a great deal but not act in a manner consonant
with these expressions.

An interesting example of the differences between cognitive and
affective components on the one hand, and behavioral components on the
other, is seen in a study of students in Thailand (Guskin, #5160). Unexpectedly, the study discovered that Thai students, who seem to be very
passive, uninterested students not concerned with asking questions, had
attitudes and values which indicated a great desire for an active, responsible role inside and outside the classroom. The difference between
their behavior and attitudes was quite striking.

"Thus, if the students have an image of a good student as
being one who is very active in the learning process, this
does not necessarily mean that they will act according to
this image. One of the reasons for this could be that
they have had little past experience in acting in this manner
and hence, the behavioral component of their attitude is weakly
developed. Also, we could say that students are unable to
express their beliefs and feelings because they are different

from those expected of them; to express them would lead to conflict. As the maintenance of smooth interpersonal relationships
is one of the most basic and most important rules of Thai social
behavior, it is necessary for Thai students to act as their
teachers expect them to act. Thus, one must be careful not to
infer the students' beliefs and feelings from their overt behavior."
(p. 108)

Such a situation produces interesting possibilities for educational
change and the use of new teaching practices--if one is aware of the
incongruity between behavioral and affective-cognitive attitudinal
components. A knowing teacher might slowly provide the context for
active student involvement in the learning process by at first gently
pushing the students to respond to questions, to present their own
ideas, and to eventually challenge the teacher. This process is
difficult because the students might question the teacher's competence
and/or motives. Once this impasse has been overcome, the classroom might
be exciting for both student and teacher.

K.   SOCIAL INFLUENCE AND ATTITUDE CHANGE

Up to this point we have placed major emphasis on the individual
and his reaction to some kind of persuasive or change attempt. Such an
orientation may give the reader some insight into the dynamics of an
individual's predispositions to change. This, however, is only a partial picture. Individuals change their attitudes or resist change not
only on the basis of their own psychological characteristics but, also,
on how these characteristics relate to the change agent's relationship
to them and how the change agent attempts to influence them. Kelman
(#6259, #1776) presents a particularly useful model for understanding
this relationship

Building on a great deal of the literature of attitude change,
Kelman proposes three influence processes and the manner in which
individuals react to such influences. Probably the most commonly used
method of influence is the manipulation of rewards or punishments--
Kelman refers to this as "means-end control." When an attempt at such control is made, the individual will typically react with external (public)
conformity but maintain his private attitudes without any significant
change. Moreover, the recipient will maintain his public conformity
("compliance") only when under the surveillance of the influencer.

However, if the recipient is attracted to the influencing agent,
a very different reaction occurs. Because the individual wants to
maintain his relationship with a desirable source he will attempt to
change his attitude so that it concurs with that of the source. A
number of well-known research projects carried out by Hovland, Kelman
and their colleagues show that when a source is considered by the
audience to be prestigeful and trustworthy there is a strong tendency
for the audience to change their attitude in accordance with the attitude
of the source. One study by Hovland and Weiss (#6281) showed a net change
three and one-half times greater when the source was high in credibility
than when it was low in credibility. Part of this study showed that these
effects were short lived, i.e., high and low credibility groups were
the same after a few weeks--this is known as the "sleeper effect."
Another study by Kelman and Hovland (#6282) showed that while the effects
of source credibility were short lived they could be reinstituted if,

after the "sleeper effect" occurred, the sources were presented again. Thus, this attraction to the influencer, which Kelman refers to as "identification", will be maintained only as long as the relationship to the source continues to be attractive and the individual is aware of the existence of the relationship. It should be noted that such an effect does not necessarily change an individual's private attitudes (Kelman, #1776).

The third major type of influence and attitude change refers to the process by which a recipient accepts an influence attempt on the basis of the congruence of the new information presented with his own beliefs and attitudes. This process--called "internalization"-- does not require the continuance of any external force or relationship in order for it to be maintained. Because the new information is accepted and internalized it is maintained by the individual without further external influence.

Each of the three processes can be considered as a different strategy of change to be utilized in different contexts or by different types of people. The "means-end" control-compliance process is common in knowledge utilization and change strategies in bureaucratic organizations or in relationships where there is a readily acknowledged inequality of power. This has also been referred to as a power model. To be effective such a strategy would require a considerable amount of surveillance. Under such circumstances the individual has little choice of alternative actions.

The attraction-identification process would attempt to develop affective ties by the individual to the desired person or institution and thereby to what the person or institution desires. This need not be seen as a sinister attempt to fool the individual, although it might be such: human relations training is often an attempt to develop either the actual identification of the subordinate with his superior or to provide the supervisor with skills by which he will be seen as an attractive source by his subordinates. Under these conditions the individual is presented with a limited number of alternative courses of behavior which he must evaluate and about which he must make some kind of decision. Either he can identify with the source either a person or an institution and thereby be motivated to perform, or he can choose not to be attracted to such a source and merely comply with orders. If a supervisor can somehow get his subordinates to choose to "identify," he will have gained a great deal more influence over his subordinates than is formally delegated to his position.

The congruence-internalization process represents the most direct knowledge utilization strategy; to the extent that information is congruent with his beliefs, a person will accept it. However, most situations are not that simple. Moreover, our previous discussion on "distortion of information" leads us to question a simplistic approach to this. While individuals will most readily internalize information which is congruent with their beliefs, they might also be willing to listen to, and possibly be influenced by, information which is incongruent with their beliefs.

L. PATTERNS OF INFORMATION-SEEKING BEHAVIOR

Different users of knowledge have different characteristic patterns of information seeking. Probably one of the most important differences between those who adopt or do not adopt an innovation is the manner in which ~~they~~ they search out information when they feel a need for more knowledge about a particular area. This search might be to solve specific problems or it might be related to general and continuous interests. An important variable involved in such a search is the reliance on friends and relatives vs. impersonal sources, or a reliance on local as against non-local sources.

Reliance upon relatives and friends for information has a generally negative effect on adoption. Lionberger (#1036) in his review of the literature on adoption of agricultural innovations states that "high dependence on relatives and friends as sources of information is usually negatively associated with the adoption of farm practices" (p. 103). This would seem to be a result of the relatives' low level of knowledge regarding new farming technology. On the other hand, he finds that there is a high positive relationship between those who are early adopters of innovation and "the use of such sources as the county agent, colleges of agriculture, and vocational agriculture teachers" (p. 103).

In his studies in the field of education Carlson (#0585) comes to a similar conclusion. He found that non-adopters were generally those individuals who relied more on local sources for advice and information while innovators and early adopters tended to rely on information outside the local area.

Rogers (#1824) refers to these non-local sources of information as "cosmopolite" and agrees that they are more important to early adopters than "localite" sources. Related to this, he states that impersonal sources of information are more important than personal sources for earlier adopters. His conclusions are derived from many studies similar to those cited by Lionberger as well as others, such as the diffusion of medical innovation studies reported by Coleman et al. (#3576)

Besides the personal-impersonal and cosmopolite-localite dimensions, a number of authors have attempted to specify the most common types of sources which early and late adopters use. Coleman, et al. (#3576) report the following:

Early adopting physicians use the following as major sources of information:
--they attend specialist (as against generalist) meetings.
--they read several medical journals (not "house organs").
--they make an appeal to several sources before making a judgment.
--they tend to visit out-of-town medical institutions which they may often use as a point of reference for their practice.
--they reside near the medical school from which they graduated or interned and use its facilities.

Late Adopters use the following as sources of information:
--they attend general (as against specialist) meetings.
--they read house organs (as against medical journals).

The general conclusions that one draws from this and the findings of others (see Rogers, #1824) is that early adopters tend to keep close contact with those sources of information which are most likely to bring them into greater contact with new ideas. Moreover, they tend to use a greater number of sources of information than do later adopters (see Menzel #3404, and Lionberger, #1036). Thus the difference between early and late adopters in their use of information is directly related to their exposure to information about new practices, innovations, and scientific findings.

This presents an interesting problem for disseminators of innovations. Due to the general exposure tendencies of individuals (particularly physicians and farmers but presumably also other professionals) which result from their general interests--e.g., their interests in medicine as scientists--those who are most likely to adopt innovations are those who expose themselves to sources providing such information. On the other hand, those who are least likely to adopt are not exposed to those sources which provide such information. How then does a disseminator reach the late adopters to convince them to adopt innovations?

This same problem exists when one uses the mass media as a medium for changing attitudes. Freedman and Sears (#6273) call this tendency de facto selectivity: i.e., "most audiences for mass communications apparently tend to over-represent persons already sympathetic to the view being propogated, and most persons seem to be exposed disproportionately to communications which support their opinions." (p. 84-90) But, it should not be concluded that this results from a desire to avoid non-supportive information. Experimental research has not uncovered a general psychological preference for supportive information.* "The simplest answer, and yet one easily overlooked, is that most of the examples of de facto selectivity come from mass communication settings in which exposure is determined by a great many complex factors which are incidental to the supportiveness of the information." (p. 90)

Another important element in an individual's tendency to search out new information involves his feelings about those who create or develop it. Beal and Rogers (#1351) report that early adopters among farmers tend to have more favorable attitudes toward the agricultural scientist and a more accurate perception of his work, as well as more interest in agricultural research, than do later adopters. In the field of education Pelligrin's review of the literature shows (#1043) that many educators do not view the scientific method as being of primary significance to their work and therefore see research as a "dubious" enterprise. This leads educators to place a low priority on the performance of research. Such a condition makes the creation of relevant scientific knowledge difficult and creates the vicious cycle in which little research of relevance is carried out. Under these conditions, in both agriculture and education, we would expect that those who are favorable do utilize research-based knowledge and those who are unfavorable will not be exposed to it and, therefore, will not be able to use it. The point of intervention may not be the reaction to the new knowledge itself but rather the reactions to those who create it.

M. EFFECT OF KNOWLEDGE, ITSELF

While there are many other factors beside the knowledge about innovations which affect adoption, the amount and type of knowledge obviously have an important effect.** In a series of studies on the early use of the Salk vaccine

*See section in Distortion of Information.

**Types and characteristics of knowledge are the primary topic of Chapter Eight and will be discussed more extensively therein.

it was found that a large amount of information related to the vaccine led to
its acceptance (Clausen et al. #6010, Sills and Gill, #1114) whereas a lack
of knowledge led to non-use (Glasser, #1385). Similarly in a study of the predispositions to accept innovation in three high schools, Lin et al. (#3903)
found a significant correlation between a predisposition to accept change and
innovations in the schools and the feeling, by the teachers, that they knew
a great deal about the innovation. Of related interest is a study of farmers (Chu,
#1937) which found that a knowledge of the causes of a problem (i.e.,
deterioration of resources) plays an important role in the decision to adopt
remedial measures; mere recognition of the existence of the problem did not
produce such a reaction.

A related point is the ignorance about the connection between the use
of an innovation and the benefits that will accrue as a result of its use.
If this connection is not seen, adoption on a voluntary basis would be quite
difficult to achieve.

Such a problem is seen in a study by   Hanks (#0346) in Thailand.
They report that diptheria vaccinations were not used by villagers even though
two young people had contracted the disease and one had died from it. One of
the reasons for this non-use by two thirds of the villagers at a time in which
there seemed to be considerable need was the villagers' lack of knowledge
of the relationship between the child's death and the contagious nature of
diptheria. This was even more striking in that one of the children was cured
by modern doctors. Most of the one-third who were immunized did so because
of the authority of the village headman who ordered them to have it done.
Complicating this issue is the villagers' general lack of concern with children's
diseases and disease in general, and the simultaneous occurrence of the rice-
planting season--a very busy time for the villagers.

In short, knowledge about, or a feeling that one has knowledge about,
a particular innovation may predispose an individual to accept the innovation.
But this is only true if the presumed knowledge is favorable. When such
"knowledge" is unfavorable it tends to lead to rejection of the innovation.
In a study of the dissemination of birth control devices in Puerto Rico, (Stycos,
 #1132) it was found that women were rejecting them because they believed the
devices caused diseases such as cancer. While this was untrue, the misinformation led to rejection of the birth control measures.

Doubts about the safety of an innovation directly affected the utilization
of the polio vaccine when it was first introduced. Even though parents were
almost uniform in their concern about polio, many did not consent because they
felt that the vaccine was unsafe for their children, that their children were
not susceptible to polio, or that the physical conditions of their children
made it unsafe for them (Clausen, et al. #6010 ; Sills and Gill, #1114; and
Belcher, #2870). While one may contest the actual scientific validity of
these reactions, given the uncertainty involved in the trial runs and early dissemination attempts of the Salk vaccine, it seems quite reasonable that many
parents would be hesitant. Probably more surprisingly, and possibly more
irrational, was the great faith that large numbers of people placed in the
medical research (of which they were probably ignorant) that supported the use
of the vaccine. It is interesting to note the comments of Clausen et al.
(#6010), in their study of the trial runs of the Salk vaccine: they stated
that people's responses to several attitude statements "indicate that consent
and non-consent should not be viewed as a sharp dichotomy, but rather as the
reflection of different weighting of the issues involved and of the evidence

with reference to these issues." (p. 1534) They also point out that non-consent was equally frequent at all educational levels, but the decision made in the light of these doubts was supported by much more evidence in the case of those with higher education.

These findings again raise the issue about the "rational" nature of the decision to adopt or reject. We have seen in this section that there is much in the literature to support the notion that "man" does make decisions based on a "rational" evaluation of the alternatives that are presented to him. Important variables that must be considered are the degree of arousal of the individual's needs and the weights that individuals use in evaluating the alter-natives. If there is low need arousal and we know the "weights" involved, then we should be able to predict the person's behavior. It should be noted that education need not be critical for a rational evaluation of alternatives. Rather, it may provide for more elaborate justifications for the decision or increase the probability that the evaluation has external validity.

Further support for this view of the adoption as a rational pragmatisn comes from a number of other sources as well. Bauer and Wortzel (#2340) in their study of the sources of information used by physicians, point out that detail men from pharmaceutical companies are very often used by doctors even though they are aware of their bias. Moreover, the personal feelings of the doctor towards the detail men is important.   However, such information is used only in low risk cases. As the seriousness of the illness increases and as the medical knowledge of treatment decreases, the tendency to rely on professional sources--colleagues and journal articles--increases.

Bauer and Wortzel concluded that doctors have too much information con-fronting them. Doctors favor sources with high information value in hopes of maximizing the information input per unit time output. The physician is said to both screen and discriminate; that is, he decides first, what he wants more information about, and second, he decides in each case who will provide him the desired amout of information in the least time.

Katz, Levin and Hamilton (#0297) in their review of the diffusion liter-ature point out that the decision to adopt or not to adopt may be a function of certainty of profitability, i.e., the greater the possible profit, the more likelihood that the innovation will be accepted. Anderson and Neihoff (#3005) make a similar point in their review when they showed the influence of practical benefit and rewards on the decision to adopt.

It would seem, then, that man is more rational than is often supposed. The question is finding out those factors which affect him and in what way they do so.

CONCLUSION

Throughout this chapter we have been presenting psychological variables related to the change or resistance to new knowledge, practices and the like. In this pre-sentation, we have not covered all the issues involved but have tried to deal with a number of important theoretical and empirical issues not usually discussed under the heading of knowledge utilization. To do this we have concentrated on the research and theoretical literature in social psychology as well as the descriptive studies of the diffusion literature, and attempted to demonstrate their relationship to individual change in the utilization process.

A discussion of such individual factors implicitly presents an image of man. We will try in this conclusion to make explicit this orientation. It should be noted that we are doing this not only to enable the reader to have a better understanding of the contents of this chapter but also to provide for the possibility of his supplementing the issues presented and applying them to his own particular setting.

The image of the recipient of new knowledge is that while he is greatly affected by such enduring characteristics as his values and deep personality needs acquired during his early socialization experiences, while he is greatly affected by the particular situation in which he finds himself, he is also a person who makes rational choices, i.e., decisions based on an evaluation of alternatives in terms of knowable priorities. These rational choices may seem to the outsider to be quite irrational, but the individual more often that not is aware of his alternatives.

For example, let us take the administrator whose position is threatened by changes: Is he irrational in resisting them? Given the nature of organizational dynamics, isn't it more rational to resist changes threatening one's position than to accept them? In a sense, one might say that the change agent who proposes changes that will present such a threat is acting without the necessary rationality if he assumes that such changes will be effective.

Another example is the expectation that sensitivity training groups for individual executives will be effective in inducing organizational change. Again, given the dynamics of organizations, how rational is it to assume that an executive who gains greater insight into his perceptions of himself and others will be able to bring about organizational changes when he returns to his company? For the newly inspired executive, an attempt to get his fellow executives to see the world his way may be terribly naive.

In short, our image of man is as a choosing person--one who makes a decision on the basis of the forces that impinge upon him. Sometimes these forces overwhelm him and he becomes a slave to them--whether they be unconscious drives or group pressures of which he is unaware. In terms of group pressures, individuals over time may come to accept others' decisions as their own.* This should not be viewed as an irrational process of influence. Often, one of the main reasons that people develop similar patterns of action is because they have similar socialization experiences; i.e., the experiences of the individuals concerned are similar, therefore, the decisions they make are based on similar foundations. These foundations have become their own and should not be viewed as external sources of control.

This leads to the formulation that one of the best--if not the best--ways to predispose individuals to change to desired behavior patterns is through experience which emphasizes these patterns. This is a costly process--both in time and effort-- and may be difficult to achieve if the desired behavior is in conflict with earlier patterns.

Another important aspect of our implicit view of man is that an individual is often placed in situations where alternatives are contradictory. Therefore, situational and, to some extent, chance factors become critical in the way he makes decisions; for example, individuals are faced with contradictory desires relating to smoking cigarettes--twenty years of smoking enjoyment vs. the possibility of getting lung cancer vs. the possibility of continuing smoking for 10 years stopping and thereby

---

*See Chapter Five for a detailed discussion of group processes.

greatly decreasing the chances of getting lung cancer. Under these conditions the presence of other people who have or have not stopped smoking may be the deciding factor. Under such conflicting alternative situations individuals may be most susceptible to external pressures.

Man does make choices based on his experience. He does seem to desire more information on which to make these decisions even if it contradicts his own desires or inclinations. If he is able he will make decisions on the basis of a considered evaluation of this information. The critical factor that determines the ability to do this is the degree of arousal of his significant attitudes, needs, values, etc. If these are aroused he is likely to make decisions which are congruent with them. If they are not aroused, he will tend to evaluate the alternatives on their merits and according to general priorities he has established for himself--congruence being only one among many alternatives.

Yet another aspect of this implicit image of man is that he often desires, above all, to interact with others and be liked by others. If a decision is not important to him he will be more concerned with maintaining his interaction with others and agreeing than disagreeing and running the risk of antagonizing them. It might be added that in some cultures the desire to remain in a group is much stronger than any other aspect of an individual's life; as a result overt disagreement with others may be quite small.*

The critical point about most of the above discussion is that individuals will, if there are alternative paths open to them, usually make a decision which is consistent with their experiences and their own priorities. On the whole, this decision in healthy individuals will not be based on irrational forces but rather will be a function of a rational weighing of the alternatives. More non-rational forces come into play when the alternatives are equal and in opposite directions. In situations where no alternatives exist--an extreme example would be a concentration camp (external forces)--non-rational forces predominate.

The image of man presented in this chapter specifies that past experiences determine the manner in which the evaluation will take place. For example, an individual develops certain expectations about how his behavior relates to that of others and how he will be accepted on the basis of this relationship. Until very recently, a Negro child who has learned that white people will reject him if his behavior deviates from the typical Negro stereotype, will, when presented with the possibility of such deviation, choose a course of action that rejects this possibility and behave in a conformist manner. If the Negro child is faced with two alternatives--deviance or conformity to white expectations--he will choose conformity because of the fear of rejection; that he had another alternative is seen in his behavior with other Negroes. Over time, the Negro child may come to believe that he is what is expected of him by whites; however, this will only occur if there is no reinforcement of his "deviant" behavior in his interactions with Negroes.

By past experiences we are also referring to the values, norms and attitudes, which an individual has internalized and which represent the frame of reference he uses when approaching events in his environment. These reference points predispose him to evaluate alternatives in a certain manner. In situations where these values and other internal forces are not greatly aroused the reference points are general tendencies or styles of behavior. In situations where they are activated they become more dominating forces. This means that to predict adoption or utilization behavior, we must know the basis on which the individual makes decisions and the degree of arousal of needs, values and other psychological factors. If a

_____
*See E. Vogel, Japan's New Middle Class, (#6294).

4-33

farmer chooses not to use a new seed this may be the result of his evaluation that the new seed is different from seed used by his father and his community. A traditional orientation may lead the farmer to reject the new seed because of his fear of rejection by his neighbors. Or, the decision to reject the seed may have been made on the basis of a very different set of alternatives. The farmer may have weighed the cost of using a new seed with the financial gains that such a seed might bring.

The importance of knowing the alternatives that an individual perceives as a basis for making his decisions is critical in any change effort. This is especially true in cross-cultural settings where differences in experiences between the national and the foreigner reduces the possibility of either accurately assessing the alternatives perceived by the other. The role of the change agent may be seen, from this image of man, as providing a new alternative for the influencee while at the same time attempting to make sure that his new alternative has greater force than the other alternatives.

In summary, we may state that the individual evaluates the existing alternative present in his environment, but he does so in a way that will maximize the perceived benefits he forsees and minimize the disadvantages. The manner in which the alternatives relate to his own priorities will determine his decision. These alternatives and priorities, can, in most cases, be ascertained by others. But, under conditions in which no alternatives are present, the individual has no choice and acts in accordance with forces prescribed by others or by his own very strong, deep, personality dynamics. These forces, whether they are under the control of the individual or not, determine the strategy that must be used to enable the individual to utilize new knowledge, or to change.

An example of how these forces operate can be seen within an organizational context. We can specify at least two different "ideal type" organizational structures which relate to the nature of alternatives present for an individual; a hierarchical organization (such as Dave Robbins' high school)*and a diffuse structure (e.g., a research institute). In the bureaucratic high school setting, middle and lower level members such as teachers and students are faced with few choices. For Dave, the curriculum may be set by his department chairman or by the state Board of Regents. The classroom structure and even the style of teaching may be similarly prescribed. The more such rules, guidelines and restrictions imposed on Dave, the fewer his degrees of freedom and the smaller his potential for responding to new knowledge as a rational decision-maker.

In the research institute, on the other hand, the alternatives for the researcher may be quite great. If the individual can secure a research contract or grant which is in the very general research framework of the institute, he has a considerable number of alternatives. He can choose the topic of his research; he can attend meetings or not, as he pleases; he can hire his own staff; he chooses his hours of work, his style of dress, the manner in which he does his research--as long as he remains within very broad ethical limitations. Under these diffuse structural arrangements a tendency toward rational decision-making would seem to be very prevalent in the individual's day-to-day operations. In the bureaucratic structure, a tendency toward non-rational decision-making would be most common, i.e., following other's orders, seeking to please others, and so on--basically decisions dictated not so much by one's own personal experiences as by the directives of supervisors and the dictated requirements of the institution.

Changing the individual's decision to utilize new knowledge is very different in these two settings. In the research institute the major target would be the individual researcher. While structural changes could limit his flexibility, the

---
*See discussion of this example in previous chapters.

norms of the institute guard his autonomy. Restrictions counter to these norms would be resisted and the researcher would probably leave. In order for any structural changes to be successful, they would require his acceptance and willingness to receive influence from others. In the more bureaucratic school setting, the change might have to be focused on the structure; without changing the structure, there probably would be little chance of changing the individual's decision-making behavior, particularly on a long term basis.*

The above discussion points out the important effects of institutional expectations--norms--on an individual's behavioral flexibility. When norms permit wide variation in behavior patterns, acceptance of new knowledge becomes a matter of decision-making by individuals; when norms are restrictive and provide little latitude in behavior, public acceptance is a direct function of the rules specified by the institutional structure.
In the latter case, any change in a large number of individuals would have to be attempted at an institutional or community level, not an individual one. (Of course, over time such norms may become internalized to such an extent that individual as well as institutional change might have to occur.)

One of the best examples of this image of man is the material presented on social comparison processes (p. 12). Individuals under conditions of relatively high anxiety and/or uncertainty will seek out others in order to compare themselves so that they will be able to properly evaluate their own ability, opinions and emotions. In this process individuals are influenced by others in such a way that they use the judgments of these people along with their own self-impressions to reach a decision about how they should behave and feel. It is important to note that while the presence of another (his attitudes, feelings, etc.) can be used as data for alternative attitudes, the manner in which the other person's presence becomes known may set the context in which an evaluation of alternatives takes place and thereby greatly affects the weights given to different alternatives and to the role of past experience factors. For example, the presence of others may cause anxiety or uncertainty which, in turn, may heighten an individual's sensitivity to their attitudes, behaviors, and so on. A sensitivity training group sensitizes an individual to the influence of others through its lack of overt norms and standards, its isolation from attitudinal and behavioral anchorages, and the feelings of group comaraderie that it engenders. Under such conditions, the weight of others opinions would be much more important than they would be in the usual day-to-day interaction setting.

We have discussed at some length in this chapter the many different ways in which individuals are affected by others. In one section, we discussed the great effect of others' expectations on an individual's self-image and the expectations he has for himself. While an individual may internalize expectations of others which continue over time and which emanate from legitimate sources, at a specific point in time they (the expectations) are data for one set of alternatives. As a result, individuals are affected by others' expectations in a specific situation but their decisions are not determined by them. It is not an atypical occurrence to see a person reject, by his behavior and decisions, the impressions others have of him. In such instances individuals show that they feel that other factors or their own self-expectations are weighed more heavily than the views of others.

---

*One of the most important aspects of attempting structural changes to produce innovative behavior in school systems is the specific provision for release-time and/or financial supplements for those who are expected to do the innovating. Such provisions have a dual purpose in promoting innovation: on the one hand they release the teacher from some of the day-to-day pressures of his routine job, giving him freedom and flexibility to "waste time" trying out new things; and on the other hand it forces the system to officially recognize and sanction such freedom.

The findings in the literature on fear arousal also directly relate to our image of man. As we stated on p. 4-14, the early work indicated that high fear situations lead to defensiveness which, in turn. lead to resistance to the information imparted by the feared object. Thus, lower levels of fear were found to be more effective in opinion change. Recent literature emphasizes that high fear presentations do not necessarily lead to resistance. If the individual is not particularly concerned or anxious about the feared object or information, the higher the fear the greater the opinion change; but if the individual is concerned or anxious, high fear would not be effective in changing opinions while low fear might be.

From our present perspective these results may be explained by the extent to which fear presents an alternative to be evaluated as against the extent to which it arouses internal or external pressures which dominate an individual. In the latter case the individual no longer is in a position to make judgments; he is in a predicament similar to the individual who faces an organizational environment which does not permit behavior that is deviant from clearly specified rules.

Again referring back to the literature presented in this chapter, we can see a rather direct relationship between the literature on attitude change and the image of man presented here. Role playing has an effect on attitude change mainly because it presents the individuals with new alternatives about his own behavior; this method of attitude change is particularly effective if it enables the individual to test out ideas and behaviors which he previously did not consider. "Side attacks" are effective because they add new information to already existing alternatives which in effect change the nature of each alternative, or the new information itself becomes a new alternative. "Preparatory communication" influence the impact of an event by either changing the context in which the alternative actions are evaluated or by presenting alternative explanations for undesirable events.

Kelman's theory of three processes of social influence and an individual's reaction to them represent the relationship between alternative courses of action or attitudes as evaluated by past experience. In the "means-end control" situation, compliance may be the behavioral result of a situation where an individual weighs the positive results of complying (reward or non-punishment) against the negative results of deviating (no reward or punishment). In the "congruence-internalization" situation, the individual may weigh the new information against what he believes to be accurate and if it agrees with his own beliefs he accepts it or if it is incongruent with his attitudes and beliefs he considers its validity on the merits of the information presented.

The third influence process (the attraction to a source and acceptance of source's attitudes--identification) also can be looked at within this same perspective: the source presents a new alternative for the individual, not in terms of the content of the attitude but in terms of the desired relationship. Under such conditions the individual may not necessarily accept the new attitudes but may evaluate whether the relationship to the individual is less desirable than the attitude change. It should be noted that such change is maintained only with the continuation of the relationship.   Over time the attitude change may become part of the individual's experience of himself and thereby become internalized.

SUMMARY

This chapter has been devoted to a review and analysis of the individual factors that relate to the dissemination-utilization process. These factors can be divided into two major groups--those characteristics which are more enduring or not easily changed and those which are less enduring and much more subject to changes in an individual's situation. Enduring characteristics reviewed were competence, authoritarianism and open-minded--closed-mindedness, values, needs, and past experience. Those less enduring characteristics reviewed were sense of threat and the tendency of individuals to compare themselves to others, the effects of fear, the self-fulfilling prophecies of expectations and how these affect attempts to utilize knowledge, the extent to which individuals can objectively process information, the processes involved in attitude change, the motivational bases of attitudes, and how influence attempts can bring about changes in an individual's attitudes.

An implicit theme that runs through much of the discussion in this chapter is that any particular characteristic does not automatically predetermine an individual's acceptance or rejection of new knowledge. An individual may reject an innovation or new knowledge because he feels it threatens his sense of competence (e.g., teacher and teaching machines) or because it creates considerable fear, or because it conflicts with some of his values. However, such resistance to new knowledge need not occur if the threat, fear or values are not seen as relevant in the particular situation. Thus, when threat, fear, or the potentially conflicting values implicit in the new knowledge and those present in the individual are aroused--that is, are relevant in the particular situation--they will lead to resistance to change; when these characteristics are not activated by the new knowledge or the situation in which it is being presented, they will not lead to resistance. It seems that the lack of arousal may lead to a more rational evaluation of the alternative actions presented by the new knowledge. For example, individuals in certain situations will seek out information contrary to their opinions, and individuals will sometimes maintain seemingly contradictory belief patterns when both serve utilitarian purposes.

Often the theoretical literature on the more enduring characteristics does not deal with the differences between aroused and non-aroused characteristics in particular situations. This is, for the most part, the result of the emphasis in psychology on the study of the unhealthy rather than the healthy personality. The literature on the less enduring characteristics also tends not to concern itself with the level of arousal; this is due, it seems, primarily to the tendency of social psychologists to limit their concerns to little pieces of an individual's behavior in very artificial laboratory settings. Hence, such researchers are not in a position to make a judgment as to the arousal of individual characteristics in circumstances different from their laboratory setting.

However, the descriptive literature does often point to instances where arousal and non-arousal occur. Some of the cross-cultural literature indicates this rather sharply--individuals who accept "seemingly contradictory" belief systems but reject "seemingly beneficial" agricultural techniques; the former do not arouse or activate the individual's needs, values, feelings of threat, etc., whereas the latter do.

This difference between arousal and non-arousal is critical to those interested in the dissemination and utilization of new knowledge and innovations. When faced with innovations that can potentially arouse the strong traditional belief systems of a farmer in a developing country, the change agent will want to create a linkage between the innovation and the belief system even if it slightly compromises the innovation. The rationale behind this is that without this linkage the strong belief system will be aroused and lead to a rejection of the innovation.

In situations where individuals are anxious about their health, one wants to avoid using high fear arousal as a strategy to convince people to use a medical innovation. Such fear may lead to defensiveness and rejection. In such situations one would want to present the objective reason for the use of the medical innovation. On the other hand, in situations in which individuals are unaware of their problems, one would want to create awareness by possibly using high fear arousal. The strategy in this case would be to create fear and anxiety and then provide a means for reducing them by use of the medical innovation. This, of course, is continually used in advertising.

An important aspect of creating openness to change and acceptance are the motivational bases on which old attitudes were developed. If one can attach the acceptance of the innovation to the motivational base by indicating the instrumental value of a new set of behaviors, then change can be brought about. The difficulty here is avoiding a conflicting attitude which might also be instrumental to the individual's desires. In such situations it might be better to create the conditions for an individual to behave in the desired manner, reward him for the behavior and, then, hope he sees its value.

These and many more strategies can be derived from the literature of this chapter. We have tried, throughout this chapter, to show the relevance of the literature to change efforts. The reader will probably see many more relevant connections.

Much of the discussion in this   chapter has not clearly differentiated the sender and receiver of influence. While this distinction is important in the diffusion literature and in an understanding of the D&U process, the psychological processes discussed in this chapter seem to apply equally to both. However, our presentation of the literature has implicitly focused on the receiver or recipient of influence--how his personality, feelings of threat, fears, attitudes, past experiences, self-expectations, etc., effect his tendency to accept or reject new knowledge.

Three themes that run throughout this chapter are as follows: (1) the openness (or closedness) of individuals to give and receive new information, (2) the potency of rewards as important elements in the D&U process, and (3) the "rational" basis by which individuals evaluate new knowledge and innovations. Relating to the "openness" factor we have pointed to the following items:

To be dissatisfied with current state.
To be ready and willing to change.
To perceive outside resources as potentially useful.
To listen, to give, and to receive feedback.
To seek out new information.
To be flexible and modern in outlook.

We have referred to reward or reinforcement as an important variable in this chapter in the following ways:

Relative advantage (return in proportion to investment in terms of effort, time or money).
The expectations of future reward may be as important as reward itself.
Rewarding encounters with new knowledge lead to self-fulfilling prophecies that future encounters will also be rewarding.
"Nothing succeeds like success."

4-38

Finally, this chapter has emphasized the fact that in most situations individuals rationally evaluate the alternatives open to them. The critical variable that emerges from this "image of man" is the degree to which enduring personality characteristics are aroused in a particular situation. If they are highly activated then the new knowledge will be accepted if it is congruent with them, rejected if it is not. If they are not activated, then congruence to personality is only one of many elements influencing the decision.

CHAPTER FIVE

INTERPERSONAL LINKAGE

Table of Contents

CHAPTER FIVE*

INTERPERSONAL LINKAGE

I.   INTRODUCTION

In the previous chapter we emphasized the effects that different psychological characteristics have on the D&U process. However, most of these characteristics were said to be susceptible to the influence of other people in the individual's environment. When reference is made to fear, others expectations, or changing attitudes we are really indicating the manner in which individuals interact with others. In this chapter, we will refocus our attention from the processes going on within an individual to the "others" or group within which the individual is interacting. We shall ask such questions as the following: How does an individual's participation in group decision-making effect his tendency to adopt innovations? To what extent will an individual's attraction to others in a group effect his tendency to adopt innovations? How can one overcome group and individual re-sistance to change through group processes? What effect does conformity have on adoption of innovation?

This chapter is divided into two major sections: one dealing with the indirect group influences on individuals and the other dealing with the direct influence attempts of others. By indirect influences we are referring to those factors which predispose an individual to be susceptible to adoption as a result of interests or forces not connected with the diffusion-adoption processes. For example, individuals are members of social groups or have friendship patterns for many different reasons, but not necessarily because of their desire to learn about innovations. A great deal of research has indicated that membership in such social units leads to greater adoption of innovations.

By direct influence we are referring to those interpersonal influence processes that directly effect the adoption process. For the most part this section will include research studies on the role of the sender and how his characteristics directly influence the adoption by the receiver. Examples of such influence processes include the perceived credibility of the sender, his expertise, his attraction to the receiver, the power of the sender over the receiver, and the resources that the sender has that the receiver desires.

A.   INDIRECT INTERPERSONAL AND GROUP INFLUENCES

1.   Participation

A major emphasis of recent social action programs has been "*participation*"; the inclusion and active involvement of individuals who are effected by decisions in the decision-making process. The War on Poverty has had as one of its major tenets the "maximum feasible

---

*This chapter was drafted by Alan E. Guskin.

participation of the poor" in the policy making process. Overseas--
U.N. and U.S.--technical assistance has often emphasized community
development with the involvement of villagers in the planning and
implementation of development schemes. Organizational change programs,
to a lesser degree, have also emphasized the role of the worker and
middle management personnel in the decision-making process.

This stress on participation is usually based on the common sense
notion that individuals who have some control over their own work will
be more committed to and satisfied with the functions required to perform
their job, as well as with the final product. Considerable research
has been conducted to establish the validity of this theory.

Probably the best known works in this area are the early studies
of Kurt Lewin and his associates (#1342) carried out during World War II
to determine how best to influence housewives to use types of foods
they would ordinarily reject, e.g., kidneys, hearts, and "bad" cuts of
meat. The results seemed overwhelming; housewives who were involved in
a group discussion and group decision-making process about the importance
of eating the "undesirable" food used it much more than those who heard
a lecture on the same topic. The process of discussion and arriving at
a decision were considered to be the major factors.

Due to methodological problems in the Lewin studies, Edith Bennett
Pelz (#6283) was concerned about what actually occurred in these studies
and set up a highly controlled laboratory experiment which independently
varied four factors that could have produced the results: the housewives'
perceived consensus, their making of a decision, the group discussion
process and the receipt of information (lecture method). She was able
to show, as Lewin did, that the lecture—informational approach was not
very effective. However, she also showed that group discussion by
itself was not directly related to the decision to participate. Her
results indicated that the two critical factors in an individual's desire
to participate were (1) the perceived consensus among their peers, and
(2) the fact that they had made a decision.

Supporting the Pelz finding, on the influence of having made a
decision on later choices, is the research of Festinger and his colleagues
on cognitive dissonance.* In experimental research studies they have
shown that individuals who make a public decision feel committed to such
a choice and resist further change attempts. Similarly individuals who
make a private commitment (Brehm and Cohen, #6277) seem to adhere to such
decisions but not as strongly as those who make their commitment in
front of others.

However, the actual value of group discussion as a facilitator of
innovation adoption remains an unsettled issue. While Pelz' findings
raise some important questions, the ease of separation of group discussion
or interaction from perceived consensus and decision-making outside the
laboratory is difficult and probably not very practical. It is much
easier to develop consensus and decisions in a group discussion atmosphere
than probably any other; the social support for such decisions is also
important. Moreover, the group atmosphere has certain important effects

_____

*See discussion in Chapter Four, section on Attitude Change.

In and of itself. Anderson and McGuire (#6284) demonstrate the lowered resistance that results from peer support. The greater the peer support the lower the resistance, and, therefore, the greater the susceptibility to influence from sources acceptable to the group. That sources unacceptable to the group lead to greater resistance under peer support has also been demonstrated. (See Jones and Gerard, #6285, p. 483.)

Thus, participation with others in decision-making groups usually leads to a commitment to the group's actions. This kind of reaction can be described as a form of indirect interpersonal influence; i.e., those group pressures which affect an individual's adoption or rejection of new knowledge as a result of his exposure to events for reasons other than those related to the innovation or new knowledge being disseminated. We shall now turn to the field literature on the adoption process to find support for this principle.

Pellegrin (#1043) in his review of the literature in the field of education concludes, among other things, that social change is more likely to be accepted if it is implemented slowly with the people involved included in discussions about the changes. Gallaher (#2613) reports that people will accept innovations more readily if they understand them, perceive them as relevant and helped plan them. Lin, et al., (#3903) report that teachers who are involved in decisions related to innovations are more predisposed to adoption. Also, Uffelman (#3838) states that involvement in the development of programs is directly related to their acceptance.

Similarly, individuals who attend meetings of direct content relevance to the adoption of an innovation--e.g., about the Salk Vaccine (Clausen, et al., #6010; Glasser, #1385)--will be in a better position to evaluate whether or not they want to adopt it. But we also find that individuals who are members of formal organizations (Coughenour, #2437) or who are more socially active (Junghare and Prodipto, #3372) also seem more predisposed to early adoption. What seems to be occurring is that individuals who participate more readily with other individuals become sensitized to being influenced by them. This sensitization would seem to result from a general openness to others with whom one interacts as well as greater facility and feeling of competence in dealing with other people. Such a sense of competence also would seem to result in greater selectivity in the acceptance of influence; not only is an individual more open to communication and influence from others, but he also is able to reject (as well as accept) without fear of rejection the views of others. General support for this notion of openness to influence is seen in a study by Polson and Pal (#0305) who report that the acceptance of modern practices is inversely related to isolation.

Another possible reason for the greater sensitivity to others' influence attempts that result from social interaction might come from the utility for the individual in adopting an innovation. In Chapter Four, we discussed the finding that individuals will accept information and will be open to information which is contrary to their views if such information has some utility for them in reaching a goal. An example of this is the following: one of the aspects of organizational membership is the member's attainment of certain policy objectives or new positions in the organization. Individuals who would ordinarily be opposed to a particular innovation or piece of information might adopt or accept it because they see that it has some relevance for an issue under discussion which they want as the policy of the group. Individuals may also desire to move up in an organizational hierarchy; in order to reach such a position they may have to perform certain functions they would ordinarily not do; thus they may adopt certain innovations or knowledge in order to enable them to get ahead.

2. Group Cohesiveness

The voluminous research on the effects of the cohesiveness of group members is of direct relevance here. Cartwright (#3341) has pointed out a number of effects which have been consistently demonstrated in the research on small groups. Basically, the literature shows that individuals, who, for any one of a number of reasons, are strongly attracted to other members of a group (cohesiveness) will be greatly influenced by the norms of the group. If the norms of the group are congruent with influence attempts, the likelihood of acceptance is very great. On the other hand, if a deviation from the group norms is required, the group will be resistant to the attempted change. Industrial research has given substantial support to these findings. Seashore (#6286) showed that groups will lower or raise their productivity on the basis of the members cohesiveness and conformity to certain norms.*

A problem related to the effects of cohesiveness on change is expressed by Havelock (#6183) when he points out that while the barriers to the flow of information within a group may be extremely permeable, there

> "is a danger that increasing intragroup cohesiveness will adversely affect _inter_group permeability. Ideally, cohesiveness should take place between groups (involved in the utilization process), but in practice this can be difficult. The individual will often see more advantage in maintaining cohesiveness with members of his own group and see a danger in alienating colleagues by fraternizing with new members." (p. 134)

3. Overcoming Group Resistance

Under certain circumstances an attempted change can be incorporated in a group even if the norms of the group are opposed to it and even if there are other barriers present. A critical variable would be the manner in which a group is prepared for the presentation of new elements. For example, a study by Coch and French (#1828) showed the effects of preparation based on participation of the targets of change in group discussions.

---

*See next section on conformity for an elaboration of this.

Realizing that a direct attempt at convincing employees in a pajama factory to change their work procedures, while maintaining their rate of productivity, would lead to a great deal of resistance, they hypothesized that the involvement of the workers in the decisions related to the change and its importance for the company would lead to a greater realization and acceptance of management's goals. They set up an experiment in which one group of employees listened to management's problems and were involved in a discussion of the implications of these problems for the future of the company which another group was merely told of the change required.

The results were quite emphatic; the group involved in the discussion not only resisted the change-over less than the other but reached the old productivity level very quickly. At the same time, there was very little employee turnover or absenteeism. In the group receiving the order for a change-over, there was resistance, a much lower productivity level, and a high turnover and absenteeism rate. While there have been recent arguments,* between a former union official (who was involved in collective bargaining with the company at the time of the experiment) and the company president, about the extent of company manipulation, the effects of preparation of a group for change are apparent. The group-- as shown in the lecture situation--would not have been favorable to the new requirements without the preparation.

One conclusion that can be reached from these findings is that the cohesiveness and norms of a group can be utilized to sensitize individuals to change they would ordinarily resist; group discussion about policy and involvement in decision-making facilitates change for individuals in a group. Four factors seem to account for this phenomenon:

1. The reduced resistance to acceptable outside sources derived from peer support;

2. The public commitment to the decision;

3. The perceived consensus of the group; and

4. The development of new norms while maintaining the cohesiveness of the group.

A number of studies carried out in very different settings indicate findings similar to those of Coch and French. Chesler and Barakat (#2248) report that teachers' participation in the policy-making process of the school leads to less alienation, greater sharing of ideas, possibly better teaching, and possibly greater receptivity to change. In a similar vein, Menzel (#2389) reports that physicians who are socially integrated into peer group structures are more innovative, i.e., more accepting of new drugs, etc. Another study reports the converse of this; that prevailing patterns of professional specialization (which serves as the establishment) block out the efforts of innovative outsiders (Barber, #2807). Another

---

*See Gomberg and Marrow (#6287) exchange in Trans-Action during 1966. Both are social scientists.

study reports that in a village on the outskirts of Lisbon, Portugal the introduction of modern medicine was directly related to the return to the village of a young physician who had been raised there but who left to get his education. A comparison village in Brazil showed the prevalence of folk medicine due to the lack of an "insider" physician. In both villages "outsider" public health doctors were present (Siegel, #3378).

The discussion in this section leads to a number of conclusions:

1. In order for innovations to be successfully presented to a group or to individuals who are closely anchored to a group, the norms, and cohesiveness of the group must be known.

2. If the innovation follows a course known to be acceptable to the group, the group will accept the innovation if the individual presenting it is himself acceptable or if the innovation is not presented in the context of other unacceptable ideas or innovations.

3. If an innovation is unacceptable to a group, special care must be taken to prepare the group to make it more susceptible to acceptance. Possible means of preparation include group discussion about the proposed change, and involvement of the individual or group in the development of the ideas, innovation, etc., in the decision to make it available to others, and in the manner in which the change will be implemented.

4. Conformity and Social Support

Closely related to the attraction that one group member has for another (cohesiveness) is the extent to which an individual feels he is accepted or threatened by the group. In the last section we mentioned a study by Seashore (#6286) which showed that cohesiveness of a group plus conformity of its members to certain norms leads to a tendency to resist or to change based on the content of the norms. More recent research has shown that the relationship between cohesiveness-attraction and conformity of individual members to the groups' norms is a function of the feelings of acceptance by the person (Walker and Heyns, #6301).

While, in general, acceptance in a highly cohesive group leads an individual to greater conformity, a high degree of acceptance also leads to greater independence for the individual. Menzel (#2389) reports that physicians who were less well accepted by their colleagues showed greater publicly expressed conformity about the use of new drugs (but not private acceptance) while those who were highly accepted showed no such public conformity, if they did not agree privately. Menzel's study supported the findings of a laboratory study by Dittes and Kelley (#6288). Similarly, Harvey and Consalvi (#6289), in a sociometric study of individuals in a detention center for juvenile delinquents, found that those who were most accepted were more independent of group norms while those who were moderately accepted were most conforming. An interesting additional finding was that those who were on the low end of acceptance showed low conformity.

5-6

In short, conformity to the norms of a group is curvilinearly related to the acceptance that individuals feel within the group as well as to the attraction that they feel towards each other. Generally, a very high degree of acceptance leads to independence, moderate degrees of acceptance tend to lead to conformity and a very low degree of acceptance leads to a lack of conformity to group norms.

Some of these findings may very well be explained by the extent to which individuals feel secure or threatened; the greater the acceptance the greater the feelings of security and vice versa. The consequences of insecurity in a group member are discussed by Klein (#3691). He states that change may threaten the sense of self-esteem, competence, and autonomy of a group that otherwise feels adequate to meet the usual challenges with which they are faced. However, Klein goes on to state that such threatened changes may force people "to confront the fact that... old preconceptions do not fit present reality". The problem in such a confrontation situation is that the feelings of threat, if too great, can lead to resistance and distortion of the new information or practice.

Janis and Smith (#6274) make a similar point in their review of research literature on group reactions to deviance. If group norms

> "are regarded as crucially relevant to the group's
> goals (they) are likely to be buttressed by stronger
> sanctions than norms having more marginal status. In
> the United States, for example, attitudes towards
> Communist China are more strongly prescribed and
> sanctioned than attitudes toward Turkey (for many
> years the subject of unfavorable imagery), because
> of obvious differences in their relevance to national
> goals and international conflict." (p. 199)

They also point out that the more closely the group consensus approaches unanimity on a given issue, the greater the resistance of individual members to communication contrary to the norm on the particular issue.

Such unanimity has distinct difficulties as shown in the classic studies on conformity by Asch (#6290). In the Asch experiments a naive subject was shown slides representing lines which were obviously different in length. The subject was placed in a room with a group of stooges who were told, by the experimenter, to say that the lines were equal in size. The subject was, therefore, placed in a conflict situation--his own judgment of the different sized lines and the unanimous judgment of what he thought was a group of fellow "naive" subjects. In 35% of the cases, the "naive" subject conformed to the stooges. The unanimous opinion of one's fellow group members apparently exerts such a strong force on the individual that he will sometimes reject the evidence of his own senses for the sake of conformity.

However, when one of the stooges was told to differ with the other stooges, but not necessarily agree with the subject, only 5% conformed to the stooges' judgment. Hence the lack of unanimity among the stooges made their judgments vulnerable. It should also be noted that many of the subjects who publicly conformed did not privately change their judgments. Apparently they viewed public conformity as expedient in that particular situation. Thus, while these studies are often cited

as an indication of the tendency of people to conform, they also
provide some evidence of the lack of conformity of most individuals
under rather extreme pressures to agree with others; 65% did not conform under unanimous opposition, 95% did not when only one stooge
broke the total consensus. The subjects in the Asch studies seem to
express a greater resilience and rationality than many reviewers have
usually recognized.

Another important aspect of an individual's relationships to others
is the effect of membership in a group on an individual's attitudes.
Two important studies in this area are the famous Newcomb (#6302) study
of Bennington College students and the Siegel and Siegel (#6291) study
of membership in non-desired groups.

Newcomb's study, carried out in the late 1930's and reported in
1943, clearly established the effects of one's reference group (the
group which one uses as a standard for his own judgments), on attitude
changes. Girls who entered Bennington College as conservatives politically
and who looked toward the liberal upper classmen and faculty members as
their "reference" groups, changed their political attitudes over the first
few years to match those of the desired group. On the other hand, those
students who still looked to their parents as their major reference group
remained relatively conservative politically--as were their parents.
The study by Siegel and Siegel (#6291) showed a similar result dealing
with students who desired to live in a sorority. Students who were unable
to join a sorority and had to live in other types of housing over the
school year changed their attitudes to be congruent with students with
whom they lived.

Under the conditions of conformity to group and reference group norms,
individuals are greatly influenced by what the group as an entity and
others as individuals believe. They are also greatly affected by the
social support that is manifested in group situations. We previously
touched on one aspect of this in our discussion of attraction/cohesiveness
but now come back to it in the context of peer group norms in a classroom.

A number of studies over the years have measured the effects of
classroom peer norms on a student's resistance to the teacher. Lippitt
(#1397) recently commented on these dynamics:

> "...there are all those supports or lack of supports
> coming from the learning group of peers. Every class-
> room group has a variety of peer norms or standards
> about such things as how active to be in interaction
> with the teacher, how much energy and effort to put
> out in extra homework. In a fairly substantial set
> of classrooms from second grade to junior high, we
> found that the majority of children in a classroom
> perceived that the majority of the other children in
> that classroom are against too active, eager collabora-
> tion with the teacher. However, on personal, private
> inventories, the youngsters also filled out how they
> personally felt. The majority were in favor of more
> active involvement and commitment, but felt that the
> normative pressures of the majority were against it.
> There had never been dialogue and never any sharing of
> data until these data were put on the board for them to

look at. This provided a great surprise. They were
maintaining for themselves a state of what the sociologist would call 'pluralistic ignorance' about the
way they thought about these particular matters of
educational involvement and commitment.

"Another interesting finding is that for a significant
proportion of children in a sentence completion study,
the meaning of helping each other in the classroom is
cheating. So the whole range of possibilities of providing assistance through interpersonal support in
learning activities becomes a rather difficult problem
if this is the kind of meaning we have been getting across
as being tied up with helping.

"Then there are the types of inhibitions to commitment to
learning tasks that come from smoldering interpersonal
peer-group problems. When we have matched children on
I.Q., but with some of them from the non-accepted part of
the classroom structure and others from the accepted part
of the classroom structure, we find significant under-
utilization of intelligence on the part of those who are
in the non-accepted or isolated part of the peer structure.
And teachers have not typically been coping with classroom
process as a basic part of releasing and supporting the
learning of the pupils in their room." (pp. 48-49)

The effect of the teacher peer support on their resistance to
innovation has also not gone without notice. Chesler and Fox (#6292)
summarize a number of studies on teacher peer support and its relation
to the investigation and acceptance of change.

"Work in a situation where one feels liked and respected
by peers and supervisors is obviously more satisfying
and fulfilling than work where one feels ignored; furthermore, it predisposes one to be positive and supportive to
others. Thus, such a setup fosters a continuing cycle of
change and support, invention and sharing of ideas.

"To establish a healthy climate for change we need first
to develop ways for individual teachers to share new ideas
with other staff members and to gain support for worthy
innovations. Further, we need to make teachers feel that
they have had some influence in developing changes by
adopting new administrative styles which decentralize decision-
making.

"The growing body of research findings about change processes
in the schools makes clear, however, that the development of
an open and supportive climate of personal and professional
relationships among the members of the school faculty carried
high priority." (p. 26)

To amplify the importance of teacher-supervisor relationships,
Willower (#0637) points out that when teachers are threatened by an
innovation instituted without their prior involvement, the resistance
to change may take the form of verbal hostility, sloppy implementation
or apathetic indifference, rigid conformity without consideration of

5-9

reason or the good of the organization and overt intra-organizational conflict strategies (e.g., warning of administrator's surveillance). Such feelings of threat also may lead to the ridiculing of students in the teacher's lounge and thereby provide a release for aggressive feelings in the context of the social support of peers. This also may legitimate inconsiderate threatment of the students.

From the above discussion on conformity to norms, the attraction (cohesiveness) of group members to each other and the support given to others through such norms and cohesiveness, we would expect that attempts to change group norms or beliefs under conditions when any of these forces were salient would be very difficult. Such a result has been amply demonstrated by the literature. On the other hand, we have seen in the Coch and French study how a sophisticated awareness of these factors could be used to introduce changes through the preparation of the individuals and groups concerned. Under normal everyday conditions such preparation does not exist and new information and practices contrary to group norms or expectations are not readily accepted.

However, under certain non-planned conditions--such as crises, social disasters, and general community upheavel--the established patterns of interaction are disrupted. Under such conditions, as Gardner (#6258) and Michael (#3892) indicate, a great deal of innovation and change is possible.

Lindeman (#2212) reports the effects of a breakdown in social cohesion of a working class community following urban renewal relocation on the acceptance of a mental health clinic. The author noted that under normal conditions such a clinic could not have gained acceptance due to the typical community member's neighborhood loyalty and anti-intellectualism. During the relocation upheaval the cohesive forces of neighborhood loyalty were gravely threatened and the clinic was able to work with the people to try to resolve some of the many problems caused by the change.

Concluding this section on conformity and social support, we may make the following points related to knowledge utilization:

1. With moderate group acceptance (and therefore some insecurity about position) there will be a greater likelihood that individuals will accept new knowledge or innovations that follow group norms. However, when use of the innovation is not readily visible to others, those who are moderately accepted and are anxious about their acceptance may publicly conform and privately disagree.

2. Individuals (or groups) who are very highly accepted are more open about their disagreement and are much more likely to deviate from group norms. Their feelings of security, as a result of their high acceptance, bolster them against the fear of sanctions. This may make them more likely to innovate. It also may lead them to reject innovations that the group as a whole wants. There is the possibility that such a situation will not occur since a highly accepted member has a great deal of influence over them.

3. Groups are less likely to accept changes which require considerable deviance from important norms.

5-10

4. Individuals are less likely to accept changes when a group consensus approaches unanimity for a different course of action.

5. The greater the social support of peers for a particular kind of behavior the greater the likelihood that the behavior will be performed.

6. Under conditions of crisis, changes can be made and accepted which would be rejected under ordinary circumstances. The major problem is the extent to which the changed behavior or structure will be continued once the crisis ends. It is probable that techniques similar to those discussed above would be necessary to assure the maintenance of the changes. It might also be that in certain, as yet undetermined, types of crises and types of changes, maintenance is assured through structural changes that produce an inability of groups or individuals to return to old patterns of behavior.

5. Social Integration

A considerable number of field studies have investigated the influence of others in the adoption process as a result of an individual's membership in groups and the influence of friends. Probably the best known and most often quoted group of studies are those carried out by Coleman and his associates (Coleman, Katz and Menzel, #3576; Menzel and Katz, #3404, and others). In their important study of Doctors and New Drugs, Coleman, et al. (#3576) found that interpersonal relationships seemed to be the most important factor in the adoption of innovations. A network of personal affiliations with other doctors was determined for each doctor in the sample. It was found that doctors well-integrated into the medical community not only used the drug earlier, but also went through a different diffusion process. Those doctors who shared offices and who had two or more friendship choices in the sociometric net had the most rapid adoption rate; lone practitioners with two or more friendship choices had a nearly identical adoption rate. Office sharers with one or no friendship choices were by far slower to adopt but the final proportion adopting was similar to the first two. Finally, lone practitioners with one or no friendship choices were by far the slowest to adopt the new drug and the final proportion of adopters was much smaller than for the other three types. The authors conclude with what seems to be a statement proposing a general sensitivity of doctors who are intimately involved in a social interaction network.

> "It is not certain just what was transmitted when one doctor 'infected' another, leading him to use the new drug. (We have) suggested that communication channels in general may play a variety of roles in a doctor's decision to use a new drug; they may, it was suggested, bring information, furnish advice on matters which are in doubt, or legitimate an action by their stamp of approval Doctors may also have affected their colleagues' decision to use gammanym (the new drug) in a variety of ways. They may have brought information about the drugs existence, composition, function, and price; or they may have told of their own experiences with it, including its efficacy as a cure and the occurrence of undesirable side effects.. Any of these transactions could have resulted in a snowball process, such as was actually observed..." (pp. 111-112)

"The data above imply that the new development diffused
through the social system in several stages. First,
interpersonal influence on gammanym adoptions operated
through professional relations among doctors who were in
contact with many colleagues through professional ties.
Next it showed its strength through the more socially
defined relations of doctors who were tied to many colleagues
through the network of friendships. During a third stage
(which actually overlapped with the second), social influence made itself felt in the more open parts of the social
structure, that is, among the relatively isolated doctors.
The fourth stage saw some additional adoptions of gammanym
by individuals who acted independently of the time at which
their associates had introduced it; social influence had
apparently ceased to be effective. Finally, there followed
a period during which virtually no further adoption occurred."
(p. 130)

Similar findings are also found in less exhaustive and systematic
studies. In studies on the acceptance of the Salk Vaccine in its early
stages of diffusion it was found that friends were important influencers
on adoption; those who knew others who had been previously vaccinated
were more likely to adopt it themselves (Clausen, et al. #6010;
Glasser (#1385).   Stojanovic (#2843) found that those people who had
knowledge of someone who had previously used a new hospital were more likely
to use it themselves.

We may conclude that individuals seem to be predisposed to accept
innovations or new practices as a result of their social interaction
with others who use them or who have knowledge about them. Moreover,
the acceptance is not necessarily a result of direct influence attempt
but rather a sensitization to others and thereby an openness to follow
their behaviors.

6.   Similarity of Background

One factor that seems to be at work in this sensitization or openness to others with whom one interacts is the similarity between the
adopter and others with whom he interacts. Newcomb, et al. (#6297)
propose, in a theoretical analysis of social interaction, that individuals
who have similar attitudes on a number of issues have a strong tendency
to like each other and to interact more. If there is serious disagreement in attitudes or behaviors on other issues they will attempt to
resolve these differences. Also, individuals who interact with each
other and have similar attitudes will be more open to influence from
other persons. They cite considerable experimental research to support
this thesis.*

The descriptive literature also supports this theory. Wellin (#2772)
states that hygiene workers have the greatest effect on those who are
most similar on economic level and cultural background. A similar finding

---

*These ideas were originally proposed by Newcomb in his book The Acquaintance Process,
New York, Holt, 1963 and in other articles.

is reported by Marriott (#2408) in his study of the diffusion of western medicine in India. He states that the western doctor is unsuccessful because his practice of medicine is directly related to western culture which is in conflict with certain aspects of village Indian culture.

> "The western ideal of personal privacy, of individual responsibility, of the dignity of certain techniques, and of the democratic nature of interpersonal trust are not intrinsic parts of scientific medical practice but are cultural accretions to it. [Before one can expect the firm establishment of western medicine in the village] its role must be defined according to village concepts and practices" (pp. 266-267).

This lack of rapport between a doctor and his patient (see also Lewis #2641) leads to a resistance to the use of western medicine. The problem results from a lack of common attitudes and values by which each could communicate to the other as well as the consistent misinterpretations of the others' actions. Similarly, Liberman (#0363) found a high degree of attitudinal consensus between "influence-influential pairs" in the use of mental health resources by families of mentally ill persons. He also found that there was greater communication among the people who had homogeneous viewpoints on the subject.

We may conclude, then, that a major variable in the communication and acceptance of influence is the similarity--attitudinally, culturally and behaviorally--between the recipient and the sender of the influence.

7. Status

Directly related to the similarity of background and its effect on adoption is the resistance or acceptance that seems to follow status differences. As was discussed in Chapter Four, individuals tend to seek out others with similar backgrounds and similar status levels for comparison with themselves, thereby enabling them to evaluate their own attitudes, abilities and emotions. We stated, in the last chapter, that the social comparison process would seem to be most operative under conditions of uncertainty or anxiety. It would seem that situations in which individuals are faced with the possibility of changing their behavior--such as is often required by the adoption of innovations--would produce some anxiety and, therefore, they would seek out others of similar status and probably avoid those of different status levels.

The study of opinion leaders (Lazarsfeld and Katz, #0294)* indicates supporting evidence for this proposition; personal influence and communication on a wide variety of matters was generally limited to individuals of about the same social status level. The tendency to stay within one's own status level becomes particularly important when status differences become great. Lionberger (#1036) reports that "even in the absence of clear-cut lines the tendency to choose persons higher on the status scale than oneself may become progressively less as distance between the seekers and the person sought increases" (p. 87).

---

*See discussion in Chapter Seven.

5-13

The theoretical propositions previously presented in Chapter Four
and the two reports just cited *differ* quite sharply with the results of
research on the tendencies of farmers when seeking advice about farm
machinery. Lionberger (#1036) reports a number of studies which indicate
that farmers generally tend to look up the status scale for advice on
matters directly related to farming.

These conflicting findings may be resolved in the following manner.
In the first discussion the emphasis was on situations having potentially
anxiety producing qualities; personal influence from high status
individuals may produce considerable tension because of the prestige
involved in one individual being higher status. Also, a large disparity
in status between individuals may create anxiety because of the tension
produced by communication between individuals of different backgrounds.
On the other hand, the seeking of advice related to new farm equipment
meant an individual was talking to another farmer who, while of higher
status, is of a similar background. Moreover, the higher status farmer
has something to offer of a concrete nature in an area in which he is
presumed to be more adept than the farmer who is seeking the information.
Generally, then, these farmers do not experience anxiety when they
communicate with the higher status farmers; rather they seem to use
them as models for their own behavior.

In summary, when status differences produce anxiety or tension
(e.g., when status itself becomes salient) lower status individuals
will tend to avoid contact with higher status individuals. But, when
the status differences do not cause any anxiety, as when the lower
status person accepts as valid the prestige of the higher status person
and/or when the lower status person needs information that the higher
status person can provide, we would expect the lower status person to
look upwards in the status scale.

An important aspect of status relationships is the extent to which
the higher status person is attempting to influence the lower status
person as against the lower status person seeking information from the
higher status individual. We would expect little resistance in the
latter case. However, there is the potential for resistance in the
former. If an individual feels that a higher status person is illegiti-
mately attempting to influence him he will most likely resist the attempt.
To the extent that the difference is seen as legitimate, the lower status
person may accept it. We shall deal with the concept of legitimate
(formal) power in the next chapter on the organizational factors which
facilitate and inhibit the adoption of innovations.

8. Community Norms

In the discussion at the end of the last chapter, we stated that not
only are individuals sometimes dominated by their internal needs but
that they are also sometimes limited in their rational judgments by
community and/or social norms. Extending this discussion we might
divide community norms along a dimension of traditionalism--modernism.

The extreme cases of traditional and modern community norms can be described, as does Rogers (#1824), in the following manner:

> "A community with traditional norms can be seen as less developed and agricultural, as having lower levels of literacy and education, as placing prime importance on interpersonal relationships over economic factors, and as having a tendency to be a relatively closed system with few outside contacts.

> "A community with modern norms can be seen as having a developed technology with a complex division of labor, usually in urban areas, as placing a high value on science and education, as having a large number of interpersonal contacts outside the community as well as receiving a large amount of information from outside the community and as placing prime importance on economic matters."

Referring back to our "image of man" we may say that the "modern" norms permit individuals in the community to choose from a considerable variety of sources and to use a large repertoire of potential decisions from which to make a judgment. The traditional community norms severely limit the freedom of the individual to make independent decisions because they drastically limit the alternatives to which he is exposed by the lack of contact with people and institutions outside the community.

Rogers (#1824) reaches a similar conclusion when he states that "an individual's innovativeness varies directly with the norms of his social system on innovativeness" (p. 71). To support this proposition, Rogers cites a study by Van den Ban (#1824) which concluded that "a farmer with a high level of education, on a large farm, and with a high net worth but residing in a township with a traditional norm, adopted fewer farm innovations than if he farmed in a township where the norms were modern" (p. 71).

There is considerable supporting evidence for the relationship between community norms and the tendency to adopt innovations. For example, Flinn (#1415) found such a relationship and Coleman and Marsh (#2406) concluded that the tendency of farmers to adopt recommended practices is a function of the farmer's neighborhood of residence: those that reside in high adoption areas, adopt more readily than those in low adoption areas.

Directly related to this is the tendency of individuals to conform
to the norms of their reference group previously defined as the group
which one uses as a standard for his own judgments. If individuals in
a community see their neighbors, whom they respect, using innovative
farm machinery, there will be a strong tendency for them to use it.

Beside the community, a source of major influence is the individual's
family. Lionberger (#1036) in his review of the literature on adoption
of agricultural innovations states that "numerous studies have shown that
family members often serve as referents or consultants in decisions
to adopt new farm and home practices". Families also serve their members
as selective screeners of new information, as direct information links
with new knoweldge (e.g., school children), as support for the performance
of new tasks (Straus, #0446), and as decision makers in the use of new
vaccine by children (particularly maternal influence, Tyroler, et al. #3263).

Concluding this discussion it seems quite apparent that community
norms and reference groups affect the adoption of innovations. Sometimes
this occurs because of a widely accepted norm; often it is the result of the
patterns (or norms) of behavior of the community members. If interpersonal interaction tends to remain within a particular community the
possibility for the acquisition of knowledge about innovation is quite
limited. If outside interaction does occur, the opportunities for knowledge
about an innovation greatly increases and with this so does the possibility
for adoption.

B. DIRECT INTERPERSONAL INFLUENCE

The influence process of senders that directly effects the adoption of
innovations has been discussed under many different headings and will be
presented in a number of different parts of this report. In the next chapter,
we shall discuss the manner in which supervisors directly affect their subordinates; and, in Chapter Seven we shall discuss the role of different types
of linking agents and structures in influencing the recipients of innovations.
In this section, we shall emphasize those characteristics of influence-senders
as they relate to direct attempts at influence.

1. Credibility

One of the most important variables that determines whether or not
a sender will be able to influence a receiver is the extent to which he
is perceived as a reliable and believable source of information. As was
reported in Chapter Four, a number of well-known experiments have shown
that when a source (a sender) is considered by an audience (a receiver)
to be prestigeful and trustworthy, there is a strong tendency for the
audience to change their attitude in accordance with the attitudes of
the source.   The field literature seems to support these
findings.

Zagona and Harter (#0527) report that the percentage of people who
agreed with information contained in a printed message on smoking and
who perceived it as trustworthy increased as the credibility of the
source increased. Also, those people who perceived the information
as unbiased retained more of it than those who perceived it as biased.

Credibility is often developed as a result of the receiver's perception of the sender's intentions. Caird (#2252) shows that agricultural advisors who live with the people with whom they are working tend to build up trust with them. Such trust not only leads to an increased ability to influence people but the presence of the advisors also enable them to be there when problems arise and make suggestions which enables the trust to be realized in the accomplishments of the people. Besides the trust engendered through living with the people to be influenced, credibility is a direct result of the competence of a change agent. Najafi (as reported in Niehoff and Anderson #3005) found that a highly motivated young and competent community development agent gained the respect and cooperation of the villagers.

But the credibility of a particular person that is gained as a result of his expertise in the past does not necessarily transfer to new situations in which he has no proven competence. Sibley (in Niehoff and Anderson #3005) reports, in a study of Phillipine villagers, that when agricultural innovations were disseminated by respected local teachers they were not accepted, as might be expected from the respect that the villagers have for teachers, because the villagers did not consider the teachers as experts in agriculture.

This study points up the difference between credibility which is based on a general attraction to another and that which is based on a specific area competence. One might expect that an individual who was revered as wise or who is very well liked would probably be influential on a whole host of items. However, those individuals who gain their credibility as a result of specific expertise--e.g., teachers--may have influence only in that area. It is interesting that the above study showed that the teacher's influence did not extend to agriculture. The impression that one gets from the behavior of teachers, families, and students in Southeast Asia, and most developing countries, is that the teacher's influence extends far beyond the classroom. What may have occurred in Sibley's study is that the villagers, whose major occupation is farming, feel that this is an area on which they do know more than the esteemed teacher. It would seem that in almost all other spheres of life this would not be the case.

2. Legitimacy of Role

The teacher's role in developing countries is probably a good example of a highly legitimated role which enables the incumbent to have considerable influence over those who accept it as such. These roles are quite prevalent in all social systems and may be considered necessary for the stable operation of a system. Without such legitimacy each role incumbent would have to prove his individual worth to the recipient and little, if any, knowledge or information could be easily disseminated. With the acceptance of roles as legitimate, those who interact with the role incumbent assume certain training and skills and, therefore, are predisposed to accept information related to these skills as accurate. An example of this is the patient's relationship to his physician and his acceptance of his advice. If each physician had to prove his worth there would be little medical care given or accepted.

The physician's relationship to the detail man from pharmaceutical companies represents the acceptance by the physicians of the skills, limited though they may be, of the detail man. While the latter is of a lower status than the doctor he, nevertheless, represents an important source of information. As was previously reported, Bauer and Wortzel (#2340) have shown that doctors are dependent upon detail men for information related to drugs used in the treatment of low risk diseases. It is of importance, however, that this study shows that reliance on detail men is much greater among doctors who are late adopters. The early adopters tend to rely much more on journal articles and professional colleagues. This seems to also confirm the finding of Coleman et al. (#3576) that early adopters tend to be much more highly linked to their colleagues in friendship relations and more influenced by them. In short, it seems as if physicians who are early adopters consider the role of detail man in a much more limited fashion than later adopters.

Probably one of the main reasons for limiting the influence of the detail man is the fact that he has a product to sell, i.e., his credibility is questionable because he represents a company which sells a particular drug. It is, therefore, assumed that he is partial. This same result was reported in the study by Zagona and Harter (#0527) where those who perceived information as biased accepted it less than those who thought it was unbiased. Another study that shows the limitation of the influence of a role incumbent as a result of possible bias is reported by Beal and Rogers (#1351). They show that agricultural scientists who work in government are considered more credible than those working for a profit-making business.

Thus, the legitimacy of a role--and, therefore, the amount of influence its incumbent can have on others--is directly related to the perceived bias (credibility) of the institution in which the role occurs. If the institution has no perceived vested interest in presenting a particular point of view, the individual who performs certain roles in that institution will have more influence over his clients.

In terms of Kelman's (#6259, #1776) theory of social influence (see Chapter Four) we would state that when an individual or a role is considered to have particular expertise or is especially attractive, the recipient will be predisposed to accept the information presented and the influence attempted; the credibility of the sender which derives from his expertise or attractiveness leads the receiver to identify with him. The sender's influence in this case is based on the receiver's desire to continue their relationship.

But there is another relationship where influence is important-- the situation where the sender controls rewards for the receiver or has the power to punish the receiver (Kelman's "means-end control"). Such a relationship exists in a supervisor-subordinate relationship and probably represents the greatest influence that a sender can have on a receiver as a result of the legitimacy of a particular role. This type of legitimacy creates a situation where the supervisor can play an important role in the recipient's adoption of innovations. Pelligrin (#1043) in his review of the educational innovation literature concludes that the superintendent's authority makes him a key element in the adoption process even though he himself does not usually create innovations because of inadequate time and other pressures. Gallaher (#2613) presents a similar argument in his discussion of the role of the advocate but questions whether an administrator like the superintendent can perform such a function due to his peace-maker role between the school board and the professionals in the schools. Whether it is the superintendent or some other administrator, there seems to be little doubt that formal authority within an hierarchical organization is very influential when used by a sender in the diffusion-adoption process. It should not, however, be concluded that such influence automatically leads to adoption. Very subtle forms of resistance are very common in such settings. We shall discuss these issues in great depth in Chapter Six.

3. Strategies of Change Agent*

Unfortunately, or fortunately, senders of innovations (or change agents) often do not have formal authority in the target organization, even if their role is accepted by all concerned. Because of this lack of formal power, they must use many different kinds of strategies to predispose their receivers to accept the innovations being presented. Three general types of strategies should be noted at this point: direct involvement, project continuity, and dealing with vested interests.

a. Direct Involvement

As might be expected from previous discussions, one of the most effective techniques is to involve the recipients in the diffusion-adoption process. Tannous (#3005)** reports that when a public health worker in Lebanon insisted that villagers must contribute something (labor, money, etc.) in order to get assistance, they did so and as a result they accepted the innovation as their own. It was not a gift or anything to be taken lightly, but something that they acquired as a result of their own actions. On the other hand, Fraser (#3005)** reports a situation in India in which the change agent assumed the task of developing new markets in order to establish rural cooperatives. This resulted in local recipients having few responsibilities and opportunities for involvement in the running of the cooperatives. In this case the recipients rejected the innovation--the cooperatives.

Involvement in competitive activities related to the adoption of innovations also can be an effective strategy. Barnett (#3005)** reported that in community development projects in the South Pacific, group rivalries between clubs, teams, districts, and families were used for constructive competition and led to the acceptance of the new practices.

A more passive form of involvement in which the sender places the recipients in educational activities as a means of creating a disposition towards adoption has had a mixed history. Shalaby (#3005)** shows how an information campaign in Egypt consisting of advertisements, informal lectures, community meetings, and demonstrations led to adoption. However, in other information campaigns (Freedman and Takeshita #1403) the results have been very disappointing.***

*For other change agent strategies, see Chapter Seven.

**Citation #3005 is a detailed review of the literature on change agents in developing countries written by Niehoff and Anderson. The authors listed are referenced only in the Niehoff and Anderson article in our bibliography.

***See Freedman and Sears (#3000) for a general review of the reasons for these results.

It might be that the difference between a successful and an unsuccessful information campaign rests with the extent to which the
receivers are personally involved in the process. Most information
campaigns are carried out through the mass media and are forced,
by the nature of the media, to be depersonalized.

b.   Project Continuity

An important element in all change attempts is the necessity
of the sender or change agent to follow-through consistently on
their promises. The recipients, especially those in community
development projects which they did not initiate, are suspicious
of the change agent's intent. In order to build up and maintain
trust, follow-through on the stated conditions of the project is
essential.

Najafi (#3005)* reports that a community development project
in Iran was successful because government and private agencies were
consistent in furnishing supplies and advising people as soon as
they were called upon. On the other hand, a project in Laos (#3005)*
failed because the U.S. Agency for International Development (AID)
did not consistently follow through on promises made for supplying
construction materials. This led to the villagers becoming apathetic
about community development projects.

Similar problems exist in the relationship between researchers
and administrators. Often researchers will accept certain deadlines
on research needed by administrators and then not meet them, or
present inadequate reports. This results in a lack of confidence
in researchers and a distrust of their intentions. It is not an
uncommon experience to find administrators who feel that researchers
are hucksters for their own ideas and are not concerned with the
utilization of the research results.

c.   Dealing with Vested Interest Groups

One of the major stumbling blocks in the effective dissemination
and utilization of innovations and new knowledge is the power of
vested interest groups. For example, Paul (#0436) concludes that
when a physician's practices in a developing country threaten someone's power or position, his efforts may be blocked; local interest
groups may sabotage the project. Similarly, Lewis (#2641) reports
that the establishment of a health clinic in a Mexican village failed
because local interest groups viewed the medical clinic as a threat
to their power. Marmor (#3160) points out that the resistance of
opposition groups can emerge either by their motivation for power,
prestige or gain or may be the result of anxieties that result from
insecurity, the feeling that their safety is best protected in
the familiar, older surroundings. Many other studies show similar
results.

---

*See footnote (**) on p. 5-19.

To deal effectively with these types of resistances, the change agent may adopt a number of tactics. One possibility is presenting the innovation in such a way as not to arouse the vested interests of a powerful group. This sounds simple but unfortunately assumes ignorance on the part of the interest group, which is often not the case.

A second more commonly used strategy is the inducement of the vested interest groups to accept the innovations in return for some desired resource. A complementary strategy is to threaten the interest group with reprisals if they do not agree to the innovation. These reprisals can be in the form of non-violent demonstrations, violent actions, punishment or the like. This also can be achieved by combining a number of interest groups in a common cause against another. Yet another variant of this strategy was reported in a study by Schweng (#3005)*. He found that the powerful landowners in Bolivia each gave an estate to a community development project and cooperated with project personnel. The reason for their "generosity" was their fear of possible govern- ment expropriation of land. A similar type of strategy is common in the dealings between federal agencies and conservative school systems. In order to get federally financed projects approved, the school system must agree to certain changes in its practices, curriculum, etc. That such change is not easy to achieve is evidenced by the difficulties of the United States Office of Education in pressuring southern (and northern) school systems to desegregate in order to qualify for federal money.

A strategy that has proven effective in some settings is the involvement of the vested interests in the decision-making process. Shalaby (#3005)* reports that a project was successful and avoided the usual pitfalls of new projects because local leaders representing various vested interests were organized into a formal village council and thereby were actively   involved in the project as well as being exposed directly to an information campaign. Sibley (#3005)* reports a project that failed due to a conflict between young, unmarried, elected officials who ignored the traditional respect for age, and the elders who felt insulted and did not cooperate.

4. Leadership

Whether or not the leader of a group represents a force for innova- tion or resistance is a point which has received considerable discussion. Many authors have maintained that the leader follows group norms more closely and more faithfully than does any other member and some have suggested that, in part, leadership results from an individual's ability to follow these norms in a more competent fashion than any other group member. This conformity has led people to assume that leaders tend to resist change.

---

*See footnote (**) on p. 5-19.

However, a number of studies have indicated that leaders often do not resist change and innovations but rather, as a result of their position, see their role as requiring them to innovate. Hollander (#5183) in a laboratory experiment shows that leadership goes through at least two stages. First, the leader becomes accepted as a result of his competence in achieving the group goals and conforming to the group's norms. As a result of these activities he develops certain "credits" of acceptance.* Second, the accumulation of these credits and his new role as leader creates in the group and in himself very different norms for his behavior. In a sense he is expected to lead and to provide the group with new activities and resources. He is not a deviant from the group norms, but rather he conforms to new norms that have been established by the group for the leader. Moreover, his accumulation of these acceptance "credits" enables him to take risks without fear of group rejection.

Support for these findings is found in a number of field studies. Putney and Putney (#0798) report that wealthy village leaders who held public office and were respected, had a reputation for innovativeness which was the basis for their prestige and which transcended the limits of their traditional culture. In another study Miller, F. (#0828) the decision-makers (leadership) in a Mexican village brought about changes through their use of social control measures. Thus, in this case, those forces which are ordinarily used to maintain traditions were used to bring about change.

What characteristics do the most effective leaders have? In recent years there has been an enormous amount of evidence which indicates that there are no common characteristics of leaders that hold up over different types of situations. The most important recent research indicates that one must take into account three key group factors in trying to assess leadership effectiveness: (1) the leader-follower relationship, (2) the nature of the group task, and (3) the position of the leader.

In the process of carrying out an extensive program of research on leadership stypes related to these three factors, Fiedler (#1718) found that the most important of these was the relationship between the leader and follower; the least important one was the position of the leader (e.g., status within an organization). Combining the characteristics of the leader with the relationship between the leader and his followers, Fiedler states that directive leadership was most effective when the leader-follower relations were either very good or very bad. However, when there were only moderately good leader-follower relations, a non-directive or human relations oriented leader was found to be most effective. These results indicate that leadership styles are important characteristics of group functioning but mainly when they are related to the interaction of leader and group characteristics.

_____
*Hollander calls these "idiosyncracy credits".

5-22

In the D&U process, like all functions that are dependent on
social organizations, effective leadership is a critical element in
achieving successful group action. This is particularly true if the
leader is seen as the "gatekeeper" for new ideas or as the innovator.
The literature indicates that if a leader is an innovator or gatekeeper
he will be effective only to the extent that his leadership style is
consonant with his relationship to the group.

5. Feedback

An individual learns of others' expectations and acceptance of
him from the ways in which they behave towards him. If he chooses
to be a member of a group and others let him do so but rarely ask him
to participate with them in important functions, he has received
important information about the way they feel about him. Feedback
that results from one's action towards another is critical to a person's
capacity to evaluate his own actions. Just as the movements of one's
body are dependent on the feedback from the physical environment in
which one lives, so too the ability to perform adequately in a social
situation is dependent on feedback from the "others" who constitute the
social environment. Nokes (#1785) writes that "...in each case feedback, i.e., information about the results of action, is essential to
a successful attainment of objectives" (p. 381). "Where this feedback
is inadequate the end result appears, in the individual, to be anxiety;
where it is available but ignored this seems to be accompanied by a
degree of autistic or wishful thinking" (p. 387). He states that these
same reactions also appear in institutions.

Laboratory studies of small groups have shown the relative effectiveness of feedback. Leavitt and Mueller (reported in Guetzkow, #6304)
state that there seems to be little doubt that feedback often improves
group performance. Guetzkow (#6304), in his review of the literature,
states that the lack of feedback creates an increase in the individual's
or group's alternative possibilities for action; when they receive no
feedback, individuals lose the ability to disconfirm any of the potential
solutions which occur to them in the course of their attempt to solve a
problem. Thus the lack of feedback makes it difficult to act with any
degree of certainty.

Feedback can by dysfunctional as well as functional, however.
Zajonc (#6305) reports that performance feedback presented to a group
has a relatively limited effect on an individual's performance, even
though direct feedback to the individual directly does have a positive
effect. When feedback is provided to the group as a unit, the individual
has no way of evaluating his own personal performance and, therefore,
has no way of correcting it. In order to change he would have to analyze
the complex patterns of interaction present in the group, assess his
contribution to these patterns, and then figure out how these contributions and patterns relate to the group product and the group feedback.
However, if he receives direct individual feedback, he is immediately
aware of the effects of his behavior and can make the necessary changes.

Let's take an example. A group of five people are asked to work
as a group to solve a problem. After much discussion, arguments, and
compromises, the group arrives at a decision. They then present this
decision to the person who requested it and are told that the solution

5-23

was wrong. The feedback generally states that their group product was not adequate for the requestor's needs. The group was not told what in their process of reaching a solution was wrong. Even if they were told the correct solution, they would not have information about how to change the manner in which they reached the decision. Moreover, it would not, by itself, be of much value to be told that the group spent too much time discussing, compromising, etc.

But, if each individual were told how his performance in the group aided or detracted from the desired solution, he would be able to correct his behavior. Moreover, it could be hypothesized that if he were given such individual feedback along with general feedback about the group decision-making process which helped or hindered a good solution, he could adjust his own behavior according to how the group was proceeding, thereby enabling the group as a whole to reach the best possible solution.

The Zajonc study (#6305) referred to above did just this and concluded:

> "The results indicated that the performance of individuals improves when they work on a group task, and that the most pronounced improvement occurs for a difficult task when information about the performances of all team members as well as of the team as a whole is made available. When information about team performance alone...is given, only slight improvement occurs," (p. 160)

Collins and Guetzkow (#6293) suggest a distinction between two different types of feedback: (1) task-environment rewards (feedback from the environment), and (2) interpersonal rewards (feedback from fellow group members). Ultimately, it is to be expected that task-environment rewards will have the greatest corrective effect on the performance of individuals. If an architect is designing a house, the rewards gained upon the completion of building have, no doubt, the greatest effect on his future performance as an architect. Unfortunately, such feedback takes a long time to occur and the time delay from the design of the house to its completion reduces the impact of feedback effects--he may have planned numerous other houses and buildings before he sees the original house built. Unless there is some drastic error or some extremely important idea he was testing, he may not be affected at all by the final product.

Because of this lag, Collins and Guetzkow maintain that task-environment rewards have only an indirect effect as feedback; these rewards usually have such a long delay that their effect on the learning process is not great. On the other hand, interpersonal rewards are often immediate and have a direct effect on learning. The approval of the client, the smile of agreement from a fellow architect, the few positive comments from the engineer working on the construction of the building--these types of feedback are felt immediately by the architect in his planning and thereby can affect the nature of his work at the moment, as well as his future plans.

While these rewards can occur at different points in time,
Collins and Guetzkow (#6293) think of them as operating together.

> "In contrast to these positions (of the separation
> of task and interpersonal rewards), we stressed that
> interpersonal rewards can be used to support task
> activities and that task environmental rewards
> can mold and maintain certain patterns of inter-
> personal relationships. Both kinds of rewards
> can support either or both classes of behavior."
> (p. 86)

However, in groups the time differences between the two different types
of rewards are complicated by the fact that:

> "...task environmental rewards are usually not
> tied to the success and failure of individual group
> members--which makes (them) of little value for
> individual learning... Interpersonal rewards,
> however, can be tied to the success and failure
> of individual group members (and) can follow the
> behavior immediately..." (pp. 85-86)

The recognition of the differentiation between task and interpersonal
rewards is extremely important in the planning and knowledge utilization
process. These processes tend to have extremely long delays (5, 10,
15 years in some cases) from the conception stage to the fabrication
and diffusion of the final product. Also, the people involved in the
early stages in a particular planning operation are often not present
when the plans are operationalized. Under such conditions, task rewards
are extremely difficult to define or to find. As a result one would
expect that planners probably rely on some type of interpersonal reward
system.

It seems that many planners have developed very elaborate friendship and acquaintance networks to support them and provide the necessary
feedback. The "invisible college" idea is just such a network. Made
up of large numbers of people who continuously correspond, phone each
other, and attend the same conferences (as speakers and attendees),
they provide for each other an approval/disapproval feedback system.
One learns not from seeing his plan put into effect but rather from
seeing how his colleagues in the invisible college react to the ideas
or plans. This support system seems to become particularly critical
when a member is involved in a government position in which he, the
planner, can be potentially overwhelmed by the operations staff who are
only concerned with the present and immediate future.

Complicating the planner's dilemma is the finding that in small
groups immediate feedback tends to displace longer range planning and
that such direct feedback may be more detrimental to performance than
delayed feedback (see Guetzkow, #6304). While one may question the
applicability of this finding to long range planning of the type
referred to above (i.e., in years, not hours) the problem it points
to may be a very real one. If interpersonal feedback, because of its
immediacy, begins to displace task feedback, planners may tend to
devote more time to satisfying their colleagues than to achieving
their ultimate goal of bringing about a desirable state for the systems
for which the plans have been made. The planner's dilemma is thus a
complicated one; how does he get meaningful feedback which enables
him to evaluate his performance when the realization of his plans are
in the distant future? And, how does he avoid an over-dependence on
those who do provide satisfying interpersonal feedback?

A less elaborate though just as critical situation exists for the teacher. The teacher's goal is to enable students to develop and grow to be creative, mature individuals; yet, he rarely can see the product of his work. The child or adolescent he teaches becomes a mature or immature adult but, especially in urban areas, he never sees his student after graduation. While there could be intermediate task rewards established on the basis of "known" effective methods or on the basis of student success or exams, etc., these situations are often not clearly defined. Complicating the problem for the teacher is his traditional freedom in the classroom--others are just not around to provide task feedback related to his classroom practices.

One attempt to provide what might be called intermediate feedback is reported by Gage, Runkel and Chatterjee (#6306). They studied the effects of providing information about the pupils' opinion of their teacher's behavior. It was found that those teachers who received such feedback from their students changed their behaviors in accordance with the information and at the same time improved the accuracy of their perception of their pupil's behavior.

Another form of intermediate task feedback that is often used by planners and administrators is simulation. Basically, simulation techniques attempt to delineate all the relevant factors in a particular projected situation and then assess the effects of different types of inputs. In planning and management situations this is usually done by computers. Recently, a number of social scientists have used human simulation situations to investigate problems in international relations (see Guetzkow, #6307).

Lippitt and his colleagues (#0791) have pointed out the importance of overcoming the traditional isolation of the teacher by a more active sharing among teachers of individually created classroom innovations. When such "sharing" attempts are made, there are usually some difficulties; this seems to be the result of a teacher's fear of being seen as arrogant if he tells others about his new ideas or a fear of being seen as incompetent if he seeks out others' innovations. If these barriers could be overcome the discussion of innovative teaching practices could serve as important feedback for the teachers. Without these discussions, however, social rewards would seem to be very important.

Summarizing the above dicussion we can state:

1. Individual performance feedback is more effective than group feedback but the combination of individual and group feedback is most effective.

2. A distinction must be made between task and interpersonal feedback. When the former is available it is most effective. Usually, however, it is delayed and has relatively little effect on performance. Interpersonal feedback is more readily available on an immediate basis and, as such, can have a great effect on performance. Both task and interpersonal rewards/feedback operating at the same time would appear to lead to the most effective action. Under conditions in which task feedback is relatively non-existent (e.g., long range planning) it has been proposed that substitute systems of interpersonal feedback will emerge.

Summary and Conclusions

This chapter has attempted to raise a number of critical issues related to the manner in which individuals interact or are linked with each other in group and interpersonal settings. Major emphasis has been placed on the role that participation of an individual in groups has on the tendency for individuals to adopt innovations. We have shown that individuals who participate in group decisions are more apt to accept them as their own. Thus, if the group decision is to adopt, they will personally adopt the innovation. The literature indicates that group participation--whether decision-making or otherwise--makes an individual more open to influence.

Another series of findings that were reported at some length relate to the nature of the linkage between individuals in a group. We have shown that if individuals in a group are attracted to one another (cohesiveness), and if the norms of the group are receptive to innovations, the individuals will tend to adopt them. But, we have also shown that this conformity to group norms is dependent on the group's acceptance of the individual. Thus, in a cohesive group which has a norm to adopt an innovation, those members who are accepted to a moderate-to-high degree will conform to the group norms and adopt the innovation. However, if an individual is very highly accepted he tends to be relatively independent of group norms and he may not follow the group. This is also the issue for those who are low in acceptance.

We also indicated that conformity is not as irrational as some of the interpretations of studies seem to indicate. Even when individuals are subjective to enormous social pressure, they will still tend to accept their own perceptions. If they do feel publicly pressured to accept the group decision, they will usually not change their private opinions.

While changing groups or individuals under any conditions is difficult, we have shown a number of studies which show the effectiveness of participation in group decisions as a way of overcoming resistance. Also, we have reviewed studies which indicate that crisis situations tend to "unfreeze" old patterns of individual and group behavior and make them more prime to change.

The proximity of individuals has also been discussed in two separate sections of the chapter. We reviewed studies which indicate that doctors who are socially integrated in the medical community tended to use new drugs earlier. In a slightly different vein, we showed that individuals who interact with each other a good deal have more similar attitudes, and vice versa. Those individuals who interact a good deal also tend to like each other and be more susceptible to influences from the others. The research literature also indicates that those people who are more similar in background (status, socioeconomic level, attitudes, etc.) tend to be more susceptible to influence from each other. On the other hand, those who are from different status levels tend to communicate less and to have less personal influence with each other.

The first part of the chapter dealt with interpersonal and group values that indirectly influenced individuals to adopt; i.e., those factors which predispose an individual to be susceptible to adoption as a result of interests or forces not connected with the diffusion-adoption process.

In the second part of the chapter we were concerned with the factors that inhibited or facilitated a sender in his influence over a receiver. We discussed such variables as the sender's credibility, his legitimacy and the strategies he ought to use. We also discussed the role of the leader and the different types of feedback--task and interpersonal--that may effect the manner in which plans are made and executed.

In conclusion, this chapter has selected some key variables that indicate how individuals interact in group and interpersonal settings and how these interactions effect the D&U process. If we relate this chapter to the "image of man" presented in the conclusion to the last chapter, we begin to see how group and interpersonal processes effect an individual's ability or tendency to rationally evaluate alternatives. For example, participation in group decision-making provides an individual with new alternatives and information which, in turn, enables him to make a more rational choice about adoption. However, if he is a member of a highly cohesive group with a strong norm which rejects adoption of an innovation, and if he is only moderately accepted, we would expect that his alternatives would be, in his own mind, severely restricted. This would be less true if he were the leader of the group. One could make a similar analysis with many of the other valuables discussed in this and the last chapter.

The next chapter will refocus our attention away from the individual and group to the organizational level of analysis. It will present an analysis of those factors that facilitate or inhibit innovations in organizations.

CHAPTER SIX

THE ORGANIZATIONAL CONTEXT OF DISSEMINATION
AND UTILIZATION

Table of Contents

CHAPTER SIX*

THE ORGANIZATIONAL CONTEXT OF DISSEMINATION
AND UTILIZATION

INTRODUCTION

In Chapter Two, from pages 2-19 to 2-31, we considered the major factors
that have to be considered in analyzing the flow of knowledge into, out of, and
through social organizations. This chapter builds directly on that outline,
once again viewing the organization as a dynamic problem-solving *system* which
maintains functionality and stability over time, by developing and maintaining
an internal structure and a protective skin to regulate and inhibit the flow of
messages from the environment.

In this chapter the factors which facilitate or inhibit the flow of new
knowledge through organizations will be discussed. We divide organizational
knowledge flow into three categories - entering (input), internal processing
(throughput), and exiting (output), noting the ways in which organizational
characteristics affect each. Yet across these categories we will be able to discern two major themes: *the drive to maintain order and certainty* tends to create
structures, hierarchies, requirements, and screening procedures which act as
barriers to knowledge flow; while *the drive to innovate and improve* tends to remove such barriers. How the characteristics of organizations specifically affect
information flow depends on the resolution of these two competing demands.

Some organizational factors appear to have particular potency in explaining
knowledge flow. In this chapter the factors of *training, leadership styles,
structure,* and *roles* have been singled out for special attention. Training
indicates to the organization member what is expected of him and how he is to
behave; the leadership style of his superior largely determines how much freedom,
responsibility and contact with others in his group he will be able to have; the
structure of the organization provides the framework of interpersonal contact
and reporting linkages; and role designations stipulate in a formal way what
position he is expected to fill in the system. An organization is an aggregate
of groups each constituted by individuals. Knowledge flow occurs, therefore,
among individuals, among groups and among organizations. We have endeavored to
understand organizational knowledge flow by examining some of the ways organizational
variables affect groups and individuals.

In Part I, we will offer some basic distinctions pertinent to the understanding
of knowledge flow in the organization. First, we will note the important distinction between information, in general, and new information. Then we will note the
various patterns and directions of flow such as *"input"* and *"output"* and the several
types of *"throughput"* (downward, upward, and horizontal).

---

*This chapter was drafted by Mark A. Frohman and Ronald G. Havelock.

Part II will be devoted to issues related to "input". We will consider what input means to an organization and how an organization copes with it. We shall see that organizations generally act to *inhibit* new inputs by developing coding and screening mechanisms, and by erecting and maintaining value and status barriers. Nevertheless, because new inputs are essential for survival, means are found for *facilitating* entry, also. As time goes on we will expect such facilitating mechanisms to become more and more important and salient to organizational leadership.

In Part III, we will move to a consideration of "output" from the organization. We will note that output is affected by many of the same variables as input and is functionally related to it. Exchange with the environment requires some sort of balance between outputs and inputs, but organizations vary greatly in their willingness and ability to improve the quality of their output by drawing on new resources in the environment. Quality output, whether it be the manufactured products of business or the human products of education, seems to be constrained both by forces in the market place and conservative forces in the organization, itself. Part III will consider both the inhibiting and the facilitating influences on organizational output.

Finally, in Part IV, we will go inside the organization to consider its internal information transfer processes. In examining these dynamics of "throughput" we will at last be able to draw upon the large body of literature which deals with "organizational change". Again a section on *inhibiting* factors will be followed by a section which discusses *facilitating* factors, the practical solutions which can be brought to bear on internal communication problems.

I. SOME BASIC DISTINCTIONS

A. INFORMATION VS. NEW KNOWLEDGE

Most authors agree that effective information flow and utilization are vital for any organization. March and Simon (#7149), for example, construct a theory of organizations on the belief that organizational members are complex information processors and that organizations are basically large decision-making units. Their major thesis is that the foundation of the organization is the flow and rational application of knowledge to problems confronting the organization. Similarly, K. Deutsch (#0903), in his discussion of governmental structures, also cites the critical nature of information flow for survival of the regulatory mechanism. Deutsch describes information channels as the "nerves of government", the essential connectors which allow the aggregate of parts to function as a whole. Other authors who stress the significance of information flow are Etzioni (#7161), Guetzkow (#6304), and Seashore (#7150).

Organizations are much more than collectivities of people. The people who belong to an organization must work together; they are interdependent. To effect such interdependence, members must necessarily communicate and utilize messages. For example, in order to fulfill the objectives of the organization, there must be communication concerning what the objectives are as well as the means by which they are to be reached. In some organizations, the information flow may be quite elementary; for instance, it may involve a message which directs that sheets of metal must be cut and that this and that lever must be pulled to achieve the various desired lengths. In other organizations the information flow is more complex: high school teacher Dave Robbins not only imparts large quantities of information to his students on

the topic of physics; he also sends and receives thousands of bits of
information on procedures, performances, and expectations. Such messages
may pertain to the curriculum, the classroom, the building, the department,
or the students and it may come from or go to other teachers, students,
administrators, parents, community leaders, and so on.

However, this sea of information which sustains Dave and the metal
cutter is not necessarily all _new_ information. Most of what they send and
receive is _maintenance information_, routine messages, redundant and familiar
is most respects. This is the kind of "information" that is usually referred
to by those theorists who concern themselves with communication patterns in
organizations, but it is _not_ the kind of information with which this report
is primarily concerned. Hence, we have a problem of extrapolation: much
has been said by organizational researchers about information flow in
organizations, but very little has been said specifically about the flow of
new ideas, innovations, and new research-based knowledge. It seems reasonable to suppose that in large part what is true for information flow in
general is also true for the flow of _new_ knowledge, in particular, but this
is only an assumption, not a proven fact. As we proceed through this
literature review we should keep this distinction clearly in mind.

B. TYPES OF FLOW

1. Input, Throughput, and Output

As noted in Chapter Two, human organizations are "open systems".
In other words they are constantly receiving messages from outside
which change what goes on inside. They maintain a continuous dialogue
with their environment, exchanging materials, information, and
personnel. We may better understand this complex exchange process by
defining three distinct phases in the handling of information. The
first phase is the flow into the organization of messages from the
outside environment, or the _input_. The second phase is the processing
or consumption of these messages as they travel through the organization;
this middle phase is often called the _throughput_. The third phase is
the export of processed messages back into the environment, or the
output.

Information transmission _into_ an organization is, generally
speaking, a function of the _openness_ of the system. Some of the
specific organizational characteristics contributing to the willingness
and readiness to accept new knowledge from outside are the leadership,
coding scheme, social structure, local pride, status, economic conditions,
linkage and capacity of the organization. These aspects will be discussed in sections II, A and B.

The passage of new knowledge _through_ the organization, from one
department to another, from one group to another, and from one person
to another depends on such organization variables as styles of leadership,
division of labor, role definition and performance, structural arrangements, reward systems and training, among others.

The third stage of this flow process is the diffusion of messages
back into the outside environment. All organizations have some sort of
output. For some the primary output may be seen as "products", for
others it may be "services" to outside individuals or groups; for still
others the primary output may be trained or educated human beings.
Most organizations send output messages in many different forms.

2.   Patterns of Throughput

In many ways the "throughput" of messages describes the life of
the organization as a system. Potentially, any member may send a
message to any other member because all members are in the same place,
working toward the same general goal, and sharing a common group
identity. In practice, however, within what we have defined as
"throughput" we need to make important additional distinctions.

    a.   Horizontal vs. Vertical

        Depending upon their positions, titles, status or responsi-
    bilities in the organization, we can speak of two individuals
    being on "the same level" or one member being "above" or "below"
    the other. The flow of knowledge can be broken down into categories
    that readily classify whether the sender and receiver are on the same
    level of the organization or on different levels: these categories
    are "horizontal" and "vertical". Horizontal information flow
    occurs between members who are on roughly the same level, either
    in the same sub-unit or different sub-units. "Vertical flow",
    on the other hand, describes the transfer of information between
    upper and lower levels according to the chain of command defined
    by the organization chart. The distinction between horizontal and
    vertical flow and their subcategories are important ones. However,
    the basic horizontal versus vertical distinctions have not been
    used often in research on information flow. Exceptions are several
    industrial studies which empirically "examine" the critical
    distinctions between horizontal and vertical flow (Simpson, #1614;
    Burns, #7151; Davis, #7152). However, even though there is an
    empirical basis for recognizing and using these distinctions in
    organizational research, two authors, after a review of the
    literature, were forced to conclude that, "There are no studies of
    distinctive types of communication which characteristically flow
    horizontally, upward, or downward in organizations, although such
    research is much needed" (Katz and Kahn, #6223, p. 247).

    b.   Vertical Message Flow: Downward vs. Upward

        Traditionally the dissemination of information in organizations
    has been viewed as a flow down the organizational structure. The
    classical theories of organization placed primary emphasis on the
    downward flow of information; in contrast there was relatively
    little concern expressed about adequate and accurate upward knowledge
    flow. Even today we see this tendency reinforced and perpetuated
    by the priorities in organizational training programs. Training
    usually focusses on improving downward information flow as from
    principals to teachers, foremen to workers. Rarely touched are
    recommendations to help a person communicate effectively with his
    own superior (Likert, #5202).

        Recently however, more and more theorists have begun to
    advocate the importance of upward, as well as downward, knowledge
    flow (Burns and Stalker, #3791; Seashore, #7150; Blake and Mouton,
    #6198 and #7153). They are recognizing that subordinates quite
    often possess the skill and knowledge essential for organizational

6-4

improvement; therefore messages from subordinate to superior
should be encouraged. Bennis states the general case that reliance
on downward flow is inappropriate for most organizations in our
contemporary society. He maintains that full and open knowledge
flow in organizations without regard to power or position is
necessary (#5082).

    c.   Horizontal Knowledge Flow: Intragroup and Intergroup

       Concurrently with this increasing awareness of the importance
of *upward* knowledge flow there has been a corresponding surge of
interest in *horizontal* flow. Some researchers have found that
knowledge flow among members on the <u>same</u> level is not only common
but is also beneficial for the overall purposes of the organization.
One researcher, tracing the flow of specific items of information
in an organization, discovered that more than one half of the
items reached their destination or end point via some lateral
flow (Davis, #7152). Another examined the flow of information
in a factory and concluded that the "vertical system would be
virtually unworkable without considerable flow of information
laterally" (Burns, #7151, p. 92). Nealy and Fiedler (#7144) have
recently reviewed a number of studies concerned with organizational
behavior. Although their primary focus was not on knowledge
flow, they concluded that, on the basis of the empirical studies
reviewed, lateral flow is much more prevalent than organization
charts suggest.

       We can also delineate two subcategories of lateral flow:
intragroup and *intergroup*.* According to the traditional bureaucratic model of organizations, intergroup information flow is sometimes
seen as unnecessary or irrelevant. Perhaps the rationale for this
view can best be presented by two theorists of the bureaucratic
school. "Reports, desires for services or criticisms that one
department has of another are supposed to be sent up the line until
they reach an executive who heads the organization involved. The
reason for this circuitous route is to inform higher officials of
things below them". (Miller and Form, #7218, p. 158)

       Even though keeping superiors up-to-date is important,
empirical evidence shows that organization members find it
necessary to have information channels among groups (Burns, #7151;
Landesberger, #6704; Walton, et al., #6720; Strauss, #6716;
Schein, #7155; Seiler, #7204; Likert, #6590). Walton, et al.
(#6720), for example, have found a very high, statistical correlation
between intergroup information flow and organizational performance
in six manufacturing plants.

II. <u>INPUT TO THE ORGANIZATION</u>

    To illustrate the entry problem we might compare the typical organization to
a giant egg encased in many shells and more or less permeable membranes. Each
of these shells and membranes has a purpose; it protects the organization against
hostile elements in the environment while allowing needed nutrients to seep
through to feed the internal structure. Together these shells represent an
intricate message filtering system; they identify messages which are needed
and helpful and allow them to pass through; they also identify messages which are
harmful, irrelevant or unneeded and keep them out. Those messages which will cause

---

*The dynamics of intragroup flow are covered in Chapter Five.

the most difficulty to this filtering system will be *unfamiliar* messages, messages containing new and unexpected information. This is the crux of the entry problem for new knowledge. What is often described as the "resistance" by organizations to new ideas or innovations is in large part the manifest sign of the struggle by this filtering system to cope with things that it does not understand. New beneficial messages may be rejected because they *look like* familiar but hostile messages, while hostile messages sometimes will be taken in because they look like familiar but benign messages. Because innovation is so vulnerable to error, it is not surprising that many organizations have a generalized resistance to all new messages.

It is possible to identify innumerable organizational shells which constitute pieces of this filtering system. Some organizations will have many protective layers and others will have an elaborate membrane laboratory* which filters, analyzes, and rechannels messages of all types in intricate detail. Still others will have only a very rudimentary filter system, being "open" to new information of all kinds, but, at the same time, also being vulnerable to exploitation, contamination, or other potentially harmful effects. In spite of these very significant variations, it is yet possible to identify at least four types of shells which all organizations are likely to possess, the shells of *survival, stability, purpose* and *membership*.

Survival is probably the first commandment for organizations as well as for people. Some messages from outside may spell doom in the form of exploitation, subversion, invasion, take-cver, contamination, etc. All organizations need to maintain a barrier to intercept these messages. When organizations are especially concerned about survival, this barrier may keep out virtually all messages from the environment.

Stability is a defining property of all social organizations. To maintain themselves and to carry out their function in a predictable manner, they must maintain some sort of internal steady state or equilibrium of forces. This equilibrium may include a steady flow of message inputs and outputs, but these messages must be predictable. Messages which contain new information content may be upsetting, constituting a threat to the established equilibrium.

Nearly every organization is bound together by some common *purpose,* usually a purpose which extends beyond survival and stability. To hold to this purpose they must erect what might be called "barriers of relevance". Educational institutions screen out inputs which might turn them into profit-making product organizations, while product organizations will avoid inputs that might put them in the position of providing services. Research, philanthropic, and fellowship organizations erect similar barriers to keep themselves on course.

Finally, we should note that the fact of *membership* in an organization creates a very complex and many facetted barrier to outside influences. Those who share common membership in one organization are also likely to share many attributes such as a common language, a common set of values, a common ideology, and a common perception of role and status.** All these attributes which tie them together also set them apart from the outside world. Anything that is common and unique to the membership of the organization is a potential obstacle to new inputs from outside.

---

*Thus all R&D "laboratories" attached to organizations act like chemical analysis laboratories, filtering and analyzing messages before they are fed into the organization.

**All examples of "norms". See Chapter Two, page 2-24.

This section will be divided into two parts. The first part will provide a review of aspects of organizations which tend to inhibit the entry of new knowledge, while the second part will focus on aspects which *facilitate* knowledge entry. Later in discussing output and throughput (Parts III and IV) we will follow the same form of presentation.

Before proceeding, one final note of explanation is in order. This section may seem redundant in many respects to what has been said in Chapters Four and Five. Such redundancy is unavoidable for two very good reasons. First, organizational systems are similar to individual human systems in many respects; organizations, like people, can be said to have values, purposes, status, size, capacity, etc. Many of these characteristics operate to facilitate and inhibit knowledge flow in organizations in much the same way that they do in individuals. Secondly, organizations are composed of people; hence the entry "point" to an organization is inevitably a person. Hence in many respects interorganizational processes can be reduced to interpersonal processes.

A.   INHIBITORS OF KNOWLEDGE FLOW INTO THE ORGANIZATION

The ten factors related to inhibition of input, discussed below, have not been ordered or grouped in any logical sequence. They are merely representative of the kinds of topics which have most frequently appeared in the literature relevant to this issue. Through these ten factors, however, we should be able to discern recurring themes related to the four "shells" discussed above: *survival, stability, purpose,* and *membership.*

1.   The Need for Stability

Several writers have commented on the general impact of order and constancy on knowledge flow. Whitney (#2063) mentioned that innovations threaten the dynamic equilibrium which characterizes the relationships of persons and groups, and since the advantages of accepting and utilizing knowledge may be outweighed by the disadvantages resulting from disturbing the equilibrium, the knowledge entry may be blocked. Schon (#6916), treating the entrance of knowledge into the organization as a function of the risk involved, states that the organization, by its very nature, is conservative. Menzel (#1386) presents a similar position. This concern for the maintenance of internal stability is a recurrent theme through many of the specific barriers discussed below.

2.   Coding Scheme Barrier

Allen (#5018, #5019), studying R&D labs, has found that members of an organization which requires loyalty and commitment tend to acquire common coding schemes or shared ways of ordering the things relevant to them. This comes from their common experience and exposure in the organization. Katz and Kahn (#6223) refer to organizational coding schemes as a determinant of communication in that they distort, reject, accept, and transform what is said. Seashore (#7150) offers similar arguments. He points out that a group establishes its own particular identity by enlarging its uniqueness. One way to do this, he states, is to define a vocabulary peculiar to the group. However, such a unique coding scheme tends to make communication with "outsiders" difficult.

It is, therefore, a barrier to knowledge flow since it engenders a lack of understanding between members of different organizations. Deutsch (#0903), studying governmental organizations, recognized this difficulty and labelled it a "communication differential" between insiders and outsiders of the organization. Likert (#7200), Campbell (#1644), and Cartwright (#6696) discuss similar phenomena.

3. Social Relationships

Another information barrier engendered by a "steady state" is the existence of enduring patterns of social behavior in the organization. These patterns serve as barriers to knowledge entry, because a change suggested by new information may threaten to alter the existing internal social structure. There is a sizeable body of literature providing case after case of resistance to new knowledge entry precisely because of its implication for change in social relationships (e.g., Steward, #3442; Schon, #6916). One author (Marcson, #2924) contends that social structure is a critical variable for knowledge influx into a society.

4. Fear of Malevolence of Outsiders

The boundaries which separate the organization from its environment (e.g., buildings, dress, rules) encourage the formation of organization myths which help members to deal with the uncertainty and ambiguity of change brought on by outside forces (Schon, #6916). Thus, knowledge from the outside can be seen as a threat to the organization, not only in terms of upsetting the orderliness as a consequence of a deliberate change, but also as a direct maligning of the organization and its members.

This belief that new inputs may represent a threat to organizational survival is in part a realistic response to the competitive win-lose psychology of many inter-organizational relationships in our society. However, the organization is not always totally rational in sustaining such a belief, and a preoccupation with this concern, amounting to organizational paranoia, may have a debilitating effect on organizational life (Nokes, #1785; Mansfield, #0786). The impression that knowledge from outside sources is "tainted" serves as a basis for an attitude of distrust and of seclusiveness from others.

One writer suggests that knowledge acceptance is, in part, a function of the psychological condition of the organization (Whitney, #2063). Other researchers have found that one major barrier to knowledge entry in communities (Lewis, #2641), in industry (Schon, #6916), and in government (Morrison, in Bennis, #1344, and Schon, #3025) is the readiness to distrust innovations and a generalized lack of interest in changing traditional ways of doing things.

5. Personal Threat

Related to the suspicion of outsiders as a threat to the organization as a whole is the belief that outsiders will say or do something that will harm an organization member. A case in point is cited by Newman (#1103). He remarks that behavioral scientists are refused admittance to organizations by members who think whatever information the scientists generate will be an indication of member failure. This fear is partly justified. New ideas may bring with them the implication that previous ways of doing things were old-fashioned, erroneous, or incompetent.

The further implication of individual failure and culpability of individuals may sometimes be inescapable. Hence the threat value of new knowledge may be realistically and psychologically high. In general, we can say that members fear outsiders whose knowledge can be seen as a disparagement of their own abilities and performance.

6. Local Pride

Almost all organizational theorists agree that to maintain the organization, members must have some degree of commitment and identification. Moreover, the organization wants its members to perceive it as an attractive place to work since such an attitude not only keeps them in the organization but also aids in attracting new recruits. This identification engenders a spirit of pride in the organization which can have an impeding effect on knowledge flow into the organization. This barrier, which we call "local pride", is manifest in several ways.

One indication of organization attachment is the distrust of outsiders noted earlier. Another is the belief that if knowledge relevant to the organization exists it will come from members of the organization itself. Evidence for this barrier to knowledge entry engendered by local pride is provided in a study of scientists in R&D laboratories (Allen, #5018) and a study of administrators in business firms (President's Conference, #3320).

7. Status Differences Among Organizations

Status discrepancies between organizations can create distrust and barriers to knowledge flow (Paul, #2925; Hoselitz, #2029). For example, Paul discusses the "status gap" difficulties encountered by medical organizations which try to reach people from lower socioeconomic groups. The fear of being judged inferior--on rational or irrational grounds--serves to inhibit the approach of a lower status organization toward another for information. This barrier may be self-perpetuating. If lack of knowledge can only be remedied by asking another for information, then the remedial act, itself, is an admission of inadequacy and of failure (Rice, #7158).

8. Economic Condition

The economic situation of an organization has a great deal to do with the knowledge it accepts and utilizes. If an organization has a very propitious financial situation, it can afford to seek out new and uncertain discoveries and innovations for experimentation (Lewis, #2641; Witney, #2603; Mansfield, #0796 and #1373).

However, being able to support innovations financially does not necessarily mean that the organization will be receptive to new knowledge. Several researchers have pointed out that an organization must feel some dissatisfaction with its present state before it can accept new knowledge (Schein and Bennis, #3383; Lippitt et al.,#1348; Schon, #6916). Thus a relatively prosperous and affluent organization such as a school district in an upper-class community may not be open to new knowledge if it does not perceive a need for it. Carlson (#0585, #0628, #1174), for example, found no correlation between per pupil dollar investment and system innovativeness in a large region of Pennsylvania and West Virginia. Carlson's findings are severely discrepant from traditional suppositions of educators and research by earlier scientists (e.g., Mort, #1191).

9. Training Newcomers to Accept the Old Ways

Many of the attitudes and operating assumptions of members are inculcated during organizational training (Schein, #7155 and #7210). If an organization member should be taught to trust or distrust outsiders, the first opportunity to teach him is at the beginning of his tenure. Therefore, training can be a potent instrument for effecting openness toward knowledge entry. Training programs all too often inculcate attitudes of "not rocking the boat" and maintaining the status quo (Schein, #7155 and #7210). In this way, training serves to perpetuate existing conditions and to inhibit the entrance of knowledge a newcomer might seek in order to change the present conditions.

10. Size

What little research there is on the impact of organization size on information flow is consistent. In a study of 294 industrial firms, Mansfield has found that the larger organizations adopt new ideas and new technologies at a faster rate than smaller organizations do (#0786). Reviewing the literature on this subject, Markham (#0805) concurs, though he does note that the relationship may be curvilinear, with the very large organization being somewhat less innovative than the medium large organization. Thus it may be that the organization which is "only number two" does try harder.

B. FACILITATING INPUT

We have seen that the organization must maintain an orderliness of functioning in order to survive, and that the mechanisms it employs for this purpose can do an admirable job. We have also taken note that the organization must continuously receive and utilize some new knowledge to survive in our rapidly changing society. Environmental changes such as competition and community pressure sometimes compel the organization to overcome its preoccupation with preserving the status quo and force it to seek out new ideas. Having enumerated some of the barriers to the input of new knowledge, it is appropriate to turn to some mechanisms that the organization uses to overcome such barriers.

1. Reward Value

Perhaps the most fundamental motive for seeking new knowledge is its potential reward value. For example, the discovery of new teaching techniques, new surgical tools and apparatus, or new industrial machines hold reward value for the organization possessing them. Mansfield (#1373), for example, in his study of 294 industrial organizations cited earlier, has found that the profitability of an investment opportunity acts as a stimulus, the intensity of which governs quite closely the organization's speed of response. With regard to business organizations, Newman (#1003) talks about fear of profit loss as a motivating factor in seeking out and utilizing new ideas.

Outside the business community the reward value of new ideas may be more difficult to assess. "Improved medical care" and "better education" are themselves difficult concepts to measure; it is therefore even more difficult to assess the potential increment in these values which might result from the adoption of this or that innovation. Nevertheless, even in these "soft" areas innovations which have highly visible reward value are much more likely to gain acceptance (see Chapter Eight for a more extensive consideration of how knowledge characteristics affect acceptance).

2. Change of Leadership

Innumerable studies suggest the critical role of the top organizational leadership in promoting or inhibiting the entry of new ideas. Of particular significance is a periodic change of command. According to Griffiths (#1183), "the number of innovations is inversely proportional to the tenure of the chief administrator". In other words, a new leader brings new knowledge and perspectives and, concomitantly, a commitment to new ways of doing things. This often leads to a shake-up at all levels in the organization so that the new leader's knowledge and policies can be adopted and adjusted to. For example, Marrow, Bowers, and Seashore (#6066) describe in detail the purchase of one organization by another and the resulting infusion of new technical and social knowledge and applications. They find that the "changing-of-the-guard" not only allows for new ideas at the top of the organization but also prepares the rest of the membership psychologically for the general changes which are to follow.

Prior location and position of the new chief are major conditioning variables on the amount of new knowledge utilization he is likely to evoke. Carlson (#0585) found that the amount of change occurring when a new school superintendent takes over is greater when he comes from outside the school system. Griffiths also mentions the effect of the prior location: "Change in an organization is more probable if the successor to the chief administrator is from outside the organization, than if he is from inside the organization." (#1183)

3. Perception of Crisis

The perception of great difficulty in the organization usually results in a hurried search for help from outside. Thus, a crisis can stimulate knowledge flow into the organization. In fact, to some theorists the changing of the top leader is perceived to be a crisis. Etzioni states "the departure or death of the non-bureaucratic head of an organization...involves a major organization crisis. The succession crisis is particularly evident in totalitarian states, and almost invariably leads to a period of instability. But corporations, churches, armies and other organizations are also subject to similar crises" (#7161, p. 55).

However, a leadership change does not necessarily produce a crisis in the full sense of the word. "The succession crisis should not be viewed as a mere loss of organizational effectiveness, a crisis from which the organization has to recover. Actually the succession period is often the stage at which needed innovations are introduced to counteract earlier deterioration of the organization or to ward off challenges it faces during the succession period." (Etzioni, #7161, p. 56)

Schon discusses the relevance of crisis perception for knowledge entry in some detail. His argument is as follows: "In individuals and organizations it is easy to underestimate the strength of the dynamisms that tend to keep things as they are. Only the strongest incentives can lead an organization to effective deliberate change. Something like a state of crisis must arise. The organization must come to feel that its survival, or at any rate, its survival as it has been, is threatened. Characteristically this perception of threat comes from the outside...Once it perceives the threat, the organization must immediately interpret it as requiring a shift toward innovation." So far Schon is referring to a real crisis, one that truly threatens the

existence of the organization. But he goes on to point out that
"crises" do not have to be real in order to have an instigating effect.
"One of the characteristics of managers capable of inducing deliberate
internal change toward innovation is the ability to create a sense
of crisis around events that need not be interpreted in this way."
(#6916, p. 127)* This is congruent with other writings which maintain
that the organization, for whatever reason, must feel discomfort
or pain before new knowledge will be sought and utilized (Schein and
Bennis, #3383; Lippitt, et al., #1343). Miles (#6056) reasons that the
increasing influx and utilization of innovations in schools has been in
part prompted by the "struggle for national survival" started by
Sputnik and the growing demand for highly trained employees.

4. Examining Other Organizations

The organization can facilitate knowledge entry by sending a member
outside to procure new knowledge from other relevant organizations.
There are several forms that such outside assignments can take, all of
which may be considered as types of training. Formal academic courses,
conferences, seminars, professional meetings and conventions often
contain knowledge inputs that are of great utility to the home organization. Carter (#0190), for example, writes that conferences on educational
innovations prove to be very useful to schools which send representatives.
Brickell (#1181) notes the value of visits to demonstrations in other
school settings, provided that those settings are similar to the home
school setting in important particulars. Governments from the national
to the local level utilize this procedure frequently to check what
other governmental bodies can teach them. Visitation can serve two
purposes: (1) to determine what knowledge the visited organization has;
and (2) to observe a "live" demonstration of the usefulness of information which has been received (Lippitt, et al., #1343).

5. Awareness

An organization customarily does not seek new knowledge in a random
manner. Rather it first is made aware that useful information exists
outside (President's Conference, #3320). Awareness of external
resources serves as a propellant or motivator to initiate search behavior, and, as such, overcomes such barriers to knowledge entry as
pride, lack of openness and status considerations.

Awareness of outside knowledge typically occurs through linkage to
outside resources manifested in visits, outside training and new leadership from the outside.

6. Training

As noted earlier, organizational training is a potent means for
encouraging or discouraging knowledge flow. Several researchers have
elucidated this point specifically in the context of facilitating knowledge entry. At least two writers have recognized the bearing of the

---

*Havelock (#7108) provides several examples of real and manufactured crises in
the highway safety field. He notes that a "crisis" strategy can also have unanticipated negative consequences especially if it is overused.

types of training teachers receive before entering the classroom on their innovativeness and flexibility in the classroom (Brickell, #1181; Quintana and Sexton, #3856). Similarly, with supporting data from several hundred industrial firms, Mansfield (#0786) concluded that the training of top and middle managers is one of the key variables determining the rate of introduction of innovations. In fact, it may be more important, he says, than the so-called "economic" variables. Since further reference is made to specific aspects of training for knowledge entry in other chapters of this report, we will not dwell on this topic much further. However, one point that should be made is that training is inextricably bound up with other factors facilitating knowledge entry. Crisis perception, awareness, linkage, and administrative changes are a few of the factors that may either be antecedent or consequent to training. Generally speaking, training that is institutionalized, i.e., a conventional part of the organizational routine, is what we are concerned with here.

7. Capacity

Earlier it was mentioned that the reward value of innovation is a major incentive to facilitating knowledge entry. It is also true that the ability of an organization to retrieve and marshall diverse resources influences knowledge entry (Deutsch, #0903). In an empirical study of a university library, Meier (#6710) documented the fact that the capability of utilizing new knowledge depends on the internal structure and mobility of the library staff. Meier goes on to present many types of adjustments libraries can make to handle the information overload presented by the publication explosion. The important point here is that the adjustments involved restructuring of linkages both within the library and to outside resources. This study, then, is consonant with previously mentioned knowledge entry facilitators.

Wealth of an organization is also an element of capacity. A President's Conference (#3320) disclosed that small business organizations with a sizeable amount of financial reserves are more apt to invest in new knowledge utilization than organizations without a strong financial picture. Following up this line of thought, the conference concluded that the availability of long-term loans is critical for small businesses to be able to seek out and utilize new research knowledge. The role of the Federal government in providing such risk capital for innovation has been greatly expanded in recent years not only to support small business but also for medicine and education through "great society" legislation including many provisions of the ESEA of 1965.

8. External Agent

Knowledge entry can also be facilitated through the actions of an outside agent. An outside person or group may perceive a need for new knowledge and undertake the responsibility of bringing this knowledge to the organization. Because this "agent" concept is discussed more fully in Chapter Seven, we will here limit ourselves to a few considerations pertinent to the relationship between the outside agent and the receiving organization.

The use of an agent does not really overcome any of the problems of entry unless the agent is, himself, an expert on the entry process. Thus, he should be aware of and sensitive to the various shell layers that constitute the organization's filtering system. He needs to know the values and self-perceptions which are most salient to the organization, the social and political forces which impinge upon it, the coding scheme it is likely to use to interpret messages, and its goals and needs, both perceived and real.

The relationship of the agent to the receiving organization can take many forms, as we shall review in Chapter Seven, but a convenient way to view the range of relationships is to characterize the extremes. On one side there is the collaborative model where both parties actively engage in examining the issue in question and exchange information and ideas; on the other side is the buyer-seller model where the agent occupies the role of expert information giver or solution maker for a more or less passive client organization (A. Frohman, #7174; Tilles, #6718). According to most authors, the collaborative model seems to be most conducive to successful knowledge flow between an external agent and another organization (Bennis, #5082; A. Frohman, #7174; Lippitt, et al., #1343; Tilles, #6718).

9. Organizational Invaders

An outsider does not always offer advice to an organization. In fact, quite frequently innovators will exert influence by "invading" the market previously dominated by more conservative organizations. Schon (#6916) argues that the infusion of new ideas into traditional organizations may sometimes be a hopeless task, particularly when the existing organizations are themselves dominating a safe and stable market. Under these circumstances change can only come from new organizations which enter the market and proceed to reap the financial benefits of their new ideas and innovations. To illustrate this invasion phenomenon, we can cite the movement of new technical firms into the educational area, the chemical firms into apparel manufacturing, and the aerospace organizations into old line industrial firms.

10. Importing Human Resources

Another way for an organization to increase the infusion of knowledge would be to hire persons who possess the expertise and competence it needs. This could be described as the importation of human resources. It facilitates knowledge entry by bringing into the organization the person(s) holding the knowledge. This, of course, is one of the many reasons why an organization will purchase or merge with another.

One theorist uses the term "cooptation" to designate this process of absorbing new members into the organization in order to preserve or enhance its functioning (Selznick, in Rubenstein and Haberstroh, #2882). Selznick differentiates two forms of cooptation. One is the inclusion of others in order to establish legitimacy of authority over them (formal cooptation). The other type, informal cooptation, occurs when the organization needs certain adjustments that the new members can execute. It is the latter form to which we are referring here.

11. Internal Knowledge Seeking Subunits

By combining the preceding two knowledge entry facilitators, external agents and imported internal experts, we arrive at another means of increasing the ease of knowledge entry, an organizational subunit whose aim is to seek out and collect knowledge. This subunit, that searches the environment of the organization for relevant new knowledge, may be a library unit (Knoerr, #2289); an "information retrieval system" (Veyette, #3301); a planning unit; a "systemic research" unit (Katz and Kahn, #6223); or a development unit. In some cases the unit may just collect already existing knowledge available from other sources; in other cases it may actually do research in order to generate new information necessary to the organization. For the latter case, Katz and Kahn offer the example of oil companies with foreign markets which "have economists and political experts on their staffs to study the development of the European Common Market, social forces in the developing African nations, and similar problems." (#6223, p. 251)

An important issue with regard to internal information subunits is location of the unit, i.e., where in the organization hierarchy it is situated. Katz and Kahn propose that such a unit should ideally report directly to the top administrators in the organization because the strategic decisions are made at that level and because ready accessibility to information is crucial for such decisions. Location near the top also denotes a status befitting the vital character of the information seeking function.

12. Professionalism

Another means by which knowledge entry can be facilitated is increased professional affiliation or identity. An organization member with strong professional ties is quite likely to be interested in applying and advancing his profession. In many cases, his organizational commitment may be less important to him than his desire to actively pursue interests in his chosen specialty field. For example, a re- search chemist for a fabric company may be more eager to synthesize a new organic compound, a feat esteemed by his professional colleagues, than to study the properties of a compound that his organization already has started to develop. Although such professional commitment is often viewed with suspicion by administrators, the proper balance of organizational functioning is usually enhanced by the knowledge entry increment which is associated with active professionalism. Increased professional striving brings with it a greater striving to "keep up" with what outside colleagues are doing. The greater knowledge which results may very well be beneficial to the organizational activities in which the person is engaged.

Utilizing this theme, Kimbrough (#0156) advocates greater professionalism among educators. He maintains that often teachers and principals do not try to improve the curriculum because they perceive themselves to be in a "poor" school system. As a result, the teachers adopt a passive "get-by" attitude. Kimbrough then points out that this attitude can be counteracted by greater professionalism be- cause it would lead to being active in the field and familiarization with educational research literature. By following this course educators would develop a strong base on which to assert their leadership as pro- moters of needed change.

III. OUTPUT FROM THE ORGANIZATION

Innovation as an output from organization is even more important than innova- tion as input, although the two processes are analogous and have many similar characteristics. Both input and output are "skin" problems; they concern the movement of information across those crucial barriers which constitute organizational identity. However, message output is of special importance because it is very closely related to the organization's primary mission; organizations exist for the purpose of providing output in the form of products and services to people. It is in terms of output, therefore, that the effectiveness of an organization is most properly measured. It is the dependent variable, the "outcome" of organizational activity, and the prime justification for organizational existence.

In this section, however, we will not be able to consider organizational output in this broad context. Rather we will focus our attention on that part of output which is "new", i.e., that which constitutes an improvement in the quantity and quality of products and services for the outside world.* The crucial question for us to ask as students of D&U is as follows: does the organization generate and continue to generate the highest quality output to the greatest number of potential users, and does it optimally utilize existing resources (research, innovations, new ideas), both internal and external, in so doing? The question, therefore, is not one of "newness", per se, but of quality and benefit to society as a whole; safer, more reliable automobiles at lower cost, more efficient and expert medical care, better educated, more responsible and more competent graduates from our schools.

It may seem surprising that these worthy and laudable goals of "output" are inhibited by organizational structures but the fact remains that they are. In the first section which follows we will consider a few of the inhibiting factors.

A.   INHIBITORS OF OUTPUT

1.   The Need for Stability

As with input, the drive to maintain stability is an overriding concern shared by all organizations which tends to make them reluctant to change *anything*. To have built and maintained a steady output is an achievement in itself. Organizations which are steady producers are thus reluctant to change what they are doing for any reason if they feel that the stability of their system would be threatened thereby. Efforts to change the quantity or quality of output, even though they may ultimately be beneficial to the organization or to society or both, initially represent a threat to this hard-won stability. For example, a mere increase in the quantity of output may be resisted internally because it requires increasing staff, retooling, altering existing facilities, or acquiring additional ones; all such changes are potentially disruptive.

2.   Inertia

In Chapter Two we spoke of "institutionalizing" (i.e., organization formation) as a hardening process. Rules, procedures, behaviors, and attitudes over time become routine, habitual, and ingrained. The simplest type of organizational barrier to new output may be this natural rigidity which is part of the organizational aging process. This is often cited as a reason for the apparent lack of innovativeness in some of our oldest product and service organizations, e.g., the post office, the railroads, and the schools, particularly the larger established

---

*i.e., for other components of the macrosystem. See Chapter Three.

systems of European education. "Tradition" is often cited as the
major factor in the relatively slow pace of innovation throughout
English society.

3. Complacency: Local Pride

Organizations, like people, help to maintain their identities by
developing a positive self-image. Usually this image is a selective
self-perception which has at least some semblance of validity. Nevertheless, it may act as a barrier to output because it blocks awareness
of the need to improve. Pervasive belief that "we are the best" or
that "our product is as good as or better than any one else's" may result
in complacency, particularly when the self-image is not based on actual
knowledge. The organization which really is "number one", on the other
hand, may indeed be so because of its innovativeness and its capacity
for self-renewal.

4. Perceived Vulnerability

All organizations are to some extent vulnerable to environmental
influences. In times of rapid social change some organizations may
feel particularly exposed to hostile outside forces which are waiting
for the chance to pounce. According to Sieber (#6228), school systems
are particularly vulnerable to such forces in their local community.
The offering of new courses, new ways of teaching, and new patterns of
classroom management may be avoided because parents or political or
church groups "might object".

5. Goal Definition

Some types of new output are not provided because they are seen
as falling outside the organization's proper function or defined mission.
For example, the automotive industry for many years has insisted that
safety is the responsibility of the driver and not something that can
be engineered into every vehicle. Similarly many educators have
insisted that certain controversial subjects such as sex education and
moral and religious training should not be taught in the public schools
because they were in the proper province of the family and the church.

"Information" as an output distinct from "product" or "service"
may be viewed as an unnecessary or irrelevant output, even when such
information would have important value to the consumer. For example,
the U.S. government withholds from the public much of its product-
testing results because it does not define itself as a product tester
for the public, but only for its own internal consumption. Recently
Consumer's Union filed a suit to get test data on hearing aids from
research done for the Veterans Administration.

In some areas the ambiguity of organizational goals may be an
additional problem. Sieber is again worth citing on this point with
respect to education:

> "The diffuseness of terminal goals reinforces the
> effects of *vulnerability* and of *status-insecurity* on
> the emergence of innovative roles. First, with regard
> to vulnerability - because it is difficult to adduce
> evidence for the effectiveness of an educational practice,
> it is often hard to oppose the naive demands of laymen,
> or to sell to the public innovations that are thought
> by educators to be of special value." (#6228)

6.   Perceived Client Readiness

    Organizations frequently withhold innovations or new information because they profess to believe that the "public is not ready". A new product line will not be marketed because it might not "sell", i.e., because the amount of energy which would have to go into production is not justified by the likely public response. Each new innovation may be viewed as another potential *"Edsel"* by the organizational leadership.* Most organizations, like most people, prefer to see others take the first plunge. If the new item catches on, then they will follow, but they are unwilling to take the risks inherent in being the innovator.

7.   Professed Danger to Clients

    Organizations frequently withhold information for the stated reason that it may be harmful to potential users, or that it is not ready for users. This claim is frequently cited by scientists as a reason for not disseminating their findings to the practice world. It is also used with some justification as a reason for holding back on educational innovations. Where the producing organization is *accountable to clients for the effects of its output* it will be very hesitant to submit a new item for popular consumption without very thorough evaluation and testing.

    When the "danger" is assessed by the organization, itself, it is usually very difficult to determine whether the risk is to the user or merely to the outputting organization. When a company fails to install a safety device in its products because the device *sometimes* might not work properly, it may be primarily motivated by the desire to avoid any legal responsibility, not by the desire to promote safety. Similarly the "barriers" of *vulnerability, goal definition,* and *client readiness* may often be only excuses or rationalizations for a more deep-seated complacency or inertia.

B.   FACILITATORS OF OUTPUT

    As much as organizations may wish to maintain stability and constancy in their output, there are powerful forces in the environment which push them forward into innovation. The world is constantly changing, the population expanding, the market fluctuating, public attitudes and tastes shifting, new groups organizing and coming to power; hence the organization in contemporary society has to run just to stand still. We live in an environment of constant crisis and upheaval in which organizational "stability" is a quaint memory for most of us. Because innovation in output is becoming an imperative for all types of organizations, it is especially appropriate that we are now considering those various forces and mechanisms which move the organization in this direction.

---

*Actually, the Edsel may have failed not so much because it was really new, but because it made the pretense of being something new when it was not.

1. Competition

Social theorists since Adam Smith have claimed that competition breeds innovation in a continuing cycle which benefits all of society, but in practice the formula is not quite so simple. Only open competition based on objective comparative quality ratings can induce organizations to improve their output, but most find such a blunt confrontation far too risky and uncomfortable to be tolerable. To avoid true competition commercial organizations will merge, fix prices, carve out exclusive market territories, scramble sizes, prices, and product lines, and advertise with pretty girls and catchy jingles. Similarly the service professions and organizations, sometimes for professed "ethical" reasons, strive to make consumer's choice a fruitless and meaningless exercise.

2. Crisis

If competition truly plays an important role in inducing innovative output, it may be because it confronts the organization with a *crisis*, sometimes a crisis of survival. The conservative forces in organizations are often such that they can be moved significantly only by major shocks from the environment which threaten their very existence. Dramatic evidence on this point has come to us in recent months from the effects of crisis in urban ghettoes and in the universities, but similar instances can be drawn from every field and every period of history, from sputnik to the world wars to the great depression and so on. Our previous discussion on the crisis effects on input apply with equal force to output.

3. Affluence and Capacity

Organizations which are successful, internally secure, and financially prosperous should logically be in a better position to take risks with new kinds of output. However, empirical studies yield very ambiguous results on this point. Mansfield (#0786), in his study of 294 firms, found that financial health, as measured by profits, liquidity, and growth rate, bears no close relationship to the length of time the firm waits before introducing a new technique. Similarly the results are unclear in education. Mort's (#1191) finding of correlation between pupil expenditures and school system innovativeness is directly contradicted by Carlson's data (#0585).

It seems reasonable to suppose that two conflicting forces in organizational dynamics are operating against each other to produce these confusing results. On the one hand we have the complacency factor mentioned earlier as an "inhibitor" when organizations see themselves as functioning at a high level already. The other is the "risk capital" factor which also comes into play as a force for innovation when organizations are functioning at a high level. Which of these opposing forces is dominant in a given situation probably is determined by additional factors such as attitude and structure which are discussed below.

4. Internal Openness

"Openness" is usually a term applied to an attitude towards inputs or throughputs, but a willingness to be open to receiving new ideas probably is related to a willingness to share with others also.

Organizations which function democratically and openly will usually
be less security-conscious and more eager to have a free give-and-
take with the outside environment. The various means by which such internal openness can be achieved are discussed in the section of
Part IV dealing with "throughput" facilitators.

5.   Values Supportive of Quality Output

To some extent an organization may be able to promote innovative
output by fostering a progressive image not only to outsiders but to
its own members. If the members of General Electric really believe
that "progress is our most important product" they may strive to live
up to the image. Similarly the reputation of a school system or a
hospital as "innovative", "progressive", or "always up on the latest"
will have an effect on the leadership and the membership. If leaders
actively promote and reward staff output of new and improved practices,
they will get it.

6.   Specialized Output Roles and Subsystems

The next step beyond the encouragement of a norm for output is
the establishment of an institution for output. Just as organizations
can promote *input* by setting up "planning" and "R&D" units, so they
can promote *output* by setting up dissemination units. Profit making
organizations have long recognized the need for separate subsystems
for advertising, promotion, and sales. Usually these units do not
play a very creative role in the output process, restricting their
concern to the maintenance of existing output, the stabilization of
the market, and the preservation of the organization's "image". Nevertheless output subsystems can sometimes act as genuine diffusers of
new knowledge and encouragers of innovation output. The National
Aeronautics and Space Administration's Technology Utilization program
is perhaps the most elaborate existing subsystem of any organization
designed to do exactly this (Lesher, #7007).

This discussion of output has been brief and superficial, regrettably but necessarily, because the literature on organizations pays
very little attention to output issues, particularly in the context
of D&U. Hopefully, by the time a revised version of this report is
produced, a much more complete and more fully referenced section can
be included.

IV.   THROUGHPUT: KNOWLEDGE FLOW THROUGH THE ORGANIZATION

Having identified several elements which typically impede and facilitate the
movement of knowledge *across* organizational boundaries (input and output), we
are now in a position to sketch some barriers to knowledge passage through the
organization. When new information has by some means entered the system, what
factors influence its dissemination within the system? Once again we will follow
the convention of beginning with inhibiting factors and concluding with facilitative mechanisms.

A.   INHIBITORS OF THROUGHPUT

Internally the organization can be seen as a complex system of filters;
each subsystem and each member has some power to block the flow of information,
to screen it, censor it, and distort it. The chief factors in internal in-

hibition are structural, e.g., related to (1) the *division of labor* into
separated components, (2) the designation of specialized *roles,* and (3) the
ordering of roles in a *structured hierarchy.* However, there are other
important organizational characteristics which have inhibitory effects
above and beyond these structural aspects. Here we will consider four:
(4) *reward patterns,* (5) *training,* (6) *physical separation,* and (7) *leadership
behavior.* Each of these characteristics will be given separate consideration
below.

1. Division of Labor

Each person and each unit typically contributes in a unique way
to the mission of the organization. For instance one high school
department teaches science, another physical education, a third shop
courses and so forth. There are several studies in industrial settings,
Walton, et al. (#6720), Strauss (#6716), and Schon (#6916), which give
ample empirical evidence of the inhibitory effect of this division of
labor on message flow within the organization. A division of labor
means that the members of each separate subsystem share interests,
experiences, problems and, to some extent, backgrounds (Landesberger,
#6704; Seashore, #7150). Such "separateness" may have negative effects
on inter-unit knowledge transfer in three ways in particular: it encourages
the formation of idiosyncratic information *coding schemes;* it stimulates
inter-unit *competition;* and it encourages the formation of separate and
incompatible group *norms.*

a. Coding Schemes

Each functional subgroup within the organization tends to
employ a unique vocabulary or coding scheme because of the members'
common specialized concerns and because of their natural desire to
enlarge the uniqueness and cohesiveness of the "in-group" (Seashore,
#7150). These unique coding schemes tend to impair flow across
groups. Jackson (#0592), in fact, calls organizational subunits
"subcultures" and states that "translation" of information is
usually necessary between subunits. Katz and Kahn (#6223) maintain
a similar stance on information transmission through the organization.

b. Inter-Unit Competition

Subunits of an organization typically compete for resources.
The competition stems from the fact that resources (e.g., money,
manpower) available to any organization are limited, and therefore
each subunit request cannot be fulfilled (March and Simon, #7149;
Landesberger, #6704; Schon, #6916). Schein (#7155), noting that
competition among organization subunits usually occurs, states,

> "It may be desirable to have work groups pitted
> against one another or to have departments become
> cohesive loyal units even if interdepartmental
> coordination suffers. Other times, however, the
> negative consequences outweigh the gains and manage-
> ment seeks ways of reducing intergroup tension.
> The fundamental problem of intergroup competition
> is the conflict of goals and the breakdown of
> interaction and communication between the groups;
> this breakdown in turn stimulates perceptual dis-
> tortion and mutual negative stereotyping." (p. 83)

In short, competition can serve to separate subunits of the organization psychologically and socially.

c. Separate Subgroup Norms

The development of groups on the basis of specialization
has significance for knowledge flow beyond the effects of competition and differences in vocabulary. Groups have norms, goals,
and values which require the adherence of all members. Moreover,
the norms, goals and values of a group are frequently at cross
purposes with those of other groups within the organization
(Dalton, #7201; Rome and Rome, #7208). Schein (#7155) epitomizes
the problem involved in the conflicting values and goals of subgroups in describing the problem inherent in forming a new inter-
departmental committee.

> "Each person is likely to be so concerned about
> the group he came from, wishing to uphold its
> interests as its representative, that it becomes
> difficult for the members to become identified with
> the new committee." (p. 73)

2. Roles

A necessary concomitant of division of labor is the segmentation
of organizational membership into differentiated positions. To these
positions are attached differentiated sets of expectations called
"roles" by sociologists. Roles potentially can be facilitative or
inhibitory for knowledge transfer; some roles incorporate specific
expectations that the role-holder will send or receive new information.
Such "knowledge linking" roles are discussed extensively in Chapter
Seven. However, most role expectations are designed to stabilize and
routinize human performance. They encourage conformity, literally the
shaping of behavior to fit into a well-defined mold. The more sharply
defined and the more limited the role, the less room there will be
for receiving and sending messages which are "new" and hence different
from what is expected.

3. Structure

The division of labor and the formation of separate roles does
not suffice to constitute an organization. The roles must be sensibly
put together and coordinated by means of an over-riding structure.
Several properties of the structure of the organization influence
knowledge throughput. The structural properties we will cover here
are hierarchy, control span, centralization, and communicative linkage.

a. Hierarchy and Differential Status

One of the most important factors influencing knowledge
transmission is the status hierarchy of the organization.
Status is derived from many sources, e.g., authority, prestige,
control over others, and responsibility. All of these variables
are associated with differential positions in the organization
hierarchy. Burns and Stalker (#3791) studied several industrial
organizations which were practically immobilized by their stress
on the importance of the hierarchical status system and by the
resistance of members to changing the structure. They found

that organization members would not recognize or utilize new knowledge out of fear of depreciating their own personal status. Gerard (#6701) and Cohen (#1760), working with experimentally created hierarchical groups, Kelley (#7198) and Read (#7197) in industrial organizations, and Allen (#5018) and A. Frohman (#7171) in R&D laboratories cite similar instances of barriers to knowledge flow because of status discrepancies. Jackson (#0592), in a general article on communication problems in organizations, cites status as a major structural barrier. Two studies report that information flow is much freer when a social structure (i.e., status hierarchy) is not in place: Larsen and Hill (#2674) studied groups of boys in a summer camp; Barnlund and Harland (#6694) reached the same conclusions in studying sororities on a midwestern campus.

Another author, discussing organizational change in elementary schools, states that when an organization divides into a hierarchical structure, "progressive segregation" occurs. He goes on to state, "the more hierarchical the structure of an organization the less the possibility of change" (Griffiths, #1183, p. 434). Maier, et al. (#7196) in several industrial settings, Blau (#6221) in a governmental agency, and others, have also noted the impeding effect of hierarchical structure on knowledge flow.

Several reasons might be advanced for the consistency of such findings, but one probable explanation stems from the power which superiors in a hierarchy have for distribution of rewards to their subordinates. Thus members are very hesitant to transmit knowledge upward through a hierarchy unless it is (1) firmly substantiated by hard data which in the case of most innovations is hard to come by (Schon, #6916); (2) reflective of only a positive evaluation of themselves (Read, #7197; Jackson, #0592; Festinger, #6698); and (3) directly relevant to the receiver.

While a tight hierarchy may inhibit innovative throughput, some authors have indicated that it might have the opposite effect on input to the organization as a whole. For example, Chesler, et al. (#7105) make the following observation from their research on innovative patterns among school teachers:

> "The objective structure of the school seems to
> have a different effect on *adoption* than on
> *innovation*. In those schools where the communica-
> tion structure was more hierarchical, teachers
> adopted more often than in schools with a diffuse
> structure."

The implication is that in a less democratic system everybody can be ordered to *accept* and *adopt* something new but that they cannot be ordered to *create* something new. Whether the *quality of adoption* is as high under the autocratic system is another question, however. Adoption directed by others is likely to be more superficial and less stable, reflecting a process which Kelman (#6259) describes as "compliance", in contrast to the more solidly based processes of "identification" and "internalization". Superiors who force change on their subordinates

in this manner will have to depend heavily on the hope that
over time and continued trial these deeper levels of acceptance
will replace compliance as the prime motivational bases of the
new behavior.

This question of *whether democracy or autocracy is more
efficient as a system for promoting the utilization of new
scientific knowledge is the most serious question which faces
us as students of D&U.* For those of us who have strong values
which endorse both innovation and democracy, the assignment is
clear: we must build a democratic society which is innovative
in both an *adopting* and an *inventing* sense, and we must build
systems and processes for innovation and utilization which are
not only efficient but democratic as well.

b.   Span of Control

The number of subordinates reporting to a superior constitutes
his "span of control". Since this concept was introduced by
Graicunas in 1933 (Gulick and Urwick, #7209), there has been much
said in the literature concerning *optimum* span of control for a
superior. How many persons can be placed under the authority of
one man so that, on the one hand, he is not stretched too thin,
and, on the other hand, he has enough to do? Although most
theorists have suggested anywhere from three to six (e.g., Dale,
#7141) under the assumption that a small span of control was
best for the organization (Porter and Lawler, #7145), there are
some writers who maintain that relatively large spans of control
are better for member performance because there is *greater
opportunity for intragroup knowledge flow.* This position is in
line with data presented by Haire (#7156) which showed that among
several industrial organizations the most successful was characterized
by the largest span of control. In any case, the optimal number of
subordinates will probably vary, depending on such factors as organizational level, technology, division of labor and personalities of
administrators (Fisch, #7142).

c.   Centralization

Many students of bureaucracy have long assumed that greater
centralization brought greater efficiency and more effective performance generally. That such is not always the case is amply
demonstrated by the inertia and backwardness of some of our largest
centralized big city school systems and by the apparent inability
of the highly centralized giants of the automotive industry to
innovate in the vital area of vehicle safety. As far as D&U are
concerned, centralization seems to cut two ways: it increases the
effectiveness of downward communication but at the same time reduces
the possibility of intra-organizational variation. Conformity and
creativity are basically incompatible. On balance, therefore, it
would seem that centralization inhibits the generation and movement

of new ideas through a system, regardless of its positive
effects on efficiency and stability of the existing structure.*

    d.   Absence of Communication Linkage

        The organizational chart which shows supervisory and "re-
porting" relationships in a hierarchy may not convey an adequate
picture of the actual communication patterns that exist within
the organization. Thus, another very significant aspect of
"structure" is the *communication linkage network*, i.e., the pattern
of formal and informal information channels which connect persons
and units both vertically and horizontally. The fewer the number
of such channels among members and among subunits, the smaller is
the possibility of effective knowledge transfer within the organization. Davis (#7152), for example, cites a case where a department
of an industrial organization often did not have vital information
merely because no formal links to it were defined.

4.   Reward Pattern

        The pattern of compensation and rewards is a key determinant of the
member's level of innovativeness. Typically he is rewarded for stable,
dependable behavior (Rothe, #7172). Katz and Kahn (#6223) state that,
"The man on the assembly line, the nurse in the hospital, the teacher in
the elementary school all know what their major job is. To do a lot
of it and to do it well are the most conspicuous behavioral requirements
of the organization". (p. 338) Thus the typical organization member
is rewarded for not "rocking the boat", for functioning in a reliable,
habitual way--a way that is not at all a facilitator of new knowledge
utilization or flow through the organization. After all, it is new
knowledge that "rocks the boat" and endangers the status quo.

        However, this pattern is not true of all organizations, or for all
members of an organization. Since the organization *must* innovate and
utilize new knowledge, some rewards for innovativeness are important
and perhaps vital. However, few writers have yet acknowledged the
importance of providing rewards for facilitating new knowledge flow
throughout the organization.

5.   Training

        Each subunit of an organization does some training of its new
members beyond that provided by the organization as a whole. As well
as becoming acclimated to the organization, it is necessary for a new
member to become familiar with the ins and outs of the group or department in which he works. Thus, just as training at the organizational
level affects knowledge flow into the organization, training at the group
level affects knowledge flow through the organization.

---

*See also the section on "decentralization" under throughput facilitators for a
continuation of this discussion.

In-group training includes learning the procedures, policies,
norms and values of the group. Some parts of the training may be
related to the task performance, other parts may not be (Schein, #7210).
Customarily the training serves to "socialize" the new member into
the group so that his allegiance and identification is with that group
and not others. This involves generating pride and loyalty and concomitantly raises the same problems for knowledge flow which were
previously discussed in the section on division of labor.

6. Physical Separation of Members and Units

The distance between organization members and between groups has
often been pointed to as a determinant of information exchange. For
instance, Gullahorn (#7195) found that distance was the most important
factor in determining interaction between employees in an office. Other
researchers found distance a major factor in the information flow among
groups in a housing project (Festinger, et al., #0982), in the military
(Caplow, #7213), in a large factory (Davis, #7152), and among sorority
houses (Barnlund and Harland, #6694). Physical separation is often
merely a function of status discrepancy, i.e., the lowest level staff
may be geographically the most remote.

Since higher status groups tend to receive more messages than lower
status groups (Kelly, #7214; Cohen, #7215; Allen, #5018), it may also be
that status and distance interact to determine the amount of message
transmission. There is some support for this notion of joint determination in Guetzkow (#6304) and in Barnlund and Harland (#6694).

7. Leadership Behavior

Leadership behavior serves both as a stimulus and as a model for
much behavior in the organization (Likert, #5202; Bowers and Seashore,
#7184), and for that reason it is a major determinant of internal
barriers to knowledge dissemination and utilization. It is not our
intention to review the massive amount of research done on organizational
leadership. Such reviews have been made by several authors, e.g.,
Cartwright, #7192; Gibb, #7188; Tannenbaum, #7212; and Stodgill, #7187.
However, a brief review of changing trends in this research and in the
conception of "leadership" may help us to understand its significance
for D&U.

At the turn of the century, there was a prevailing conception that
leadership consisted of accurately and clearly telling subordinates
what their tasks were and of specifying how to accomplish them. Like
machines, the organization members were to obey to the letter what the
leader decreed. It was also assumed that organization members worked
solely for their own economic self interest; therefore, superiors merely
had to pay a living wage and tell subordinates the best way to do their
jobs and the jobs would be done (Taylor, #7214).

These assumptions were discredited in the late 1920's when they
were subjected to empirical research by Mayo (#7190), Roethlisberger
and Dickson (#7193), and others. The findings of these pioneer studies
can be summarized as follows:

The members of an organization:

(1) are motivated by social needs,
(2) seek satisfaction in social relationships on the job,
(3) are more responsive to the social forces from their
    peer group than to the demands and constraints of
    their superiors,
(4) will accede to superiors to the extent that they can
    meet their social needs, and
(5) will create informal organizations that satisfy their
    social needs.

Two researchers state that, despite the depersonalized atmosphere,
"large groups tend to develop subcollectivities--subordinate, small,
face-to-face, informal groups or units--within them (Rome and Rome,
#7208, p. 258). These informal structures may act at cross purposes
with the formal organization and serve as barriers to information flow.

Partly as a result of the research of the 1930's, a new conception
of leadership has since developed. According to this new view, leadership is the ability to integrate the objectives of the organization
with the personal needs and goals of its members. Rice states that
"leadership involves sensitivity to the feelings and attitudes of others,
ability to understand what is happening in a group...and skill in acting
in ways that contribute to, rather than hinder, task performance" (#7216,
p. 5). As this new conception of leadership becomes more widespread,
the inhibitory effects of leadership behavior on knowledge flow should
diminish.

B. FACILITATORS OF THROUGHPUT: OVERCOMING BARRIERS TO KNOWLEDGE FLOW
   THROUGH THE ORGANIZATION

Just as it is imperative to receive messages and new ideas from outside,
it is also critical to transmit ideas and information through the organization.
To state the obvious, it is not enough for one person in the organization to
have an idea; he must relay it to others and have them cooperate in testing
its utility. We have discussed in some detail the organizational features
that may inhibit the process of knowledge D&U through the organization and
it is now appropriate to enumerate some ways by which the flow-through is
encouraged.

1. Leadership

The potential impact of different administrative styles on knowledge dissemination and utilization is probably obvious. An administrator
can (1) exhort his subordinates to seek out more information from other
subunits, (2) direct subordinates to use understandable terms when
communicating with others (Lawrence, #2832), (3) amend role demands so
that his subordinates are more functionally interdependent, (4) manipulate rewards to favor knowledge flow among subunits, (5) train subordinates to value and utilize knowledge from other subunits, and (6) create
structural modifications to stimulate information passage by greater
number of linkages and channels.

Whether or not a leader will be able to employ these mechanisms of knowledge facilitation is dependent on both situational constraints and on his reportoire of leadership skills. R. Katz (#7186), Katz and Kahn (#6223), and Mann (#7217) suggest that three sets of skills are essential for effective leadership: technical proficiency, organizational or administrative ability, and an understanding and ability to relate to people (human relations). Some mix of all these leadership dimensions is probably required to promote message flow.*

2. Training

Certain types of training can teach the leaders and members of an organization to value innovative behavior and knowledge exchange. In fact, many currently used organization development programs are intended to improve the process of communication within the organization, and thereby such programs are relevant to the improvement of D&U processes also. According to Buchanan (#3618):

> "The function of organization development (OD) programs
> is to help an organization improve the extent to which
> it accomplishes its intended goals or carries out its
> functions. In the case of school systems, this means
> improvement of the school's contributions to the learning
> and development of children. But OD also has an objective
> which goes beyond that of facilitating improvement, and
> that is to help an organization attain a condition of
> "self-renewal"--to become sufficiently viable to con-
> tinuously adapt to its changing environment and its own
> internal forces: thus, the concept of organization *develop-
> ment* rather than *improvement*. The distinction is similar
> to that made by educators between *learning* and *learning how
> to learn*. OD, when effective, results in an organization
> which has processes, norms, procedures, and member skills
> required for continuous adaptation and thereby continuous
> optimal fulfillment of its goals." (p. 2)

Three of the better known programs are: (a) the Grid program; (b) Survey and Feedback; and (c) Sensitivity Training.

a. The Grid Program

The Grid is a training program created and promulgated by Blake and Mouton (#6198). It emphasizes the importance of interpersonal relations and of task performance as independent yet major contributors to organizational effectiveness. The goal of this program is to change patterns of relationships among members and groups so that more effective problem-solving and decision-making can occur throughout the entire organization. The term "grid" comes from a diagram Blake and Mouton use to depict types of leadership styles; this diagram is shown in Figure 6.1.

---

*The potential significance of various types of formal and informal leaders as knowledge "linkers" is thoroughly explored in Chapter Seven.

FIGURE 6.1   The Managerial Grid (Blake and Mouton, #6198)

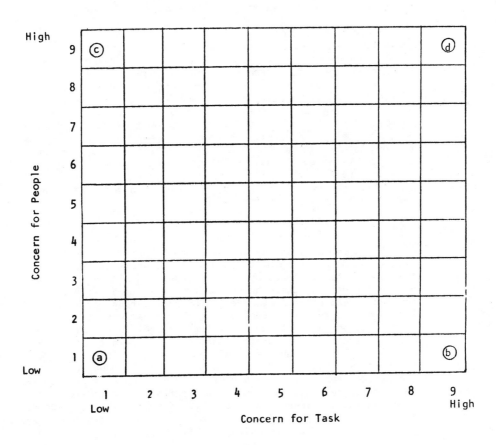

Assumptions of Management Styles:

a.   1,1 management = exertion of minimum effort to get work done; little concern
      for people.

b.   9,1 management = organization efficiency obtained by working conditions that
      are structured so that human elements interfere to a minimum.

c.   1,9 management = thorough attention to social needs of people, which leads to
      a comfortable friendly organization climate and work tempo.

d.   9,9 management = organization performance is perceived as best when members
      are involved in the activities of the organization and feel committed to it.
      Members' interdependence and common goals create relationships of trust and
      respect.

The objective of the program is to train "9,9" leaders,
i.e., leaders who show high concern for their subordinates as
social beings as well as for organizational performance.

There are six phases to the training program. The first
phase is a behavioral science "laboratory" where general problems and concepts of interpersonal relationships are discussed.
The second consists of team training where members of organization
subunits work together to apply the behavioral science knowledge
to their own group. Problems of knowledge flow, influence,
decision-making, and authority are among those handled. The third
phase concentrates on improving information flow among subunits
of the organization, i.e., creating linkage among groups. Thus,
intergroup problems are surfaced and processed. The fourth phase
concentrates on the establishment of new goals for the organization and its subunits. The fifth step is the implementation of
planned change toward new goals. In the sixth and final phase,
stabilization and review occur.

b.   Survey Feedback

Organizational survey research can be applied directly as a
training and "OD" program through a method known as "survey
feedback". As developed by Floyd C. Mann and his associates,
this procedure includes the systematic collection of data from
the membership of the organization on a wide range of issues
including supervisor perceptions, work motivations, aspirations,
communication patterns, and satisfactions. This data is summarized
and fed back to administrators and their subordinates as a means
of confronting serious human and managerial problems. Such a
procedure has been found to stimulate discussion and subsequent
productive problem-solving behavior. The method has been applied
in numerous business and government settings with considerable
reported success (Mann and Likert, #2068; Mann, #5222; Seashore
and Bowers, #7184). In one reported application in a school system
it had mixed results (Benedict, et al., #6751).

A survey feedback program, when used most effectively, can
do five things for an organization. It can (1) identify general
problems in the organization and in its various subunits; (2) make
organization members aware of the problems; (3) help identify
the causes of weaknesses; (4) create an environment for discussion
of the deficiencies reported in the survey; (5) facilitate finding
solutions for weaknesses.

Likert (#5202, #6590) has also suggested that a well-constructed
survey instrument can detect the presence of a problem before it
reaches major proportions. He therefore recommends that organizations
institute a regular procedure of periodic surveys to facilitate
a continuous process of self-renewal.

c.   Sensitivity Training: The "T-Group"

The National Training Laboratories of the NEA (now renamed
the NTL Institute for Applied Behavioral Science) has developed
several models for improving the problem-solving capacities of

individuals, groups, organizations, and communities. These "laboratory" programs stress the development of greater openness and interpersonal competence as the prerequisites of both effective problem-solving and meaningful innovation by individuals and systems. Laboratories may be conducted for individual self-renewal ("stranger" labs) or for team and system development ("cousin" and "family" labs) and they may be conducted on-site or at off-site "retreats". The most elaborate laboratory strategies employ all these variants in various combinations.

At the heart of most "laboratory" training programs is the "T-Group" or sensitivity training group. T-group training is primarily designed to help participants more fully realize their own potential for improvement and to enhance their ability to work with others. Basic to this training in organizations is the belief that the development of effective teamwork is, at the very least, a prerequisite of organizational improvement. This does not mean that the focus is solely on group processes; rather there can be multiple foci: self-insight, interpersonal relationships, group processes, the characteristics and properties of organization, and the dynamics of change.

T-groups can be conducted in many different ways, although some common elements have been identified (Bradford, et al., #6196; Schein and Bennis, #3383). They are usually unstructured with regard to agenda, goals, speakers, and even length, in order to facilitate learning. Willingness to indulge in self-inquiry and experimentation is encouraged by relative freedom to do and say what one wants. The leader or trainer of a T-group behaves passively, taking a "permissive, nonauthoritarian, and sometimes almost completely nonparticipating role. By refusing authority, the leader thus presumably encourages group members to define and solve their own problems" (Leavitt, #6705). Bennis and Shepard point out that one of the principal obstacles to valid communication is orientation toward authority (Bennis, et al., #1344). In a T-group, however, the "authority" role is rejected by the "leader", himself; the group is thereby forced to establish norms and procedures for itself without regard to the presence of an authority.

Whereas the two training methods previously mentioned concentrate on what goes on inside the organization, the sensitivity training group uses the on-going interactions of the people in the group as "data" to be analyzed by the group. To use this "here-and-now" data in a constructive fashion, the group first must build an atmosphere of mutual supportiveness and trust, what Schein and Bennis (#3383) call "psychological safety". Thus, with the supportiveness and permissiveness of the trainer as a model, the group members must develop openness and supportiveness toward one another. As members, to varying degrees, undergo the transformation from the formal, status-loaded, impersonal, role-defined world to a climate of informality, trust and equality, and group "building", they are supposed to learn first-hand and spontaneously the value of full and open interpersonal communication. The paradigm can be seen in terms of three steps: unfreezing old behaviors and attitudes, learning behaviors and beliefs, and freezing the new behaviors and beliefs into the permanent repetoire of the participant.

Transference of T-group learning back to the organizational setting is a major problem (Bradford, et al., #6196). The setting of the T-group is a free and open climate; however, what is useful behavior in this type of climate may not be useful behavior in the organization. Although Davis (#7203) has made some important strides in overcoming the barriers to application of T-group training in the organization, questions about the possible limitations of this training in application to the organization have still to be completely resolved. Insights about self, others, group processes, and organizational characteristics are presumably of value for facilitating knowledge flow, and an implicit goal of all T-groups is improved communication (Bennis and Shepard; and Miles, in Bennis, et al., #1344). Nevertheless, some recent and exhaustive reviews of the literature on this topic (House, #7170; Campbell and Dunnette, #7140) leave room for considerable doubt about the feasibility of transfer of training back into the organizational setting. According to Campbell and Dunnette (#7140), "examination of the research literature leads to the conclusion that while T-group training seems to produce observable changes in behavior, the utility of these changes for the performance of individuals in their organizational roles remains to be demonstrated".

3.   Shared Perceptions

Intergroup knowledge flow can also be facilitated by giving salience to superordinate goals which subunits perceive as shared (Blake and Mouton, #6198; Schein. #7155). For example, the discovery of a "common enemy" often leads subunits to circumvent communication barriers and to reconcile their internal differences. For example, teachers may become unified in the face of an oppressive, tyrannical assistant principal; players on a football team can overlook their differences when playing an all-star game against another league; differences between purchasing and production divisions of the industrial organization are suppressed when the organization must vigorously compete against another organization in its field. Regrettably, however, such superordinate goals may only represent a temporary shift of conflict to a different level; once the common enemy is disposed of, the old barriers to knowledge flow and collaboration will probably return (Blake and Mouton, #6198; Schein, #7155).

Superordinate goals may be instituted in various ways. The goal itself can be a new task which requires collaboration of subunits, or it can be a goal the groups have in common which previously had been overlooked. Even if groups do not actively work together toward a common goal, the acknowledgement of a shared goal will increase the openness and remove some of the defensiveness between parties (Mann, #7175).

The appeal to a superordinate goal is used with some success by Blake and Mouton (#6198 and #7153) in their strategies to improve communication and cooperation. However, they note that once task goal attainment occurs, the heightened knowledge flow may be cast aside for the rekindling of competition.

4. Participation*

    One of the best ways to overcome intraorganization barriers to know-
ledge flow is to routinely convene groups of organization members to
discuss relevant issues. Guest (#0861) calls this "institutionalized
interaction". If interaction accompanied by a *genuine sharing of
influence* can become a normal procedure throughout the organization, it
can work toward effectively mitigating poor vertical and horizontal
knowledge flow.

    The staff meeting where problems are surfaced and discussed, and
where all group members are encouraged to participate, can be a primary
vehicle for overcoming barriers to knowledge flow (Habbe, #7194; Likert,
#5202). It has been noted that supervisors who utilize group meetings
to enhance knowledge dissemination and utilization should "display
an interest in the ideas of their subordinates and make use of these
ideas" (Likert, #5202).

    Participatory group methods have been shown to improve cooperation
(Morse and Reimer, #6712; Katz, et al., #7176), lower abseteeism (Mann and
Baumgartel, #7178), and improve attitudes toward the organization (Likert,
#5202).

5. Overlapping Groups

    The use of overlapping groups in which some individuals have dual
memberships has been advocated as a mechanism for increasing intra-
organizational communication by several authors. This idea was first
proposed by Likert (#5202) and has been developed by him (Likert, #6590,
Chapter Ten). Some useful techniques for instituting overlapping groups
are also proposed by Allen (#5018) and Lorsch and Lawrence (#2281).

    Three principal patterns of overlapping groups are suggested in
Figure 6.2. In vertical overlap, the leader of each subordinate group
is seen as a member of two "teams", one composed of him and his subordinates,
the other composed of him, his superior and his peers. If communication
within each team is open and if true participation takes place, then
information can flow smoothly up and down the hierarchy through these
key "link pin" members. The same rationale can be used for horizontal
overlapping groups.

                      [Insert Figure 6.2 here]

    Another variation of the overlapping group principle is the
temporary ad hoc task force, a team composed of members of the different
units that would be involved in consumating the overall task. After
accomplishing their primary task, members of these teams return to
their regular units. Lorsch and Lawrence (#2281) see this as an

_____
*The term "participation" has been used often and abused almost as often. R. Miles
 (#7221) and Mann and Neff (#3913) list some of the meanings. Following Likert
 (#5202, #6590), we see "participation" as an aggregation of two processes essential
 to the internal functioning of the organization, *communication* and *influence*.

FIGURE 6.2   Vertical and Horizontal Overlapping Groups

a. Vertical: Superior-Subordinate Co-Membership

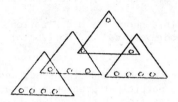

b. Horizontal: Peer Co-Membership

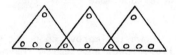

c. Horizontal: Coordinating Committees and Ad Hoc Task Forces

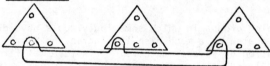

important way to improve collaboration. They also point out that
such teams must be composed of members low enough in the organization
to have detailed knowledge bearing on the project.

Members of subunits can be drawn into a new group for the
purpose of coordination, as well as for project teams.   A team
established to serve as a coordinator unit for several task units
stimulates knowledge flow by gathering from each functional unit
representatives who can receive and transmit information to representatives of other functional units. Lorsch and Lawrence (#2281) point
out that "such a unit is most effective when its members have a
balanced point of view which enables them to work effectively with
each of the specialist groups".

6.   Job Rotation

Job rotation is another way to facilitate knowledge D&U among
subunits of the organization (Allen, #5018; Guest, #0861). Rotation
is useful mainly where totally different technical knowledge and
skills characterize different subunits. Rotation of members among
subunits facilitates an awareness and understanding of the problems
facing other departments. Then, if knowledge from other departments
is relevant, it can be provided by the man who is "on rotation".
Allen also suggests that a policy of job rotation does not carry
with it the implied status differential of "consulting" which tends
to impede the message exchange.

7. Link Pin Specialist

Bennis (#5082), forecasting the organization of the future, offers the vision of the leader being replaced by specialists in the organization whose primary purpose is to facilitate knowledge flow from one subunit to another. "The function of the 'executive' thus becomes *coordinator* or 'linking pin' between various project groups. He must be a man who can speak the diverse languages of research and who can relay information and mediate among groups. People will be differentiated not vertically according to rank and role but flexibly according to skill and professional training" (Bennis, #5082, p. 12).

8. Restructuring

We can extend the idea of overlapping groups and dual memberships to the point where the organizational structure is changed. This provides several additional ways to facilitate knowledge dissemination among groups.

Price (#1780) suggests that where there are two groups in the organization not communicating, another group should be added which is mutually appealing to both. He suggested that a major communication gap between biologists and hatchery workers, which he observed while studying the Oregon Fish and Game Commission, could be bridged by applied scientists to whom both groups felt some affinity. Price proposed giving applied scientists responsibility for maintaining contact between the biologists and the hatchery workers by relaying information back and forth. This method of changing the knowledge flow network is probably most useful in organizations where an in-between group exists to which other groups have good communication channels.

Another way the structure can be modified to facilitate knowledge flow is to increase the average span of control. As noted by Barrett and Tannenbaum (#7219), "while the addition of individuals to a group is an arithmetic function, the increase in number of relationships between individuals is geometric. Hence, the number of relationships increases very rapidly with only small increments in the span of control" (p. 5). An enlarged control span therefore offers subordinates many more sources of information within their own group. An example of such a restructuring with favorable results is reported by Worthy (#1750) of the Sears, Roebuck organization. (This method removes intergroup barriers by collapsing the groups. Whether it destroys the barriers or makes them intragroup obstacles is an interesting question and one that remains to be studied.)

Another potential effect of increasing the average control span is to reduce the number of organization levels. Reducing the height of the organization would occur if enough supervisors at a level are removed so in turn their coordinators, at the next highest level, are not needed.

9. Decentralization

Decentralization offers increased capacity for knowledge flow and utilization among the members of the decentralized unit (Griffiths, #1183; Katz and Kahn, #6223). However, decentralization is also likely to hamper dissemination between parts of the organization. For example, the decentralized units and the organization headquarters may not have adequate message flow because the subunit may perceive itself as self-sufficient or the headquarters may not want to "interfere" (Likert, #5202; Rice, #7158).

Nevertheless, several authors stress the facilitative effects of decentralization. Pelz (#0636), from his research on scientists in organizations, suggests that innovation is prompted by a decentralized atmosphere. Griffiths (#1183) recommends decentralization for school systems, Beckhard (#7180) and Schon (#6916) for industrial organization. Worthy (#1750) cites his experience in a decentralized sales organization, Sears, Roebuck Company, as validation of the utility of decentralization.

10. Geographical Arrangements

Morton (#6840) suggests that not only organizational but spatial mechanisms be used to facilitate knowledge transfer. Thus, physical distance and proximity becomes a mechanism to impede or increase communication between groups. He specifically discusses the utility of locating certain organizationally separated departments together in a building to facilitate knowledge flow, and he describes how such arrangements are employed to good effect in the Bell Telephone Laboratories.

Burns and Stalker (#3791) also suggest that location can have a large impact on the amount of information flow to and from the group; Davis (#7152) gives support to this position with empirical data from an industrial plant. He found that the group processing the least information was furthest away from the center of the organization.

11. Social Engineering

Another approach described by Rice (#7158), Marrow, et al. (#6066), and Trist, et al. (#5367) uses changes in technology as well as in the social system of the organization to improve organizational functioning. These authors contend that the structure of the work flow as well as the social groups of organization members has an effect on behavior, on knowledge flow and on task accomplishment. This approach has been described as "social engineering".

Social engineers view the organization as an interaction of two major factors, the technology and the organization member. In planning or changing one factor, the implications and repercussions on the other must be considered. For example, in weaving mills (Rice, #7158) and in coal mines (Trist and Bamforth, #7165) advances in technology met with lowered productivity because stable and satisfying social systems had been destroyed by the work flow changes. When the technical system was modified by assigning groups of men to several machines, and by eliminating the one-man-to-one-task work assignment pattern, performance increased and absenteeism decreased. From such cases, social scientists are coming to realize that organization members typically have the knowledge and ability to be fully responsible for their jobs. Given the flexibility and freedom to arrange their work as they see fit, they are likely to find the optimum pattern and maximize their performance. Moreover, since there are frequently several ways work flow can be organized, the issue becomes one of choosing the best system so that both technical and social requirements are met.

6-36

The solution seems to be the autonomous work group where a group of members can share responsibility and knowledge for a meaningful part of the "organizational mission" and can maintain satisfactory social relations at the same time (Rice, #7157; Trist and Bamforth, #7165; Trist, Higgin, Murray, and Pellock, #5367; Marrow, et al., #6066; and Bucklow, #7220).

12. Reward Structure

The most potent means of governing human activity is to reward desired behavior. In line with this reasoning, Allen (#5018) suggests allocating rewards for intergroup knowledge transmission. In a similar vein, Schein (#7155) suggests that intergroup collaboration can be increased by "organization rewards given partly on the basis of help which groups give each other" (p. 85).

Summary

Organizations play a vital and pervasive role in the dissemination and utilization process. Most new knowledge originates in organizational settings; most knowledge is processed by organizations; most knowledge is transmitted by organizations and through organizations and most knowledge is consumed by organizations and by people who are living in an organizational environment. Most organizations are engaged in all four processes, i.e., *creation, processing, transmission* and *consumption*. It is therefore imperative that, as students of the D&U process, we understand the organizational context thoroughly.

To simplify this task we found it convenient to subdivide the chapter into three major sections, each concerning itself with one phase in the overall flow process. Each of these three phases, *"input"*, *"output"*, and *"throughput"*, seems to pose a distinct set of problems and offer a distinct set of challenges for D&U. At each point it was possible to discern certain organizational features as "inhibitors" and others as "facilitators" of the movement of new knowledge and innovation.

We found that "input" and "output" have many similar features and present many similar problems because they are "skin conditions". They concern the penetration of the shell of the organization; the organization is something like a giant egg, surrounded and protected by many types of membranes, hard and soft, elastic and brittle. All these membranes are functional in preserving and nurturing the organization as a living system; they are all semi-permeable, allowing some messages from outside to come in while screening out others, and allowing some messages from inside to go out while holding in others. We noted that while this system of filters is effective for maintaining the stability of the system in the short run, it must be highly adaptive and must be able to admit and export new messages if it is to survive in a rapidly changing and crisis-torn environment.

Specifically we identified ten factors related to the *inhibition of input*. These were (1) the need for stability, (2) the organization's unique input coding scheme, (3) internal social cohesion, (4) the fear of malevolence of outsiders, (5) the fear of personal threat to particular insiders, (6) local pride, (7) organizational status, (8) the overall economic condition of the organization, (9) the training and socialization process for new members, and (10) the size of the organization as a whole.

Countering these inhibiting forces we were able to name twelve potential *"facilitators"*, including the following: the reward value of the new knowledge, itself, a change in organizational leadership, perception of crisis, specialized "input" training, the importation of new staff members who already have new ideas, and the installation of specialized knowledge-seeking and innovating subunits such as "R&D laboratories".

For *output* we found seven major *inhibiting factors*. Again, an overriding theme seemed to be (1) the need for stability. Other potential factors were (2) inertia, (3) complacency, (4) perceived vulnerability, (5) inadequate or over-limited organizational goal definition, (6) perceived client readiness, and (7) professed danger to clients. It was suggested that some of these latter "reasons" might also serve as publicly acceptable rationalizations disguising an underlying inertia and complacency.

Output can be facilitated by (1) free and open competition, (2) crisis, (3) affluence, (4) internal openness, (5) organizational values which support quality output, and (6) specialized output roles and subsystems.

The problem of "throughput" is far more complex than either "input" or "output" but can be simplified by viewing the internal substances of the organization as a complex of separate but coordinated subunits and individuals. Hence, many of the internal "barrier" problems are similar in kind to the barrier problems between organizations.

Of seven identified *inhibitors to throughput,* three were explicitly structural, i.e., (1) the division of labor and subgrouping of membership stemming therefore, (2) the specification and separation of specialized task roles, and (3) the formation of an organizational hierarchy. Other potential inhibitors of throughput were (4 & 5) innovation-suppressive reward patterns and training, (6) physical separation, and (7) traditional bureaucratic patterns of leadership.

To *facilitate the throughput* of new knowledge we suggested twelve possible strategies. Among these we devoted most attention to the following: the organization could (1) develop a newer style of leadership which includes a mix of technical, organizational, and human relations skills, (2) conduct any of a variety of "organization development" training programs, (3) develop shared perceptions and superordinate goals with which all subunits could identify, (4) increase genuine participation and influence-sharing up and down the hierarchy, (5) build overlapping subunits with multiple shared memberships, (6) provide for periodic job rotation, (7) create specialists in the linking process, and (8) generally restructure itself to optimize the knowledge flow function.

[Insert Figure 6.3 here]

In Figure 6.3 we attempt to sum up graphically much of what has been said in this chapter. The figure shows the three main phases of input, throughput, and output, the various structural patterns of flow within the throughput, and some of the structural arrangements which can be used to facilitate knowledge flow, e.g., specialized input and output subsystems, and overlapping vertical and horizontal groupings.

In conclusion, it should be stressed that as yet we know very little about the organizational context of D&U, and we must learn very much more. Unfortunately, the bulk of the diffusion literature heretofore has ignored the internal dynamics of the organization, even though the organization is sometimes taken as the

6-38

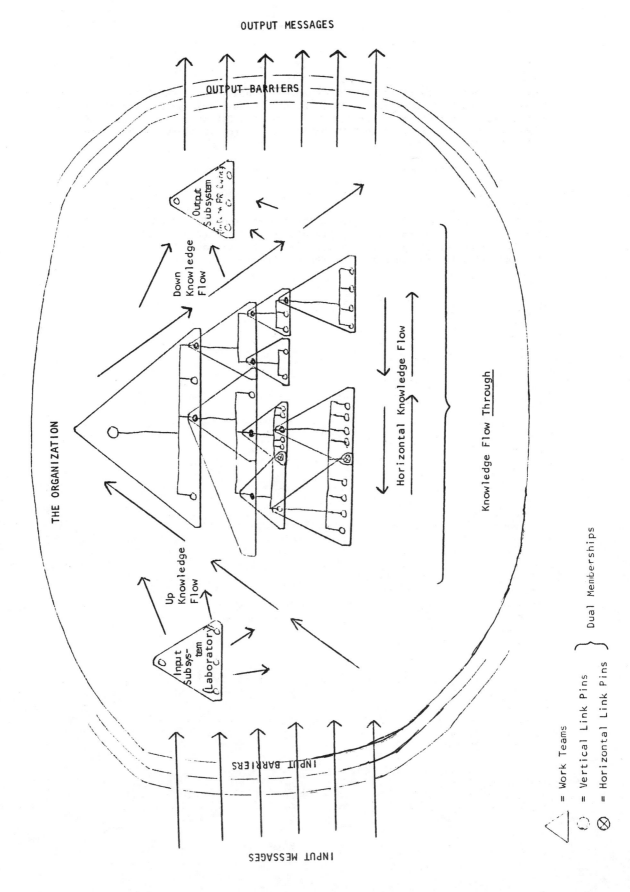

OUTPUT MESSAGES

FIGURE 6.3   Summary of Knowledge Flow Patterns in the Organization

OUTPUT BARRIERS

Output Subsystem

THE ORGANIZATION

Down Knowledge Flow

Horizontal Knowledge Flow

Knowledge Flow Through

Up Knowledge Flow

Input Subsys- tem (Laboratory)

INPUT BARRIERS

INPUT MESSAGES

= Work Teams

= Vertical Link Pins   } Dual Memberships

= Horizontal Link Pins

"adopting unit". Therefore, in this chapter we have had to rely heavily on a body of literature which is only partially relevant because it was compiled by organizational researchers who have had little interest in D&U as such. Because of the importance of organizations to D&U and of D&U to organizations, we hope that future research will soon fill this void.

Of all the substantive issues identified in this report none is more critical nor more fundamental than the question of autocratic vs. democratic organizational structure as a facilitator of innovation and effective knowledge dissemination and utilization. Autocratic structures seem to have some distinct advantages for rapid system-wide adoption,while democratic structures probably engender more internal variation and innovation. The top "development" priority would appear to be the creation of democratic processes which allow for rapid and efficient adoption where such is called for by the nature of the new knowledge at hand.

CHAPTER SEVEN

SPECIALIZED KNOWLEDGE LINKING ROLES

CHAPTER SEVEN*

SPECIALIZED KNOWLEDGE LINKING ROLES

Any detailed consideration of the dissemination and utilization of knowledge must sooner or later focus on the question of linking roles. Who sees
to it that knowledge gets to the user? Who is charged with the responsibility
of retrieving basic or applied knowledge, deriving practical implications
from it, and distributing it to people who need it and can use it?

A natural starting point for a discussion of linking roles is a birds-
eye view of what is often termed "the knowledge gap": the situation for which
linkage is required. Figure 7.1 depicts this gap: the two enclosures represent

FIGURE 7.1   The Knowledge Gap

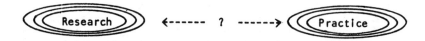

two social systems each defined and identified by its own set of rules, values,
languages, and communication patterns. Those norms which are shared within
each system also define their separateness from each other. There is an
inadequacy of shared values, common perceptions, and inter-system communication
patterns.

The linking role argument is that this gap can be bridged effectively if
additional persons or groups are interposed between the two systems as in
Figure 7.2, these additional intermediaries being specialists in the process of
linking itself.

FIGURE 7.2   Filling the Knowledge Gap

The question which really should be asked first is this: are linking
roles necessary? Is it not better for knowledge builders to pass their findings directly to potential users? Do we really need someone in between to
translate (and possibly distort) the researcher's knowledge? Isn't this the
simplest, most efficient, solution we could possibly come to for the linkage

*This chapter was drafted by Ronald G. Havelock. It also appears in Eidell,
T.L., and Kitchel, J.M. (Eds.) Knowledge Production and Utilization in Educational
Administration, University Council for Educational Administration, Columbus, Ohio
1968.

problem? There is no easy answer to this question, but in this chapter we
will try to address outselves to it. We will try to show what all the
components of the linking function are and with that understanding we will
return to ask this question again.

This chapter will begin with a review of the various roles which do
seem to serve the primary function of knowledge linking. Following this
review, these same roles will be cast in their institutional context with consideration given to the institutional barriers to knowledge flow both on the
knowledge builder and knowledge user sides, and to the institutional arrangements which facilitate the linker's activities. The presentation will conclude
with a summary analysis of what appear to be the endemic problems in the linker
concept and some thoughts about how it ought to be developed in education.
We will endeavor to be practical, indicating what types of linking roles seem
to be most suitable and effective for what linking tasks, what characteristics
and skills need to be considered in recruiting and training linkers, and what
kind of institutions need to be created to secure these roles and to make
knowledge linkage an embedded feature of our national educational system.

I. A TYPOLOGY OF LINKING ROLES

One of the first facts we should be aware of when we discuss linking
roles is that there are a great variety of roles which could be said to be
linking in one way or another. Indeed, connected to every phase, every aspect,
and every problem in the dissemination and utilization process, one could
conceptualize a specific role; someone responsible for retrieving knowledge from
basic research; someone responsible for identifying new innovations in practice;
someone responsible for writing handbooks and producing packaged knowledge for
potential clients of various sorts and so forth. The range of such roles is
suggested by some recent attempts to classify them. A well-known typology
current in education is that developed by Clark, Guba, and Hopkins in a
number of recent articles (e.g., #3586). They have posited a sequence of
interrelated roles which correspond to various stages in a research, development, and diffusion sequence. Under "development" they include roles for
"inventing," "packaging," and "evaluating," while under "diffusion" they list
"informing," "demonstrating," "training" and "servicing" or "nurturing."
Another educator (Hencley, #6032) offers a "taxonomy" of research and development roles which includes "quality controllers," "social bookkeepers," "design
engineers" and "researchers who concentrate on diffusion." One could go on to
other theorists and taxonomists in education and other fields to find similar
lists. Each list has its own special logic and its own special elegance. It
is, therefore, with considerable trepidation that we set out to compile our own
typology, piecing together from diverse sources those concepts pertaining to
linking roles which seem to be non-redundant and conceptually additive or
integrative.

A cautionary note may be in order before we proceed, however. As in any
classification, the "types" offered here are all somewhat fictional, something
on the order of "ideal types." When we look at the linker *in vivo* we find that
he is a mixture, playing several linking roles in sequence and simultaneously
and indeed sometimes not playing the linker at all.

Here, then, in Table 7.1 is a typology of linking agents drawn from a wide
spectrum of sources across many fields of knowledge, and grouped under major
headings which suggest their most salient functions or the assumptions about the
transfer process which each set seems to imply. The discussion of the next several
pages will follow this table closely.

[Insert Table 7.1 here]

A.   THE CONVEYOR ✓

The most rudimentary and simplistic linker concept is the "conveyor"
(Havelock, #3041) or "carrier" (Jung, #6029), one who takes knowledge from
expert sources and passes it on to non-expert potential users. The
"knowledge," of course, could be in the form of research data, information
derived from research, "packaged" knowledge derived generally from scientific knowledge in the form of curricula, printed materials, and training
programs, or it could be supplies, products, services, or practices founded
on or derived from scientific knowledge in one way or another. The pure
conveyor concept suggests that such knowledge is passed on pretty much in
the form that it is received. It seems doubtful, however, that anyone in
a linking role performs in such a limited capacity. Perhaps the salesman
comes as near to this pure linking role as anyone, taking from the producer
a fully developed, fully packaged, and fully usable product and placing it
in the hands of the user. There is very little question that salesmen in
all fields play important knowledge linking functions (Stein, #6062;
Abell, et al., #3886; Bauer and Wortzel, #2340; Wilkening, #5385; and
Elliott and Couch, #1447). Even the salesman, however, may be helping the
user in a more complex manner than is usually conceived. The drug detail
man may give the doctor samples and literature of various sorts and he
may, in addition, tell him what drugs Dr. X in the next town is ordering
(Bauer, #2340). The grain elevator operator (Elliott and Couch, #1447)
may pick up items from agriculture experiment station bulletins so he can
pass on useful bits to farmers and thereby develop firmer ties of friendship
and respect.

Another role which may come close to the pure conveyor type is the
extension subject matter specialist in agriculture. A full time agent of
the Cooperative Extension Service, he is usually based in the university and
is responsible for keeping the county agents informed and up-to-date on new
developments in his special area. There is some research evidence that
these extension specialists do indeed see their role primarily as that of
one-way communicators of university research to the counties (Brown, #2866).
Nevertheless, the linking task of this specialist is a sophisticated one.
He must take research findings in raw form and package them into pamphlets,
programs, projects, lectures, training courses and other forms which are
readily digestible by the county agent and his farmer clients. Such a
variety of tasks would in industry involve such varied roles as research
retrieval, engineering, production, packaging, advertising and marketing.

A similar linking role is played by the science reporter (e.g., Wood,
#3897), who retrieves and interprets knowledge from a wide range of scienti-
fic sources, even if he specializes in one field, and draws forth items which
appear to be of interest to the general public.

Of all conveyor types, the one most frequently cited and viewed as a
classic is the county agent of the CES, who is most frequently viewed as a
one-way communicator of new technical information from the state university
to the farmer. Various studies of the "image" of the county agent indicate
the prevalence of this limited conception (Wilkening, #3052; Abraham, #3516).
This view is not shared by the county agent, himself, however, and is not
confirmed by researchers who have studied the role in depth (e.g., Stone,
#1129; Wilkening, #5385). In fact, the county agent serves as communicator,
teacher, consultant, demonstrator, helper, and community leader, culling
information from a variety of sources and disseminating it in a variety of ways.

TABLE 7.1　　　　　　　　　　　　Knowledge Linking Roles

ROLE TYPE	FUNCTION	FIELD	EXAMPLES	SAMPLE REFERENCES
A. Conveyor	To transfer knowledge from producers (scientists, experts, scholars, developers, researchers, manufacturers) to users (receivers, clients, consumers)	Agriculture	County agent (especially as seen by others)	Wilkening, #3052 Abraham, #3516
		Agriculture	Extension Specialist	Brown and Deckens, #2866
		Agriculture Medicine	Salesman, retailer, drug detail man.	Elliott & Couch, #1447 Anderson, #2535 Bauer & Wortzel, #2340
		Psychology	Science reporters	Wood, #3897
		Education	Trainers Informers Demonstrators } Disseminators	Clark & Hopkins, #3586
		Education	Teacher	
		Gov. Policy	Scientific expert	Moulin, #3382; Schilling,#3402; Sponsler, #3422; Leiserson,#1146
		Industrial R & D	Systems engineer	Havelock & Benne, #3872
B. Consultant	To assist users in identification of problems and resources, to assist in linkage to appropriate resources; to assist in adaptation to use: facilitator, objective observer, process analyst.	Various	Mental health consultant	Bowman, #1319; Berlin, #2079; Binderman, #1335; Kaufman,#3947; Glaser,#6097
		Various	Change agent	Lippitt, et al., #1343
		Organization	Change agent	Schein & Bennis, #6077
		Education	Change agent	Watson, #6194 & #6195
		Agriculture	County agent (as he actually operates much of the time)	Penders, #6042 Stone, #1129
		Urban	Expeditor	Reiff & Reissman, #3218
		Psychiatry	Legal mediator	Tershakovec, #3251
C. Trainer	To transfer by instilling in the user an understanding of an entire area of knowledge or practice.	All Fields	Teacher Professor of Practice	
		Education	Trainer	Clark & Hopkins, #3586
D. Leader	To effect linkage through power or influence in one's own group, to transfer by example or direction	Education	Administrator: superintendent, principal	Carlson, #1174 Richland, #3698 Chesler, et al., #2607
		Various	Gatekeeper	Lewin, #2640
		Medicine	Opinion leader: physician	Katz, #0295
		Agriculture	Opinion leader: "good farmer"	Blackmore, et al., #2492 Wilkening & Santopolo, #1923
		Community (urban)	Opinion leader: informal power structure	Angell, #6193
E. Innovator	To transfer by initiating diffusion in the user system.	Agriculture	Innovator	Rogers, #1824
		Agriculture	Demonstrator: farmer	Blackmore, et al., #2492 Wilkening & Santopolo, #1923
		Industry	product champion	Schon, #3025
		Industry	Entrepreneur	Nader, #6094

Continued on following page

Role Type	Function	Field	Examples	Sample References
F. Defender	To sensitize the user to the pitfalls of innovations, to mobilize public opinion, public selectivity, and public demand for adequate applications of scientific knowledge	Various	Defender	Klein, #3691
		Agriculture	County agent	Francis and Rogers, #1409
		Education	"Quality controller"	Hencley, #6032
G. Knowledge-builders as linkers	To transfer through gatekeeping for the knowledge storehouse and through defining the goals of knowledge utilization.	Various	Scholar: scientific leader	Znaniecki, #6033
			General educator	
			Definers of human values	
		Various	Futurists and future planners	Wright, #6199
	To transfer through maintenance of a dual orientation: scientific soundness and usefulness.	Industry	Applied researcher-developer	Stein, #6062
		Education	Applied researcher-developer	Clark & Hopkins, #3586
		Medicine	Clinical researcher	Havelock, #6183
		Industry	R & D Manager	Krugman & Edgerton, #2573 Pelz & Andrews, #6067
		Education	Res. coordinator	Sieber, #6187
		Education	Res. director	Sieber, #6187
		Education	Engineer	Anderson, #1059
		Education	Curriculum developer	Clark, #1172
H. Practitioner as Linker	To transfer to clients and consumers through practices and services which incorporate the latest scientific knowledge.	All		
I. The User as Linker	To link by taking initiative on one's own behalf to seek out scientific knowledge and derive useful learnings there from.	Agriculture	Most advanced farmers	Havelock & Benne, #3872 Rogers, #1549

When planners and policy makers in education discuss the need for more disseminator and diffusor roles in education (e.g., Clark and Hopkins, #3586) they should be sensitive to this distinction between "conveyor" and a more complex conception of linker. There is, nevertheless, a distinct logic to the simple concept and a distinct utility if it could be made to work in practice. The trouble with the concept may be in large part one of "image." The fact is that terms like "disseminator" or "conveyor" sound to most people like "errand boy," and "runner." Znaniecki (#6033, p. 150), for example, describes the disseminator function thus: "while important socially (to develop support for scholars), it is scientifically unproductive". Halpin (#0641) puts the matter bluntly:

> "I can only writhe as I watch the fatuous and condescending
> attitude of both the scientist and educational practitioner
> toward prospective middlemen. Even the advocates of the
> middleman plan imply that the middleman should serve as a
> type of editorial assistant, at a status level only slightly
> above that of the average secretary and certainly below that
> of the research technician."   (p. 198)

Such comments may well be valid in the main. There are some conveyor-type linkers, however, who escape stigma altogether. In particular we can cite the by now well-established role of scientific expert or advisor. Perhaps beginning with the mobilization of brainpower in the Second World War, there has been increasing interest at the highest levels of government for advice and presumably expert information from distinguished scientists. In repeatedly answering this call, some of our most renowned scientists have, in effect, turned themselves into knowledge linkers of the conveyor type. Unfortunately, there have been no quantitative and thorough empirical studies of this role of scientific expert, although much has been written in a journalistic vein. Most writers focus on the question of the legitimate or proper role of the scientist in the policy-making and decision-making process. Many warn of the dangers of too much reliance on experts. For example, Moulin (#3382) notes that experts are replacing public opinion as guiding forces in political decisions (hence possibly subverting democracy). Schilling (#3402) and Michael (#6190) warn that scientists may disguise personal values and partisan viewpoints in the form of "expert advice," while Penders (#6042) cautions us that expertise at the top, while indispensible, should only be used in conjunction with heavy local responsibility. On the other hand, some writers deplore the relative powerlessness of the scientist-expert. Sponsler (#3422), for example, contrasts the influence of scientists in the Soviet Union and the United States: there they are "on top," in significant policy roles, but here only "on tap," and therefore functioning in a marginal and less-than-optimum capacity. On the other side of this argument, Leiserson (#1146) says that as we move from "technical" to "policy" advice, the scientist's role becomes less vital and this is as it should be to protect and maintain his status as an objective knowledge source.

Another successful, if less exalted, linking role is found in some sectors of industrial R&D in the title of "systems engineer." As this role is depicted operating in the Bell Telephone Laboratories (Morton, #6840; Havelock and Benne, #3872) it allows basic researchers and development engineers to pursue their separate special interests without "interference" from management. The systems engineer looks over their shoulders, pulling out ideas and popping them in when it seems appropriate, but not disrupting their ongoing creative efforts. One might assume that such a person would be subjected to second class status as depicted by Halpin. In fact, however, he survives and prospers to the point where upper management looks to this group for future leadership positions.

To sum up, the conveyor concept of linkage is a very limited one but has wide-spread currency; it is what people usually think of when they think about special roles to disseminate knowledge. Very low valuation, by researchers and practitioners alike, suggest that it is a problem role under most circumstances. There are instances, however, where conveyor-type linkers are accorded high prestige and are able to operate with high effectiveness.

B. THE CONSULTANT

In its purest form the consultant role is not necessarily a knowledge linking role at all. The consultant is, rather, a facilitator, helper, objective observer, and specialist in how to diagnose needs, how to identify resources, and how to retrieve from expert sources. He tells "how" in contrast to the conveyor, who tells "what" (Havelock, #3041; Jung, #6029). The underlying rationale for consultation is that only the client, himself (the user), can determine what is really useful for him. Therefore, when others come to his aid they should do so as collaborators (Thelen, #3692) or encouragers (motivation builders, Bowman, #1319). It is up to the consultee to take initiative (Boehm, #3550) and when information is given, he is in a position to take it or leave it. Bidman (#1335) notes that five characteristics distinguish consultation from education (the conveyor role): first, the consultee initiates; second, the relationship is temporary and specific; third, the consultant is from a different professional discipline than the consultee; fourth, he is advisory only, having no responsibility for implementation; and fifth, he has no administrative relationship to the consultee.

Consultation is often depicted as a second best procedure, a very passive, impotent, almost bystander role (Huessy, #6012; Fry, #2993), but two relatively recent developments have added considerable depth to the concept. One of these has been "mental health consultation",* first advanced by Coleman and later refined by Gerald Caplan (#2079). From the psychiatric interview came the insight that "help" really starts with "help me to understand myself" and "help me to define for myself why I need help and what help I need." This concept has been generalized from the mental health professions to all forms of helping and applies equally to knowledge linking. When someone comes to someone else for "advice", what he needs first and foremost is an understanding of what his problem is and how he is reacting to it. The consultant, therefore, should allow the consultee to tell his story, not so the consultant may be informed, but so he himself may be informed. This type of relationship calls for restraint and a non-directive stance by the consultant and a withholding of advice, expert information, and a minimum of programming for the consultee.

A somewhat different concept of consultation has been developed over the last twenty years by the staff of the National Training Laboratory under the label of "change agent" (Lippitt, et al., #1343). The "change agent" consultant, like the mental health consultant, emphasizes the need for client self-diagnosis and problem definition, but the change agent is flexible in what he gives. He may assist in the diagnosis by showing the client how to conduct a self-survey (Selltiz and Wormser, #6181), or by conducting a self-survey for the client (Mann, #5219; Mann, #5221; Mann and Neff, #3913). He may provide the client with skills in problem formulation and problem solving and he may make the client

---

*This should not be confused with psychotherapy, psychotherapeutic counselling or other varieties of treatment for mental illness in spite of some similarities in historical origin and assumptions.

7-6

aware of various change strategies. The change-agent consultant is, therefore, an active participant and collaborator and a conveyor of knowledge about the process of change itself.

Both of these developments in consultation have come a long way in their twenty year history, each developing as a distinct profession with its own rules and institutions. Most recently, however, there are signs of a merging of, or at least a mutual learning between, the two movements, the change agent group becoming more clinically sophisticated and the mental health consultation group more concerned with active helping and collaborating with the client (Chin and Benne, #6113).

While such refinements in the concept of consultation are now widely understood and accepted, the reader should be cautioned that the actual term "consultant" is still used very loosely to describe any type of advice-giver or expert, including the "conveyor" type discussed earlier.* Many writers use the term to describe someone who is peripheral to the mainstream of decision-making, either because his expertise is not recognized or valued,** or because he needs to retain the onlooker's objectivity.*** The term is used by Schein and Bennis (#6077) merely to distinguish the outside change agent (the "consultant model") from various other change agent roles which operate within the client system.

We may be able to gain some perspective on the concepts of "conveyor" and "consultant," as used here, by a comparison of some of their attributes. Table 7.2 illustrates some important advantages of the consultant's role definition. However, we do not wish to stress the value of the consultant over the conveyor as this table may imply. The emphasis should be placed on the unique

[Insert Table 7.2 here]

contribution which each type of role may play in a total program of knowledge dissemination and utilization. The two roles may be and can be used effectively in a coordinated development program, with the consultant type preparing the client or client system, building a readiness to change and an openness to outside expert knowledge and an understanding of how and when to use such knowledge. Glaser, for example (#6097), in a carefully controlled field experiment, found that psychological consultation developed greater client receptivity to "research, demonstration and innovations developed by others."

On the other hand, the conveyor is needed to provide crucial technical information at the time when the client is ready for it. Wilkening (#5385) found that the county agent was relatively ineffective as an introducer of new ideas, but when it came to translating innovations into practice and adapting them to personal use, he was crucial. As we have mentioned previously, detailed studies of the effective county agent show him taking a variety of roles at different stages in the adoption process (Stone #1129; Penders #6042), sometimes encouraging and assisting the client with self diagnosis, sometimes providing new information, sometimes training or retraining, sometimes providing encouragement and reinforcement.

---

*Fairweather (#6189),"Social Action Consultant."

**Early use of mathematicians in industry (Fry, #2993).

***Peter summarizes the viewpoint of social scientists about their action role: "observe and do research but remain essentially aloof from action programs" (#6057).

TABLE 7.2   <u>Five Difficulties With the Linkage Role:</u>
                       <u>A Comparison of Two Approaches</u>

Problem	Conveyor	Consultant
(1) Marginality	Because he is not "one of us" he may be excluded from inner circles of both research and practice where most sophisticated and appropriate formulations of knowledge and problems may reside.	Doesn't need to belong to "inner circle" because he doesn't need special knowledge.
(2) Two Masters	If he is seen as serving special interests of one client, the other client may not be open to him. May see his information as biased or illegitimate in one way or another.	Does not put himself in position of "selling" anything from someone else.
(3) Pain Remoteness	Must know the nature of the need in order to bring relevant knowledge to bear.	Makes sure initiative develops from client himself.
(4) Super-expertise	Over-strains the capacity of the linker. Over-isolates researchers. Builds dependency and problem-solving incapacity in client.	Required to have only general knowledge of retrieving information, deriving solutions, and diagnosing problems. Avoids being seen as a "walking encyclopedia."
(5) Structural Redundancy (channel inefficiency)	He is "on-line." If he pulls out he is in danger of disrupting flow, may not leave client with adequate skills. If he stays "on-line" we have lost manpower and we have created an additional potential source of error in the system.	Never puts himself "on-line,": ...doesn't constitute a direct block. (See Figure 3 also)

There are a number of other roles which are akin to the "consultant" in that they are not directly providing knowledge but rather facilitating the process. Reiff and Riessman (#3218) discuss the role of "expeditor" as an ideal role for the indigenous non-professional. The expeditor is one who "sees to it that service is given" to the user. Such a person would be able to identify with client needs and concerns and yet be influential and know-ledgeable about the resources of the serving system. Where this type of role deviates from the consultant concept is in the idea that partisanship (on behalf of the client) is a useful and in most cases necessary stance for the linker. We will return to this question later in discussing the role of "defender."

At the opposite extreme is the "mediator," one who is officially and legitimately objective. This notion of linkage is thoroughly legal. It assumes that knowledge producers, conveyors, and clients are all basically partisans and potential adversaries. Thus, relations between doctors and patients, seller and buyers, writers and readers, and teachers and students are regulated by specific norms and rules which are codified in our legal system. This system, in turn, is administered by an officially "objective" group: the judiciary. Probably the role of the judiciary has been most prominant in the field of psychiatry (Tershakovec, #3251). The marginal status of psychiatry as a medical science leads to considerable conflict and confusion between psychiatry and the public on such critical questions as "what is mental illness?", "what is the proper treatment for mental illness?", and "what is the differenee between mental illness and criminality?". Decisions on these questions are not made by the "experts" but by the judges after listening to experts and reflecting on the needs of society. The utility and appropriate-ness of this sort of middleman may be disputed in specific cases, but it is probably an indispensible last resort when problems of linkage have turned into conflicts.*

C.   THE TRAINER

There is probably a need to distinguish the specialized role of "trainer" or "teacher" from both conveyors and consultants despite some overlap in meanings. The trainer works on the assumption that underlies much of formal education, namely that a body of knowledge can be conveyed and stored for future use in an extended, intensive learning experience, usually in a special-ized learning environment (e.g., a school, institution, university, summer camp, etc.). The trainer is an expert who is capable of conveying large quantities of knowledge and/or complex skills but he does not typically convey this knowledge to people who are in the work setting. In contrast to the "conveyor" he tries to inculcate new knowledge prior to the time the practitioner enters the work setting. Thus the farmer's son may attend the agricultural college to be taught by professors of agriculture (trainer). Later, back on the farm he may learn from the county agent (conveyor).

The trainer is also distinguishable from the conveyor in having a greater control over the learning environment. Typically, he has some position of authority over the learner (as teacher to student), and can use various coercive and/or reinforcing techniques which neither the consultant nor the conveyor have access to (grades, flunking and passing, diplomas, certificates, letters of recommendation, etc.)

_____

*Many readers may see this inclusion of judicial and legal roles within the linking role concept as rather muddy. It must be agreed that such persons are not primarily knowledge linkers, but only serve this role on occasion.

This review did not include any extensive consideration of the literature on teaching or the role of the teacher or trainer, and no literature
is cited here, for although it is important and deserves a place in any
taxonomy of linking types it is a role thoroughly understood by most readers
and effectively described in other sources.

For knowledge utilization among practitioners in all fields the most
vital trainer role is probably the professor of practice. Particularly since
the eclipse of the apprenticeship system, our culture has relied almost
exclusively on the professor of practice in the university to pass on or
inculcate an understanding of a profession in the next generation of practitioners. Because of his strategic role in the socialization of the
practitioner, the professor's attitudes, training, skills and orientation toward
change will have a major impact on the progressiveness and innovativeness of an
entire profession.

The chief limitation of the trainer role is the lack of continuing
contact with the practitioner, especially contact in the field setting. The
trainer prepares the new practitioner and sends him out into the world as
if he were somehow a finished product. Perhaps he will need occasional
servicing or recharging in summer institutes or refresher courses but
essentially the trainer relinquishes any linking function after a designated
training period is over.

D.   THE LEADER

Both the conveyor and the consultant are typically outsiders as far as
the receiver-user is concerned. They are not likely to be linked to him in
a formal organizational sense, nor are they likely to be related in a reference group sense of being "one of us." There are, on the other hand, a
great number of roles which create effective linkage through power or
influence within the receiver's own group. We discuss these various role
types under the designation "leader."

To begin with, there is a good evidence that formally constituted leaders
(administrators, supervisors, directors, presidents) do have a major effect
on utilization of new ideas. Carlson has shown this with respect to school
system superintendents (#1174), as has Richland (#3698). Just how the administrator brings about utilization, and what sort of role he plays in the
process, is more problematic, however. Some authors (e.g., Ashby, #1279)
seem to suggest that he is sort of a funnel through which all information
comes to the users. Others* indicate that administrators function as
"facilitators" or "supporters" of the user's efforts to retrieve and utilize
new ideas.

A concept related to formal leadership, but used more typically in the
area of planned change and diffusion, is that of "gatekeeper." This term
was first introduced by Lewin (#2640, #1342) in describing housewives as
the focal persons through whom influence on household eating habits had to be
channeled. Many receiver systems may be so organized that there is a distinct

---

*Chesler (#2607) on the role of the school principal, and Carey (#3602) on the
role of the University president in the development of evening colleges.

"gate"(specific set of rules, norms, etc.) which must be passed to get free access to a group of receivers. In bureaucratic organizations this "gate" may be controlled by the "boss," the formally designated leader, or it may be controlled by some other officially designated person (e.g., editor).

The "gatekeeper" concept is significant in that it reminds us to note the channels and barriers which represent the client-user system and the access routes to it. The gatekeeper is the one who holds the strategic position. The gatekeeper can be the formal leader, but organization charts and official power may be misleading. In most parts of the world, for example, the oldest male is the head of the household and is accorded the highest prestige. Nevertheless, it may be the female who controls access to those critical areas of personal life which are of most concern to the development worker, as for example, in the dissemination of birth control information, sanitation procedures, food preparations, etc. Cama (#6044), for example, notes the great potential of utilizing women in development programs for these reasons.

The formal leader and the gatekeeper (strategic role holder) are both to be distinguished from the opinion leader (Katz, #0295). There is a large body of literature supporting the view that the vast majority of those who eventually adopt new ideas do so because they are influenced by some other member of their own group. When this pattern of imitation is focussed on one particular person and is stable over time and across a number of innovations, we can speak of "opinion leadership."*

That judgements and attitudes are influenced by the social environment is a well established fact in social psychology. People do have a tendency to conform to the opinions and behaviors of those around them, not only in unstructured situations,** but even where there is direct sensory evidence which contradicts those opinions and behaviors.*** This phenomenon of conformity in itself may be responsible for many kinds of adoption behavior, but there is considerably more which should be understood to appreciate the opinion leadership concept. For one thing, conformity is not typically blind acceptance of what anybody who happens to be present is doing or saying: there are spheres of conformity, specific kinds of groups, often called "reference groups," within which there is likely to be high conformity on certain issues. In other words, people are distinctly selective in their acceptance of the opinions of others, and their selectivity is based largely on prior experience and background. For example, most farmers have most of

---

*Actually, this definition is not universally accepted and there is a need for clarification. See Rogers' discussion (#1824), especially pages 209-214.

**Sherif's classic experiments using the autokinetic phenomenon. Sherif, M., The Psychology of Social Norms, New York: Harper Brothers, 1936.

***Asch experiments asking subjects to compare lines of various lengths. Asch, S.E., "Effects of group pressure upon the modification and distortion of judgements" Maccoby, E.E., Newcomb, T.M. and Hartly, E.L. (eds.) Readings in Social Psychology, New York: Holt, Rinehart and Winston, 1958, pp. 174-183.

their discussions and exchanges about farming with other farmers. Therefore, naturally, "other farmers" are their reference group for new ideas on farming. Some farmers, however, have had many successful encounters with the extension service. In these cases the county agent may become a member of the farmer's reference group and the conveyor and opinion leader functions can be fused. Thus Beal and Rogers find that the agricultural scientist is a significant referent for the most innovative farmers (#1351).

The county agent example is offered to make a point: reference groups can form on a rational as well as non-rational basis. There are certain people one trusts for new information and there are certain people one doesn't trust for information, but this kind of trust may have little to do with personal friendship or liking. There is no doubt, of course, that friends and neighbors do play a critical role in the adoption process (e.g., Lionberger and Hassinger, #2690; Abell, et al., #3886; Anderson, #2535). Yet the influence they exert may not be based soley on "good fellowship." Indeed, if experience has told us that our friends are not reliable sources of information, we will often ignore their advice. What counts is our perception of others as relevant information sources and relevant role models and/or exemplars. It is not so much "being like me" as "being what I aspire to be" or "being what I would be if I could." Thus both Blackmore (#2493) and Wilkening (#1923), in different settings, found that test demonstrators who were effective were seen primarily as "good farmers."

Discussions of opinion leadership have typically focussed on what is known as the "two step flow of communication" hypothesis, first introduced by Lazarsfeld and others in an analysis of voting patterns in 1940 (#6182). According to this hypothesis, mass media of communication, which are presumably beamed at the public as a whole, are actually only influential with a small portion of externally oriented, media-oriented, people. It is these people who in turn influence the remainder of the public through their opinion leadership.

The theory has proved to be problematic in many ways (see Katz, #0295, and Rogers, #1824), particularly in implying: (a) that there are only two steps; (b) that there is only one channel through which a given individual may be influenced; and (c) that those who are influenced by media are in fact the most influential people, i.e., that media-oriented people are opinion leaders. Extensive literature surveys of the diffusion process (e.g., Rogers, #1824) emphatically contradict all three of those assumptions.

The point which should be made here is the need to know how the opinion leadership is constituted and organized. We should recognize above all that opinion leadership is something which is present in every social system and every reference group, but we should not assume that such leadership, when found, will be progressive, i.e., that it will encourage the adoption of new ideas. Hoffer (#1852) notes that "high quality and quantity of well-recognized extension-oriented leadership were all found to be positively related to success of the extension program." In other words, the extension service depends for its success on a core of progressive leadership in the client system. This same point is made by many who have discussed the problem of national development. For example, Hull (#1768) states that there must be an elite of powerful modern-ization proponents before technical assistance will "take." Otherwise, advice will be ineffectual. Interestingly enough, the same point has been made about introducing change in our own urban communities in the United States. There needs to be a stratum of informal (as distinct from purely political) leadership in the community which is not only effectively oriented toward new ideas from outside but which is also effectively linked to the "followers" within their own community. This has been demonstrated in survey studies of the social integration of American cities (Angell, #6193).

The importance of opinion leadership, in contrast to formal leadership, probably relates to the degree of formal coordination of the user social system. Presumably, the more loosely structured the system the more important is the role of opinion leadership. Thus, in farming (individual land holdings), in much of medicine (individual physicians working out of their own offices), and in the academic world (individual scholars working on independent self-determined research projects) colleague influence may play a determining role. It is less clear what constitutes opinion leadership within bureaucratic structures, i.e., among organizational scientists, hospital staffs, government departments, corporation employees, and school system personnel. It might be argued that opinion leadership is an important concept for these groups also, but only among the leaders of more or less autonomous units (e.g., among directors of laboratories, hospital administrators, corporation executives, and school system superintendents).

Before leaving the concept of "opinion leader" we should also see how it relates functionally to the "conveyor" and "consultant" described above. Katz (#0295) suggests that the opinion leader serves three purposes for the receiver-users: he provides (1) information (conveyor), (2) a standard to follow (conformity to reference group norms), and (3) social support for adoption decisions. In other words, he seems to serve similar or overlapping functions to those of conveyor and consultant. It would appear, however, that the distinctive aspect of the opinion leader is his insideness. The opinion leader is above all a legitimator of new ideas and practices.

Anyone contemplating a program of diffusion should consider the implications of opinion leadership and legitimation. In a stable client system with identifiable and strong indigenous opinion leadership, it may be a wise strategy to take the opinion leaders as primary communication targets. But when this leadership is not strong, the attempt to make them inside change agents may alienate them from the rest of the client system and disrupt whatever community coordination may have existed previously. At the same time, to select members of the client system who are marginal in status and isolated from other members is equally fatal to a change program, unless some means are found for legitimating these insiders to their colleagues.

E.   THE INNOVATOR

Another type of role sometimes confused with the opinion leader but clearly distinct both conceptually and empirically is the "innovator", the first person in a social system* to take up a new idea. The "innovator" may or may not be original in an absolute sense as an inventor but he may be the first to adopt a new idea within a particular social system and hence the originator as far as that system is concerned.

One might ask why the "innovator" has been included as a "linking role". Does he really link to anyone, or is he simply an accidental by-product of the diffusion of knowledge? It seems that the innovator may indeed be a linker in several ways. First, he may be a latent opinion leader, perhaps through the success and the prosperity which may result from being an innovator. This may

---

*This definition is very close to Rogers (#1824, p. 193).

be the way in which Blackmore's (#2492) and Wilkening's (#1923) test demonstrators came to be known as "good farmers". Through innovation they developed well-run profitable enterprises; other farmers, seeing them prosper, wish to emulate them.

A second way in which innovators serve as linkers is as demonstrators and quasi-opinion leaders for the real opinion leader. The opinion leader may be reluctant to stake his reputation on an untested product or practice. If he is able to see how someone else (the innovator) fares before he starts, he is in a safer position. This type of flow pattern depends, of course, on adequate linkage between innovators and opinion leaders. If it is true that innovators are isolates, viewed as cranks and oddballs by the rest of the social system,* then there is little hope for this type of linkage. Under these conditions opinion leaders would avoid innovators. Such may well be the case, particularly in very conservative social systems.

The relationship between opinion leaders and innovators still needs clarification. Menzel and Katz (#3404) found an inverse correlation between early adoption of a new drug (innovation) and opinion leadership among doctors. They use this finding to suggest that the innovator acts as an "advance scout" for the opinion leader in much the same way as we have suggested here, but the linkage between the two (the innovator and the opinion leader) is left unexplained. They note that rural sociologists have found similarly inconsistent relation-ships between opinion leadership and innovativeness. To this knot, another loop is added by noting that those contacted directly and those influenced indirectly may be in the same group. Innumerable studies have shown (e.g., Rogers and Capener, #1534, and many others cited by Rogers, #1824) that such factors as higher education, higher social class, larger farms, larger income and cosmopolitan orientation, characterize the farmers who have more contact with the extension system. If these correlations represent a cluster of attributes which define a very special subgroup, one implication might be that linkage between this group, loaded as it is with potential opinion leaders, and the larger group of low education, low income, small farm, localite farmers, may be a real problem. Research clearly is still needed to untangle this problem, to discover if and how the chain of influence from innovator to opinion leader to opinion follower works.

A third way in which the innovator may become an effective linker is through the active advocacy of the innovation. The innovation advocate may be a particularly useful role within large bureaucratic structures where profit does not depend exclusively on self-initiative but more on one's reputation in the system and one's contribution to the success of the group.** Schon has given us some illuminating case examples of how "product champions" operate in industry (#3025, #6094). It is sometimes the case that the inventor, himself, champions his own product, becoming sort of a missionary on his own behalf. Schon finds, however, that at least two and possibly three roles are involved in adoption of innovations in an industry. First, there is the inventor; second, there is the champion, a man who sees the value of the invention, comes to believe in it, and decides to devote all his energies to

---

*As Barnett would have us believe, #0620.

**A situation which does not hold in agriculture or in private medical practice.

selling it to top management; and finally, there may be a third role of backer or "patron", someone in high power and high monetary position who is persuaded by the champion and allows him to become an entrepreneur by giving him risk capital.*

Although Schon to a great extent is bemoaning the inadequacy of the utilization of new ideas in industry, particularly when they are from "outside", the "champion" concept may provide an important key to effective utilization in many fields, especially education. The big factor here is motivation, the total involvement and investment of self in the innovation. This is what separates the champion from the bureaucratic errand boy concept of the conveyor, which we discussed earlier.

F.   THE DEFENDER

As discussed up to this point, the linking role has always been viewed positively; facilitating, speeding, easing, expanding the flow of knowledge. There is another side to the coin, however. We know that not all change is good, and not all resistance is misguided and perverse. On the contrary, it may be that all new ideas and changes bring with them some problems and some reasons why adoption is not advisable. It is partly for this reason that sophisticated knowledge-linking systems require barriers, checks and balances.

Previously, mention has been made of the "gatekeeper", one who stands guard over the entry points to the client system, but there is also a more active role of defender, one who champions the client against innovations.** It has been traditional to think of individuals filling such roles primarily in a negative way, as blockers, unwanted nuisances and hinderances in the path to progress. Some authors (e.g., Klein, #3691), however, see the defender as having a more benign influence on the process. The fact is that some clients and some client systems are too open to change and adoption of new ideas, too unaware of the pitfalls of innovations, too vulnerable to the dangers. The defender is always on watch for these dangers, always ready to sound the trumpet to awaken the public. In so doing, he may, of course, merely compound the linkage problem by making the client more defensive, more suspicious, and more hostile to anything new. On the other hand, he may be playing a creative role in: (a) sensitizing the consumer to important value concerns (e.g., fluoridation: the involuntary medication issue. Even groups sometimes seen as lunatic fringe may be functional in this way on some issues); (b) spurring a re-examination and re-diagnosis of needs (e.g., Upton Sinclair, on need for pure food and drug legislation); (c) mobilizing public opinion to demand more adequate products and services (e.g., Nader on automobile safety); and (d) developing a greater public sophistication and selectivity in evaluating the quality, value, relevance, and feasibility of innovations (e.g., the role that the Consumers Union is able to perform on a limited scale). Large scale attempts to institutionalize "defender"-like roles in the urban ghettoes using indigeneous recruits have been noted by Kahn, et al. (#0020) and Reiff and Reissman (#3218).

One of the most vital tasks in the utilization of knowledge is the communication of negative information. To forestall and especially to reverse an adoption process once begun may be a more important and yet more difficult

---

*Columbus must be rated as the classic case of this type.

**Contrast Schon's "product champion", #3025.

task than bringing about the acceptance of innovations. The history of smoking would appear to be the classic case of this. The first part of the twentieth century witnessed one of the most effective diffusion campaigns of all time. Hundreds of millions of men and women of all classes in many countries adopted cigarette smoking. Now in the 1960's we are struggling to utilize scientific knowledge on the hazards of smoking, with very little effect. The defender tries to prevent these situations from happening by forestalling change until such irreversible risks are thoroughly examined. Francis and Rogers (#1409, #1410) have noted that this is one important function of the county agent. Tracing adoption behavior for a non-recommended innovation which was on the market (the "grass incubator"), they found that non-adoption was correlated with agent contacts. In this case the county agent was an effective defender against pseudo-innovations being pushed by commercial conveyors.

Although the imagery is legal, the implicit assumption behind the "defender" concept is thoroughly scientific: i.e., the critical and objective <u>evaluation</u> of all practices, products, and ideas, regardless of the claims of their champions. This concept has a kinship with such scientific roles as the <u>evaluation researcher</u> (e.g., the role of social scientists in community development projects, Hendriks, #6045), Hencley's "<u>quality</u> controller" (#6032), and the "development" role of "testing and evaluating solutions and programs" included in the Clark-Hopkins paradigm of R&D roles in education (#3586). The Consumers Union and its publication <u>Consumers Reports</u> play such a role for our society at large.

Of course, this role is not always a benign influence. The defender may sometimes be <u>committed</u> to resistance to the point that he is still resisting and preventing diffusion long after the value, relevance, and safety of an innovation have been clearly demonstrated. Even the most perverse manifestations of the role may <u>still</u> be functional, however, is serving as markers of latent resistance in the client system. The skillful change strategist can steer a course around these markers, avoiding what might be icebergs of latent hostility and anti-change sentiment.

G.   KNOWLEDGE BUILDERS AS LINKERS

In discussing the "defender" role above, it was noted that the scientist plays a key defense role by evaluating and critiquing new knowledge. We should now like to turn to a more detailed consideration of the part played by scientists, scholars, engineers, and other knowledge builders in the processes of dissemination and utilization. To the extent that such people operate as linkers to the world of practice or to the consumer, they may do so half-consciously (and sometimes, we fear, half-heartedly) because they see their primary functions as builders, not transmitters.

But do these builders, in spite of themselves and their own self-images, assist in the knowledge linking process? Some good evidence suggests that they do often, depending on how they are positioned in the social system and how they are used by others.

1.   The Basic Scientist and the Scholar as Linkers

Earlier in this chapter we noted how the basic scientist who is a star, among the most respected in his field, comes to be known as an "expert" and is called upon by government policy makers and others in the world of practice. The importance of these distinguished leaders of science goes beyond this, however. The high ranking basic scientist is in a real sense the gatekeeper to the world of science. He defines what is scientific and what is not, and he is responsible for the maintenance of the standards of science and empirical "truth" (Znaniecki, #6033).

At the very least, it must be said that such a role of defender and champion of basic knowledge is indispensable. Without it, we would have no scientific knowledge at all.

Another equally important role for the basic scholar is that of supreme generalist and general educator. Partly because he is removed from the hustle and bustle of everyday dealings with everyday problems, the scholar can consider the basic implications of new knowledge and can integrate disparate findings into theories that make sense out of the whole and show us where we are going. These sweeping overviews of knowledge are disseminated to the next generation through classroom teaching and textbooks in the university, indirectly, and through curricula in the schools.*

Yet another way in which some scholars, particularly philosophers and some social scientists, may influence the utilization of knowledge is in being the definers of basic human values and directions. These are the people who help us answer questions such as: "Knowledge for what?"; "What is progress?"; "What is well-being?". There is, to be sure, some dispute about who ought to be the definers of such fundamental questions. Ayn Rand would have us leave it to the philosophers. Traditionally, it may have resided in theologians, mystics, and prophets (Znaniecki #6033). Perhaps there should be no final arbiters on such questions. Nevertheless, it would seem that someone should be helping us to think through these weightiest of all knowledge utilization questions.

Finally, there is the semi-scholarly role of "future planner" or "futurist". Knowledge utilization systems must not consider only the short run in terms of months and years. There must be some individuals devoting a large amount of their time to a more long range future a decade or a generation beyond the present. Very recent developments in education indicate a growing recognition of this planner role. Recently the Office of Research in the U.S. Office of Education commissioned a number of scholars in various institutions to prepare descriptions of society and societal needs in the 1980's. Even at the local level there may be a role for futurists, however. Kurland (#3447) believes that State Departments of Education are the ideal locus for future planners, and some California experiments now under way may show us that even at the school district level long-range planners can be functional (Miller, #6191). Thus the planner concept is now definitely with us. Where the role belongs in the structure of education and what its focus and range of concern are to be are issues yet to be resolved.

---

*It is important not to confuse this scholar role with the role of educational researcher Ironically the basic scholar may be responsible for more innovation than the applied man. For example, Carter and Silberman (#6096) note: "the moving of advanced topics down to earlier grade levels and the new curricular materials are the products of the subject-matter scholar rather than the educational researcher".   (p. 4)

2. Applied Researchers, Developers, and Engineers .

When we move from basic to applied research the implicit linkage
assumption becomes inescapable. An applied researcher is inevitably
someone with a dual orientation, looking toward "research" on the one
hand and "application" (making something practical, something useful)
on the other. The necessity of facing simultaneously in two directions
may make life difficult for the applied researcher but it does allow
him to fulfill a linking role. The importance of applied researchers
as linkers is related in part to the inadequacy of the conveyor concept.
The fact is that few conveyor-type linkers are capable of retrieving
knowledge from basic research, screening, and packaging it, and at the
same time transmitting it to the user. There is a great need for a
division of labor between the processing and the transmitting aspects of
this job. Earlier we saw this in the division of labor between the
county agent and the extension subject matter specialist. Even the
specialist, however, by his own admission, does not feel competent to
interpret research findings as such to practitioners and county agents
(Brown and Deckens, #2866). Hence, for many kinds of research dissemination, the researcher, himself, may be the only competent conveyor.

The types of activity listed by Clark and Hopkins (#3586) under
"development" give a good idea of the range of activities in which
applied research and development people are engaged: "inventing
solutions to operating problems", "engineering packages and programs
for educational use", and "testing and evaluating solutions and programs".
All these definitions imply that the R&D man translates research into
usable services and products. Through this translation-adaptation function
the R&D man does truly serve as a linker between research and practice.

Most of the literature on these applied research and development roles
comes from industry (e.g., Abrahamson, #1163; Stein, #6062; Morton, #6840),
perhaps because the concept of the R&D laboratory really originated here.*
What the literature emphasizes is the constant struggle between company
goals on the one hand and individual research and professional goals
of the scientist on the other. The fact is that industry still does not
really know how to utilize science effectively. Much of the problem may
be traced to the socialization and the self-image of the scientist. The
organization expects effective dissemination and linkage to them, not to
the scientific fraternity. The scientist, on the other hand, is reluctant
to see practical concerns as paramount or co-equal to scientific ones.
Nevertheless, we want to emphasize that the scientist who is successful
in industry is a true linker; he is creating a bridge from scientific
knowledge to use.

3. The R&D Manager

The linking function of R&D is most fully realized in the role of R&D
manager, the man who must attract and hold high calibre scientific talent
and at the same time justify the work of the laboratory in terms of improved
product quality and new marketable products. His job depends on the lab

---

*However, with the growth of the regional educational laboratories and educational
R&D centers which have U.S. Office of Education support, we can expect this picture
to change.

being useful to the company. To fill the role it is not enough for him to simply have background and training in management. He also needs to have an understanding of scientific values and methods (Krugman and Edgerton, #2573; Neff, et al., #6192).

Within education the concept of R&D management is still under-developed, but the review by Sieber, of the organization of educational research, highlights the importance of the roles of "director" of educational research bureaus and "research coordinator" within the school of education, role designations which have only emerged within the last decade (#6187).

The power of the applied research and applied research management roles, in contrast to the pure conveyor discussed earlier, resides in the potential for genuine two-way flow. The R&D manager is capable not only of translating research into practice, but also of translating practice needs and concerns into researchable problems. He provides the vital stimulation which the research world needs from the everyday world. In this connection the consistent findings by Pelz and Andrews (#6067) are worth noting: that scientists and engineers who participate in management and dissemination activities are more effective and more productive as scientists, judged by criteria of publications and ratings of scientific excellence and overall usefulness. These findings are in sharp contrast to the popular view that scientists are most effective only in cloistered and strongly protected environments.

The advantages of diversity may not apply to all types of non-research activity, however. In his research, Sieber (#6187) found that educational research directors who are assigned the role of providing services in addition to research were less productive than those who could spend full time on the research mission.

4. Engineers

Hardly distinct from other applied research and development roles is that of the "engineer", a term which has an increasingly hazy meaning within the industrial world.* The engineer is someone who has a broad scientific and technical training and who can be used by industry in a great variety of roles, e.g., as applied researcher, developer, conveyor, and consultant. Largely, what an engineer has in the way of specific skills he learns on the job. It is not clear, therefore, what some educators mean when they say we must have "educational engineers" (Anderson, #1059). In fact, we probably have them already in the form of "curriculum leaders" (Babcock, #0212), curriculum developers (e.g., PSSC, Clark, #1172), curriculum coordinators, school psychologists,** and many other existing roles in the educational establishment.

Deploring the knowledge gap between the learning researcher in experimental psychology and the training practitioner, Mackie and Christensen (#6237) urge the formation of a "corps of professionals who may be described as learning engineers". They say that these engineers should be highly trained and qualified as critics of learning research, should

---

*As noted by J.W. Forrester of M.I.T. in a recent address to the National Academy of Engineering.

**Especially as envisaged in the Chicago plan of COPED, The Cooperative Project for Educational Development.

be experts in the learning process, and should be able to relate "theoretical, laboratory, and real-world variables", to assess the meaning of research findings, and to invent applications.

Emerging roles in educational engineering are too numerous and as yet too recently conceived to be listed here in detail. The newly established regional laboratories, ERIC Centers, "Title III" Centers,* and IDEA Centers** have spawned numerous role-types which fit within "engineering" or "development" or "linking" designations. John E. Hopkins and others at Indiana University have tried to bring together a number of these in the working paper: "Exemplars of Emerging Roles" (#6188).

H. PRACTITIONERS AS LINKERS

As we have used the linking concept in this chapter, we have typically been referring to linkage to the practitioner (e.g., the physician, or the teacher). Yet we realize that the practitioner is not the user in any ultimate sense. We only wish to help the practitioner to become more effective in serving his clients, the general public, the consuming public, students, patients, the needy, or whatever. It is appropriate, therefore, to view the practitioner, himself, as a linker of knowledge to the ultimate consumers. Earlier we listed the teacher-trainer in this role, but it is equally true that anyone who provides specialized services, whether he be a plumber, a manufacturer, a physician, or a mechanic, is imparting to the public some elements from our vast collective cultural knowledge bank. To the extent that such services reflect new and scientific knowledge these practitioners are serving as linkers.

It may be important for us to look at the practitioner from this angle in assessing some of his deficiencies. There can be an overemphasis on professionalism and specialization in some occupations, which may weaken the linkage to the consumer (e.g., by making it more difficult for him to know where to go to be served for particular needs). In medicine, where these trends are particularly marked, some have advocated the revitalization of the general practitioner role, someone who would be able to interpret the needs of the patient as a whole to the various specialists (World Health Organization, #1973). In education, efforts to make the classroom "student-centered" reinforce the image of the teacher as a linker (conveyor, consultant, trainer).

An alternate solution would be to develop a special kind of linking agent for the consumer, a role already existing in Britain's Citizens Advice Bureaus (CAB's, #0020), and in the early stages of development in recent federal programs for the poor. To be effective, these generalists must be equipped not only to provide information but also to provide emotional help, referral feedback, and, at times, to undertake advocacy of the client's interests.***

Actually, these most generalized consumer-linker functions have been part of the CES county agent role repertoire for many years. Not only does the county agent provide information on specific agricultural practices, but he serves also as a youth worker, home economics expert and advisor, and organizer and coordinator of multitudinous community events (e.g., Stone's analysis, #1129).

---

*All of these sponsored by the U.S. Office of Education.

**Sponsored by the Kettering Foundation.

***See again the section on the "defender" role in this connection.

I.   THE USER AS LINKER

With the brief analysis of the generalized linkers just presented, we
have now come full circle to the question with which we began. Are linkers
necessary? Can the user serve as his own linker? Reviewing the various
functions which seem to have been necessary to bring knowledge to the user,
translating basic knowledge into useful products and practices, retrieving
and transmitting, screening, adapting, testing, and so forth, one might say
that the task of the user doing his own linking would be overwhelming. Even
so, there is merit in the argument that the user should be his own linker
and it is based on one central fact: the user is the only locus of primary
need. It is for him and only for him that the knowledge is useful.

In order to be his own linker, the user must have or acquire three things:
knowledge of resources, access to resources, and diagnosis of his own need. It
is possible to give people knowledge of resources through training, a good
"general education". It is possible, in a technologically advanced society,
to provide many people with ready access to these resources, and it is possible
for sensitive, self-aware, self-critical, and secure people to make pretty
good diagnoses of their own needs. But it is very rarely that we find people
fully equipped in all these respects. Moreover, when we speak of "underdevelopment",
at home or abroad, in the ghettoes, in the countryside, in hospitals, industries,
or schools, we mean that there is a serious deficit in all three of these areas.

It is probably true that as knowledge utilization in a particular field
improves over time, the need for intermediary roles declines. Thus we find that
the most sophisticated farmer, with long experience with the extension service,
and training at the agricultural college, does not rely on the county agents
quite as much as some other farmers do. If he wants something new, he knows that
he can pick it up from the university and from the research literature long
before the county agent is likely to come around with it (Rogers, #1549;
Havelock, #3041). But even in a very advanced system, like U.S. Agricultural
extension, this pattern is the exception, not the rule. Hence the general
conclusion must be stated emphatically: For the forseeable future all fields
of knowledge will require the installation and support of a variety of linking
roles if effective utilization is to be realized.

Summary of Discussion on Linking Role Types

In offering this typology of linking roles we have tried to cover all the
important functions which, together, are needed to establish and maintain linkage
between knowledge sources and resources on the one hand, and users, consumers, and
clients on the other. We say "together" because we believe that they should be
seen together, forming among themselves an interlocking chain. Figure 7.3 tries to
illustrate this story.

[Insert Figure 7.3 here]

On one side of this figure we have a vaguely defined network of roles which could
be described as the "resource system", including the knowledge builder, the experts,
and the producers. Many of the roles within this system are capable of several kinds
of output to several kinds of audiences. Experts are influential largely through
their contact with community leaders, including the top layers of government. Scholars
and basic researchers, of whom the experts are essentially a sub-class, exert their
influence largely through applied research and development but also influence the

FIGURE 7.3

Relationships Among Linking Roles

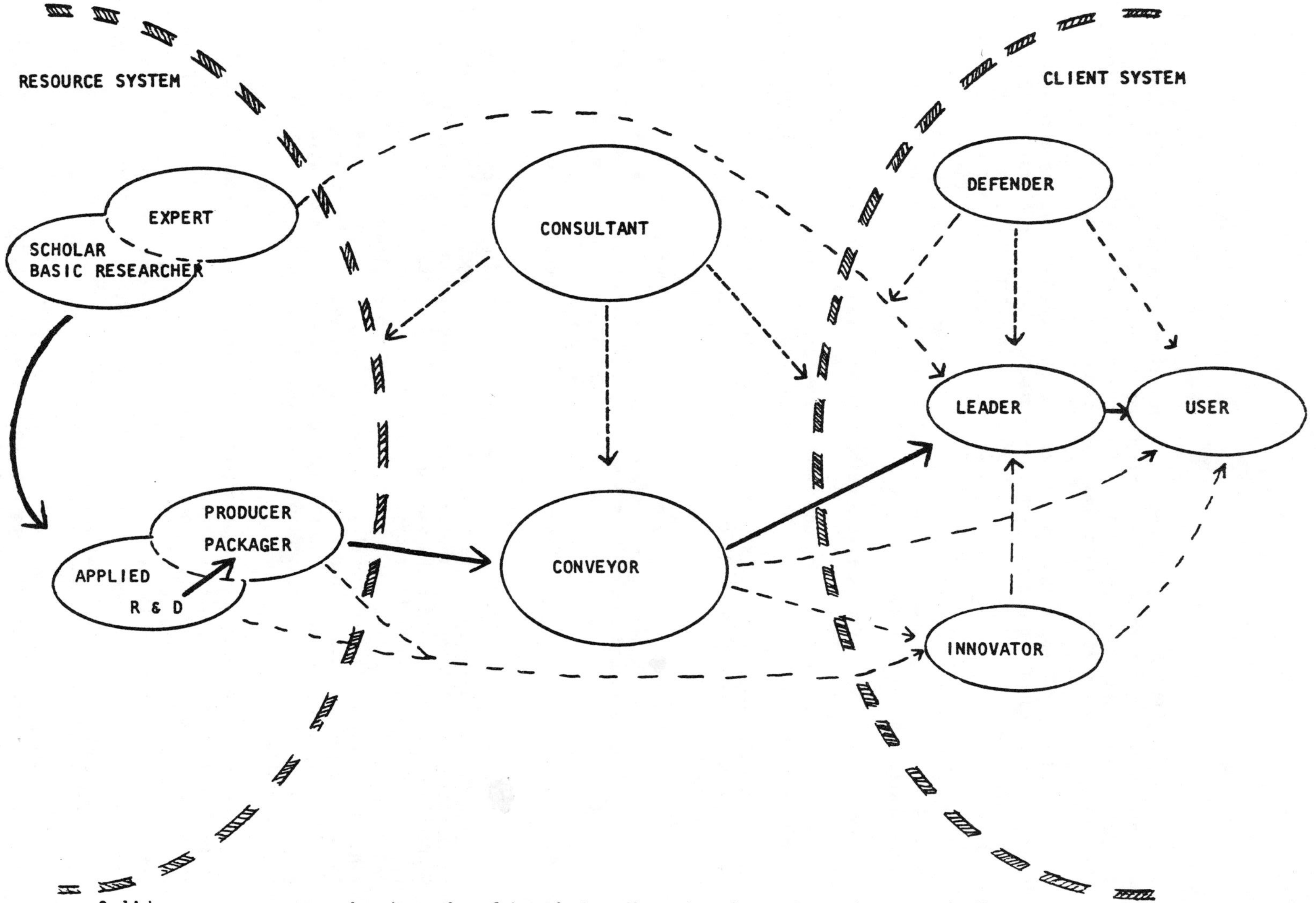

Solid arrows suggest main channels of knowledge dissemination. Dotted arrows indicate subsidiary or secondary channels.

general public (all consumers) through their guardianship of general education and academic curricula, and through their participation in the training of the next generation of practitioners and users. They may also influence the public through intermediary conveyor roles such as the science reporter.

Applied R&D influences the user either through conveyors, such as extension specialists and county agents, and perhaps now also through the regional laboratories in education, or, more commonly, through producers (manufacturers, publishers). The producers in turn rely on such conveyors as advertisers, salesmen and retailers to move their products on to the consumer. Since much of applied R&D takes place in the professional schools attached to the university, by people who wear two hats, researcher and trainer, the trainer-linker also needs to be seen as an important dissemination channel for applied R&D.

On the other side of this figure we have another vaguely defined region which has been called the "client system". It includes first of all the "user". He could be the ultimate consumer, the patient in medicine, or the student in education, but for the most part within this presentation he is seen as the individual practitioner, the practicing physician, the teacher. Just who the "user" is, of course, depends on the type of knowledge conveyed. If the knowledge to be disseminated and utilized is on educational administration, then the typical superintendent and school principal are the "users", and so forth.

Relating to the user in a very direct way is the "leader", whether he be the officially designated leader or the informal opinion leader. For the most part, the majority of users depend on the leaders of their reference groups for decision making on adoption of innovations. Users and leaders depend to some extent on "defenders" to screen new knowledge for them and to alert them to hidden dangers, and they may also depend on "innovators" to advance-scout and pre-test new ideas, to be their guinea pigs.

Between the resource and client systems we have positioned the conveyor, the consultant, and the trainer. The conveyor receives knowledge in various degrees of packaging from all parts of the resource system and transmits it directly to leaders and innovators within the user group. He is aided by the consultant, who prepares the client system for acceptance of new ideas, helping to diagnose the needs and giving help in adapting new ideas to local conditions. The consultant can also aid the conveyor by advance scouting, indicating the most favorable times, places, and persons for introducing innovations to the client system. The trainer transmits new ideas, skills, and innovations through education, especially education of the next generation of practitioners, but also through retraining and in-service training of past generations.

Finally, it was also noted that effective linking agents, in reality, are able to perform in several ways, as conveyors, consultants, defenders, and leader-coordinators for the client system. In particular, we find this multiple role capability in the county agent of the agricultural extension service. However, questions about the optimum division of labor in the linking process and the methods by which several linking roles can be coordinated will be put off until the next section.

II. THE LINKING ROLE IN ITS INSTITUTIONAL CONTEXT

It is probably not very meaningful to discuss linking roles outside the institutional - organizational context in which they are embedded. In the preceding section we had occasion at several points to touch on institutional questions, particularly in the discussion of leadership, and wherever mention was made of in-stalling, coordinating, and combining roles and building lasting interrelationships among them. We also touched on institutional issues when we spoke of where roles come from: the "Cooperative Extension Service", the "Office of Education", the "industrial corporation", the "university", and so forth. Indeed, institutional factors are ubiquitous in any analysis of the utilization process. In this section we will try to nail down some of these issues as they pertain to linking roles.

There are three institutional questions of highest relevance to the topic of linking agent: first, what sort of institutional barriers, both in the resource system and in the client system, most frequently affect knowledge dissemination and utilization? Second, what kind of institutions are most effective for fathering (supporting, controlling) linking roles? And third, what kinds of institutions serve as linkers?

A. INSTITUTIONALIZATION IN RESOURCE AND CLIENT SYSTEMS: ITS EFFECTS ON KNOWLEDGE LINKING

In Figure 7.3 the resource and client system were presented as two large and vaguely defined regions between which knowledge must pass. We now ask: how are these regions defined and how do these definitions affect knowledge flow? Institutions are more or less permanent structures through which society assures the performance of certain functions. Thus the existance of institutions should be the proof of society's good intentions with respect to knowledge utilization. If knowledge utilization is seen as an important function, there will be institutions which directly and indirectly facilitate it.

1. Institutional Barriers in the Resource System ✓

When we look at existing institutional structures in our society the vista is not too encouraging in this regard. The primary institutional form in which the resource system is realized is the university. The university is the focal center of all the expert resources, stored cultural heritage, scientific knowledge, and scientific knowledge-building capacity of the of the entire culture. Yet, as it is typically structured, access to the university and utilization of university resources by non-academic people is strictly circumscribed. The primary repository of all the expertise of universities is the faculty, a very tight reference group with the highest standards of membership (most advanced degree offered in the specialty and proven expertise through publication and recognition). Within the faculty, knowledge may flow relatively freely, but informally. Faculty members view themselves as autonomous and guard their "academic freedom" vigilantly. As a result, any attempts to coordinate their efforts or systematize their communication patterns are resisted with vigor.

The typical faculty member probably does not like to think of himself as a linker and probably has the image of the linker which Halpin describes (see again the discussion of "conveyor"). There are, however, two thoroughly legitimate ways for academic faculty members to dispense knowledge: first, through the courses taught in the academic curriculum (i.e., as trainers) and second, through publications and papers addressed primarily to colleagues. Even in teaching, however, favored treatment is generally accorded students who are concentrators, especially honor concentrators, and graduate students, since these are potential recruits into the academic world, hence future colleagues.

Linkage of a sort does occur through the establishment of professional schools as a part of the university establishment. Here too, however, faculties operate on very much the same norms, addressing their primary efforts to communicating among colleagues and to training neophytes. Extension and continuing education are relegated to secondary status if they are handled at all. Carey's account of the development of evening colleges within this university illustrates the marginal status accorded extension activities by all other university divisions ((#3602).

Ironically, in spite of its mimicry of basic academic norms, the professional school remains as a marginal component of the university in the eyes of many academicians. Faculty members recruited from academic departments to professional schools are treated as lepers by former colleagues even when they join the established and prestigious faculties of medicine. The fact is that the typical university is pervaded by an attitude which denigrates practice and practical concerns. On the one hand, this attitude makes the special role of linker all the more vital since the resource persons themselves lack the motivation and cannot be relied upon for effective linkages. On the other hand, the attitude makes it all the more difficult for the linker to link effectively to these expert resources. Even such models of effective linkage as agriculture's extension subject matter specialists are likely to be accepted as only marginal members of the agricultural college. Richert notes that in spite of an official pattern of trifunctional units, including resident instruction, research, and extension, the extension specialists (in home economics) were a part of this team in only one third of the nation's fifty land grant colleges (#3835).

2.   The Client System: Two Patterns: Colleaguial and Bureaucratic

Turning now from the resource system to the client system, two principal institutional patterns emerge. The first, not unlike the university in some respects, is the "profession", a high status group of independent operators bound together in a reference group with exceedingly tough membership prerequisites. Specifically, this pattern is exemplified by the legal and medical fraternities. But there are major differences between these groups and the university: first, they are dispersed throughout the community and are likely to have extensive contacts with a great variety of clients. Second, they are not primarily oriented to sharing knowledge with colleagues or to building knowledge as such. Thirdly, they are primarily oriented to providing service and to being practical. There is, therefore, motivation to receive knowledge and a capability of understanding it in relatively complex unpackaged forms.

In spite of those factors which would make them ready targets for new knowledge, lawyers and physicians in private practice are not linked to the university-based expert resource system to any extent. Apart from the drug detail man, the practicing physician has no ready access to such expert sources through any medical extension service. For lawyers, the lack of linkage may be partly a problem of orientation. The law is seen as based on tradition and statute rather than on science, so that the needs of lawyers are most likely to be perceived in terms of ready access to court cases and laws. To some extent lawyers are adequately serviced by publication of all court cases and continuously updated legal encyclopedias to which all lawyers have ready access. It seems doubtful, however, that these devices substitute for a fully developed network of legal extension specialists.

When we compare these more exalted professions with the farmer, it appears that the latter is well served, indeed. In spite of barriers and hurdles represented by geographical dispersal, relatively low educational background and scientific competence, and the vast cultural separation from the academic world, the farmer has access to and uses a great number of innovations directly based on scientific knowledge. He is able to do this largely because of a system of linking roles, both governmentally and commercially supported, designed to serve him.

But practice in the client system is also institutionalized in another way, in bureaucracies, and it is probable that the problems and opportunities for linkage under these circumstances are quite different. Bureaucracies, whether we are talking about businesses, schools, or hospitals, are characterized by a formalization of division of labor, leadership, and interdependence, which are absent in the organization of the professions discussed above and only vaguely present in the university. The presence of any of these three attributes, (1) specialization; (2) leadership, and (3) coordination, should, in theory, facilitate linkage:

(1) With specialization there should be an increase in competence within the specialty, a better definition of the requirements of the role and its resource needs, and an easier task of retrieval from a more limited knowledge store.

(2) Where effective leadership exists, as noted earlier, it is possible to influence more people more successfully. An effective leader in a well-organized system is related to all other members through overlapping group memberships* which allow influence to be shared and to flow downward and upward easily. If the leader in such a system is made aware of new and useful knowledge, he can become an inside change agent or catalyst.**

(3) Influence through leadership may be relatively ineffective, however, if the organization is poorly coordinated. Such lack of coordination could be reflected in mutual distrust and hostility between hierarchical levels or across specialities and among colleagues. A major aspect of organization health is the ability to cooperate and to keep lines of communication open.

Bureaucratization of the client system does not necessarily make dissemination of new knowledge more difficult. On the contrary, if the client system bureaucracy is in a healthy state with respect to the three dimensions listed above, then dissemination and utilization will be far more rapid and effective than it ever could be under the colleaguial pattern.

B. EFFECTIVE INSTITUTIONAL FATHERS FOR LINKING ROLES

Having considered the types of institutions with which linkers have to cope, we can now turn to consider the types of organizations in which they should be

---

*Well described by Likert, #5202.

**Schein and Bennis, #6077, note the success of this model exemplified in the organizational effectiveness of a clothing manufacturing concern headed by a social psychologist in close contact with outside social action researchers.

based: first, the general type of base or parent organization in which they should be embedded, and then in Section C, below, the type of sub-unit or "linking institution" in which they can be organized will be discussed.

Five primary types of institutional base should be noted: university, government, commercial, practice, and independent. Let us look briefly at each in turn.

1. The University

The university, as discussed earlier, is not the most hospitable home for the linker, particularly if he is unable to show many credentials to back up his claim to expertise. The weakness of extension services run by universities seems to attest to the unwillingness of the university to indulge in the kind of linkage to practitioners and consumers which comes under the loathed heading of "service".

There are some kinds of linkage which do typically come under the university wing, however. One of these roles is that of the high level expert. He has the credentials and his status within the university is secure enough that he need not be very concerned about engaging in marginal activities. The other role is that of the applied researcher attached to university centers and professional schools. But many questions need to be raised about the university's role in knowledge utilization. Is the university the proper locus for the kind of applied research which is useful to practice and disseminable to practice? Certainly in agriculture this does seem to work. In technology and medicine it is more difficult to say. In education, even with the recently established R&D centers, the production of useful knowledge seems to be a pitiful trickle in proportion to the investment.

Part of the dilemma centers on the difficulty of assessing the utility of knowledge generated within the university: there is no accounting, no assessment of what is done in terms of value to society, nor is the research administrator in the university under any pressure in this regard. The orientation is inward toward the university and to evaluation by academic colleagues. Productivity is measured in terms of number of articles in "prestige" journals, not in terms of the number of people helped or number of people informed. (See again Mackie and Christensen, #6237, on learning theory research.)

2. Government

Knowledge linkage is a serious problem and a massive problem. Effective retrieval alone, disregarding dissemination, is becoming a problem with which individual universities and companies can no longer cope. Add to this the dissemination needs, including packaging, conveyor and consultant services, and effective opinion leadership, and we are then talking about a multi-billion dollar enterprise involving the coordination efforts of tens of thousands of skilled professionals. This is what is represented to a degree in the Cooperative Extension Service. We have no equivalent in any other field.

It is difficult to envisage a coordinated system of linkage without heavy government involvement either by itself, or in partnership with the university and private profit and non-profit organizations.

7-27

At the present time the government is dabbling in the extension-knowledge linking business in technology, medicine, and education, with rather mixed results. The technology information program undertaken by the National Aeronautics and Space Administration has been very well financed and elegantly organized, but so far, evaluation studies* indicate the instances of genuine knowledge transfer resulting from this system are negligible. In medicine, the government has been less ambitious so far but the funds expended on such projects as the National Library of Medicine's automated information retrieval system (MEDLARS) have not been clearly justified.**

In education there has been considerable activity, particularly in institution building, in the last three or four years. First came the R&D centers established with firm university bases, and perhaps suffering in effectiveness as linkers for that reason. Then came the ERIC centers, university-based and coordinated at the federal level, but so far equipped primarily to service the information needs only of researchers. Finally, we now have the Title III centers at the school system level and the regional laboratories originally created as semi-autonomous research, training, and service centers to serve groups of states on a regional basis. In spite of this flowering of institutional structures and substructures, and in spite of planning and funding from one source, there is no explicit relationship among these various units. This would appear to be in contrast to the system in agriculture.

There may never be a day of reckoning for this government supported non-system for development and diffusion in education, especially when we are still struggling for satisfactory criteria for success in this area. Nevertheless, some comments are in order on how it will affect the evolution of linking roles. First of all, it doesn't seem possible in light of our experience in agriculture and elsewhere that linking roles could be established in education without heavy federal support. David Clark's comment that "the total cost of such an educational extension service would not be great" (#6085, p. 117) would appear to be questionable. The total cost of the CES and the subsidies to the associated land grant colleges over the last 100 years would be hard to compute in today's dollars, but it is undoubtedly on the order of several billions.

Secondly, it would seem advisable for the government to involve itself directly as well as indirectly in the diffusion process. County agents and extension specialists are government employees. While this is disadvantageous in some respects, it does provide a unique home base and an independence from university and commercial requirements. The farmer looks on the county agent as a reasonably objective information source. The same cannot be said for the detail man, the publisher, or the seed salesman.

One of the problems in installing government employees as linkage agents is the tendency for them to be used as and seen as control agents or policemen. Apparently the county agent has managed to avoid this image and

*Denver Research Institute, #6111; Wright, #6199; Arthur D. Little, Inc., #6200.

**Atwood notes that it is far too expensive and time consuming for even small scale research use. For very large research projects it appears to be useful. Apparently, the individual practitioner is not yet viewed as a possible user (#2342).

It is possible for education's linkers to move away from such an image also, as this observation by Featherstone on some reforms in the British primary schools indicates:

"Another element in the reform was a different emphasis in the work of the HMI's (government inspectors). As long as the inspectors acted as educational policemen, making the schools toe the mark, their effect over the years was to dampen inno- vation. But as their role took on more and more of an advisory character, they became important agents for disseminating new ideas. There is a clear moral here: external rules enforced from without not only have little positive effect on schools, but they tend to make their practices rigidify through fear. Where government and local inspectors have ceased inspecting and taken up advising, the results have been excellent. Some of the lively authorities, such as Leicestershire, set up district advisory offices, with no administrative responsibilities except to spread ideas and train teachers in new methods." (#6388)

Thirdly, the government should be specific in defining the roles it wishes to establish. This should be a matter of public policy. Thus far the varolus roles generated by different centers have been richly innovative but they hardly give a chance for the development of a professional identity and esprit de corps, which are essential to put a new role on a solid footing. Having allowed these various roles to flourish for a time, the government should decide what specific linking role or roles are best and devote its resources to the development of such roles, to the exclusion of others.

3. Commercial

Having said that government involvement is essential, we would now add that commerical involvement is probably essential also. Nowhere can one gain a greater appreciation for the mixed economy than through the study of processes of dissemination and utilization. In agriculture, the county agent, the farm magazines, commercial agents, and other farmers all seem to play complimentary and important roles in the ultimate adoption of new ideas, products, and practices.*

Both the strengths and the weaknesses of the commercially based linker are related to his special motivation. On the positive side, unlike other linkers he has a real stake, a direct survival stake, in adoption. While this may infuse him with greater zeal it also stands in his way because the client generally does not give him high credibility for this reason. Beal and Rogers, for example, found that farmers were generally suspicious of the motives of the commercial agent, and even innovators did not use him as a short cut to new ideas (#1351). The dangers of doing so are illustrated in the story of the grass-incubator, a useless "innovation" pushed by some dealers. Farmers who were in good touch with the county extension service as well as commercial agents were not taken in (Francis and Rogers, #1409; Francis, #1410). Hence they successively utilized the more truly scientific counter-knowledge of the CES. In contrast, adopters of the incubator were

---

*Abell, #3886, cites his own work and 13 other works to illustrate this fact. Research by Lionberger, #2690, and Wilkening, #5385, testify to the same point.

found to be farmers who had great faith in the salesmen, relying on them for information which could have easily come from other sources.

When other expert sources are easily available within one's working environment the commercial agent is probably least influential. Burkholder, for example, found that the drug detail man's offerings were scorned and ignored by physicians working within the context of a large teaching hospital (#0671).

Increasingly in recent years the government has taken to contracting out much of the research and development work that it needed for space and military programs.* This has been used in part to circumvent bureaucratic roadblocks such as fixed salary schedules. There are some signs that in education, too, the government is beginning to move in this direction. There is no question that private enterprise should be heavily involved in diffusion to our educational system. It would appear from the above findings that the government would be ill-advised to leave the field entirely, however.

4.   Practice Institutions as Bases for Linkers

Should the linking agent be especially supported by the individual hospital, school system or business organization? Such a proposition is attractive in some respects and is actively endorsed by a number of authors. Anderson (#1059) argues that his "educational engineer" must be hired by and be responsible to the local school system. The "Research Implementation Teams" now being developed by Research for Better Schools, Inc. (a regional lab) are founded on the same philosophy (#6065).

The advantages of such an arrangement would appear to be related primarily to the concept of "insideness". The linker is right there at the locus of need. He understands the client system in all its uniqueness.

On the other hand, there are many tough problems associated with this arrangement. One is recruitment; how do we attract people with the requisite skills to work on such a local and presumably lowly level? Another is access to resources: from such a base how does the linker keep himself in touch with new developments? How does he stay linked to the resource system, itself? Finally, how does he gain acceptance in the local system, itself? We cannot assume that, having a local practice base, the linker will be seen as a legitimate source. We cannot create instant opinion leadership, and we cannot prevent this inside linker from being viewed sometimes as an interloper, a policeman, or a busybody.

5.   Independent Linkers

There are probably innumerable bona fide knowledge linkers in our society who do not go under any official title as linkers. The informal role of opinion leader is a case in point.

Although there is a place for independent and free lance linkers, there are major limitations. First of all, they cannot serve as linkers on a full time basis. Secondly, their efforts are likely to be sporadic and their

---

*See Marx, #5231, and Lindvelt, #2836, for analysis of this trend.

influence haphazard. Thirdly, they cannot be relied upon to provide
training, special skills, and equipment and supplies which are often the
necessary accompaniments of innovations.

Nevertheless, there are some outstanding cases in which free lancers
have played a major role. B.R. Clark (#1172) notes a pattern of "private
committees serving as connectors between public authorities notably between
federal agencies, and local authorities in the curriculum reform movement".
He goes on to cite the Physical Science Study Committee as an example.

As inventors of new products and practices free lancers play a surprisingly important part even in technical areas (Jewkes, et al., #0941;
Nader, #6094). In one study (#0941) it was found that 33 of 61 inventions,
when traced to their source, turned out to originate with independents.
When it comes to diffusion, however, it seems doubtful that individuals
working alone without legitimation and without financial and organizational
support can play a major role.

To summarize this discussion, there appear to be four principal
institutional bases for the linker: university, government, commercial,
and practice. University and practice bases may be facilitative in gaining
entry to the resource system and the practice system respectively but there
is little evidence that outsiders are less effective or less influential
than marginal insiders. Both government and commercial linkers were seen
as operating very effectively from the outside and in complementary ways.
A well functioning knowledge diffusion and utilization network includes
government and commercial channels. However, when one is used without the
other, distortions and imbalances which affect the process adversely are
likely to result.

C.   LINKING INSTITUTIONS

From the broader question of institutional parentage or base we now move
more specifically to a consideration of the types of institutions which could
in themselves be called "linking institutions". Throughout this chapter the
linker has been viewed as an individual person and when we have talked of
several linking functions we have seen them as roles which acted in complementary
ways to help build a knowledge linking chain or system. (See again Figure 7.3.)
We also noted how these ideal role types defined by function could be combined
in one actual linker, the county agent being a prime example of this. At this
point, however, it should be recognized that a number of individuals serving
complementary linking functions can combine organizationally to serve as one
unit. Thus the extension subject matter specialist and the county agent both
belong to one institution, the Cooperative Extension Service, which as a whole
is the knowledge linker between the university and the farm family.

Overriding other aspects of a typology of institutions is the distinction
between permanent and temporary organizational units.* Institutions of the
permanent type include such entities as "centers","institutions", "laboratories",
"companies", and "associations", while those of the temporary type include such

---

*This distinction is most fully developed and utilized by Miles, #1189.

entities as "projects", "programs", "committees", "courses", "conferences", and "conventions". The effective installation and manipulation of both these types of institutions plays a major part in insuring the viability and the effectiveness of the individual linking agent.

1. Permanent Linking Institutions

Permanent linking institutions provide three important possibilities for the individual linker: (1) security, (2) identity, and (3) coordination. Security means a home base and a degree of independence from both the practice world and the university research world demands and dependencies. These seem to be basics of survival for any role in a social system. A chronic problem is the perception of the linker as an adjunct, not a necessary part of either research or practice. This means that inclusion of linkers in these other institutional homes would perpetuate insecurity.

Identity comes from the awareness by the linker, himself, and by those with whom he deals that he is somebody; somebody who does something not only valuable but clearly distinguishable from what other people do. In some degree identity is something each individual has to achieve by himself through his own labors, but in face-to-face interactions with others, role holders depend heavily upon the generalized impression or "image" that their own role has attained. This is an especially severe problem when we are attempting to introduce new roles and when we are attempting to introduce roles which overlap and interconnect with well established existing roles such as "researchers" and "practitioners". How the linker is judged and how well he is welcomed will depend greatly on the image of the organization of which he is seen to be a part.

Coordination serves what might be called the rational function of organizations: through division of labor to accomplish as a group what the individual alone cannot accomplish. In terms of linking roles, coordination means the capacity to fuse the many functions discussed earlier in this chapter while allowing individuals to specialize in providing those functions with which they are most skilled. Some can concentrate on the task of retrieval of knowledge from research, some on translating and packaging this knowledge, some on conveying it to clients. Still others can specialize in consultation, helping clients diagnose needs, helping them adapt, building openness, providing reinforcement and so forth. If all these functions had to be performed by one person, or through one role, they probably could not be done. Certainly, they could not be done well.

Unfortunately, coordination works better in theory than in practice. As noted earlier in the discussion of leadership in the R&D laboratory, there is a constant tug of war between independent basic research and application concerns, between science and management within the industrial laboratory. Conflicts of the same order might well arise in linking institutions, let us say between those who believe the conveyor role is paramount and those who believe the consultant role is paramount. In settings where there are no external pressures to produce, for example in university applied research centers in contrast to industrial R&D centers, the manager is likely to escape from such conflicts by letting each man or each sub-group go his own way. It would be unfortunate if the directors of linking institutions took this completely laissez faire attitude. Coordination is difficult to achieve but it is a prize worth the struggle. When a manager evades his responsibility in this area his organization will fall far short of its potential.

2. Temporary Systems

With the advantages of the permanent institution's security, identity, and coordination go corresponding disadvantages of isolation, self-satisfaction, and rigidity. These would be fatal shortcomings for any organization trying to be a linker. It is largely through a sub-organization into temporary systems that linking institutions avoid these pitfalls and maintain their vitality.

The actual work of linkage is not a continuous routine process. It simply doesn't work that way. Even the conveyor is not a conveyor belt. The work of a county agent, for example, is structured around programs, special projects, campaigns, etc. (Stone, #1129; Penders, #6042), as is the work of the Extension Subject Matter Specialist (Brown, #2866), and as is the work of the cross-cultural development worker (Schmitt, #0816; Holmberg, #2030). It is important for the motivation of the linker to see his work in time-limited segments which follow a meaningful sequence from initiation to completion. These time-limited sequences or projects are one form of temporary system.

The temporary system is also important in being the vehicle through which interaction and exchange with clients and researchers is carried on. The training course, the conference, and the convention are traditional types of temporary systems in which knowledge linkage of a sort takes place. Most recently, however, many new models of temporary systems for linking to new knowledge are taking shape. Human relations training laboratories (Bradford, et al., #6196), "grid" management training programs (Blake and Mouton, #6198), organizational survey and survey feedback projects (Mann and Neff, #3913), traveling seminars (Richland, #3698), and collaborative action-inquiry projects (Thelen, #3692), represent a few of the unique temporary systems which have evolved in the last decade to bring the linking agent (often called "trainer", "consultant", or "change agent") together with the client in a meaningful sequence of steps designed to help the client by making him more expert, more open to new ideas, more adaptive, and so forth.

Another type of temporary system, this time bringing researchers (at least social researchers) more into the picture, is the action research project. Here the program or change activity is experimental and the researcher's involvement, at least initially, is restricted to evaluation and creating instruments and a design which allow for evaluation. As a method for linking researchers to practice this model of action research has some problems, however. Relations between the research and action roles can be stormy and there is always resistance on the part of the researcher to "getting his hands dirty" with application and utilization activities. Schmuck's paper (#6229) sheds considerable light on various aspects of this barrier problem between social scientists and practitioners in education.

It has been suggested by Jacobson (himself citing Palmer Johnson) that very large scale experimentation in education, whatever its value scientifically, is an effective means of disseminating new knowledge. The more people who take part and the more disciplines and different knowledge sources they represent, the better the chance for cross-fertilization and new learnings by all and the better the chances of publicity and hence diffusion to non-participants (Jacobson, #6086). The same type of research is criticized by Blackwell (#1218), who believes that enforced "togetherness" restricts productivity and creativity, reducing everything to the lowest common denominator. Massive inter-university inter-disciplinary research action projects such as the Cooperative Project for Educational Development (COPED), when they are evaluated, should answer such questions for us.

There are other temporary systems which do involve the researcher directly in a collaborative knowledge retrieval and application activity with linkers and practitioners. At the highest level we have seen this in the Physical Science Study Committee.* There is yet another model, however, which seeks to involve not only researchers and linkers, but also policy makers, administrators and practitioners ("direct workers") in a sequential activity of problem diagnosis, research retrieval, derivation of implications and future action planning. This is the "derivation conference" now being pioneered by Jung and Lippitt (#6197).

It has not been our intent to dwell on these various temporary institutional forms in any great depth, but this brief summary should give an indication of the many tools which the linker potentially has at his disposal. A permanent linking institution should have a capability of generating a great variety of temporary systems to suit specific occasions, clients, and topics, for it is largely through the overlapping group memberships and collaborative activities of these temporary systems that linkage between resources and user can be achieved. Figure 7.4 is intended to be a schematic representation of this pattern of inter-institutional linkage.

[Insert Figure 7.4 here]

III. ENDEMIC PROBLEMS IN LINKING ROLES: A SUMMARY

Throughout this chapter, we have seen certain issues which seem to keep coming up again and again, problematic aspects in the linker role which run as themes through the discussion of function, coordination, institutional context and so forth. These problems were suggested in Table 7.2 where a comparison of conveyor and consultant linkers was presented, but they can probably be summarized under just two headings: overload and marginality.

A. OVERLOAD

The linker's activities can be grouped into three kinds of processes: getting information (input), processing information (thruput), and distributing information to others (output). In each of these processes the linker may have too much to do. He may have too much information to handle, too many people to get it from, too many steps to put it through, and too many people to give it to. In Table 7.3, the various problems related to overload are summarized.

[Insert Table 7.3 here]

Table 7.3 shows us the complexity and magnitude of the job of the linker. It highlights the need for a drastic division of labor and a clear definition of sub-function which can only be accomplished through institutionalization. It also highlights the need for the linker to focus his activities in projects, time-limited and objective-limited sequences.

---

*It was perhaps the most successful knowledge utilization project of all times in education, although this could not all be attributed to its structure. Within five years, 50% of the schools in the U.S. had adopted it, an extraordinary record (Clark, #1172).

FIGURE 7.4   Linking Institutions: Separateness and Togetherness

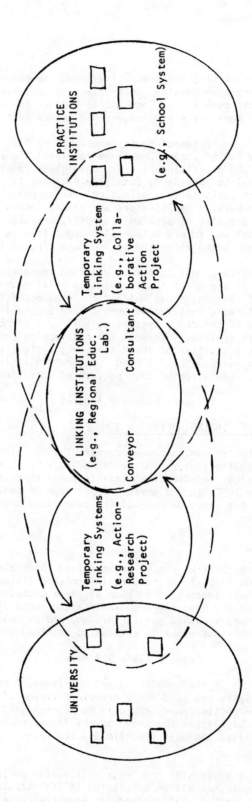

TABLE 7.3   Overload Problems for the Linker

	Number	Complexity	Difficulty
Input	Information has to be assembled from too many sources	Sources are highly technical, requiring high degrees of scientific competence.	Information is inaccessible.
Through-put	Too many pieces of information need to be assembled.	Information has to be taken from a high-ly technical form to a highly simplified and packaged form.	The forms into which the know-ledge must be assembled require a great expenditure of effort (e.g., construction of a complete training course).
Output	Information has to be distributed to too many people.	Information which is complex and difficult to understand must be communicated to the user.	Users are very hard to reach and to influence.

With all these potential overload problems and a job to be done, one might ask: how can it be done, and how is it done now? The answer is: "not too well!" When we can't do something right we muddle through; we cut corners; and we do "something" even if the something doesn't work, isn't useful, even if it raises expectations which can't be met or casts the client adrift.

What compounds the problem is our human tendencies: (a) to avoid defeats and failures by thinking of them as victories; (b) to disguise the inadequacies of our knowledge by saying that there is nothing more out there worth knowing, and (c) to hide the inadequacy of our range of skills by saying that what we know how to do is the only important thing which needs to be done.

These human tendencies to hide or paper over limitations have serious effects in producing divisiveness between linkers with different skill mixes and knowledge bases. The learning people disparage the human relations trainers, who disparage the survey researchers and so forth. Thus, people who should be getting together go separate ways, forming their own competing models of "the" change process and their own institutions and programs for linking. The practitioner's reaction is often the justified cry of "a plague on all your houses".

B. MARGINALITY

The second problem theme which seems to be present whenever we discuss knowledge linking roles is "marginality". Marginality may well be inherent in the linking role for strategic reasons. The linker is necessarily and by definition an in-betweener. He takes from the research world but he is not clearly a part of that world, and he gives to the practice world while not being clearly a part of that world either. He can attain partial membership in either the practice or research world by overlapping memberships while not achieving full membership; these associations only partly legitimate his presence.

This marginality is not entirely in the nature of things, however. The linker may be fortunate in belonging to an independent linking institution with a long and distinguished record and a good image. If he is, his structural marginality, his outsideness, will be more an asset than a hindrance.

Another element which often causes the marginality is recency. Any role is marginal when it is first created and developed. Thus in education where the knowledge linking role is only now emerging we may expect more difficulties related to marginality than we find, let us say, in agriculture where the county agent is so well established. As we all know, anyone who has a new job is marginal to the organization, and if the job itself is newly created it is just that much more of a problem. It is compounded by suspicion by various persons and groups who feel infringed upon (role-conflict) and others who are in the "same" roles as we are but seem to be behaving very differently (role-consensus).*

*For a more adequate definition and discussion of the problem of marginality in organizations and how it affects the role holder see Kahn et al., #3072. The classic study in role analysis is, of course, that of Gross, et al., of the school superintendant, #5169. Additional empirical studies of that calibre and that depth are now needed to evaluate the role of knowledge linker.

These are some of the causes of marginality,* but what about its effects?
Here we must confront the basic fact of viability. Marginality of the role
means stress for the role holder. Put this together with the stress which
results from overload and we have a completely untenable position. Nobody will
get in it and nobody will stay in it. The social engineers who are designing
linking roles will have to find ways to reduce either marginality or its ill
effects.

IV. IMPLICATIONS FOR EDUCATION

We come at last to the implications of this analysis for education and for those
who would foster the development of linking roles in education. Our prescription
revolves primarily around solutions to the two big problem themes: overload and
marginality. Looking at this from the point of view of planning and administration,
there are four things that have to be done to build a functioning system of knowledge
linkers: (1) we need to build an institution which includes and supports the required
roles; (2) we need to recruit candidates to serve in these roles; (3) we need to
train these recruits to fill the roles; and finally (4) we need to supply them with
the equipment necessary to help them do a good job. We will discuss these four
requirements under the headings: installation, recruitment, training, and equipping.

A. INSTALLATION

We need to build a secure base for the linker, a permanent institution which
includes a mix of interdependent complementary linking roles, especially those
described earlier under "conveyor" and "consultant". We must make certian that
these roles are not only included but are coordinated by a director who appreciates
the need and importance of each role and is motivated to work hard at bringing
them together.

This linking institution could be based in a university or a school system
but neither of these alternatives is entirely satisfactory. An independent base
not identified with either the research world or the practice world is probably
preferable. In any case the institution will be expensive to operate if it is
to be an effective linker and will, therefore, require federal support either
directly or indirectly through contracts and grants to universities, school
systems, and commercial firms. The part played by the federal government should
not end with financing, however. There is a more definitive, directive, and
coordinative function which the government should not avoid. Eventually, in the
not too distant future, the government should come up with an overall plan for
an educational extension service which includes well-defined linking roles at
various levels. Furthermore, it should not shy away from coordination of state
and regional services to reduce redundancy of effort and to insure that knowledge
packages and programs developed in one area are effectively diffused throughout
the national extension system.**

---

*In a previous paper, Havelock (#3041) suggested that transiency was also a problem,
i.e., the possibility that one's role would become obsolete as the user sophistication approached that of the linker. Further review of the literature does not
yield any information to indicate that this by-passing phenomenon is a real problem.
There always seems to be plenty of useful work for the linker still to do, even after
his most sophisticated clients have learned to do without him.

**Duplication of effort is probably one of the most wasteful aspects of our national
effort in Agriculture, divided as it is into 50 separate research-development-
diffusion systems.

B. RECRUITING

The question of how we can fill the need for a large number of linking agents in the next decade is of concern to many educators (Clark & Hopkins, #6241) but we feel that there are ways of filling this gap. In part, we are inclined to go along with Pellegrin's observation (#6030) that the roles get filled if the money is there, but in any case there are still many manpower resources which could be tapped for this role if it were adequately institutionalized. First of all, it should be an attractive role for the young teacher or teacher-in-training who wants a little more challenge and variety than he is likely to get in a routine teaching assignment. Secondly, there is the large reserve of female talent in this country which is becoming partially liberated from the housewife role. Finally, we should not forget the retired teacher who might be an exceptionally valuable change agent in working with older and more experienced client teachers.

If the need is for people with top-flight research backgrounds and credentials, then the recruitment picture is dim if not hopeless. However, the need for highly educated people will not be great if we can provide talented candidates with training to make them proficient as knowledge retrievers and research assistants.

C. TRAINING

This brings us to the third task: training for the linking agent. We need to develop a new curriculum in our schools of education specifically designed to develop linking agents. We see at least four elements that would have to go into such a curriculum: (a) an understanding of the knowledge dissemination and utilization process as a whole including some awareness of various models of planned change, empirical studies which have been done, and research methods for studying it; (b) an understanding of how to work with client systems including strategies for collaboration, help on diagnosing of needs, and help in self-evaluating of effort; (c) an understanding of the resource system including an appreciation for research values, concerns and methods, and a review of knowledge storage and retrieval methods and tools; and (d) an appreciation of the need for role-complementarity and coordination in the fulfillment of dissemination objectives.*

D. EQUIPPING

Lastly we come to the important matter of equipment. It is not enough to train a man and send him out into the field. We must give him tools with which to work, and if we don't have these tools now, we should get busy and develop them. Again here we find that experience in agriculture and other fields points up the importance of putting well-designed, well-prepared working materials in the hands of the linker. At least six types of tools need to be developed for his use: (a) first he needs to have at his disposal a range of linking strategies or project designs for work with various clients under various circumstances so he can build the most suitable temporary systems for the task at hand; (b) second, if he is in a conveyor role, he should be provided with a handbook of new practices, innovations, and usable research knowledge equivalent to the loose-leaf handbook which is the basic stand-by of the county agent; (c) thirdly, especially if he is a consultant but even if a conveyor, he should have a handbook on linking problems and solutions, possibly accompanied by a checklist of problems to look

---

*Lippitt, et al., (#1343) provide a number of useful suggestions on the possible content of a "curriculum for training change agents" (pages 287-298).

for in utilization activities; (d) fourth, he would be helped by having a guide
to the retrieval of knowledge in his particular area so that he can have access
to knowledge beyond that contained in the handbook; (e) fifth, he needs to have
at his disposal simple instruments to measure the success of his dissemination
and utilization efforts. Such instruments, which might be in the form of checklists, questionnaires, or interview questions, would be invaluable in giving him
feedback so that he can change his behavior and improve his performance as a
linker; (f) sixth, and finally, particularly if he is a consultant he needs to
have at his elbow client self-diagnostic tools, again including checklists, formats
for making force-field analyses, and self-administered questionnaires.

Any or all of these tools will be important in building a sense of security
and competence in the linker and in reducing his overload.

There may yet be a nagging question to some educators on these proposals
for the development of linking roles, a question which is raised again and again
at educational research meetings. It is: "Do we have any knowledge worth
disseminating?" We think that the answer should be an emphatic "yes". We have
knowledge in the form of programmed instruction, driver training films, computers,
texts in innumerable formats covering innumerable topics in innumerable ways,
films, vidio-tape recorders, classroom feedback exercises, and so on.

The trouble is that this "knowledge" in most cases is untested, unevaluated.
Its status as "scientific" knowledge is questionable, or its status as useful
knowledge is questionable, or both. Broadly what we need to do is to upgrade
our store of knowledge in education through translating it, evaluating it, trying
it out and re-evaluating it. Our educational researchers must be involved in
this process and a significant number of our educators and educational administrators and practitioners must be involved in it, too. This can be done through
a coordinated extension and knowledge linking system.

CHAPTER EIGHT

THE MESSAGE: TYPES OF KNOWLEDGE AND INFORMATION
AND THEIR CHARACTERISTICS

Table of Contents   Page

CHAPTER EIGHT*

THE MESSAGE: TYPES OF KNOWLEDGE AND INFORMATION
AND THEIR CHARACTERISTICS

In this review we have gathered together an enormous range of phenomena under the heading "dissemination and utilization of knowledge" D&U, and we have done this on the assumption that all D&U processes have common properties which justify looking at them in the same way. Nevertheless, there comes a point at which we must ask the question: "What knowledge?" What range of phenomena deserve the label "knowledge" or "scientific knowledge" or "innovation"? In this chapter we will attempt to sort out the major issues which relate to this critical question of content of the message. It will start with a categorization of the different types of messages that play a significant role in the knowledge flow process as we have discussed it in chapters Two and Three. At the same time we will note the major differences between these knowledge types as they have been brought to our attention by various authors.

A major purpose of this chapter is to address those scholars who take a *particularistic* point of view toward D&U, by holding that every type of knowledge is uniquely different from every other type. These authorities maintain that each piece of information has its own unique characteristics, so that general principles of d and u can never be developed. This chapter is addressed to those particularistic scholars. It points up the differences and the commonalities across fields, across subject matter, and across various forms·

There is a need, of course, to distinguish the important from the trivial. Obviously, we cannot discuss the special characteristics of every piece of knowledge. However, in this chapter these particularistic viewpoints will be given serious consideration. *There are vast differences in knowledge* and knowledge characteristics, and these differences do suggest different processes and strategies. Just as people (Chapters 4 and 5) and institutions (Chapter 6) have differing characteristics which make them differentially open to the same knowledge, so too, different types of knowledge have characteristics which affect the same people differentially.

This Chapter will be divided into three major parts, each part looking at the message from a somewhat different perspective. The first part will be an attempt to subdivide messages of "knowledge" into major *types* which have some relevance for utilization questions. Thus, in Part II we will present some of the important characteristics of knowledge which are known to affect diffusion rates and utilization patterns. This part will include a brief review of those factors of knowledge most thoroughly discussed by diffusion researchers, e.g., cost, profitability, divisibility, and congruence.

Finally, Part III of this chapter will focus on one crucial characteristic: the type of *behavioral adaptation* which utilization of the message requires. Does it require merely a reinforcement of existing modes of behavior, or does it require taking on a new role, a new value orientation, and/or a complex set of new skills? These considerations will remind us of the adaptibility of people (Chapters Four and Five) and organizations (Chapter Six) which must be taken into account. They will at the same time lead us into Chapter Nine and a consideration of how the knowledge is actually transformed and transmitted so that it does become useful.

*This chapter was drafted by Ronald G. Havelock.

The chapter as a whole will subdivide knowledge into many types and categories but the theme will be interrelatedness. Messages of all types relate to one another in many ways: e.g., the *fusion* of several pieces of knowledge from several different disciplines; the *integration* of knowledge from "science" with knowledge from "practice"; the inseparable bond between *message and medium, fact and method;* and the coincidence and covariation of characteristics; the interdependence of *practice and product* and the interdependence of *social science and physical science* applications. The goal of this chapter is to provide a broad framework within which we can analyze the "message" and study its effects.

I. A TYPOLOGY OF MESSAGES

In this review the term message has been defined very broadly. An anchor point has been the concept "scientific knowledge", but this expression has also been construed broadly and perhaps loosely. We have found it very difficult to draw the line between information which is and is not scientific. Moreover, when we look at what happens to knowledge as it moves from the hands of the scientist-creator to the hands of the various others who "use" it, it seems to go through a kind of metamorphosis; the form changes. Thus, what may have been a basic law to a physicist becomes an operational guideline to an engineer; and what was a theory of personality to the academic psychologist becomes a theory of psychotherapy in the clinic. Theories become models and models become products. Whereas we collected data in the physicist's laboratory *to test hypotheses,* we may be collecting data in the R & D laboratory to test *models* or *prototypes* and we may be using data in the field to look for *problems and defects* in cars, tires, and people. The first task of this chapter will be to understand this metamorphosis of knowledge as it flows from specialist to specialist, from research to practice, from creator to user.

At the outset it will be helpful to remember once again the four major functions or system groupings that have been used in this text in describing the flow of knowledge. This time the headings are amended so that instead of functions, or people, or institutions, only the message outputs of these various systems are considered. Figure 8.1 depicts this arrangement in a skeleton format. In the pages which follow, the types of message output under each of these four headings will be defined and discussed in turn.

FIGURE 8.1   Overview of Message Types

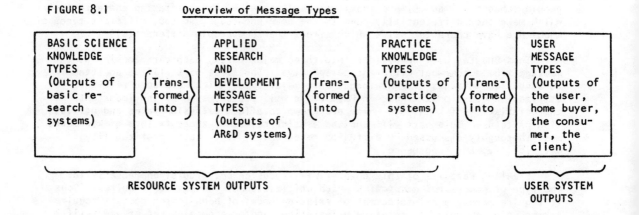

Woven into the discussion will be consideration of differences between *fields* with respect to the relative frequency of certain knowledge types and the special problems or advantages of D&U in such fields. However, no attempt will be made to take up the various fields of knowledge one by one to indicate their unique properties and problems. Rather, mention will be made of particular fields where it will allow a clearer understanding of the "message" as an aspect of D&U analysis.*

Each section below will begin with a listing and definition of the various types and conclude with a discussion of the issues or problems raised in the literature which seem to relate to these types. Following the analysis under the four headings of Figure 8.1, some additional types of knowledge which don't fit this paradigm as clearly will also be discussed. Part I will then conclude with an attempt to illustrate interrelationships among types as a part of the overall picture of knowledge flow.

A.   BASIC KNOWLEDGE TYPES: THEORY, DATA, METHOD

   1.   Definitions and Distinguishing Features

      The word "science" undoubtedly has special and divergent meanings to different scholars. However, all definitions seem to include three ideas which are summarized here as "theory," "data," and "method."

      First there is *theory*, the idea of orderliness; it is the proposition that there is a relationship among parts and of parts to the whole, that there is *system*, regularity, and connection between events which can be formally stated as laws or hypotheses.

      Second, there is *data*, the idea that there are identifiable elements or units into which the phenomena of experience can be segmented and from which theory can be generated. These are the factual or empirical elements of science.

      Third, there is *method*, the idea of verification, of determining the validity and reliability of data and of theories, defined procedures by which the "truth" value of knowledge can be determined.**

---

*Field designations,too, obviously are different at different points along the research--to-use continuum: thus the "basic" fields of "physics," "chemistry," "biology," "psychology," "sociology," etc. have no direct counterparts in applied research and development where we find the more practice-oriented labels of "engineering," "educational research," "bio-medical research," and so forth.

**These three themes are evident in various dictionary definitions of science, e.g., American College Dictionary, Random House, 1950:

  "1. A branch of knowledge or study dealing with a body of facts or truths system-
      atically arranged and showing the operation of general laws: the mathematical
      sciences.

   2. Systematized knowledge of the physical or material world.

   3. Systematized knowledge in general.

   4. Knowledge, as of facts or principles; knowledge gained by systematic study."

The term *basic knowledge* is taken to be more or less synonymous with "basic research," "basic scientific knowledge" and "pure science." It is here defined as the knowledge which builds a fundamental understanding of the environment from the microcosmos (atomic physics) to the macrocosmos (astronomy), an understanding which may be purely descriptive and empirical (e.g., some branches of botany, zoology, and geology) or purely theoretical (e.g., mathematics) or both. The words "basic" and "pure" define a segment of science which is explicitly divorced from considerations of usefulness, application, and practical significance. Since this is knowledge for the sake of knowledge, its primary users are scholars and basic researchers within the academic scientific fraternity.

Although practical utility may be far down the list of reasons why basic knowledge is gathered, such knowledge does, nevertheless, find its way into practical applications in many forms and by many routes.

2. *Issues and Implications for Utilization*

a. *Theory: General but too general*

Basic knowledge in the form of general theories, laws, or principles ought to be applicable across many phenomena and hence probably useful. This presumably is the rationale for including so much basic science in the school curriculum; it is seen as something all of us should learn to become adult members of our culture. Zetterberg's (00526) characterization and justification of sociology is typical: "there is a body of seasoned sociological knowledge, summarized as principles of theoretical sociology, which is superior to our common sense notions about society" (page 22).

Yet, when it comes to practical applications, knowledge in this basic form comes in for much criticism. Thus, for example, Golden (00691) recommends that theory be avoided in explaining psychological and psychiatric principals to physicians. Instead of confusing the listener with generalities or strange and esoteric concepts, the communicator should stick closely to specifics which have meaning in the everyday experience of his audience. Michael (01693) notes the same problem in discussing the utilization of social science knowledge in the military establishment. The social scientist, he says, simply doesn't have "data" on military systems problems, and may run into trouble if he has to stretch theory derived from artificial situations.

Guetzkow (00202) notes the same problem in the direct dissemination of the tested theories of social science. He says that these general statements must be converted into *predictions of what would happen in concrete situations:* the basic variables have to be redefined and remeasured and the appropriate and relevant theoretical models have to be selected from the many available.

This problem of moving from general laws to concrete user circumstances is claimed by some authors, including those cited above, as a unique affliction of knowledge utilization in this or that particular field. Typically, those who write in this vein are speaking for social science or behavioral science, generally the so-called "soft" sciences. Mackie and Christenson (06237) for example, try to explain the woefully inadequate use of the well-supported and rigorously tested theories of learning:

"There appears to be a fundamental difference between theoreticians and practitioners in psychology and their counterparts in the physical sciences. Physical scientists and engineers have the advantage of common technical terms and mathematical laws describing <u>natural</u> phenomena. Psychologists, on the other hand, are <u>inclined</u> to <u>invent</u> or <u>contrive</u> behavioral phenomena through the use of tasks that suit experimental convenience. The result is that it is extremely difficult to identify the learning processes involved in the laboratory as either similar to, or different from, those in a given educational environment."

Without questionning the fact that translation from theory to practice is difficult in these fields, we may ask if it is not equally difficult in the so-called "hard-sciences." Is current theory in biology and chemistry easily absorbed in everyday medical practice? Do engineers have no trouble applying the theories of physics in the development of nuclear reactors and space satelites? Marquis and Allen (#S230) for example, conclude as follows: "There is little evidence for direct communication between science and technology. The two do advance quite independently and much of technology advances without a complete understanding of the science on which it is built." Translation from basic to applied concerns is apparently a tough problem in all fields, "hard" or "soft."

b.   Data: Irrelevant and Artificial

Data as basic knowledge* is collected primarily for the purpose of demonstrating theories or measuring phenomena which are basic to our understanding of the environment. One major problem for utilization, therefore, is the transposition of data collected for one purpose (theory building and theory testing) into a context where it must be used for a different purpose (specific practical applications). The mental gymnastics required to achieve this type of transposition makes it a difficult feat, if it is attempted at all, and one that is seldom rewarded by applause from either researchers or practitioners.

The typical context for the collection of basic data is the *laboratory experiment,* a highly restricted environment which is easily controllable, observable and measurable. Herein lies another of the problems for utilization: *artificiality.* The restrictions of experimental science lead the practitioner to question the practical relevance of scientific findings. There is a certain irony in this complaint, however; the very conditions which lead to the charge of artificality are imposed in order to insure the *reliability* and *validity* of the findings. The scientist wants to make sure he has <u>real</u> knowledge, yet the very steps he takes to make sure it is real create suspicion in the practitioner that the knowledge is unreal! Although it might seem that any procedures which increased reliability and validity would make data <u>more useful</u> to anyone, they may have the opposite effect.

One important issue which needs to be unravelled here is the distinction between *perceived artificiality* and *actual artificiality.*

---

*We will consider other kinds of data at a later point.

As we recall from previous chapters, various attitudinal barriers separate the scientist and the practitioner. Hence, since the whole world of the scientist may seem strange and alien to the practitioner, the resulting data may be seen as "artificial" whether it is or not. If people in the world of practice can be led to understand why these procedures are imposed, they may come to appreciate the quality of scientific data and may be more prone to use it (or to ask for help in using it).

Because of real or perceived irrelevance and artificiality, it is doubtful that basic research data will often be effectively transmitted to application-oriented receivers in anything like its original form. Rather it will typically be offered in conjunction with the theories and principles it is intended to support. This is unfortunate in at least one respect: the applier may be shielded from data which do not support the theory being presented. All too often, scientists have a vested interest in their theories; therefore, when they present data with their theories, they are likely to select or emphasize confirming data at the expense of disconfirming or ambiguous data.

Just how much basic research data ought to be disseminated is perhaps another question. Marshall (01012) points out that contradictory findings (which tend to be the rule rather than the exception in a field like sociology) lead to rejection by the public and selective perception based on common sense interpretations.* Thus in the absence of clear theoretical guidance from the researchers, the user may impose his own "implicit theory," and accept as valid only those research findings which fit this personal theory.

c. *Scientific Method: A Very Diffusable Product of Basic Research*

The scientific status of knowledge depends largely on methodology; the rules of evidence, the "operational" definitions, the instruments of measurement and analysis and the rules of scientific reasoning. This methodology is what distinguishes science from theology, from the humanities, and perhaps from the world of practice. It is curious, therefore, that we so often think of the "body of scientific knowledge" as including only the theory and empirical description of our environment, neglecting this third aspect as if it were taken for granted or merely an assumption within the other two. A number of studies in the literature suggest that the method of science deserves more recognition as a separate diffusable item in and of itself. Of all the outputs of basic science, *methodology*, defined broadly to include scientific attitude and orientation, is probably the most significant message for potential users inside and outside the scientific fraternity.

First of all, it appears from at least two studies of communication among scientists (Menzel and American Psychological Association both cited by Paisley, 01240, p.111-22), that most scientist-receivers are

---

*The survey of attitudes of state legislators cited in Chapter Seven (Blum and Funkhouser, 02235) shows that conflicting and/or highly qualified testimony by social scientists is a major reason for their rejection by policy makers.

tuned in to get information from colleagues, not on what they are doing and finding out, but on *how* they are doing it. When scientists are asked what they get out of professional conference sessions and informal communication channels, they respond that their major interest is in information on methodology: "know-how," apparatus, new statistics and measurement instruments.

Such findings are not so surprising, however, when we consider how new knowledge is built and understand the great dependence of new knowledge on new methodology. Ben-David (01736), looking at the history of scientific discovery, finds that existing methodology at any given time defines the scope of problems which may be asked.

Methodology as an output assumes equally great significance in dissemination from the scientific community *to practice* and *to the general public*. More important, and perhaps necessarily preceding the understanding of facts and theories, is an appreciation and an acceptance of science as an orientation to the environment and a method of discovering and understanding nature. Brooks (00810) observes that scholars and practitioners in many non-scientific fields have increasingly adopted the spirit and mode of thought of the natural sciences. The importance of this trend for general technical advancement is well stated by Rummel (Campbell, 00642): "Before we can do very much on the implementation of research (in school settings) we have got to make our body of consumers more aware of the concepts and principles of research methods." The impact of scientific method on modern man has been eloquently described by classicist Eric A. Havelock:

> "To describe the scientific method, as it is understood in
> the present age, can be an endless task. Suffice it here to
> say that it has created a definition of the intellect of man
> more precise and more formidable than man in the past has
> been willing to entertain. The thing has not taken place in
> a social vacuum. To support and extend the power of intellect
> has meant the creation of a vastly extended apparatus of higher
> education. The university, along with the training and tech-
> nical school, has ceased to be the support of culture for the
> few, and has become a functional institution in society, and
> part of its day's work. In ten thousand classrooms and
> hundreds of laboratories, by the use of millions of printed
> words read and written, the process of training men in the
> habits of measurement and calculation and analysis and hypothesis
> goes on over most of the civilized world, and it is still acceler-
> ating. The methods and procedures, though developed mainly in
> the struggle to control physical nature, have been applied back-
> ward to the behavior of man himself, and even to his literature
> and his art. The total effect has been an enormous extension,
> in western culture, of what for a better word can be called
> "intellectualism." (7106, p. 20-21).

We cannot leave the dissemination of methodology without a special note on the *methodology of the social sciences*. During their first century of development, the social sciences had to fight for their right to exist as scholarly and scientific disciplines. Because of this struggle there may have been a tendency to withdraw or hold back from the practical world and to develop a methodology in the isolation and

security of the "laboratory." In the last dozen years, however,
the various methodologies of the social sciences seem to have
sprung loose from their academic moorings.* Such devices as sample
surveys, attitude questionnaires, focussed interviews, group process
analysis and role-playing have ceased being special esoteric equipment in the hands of the basic researcher; they have become familiar
and legitimate tools for the industrial firm , the government department, the school, the advertising agency and the television network.
There is a growing recognition, even among the general public, that
information about our social environment and about ourselves can be
obtained more precisely and accurately by the use of these new tools.

The effects of this diffusion undoubtedly go beyond mere expansion
of our technical powers to measure the social environment. Just as the
diffusion and acceptance of physical science led to changes in cultural
attitudes (e.g., a greater acceptance of rational thought and empiricism,
at least among the educated classes), so the diffusion of social science
is changing the orientations and perhaps the basic values of the general
population.

With the intrusion of scientific method into the areas of social
life and organization which were formerly the province of common sense
and everyday experience, it may be only a short step further to
realize that scientific method can be used to study *anything*, even the
most cherished religious and philosophical precepts. Sanford, for
example (0503) shows us the impact of scientific method in the study
of values:

"Science of value assumes that values are held by men, that value
judging is a mental process that can be studied. Instead of putting science in the service of what is thought to be good, it undertakes the scientific consideration of goodness and badness. I
need only remind you of the solid achievement of this familiar
approach. It has demonstrated that certain things widely thought
to be good, like ethnocentrism, or a rigid super-ego, are not
good, and that things widely thought to be bad--like some of the
less orderly instincts, are not really bad, and it has lent the
support of science to the great ideas of various ethical systems--
for example, justice, truth, beauty, courage and love. It has
undoubtedly improved the quality of value judgements by supplying
knowledge of what enters into them, and not least, it has revealed
much about the conditions of moral behavior." (p. 64).

------

*A number of ramifications of this development are discussed by Schwartz, 0486. Three
groups whom he sees as being especially influenced are (1) other scientists, (2) social
action professions, (social workers, Peace Corps Volunteers, Poverty Program Workers),
and (3) high school and especially college students who are enrolled in social science
courses in growing hordes.

d. The Special Problems of Social Science

In investigating the literature on utilization, one is struck by the preponderance of studies and commentaries by social scientists on themselves and their own process. Since it is probably inevitable that self-analysis leads to some degree of self-criticism and self-pity, it is not surprising that most of this testimony stresses the problems, difficulties, pitfalls and disadvantages of social as against other kinds of science. In the absence of equivalent self-analysis in natural, physical, biological and other sciences, the reviewers feel that such claims should be considered with caution. Here, then, are a few of the frequently cited special problems of the social sciences as they might affect D&U.

Young (1223), cites four characteristics of sociology which he feels reduce the capability of meaningful collaboration with the practice professions. First, sociology is very young as a science and has a relatively small amount of hard knowledge built up. Second, sociologists have been anxious to build and maintain an image as a real basic science and in so doing have stressed their non-involvement in practical concerns and their distance from them. Third, the training of sociologists does not include subject matter which has direct bearing on applied problems. Finally, Young notes as a difficulty the unrealistically high expectations which the practitioner is likely to entertain for the usefulness of sociological knowledge once he has come to accept it. Likert (5202) also gives special mention to *over-optimism* as a problem in the utilization of behavioral science knowledge to improve organizations.

These difficulties sound reasonable enough. What is not clear is how some of these problems are unique to the social sciences. It seems reasonable to suppose, for example, that the "basic" orientation of the physical sciences builds equally high barriers to practice or that many optimistic hopes for practical uses of physical science are equally misguided.

A number of authors note that the special subject matter of the social sciences makes them more of a threat to existing institutions and practices than was true for natural sciences.   Fukuyama (0981) believes this is especially true when they are focussed on religion. He believes that clergymen are unwilling to turn on powerful tools of sociology loose on the institutions of the church for fear that they will "subvert the sanctioned beliefs and undermine the existing order of the religious establishment."

Some argue that social science can and should sidestep such problems by a declaration of neutrality on value questions. Thus Garfinkel (0961), in discussing the proper role of social science in school desegregation cases, says that social scientists should clearly distinguish "fact" questions from "value" questions and deal solely with the former. He goes on to say that we must still turn to politics "to resolve conflict of interest and the ancient problems of justice and civic morality." However, in view of the obvious relevance of the social sciences to the study of values we may wonder whether it is feasible to draw the lines so clearly.

8-9

This question of how far social science should involve itself
in public policy has been discussed for some years. Lynd (6098),
writing in 1939, took his fellow social scientists to task for
their reluctance to respond to public demand for social problem
solutions: "If the social scientist is too bent upon 'waiting until
all the data are in,' or if university policies warn him off controversial issues, the decisions will be made anyway--without him"
(p. 9). Immediate social problems call for immediate solutions and
policy makers will act with or without facts. Taylor (2039), in 1941,
made the same point with respect to the role of rural sociologists
in the Department of Agriculture. He urged them to collaborate with
administrators in such matters as planning community resettlement for
the Columbia Dam project regardless of the shallowness or incomplete-
ness of their data because, as he noted, such planning would be done
by someone in any case. It might just as well be the people who
possess the only expert knowledge, regardless of how inadequate or
incomplete such knowledge might be.

Finally, Lippitt (3873) notes that social science utilization
suffers from a generally *underdeveloped concept of social engineering*.
He feels that there exists no clear conception of social "invention"
equivalent to the technologies that appear to have developed from
the physical sciences. While we have highly developed social practice
professions in some cases (e.g., law, social work) these professions
have no clear self-perception as being social science-derivative or
social science-based.* This point leads naturally into the next topic
of this chapter, the types of knowledge which belong to the "Applied
Research and Development" segment of the message spectrum.

B.   APPLIED RESEARCH AND DEVELOPMENT KNOWLEDGE TYPES: THEORY, DATA, METHODS,
     DESIGNS, AND PROTOTYPES

Discussions of utilization which contrast knowledge which is "practical" on
the one hand to knowledge which is "basic" on the other may obscure the fact that
a vast array of knowledge types exist between these two poles: there are many
kinds of knowledge which are both research-based and use-oriented at the same time.
In this section these types will be discussed under the combined heading "Applied
Research and Development." (Hereafter designated AR & D)

1.   *Definitions and Distinguishing Features:*

"AR & D" is a general designation for knowledge types which lie somewhere between basic knowledge and practice knowledge.** Such knowledge has
some degree of scientific status--being founded on or derived from scientific
method and produced largely by people who have scientific training--but it
is also knowledge which is oriented to and dependent on the practice professions. Not only is it identified by practice field designations, e.g.,
"medical research," "educational research," but it is usually undertaken
in institutional settings where research is secondary to an overall practical function: e.g., the medical school, the university hospital, the
product manufacturing concern.

---

*It may be, of course, that we have a tendency to assume more connection between
 basic and applied areas than actually exists even in hard science fields.

**See again Figure 8.1.

It might be said that knowledge in the AR & D category is "marginal" because it is both *marginally* scientific on the one hand and *marginally* practical on the other. It looks enough like basic knowledge for an analagous subdivision into "theory," "data," and "method" to make some sense; however, its data is not necessarily theory-oriented and its theory does not propound universal laws on the nature of things. In addition, there are other creatures in AR & D such as "working models," "designs" "blue prints," "mock-ups," "prototypes," and "inventions" that have no real counterpart in basic knowledge. However, AR & D knowledge is not *directly* practical either. Rather it is <u>knowledge in evolution</u> on the way to becoming practical. It is tentative and partial, not quite ready for unrestricted use. If it is taken up by practitioners it is on a "use-at-your-own-risk" basis.

The present conception of AR & D has an interesting ancestry, that may sharpen its meaning for some readers. Although the expression "R & D" is quite recent, the origin of the underlying concept is probably as old as science, itself. Certainly, the Greek authors of the fifth century B.C. saw their scientific philosophy as a body of knowledge having direct relevance and applicability to everyday affairs, and many "philosophers" were inventors and developers of new technology at the same time.

In the modern era, according to Kranzberg* "the concept was articulated as far back as the 17th century in the work of Francis Bacon, whose scheme for a utopian society in <u>The New Atlantis</u> embodied the notion of scientists (in Salomon's House) attempting to discover new knowledge regarding the physical environment and making it usable for mankind. The scientific societies formed during the 17th century and later particularly the Royal Society in England, were a direct outgrowth of Bacon's ideas, and they had as their original aims the discovery of new knowledge and its application to human affairs. In our own country, the American Academy of Arts and Sciences and the American Philosophical Society provided examples of this. *Most of the scientific societies soon found themselves involved in "pure" science and neglected the utilization aspects of their work,* leading to the formation of other societies in the 18th and 19th centuries, such as the Royal Society of Arts, which were primarily concerned with the utilization of scientific knowledge.

Another application of this same concept grew out of the industrial research laboratories, which first became prevalent in the German chemical industry during the latter part of the 19th century. The first industrial research laboratories in the United States date from the first part of the 20th century--the General Electric Laboratory and the Eastman Kodak Laboratory--and they were really doing R & D even though they did not call it that."

The origin of the actual expression "R & D" is unclear but it seems to date only from World War II. Again, Kranzberg:

---

*Melvin Kranzberg of Case Western Reserve University in personal communication to the author, February 28, 1969.

"...The term was embodied in the name of the OSRD (Office of Scientific Research and Development), which was established within the Office of Emergency Management in 1941. The director of the OSRD, Vannevar Bush, did much to popularize the term. By 1948 it was certainly a part of our vocabulary, as evidenced by the founding of the RAND Corp., with the term "RAND" being a form of acronym for R & D."

In education the concept has been put forth most forcefully in resent times by Egon Guba and his co-workers. For example, Clark and Hopkins (6241) have provided us with a set of categories of R & D activities which they call "functional emphases in relation to the change process." Their focus of concern is education but their typology is equally applicable to other fields. They start with what they call "conducting basic scientific inquiry." This would correspond to the "basic knowledge" previously discussed here. Their remaining two categories under "research" and three categories under "development" belong within the knowledge form we have chosen to call AR & D. These are as follows:

"2. Investigating (educationally) oriented problems.
 3. Gathering operational and planning data.
 4. Inventing solutions to operating problems.
 5. Engineering packages and programs for (educational) use.
 6. Testing and evaluating solutions and programs."

In this review, a somewhat different breakdown is attempted with the recognition that there will be considerable overlap and redundancy with the Clark-Hopkins list. The major AR & D types which will be identified and discussed here are as follows:

a.   AR & D Theory
b.   Data: AR & D Theory Testing
c.   Data: Diagnostic
d.   Data: Evaluation
e.   AR & D Method
f.   Designs
g.   Prototypes

a.   *AR & D Theory*

Just as there is "theory" in basic knowledge, there are broad generalizations or principles in AR & D which can also be designated as "theories." The difference lies in the avowed purpose of the theory. AR & D theory is intended to provide broad <u>principles to guide the behaviors of practitioners</u>. Thus we have theories of building design and construction, theories of epidemiology, theories of pathology of various diseases, theories or principles of good medical or surgical practice, theories of psychopathology and of psychotherapy, theories of child care, and theories of teaching and educational administration.*

---

*Curiously and somewhat ironically, that branch of psychology known as "learning theory" is not, as the name implies, a theory of practice in the sense used above. With a few exceptions, there is very little concern among scientists in this area for improvement of educational practice or human learning practices in general (Mackie and Christenson #6237).

Many readers may want to further subdivide these theories into those which are <u>descriptive</u> and those which are <u>prescriptive</u>. In other words, some theories e.g., theories of pathology or of the "natural" processes of socialization, learning, plant chemistry, etc. may be seen as building our descriptive understanding in a domain of special concern to practitioners (medicine, education, agriculture, etc.). Others are more specific in defining what the practitioner should do, what principles of prevention, healing, teaching, or soil tillage he should follow. These latter might be dubbed "theories of practice."

b. *Data: AR & D Theory Testing*

A large part of the research energies of university-based applied researchers seems to be channeled in the direction of theory testing. In this category, for example, we would find the various research efforts designed to demonstrate the efficacy of psychoanalytic psychotherapeutic principles, the value of "progressive education," the validity of "Keynesian economics," and so forth.

c. *Data: Diagnostic*

Theory-testing data is only indirectly useful to the practitioner in giving him reassurance (or greater uncertainty) that his general way of operating has some efficacy or that his philosophy of practice is right. However, there are other kinds of data collected for different purposes which he may see as more directly relevant. Most particularly, in this category would be data which is *Diagnostic* or purely descriptive. Such data is collected simply to describe something using the instruments and methods of science. The "something" may be a problem or a "pain" which has made itself known, or it may be an area of practical concern where knowledge is lacking. The need for accurate, scientifically based diagnostic data has long been recognized in medicine and engineering but only recently in the social sciences, starting perhaps with intelligence and skill-testing half a century ago, followed by the economic measures and indices of the New Deal era, and finally in the 1960's indicies of social pathology in the family, the work group, the organization, and the community.

There may be some question concerning who should generate and who should rightfully "own" this type of knowledge. Inicially only the scientist can generate knowledge of this sort because he is the only one who has the methodology. As the procedures for collecting diagnostic data become routinized, however, the practitioner is more likely to be collecting and using such data himself (e.g., as in diagnosis of illness by a physician). Ultimately the methodology of diagnosis in a particular area may become so systematized and simplified that the ultimate consumer (e.g., the patient, the worker, or the student) may be able to administer his own tests and interpret the results for himself.

d. *Data: Evaluation*

A third "data" category within AR&D is that which we call *Data: Evaluation*. This is roughly equivalent to what Clark and Hopkins call "Testing and Evaluating Solutions and Programs." It also could be called "engineering data" or "quality control data." It is, in a sense , diagnostic data, i.e., diagnosis of a <u>solution</u>, the information on whether or not an innovation "works," or meets our needed specifications. It is a very focussed, non-exploratory kind of knowledge intended for the measurement of specific interventions, practices, and products (in contrast to data which tests theories of practice).

e.   AR & D Method

Again, as in basic science, a very important subset of AR & D messages belongs in the *method* category: technique, test, index or instrument. What has been said of this already under "Basic Knowledge" applies equally here, although the methods of AR & D will be more specific, more <u>ad hoc</u>, more relevant to immediate operting problems. The diffusion of scientific method from basic research to various fields of practice is really what created AR & D and it is also what makes it so difficult to define what "scientific knowledge" means in the contemporary world. The fact is that anyone, whether he be an academic, an entrepreneur, a practitioner, or a consumer, if he understands scientific method and can apply it meaningfully, can be said to be a scientist and a producer of scientific knowledge. There may indeed come a time when being a good scientist is seen as an important part of being a good citizen. Already we can note this sort of evolution for certain scientific methods, e.g., the evolution of interviewing techniques from (1) experimental research tools to (2) therapeutic and personnel evaluation techniques to (3) ways of relating to one another in everyday interaction. It is possible that further diffusion of the methods of science will eventually lead us to a *scientific culture* in which the average consumer will have the ability to apply scientific methods to evaluating the stream of products, services, and political and social information which is daily directed at him. Already there is some suggestive evidence that those who have a scientific orientation are more effective consumers (Morgan, et.al., 6326); science-oriented consumers are more likely to use seatbelts, want fluoridated water, and reject scientifically valueless innovations. Whether those who have this pro-science orientation also have some actual understanding of scientific method may be debatable without more research on this topic, but the presumption of a relationship seems at least reasonable.

f.   Designs

A critical phase in the translation of research knowledge into practical knowledge is the fusion of theory, data, and method into the *design* of something that might eventually become a useful innovation. The *design* however, is not to be confused with the innovation, itself; the design merely is a clear delineation of the idea behind the invention, usually set forth as a description on paper, a drawing, a diagram, an outline, or a rudimentary model which suggests the form and major features,sometimes described as a "mock-up." In later stages of the development process designs may include exact instructions and specifications for the fabrication and assembly of finished products.

g.   Prototypes

Finally, the term *prototype* * is used here to describe a large
number of knowledge types or knowledge packages which are the earliest
experimental versions of specific practices, services, solutions,
treatments, and products. From the Guba-Clark-Hopkins schema, very
rough equivalents might be "investing solutions to operating problems"
and "engineering packages and programs for use."

Although prototypes are usually based on *designs*, neither designs
nor prototypes are necessarily derived from basic knowledge or other
kinds of AR & D knowledge. When they are so derived, they are likely
to be derived in a very complex way. A prototype is likely to be a
knowledge "package," a concretization of a *theory* of practice made to
fit the empirical realities of *diagnostic data* and modified and rebuilt
on the basis of *evaluation data*.

Often, however, prototypes are not derived from other research
(basic or applied), but arise as "inventions" generated by creative
people without scientific training, stimulated perhaps by knowledge
of some obvious unmet consumer needs. Once generated, of course,
these inventions may interact with the other more scientific brands of
knowledge (theory, evaluation, and diagnostic data) to produce more
refined prototypes. In any case, the *prototype is probably the most
practice-oriented form of AR & D:* It looks like a practice or a
product; it is easily recognized and understood by the practitioner;
and it is probably something the innovative practitioner would like to
get his hands on and try out.

Although prototypes are concrete and specific, in contrast to
theories, they are not necessarily "hardware." The experimental
computer program is equally a prototype along side the experimental
computer. The experimental teaching routine is just as much a prototype as the experimental teaching machine. In short, a prototype is
simply a package of knowledge ready to test or almost ready to use.

2.   *Issues Among AR & D Knowledge Types*

a.   *Applied Research Versus Development*

In the above paragraphs we have attempted to delineate six knowledge types belonging under the heading "applied research and development."
It should be obvious from this discussion, however, not only that these
types cannot be clearly separated from one another, but also that they
are interrelated and interact with one another. This is the primary
reason why the term "applied research" and the term "development" were
grouped together for this analysis. Although "development" is often
seen as a step which *follows* applied research, there are also certain
types of activities deserving the "applied research" label which

---

*In early drafts of this review, the term "model" was used here, but was replaced in
an attempt to avoid the confusion of overlapping meanings. The word "model" has
several meanings which range from "basic conceptual framework" to "miniature copy"
and it is used at other points in this review to signify "abstract version" or
"idealized version" as in "model of planned change." It is hoped that the less
familiar word, "prototype," will avoid these confusions.

necessarily come after development; testing and the collection of
evaluation data are often associated with the "development" of
prototypes, and a new kind of diagnostic data may lead to the
development of new theories of practice. In such evolutionary
processes it is rarely, if ever, clear just where development leaves
off and applied research begins, and vice versa.

b.   *Invention Versus Derivation*

Another issue which is often seen as important is the distinction between *invention* and *derivation*. The causes and sources of
creativity in AR & D are a matter of consuming interest to many
writers and some researchers, and the balance of the findings seem
to favor invention. That is, the bulk of innovations which pour forth
from AR & D centers have no discernable direct parentage either in basic
knowledge or more abstract and scientific forms of applied research
knowledge. Thus, in "Project Hindsight," an attempt to retrace the
development of successful naval weapons systems, very little credit
was given by the developers to "up-the-line" or remote knowledge
sources. Only 10% of the discovery "events" could be traced clearly
to origins in basic scientific research. (Carter, 6226). Similarly,
the very meager results of technological knowledge dissemination networks (e.g., Denver Research Institute, 6111) suggest that scientists
and engineers are more likely to invent or reinvent something than to
derive it from the research or development work of someone else,
especially someone they don't know, in a different organization and
in a different discipline. In reviewing 50 case histories of specific
inventions over the 19th and 20th centuries, Jewkes, et.al. (0941)
are equally skeptical of the drivation hypothesis:

> "...chance still remains an important factor in invention and
> the intuition, will and obstinacy of individuals spurred on by
> the desire for knowledge, renown or personal gain are the great
> driving forces in technical progress." (p. 223).

> "The theory that technical innovation arises directly out of,
> and only out of, advance in pure science does not provide a
> full and faithful story of modern invention." (p. 224).

It is important, however, to view these findings within the context
of other studies and analyses contained in this review, One fact to
keep in mind is a psychological one, namely, the reluctance of people
to see themselves as dependent upon others and hence somehow *incompetent*.*
Thus an applied scientist or developer will not want to view his work
as *derived* and hence somehow less important than the work of the basic
scientists. Another factor here may be the non-recognition of method
as a genuine knowledge product. Thus the "inventor" may immediately
test out his invention using all kinds of elaborate laboratory set-ups,
measuring devices, and statistics without seeing these as derivations
from science. For example, Dennerll and Chesler (5121) report on a
project in which innovative classroom practices of teachers (i.e.,
inventions) were identified, evaluated, and distributed in booklet
form to other teachers. In a sense, the teacher inventions did not
originate in a research environment, but the inventions as packaged

---

*For a consideration of the variable of *competence* as a factor in receptivity to new
knowledge, see Chapter Four.

8-16

and ultimately received by other teachers did: a university-based research team collected the information, ordered it, and distributed it, in addition to conceiving of the whole project in the first place. Hence, the "inventions" which were distributed had a non-scientific origin but a very scientific development history. Processing and evaluation using scientific methods and tools makes all knowledge "scientific" to a degree. In such cases, the distinction between "invention" and "derivation" becomes somewhat obscure.

c.   *When Is It Ready to Use?*

A third issue which beclouds discussions of AR & D is the difficulty of drawing a dividing line between what is still tentative and what is tried, proved, and ready to use. Part of the role of applied research is to act as a policeman or a brake regulating the dissemination of untested innovations. Increasingly in our society "regulation" is coming to mean "subjecting to scientific scrutiny."

Conflict may arise when over-zealous practitioners, seeing great new opportunities to fill pressing needs or perhaps the chance of windfall profits, push for the immediate use of new knowledge but are prevented from doing so by applied researchers who claim that testing is not completed. Ambitious and innovative farmers, for example, have been known to bypass the county agent with his tried-and-true knowledge carefully screened and tested by the extension service to snatch new items directly from the state experimental farm (Havelock 6183). Likewise, the drug manufacturer (a practitioner of sorts) may be eager to get a new drug on the market first, if he has reason to believe that it will be popular, even though all the test results of the more conservative and compulsive researchers are not in. The Thalidomide or Krebiozen cases of a few years ago should serve to remind us that these conflicts are real and important. Stories like the Thalidomide case, however, should not blind us to the fact that researchers can also be super-cautious, obsessively refusing to admit that the extensive knowledge they now possess is anywhere near ready for application.

C.   **PRACTICE KNOWLEDGE: PRACTICE AND PRODUCT: HARD AND SOFT**

We now turn our attention to the third message type in Figure 8.1, the knowledge which is the property of the practice world.

1.   *Definitions and Distinguishing Features of Practice Knowledge*

In developing the typology presented in this chapter the authors hesitated before separating "AR & D" from "Practice" knowledge types, realizing that the *final* product of AR & D was inevitably knowledge in a form in which the practitioner could use it. However, it is important to make a distinction between *knowledge in process and knowledge after processing*. This distinction makes especially good sense in studying the literature on diffusion, where interest has been concentrated almost exclusively on fully developed products and practices (i.e., practice knowledge). There are good methodological reasons for this; knowledge in this finished state is more easily definable, recognizable and observable. But partly for these very reasons it is *different* from the research types of knowledge discussed above and it may provide *different* problems (whether easier or harder) than those we find in the utilization of research in less polished forms. These reasons seem to suggest the need for separate classification.

Practice knowledge, then, is the newest, most effective, most appropriate usable knowledge which is available in a particular practice field at a given time. "Practice field" is intended to signify any domain which supplies or services a significant area of human need. Thus, it could be food production, medicine, education, law, transportation industries, housing industries and so forth.

a.   Service

Any and all of these practice fields are engaged in supplying the consumer with knowledge in several forms. First of all, they provide their own labor, usually purchased by the consumer or sought out by him because it is seen as expert or specialized and therefore something that the consumer cannot provide for himself. Such labor is here designated as "service."

b.   Product: Hardware

Service representing direct rendering of labor to the consumer is to be distinguished from *"product"*, knowledge which has been developed, prepared, and, packaged in such a way that the consumer himself can use it. This product form of knowledge can be further subdivided for analysis into two broad categories: *"hardware"* products and *"software"* products. The term "hardware" is used here to refer to tangible and usually manufactured items; they may be either consumable (e.g., a pill) or durable (e.g., a wheel chair), simple (e.g., a brick or a wire) or complex (e.g., a school building or a computer).

c.   Product: Software

Even broader and more obscure in meaning if the term *"software"*. In this review it is taken to mean products in ideational, verbal, or symbolic form, such as instructions, curricula, courses, training programs, computer programs, plans, or even concepts. Typically, but not necessarily, these software products are contained in tangible packages (such as books, brochures, manuals, card decks, videotape, blueprints, etc.). Although the packaging aspect is often intricately related to the software itself, specific discussion of packaging will be postponed to the chapter on the technology of knowledge flow, where it will be considered as a topic under "media."

d.   Combinations

Practice knowledge also is likely to occur in combination: the physician may treat the patient but also give him a pill and provide him with a set of instructions; the automobile dealer sells the car together with a manual on its use and at the same time he may provide services in the form of checkups and repairs; the manufacturer sells a computer but also provides service personnel and programs of various sorts; and so it goes. On close examination we find that one type of practice knowledge is rarely provided entirely independently of other types. The county agent provides new information on weed sprays, but he has to assume that the weed spray is available or soon will be. The physician prescribes a medicine, but he must assume that the patient can obtain the medicine, that he knows where there is a drugstore, that the drug store will have the medicine, that the patient will know how to take the medicine, and so on. Any product or service, at least in an advanced culture, is likely to be related to a long chain of other products and services which have to be available and readily accessible before utilization of the new product or service can be effected.

2. *Issues and Implications for Utilization*

Four principal issues emerge from the literature relevant to practice knowledge types. First, there is the question of the relationship between *practice knowledge* and *research knowledge,* (already partially discussed under AR & D). A second major concern is the relationship between *service and product* and the effects of the dissemination of one without the other. Related to this is a third issue, the perennial question of "lag," the dis-equilibrium in the relationship between *hardware and software* knowledge. Finally, in this section there will be a brief consideration of that strange new creature, *the social science "product"* and the new problems and new opportunities presented therein.

a. *Practice: Is It Based on Scientific Knowledge?*

When we examine practice fields in detail, we will find that few, if any, are based entirely on research knowledge as a whole and that none are founded exclusively on basic science. Most practice profes-sions have historical roots which run deeper than any research disci-pline and have evolved rules, norms, methods, and procedures which have no scientific antecedents. More than this, the traditions and the values of most practice professions since Hippocrates commit their members first and foremost to serve the consumer. Thus, when science enters the picture, it enters first as a guest and later perhaps as a junior partner. Even at the optimum, the linkage between science and practice should probably not be all-embracing, particularly if the practitioner's ties to the consumer are thereby weakened.

There is within most practice professions a split between *pro-gressives,* those who have a greater concern for the infusion of new knowledge from science into their field, and the *conservatives,* those who view the profession as an "art" which must be learned on the job and by insight and intuition. Hence, a large number of managers and administrators do not recognize any "science of management"; a large number of military men still see the infantry soldier (or the aircraft carrier or the strategic bomber) as the only weapon of importance; a large number of social workers still see the Christmas basket and the welfare check as the primary tools of the trade; and a large number of teachers and other educators still view the three R's in the traditional classroom as all that education ought to be. To all such individuals science has only a trivial tangential relationship to practice; it is not a foundation of practice. Yet, such "conservative" attitudes are obviously withering, so that even those who reject new science-based innovations are now likely to look for and cite scientific data of some sort to defend their positions.

One profession, however, stands apart from all the others in being curiously immune to the scientific ethos of our time. This field is law. Marshall, for example, (1021) notes that law has ignored scientific method, clinging to such quasi-theoretical concepts as "right and wrong" and rarely utilizing "scientific concepts of the relative and situational qualities of happenings, events, and relationships..." In a similar vein, Ulmer (2043) states: "any discussion of scientific method on legal research must recognize at the outset that the goal of judicial processes is not always knowledge, Indeed, the judicial process in innumerable ways, actively suppresses the search for 'truth.' In choosing among hypotheses concerning historical fact, the lawyer seeks victory, not truth." Reliance on both *precedent* and on the *adversary system* are

blamed by Schur (1981) for the lack of influence of science on law.
A true "science of law" he deems to be nearly achievable in the
face of these traditions.

One might ask if there are lessons to be learned for knowledge
utilization in other fields from this state of affairs in law. There
are discernible trends in such areas as race relations and urban
community development to move toward an adversary system.* Do these
trends pressage a retreat from a scientific knowledge orientation in
such fields? Or, is it possible to maintain a scientific orientation
while mobilizing to do battle?**

In the last analysis, of course, it should be remembered that the
progressives who push for the utilization of the new scientifically-
based expert knowledge may not always be promoting the best practice
for particular circumstances. There are many occasions on which the
old ways or the local ways of doing things are still the best ways.
Thus development workers in other countries remind us of the need
to look at what the local nationals already are doing before plunging
in with our new expertise (Public Administration Clearing House,
1045, p. 339, para. 68).

> "some consultants state that many techniques currently most
> suitable for extensive use in a country have already been
> developed by indigenous professional leaders or the common
> people. The first task of the outside expert is to familiar-
> ize himself with what has been done or invented by the local
> people, by indigenous specialists or by other outsiders
> already operating technical assistance projects. It is unwise
> to ignore or to fail to tap the practical wisdom of the people."

b. *Service Versus Product*

As stressed earlier, there would appear to be an organic inter-
relationship between service and product and between hardware product
and software product. To begin with, it is important to recognize that
service by itself is likely to be an extremely expensive and inefficient
way to serve the consumer because it means that expert labor, always
in short supply, is continuously tied up in tedious and redundant
interaction with the consumer population. If the expert practitioner
performs service for the consumer without passing on to the consumer

---

*e.g., comments by Clark, (6323), on the strategy of his Metropolitan Action Research
Center, an approach long advocated by Saul Alinsky for organizing community action.

**Possibly these questions could be studied empirically by carefully reviewing the
history of the interaction between labor-management relations and utilization of social
science knowledge and techniques to effect change in organizations. See for example,
a dialogue between union and social research viewpoints on the famous pajama factory
experiments; Trans-action, 1966, (Gomberg, Bennis, Marrow, 6316, 6317, 6319, 6320),
Adversary relations and power as strategies of deliberate change will be discussed
more fully in later chapters.

information (software) and tools (hardware) which enable him to help himself, at least three unfortunate consequences are likely: first, the practitioner is *overloaded* because he has to serve the same needs of the consumer over and over again; second, his *services become scarce* because of this overload and *expensive* because they are scarce; and, third the consumer is trained into an unhealthy *dependence* on the practitioner instead of developing his own capacity to seek out resources and help himself.*

Just as service without product creates problems,so does product without service. Again the experiences of those who must deal with other cultures is most instructive. Lachman, (0351) among others, notes the folly of what he calls "technology-import without implantation." The technical and managerial skills and know-how upon which industrial technology depends must be communicated to local practitioners before a firm market (and hence effective utilization) can be developed.

c.   Product-Hard Versus Product-Soft

Parallelling the previous discussion and probably not distinct from it are the frequently discussed differences between hardware and software knowledge.** The context in which these differences are most often discussed, is the venerable but highly debatable "lag" hypothesis. Roger's brief review on this topic deserves quoting (1824, p. 133).

> "Ogburn (1364) claimed that material innovations diffused and were adopted more readily than non-material ideas. Linton (6390, p. 337-338) pointed out that one reason for this cultural lag (of non-material behind material innovations) is greater visibility and communicability of material ideas. He stated, "the material techniques and their products are probably the only elements of culture which can be completely communicated, and it is significant that it is usually these elements which are accepted most readily....' The culture lag theory of Ogburn has fallen into academic disrepute in recent years. In fact, Boskoff (6391, p. 296) labeled the distinction between material and non-material ideas as a theoretical *cul de sac* and recommends a hasty exit."

---

*In some professions, medicine, and psychiatry in particular, some practitioners view this dependence as healthy and necessary to their practice. Gebhard (0232) notes that faith and confidence in the physician is maintained by keeping a large knowledge gap between himself and his patient, a gap so large in fact, that the physician is viewed as some sort of magician or miracle worker. One may wonder if medical practitioners have every seriously considered and balanced the negative against the positive consequences of this state of affairs. (See again, in this connection the contrasting roles of conveyor and consultant discussed in Chapter 7 on linking roles. The dependency problem is nowhere better understood than in the field of international development where building a self-help orientation is fundamental to change. See, for example, the summary of experiences of personnel of U.S. Voluntary agencies in other countries, Public Administration Clearinghouse, 1045, p. 330.

**Also intertwined with this topic is the previously discussed "social science versus natural science" question.

It seems doubtful that this topic can be dismissed as readily as Boskoff would have us believe, however, because large and at least superficially obvious differences exist between hardware and non-hardware knowledge which many authors still see as affecting utilization. Schwartz, for example, (02893) notes that research related to bringing about peace has focussed on such hardware items as detection devices at the expense of research into the social causes of war which might bring forth new policies and diplomatic strategies (software knowledge) specifically engineered to lower the probabilities of military conflict. Among the other presumed attributes of hardware as distinct from software are greater glamor, less cost (superficially at least) and likelihood of being less controversial and less threatening (which could be secondary effects of complexity and communicability).

In addition to and in contrast to these presumed advantages of hardware, however, certain points should be kept in mind. First of all, we need to remember that hardware does not diffuse easily when it is introduced into new settings. Barnett (2510) for example, points out that we use different criteria for "acceptance" of material and non-material innovations, and that if we required that acceptance of a technology include manufacturing, as well as using material items, we would eliminate the often-observed "cultural lag." Responding to comments by Drucker (6361) that "tools, in sharp contrast to ideas, are widely welcomed everywhere," Pi-Sunyer and DeGregor state (2098):

> "Tools are not autonomous artifacts; they have their 'ecology'. They are elements in three distinct but related complexes; technological, cultural and environmental. Tools are related to other tools in a problem-solving process. Tools also imply behavior. Finally, because Tools are part of a problem-solving process, different climatic or cultural environments create different problems whose solutions require different tools or different use of the same tools. ...to distinguish between ideas and tools as Dr. Drucker does, and to assume that one will be borrowed without the other, is a misunderstanding of both culture and technology." (p. 248).

This statement corresponds closely to the point of view which we have put forth and wish to stress in this chapter, that hardware and software are intricately related   knowledge products. One implication for the student of diffusion is to look for gaps and inadequacies in software and service components wherever he finds instances of "unaccountable" resistance to hardware innovations, and vice versa.

Before concluding this discussion, two points should also be made in favor of hardware knowledge. First of all, it may well be that advanced hardware technology provides the opportunity to bypass immense and complex problems which might otherwise require endless training and servicing. This is surely the promise of automation. The mechanical loom obviates the necessity of training thousands of weavers; the automatic sensing device obviates the need for training countless observers and nightwatchmen; the computer obviates the necessity of training people of follow long and complicated accounting routines; and so on. Thus, hardware technology always holds out the hope of what Weinberg (0539) calls "quick technological fixes" on problems which would otherwise require massive doses of social control, attitude change, education, and the like. He cites the intra-uterine device as a birth control measure which exemplifies this kind of product, and looking forward, he sees the desalination of sea water as another dramatic development which would have this by-passing effect on a host of difficult social control problems.

Finally, hardware technology may lead the way for software technology and new practices. If it is true that there is a lag, according to this view it is only because hardware knowledge is forging ahead and may well by pulling software knowledge along behind at a much faster rate than could otherwise have been hoped for. Certainly, the acceptance of responsibility to support natural science research seemed to open the door to a willingness by government to begin supporting social research also. Moreover, hardware advances in such areas as communication and computers have been prerequisite to the development of many forms of social engineering including the opinion poll, the organizatinal survey, and many tools of economic and social analysis and prediction.

d.   Social Science "Products."

A special word is probably in order about a new kind of product which is just now beginning to come on the market which may change our society and our lives more radically than any of the inventions of hardware technology have up to now. This is the *social science invention*. Until the middle 1960's most social science utilization efforts were experimental and tentative. At most they were working models or prototypes (see again discussion of prototypes under AR & D). But now some of these models have been tested and refined to the point where they are at or near the production stage. One example of this development is Blake and Mouton's "Managerial Grid" program (6198), a comprehensive "package" program for bringing about change in organizations. The "T-group" human relations training technique (developed largely by the National Training Laboratory, see Bradford, et.al., 6196), is another item that is moving rapidly from the experimental and trial stage into a mass dissemination stage. Other social science engineering developments which may be reaching this point include the organizational self-survey, the conflict management lab, classroom interaction analysis (Flanders, 2863), instant audience feedback and many more.

These new "products" confront our society and even our researchers with perplexing new problems. One pressing need is to find out at an early date as much as we can about the effects of these innovations on people, organizations, and our culture. Only with such knowledge will we as a society be able to apply to these phenomena the appropriate controls to safeguard values that we hold to be fundamental. It has been said many times that the biggest problem in the so-called cultural lag is the inability to assess the social and psychological effects of technology until long after they have been introduced, so that change is no longer within our control.* Ironically, this may be even more true of the social innovations.**

---

*This point has been stressed several times by Michael (6190) and is also noted by Vickers, (6362, p. 386).

**See Carlson, 0585, Chapter 6, for discussion of unanticipated consequences of programmed instruction in the classroom.

D.   USER MESSAGE OUTPUT: FEEDBACK

With the discussion of practice knowledge, we may have covered the full gamut of what most people would consider "knowledge," but in an effort to follow through on the systematic analysis of message transformations presented in Figure 9.1, it seems appropriate to deal with the messages which the consumer produces, as distinct from those which he takes in.

We have noted at various points in this review that knowledge utilization is a partially closed system of reciprocal relations between a "user" sub-system and a "resource" subsystem (see Chapter Two). Thus while it is true that knowledge which gets to the user has reached the "end of the line," it is equally true that the system requires return signals or "feedback" to the resource systems, not only to keep knowledge flow going but also to provide the resource sub-systems with creative stimulation. This feedback in a very real sense is knowledge, *the knowledge output of the user.*

1.   *Need Expressions.*

Users generate two kinds of messages which are of importance to practitioners and researchers. These are: (1) need expression and (2) consumption reactions. A principal distinction between the two is the point at which the information flow cycle is seen to originate. Among many authors,* it is popular to view this cycle as starting inside the consumer with his needs, perhaps even his basic needs. To some extent this view depends on a conception of motivation as an internal self-starting process within the individual person. In any case, it is treated as the *given,* the starting point in the long process which leads to the statement of problems, the development of solutions and eventually the dissemination of these solutions in usable form.

Needs can be classified in innumerable ways (see for example Murray, 6328, or Murray and Kluckhohn, 6329, for a very thorough classification), and some authors (e.g., Maslow, 6327) have attempted to place needs in some sort of hierarchy whereby certain classes of "higher" need only become salient when other more "basic" needs have been provided for. Havelock (6183, pp. 220-223), and Havelock and Benne (3872) have tried to provide classifications of needs with specific reference to the D & U Process.

In this section we will try to indicate the various ways in which these needs become *articulated;* i.e., how they are transformed from "feelings" to *expressions.* Probably the most familiar distinction among need expressions is between *pain and pleasure.*   These may be stated more precisely as *"expressions of need for pain reduction; the alleviation of an unpleasant condition"* on the one hand and *"expression of desire to achieve pleasure or to produce a pleasant or a better condition"* on the other hand.

---

*The problem solver (P-S) perspective discussed at length in Chapters 10 and 11.

a.   Pain

There is no more important nor more useful message from consumer
to practitioner than an explicit, pin-pointed expression of *pain*.
The pain message   is the essential starting point of problem identification and problem solving. However, it is not always easy or
even possible for the consumer to emit such an expression. Typically,
it can only be expressed when it is an *acute pain*, that all-too-
transient phase of a problem when the consumer is explicitly and loudly
aware that something is very wrong with himself.

Therefore, it may well be that acute expressions of need represent
only the visible portion of an iceberg of humanity's ills. Many of the
things that afflict us eventually become *chronic* conditions; we learn
to live with them, to forget or repress or become numb to them. In this
buried form of *chronicity* they become more difficult to communicate,
to understand, and to treat.

Part of the task of the change agent who is faced with endemic
chronic need situations is to reawaken and revitalize the client's
awareness of pain. In so doing he may be said to be transforming the
need expression from the chronic state back into the acute state. As
acute·needs they can be identified, diagnosed and treated more easily.
This is a cardinal principal of most forms of psychotherapy (subjecting
chronic problems in a person's life to intensive scrutiny and historical
review to reidentify the acute pain points and start rebuilding from
them) and is recognized by some authors as a key element in planned
change in client systems.*

b.   Pleasure

Need expressions on the *pleasure* side may seem less important or
less deserving of attention, but as our society becomes more affluent
and more concerned with reaching higher levels of need satisfaction
(as in Maslow's concept of *"self-actualization"*) the need expressions
in this area may loom larger in importance. It may also be that expressions of a desire for *better* conditions are more readily evoked than
expressions of pain. Furthermore, they may be more effective than pain
messages as forms of communication because, as positive messages, they
do not evoke defensive, pain avoidance behavior in receivers.

The changing nature of needs and need structures is an important
fact which needs greater recognition. *New areas of need* emerge and
new areas of need are *created* as people grow, as they become affluent,
and as they become more aware and more understanding of their environment. These new areas of need and new definitions of need represent
additional important message outputs from the user; these messages are
especially relevant as inputs to the researcher and to the inventor who
must be able to predict what will be needed by large segments of society

---

*Lippitt, et.al., 1343, repeatedly cite the evocation and utilization of awareness
 of pain in the client as a major task of the change agent.

five and ten years hence. An important aspect of the new role of "futurists" in the R & D process is the prediction of such changing need patterns.

2. *Consumer Reactions*

Need expression is only one half of the story of User Output. If they are to be effective problem-solvers, the practitioner and the researcher also need feedback on what they have done; they need to know if they have been effective or ineffective, helpful or hurtful to the consumers; and they need specific and detailed knowledge on what parts of their output seem to work better or worse. These feedback responses to practice by the user can come in a number of ways which we can conveniently subdivide into "good news," i.e., *need reduction expressions* and "bad news," i.e., *need continuance and exacerbation.*

a. *Need Reductions.*

(1) Satisfaction

The general term for an articulation of need reduction is *satisfaction,* and there are situations where a statement by the user that he is now "satisfied" is sufficient feedback for the practitioner. However, such testimonials have a number of shortcomings as feedback. First of all, they are restricted to situations in which direct face-to-face feedback is possible, i.e., they do not apply when large numbers of users are affected or where the information is transmitted through mass media or through commercial channels. Secondly, such feedback does not provide detailed information on which the practitioner can change his behavior. Thirdly, statements of "satisfaction" are notoriously unreliable particularly where "satisfaction" responses are deemed to be socially desirable. For example, it is often viewed as *polite* to express only satisfaction especially when the practitioner has endeavored to do something for us (i.e., we should be grateful for his concern whether he helps us or not) and when he has high status. Thus, one physician (cited by Hubbard, 0751) notes that patients will lie about following a prescription in order to please the doctor.

(2) Symptoms of well-being and improvement

More reliable but sometimes less visible than signs of satisfaction are various signs or *symptoms of well-being* which truly satisfied users may exhibit. If children in a town which has adopted fluoridation show up less often at the dentist or have fewer teeth filled, this strongly suggests that a genuine reduction in tooth decay has taken place; if infant mortality declines, this is a sign of improved health standards; if workers in a factory stay on the job longer and show up less frequently at sick call, these are material signs of improved job morale. The principal problem with such signs is that they may be difficult to read or interpret. In a sense they are not messages given off by the user, but messages which the alert practitioner needs to *retrieve* from the user. (See also discussion of unobtrusive measures for feedback in Chapter Nine).

Of more immediate use to the practitioner may be the specific
and short-run *signs of improvement* in a specific condition which is
under treatment: the patient who shows a reduction in hallucinations
after the tranquillizer is administered; the farmer who shows an
increased crop yield after using the new soil conservation practice;
etc.

(3) Payment

Perhaps the most common and effective form of feedback to
practitioners is *payment* usually in the form of money. Payment
is the substance which keeps people working and keeps knowledge
flowing to the user at least in a commercial economy. Certainly, no
understanding of utilization is complete if it leaves out the
important element of financing. Payments may be offered directly
to the practitioner in return for products and services; or they
may be rendered indirectly through taxes which are distributed as
payments, grants, subsidies, and contracts by government. However,
the indirect payment* is far less effective as a feedback message
on actual performance.

As utilizable feedback, however, payment has many deficiencies.
In the first place payment if often *not contingent* on adequate
service but simply on service. A physician gets paid whether or
not he helps us, and typically we pay for a product before we
know whether or not it works properly (at least if it is a major
product like an automobile). If the payment is not contingent
on adequate performance, it follows that it is not useful feedback
any more than the feedback of the user who always says he is
"satisfied"whether he is helped or not.

A second limitation of payment is the extremely slow feedback
cycle that may be involved in any one exchange. The manufacturer
must gamble that his product will sell, for he cannot afford to
wait for actual repayments before he starts mass production. Even
less can the researcher wait to discover whether or not the
general public and its elected representatives are satisfied with
research payoff before he continues his studies. All of us in
reality float on a *sea of credit*, investments, and gambles in
which payments are only loosely contingent on specific performances.

The authors of this report are not economists so we will
avoid discussing this complex topic further, but we move on with
a realization that economics is a big and, to us at least, puzzling
part of the equation of knowledge flow.

There may well be other rewards to the practitioner and the
researcher which stand in place of immediate payments. Indeed
there may be a natural tendency to seek out feedback, to learn
specifically what one is doing right, and this drive may be
related to the general striving for competence discussed earlier
(Chapter 4). To be truly useful this feedback must be specific; it
must tell the practitioner what worked, how it worked, where it
worked and why it worked.

---

*Most research activities are supported in this indirect fashion.

b.   Need Continuance and Exacerbation

Even though we usually have trouble hearing it (see Chapter 4) bad news is probably more useful than good news as feedback for many of our endeavors. An analysis of this negative feedback essentially parallels the analysis of positive feedback presented above, but it is worth discussing separately because of some rather distinctive issues that it raises for us.

(1) Signs of Dissatisfaction

In the first place, even though *dissatisfaction* may be a much harder message to convey than satisfaction when certain kinds of social constraints are in force, once expressed, it may be *more visible* and may be perceived as more "urgent" by resource persons. People who know they are dissatisfied and have decided that they want to express their dissatisfaction are capable of expressing it quite loudly and flamboyantly whether it be a screaming tantrum, a sit-in, a strike, or a march on Washington. A consumer reaction of this type stops the action for the practitioner, forcing him to to pay attention to the consumer and forcing him to reexamine his "helping" role.

(2) Signs of No Change

In contrast, most difficult to identity are the *signs of no change* in a pre-existing condition, particularly where there is no concommitant awareness of dissatisfaction on the part of the user. "No change" almost looks like "no information" *but it is not the same* as no information; indeed it should be a clarion call to action on the part of the practitioner. It may be difficult for the practitioner to stir himself to action when he gets only "no change" information, but if he does not act on this sort of "non-message" he may soon find himself with a dead patient, a closed school, a struck factory, or a shut-down university.

(3) Signs of Deteriotation

Equally insidious but perhaps more visible are *signs of deterioration*. Like chronic conditions which have suddenly turned acute again, signs of deterioration are likely to send loud signals to practitioners who are immediately involved. This was evidently the case when pediatricians began noticing a high evidence of blindness in premature infants who had been in incubators. Alerted to this grim side-effect of their own labors, they worked rapidly and hard to identify the problem and remedy it.* It may also explain why state governors act on highway safety matters when they are faced with the "crisis" of a particularly high fatality year   after years of inaction on this dreadful but chronic social problem. (Havelock, 7108).

---

*The problem turned out to be the high oxygen environment of the incubator. By diluting the mixture, they were able to achieve the same benefits without harmful side effects (see discussion of this case in Havelock, 6183, pp. 41-42.)

(4)   Non-Payment

Non-payment is probably the least reliable of indicators of
negative feedback, partly for the same reasons that payment is
inadequate as a measure. To start with, non-payment, is a relatively rare event. Typically we commit ourselves to pay for
products prior to the time we are able to try them out. Hence,
non-payment has little meaning except as it applies to buying
the same product *again* from the same manufacturer at a later time.
At best, this "next time" feedback is slow, indirect, ambiguous,
and difficult to interpret as a response to specific items.*

The same strictures about payment-in-advance seem to be
applying increasingly to service areas such as medical treatment,
dentistry, and law. Whether this situation applies because of the
unequal power balance between consumer and practitioner may be a
topic worth investigating. It does seem that consumers who act
in concert or as large organizations (corporations or governments)
are more able to pay through contract on a <u>contingency</u> basis (i.e.,
only if it works). Presumably, in these contractual relations
between consumer and practitioner the threat of non-payment <u>does</u>
constitute meaningful feedback on inadequate performance.

(5)   Non-Adoption

Related to non-payment is the implied message inherent in
"non-adoption". This is a very difficult kind of "feedback" to
measure and is perhaps the least specific form of feedback since
it tells the practitioner nothing about <u>why</u> he is failing. The
fault may lie in the product, the marketing or advertising techniques, the price, the label, or perhaps even the mood of the
consumer. Famous cases of non-adoption such as the Edsel
Automobile in 1958, indicate how baffling and trouble-some the non-
adoption phenomenon can be.

In the previous chapter, the "defender" was discussed as a
troublesome but possibly functional role in many utilization
chains. Also in Chapter Four various defensive and self-protective
behaviors were analyzed as these contributed to our psychological
understanding of the receiver. In this chapter it should be noted
that such *defensive and self-protective behaviors* constitute a
form of feedback knowledge to the practitioner. If the practitioner
(or the researcher) can "read" these signs and if he can heed the
"defender," he may obtain useful information on which to change
and improve his own output.

(6)   Control

User behaviors which are usually not recognized as "feedback"
are the various attempts which the user makes to <u>control</u> the
behavior of the practitioner and the researcher through government
action. Government regulations, restrictions and laws which are
designed to insure safe drugs, accurate advertising, uncontaminated
food, safe airplanes, and (most recently) safe automobiles

---

*The inadequacy of payment as a feedback mechanism is probably a major factor in the
rise of market research, the purpose of which is to provide consumer reactions before
mass production is risked. Regrettably very little market research has been surveyed
for this report because most such research is not in the public domain.

constitute information to manufacturers, researchers, and practitioners. Behind many of these laws we find a history of gradually increasing awareness of a problem by consumers (usually assisted by *defenders* who are somewhat contemptuously referred to as "muck-rakers"), with a concomitant increase of pressure on elected officials, until, finally, legislation is enacted, usually representing a compromise between practitioner and consumer interests. These changes can well be understood as efforts by the *macrosystem* (see Chapter Three) to regulate its own behavior. In effect control legislation, when it is well-conceived and well-enforced, constitutes a most useful feedback message from the user subsystem to the resource subsystem.

(7) "Bugs"

Finally under this heading of "need continuance and exacerbation" we should also include those specific and detailed indicators of trouble which are known in engineering as "bugs,"* specific and localized indicators of *things not working*. This is the kind of feedback which is potentially the most rewarding to the practitioner and the researcher if they can get it. To be most useful, information on "bugs" must be detailed, accurate, and immediate. It is usually very difficult to derive information that meets these three standards simultaneously.

This brings us to the end of our discussion of user message output. In this section we have tried to convey some idea of the vast range of possible feedback message types, and we have also tried to indicate that these types should be considered along side the message outputs from the researcher and the practitioner as equally important parts of the total *knowledge flow system*.

E. ADDITIONAL MESSAGE TYPES

An analysis of knowledge types would not be complete without a listing of certain kinds of changes which do not constitute "knowledge" in the usual sense. Four types of phenomena which fall within this area are: (1) *attitudes, values, and orientations*, (2) *resource identification and retrieval information*, (3) *people*, and (4) *media*.

1. *Attitudes, Values, and Orientations*

The social change literature both in psychology and in anthropology is focussed on *attitude change* and *value change* without regard to questions of utility. It is on this ground that we have excluded much of this literature from our review.** There are, however, points at which these phenomena cannot be ignored. In the first place, we have noted at various points in this text that the *attitudes* of receivers towards new knowledge strongly

---

*See for example, Ames 3294, for a discussion of the importance of "bugs" as information in the development process.

**Although major sources on such topics as the social psychology of attitude formation and change are discussed in Chapter Four.

affect their adoption behavior. To succeed in diffusing a new product or practice where resistant attitudes pre-exist, it may often be necessary to *diffuse a new attitude* toward the innovation prior to the actual innovation diffusion effort; the diffusion of new attitudes and sometimes *even new values* may be the first step in any sort of technological advance.

The largest potential positive result from attitude change might come about from the successful diffusion not of new attitudes about *specific* products, but new orientations and new values concerning scientific knowledge and innovations *in general*. We have noted the phenomenon of the science-oriented consumer (Morgan, et. al., 6326). This may be especially important in the field of education. As Michael states (3892, p. 13):

> "The enlargement of knowledgeable and committed concern about education may prove to be most important education innovation of all."

2. *Resource Identification and Retrieval Information as a Type of Knowledge*

In this report we have presented a conception of the utilization process as a reciprocal interaction between the "user" and the "resource system". However, before such an interaction can be initiated, the user needs to know something about resources. He needs to be able to identify for himself *where the resources are,* how they can be used, what they cost, and whether they are appropriate for his special needs. The most valuable information that the user can be given is sometimes knowledge about where to go and who to see. Although "resource retrieval" as a process will be discussed more fully elsewhere (especially in Chapter 9) it should be noted here that information about resource retrieval is a very important type of resource.

Information about how to identify resources may be conveyed unwittingly as a side-product of other attempts to diffuse knowledge. Hence, the man who gives us a detailed lecture on computer programming may not teach us anything about computer programming but he may teach us who to go to if we should need expert advice in this area. An instance of this type of learning apparently occurred in a seminar on psychiatry for general practitioners reported by Golden (0691). What the physicians learned about psychiatry wasn't very impressive, but there was a subsequent dramatic *increase in psychiatric referrals from* these G.P.'s.

3. *People As Knowledge Packages.*

People who have knowledge can be hired and used almost as if they were knowledge packages. Within competitive industries it is a common practice to buy the inventor if you can't buy the invention. Likewise, when the government hires a scientific advisor or pays a scientific consultant, it is really obtaining scientific knowledge and expertise which it cannot generate internally. The consultant-expert thus becomes a kind of handy reference tool, a portable fast-retrieval knowledge bank. As Chin (2612) comments: " 'Have Knowledge, will travel' for hire, might well be the slogan of the consultant who attempts to distill, refine, and apply his knowledge to serve a specific purpose of a client" (p. 7).

Related to this "buying of people" is the *training of people* within one's own group to be expert resources. However, both training and recruiting are forms of knowledge acquisition available only to wealthy consumers or large groups of people acting in concert (e.g., government, corporations, very large and affluent schools systems.) The relative advantages of retrieving

knowledge versus retrieving knowledge *holders* for various sized groups of
users are unclear. Allen and Cohen (6737) have obtained some evidence
that in a R & D laboratory human sources are more useful for discovering
particular techniques while impersonal literature sources are more important
for reviewing the state-of-the-art in a given area. In general, however,
the trade-offs between using people and using other types of resources are
not known.

4.   *The Medium as Message*

Marshall McLuhan has captivated the intellectual community of the 1960's
with his provocative thesis that "the medium is the message," (6503). This
proposition has special significance for students of knowledge utilization.
Until there is a clear channel between resource and user, D & U is a
terribly slow, difficult, and expensive process. However, the acceptance
by the user of a *medium* opens vast opportunities for the diffusion of
innumerable separate innovations. The medium, therefore, is at least one
type of message and a very important one because the medium can be thought
of as including the information that it is capable of conveying. If the
consumer "buys" the medium, he necessarily buys the things that the medium
sells. Inevitably, also, the more he is sold on a medium, the more of its
messages he buys and the more dependent he is on it; it changes his way of
thinking and looking at the world; it makes him an integral part of a new
system, (the network of the medium); and it puts him under the influence and
control of those who control this system.

At times McLuhan seems to be telling us that different media compete
with each other in a kind of dialectic process (see Chapter 10); one
medium (e.g., the printed page) remains dominant over culture for a period
of time until a new and more potent medium gains ascendance and comes to
dominate (e.g., radio - T.V.). From our understanding of the utilization
process, however, we would doubt that this dominance ever takes place to
the extent implied in McLuhan's writings. Fortunately, few if any of us
are utterly addicted to any one medium, and no medium is 100% successful in
this sense. Rather we are influenced by several media representing several
different kinds of networks: television, with its attendant reporters,
commentators, ad men, executives, and sponsors; school classrooms and their
attendant teachers, administrators, school boards and regents; our face-to-
face relations with our peer group with its attendant opinion leaders, socio-
emotional specialists and gatekeepers; our work group with its attendant
supervisors, vice presidents, personnel managers, and board members. These
are all influence networks, controlled by particular "media" which impinge
on us daily, bombarding us with messages, competing for our attention. The
vital fact is that *they do compete* and continue to do so; no one medium ever
seems to win out completely, so we remain at least partly free; the consumer
does retain some control of the decision-making process.

F.   THE METAMORPHOSIS OF KNOWLEDGE

The major classes of "message" which have been discussed here are functionally
and logically related to one another. In this section we will try to spell out
these interrelations, suggesting a step-by-step metamorphosis from "basic knowledge"
to "utilized knowledge" and from "user messages" back to "basic knowledge."

In order to simplify this presentation, let us take *practice knowledge* as a point of departure. This is the knowledge which has come through the development phase and has been tested and packaged for diffusion. It is knowledge which has reached the point at which it is definitely useful and immediately relavant to the user. Where do the other types of knowledge we have discussed stand in relation to this practice knowledge? Figure 8.2 sketches a rough outline of these relationships.

FIGURE 8.2   Elements in the Generation of New Practice Knowledge

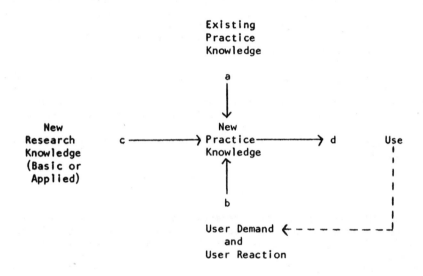

As Figure 8.2 indicates, new practice knowledge is generated from three primary sources. First of all, it grows out of (and is embedded in) *existing* practice knowledge (relationship "a" in the Figure). In this sense it is only partly "new." New knowledge simply is not practical if it takes no account of the practice knowledge already in use. Changes in practice are likely to come about through an evolutionary process, an integration of new elements into a pre-existing whole, rather than through revolution, or wholesale substitution.

Existing practice also has an important impact in another sense, when it represents the diffusion of good practice from one practitioner to another. Usually the term "practice innovation" is a relative one; that is, the practice is new only to the practitioner who makes the decision to adopt for the first time. He may, however, learn of this "innovation" from another practitioner who has already used it for years.

New practice knowledge is also based partly on inputs representing user demand ("b" in Figure 8.2) in its various forms. These were previously analyzed (in the section on "user messages") into need expressions and reactions to previous practice knowledge, and they include immediate feedback to the practitioner on the effectiveness of his craft.

Finally, we have the input from research ("c" in Figure 8.2), whether "basic" or "applied" or in the form of "developed" prototypes. Research inputs are undoubtedly an important and unique part of this equation and represent knowledge which is not only new but also *validated* according to specified rules.

In Figure 8.3 we have tried to spell out these same relationships among knowledge types in much greater detail.

[Insert Figure 8.3 Here]

To begin with, this figure reassembles the four major categories of knowledge with their most prominent sub-types. In the center and at the focus of our concern is *"practice knowledge."* At the left are AR & D and more remotely Basic Knowledge. On the right is pictured the ultimate recipient, the "user", and emanating from him are the various forms of feedback described in the section and "user message output."

The figure also identifies sixteen important relationships among knowledge types (designated by letters "a" to "p"). These sixteen relationships are described briefly as follows:

1. Basic Knowledge Transformations:

    a. Basic Knowledge may be disseminated in the form of *theory, data,* or *methods.* Typically, it is considered to be in a final, disseminable state only when all three are synthesized as formal research reports. However, potential users do not necessarily retrieve all three simultaneously or use them in this synthesized form.

    b. The major movement of basic knowledge is most typically from scientist *to scientist,* presumably for the generation of additional basic knowledge. However, the applied researcher and the developer (AR & D) are probably the second most frequent receivers of this kind of information, and a large part of AR & D is derived, in part, from at least one of the three types of basic knowledge.

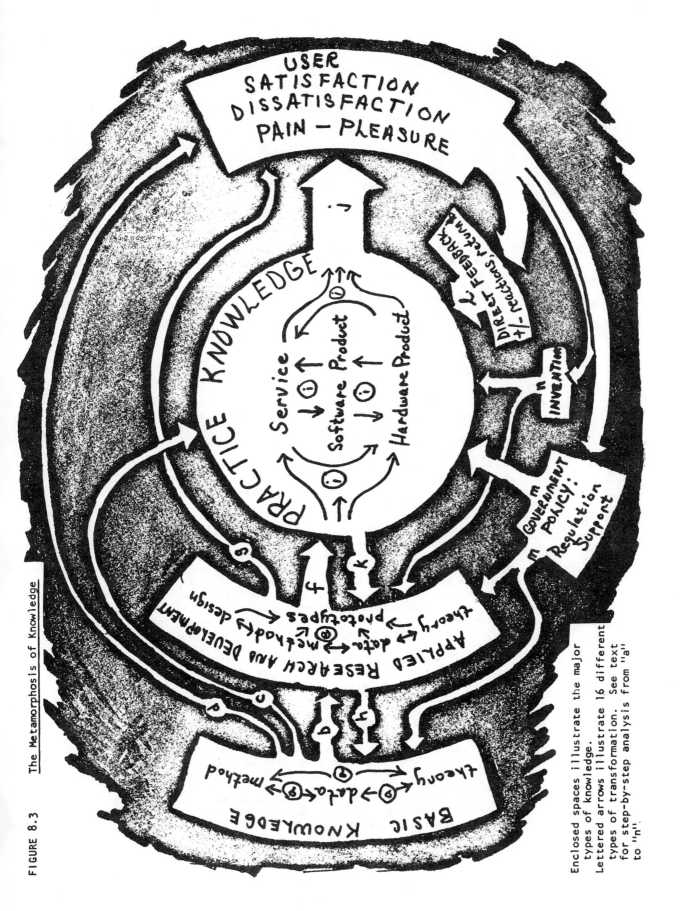

FIGURE 8.3 The Metamorphosis of Knowledge

Enclosed spaces illustrate the major
types of knowledge.
Lettered arrows illustrate 16 different
types of transformation. See text
for step-by-step analysis from "a"
to "n".

c.   A lesser amount of basic knowledge is also transmitted directly to the practitioner, typically in his early training for his profession (e.g., biochemistry for the pre-med student, sociology for the pre-law student, etc.). Probably very little of what is *transmitted* actually gets *translated* and *transformed* into practice, but the effort to transmit continues to be made largely with the rationale that it provides a foundation for later more applied learning. Undoubtedly some basic knowledge also gets transformed into *operating principles* or even *values* which the well-grounded practitioner can apply to problems in his everyday work.

d.   Finally, some basic knowledge finds its way directly to consumers through such mechanisms as science reporting (see Chapter 7). This type of knowledge transformation is important in at least two ways. First, it allows the consumer to develop a *scientific orientation* toward his environment which, in turn, gives him a broader and more meaningful perspective within which to view his own needs and the resources available to him. Secondly, it may get transformed into consumer expectations and consumer demand for better practice founded on valid scientific principles.

2.   AR & D Transformations

e.   The several forms of AR & D knowledge may be transmitted separately or in various combinations. The *"prototype,"* in particular, represents a complex package of *data, applied theory,* and *method,* which is in some sense, the end product of the AR & D process.

f.   The major receiver for AR & D knowledge is the practitioner. The AR & D process culminates in the prototype but as the prototype is tested and adapted in more and more practice settings it gradually becomes "practice knowledge."

g.   Some AR & D knowledge also is disseminated directly to the consumer. This is the type of knowledge which is most likely to be transformed into consumer awareness, readiness, and demand for new practice knowledge. For example, an awareness that two-way video-telephones are now being developed undoubtedly is preparing the public for later acceptance and even demand for this innovation. Similarly, kidney and heart transplant operations performed on an experimental basis but highly publicized by the press are likely to be translated into expectations and pressures by patients on their own doctors to provide similar services.

h.   Finally, an important direction for AR & D output is feedback to basic research either in the form of field tests of basic theories or in the stimulation of the new basic research inquiry arising from AR & D discoveries.

3.   Practice Knowledge Transformations.

i.   As was indicated in Figure 8.2, practice "innovations" frequently come not from research or development but from *other practitioners*. Moreover there is a frequent *blending* of various types of practice knowledge. New products may require the development of new practices; an artificial heart (hardware) obviously must be accompanied by surgical skills (practice) and procedures (software), and possibly new surgical instruments and supplies (more hardware) before it can be meaningfully utilized; a teaching machine (hardware) requires new teacher skills on how to introduce it to the classroom (service) and programs to be used in it (software).

j. The primary receiver for practice knowledge is the ultimate consumer. In total volume this is by far the largest knowledge transfer in the D & U macrosystem. It is also the most critical.

k. Current practice knowlege together with the needs expressed by practitioners, and reports on problems they encounter, are prime sources of stimulation for AR & D. The relationship between these two types of knowledge has to be close and feedback between them extremely rapid if either is to be optimally useful.

4. User Knowledge Output

The various forms of knowledge--basic, applied, and practice--which are absorbed by the user are translated into *satisfactions* and *dissatisfactions*, articulated in at least three forms: "l" direct feedback, "m" government activities; and "n" inventions.

l. Practitioners are the prime target of *direct consumer feedback* in the form of positive and negative reactions, statements of satisfaction and dissatisfaction, and dollar return.

m. On a larger scale and for larger issues the government represents the most important channel for *indirect consumer feedback* and consumer *control* over the resource system as a whole. It would appear to be the only way in which the general public can affect the work of basic knowledge builders.

n, User demand is also a powerful incentive to invention, especially for independent free-lance inventors identified by some authorities as being highly significant sources of innovations (e.g., Schon, 6092). Inventors in turn supply important inputs for AR & D; their "inventions" represent first approximations of prototypes which can be screened and further refined through the AR & D process. However, untested inventions also may find their way <u>directly</u> to practice, particularly in areas where AR & D knowledge is primitive (e.g., in knowledge about management practices). This type of transformation opens the door to all kinds of quackery and mal-adoption.

Figure 8.3, complex as it is, does not begin to describe all the transformations of knowledge but it does give us a notion of the cyclical process by which knowledge is transformed and evolved. It is a process that can be, and typically is, composed of much briefer cycles of output and feedback; these shorter loops may entirely leave out basic knowledge or AR & D--as when inventions lead to new practices or when immediate feedback from users leads a practitioner to improve what he is doing.

This summarizes and concludes Part I, A TYPOLOGY OF MESSAGES. In Part II, we will consider the characteristics of messages which affect their disseminability and utilizability.

II. CHARACTERISTICS OF KNOWLEDGE AND INNOVATIONS

As we have noted, a traditional approach to the classification of various types of knowledge is one which focusses on those characteristics which permit comparisons of diffusibility. In reviewing the literature we have found it helpful to make the distinction also made by Barnett (0620) betweem *intrinsic* and *extrinsic* characteristics. Intrinsic characteristics are those which are inherent in an innovation, while extrinsic characteristics are those which have meaning only in the context of specified audiences or adoption settings, as with the "congruence" of a message with the values of the receiver.

A. INTRINSIC CHARACTERISTICS

Five intrinsic characteristics are expecially worth noting. These are: (1) Scientific Status of the Knowledge; (2) Value Loading; (3) Divisibility; (4) Complexity; and (5) Communicability.

1. *Scientific Status of the Knowledge*

Knowledge is considered to be more or less "scientific" according to the degree of its *reliability, validity, generality, internal consistency,* and *congruence with other scientific theories* (see again first pages of this chapter). Despite the presumed importance of these attributes to *scientists,* the literature contains few reported attempts to assess the effect of the dimension on diffusion or utilization. An initial problem here may be one of deciding what is "scientific" and what is not, a question which becomes increasingly problematic as we move from basic "hard" science into the "softer" social and behavioral science areas. Also complicating this picture is the fact (noted in Part I of this chapter) that information changes as it flows from one stage to another in the development process; hence criteria of scientific evaluation appropriate at one stage (e.g., when it was published in a research journal) may be inappropriate at another (when the same knowledge is applied and emerges as the prototype of a new product). Products based on scientific findings may need to be evaluated in terms of such design features as "utility," "durability," "precision" and "cost." Hence the terms "reliability" and "validity" may have different shades of meaning to the engineer than they have to the scientist . Evaluations at these later development stages may no longer be viewed as measures of the degree to which the knowledge is "scientific". In any case, the stamp of approval or disapproval from scientists may not be a decisive factor in adoption behaviors as the many community rejections of fluoridation and increasing cigarette sales indicate.

A few studies in the rural sociology diffusion tradition may throw some further light on this dimension. We have the study by Francis (1410) of the diffusion of a non-recommended innovation, the grass incubator.* This device was evaluated and declared useless by agricultural economists, animal nutritionists, the U.S.D.A., and by state extension services, yet *some farmers chose to ignore this advice.* For these farmers apparently the salesman was a more influential and credible source than the scientists. Rejectors, on the other hand, were those who relied on scientific sources, as translated by county agents.

Rogers (1824, p. 143) points out that it may be difficult to determine whether an individual should or should not adopt an innovation. If it is assumed that the innovator's behavior is subjectively rational,** we can only rely on expert opinion for the determination of under- or over-adoption. The "scientificness" of the innovation may be the criterion on which this

---

*Also mentioned in Chapter 7

**See again Chapter Four for our analysis of the receiver as a rational chooser.

judgement is made, and thus the basis for determining rationality of adoption. A number of studies illustrate the fact that scientific judgements of rational adoption are not necessarily the determinants of adoption rates. Toussaint and Stone (1070) report a study of North Carolina farmers who had purchased self-propelled tobacco harvesters, a scientifically validated useful innovation; but because they did not use them to full capacity, they did not meet a criterion of rational adoption as determined by economists. Goldstein and Eichhorn (1835) studied the adoption of four-row corn planters which experts had described as economically justifiable only for 60 or more acres of corn. Using this criterion, they found 37% of the Indiana farmers whom they studied to be rational adopters, 30% irrational over- or under-adoptions, and 33% rational rejectors. Further analysis by Goldstein (6313) indicated differences between the rational and irrational adopters in terms of both education and tradition-oriented beliefs. Thus, education may well be a factor which gives meaning to the "scientificness" of an innovation (Rogers, 1824, p. 142-144).*

Clearly, the scientific status of an innovation or the scientifically rational basis for its adoption, are not necessarily important factors in diffusibility. Factors which may over-shadow scientific status include education of the receiver, perceived credibility of the information source, and other characteristics of the innovation, to be discussed below.

Even among scientists, perceptions of "scientificness" may be discrepant. Simons, et.al. (1739) pointed to this as a problem in their analysis of problems of interdisciplinary research on mental illness. They found a major "hang-up" in communication between "clinicians" and "quantitative researchers" to be the question of the validity of each groups' findings as perceived by the other. In this case, "scientificness," as defined by each group, became an integral criterion for adoption or rejection of new information, but it failed as an objective standard for arbitration between the two groups.

There are some undocumented observations that being viewed by the receiver as "scientific" may have a negative effect on diffusion of an innovation. Beal and Rogers (1351) found that early adopters in agriculture tended to have more favorable attitudes toward the scientist and his products than did late adopters; for the latter the scientist was a "distant referent." Handlin (6025) describes "respect and deep underlying distrust" toward science as being popular attitudes. Kirscht and Knutson (1769) found that a group opposing fluoridation tended to fear the "diffuse unanticipated consequences plus the overemphasis put on scientific endeavor" in reacting to inputs from scientific experts.

2. *Value Loading*

Almost every innovation contains either an implicit or an explicit value message. Even the most objective "facts" may have value implications, if only because "objectivity" itself, is a value and it is a part of an ethical system which defines what is a "fact," and how "fact" is different from other information. Sanford (0502) points out that science is partly an ethical system which dictates respect for truth, and even defines truth. (See again Sanford quote earlier in this chapter).

---

*See also discussion of "education" as a receiver characteristic of some importance, Chapter Four.

Value loading is frequently cited as a problem inherent in psychological and sociological data on racial differences. It is widely known that social scientists as a group strongly identify with such liberal values as equality and democracy. Hence they are often seen as unwilling to present facts about racial differences without at the same time "moralizing" that observed differences are the result of unequal treatment and/or culturally biased instruments. This value loading may make the information more acceptable to some groups,(e.g., their own peers with similar values)and at the same time less palatable to those who hold opposite values.

Value loading is one feature of information which makes it biased or unscientific in the eyes of those who hold most strongly to *scientific values*. If, however, science itself is viewed as a value system, value loading may be an inescapable characteristic of knowledge.*

3. *Divisibility*

Some innovations require acceptance on a once-only, all-or-none basis while others can be sampled, tested, or tried out before final decisions have to be made about adoption. This is the dimension which Rogers and others call "divisibility"; Rogers defines it as "the degree to which an innovation may be tried on a limited basis." (1824, p. 131). The literature clearly indicates that innovations which can be adopted on a limited basis (either in terms of adopting on a small scale or for a limited trial time period) are more readily diffused than those which cannot. For example, a tractor is an "all-or-none" proposition. Once it has been purchased, discontinuance of use is highly unlikely. On the other hand, Katz (0298) points out that some innovations, such as hybrid corn and new drugs are innovations which may be adopted by installments. Gammanyn could be tried out on a small number of patients, and hybrid seed corn could be planted on a small amount of acreage. In either case, neither adoption nor discontinuance require a maximum effort. Mansfield (0796) points out that this principle holds in industry; the probability that a firm will introduce a new technique of production is, in part, a function of the size of the investment required.

Rogers (1824) cites studies which indicate that divisibility of innovations is more important for early than for late adopters (Gross, 1863, Ryan, 1749; Katz, 1390). In this case, it is clear that the early adopters have served a useful function for the community as a whole by acting as "demonstrators." This allowed late adopters to evaluate the innovation at no risk to themselves. If the later adopter correctly judges the relevant similarities between his own needs and those of the early adopters, divisibility will not be an important element in his decision to adopt.

Divisibility may also be regarded as the *number of individuals* or the proportion of a social system who must be involved in adoption. Barnett (2510) indicates that an innovation which requires group consent will diffuse less readily than one requiring an individual decision. In his terminology, a divisible innovation is "unencumbered"; it does not require changes throughout a system. Some innovations are divisible in both the "partial adoption" and "individual decision" sense. For example, birth control is divisible both in terms of limited utilization by one person, or use by a limited number within a population. Fluoridation of water supplies on the other hand, is

---

*See Havelock, 6183, pp. 160-179g, for an extended discussion of the role of values in the utilization process and a partial taxonomy of value issues. This discussion is summarized in Havelock and Benne, 3872.

an innovation with low divisibility; the entire community must adopt it
simultaneously. This fact has been cited as one of the major obstacles
to its diffusion.

4.   *Complexity*

The word "complexity" subsumes a number of attributes of innovations
which contribute to making them difficult to disseminate. It may refer to
the number of parts of the innovation, the number of behaviors or skills
which must be learned or understood before adoption is possible, or the
number of procedures required for effective maintenance over time. Rogers
summarizes by defining it as "the degree to which an innovation is relatively
difficult to understand and use" (Rogers, 1824, p. 130). It is generally
suggested that the degree of complexity of an innovation is negatively related to adoption. Kivlin (2697) found that complexity of farm innovations
was negatively related to adoption, a finding confirmed by Fliegel and
Kivlin (2582).

As Rogers notes, it is not so much the objective complexity of an
innovation which determines its diffusibility as the amount of *complexity
as perceived by the reciever* (suggesting that this perhaps should be viewed
as an extrinsic rather than an intrinsic characteristic). Belcher (2870)
found that polio vaccine was more readily accepted by less educated and
poorer Negroes in Georgia. He attributed this finding in part to the fact
that better educated people were more able to recognize possible complexities in its use and were more uncertain about the safety of the vaccine.
The notion that complexity has differential effects on different socio-
economic groups is illustrated by Graham's (1763) study of the diffusion of
five innovations in six socio-economic strata of New Haven. He found that
no class was either innovative or conservative on all five innovations.
Canasta, for example, was adopted rapidly by the upper, and TV by the lower
classes. He attributed the difference to the relative complexity of the
two innovations, with the simplicity of TV appealing to the less educated
adopters. Here, again, the complexity of television as a medium and as an influence on family life patterns was probably not apparent to the lower
class receivers who viewed it merely as a product they could acquire for
"X" number of dollars.

Complexity may also bear an *indirect* relationship to adoption, in that
it is sometimes difficult to understand the *relevance* of a complex technique
to the problem at hand. For example, in under-developed countries those
methods of birth control which require little sophistication and which are
easily understood as relevant will be most acceptable. Thus, if conception
is thought to have supernatural aspects, as is true in some Australian
tribes, it may be necessary to simplify birth-control measures by explaining
them in partly supernatural terms. Many attempts to make complex innovations
appear relevant to specific problems are found in the literature involving
employee participation in planning for change, e.g., Coch and French (1828).

Finally, it should be noted that the introduction of complex innovations
may require complex skills. This is a particularly important problem in
under-developed countries where, for example, literacy is often a requirement
which must be met in order to prepare the ground for further innovations.
This point will be discussed in depth in Part III of this chapter.

5. *Communicability*

Even less explicit and more general than "complexity" is the characteristic which Rogers calls *"communicability."* Communicability is the sum effect of a number of characteristics which make an innovation easy or difficult to explain or demonstrate. Presumably it is related to *complexity*, to the *adequacy of packing and labelling* and to the *visibility* and demonstrability of its effects.

Rogers (1824) cites three studies to support the presence of a communicability factor: Hruschka (6404, new haymaking technique versus keeping farm records); Erasmus (0114, spectacular results of Cuban yellow corn seed introduced in Bolivia); and Menzel (1386, drug adoption versus adoption of modern patient management).

Very little distinction is made in the literature between *communicability* and *complexity*. While it is true that complex ideas are more difficult to communicate, the two concepts are not the same. It may be helpful, therefore, to conceptualize communicability as a dependent variable, the result of the complexity, visibility, and demonstrability of the innovation. Thus, an innovation which is not complex and is both visible and demonstrable will also be readily communicable.

Katz (1398) attributes the successful dissemination of both hybrid seed corn (Ryan and Gross, 2621) and Gammanym (Coleman, 3576) in part to visibility of results. Both seed and drugs are , he says, "...the sorts of products whose effects can be measured with a rational yardstick which enables users to see for themselves, more or less, whether the innovation serves better than its predecessor."

Communicability of ideas has been of great interest in the study of anthropology. Barnett (0620) has suggested that material items find more acceptance than ideas because their utility is more easily demonstrable. Menzel (1386) makes a similar observation when he says that, "some cultural elements can be more easily verbalized, or otherwise communicated than others, and those which can be most readily and completely expressed are most readily available for acceptance" (p. 708).

Visibility and demonstrability seem to be important factors in diffusibility of any innovation, but there is not conclusive evidence as to how much of a role they play. Communicability, like all other intrinsic characteristics is subject to modifications imposed on it by extrinsic, situational characteristics. It is only in the context of a diffusion situation that intrinsic characteristics assume meaning. Thus the congruence between the value loading of a new idea and the values of a receiver system may become a factor completely overshadowing visibility or complexity.

B. EXTRINSIC CHARACTERISTICS

The extrinsic characteristics of innovations are classified here in terms of (1) compatibility with the receiver's system; and (2) relative advantage.

1. *Compatibility*

Compatibility with the receiver's system is the degree of congruence between the intrinsic characteristics of an innovation, and various aspects of the user system. In previous chapters (4, 5, and 6) we have discussed the effects of basic congruence between the value load of an innovation and

the value system of the receiver on the diffusibility and adoption of new
ideas. An example is the case cited by Barnett (0620) of the introduction
of rice by the Japanese to the men of a South Pacific tribe. Rice was
initially accepted because it involved a positive identification with the
Japanese. However, the innovation was eventually rejected because cultivation in that tribe was traditionally the task of women, and the men would
not accept the feminine role of rice cultivation. An often-cited example
of conflict between the value-load of an innovation and the values of society
is the failure of attempts to introduce beef-eating as a means of reducing
starvation in India. The value of the cow as sacred is overriding, and
there has been complete rejection of the idea of killing cattle to provide
food.

Rogers defines compatibility as "the degree to which an innovation is
consistent with existing values and past experiences of the adopters"
(1824, p. 126). He reviews a number of studies (p. 127-130) which support
his hypothesis that "the compatibility of a new idea as perceived by members
of a social system, affects its rate of adoption.

It is important to bear in mind that "compatibility" of an innovation
with different parts of the receiver system can be judged only by the
perception of its members and may or may not have any objective validity.
As Katz, et.al., (0297) have pointed out, the meaning of a given item for
one system (individual or institution) may differ from its meaning for
another. In Chapter 6 we discussed the importance of contextual and background factors for giving meaning to any piece of information.

In some situations we find that innovativeness, in and of itself, is
held as a highly praised value. When this is the case, "newness" becomes
the criterion against which information is examined and interpreted. Watson
(6364) describes our present society as basically change-oriented, and
cites the role of scientific method in bringing about this orientation:
"the norms of science,--problem solving, search for new truth, holding hypotheses tentatively while testing them critically--increasingly pervade other
areas of life." (p. 560)

Congruence with cultural values need not be a positive factor in adopting
innovation, however. When receivers are deviant from the general culture,
a novelty which contradicts and counteracts a despised norm may be welcomed
(Barnett, 0620, p. 358). This is particularly applicable to the current
phenomenon of the aliented "hippie," who innovates by rejecting the norms of
the scorned larger society, and often adopts practices largely because they
are *not* compatible with the general culture.

Although compatibility is usually discussed in terms of general cultural
values, it may also refer to perceived congruence with previously accepted
practices. Brandner & Bryant (2076), for example found that sorghum hybrids
were most readily accepted in a particular area where hybrid corn had
previously been accepted, even though this was not the area where sorghums
had the best profit potential. This study has a bearing on the "profitably
versus compatibility" dispute described and documented by Rogers (1824,
p. 136-138). The studies he cites provide no solution to the conflict, and
indicate only that both social and economic factors are important determinants of adoption.

2. *Relative Advantage*

It is possible to identify several economic and non-economic *cost
factors* and several economic and non-economic *reward factors* which could
affect knowledge utilization. On the cost side there are such variables as

*initial cost, cost of try-out, cost of maintenance over time, risk, and
trouble* to make the investment. On the reward side can be listed *rate
of cost recovery, immediacy of return, regularity of return, amount of
return, amount of time and labor saved, amount of pleasure* afforded and
so forth. In theory, at least, it should be possible to make a balance
sheet of all these plusses and minuses to arrive at an over-all benefit
ratio. This is the kind of index which Rogers is reaching for when he
discusses the "relative advantage" of an innovation.

Any assessment of relative advantage requires balancing by the
receiver, between the costs of adopting an innovation and the rewards he
expects to derive from such adoption. We shall outline some determinants
of cost and reward, and discuss how the "relative advantage"
of an innovation can be computed from them.

    a.   *Cost Factors: Cost Factors in Adoption Include Both Initial and
Coninuing Costs.*

        (1)   *Initial costs* are human and material resources which are
required in order to try out an innovation. They include
such costs as capital outlay, training of personnel, changes
in spatial arrangements, changes in social structures,
variations required in the value system, and other psychological hurdles. (See Wilkening, 2813; Barnett, 0620, Chapter
13; Rogers, 1824, pp. 124-126, and Katz, et.al., 1398).

            Financial resources necessary to implement a new idea often
determine its diffusibility. Limited resources and limited
capital expenditure are reasons for the lag between basic
research findings and their application ("Appli..etc." #5052. Such
expenditure may also include the resources necessary to acquire
new skills, or to train workers. We shall discuss these
points in more detail in Part III of this chapter.

            Psychological discomfort directly related to adoption of
unfamiliar practices may also contribute to cost. Negative
sanctions or penalties, and fear of such penalties, are
included in this category (Barnett, 0620, Chapter 12). Among
these penalties, social repercussions are the most easily
notable. When accepting a novelty involves an individual's
associates, fear of being condemned may lead to a reconsider-
ation. If mastery of an innovation requires concentrated and
prolonged effort (high resource investment and psychological
costs), then that innovation will be less diffusible than one
which requires less effort. Thus complexity of an innovation
contributes to the cost of its adoption.*

            The *effect of crises* on diffusibility can be considered in
terms of cost. One of the major effects of crises on social
institutions (and for that matter on most individuals) is
its loosening of structures and value systems. Such loosening

---

*Again, perhaps the best example is the need for literacy to precede industrial
development in underdeveloped countries.

reduces the cost of changes which require concomitant changes in values and long established beliefs and orientations. To alter a relatively weaker structure requires less effort and produces less tension and psychological discomfort. Rogers cites a number of reports on the effects of crisis. For example, he describes Wilkening's study of the effects of a climatic crisis on adoption of grass silage by Wisconsin farmers; Mulford's (1959) observations of the effects of economic crises on the rate of adoption of industrial development commissions by Iowa communities, and Sutherland's (1959) and Bertrand's (1951) reports of similar findings for English industries and American farms

    (2)   *"Continuing costs"* are those costs which continue to exist even after an innovation has been adopted. A simple example is the cost of *maintenance* of farm machinery over and above the initial purchase price. These costs may forestall the adoption of many new innovations, but it is more likely that they will be underrated by the adopter because they are less visible at the time of adoption. If car buyers were presented with a listing of all future maintenance charges and gas bills at the time of purchase we doubt if it would result in an increase in sales.

b.   *Reward Factors*

Reward factors are material or non-material benefits which the adopter expects to achieve as a result of using an innovation.

    (1)   *Material rewards* and savings include such factors as the rate of profit expected from adoption of an innovation. Nelson (1004) believes that expected profitability of an innovation is one of the major factors in its diffusibility. Katz, et.al. (1398) reviewed several reports and concluded that the extent and certainty of profitability or efficacy of an innovation were among major factors in its diffusibility. Mansfield (1373) (0786) discusses the effect of profitability on adoption in industry.

    (2)   *Non-material rewards* and savings, include both expected pleasures to be derived from adoption and also discomforts and conflicts averted by such adoption. For a teacher, the expected psychological pleasures of being more effective in the classroom may be an important factor in adoption of new teaching methods, but these rewards may be counterbalanced by the expectation of colleague and student disapproval for being "different," "eccentric," or "odd." The expectation of probably failure is likely to tip the scales against innovation.

SUMMARY OF CHARACTERISTICS OF KNOWLEDGE SECTION

Intrinsic characteristics--scientific status, value loading, divisibility, complexity and communicability--are those characteristics which are by-and-large inherent in innovations, and can be measured independently from the diffusion setting. The literature, although far from conclusive, suggests that the more complex and the less communicable a new idea, the less diffusible it is. Scientific status and value loading seem to be factors of less concern to scholars in the field, but are presumably important also.

8-45

Especially important for the diffusion of innovations are *extrinsic* characteristics, those factors which are generally the result of an interaction between intrinsic knowledge characteristics and the characteristics of receivers (Chapter 4 & 5) and receiver systems (Chapter 3 & 6). In this category we find that relative advantage and compatibility with the receiver system are of major importance.

III. KNOWLEDGE AS IT AFFECTS THE RECEIVER: THE ADAPTIVE DEMANDS OF DIFFERENT KINDS OF MESSAGE INPUTS TO THE USER.

About the best way to understand characteristics of the message is to observe and analyze the changes it requires in the receiver. Different kinds of knowledge call forth different kinds of behavioral responses and different kinds of adaptations to what is new. In this last section of Chapter Eight, Knowledge will be looked at from this point of view and the question for analysis will be: what kinds of change or adaptation are called for by different types of knowledge?

In the discussion of characteristics in Part II we have already developed some idea of this dimension of analysis: the characteristic of "complexity" suggested the requirements of more complex responses by the receiver; the characteristic , "pervasiveness" suggested that there was a dimension of magnitude of impact; and the dimension of "cost" signified a requirement of financial resources in sufficient quantity before successful adoption was possible. In the previous discussion of these topics the analysis of *behavioral consequences* was not carried very far. Some authors, however, have tried to focus their concern on the behavioral side. Wilkening (2817), for example, thinks that we should classify innovations by asking what kind of receiver changes are required. Similarly, Lippitt (3873) stresses the importance of looking at social science utilization as a process of *adaptation* where the receiver takes an active role in incorporating new knowledge. Thus, he sees amount and type of receiver involvement as a most significant dimension of analysis.

There are at least ten distinct types of change which roughly fall into two groups. We shall call these two groups: *"How much change in receiver?"* and *"What kind of change in Receiver?"* The ten categories break down as follows:

A.   How Much Change in Receiver

   1.   Change in Size and Scope of Operations

   2.   Acquiring New Skills

   3.   Changing Goals

   4.   Changing Values and Orientations

B.   What Kind of Change in Receiver

   5.   Substitution of Parts or Elements

   6.   Alteration

   7.   Addition without changing old elements or patterns

   8.   Restructuring

   9.   Eliminating old behavior

   10.   Reinforcing old behavior

8-46

A.   HOW MUCH CHANGE IN RECEIVER

In the most general sense the question raised here is one of expansion: is some sort of expansion required on the part of the receiver? One way to look at this is to see the receiver as occupying a certain *psychological space* at any given point in time, a space which represents the limits of his awareness, understanding and capability of action. All innovations in some degree and some innovations in large degree call for an *enlargement of this space*.*

1.   *Change in Size and Scope of Operations*

Wilkening (2817) among others notes that innovations may require massive outlays of capital, labor, land, materials, and equipment. Where such requirements are not prohibitive, they may nevertheless have considerable impact on the receiver's life style, changing him from a small-time operator to a big-time operator; turning him from a subsistence farmer into an entrepreneur or risk capitalist; from an independent operator into an employer--manager, and so on.

2.   *Acquiring New Skills*

Earlier in this chapter we discussed the characteristics of "compatibility" from several points of view, one of which was compatibility with existing skills of the receiver. We approach this subject again now asking what new skills are required and how much skill development is needed before utilization is possible? Wilkening (2817) again notes this as an important consideration. Lippitt (3873) points out that social science utilization may be especially difficult in that it calls for the development of new skills by the social practitioner.

3.   *Changing Goals*

When the adoption of new ideas changes a farmer's self-conception from a tiller of the soil to the manager of a profit-making enterprise, when it encourages the nurse to see her role as supervisor of a patient-care "team" instead of the doctor's assistant, or when it suggests to the teacher that she is a helper in the learning process rather than a conveyor of facts, in all such cases the receiver of the new knowledge is changing not only his self-image but also his goals. Typically, we think of utilization of new knowledge as more effective, more efficient means for arriving at our pre-established ends. But innovations may often carry with them new "images of potentiality," and the hope of achieving goals even more desirable than those toward which we had been striving previously. Wilkening (2817) for example, cites changes in the types of product that a farmer produces as an especially significant aspect of innovation. In industry new market conditions and new inventions require companies to constantly shift to new products and to new definitions of purpose; the railroad, the automobile and the airplane each in turn required a changing or a broadening of goals on the part of a large spectrum of business enterprises (e.g., from providing "horse-drawn buggies for hire" to providing "transportation services for hire.") Companies in the transportation business who defined their goals concretely and narrowly in terms of the previous mode of transportation quickly found themselves going under.

---

*See Lewin's exposition of the concept of "life space" and especially his discussion of the "extension of the life space" (6500, 1951, p. 127).

The increasing rate of technological change and the increasing difficulty which our society is having in tracking the effects of this change
become especially important and ominous facts when this goal-changing aspect
of innovations is considered.

4. *Changing Values and Orientation*

Very much related to changes in goals are changes in the more generalized and more deep-seated aspects of the receiver's life-space. Earlier
in this chapter we noted how the diffusion of science may be creating a
science-oriented and science-valued culture. We also noted in Part II that
some knowledge may have value-loading as an intrinsic property. But the
point here is somewhat different. New knowledge may not have any explicit
value loading and still it may force us to change certain values. Several
authors have commented on the importance of this type of change including
Chin (2612, p. 14) and Lippitt (3873, noting that social science utilization
most frequently requires value shifts.) Miles, in summarizing from a number
of contributors in his reader, "INNOVATION IN EDUCATION," cites three authors
in support of the generalization that "any innovation implying or requiring
important *value changes in* acceptors....will encounter difficulty, since much
more than the nature of the innovation itself is at stake," (0580, p. 639).

Meierhenry (5235, p. 423) notes two major areas of change in education
which require value changes:

> "The desegregation of schools is an excellent example of this
> type of change. The struggle through which almost all Americans
> are going in this regard indicates the difficulty of making
> changes which pertain to deep-seated beliefs. To a somewhat
> lesser degree the place of religion in public education has many
> of the same overtones of basic value judgments. Changes which
> involve values probably require a change of what is in the heart
> as well as what is in the head."

B. WHAT KIND OF CHANGE IN RECEIVER

In this second section we move somewhat further into the psychology of the
receiver to try to specify the type of processes of learning and unlearning
which may be involved in "adoption" or "adaptation," regardless of whether we
are talking about change in products, skills, goals, or values.

5. *Substitution*

Probably the commonest and most easily adoptable innovation is one than
is seen as merely a replacement for another item already adopted at an earlier
time. When we trade in an old car and get a new one--one which has a collaps-
ible steering column, shoulder harness, emergency flashers and so forth--
we are actually adopting a host of innovations often without being aware that
we are doing so. Noting that this is the simplest form of change, Chin
(2612) hopes that educational innovation will eventually have an equivalent
status in the public mind so that each new year's textbook is anticipated
with the eagerness of the new model car. Meierhenry (5235, p. 422) adds that
substitution may be particularly advantageous in education because it generally
does not involve relationships among teachers "so that the person introducing
a new practice is not concerned with either antagonism or support from his
colleagues."

In contrast, Eash (6024) finds much to criticise in the substitution
process (which he calls the "displacement model") particularly when it is
utilized on a large scale in educational settings. He states:

"It would be a comfort to harrassed school administrators
if the displacement model effortlessly implemented change
in classroom practice, minimized conflict, and guaranteed
the preservation of the integrity of the innovation. Basically, however, it is a mechanistic view of the instructional
process, conceptualizing it as an assembly line, a conceptualization that overrides the human components and leaves
basic problems (of utilization) unresolved."

6. *Alteration*

Some innovations consist primarily of changes or alterations in existing
structures rather than complete substitutions of parts or elements. In this
form one might think that change would have no trouble gaining acceptance.
There are some problems, however. Miles (*1481*) comments on Forsdale's discussion of eight millimeter film utilization in education as follows: "...the
spread of an innovation may be retarded when the potential user regards
it as *familiar*--as only a slightly different version of an existing procedure or practice--and thus not worth the extra cost required to shift over
to it." Forsdale (1176) had noted the very slow development and diffusion
of 8mm sound systems in spite of the enormous potential
of this alteration in a familiar medium (much cheaper and more convenient
than 16mm sound now in use and much more satisfactory for educational
purposes than silent 8mm).

Chin (2612) reminds us that many so-called innovative alterations
may in the course of time turn out to be what he calls only *"perturbations
and variations,"* transient oscillations or disturbances in the over-all
equilibrium of the receiver system. In this category might fall the many
ambitious human relations training programs which seem to awaken people
momentarily to an awareness of their interpersonal environment and their
impact on others but which seem to leave hardly a trace after six-months
back on the job.

7. *Addition Without Changing Old Elements or Patterns*

Some innovations represent entirely new elements to the receiver and as
such present a different set of opportunities and problems in contrast to
substitutions or alterations. On the plus side they do not encounter the
resistance which is usually faced when old ways have to be changed and long
established prejudices and defensive attitudes overcome. As Miles states,
generalizing from his contributors (*1481*, p. 638): "...other things being
equal, innovations which are perceived as *threats* to existing practice,
rather than mere additions to it, are less likely of acceptance..." and
"more generally, innovations which can be added to an existing program without
seriously disturbing other parts of it are likely to be adopted."

On the minus side, however, innovations which are entirely new are also
entirely *unfamiliar*. The receiver may have no adequate way of assimilating
them. Thus, for example, Brickell (writing in Guba,6118) notes that research
findings, when they are the only source of information on a topic, probably
have a rougher time gaining acceptance than research findings which merely
substantiate everyday experience or prior folk knowledge.

There may also be generalized hostility or defensiveness in many people
to anything different, strange, or novel. The success of "additions" may
therefore, depend largely on the orientation toward change and toward
innovation-in-general in the particular receiver or receiving culture (for
which see discussion in Chapter Four and Five).

8-49

One problem with the concept of "addition" from a research standpoint might be the difficulty of identifying pure cases. The telephone, when initially introduced, would seem to have been an addition; but was it really a substitution for the letter, the over-the-back-fence chat and other modes of communication of the time? Were there forerunners to the automobile? to the cigarette? to the computer? to the motion picture? All these apparent cases of "additions" might have to be reclassified as substitutions or alterations once we delved more deeply into their history of development and diffusion.

8. *Restructuring*

There are certain kinds of changes which many authors feel are much different from what is usually thought of either as addition, substitution, or alteration, to which they give the term *"restructuring"*, meaning changing the structure of the receiver system in some significant way.

Psychologically, restructuring may be very much the same sort of thing that we discussed earlier as *goal changing and value and orientation changing*. Lewin (6500, p. 72-84) noted the significance of cognitive restructuring as a major aspect in human development, and he defined it as "the differentiation of previously undifferentiated regions." Through such restructuring we become able to make more accurate judgments and to perceive finer distinctions.

At the material level "restructuring" may amount to a rearrangement of work space. For the farmer this may be change in land use patterns, or change in how he distributes his time during the day. For the school it may mean changing the composition and size of classes, the loci in which various subjects are taught, or the actual layout of the school building. Likewise changes in the curriculum may involve reemphasis and rearrangements which amount to restructuring. Meierhenry gives the example of the teaching of foreign languages to younger children (5235, p. 423) as an innovation requiring not only attitude change by teachers and parents but also a shift in how the elementary curriculum was conceived.

Finally, at the level of the receiver social system, there are many obvious examples of restructuring innovations. Meierhenry (5235) lists team teaching and the introduction of departmentalization in elementary schools in this category. In the field of management of organizations there are numerous examples of changes such as the introduction of new roles, stripping or adding layers of supervision, and the creation or elimination of various staff and line units, all of which fit under the heading of "structural" changes. Perhaps surprisingly, Miles concludes (1472, p. 638) "it does not seem automatically clear that substantial structural innovations, such as changes in teacher role definition, diffuse at lower rates than technologically based ones." In any case it seems clear that the specific problems of restructuring in contrast to other types of change deserve further investigation.

9. *Eliminating Old Behavior*

Perhaps the most troublesome knowledge of all from the point of view of D & U is that which tells us to "stop." There are mountains of research evidence which seem to be telling us to stop smoking, stop eating, stop taking drugs, stop committing crimes, stop having accidents, stop fighting, stop distrusting one another, and so on. The human being seems to indulge in many kinds of behavior which seem to be bad for him and/or bad for his fellows, and the biggest problem is that he has the wrong behavior or the wrong attitude or the harmful product before we ever reach him. Under these circumstances the would-be-diffuser of knowledge is always in the position of <u>accentuating the negative</u>, applying negative reinforcement, or negative sanctions. However, as Skinner and other researchers on the psychology of learning have noted time and again, this type of behavioral change is very hard to bring about, and even when adopted, it is likely to be only a temporary suppression rather than a true elimination.

In spite of its obvious importance this topic has received relatively little attention in the research literature on diffusion and utilization. Weiss (2629) has done some pilot work towards a study of the effectiveness of evaluation research studies indicating that when the evaluation is negative it is ignored by those responsible for administering the programs being evaluated. Brickell (in Guba, 6118) in a similar vein notes that "in the United States today, research findings do not compete well against such established, persuasive information sources as one's personal experience or knowledge of what other schools are doing."

10. *Reinforcing old Behavior*

Finally, we come to the kind of knowledge which is probably the easiest to transmit and "adopt," knowledge which reinforces what we are already doing, confirms past decisions, and shows the wisdom of prior adoptions. Brickell again notes (in Guba, 6118) that research findings which confirm the folk wisdom and "experience" of the practitioner will be well received. His observation is confirmed by basic research in social psychology which indicates that people seek out confirming information so that they can resolve lingering doubts about irrevocable past decisions (see, for example, Festinger, 0264, Brehm and Cohen, 6277).

What may be a problematic twist to this dimension is the situation in which *non-behavior* needs to be reinforced. There are many situations in which the best scientific knowledge suggests non-action or non-adoption as the right course of "action" as when we want to urge young people not to take up smoking. This kind of knowledge may require rather different kinds of strategies of D & U. We presently know very little about how to develop such strategies.

This discussion in Part III, focussing as it has on the behavioral effects of various types of knowledge, forms a natural bridge to the next chapter in which we will take up in detail the various mechanisms or strategies by means of which all these types of knowledge can be successfully diffused and utilized.

CHAPTER NINE

THE TECHNOLOGY OF KNOWLEDGE FLOW:
ONE-WAY AND TWO-WAY MEDIA, PROCESSES, AND STRATEGIES

CHAPTER NINE*

THE TECHNOLOGY OF KNOWLEDGE FLOW:
ONE-WAY AND TWO-WAY MEDIA, PROCESSES, AND STRATEGIES

I. INTRODUCTION

    A. PURPOSE OF THE CHAPTER

        1. Answering the Question: "How?"

            The purpose of this chapter is to answer the question "HOW?" How
        is knowledge transmitted? What channels and media can be employed
        to carry the message? What tools and instruments, human or otherwise,
        can be used in the process? What approaches, techniques, or strategies
        are most successful or most appropriate for given situations? These
        are the questions for which future social engineers will have to know
        the answers.

            As we proceed through this chapter, it will become apparent that
        there are not many answers to these "technical" questions. Information
        about them is scattered and where it exists it is often ambiguous.
        Nevertheless, it should also become apparent that we can get answers
        to these same questions by applying existing social and behavioral
        science methodologies to the buzzing confusion of ongoing dissemination
        and utilization activities throughout our society. In other words,
        we do know how to know how.

            Finally, it should become apparent that the answers to these
        questions would be of tremendous value to our society, worthy of the
        highest priority in our national research goals for education and
        other fields. A comprehensive and a codified understanding of these
        technical details of knowledge flow are prerequisite to a meaningful
        national effort to spread the benefits of progress. Today, we simply
        cannot say, with any degree of objective certainty, that we have this
        understanding.

        2. Relevance of This Chapter to the Rest of the Review

            In previous chapters we have been building a concept of knowledge
        flowing, moving through people (Chapters Four, Five and Seven) and
        through institutions of various kinds (Chapters Six and Seven) and
        along the way becoming transformed from needs to problems, from problems
        to research, from research to development, from development to practice,
        etc. (Chapter Eight). So far, then, we have considered the people,
        the places, and the knowledge involved in this flow. Now we turn to
        the process.

_____

*This chapter was drafted by Janet C. Huber in collaboration with Ronald G. Havelock.

3. Levels of the Discussion in the Chapter

    It should be helpful to understand and keep in mind the level of
discourse that is employed in this and the subsequent chapter.
Chapters Nine and Ten both concern themselves with process but each at
a different level of analysis. This chapter starts with specifics,
the tools: channels, media, mechanisms, and techniques of knowledge
flow. Later in this chapter, under the heading "strategies", we will
climb one step up the abstraction ladder to look comparatively at the
various ways in which these specific processes can be put together,
depending on the utilization goals we have set for ourselves and the
kind of knowledge we have to transmit. Then in Chapter Ten we will
take a broader comparative view, looking at different conceptions of
the whole process; the sequence of stages or phases through which
knowledge passes as observed and understood by various authors.
Finally, in Chapter Eleven, we will climb to the top of the abstraction
ladder to look comparatively at different models of the process,
theories of planned change, dissemination, and utilization, attempting
to determine where there is concensus and where divergence among
theorists. Throughout this climb up the ladder, we will also try to
distinguish between description and prescription, i.e., between analysis
and facts about the process *as it is* on the one hand, and recommendations,
remedies, and solutions for improving it on the other.

B. GENERAL CHARACTERISTICS OF THE TRANSMISSION PROCESSES

    1. Directional Differences

        Throughout this review we have stressed the importance of two-way
communication between knowledge users and resource persons. The
"linkage" concept (see again Figure 1.3) implies that the communication
of new knowledge will not be effective unless senders and receivers
are interdependent, mutually giving and taking. However, actual
knowledge communication processes can be distinguished by their direction
and by their ability to incorporate interaction. We, thus, find it
appropriate in this chapter to direct our attention separately to three
types of transmission processes:

    a. In the ideal model of the knowledge flow chain, as
        delineated in Chapter Two, "solution" messages flow
        from research to practice to consumer. These can be
        designated, *diffusion transmissions*.

    b. In that same model, messages indicating "needs" flow in
        an opposite direction, from consumer to practitioner
        to researcher. These we will call *feedback transmissions*.

    c. Many communications do involve almost simultaneous
        diffusion and feedback. In such cases it becomes
        impractical to separately distinguish the unidirectional
        components of such an exchange. These are the
        characteristically *two-way transmissions*.

Figure 9.1 illustrates this three-part subdivision of transmission
types which will structure the discussion that follows.

FIGURE 9.1   Direction of Transmission Processes

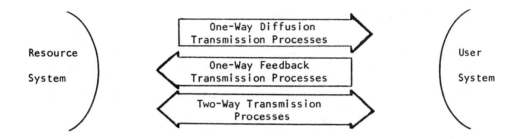

2.   The Medium as a Focus of Discussion

       Other chapters in this review have focused on some of the
individual components in the communication of knowledge (e.g., sender
and receiver, Chapter Five: message, Chapter Eight).   This chapter's
goal is to provide the reader with an understanding of the impact of
media on communication, in order that he may adequately deal with
this component of the knowledge transmission process. In evaluating
the impact of media it is necessary to isolate its pertinent intrinsic
characteristics and their consequent effects. Most of the studies
reviewed and reported here have attempted to study media impact, but,
unfortunately in so doing, have not taken care to distinguish the
intrinsic characteristics of the medium, per se, from the characteristics
of the sender, the receiver, or the message.

       It is generally true that a combination of media or transmission
mechanisms is more effective than any one used singly if the characteristics of the selected media complement one another. Marshall McLuhan
has stressed this principle for educators:

               "...it is important that we understand cause and process.
               The aim is to develop an awareness about print and the
               newer technologies of communication so that we can
               orchestrate them, minimize their mutual frustrations
               and clashes, and get the best out of each in the educational
               process. The present conflict leads to elimination of the
               motive to learn and to diminution of interest in all pre-
               vious achievement: It leads to loss of the sense of
               relevance. Without an understanding of media grammars,
               we cannot hope to achieve a contemporary awareness of
               the world in which we live." (Carpenter & McLuhan, #7017, p. xii)

In the discussion which follows we compare the impact of the various
media, point out the strengths and weaknesses of each, and finally,
attempt to demonstrate how they can be orchestrated to bring about
a successful knowledge utilization process.

II. ONE-WAY DIFFUSION TRANSMISSION PROCESSES

Most knowledge is packaged and disseminated in such a manner that the potential user has little or no opportunity to influence the originator or to change the nature of the message. The user is a receiver, only; not a sender, and he cannot enter into a dynamic relationship with the sender. He can accept the message, or ignore it; sometimes he can even turn it on or off, but he cannot alter the essentially one-way character of the medium. Nevertheless, these "one-way" processes have some distinct advantages when they are used appropriately. When the audience is just right and the message is just right, there is probably no more effective way to transmitting large quantities of information to large numbers of people in the shortest possible time. In this section we will consider both the advantages and disadvantages of the most frequently used one-way channels of communication.

A. WRITTEN MEDIA

1. For the Dissemination of Knowledge to a Mass Audience

The written word has long been the prime vehicle for the *mass* dissemination of new knowledge, and has been presumed to be an effective medium for this purpose. Some recent research, however, has cast considerable doubt on this assumption. Written media, in fact, are rarely suitable for indiscrimate distribution of knowledge to large numbers of people. At least three major receiver variables condition the effectiveness of written media (1) education and socio-economic status, (2) cosmopoliteness, and (3) innovativeness.

The most widely reported characteristic of written media users is their relatively high educational attainment and socio-economic status. (Schramm, #0878; Swinehart and McLeod, #1779; Davis, #5119; Myren, #0397.) For example, in studies conducted during the Salk polio vaccine tests of 1954, one report confirmed a substantial difference in educational level between those mothers who consented to have their children participate and receive the vaccine and those mothers who did not. (Clausen, Seidenfeld, and Deasy, #6010.) An entirely separate study related these same differences in mothers' responses to the vaccine to "status", a factor combining education, income, and social/professional position. (Youmans, #2868)

Another characteristic distinguishing mass media readers from non-readers is their tendency to be cosmopolitan and, generally, outstanding consumers of all the media. (Swinehart and McLeod, #1779; Davis, #5119; Schramm, #0878.) This was found to be a particularly crucial point during the polio vaccine tests of 1954. Parents who ultimately allowed their children to participate in the tests not only had higher education and professional status than those who did not, but they also (1) knew more about both the positive and negative aspects of the vaccine, (2) had first heard of the vaccine through newspaper reports and then had sought out secondary sources in order to learn more, and (3) relied more on *newspapers* for information than on radio or TV, in contrast to parents who refused to let their children have the vaccine. (Youmans, #2868; Clausen, Seidenfeld, and Deasy, #6010.)

9-4

A third characteristic attributed to readers of the mass media ——— is their high willingness to try out new things, i.e., to be "innovative". Davis (#5119) noted the written media consumer's positive attitudes toward science and scientists; readers see science as beneficial and scientists as dedicated and trustworthy men, in contrast to non-readers, who view both with general mistrust.

A further aspect of the "innovativeness" of mass media readers is reported in two separate studies of agricultural extension, one in northern Japan and another in southern Brazil. In these relatively isolated areas where literacy rates are lower and farm journals less abundant than in the United States, early adoption was found to be directly related to farm journal reading. (Tajima, #1066; and Fliegel, #1424.) However, this study seemed to indicate that the correlation between media reading and innovativeness might be eliminated if other media for communicating farming information were substituted for the written word.

These three characteristics associated with mass media readership appeal to common sense and seem to have attained a legitimacy apart from the empirical support for their validity. However, as clearly suggested in the Brazilian study, the easy assumption of causality in the relationships of education and socio-economic status, cosmopoliteness, and/or innovativeness with media readership is premature.

2. For the Dissemination of Knowledge to Special Interest Groups

Written media which are designed for the interests of particular audiences are more likely to have mass readership among such audiences. These include messages aimed at any sub-portion of the population: from hi-fi buffs to lawyers to psychologists. For example, Myren (#0397) found that although non-farm magazines were only subscribed to by the farming elite (cosmopolite, high income, high education), the great majority of U.S. farmers subscribe to *farm* magazines.

Even among highly specialized groups, however, written media are not uniformly effective. Within professional groups, it has been generally found that the written media are prime channels for opinion leaders and those sociometrically central to the group. The Menzel and Katz study (#3404) of the diffusion of a new drug through the informal social communication network of physicians in a given area is widely cited for demonstrating that doctors who are opinion leaders among their peers tend to rely heavily on professional journals to learn about innovations, whereas other doctors most often get such information from drug company detailmen (salesmen) or advertisements. Similarly, Bauer and Wortzel (#2340) found that advertisements and detailmen were major *sources of information* about new drugs, but that the decision to use and prescribe such drugs involved a complex series of influences. For example, as the seriousness of the illness increased and the treatment knowledge decreased, the tendency to rely on 'professional' sources -- colleagues and professional journal articles -- increased. Interestingly, too, doctors who tend to be consulted by their colleagues cite journal articles as their most important source of information, unlike others who rely mostly on detailmen.

Within another professional group, industrial technologists, Scott (#2120) identified a similar pattern of information diffusion. Journal readers also tended to be advice-givers to the extent that they recommended specific articles to others. In Scott's study, 43% of the articles reportedly read were located in this manner.

3. Limitations of the Written Mass Media

Excessive reliance on the written word often constitutes a severe problem. Inundation may undermine the effectiveness of the channel. It has been estimated that doctors would have to read 27 books a day to keep up on the new discoveries in medicine (Neal, #6160). Moreover, archaic classification and retrieval operations have stubbornly resisted attempts to economize. This resistance to change probably reflects the massiveness of the task of reclassification and retraining, not a lack of creativity in the attempts designed for its solution. The difficulties confronting the MEDLARS attempt to organize medical literature (Atwood, #2342), LITE in the field of law (Allen, #3787 and Kelley et al., #0292), and ERIC in education (Guba, #6118) attest to the immensity of the problem.

Because complete and functional computerization of retrieval systems is still a distant possibility, our attention must also be directed at temporary alternatives. Magazines, newspapers, even scientific journals, and their various indices are inadequate for the *storage-for-retrieval* of already existing information. (Scott, #2120) The development of flexible and appropriate reference works (loose leaf handbooks, manuals, etc.) for use in the interim would be a feasible response to both the continuing explosion of knowledge in a field and the current input overload on the individual receiver. (Havelock, #7111)

4. Effectiveness of the Written Media in Dissemination

Within that group which we have defined as the "reading public", written communications serve most widely in their *information-giving* function. For transmitting knowledge to all members of a profession or a field, the written word has yet to be surpassed; it is easily disseminable, is privately retrievable for reference purposes, and can be absorbed at the individual receiver's own rate. Psychologists, for example, list journals and books as the most useful "sources" of new information. (American Psychological Association, #2126) Legislators, too, utilize a broad range of written communications as sources of factual information. They list channels as diverse as the Legislative Reference Service and "correspondence from constituents" as relevant. (Hattery and Hofheimer, #1214) Farmers cite the written media as their principle source of information about farming innovations, although agricultural extension possesses one of the most elaborate and advanced systems of information dissemination. (Smith and Sheppard, #1090; Lionberger and Hassinger, #2690.)

Though written messages are widely disseminable among a chosen audience, their success in *arousing interest* or in precipitating *adoption* behavior depends, more than for other channels, on the high relevance, functionality, or salience of their information for the intended receiver. These crucial content factors influence not only subsequent *utilization* of the communication by the receiver (Back et al., #1677), but also his very decision to make the effort to read it in the first place. Greenberg (#1860) found that people highly interested in a particular topic sought information from newspaper accounts as well as from personal sources, while those who were less involved relied solely on social contacts for their knowledge.

Conversely, an individual's interest in a topic may be influenced by the character of its original presentation to him. In this respect, written communication may not be as effective an arouser of interest as other media considered below -- even for highly educated, cosmopolitan, and innovative groups. However, of notable success in arousing interest and effecting openness to an innovation was a pamphlet developed by Edward Glazer (#6097) for the Division of Vocational Rehabilitation directors, regarding some new vocational rehabilitation practices. When this carefully conceived package was combined with subsequent personal communications and conferences, the new techniques received an impressive degree of adoption. The further refinement of packages of this type could profitably absorb the efforts of interested media researchers.

B. LECTURES, SPEECHES, SYMPOSIA · ORAL PRESENTATIONS TO LIVE AUDIENCES

1. A Multitude of Conditioning Variables

Determinants of the success or effectiveness of the spoken word in the communication process are infinite. The ability of presentations to live audiences to maximize change among receivers depends not only on the variables of message salience and receiver receptivity to the medium (discussed also in the preceding section), but to a large extent on the interaction of the individual personality of the speaker with the collective personality of his audience. The rapport a lecturer may establish with his listeners is a crucial, but elusive, variable in the analysis of such communications. The extent to which the audience is "turned on" and "tuned in" to the speaker and the message probably is the major determining variable (see e.g., Zajonc, #6275, for experiments on cognitive tuning).

2. The Structure of the Message: What Should Be Said When

Hovland's experiments with influence attempts through the lecture medium (#7009) give helpful insight into how the *structural variables* of a lecture or other communication can influence the acceptance of its message. He verified the hypothesis that for optimal acceptance of a message, need arousal must precede factual information on how such needs might be satisfied. Advertisers have apparently had sufficient reinforcement to continue to operate on this principle.

Hovland made a further contribution to our understanding of the structural make-up of an oral communication with his clarification of the "law of primacy": information which is presented first in a communication has disproportionate influence. This principle applies to communications in which conflicting arguments are to be presented, and functions in a lecture when (1) the contradictory sides are presented in a single communication by a single person, or (2) when

the receiver has made a public expression of his opinion directly after
the first bit of information has been presented, and prior to the presentation of the second. The "law of primacy" is least operative,
according to Hovland, when the conflicting information is presented
(1) by separate people, (2) with any intervening activity between the
two presentations, (3) to an audience who has been alerted to the fallibility of 'first impressions', and (4) to receivers who have relatively
high cognitive need and are, thus, apt to organize the material logically,
regardless of its original form.

A commonly perceived danger in primacy effects is the potential
for undue biasing or brainwashing of a public through propaganda or
irresponsible news releasing or reporting. Hovland, himself, derides
the possibility:

> "For important social situations in which primacy effects
> have been considered a danger, for example, legal trials,
> election campaigns and political debates, the issue is
> usually clearly defined as controversial, the partisan-
> ship of the communicator is established and different
> communicators present the opposing sides. These factors
> should give rise to relatively little primacy effect.
> Our concern might then be concentrated on preventing
> premature commitment on the basis of the first presenta-
> tion alone and on developing interest and responsibility
> on the part of the citizen to ensure objectivity and a
> genuine desire to reach the heart of the issue." (#7009,
> p. 155)

At any rate, existing research does not give adequate guidelines
for practical application of the "law of primacy". Even in highly
controlled research settings, the possibility of prior knowledge about
a topic by individual members of the audience cannot be entirely
eliminated. Certainly, then, this is not a realistic expectation for
practice. Moreover, outside the laboratory the individual receiver
can choose whether or not he will even expose himself to the second
side of any controversy. We know neither how to prevent this nor how
to even predict which, for him, is the 'second side'.

All this suggests that the "law of primacy" may be a weak base
on which to build a practical model for oral communication attempts.
Future research might be more profitably directed at discovering methods
which could circumvent this variable.

3.   The Goal of the Speaker

The appropriateness of the choice of a lecture or of some other one-
way presentation to a live audience will depend on the goals of the
speaker, and will be limited by the character of the knowledge he is
presenting (Chapter Eight). If mere transmission of the information
is all that is required for the listener to receive it, a lecture may
suffice for a "tuned-in" audience. However, if higher cognitive
functions are involved, as the development of concepts or of problem-
solving skills, two-way interaction is needed. (McKeachie, #6439,
and Bloom, #7085.)

C.   TELEVISION

1.   Conflicting Reports on Effect and Effectiveness

The effectiveness of television as a medium for communicating new
knowledge is much in controversy. Again, this variance in opinion seems
to be a function of variations in format, or "programming", which range
from commercial entertainment to educational programs. Thus, studies
of commercial TV, though plentiful, have not adequately defined its
influence; exposure to TV has separately been held responsible for non-
acceptance of the Salk vaccine by parents (Clausen, Seidenfeld, and
Deasy, #6010); aggression among children (Maccoby, #5395); and the
promotion of segregationist attitudes (Tumin, #0337).

TV in the "classroom", on the other hand, has been adopted and
adapted in a host of creative ways, and with apparently unlimited
potential for success. By far, the greatest amount of documentation
of the effectiveness of educational TV programs in our literature survey
comes from the field of medicine. Open and closed circuit TV has been
utilized extensively, often in combination with radio and telephone
feedback, in both the programs of medical schools and in the postgraduate training of practicing M.D.'s. Medical school instruction
in both the basic sciences and the clinical sciences has benefited
from the TV camera's ability to magnify the image, multiply it, or
transport it; and thus, to optimize the observation point of the
student. (Ramey, #6208)

Perhaps of greater significance to the medical field as a whole
is the postgraduate training being done by TV. It seems to be favorably
accepted by the viewing doctors, and can be fairly economical: using
existing network or ETV station facilities at unannounced times for
privacy, and allowing feedback through telephone, mail, or hospital-
based radio transmitters. The two primary advantages of this new
technology are related to its *convenience* for the target doctors. First,
many more practitioners tune in to a broadcast than would take the time
to attend a hospital lecture, and, secondly, doctors in *isolated areas*
can participate as readily as those in metropolitan centers. (Neal,
#6160; Robertson, #6159; Castle, #0672.) These advantages would pre-
sumably have equal value in education, law, and other fields.

2.   Range of TV's Uses in Education

The adequacy of the programming seems to be a major factor in the
ready acceptance educational television has reportedly received.
Commercial television has not placed major emphasis on programming
which attempts to educate by focusing on specific topics for specific
audiences. However, some research indicates that television used in
combination with more personal methods, such as group discussion,
might be very successful. One study demonstrating the effectiveness
of this combination approach used parent-child relationships as the
topic with an audience of mothers (Tamminen, #1681); in another study,
the topic of cattle feeding was chosen for an audience of dairymen
(Alexander et al., #1352). The opportunities for manipulability inherent
in the classroom situation suggest that even higher returns than those
reported in these studies might be obtained for the technological

blending of TV and other techniques. The Far West Laboratory for Educational Research and Development in Berkeley, California, is currently experimenting with such combined TV-discussion series packages in its communications program.

Television has already contributed to the solution of several of the knottiest problems in education today. In the field of general education, and especially at the college level, TV has demonstrated that it can function efficiently as a *labor saving device*. Its use can alleviate classroom crowding or teacher overload due to the rapidly increasing influx of students. It can enable faculty members to be flexible in their scheduling so that they may more conveniently handle the diverse demands of both on- and off-campus responsibilities. It can also maximize the exposure of the reknowned scholar and the superior teacher. (EDUCOM, #7010)

Moreover, through the use of videotape and in combination with other media it can provide complex *audio-visual learning* packages whose effectiveness is far superior to the best teacher. (Fuller, #6092) For example, in the training of future teachers, it can be used most effectively for self-evaluation and for supervisor critiques of the student teacher's classroom behavior. (EDUCOM, #7010)

The evolution of commercial advertising on TV may provide many clues to new and more effective ways to package and disseminate information. The National Safety Council, American Cancer Society, and other scientific knowledge disseminators have already adopted Madison Avenue techniques.

The very fact of television's adaptability and potential for handling the 'overload' for live teachers may, ironically, be an inhibiting force in its adoption. TV's ability to usurp the teacher's role or to invade her traditionally sacrosanct privacy is an initial threat to the teacher-user. Guba has noted, however, that such fear is overcome with experience (#6089). Many creative uses of TV, which do not directly infringe on the 'conveyor of knowledge' function of teaching, could be stressed in the initial phases of adoption to ease the acceptance of this technology. Dramatizations, role playing, student self-evaluations of public speaking, and the recording of field trips and unit reports are several techniques which have successfully introduced the use of TV and videotaping.

3. Factors Influencing the Potential of "Educating" TV

Television's excellence for transmitting learning packages, its ability to incorporate feedback, and its labor-saving potential make it unquestionably a medium to 'watch' for future communications of scientific knowledge. Its currently prohibitive expense is being somewhat lightened by new government support for educational technologies. If TV promoters and producers can, themselves, be "educated" in its varied potential uses, it may revolutionize the transmission and utilization of knowledge. The lesson of this section is that extensive and, perhaps, costly development, including programming and packaging, of software is still needed before the potential can be realized.

D.   FILMS

1.   Conflicting Reports on Effectiveness

The research on the effectiveness of films, like that on the effectiveness of TV, has arrived at conflicting conclusions. As an example, films seemed to be an appropriate and somewhat successful means of communicating new knowledge to practicing doctors in attendance at medical conventions (Hackel, #0753), but a dismal failure when used to inform adults of research information pertinent to a proposed school board reorganization. (Kreitlow, #3868)

2.   Potential for Educational Purposes

With'n this medium, as in television, such divergence of opinion is a result of the specificity of the research, not the vagaries of the technology. Under more controlled conditions, films used in combination with other techniques can *stimulate interest* and *educate* for change. For example, Tucker cites the use of a mental health film with in-patients in facilitating group therapy (#3141). Educationally, the films served to orient "psychiatrically unsophisticated patients toward the interests and in methods of psychotherapy much more rapidly than previous experience with such patients would have lead the writers to expect" (pp. 280-281). It also legitimized for the group the acceptability of sharing experiences and broaching topics which previously had been avoided. In another setting, films were satisfactorily used in an educational series on 'mental health aspects of patient care' for the staff of a hospital that was characterized by high rates of turnover. (Verhaalen et al., #3954)

3.   Advantages for Immediate Use

The *economic advantages of films* make them an especially important tool for education in the immediate future. Cartridge-loading 8mm. films, though not as flexible as videotapes, are cheaper and superior in picture quality and convenience. (Forsdale, #1176)

E.   RADIO AND RECORDINGS

1.   Reaching a Mass Audience

The radio has functioned in the communication process mainly at the awareness stage of knowledge diffusion. Its impact as a first source of information is difficult to distinguish in the literature from that of television. In recent studies of mass media effects in general, radio is usually considered together with TV and/or newspapers, if it is mentioned at all. Recordings, transmitted over either of the broadcast media, have largely been ignored. This is undoubtedly due to the wide diffusion of all these media, but also to researchers' apparent fascination with that newer medium, TV.

2.   Potential for Education: Two-Way Communication and User Control

Again, the field of medicine has been a leader in its adoption of the *two-way* radio systems in their training programs. In this field, radio has been used singly or in combination with a video transmission, and on both the medical school and postgraduate level. (Ramey, #6208; Neal, #6160) Apparently, too, the radio classroom is used with great effectiveness in the very sparsely populated "bush" regions of Australia, although no research studies verifying this innovation were identified in the literature surveyed for this report.

The major advantage of radio is economic; a receiver and transmitter cost only about $500 per year per participating hospital, and the programming is available to all doctors on the staff. (Woolsey, #0746) However, a special advantage of two-way radio is the individualization of the teacher-student contact. This is a matter which deserves further attention from educators.

Tape recordings have also been used successfully on a limited basis in the medical field to distribute abstracts of the literature. (Neal, #6160) However, the primary source of research on the utilization of recordings in educational settings has been done with foreign language laboratories. This particular innovation has not met with exceptional success. Much of the resistance to language labs has undoubtedly stemmed from the size of the initial capital outlay required for adoption. Moreover, the fact that it was one of the first intensive and expensive technologies introduced into school systems meant that it ran much of the interference for subsequent innovations against teacher resistance and misapplication. Even among later studies, however, its ability to increase learning by language students was found to be negligible, and among the more capable students, language lab time was even termed a hinderance to learning. (Keating, #3733) In this case the failure of the innovation was due not simply to inadequacies in the technology, but also to those in the theory behind "language labs". Pre-taped or recorded lessons are limited to mere rote memorization and repetition as teaching techniques. They are one-way channels, not designed to provide feedback of progress in process, nor to ensure that one knowledge "bit" is thoroughly digested before proceeding with instruction on the next. Such methods would understandably quell the enthusiasm of the better student. In contrast, when taped lessons are incorporated into programmed learning *packages*, where the rate of proceeding is controlled by the student and where feedback is constantly available to him, they perform quite satisfactorily. (ITM, #7014)

F. MAILING

1. Effectiveness in Dissemination

The communication of scientific knowledge through the mail may be seen as a sub-topic of "Written Media". In fact, however, it functions as a unique channel for knowledge dissemination and, hence, deserves separate mention. The use of direct mail to advertise or to inform people of new products or processes seems to have its greatest potential among specialized target audiences for whom it may serve a secondary, supportive role *to other communication media*. Its advantage is its effectiveness as a secondary in-put for material communicated over the mass media. With properly chosen receivers a mail campaign can be quite effective.

2. Targetted Mailings

An excellent example of this type of usage appears in medicine, where much drug advertising is channeled through the mail as well as through professional journals and through the drug company detailmen. (Jeuck, #0752) The journal in this situation enhances the usefulness of the direct-mail advertisement. For a firm which does not have an established reputation, the prestige of an accepted journal can lend respectability to its mail campaign.

The choice of receiver is a relevant issue whether or not the advertiser is a well established firm. General practitioners are the group most receptive to mailed advertising (#0752), but certain products are obviously most appropriate for particular specialists. Communications concerning such products should be limited to these specialists, for the sake of economy and to prevent saturation of both the receiver audience and of the medium with irrelevant messages.

3. Mass Mailings

Within a consumer population of high purchasing potential, market researchers have studied content and format variables in direct-mail advertisements. (Lucas and Britt have reviewed these researcher's findings, #7013.) The usual purpose of such study is the identification of the most appealing layout, so that it may be used subsequently in a nationwide campaign which would not be limited to advertisements sent through the mail. Although a substantial amount of money is spent annually on mass mailed ads, researchers have not found this medium to have any particular advantage over the other media used for advertising.

G. DEMONSTRATIONS

1. Why Demonstrations are Effective

Demonstrations can be very successful mechanisms for inducing change in both the demonstrator and his audience.* The demonstration seems to function in at least three important ways: (1) it stimulates interest and involvement in the audience; (2) it provides an opportunity for pre-trial evaluation by observers; and (3) it reinforces prior adoption for the demonstrator, himself.

The "traveling seminar", a demonstration technique developed and popularized by Malcolm Richland (#3698), has been most effective in familiarizing educators with innovations being successfully attempted in other school systems, and in motivating them to begin innovative projects and similar visitation exchanges 'back home'. The traveling seminar has been adapted by other educators for their own change projects (Kaser, #3905; Carr and Meyer, #5102).

_____

*The pilot project sometimes serves the same purpose.

The demonstration facilitates acceptance by giving potential adopters the opportunity to watch the innovation in action before large investments in time, money, and staff are committed. This opportunity to observe and evaluate a working model before trying it is an asset to the potential adopter not only because he can better determine the appropriateness of the innovation to his situation but also because seeing the operation of the innovation often brings to the surface important issues in installation which the potential adopter will need to consider. Some innovations can only be fully evaluated by actually "trying them out". A pilot model, which necessitates only a small investment, can help the adopter evaluate the innovation's appropriateness and the requirements for its installation on a broad scale. Schon found, in fact, in a study of the military and of private companies participating in government contracts, that the most feasible of the proven methods for introducing innovations was the construction of a pilot model of the change prior to requests for total acceptance of the innovation. (#3025)

Demonstrations may be especially effective to reinforce adoption by the demonstrator, himself, because it compels him to make a public commitment to the innovation. Change agents have often induced their clients to demonstrate newly adopted innovations to other groups in order to produce greater dedication or internalization of the change. (Lippitt et al., #1343) Festinger notes how public commitment puts the communicator in a cognitive "box"; he cannot henceforth reject the message that he has advocated to others without feeling "cognitive dissonance" from the discrepancy between his advocacy and his behavior. (#0264)

2. Impact of Demonstration on Long Range Policy Making and Goals for Change

According to Rein and Miller (#7029), the demonstration or demonstration research project is a powerful method of bringing about change in the face of budgetary or legislative scrutiny. There are several advantages of such a method: (1) it encourages activity, (2) it is a highly visible and publicizeable technique, and (3) funding agencies that could not be induced to support operational projects will often consider funding demonstrations. On the other hand, demonstrations: (1) postpone major change, (2) affect relatively few people, (3) as instruments of change, do not severely threaten established institutions, nor demand immediate action, (4) promote the unequal distribution of resources (money, etc.), (5) distract from long range policy by creating substitutes for broad-based programs, and (6) over-emphasize success and play down failures. (#7029) Because of these broader considerations, one should take particular care in selecting goals for a demonstration project and in pursuing them. "The ultimate test of the success of a demonstration is whether it can actually influence long term and large scale policy". (#7029, p. 33)

3. Status and Proximity Factors in the Success of a Demonstration

A field in which the demonstration is particularly adaptable, and also highly developed and widely used, is that of agriculture. Selected farmers in an area try out new farming practices and methods, demonstrate good farming, and encourage others to do so as well. (Blackmore et al., #2492) Their 'demonstrated' success seems to lie in their ability to serve as in-group opinion leaders. They are perceived by their neighbors and peers as 'good farmers', not necessarily as members of the extension service team. The degree of effectiveness that a demonstration has in influencing potential adopters has even been correlated with the geographical proximity of the demonstration farm to the target farmer's property. (Blackmore et al., #2492) Even those studies whose conclusions about the effectiveness of the demonstration farms were most conservative, admitted that they had been an "important" source of innovation communication. (Smith and Sheppard, #1090; Anderson, #2535)

4. Demonstrations that Fail

While a successful demonstration may provide strong positive impetus for change, a demonstration that fails may have an equally strong negative impact. Change agents have learned from painful experience that if direction and guidance are not sustained through-out a demonstration project, failure, leading to increased resistance to future innovations, is the result. For example, in one agricultural improvement project in the Punjab, lack of attention by the change agents allowed such essentials as the care of the growing crop and the publicizing of the fact of the demonstration to the local farmers to be neglected. (Sinha and Yadav, #1142) Similarly, if available funds are used up in the engineering and production of the project, and educational-social acceptance aspects are neglected, or if those phases are not synchronized, the innovation will ultimately be rejected by the client system. (Sasaki, #1106)

Considering these disadvantages, it must be recommended that one should not attempt a transmission process as complex and expensive as the demonstration unless ample time and resources are provided for preparation, coordination, and completion. However, if the complexity of the innovation, itself, contributes to the demonstration's failure, then the intended users will be fairly warned about the difficulty of the procedures in which they might be involving themselves. Obviously, if the innovation is truly ineffective or unworkable, the demonstration that fails plays a very healthy role in inhibiting diffusion.

H. PROGRAMMED INSTRUCTION AND TEACHING MACHINES

1. Sources of Controversy

Some of the most interesting and controversial innovations in education are those involving programmed instruction or teaching machines. The experience of those systems which have attempted to introduce these innovations has repeatedly demonstrated the difficulty of altering role concepts, a change which they necessitate. The propensity and ability of the classroom teacher to consciously or unconsciously sabotage a threat to her long-standing role as "knowledge conveyor" and, hence, her perceived competence as a teacher is now a widely recognized problem. (Chesler et al., #2607; Guba, #6089)

However, convincing data does exist to support the effectiveness of programmed learning although such evidence has been obtained in settings which are located outside the traditional public school system. In an industrial setting, for example, the feasibility of remote computer-assisted instruction for training newly hired electronic technicians was compared with that of a programmed text. Trainees rated both techniques as being as effective and desirable as traditional classroom instruction. Moreover, the use of the computer, the teaching machine in this instance, allowed a 10% reduction in the time required to complete the course. (Schwartz and Haskell, #3189) This finding is typical among motivated learners.

2. Advantage of Divergence from Traditional Education

Programmed instruction is uniquely appropriate for use with problem students. A major reason for the cycles of academic failure and disillusionment among these students may be their inability to relate effectively to authority figures (teachers) and to peers. Programmed instruction offers an instructional attack on these handicaps where intensive psychological analysis is impractical. Programmed instruction potentially is able to inculcate new knowledge and skills while circumventing many of the stumbling blocks to learning inherent in the authoritarian nature of the traditional teacher-student relationship.*

For the most profitable application of programmed learning in the immediate future, the advantages of the isolated educational setting may be worth exploiting. Moreover, the appropriateness of this technique for students with learning problems stemming from an inability to adjust to our traditional educational system could be a potent motivation for teachers who would be induced to use it.

I. SUMMARY OF ONE-WAY DIFFUSION TRANSMISSIONS

The main advantages of using one-way channels in the communication of innovations are, (1) the packageability of messages for this form of channel, and (2) the disseminability of such communications to large audiences. Such assets make the one-way technologies practical for wide usage. Also, they are perfectly adequate for the transmission of knowledge (a) when the message is not likely to elicit audience resistance, or (b) when the goals of the communicator focus on informing the receiver, making him aware of certain information, or arousing his interest. One-way media certainly can make major contributions in dissemination campaigns where several techniques are used in combination and in sequence to bring about the ultimate adoption of an innovation.

III. ONE-WAY FEEDBACK TRANSMISSION PROCESSES

A. THREE BASIC DISTINCTIONS

It is probably axiomatic that any kind of transmission effort, even if it is one-way, will evoke some kind of response, some sort of activity which represents a return message from the receiver of the transmission to the original sender (see Figure 9.2 below). In the previous chapter such messages were analyzed as "user knowledge". (See again pp. 8-43 to

*Discussion of a Programmed Instruction program with this specific aim appears in ITM, #7014.

8-54.) We now refer to it simply as *feedback*. The channels utilized in feedback communications are not entirely distinct from those which might carry messages to the consumer (e.g., written reports, mail), but such channels serve a distinctly characteristic purpose when flowing back in the direction of the resource.

FIGURE 9.2

The utilization of feedback is an integral part of the knowledge utilization process. The researcher, developer, and practitioner must "hear" and respond to expressions of "user need" and "user reaction" if effective utilization of new knowledge is to take place. In order to understand and appropriately respond to feedback messages, the receiver of these communications (i.e., the 'resource') must know how to interpret user information. Three important aspects of the feedback message must be evaluated:

1. Was it *elicited* by the resource or *initiated* by the user?
2. Was the user *aware* that he was providing feedback?
3. Does the feedback reflect the user's *behavior* or does it reflect his *attitudes*?

1. Resource-Elicited vs. User-Initiated Feedback

Sometimes researchers from corporations, governments, etc., elicit feedback through such mechanisms as surveys, polls, and elections. At other times the user takes the initiative and his feedback arrives 'on the doorstep' of the resource system unrequested and, perhaps, unwanted, in the form of letters, petitions, and protest demonstrations.

In elicited feedback the resource can control, through its sampling procedures, the representativeness of the population being heard, or it can select a relevant sub-population for survey. On the other hand, if the primary need of the resource system is the assessment of the *strength* of the user's attitude, then user-initiated responses are probably more valid. It has been shown that the person who submits feedback unrequested is highly motivated in holding his opinions on an issue, and maintains them consistently throughout the cognitive, affective, and behavioral levels of his personality. (Krech, Crutchfield, and Ballachey, #7130; Bettelheim and Janowitz, #7129)

2. <u>User Awareness of the Feedback: Direct vs. Indirect Procedures</u>

A user is aware that he is providing feedback to the resource system (1) when the resource questions him directly about his needs or reactions, or (2) if he purposely sends an unsolicited message to the resource. He is unaware that the resource is receiving feedback from him (1) if information about his needs or reactions is obtained through secondary sources, or (2) if the feedback heeded is that discovered in the latent content of his message. In other words, *direct feedback* is that information received from a user who is aware of the "what and why" of its collection. *Indirect feedback* consists of the information collected from a user without his knowledge, or when the purpose of its collection is not specified for him.

a. Direct Feedback

Messages that travel 'up the line' from the consumer are, more often than not, overt attempts to influence. For example, the consumer is aware that his elicited responses will be considered, or he may initiate the communication himself with the intention of altering the behavior of the receiver of his message. Probably, the great majority of <u>utilized</u> feedback is of this type.

An advantage of the direct methods is that they provide information to the resource person which would be unavailable through even the most adroit manipulation of archival records, one technique for obtaining indirect feedback. A further consideration in selecting direct methods is that in some cases the subjective selection of the respondent may introduce no greater degree of error than would that of the researcher. Statistical support for any such assumption is, unfortunately, lacking.

It is true that the responses elicited through direct feedback may be biased in part by the user's reaction to the collector or to being in the position of 'typical consumer'. However, at the present time direct feedback is probably the simplest and most economic means of getting at certain kinds of information.

b. Indirect Feedback

The strength of indirect feedback, also termed "non-reactive research" (Webb et al., #6919), lies in its ability to evade subjectivity in the response. Indirect techniques are necessary to measure certain categories of information which more obvious methods of collection would prejudice. They are most appropriately utilized where tendencies toward socially acceptable responses are likely; when honesty is incalculable; and where inaccuracies in self reports, due to memory lapses, misunderstanding of the question, etc., are probable. For example, in their study of sociometric influences on the diffusion of a new drug among physicians, Coleman, Menzel, and Katz (#3895) went to pharmacy records to identify the approximate date on which various doctors began prescribing it. This use of records circumvented the error inherent in direct reports by physicians attempting to recall what they had done.

9-18

Webb and his associates (#6919) have suggested that attention be directed toward the development of appropriate combinations of both direct and indirect techniques. Hopefully, the short-comings and imprecisions in each method could be eliminated through such cross-validation, and a high degree of accuracy could be obtained.

3.   Feedback on Behavior vs. Feedback on Attitude

It is not always easy to determine whether feedback reflects the user's attitude or, simply, his behavior. If, for example, a social scientist wants to know about a user's attitude, he can ask the user directly what his attitude is or he can infer it from the user's behavior. Because it is difficult to avoid bias in direct measures of attitude, the researcher may need to use indirect methods. In a classic design for studying the preference for male children among upper-class parents, Winston (#7018) searched the birth records of children from families estimated to be complete, and from these obtained the occupational status of the father, number and sex of the siblings, and sex of the 'last child'. His hypothesis was that a preference for males would make the male-female ratio for 'last children' greater than that for 'all children' of these families. This was confirmed by the data.

Such sophisticated manipulation of records is not always necessary, for attitude is often only secondarily important to the retriever of feedback. The market researcher, for example, is interested in the consumer's 'attitude' about the product only as it affects his buying behavior.

It is tremendously important that the person receiving feedback be aware of whether it is a reflection of attitude or of behavior. It is very easy to interpret feedback incorrectly; two examples from the political sphere can illustrate this:

a.   A national election, the primary mechanism for political feedback in a democracy, is intended to be a measure of the sentiment and will--the attitude--of the people. The results of an election are often interpreted as a "mandate from the people" for some political program. However, extensive research on voting behavior has determined that a number of causal factors, extrinsic to the issues of the election, have an inordinate amount of influence on the choice of the candidate and even the decision to vote. Such factors as the party preferences of the voter's family and the relation of these to the dominant political attitudes of the local community, the presence of an influential other (e.g., the spouse), and personal experience with the previous administration regularly demonstrate their ability to decide the action of the voter. (Campbell, #7021) Thus, elections, in fact, reflect only the lever-pressing behavior of the public, though the elected candidate may claim that they signify public attitude.

b.   Protest demonstrations present a contrasting example.
They are not a legitimized means of feedback to government
or other institutions, though they are used and they do
elicit responses from the organization they intend to
censure. Protest demonstrations are direct manifestations
of attitude. However, we frequently tend to interpret the
protest only in terms of the protestors' behavior. The
fact is that much attitudinal feedback is ignored when
the receiver of the feedback focuses merely on the behavior
of the sender.*

There is, among collectors and users of feedback, an ever-
growing appreciation of the complexity of interpreting this
retrieved user knowledge. Considerations involving both
methodology and ethics are currently unresolved. A thorough
enumeration of these ethical issues and methodological
problems, specifically as they pertain to survey research,
appears in Webb et al. Unobtrusive Measures: Nonreactive
Research in the Social Sciences (#6919).

B.   FEEDBACK MECHANISMS

   The channels through which a resource system may receive feedback
from its users are numerous. Some are more 'useful' than others, depending
on the kind of user information to be retrieved and the purposes for which
the feedback is needed. The feedback mechanisms listed below are the major
one-way channels through which user information is currently flowing.

   1.   Public Archives

   The use of the public archives of record-keeping societies has
long been a fruitful technique for the researcher attempting to learn
about the behavior or attitudes of a particular group of people.
Getting feedback data through public records is usually the least
expensive means of eliciting this kind of information, and in many
cases it is entirely adequate for the researcher's purposes. Of course,
one may encounter gaps in the records due to circumstances or to the
subjective selection of the recordkeeper. These inadequacies can be
overcome if the researcher can supplement the information in the public
records with feedback retrieved through other channels.

   Winston's creative analysis of birth record data in verifying
the preference of upper-class parents for male offspring (#7018, Section A.3. cited above) is an example of eliciting feedback indirectly
from the public archives in order to obtain information about attitudes.
Other governmental and scientific records (e.g., budget, weather) may
be useful sources of indirect feedback for the researcher.

---

*There are, of course, many other complex issues surrounding the purposes and
 reliability of such demonstrations. (See section B.8. below.)

2. Private Records

The research on advertising effects and consumer behavior being done by private companies comprises a considerable proportion of the statistical knowledge about user behavior and attitude that currently exists in our recordkeeping-oriented society. Data from such private records is, however, frequently less accessible than that from other feedback channels unless the researcher is associated with the organization that originally collected it. If the researcher can gain access to them, private records usually provide more detailed information than do public records and may, consequently, be more useful to the researcher.

3. Attitude and Opinion Surveys

One major concern of social survey research is feedback to the society about its own functioning. Attitude and opinion surveys are those channels by which researchers determine reactions to or preferences for change and innovations. The most carefully considered and scientifically controlled feedback is to be found in opinion polls and social research designs. By providing legislatures with data on the temper of the people, they have become important tools of government and administration. (Likert, #5202)

These surveys rely primarily on the questionnaire and the interview as mechanisms of feedback. These two mechanisms are, perhaps, the most vulnerable of all the obtrusive measures to the source of error popularly known as the "guinea pig" or "Hawthorne" effect. The knowledge that, "what I say is important and will be taken under consideration," confounds these measures to a large, but as yet undefined, extent. Moreover, the questionnaire and interview are also the mechanisms most widely criticized for their dependence on the fallibility of the data collector. Given such dim views of their qualifications, the overwhelming advantage of these feedback channels is their ability to collect certain information which is not available from less direct sources, such as public records.

4. Observation

Valuable feedback which is not contaminated by "user awareness" can often be retrieved from the user through direct observation of his behavior or, indirectly, by observing the results of his behavior. For the person concerned with knowledge utilization, such feedback about the on-going reaction of the user to the knowledge disseminated to him helps in the evaluation of the process in progress.

There are three distinct types of "observation" which can bring relevant indirect feedback to the researcher:

a. noting the latent content of the user's communication
b. studying the user's behavior or performance, as affected by the dissemination effort
c. measuring physical signs (traces) that are indicative of behavior that has taken place

Each is discussed in greater detail below.

a.   Latent Content of Responses

The utilization of the latent content in a feedback message
is one method of obtaining an indirect measure of attitude. An
open-ended interview, as in survey research, is often designed
to pick up more than just the manifest content of the inter-
viewee's responses; his words are noted, as are the pattern of
his associations, and the underlying attitude reflected is
interpreted by the interviewer. Much criticism has been leveled
at this type of data collection because of its ordinate reliance
upon the reliability and validity of the human factor: the
interviewer's interpretation of the reactions of the respondent.
On the other hand, the use of gross statistics, as found in archival
records, in many instances may merely succeed in replacing the
researcher's subjective perception with the subjective perception
of the recordkeeper.

b.   Performance/Behavior

By unobtrusively observing the user's behavior in response
to an information input, one can easily determine the effectiveness of the dissemination effort. The example of this type of
observation which comes most quickly to mind is the advertising
technique of studying the comparative effectiveness of two or
more kinds of product displays or advertising layouts by measuring
the increase of sales or "coupon clipping" resulting from each.

In the educational setting the awareness of being observed,
or of having one's behavior measured (i.e., the previously mentioned
"guinea pig effect" or "Hawthorne effect"), is presumably less
of an issue because of the long tradition of routine testing.
Hence, the teacher-administered exam is an indirect measure of
whether or not the student has studied.* Unfortunately, as all
teachers know, the classroom test has all the shortcomings of
interpretor subjectivity that other indirect feedback techniques have.

c.   Physical Signs

Sometimes it is possible to use physical signs or "traces"
as sources of feedback information. Although the collection of
this type of feedback can be both time-consuming and costly,
such methods can be more revealing than can direct questioning
of the user and, perhaps because of their uniqueness, they can
also have a stronger impact on the system receiving the feedback.

A broad range of topics are amenable to study through
tabulation of their physical traces. One enterprising researcher
kept a tally of trash can contents to measure the liquor consumption
in a "dry" town and found that the behavior of the townspeople
belied their publicly-expressed "dry" attitudes. (Webb citing

---

*The "direct" approach to feedback would be to ask him.

Sawyer, #6919) In another case an automobile dealership selected
a radio station for its advertisements by keeping a count of the
dial positions on the radios of cars brought in for service.
(Anonymous 1962, #7015) In a third, the comparative relevance
of sections in the International Encyclopedia of the Social
Sciences was measured by noting the varying occurrence of finger smudges
and frayed edges among pages of editions in six university libraries.
(Mosteller, #7016) And, finally, at Chicago's Museum of Science
and Industry the popularity of the 'hatching chick' exhibit has
been verified for the maintenance crews by the need for replacing
the vinyl tiles in front of that display every six weeks. The
flooring in the rest of the building lasts for several years.
(Webb et al. #6919)

5. Referenda-Elections

Elections are the basic mechanism for political feedback in a
democracy. Their serviceability as a valid representation of the public
will is, however, very difficult to measure. As mentioned previously,
many factors extrinsic to the issues or candidates in the election
operate on the decision of the voter. (See again Section A.3.a.)
The validity of the election results is more of a concern in elections
on a national level than in local elections and referenda. The extrinsic
influences on the voter serve to fractionate the vote across the country
by interest groups and regions. In local elections where issues are
more directly related to the personal interests of the voters, the
results reflect to a greater degree 'the sentiment of the people'.
(Campbell, #7021)

6. Petitions

The petition is a popular and legitimate means of citizen feedback in a democracy. In theory, its usefulenss for measuring the will
of the people is not unlike that of the election: its power rests
on voter initiative. Also, because duplication can be eliminated by
verifying signatures against lists of registered voters, a petition
can be proven to be more representative of public opinion than can
"number of pieces of mail from constituents". (Webb et al., #6919)

Research has shown, however, that petition-signing is even more
apt to be biased than is voting, probably because the signing of a
petition is a public act. Various studies have confirmed that the
decision to sign is influenced both by the strength of the plea and
by the reaction (refusal or endorsement) of the previous person
approached by the petition circulator. (Blake et al., #7023; Helson
et al., #7020) One can imagine the use of a confederate in attempts
to sway the decision of a potential signer. The real question about
obtaining signatures in such a manner is, how permanent is the attitude
expressed in the public act of signing the petition? Hovland's
discovery that "public commitment" has a significant influence on the
individual's retention of change (#7009) may be an important factor
operating here. Further research should clarify how the mechanism of
petition-signing affects the future behavior of the signer.

7. Letters

Letters from a consumer or a constituent are often sources of
stimulation for change. In a survey of U.S. Senators and Congressmen,
"personal correspondence from constituents" was claimed as a major
source of relevant 'new information'. (Hattery and Hofheimer,#1214)
However, when such correspondence takes the form of exhortations to
support one measure or another its validity as feedback is disputable.
One Senator, whose curiosity was aroused by a deluge of mail urging
his support of a measure for which, in fact, he had worked quite actively
since its introduction, had his staff trace the correspondents. They
found that only 33% of the letters were from registered voters.
(Dexter and White, #3624) This illustrates the persisting dilemma
which confronts legislators in their evaluation of and reaction to
constituent feedback. Their daily mail must be identified as (1) "junk",
i.e., form and duplicated letters; (2) "stimulated mail", that the
employer, union, etc., of which the correspondent is a member has
suggested he send; or (3) "genuine" reactions from the public.

8. Protests, Riots, and Revolts

These three types of direct public feedback differ in intensity
and finality, but they represent similarly strong reactions against
the status quo and they are all pointed mandates for change. In
contrast to voting and petition-signing, protests, riots, and full-
blown revolts are not institutionalized mechanisms of feeding back
information in a social system. Consequently, as might be expected,
the interpretation of such feedback is a problem; the message is
usually quite clearly heard, but not clearly understood. Their
effectiveness as mechanisms is limited by their blatancy. The directness of the attack on a society or on an institution which characterizes
these methods brings about the most intensive kind of confrontation
with conflicting vested interests. Such directness, however, is a
symptom of the futility and frustration of the participators. It is a
seemingly unavoidable consequence of previous failures with less
belligerent or violent means of inducing or accelerating change. Hence,
the usefulness of these phenomena as 'feedback' per se is doubly
questionable.   The value of a mechanism for providing relevant information about popular sentiment is negated (1) if the mechanism itself
blurs the message, (2) if it is ignored by its intended audience, or
(3) if it destroys the institution it was designed to censure.

C. SUMMARY AND CONCLUSIONS ABOUT ONE-WAY FEEDBACK

One-way feedback can be very helpful if properly evaluated and kept
in perspective. It is an essential mechanism for obtaining receiver information in large systems where two-way communication efforts are impractical,
and it is especially appropriate when major status or power differences exist
between the sender and the receiver of the feedback. This is most typical
in the relations of employees to management, patients to doctors, and the
general public to the government.

In order to achieve optimal usefulness of a channel, several major
developments should be considered in the near future. There is a need for
immediate and effective ways for large audiences to give direct feedback.
The telephone is a mechanism of potentially vast significance in the solution
of this problem.

There is a concommitant need to protect both the sender and the resource system from *feedback overload*. In complex innovations, for example, it may take time to complete the change and to make results visible. Having a great deal of feedback in the early stages may provide only redundant information and, more importantly, it may contribute toward resistance to sending or receiving feedback at a later stage. Early feedback may also be confounded if the change in process is initially undesired and unappreciated but is important in the long-run for the welfare of the consumer.

IV. TWO-WAY TRANSMISSION PROCESSES

It is often vital that information about certain changes or innovations be transmitted in a setting where free and immediate feedback can be received and responded to. Although the large number of senders needed in comparison to the size of the audience reached is a factor which is often criticized as inefficient, such two-way communication is needed to bring about complex change. (Schramm, #5396) When the complexity of the message requires detailed clarification or when major attitude, behavioral, or value changes are required, two-way communication is most helpful. In these cases the communications generated from the consumer system could take the form of a statement of needs, diagnostic information, evaluation of the new ideas, or indications of comprehension of the original message.

Within the two-way transmission process there appears a natural division among the techniques or channels which reflects the number of people interacting: two, a few, or many. In this discussion we will arbitrarily make a concurrent distinction among these groups of our emphasis on (A) the interaction of individuals, (B) the effect on the individual of mere membership in the group, and (C) the organizational or systemic factors relevant to the transmission of communications.

A. DYADIC EXCHANGE

A dyadic relationship, signifying the interaction of two people, may be identified within a group of any size or composition if one is focusing solely on variables affecting interpersonal interaction.* Dyadic exchange, by far the most common type of two-way communication, has the potential to support the deepest kinds of change in individuals. The patient-therapist and parent-child relationships are the obvious examples of the potency of dyadic interaction to influence for change.

One of the advantages of this and other kinds of two-way oral communication is the *immediacy* of perceived reaction. Without this availability of feedback, two-way channels function no more effectively than do unidirectional ones. For example, psychologists rank 'personal discussions' with colleagues as more effective means of communicating than two-way written correspondence with these same people. (American Psychological Association, #2126) The importance of immediate reaction has also been substantiated in the field of medical continuing education. Many designs have been tried for broadcasting information about medical innovations to practicing doctors over radio and TV. In these designs a number of ways to incorporate the M.D.'s questions into the program

---

*The *personality variables* influencing human interaction have already been discussed quite fully in Chapters Four and Five.)

have been attempted: mailing forms were given to the doctors, telephones and two-way radios were installed in hospitals, etc. (Robertson, #6159; Neal, #6160) It is notable that the recent developments in this field have shown the increasing use of some form of *two-way audio hook-up* in the programming. (Ramey, #6208)

1. Traditional Uses of Oral Informal Exchange

Some of the more specific of the reviewed studies on dyadic interaction have been done by the American Psychological Association. Their findings show that informal discussion among peers serves diverse uses. Psychologists report dyadic exchange to be a most useful communications medium for: (1) learning about new ideas (#2126), (2) locating pertinent written resources (#1206 and #2125), (3) getting information about new methods and procedures for research (#2123), and (4) receiving feedback on their own new ideas (#2124).

2. The Impact of Involvement

Face-to-face confrontation, with all its advantages, does evoke a number of secondary reactions to a communication which may be detrimental. The affective proximity of the 'other' and the 'involving' capacity of the act of participation also elicit more complex and total responses within an individual. Under these circumstances the *personality variables* discussed in Chapter Four may become salient. The *roles* held by the people participating in two-way transmission processes are interdependent with their personalities in determining the success of the communication.

There is evidence that in collaborative work among researchers from different fields, discussion and coordination with another researcher is seen as detracting from time and energy that should be spent in *the solitary pursuit of knowledge*. (Blackwell, #1218) This finding reflects the perceptions and expectations researchers hold regarding their own role. It suggests that attempts at team organization and task consolidation will be handicapped from the outset, and it warns that the obviously momentous task of developing an appropriate status relationship among the disciplines should take account of their mutual *independence*.

In an initial meeting between people representing different status levels (roles) within a single field, mutual suspicion is often aroused regarding the other's conflicting goals and/or questionable commitment. One or the other or both individuals may see collaboration as inadvisable. A clarification of misunderstandings between them and an openness to the reevaluation of goals other than one's own can be achieved through a continuing dialogue that attempts to see each role in perspective and to increase respect for both. (Poser et al., #2210)

A real difficulty develops when there is a difference in both the status level *and* the professional field of collaborators; e.g., educational researchers and government administrators. (Guskin, #5162) The sheer magnitude of the distance between two such roles creates a "credibility gap" which easily generates suspicion; hence, voluntary cooperation is unlikely. If it were obligatory, one could expect "compliance" without private acceptance or impermanent "identification" from the subordinate, but not "internalization" a la Kelman. (Hovland and Weiss, #6281)

3.   Establishing Successful Dyadic Exchange

Several recognized techniques have been developed which circumvent or overcome potential conflicts in face-to-face exchanges. Two successful ones are presented below.

   a.   Consultant Relationships

      The "consultant" relationship is an example of a generically unique type of association between people on different status levels, who may also be in different fields. It is a functioning model in which successful communication has been achieved. The key to its effectiveness lies in the fact that the potential user, or subordinate in this relationship, is the initiator of the inter-action, i.e., he seeks the consultant's expertise. Moreover, the consultant by definition, has no power over the behavior of the consultee or the adoption of the innovation.*

      The consultant relationship, because it is user initiated, also has the advantage of user "openness", or readiness for change. The user decides to seek consultant help only after he has had a chance to do some preliminary exploration of the topic on his own. This was discovered by Wilkening when he studied agricultural extension agents. (#5385) The county agent was ineffective for introducing innovations to farmers. However, after they had become interested in an idea or product (possibly through reading of it in a handy extension bulletin or journal article) the use of his consultation was highly coordinated with adoption. Stone (#1129) confirms Wilkening's finding for dyadic consultation and advice-giving by county agents or "other farmers" to farmers during the trial or adoption stage of diffusion.

   b.   Roger's "Rule"

      Floyd Mann (#7022) and his colleagues have developed a technique for dealing with misunderstandings and verbal conflicts in human interaction. Such misunderstandings may lead to pseudo-dyadic one-way discussions. The method builds on the premise that conflict begins with misunderstanding, and that misunderstanding stems from failure to listen to the other person: frequently the "listener" pays very little attention the the words of the speaker, being pre-occupied with planning what he will say at the first opportunity to interrupt. If he is, in fact, aware of what is being said, he may only be evaluating it from his own point of view, not trying to understand it from the other fellow's position. Hence, the discussion degenerates to the point where people are no longer talking to each other, but past one another.   The "rule"** that can be used to intervene and halt or avoid an argument requires that each person *accurately* restate the ideas and feelings of the previous speaker before he presents his own. This "reflecting" of the other's

---

*A complete discussion of the consultant role appears in Chapter Seven.

**First proposed by Carl Rogers #3809.

message serves both to reduce misunderstanding and to lower the emotional level of the discussion. If, when resolution of misunderstanding has been achieved, real value disagreements are found to remain, these can be related to broader value systems or goals that are held in common, and an action decision can be made in the light of these. If no such broad values are found, and one of the alternatives must be selected, a mutual commitment to a thorough evaluation of the chosen course of action should be established and carried through.

4. Conclusions about Dyadic Exchanges

It is clear that much remains to be done in the development of means to measure and to increase the success of dyadic exchange. The numerous variables to be considered have limited the definitiveness of research in this area. Nevertheless, much of the effort up to this time has been directed toward projecting costly and elaborate solutions for specific dyadic situations (e.g., the broad adoption of expensive one-to-one consultation). The practicality of expending energy in deriving such solutions is disputable. Even if they could be operationlized, the length and cost of commitment required from the consultee could only be supported by a very stable or wealthy "system". The benefits would still remain unavailable to the general public. Information on the dyadic interaction process should be made more widely distributable to potential users. As exemplified by the work of Mann et al. (#7022), attempts to move toward generalizable and easily applicable models for interaction are beginning to emerge. In future development work in this area, we need to put even greater emphasis on such economical and efficient means of training people to interact effectively.

B. SMALL GROUPS

It is advantageous to communicate certain kinds of innovation messages within the context of a small group. Mere membership in the group can facilitate an individual's acceptance of a message. Most simply stated, the group and group discussion methods have been found most useful in the latter stages of the "communication of change" process. Because small group discussions utilize a comparatively high number of "sender" resource persons in relation to the number of users reached, they are not a practical technique for creating awareness about an innovation or for arousing interest in it. The one-way mass media can adequately handle these functions. However, when a potential user has reached the point of considering the relative merits of his own adoption of the change, when he needs to understand it thoroughly, when he needs answers to his specific questions about it, and when he needs supportive feedback on his newly-adopted behavior, small group interaction can be highly effective.

Along these lines, McKeachie (#6439) has suggested that a lecture method is more satisfactory than discussion for the mere transmission of facts, but that if one is concerned with developing or changing attitudes or with the retention of such changes (i.e., "moving" and "refreezing"), then discussions have substantial superiority. (pp. 1126-1127) The superiority of group discussions to lectures in bringing about changes in attitude and behavior is further supported by the data from the experiments of Lewin and his students (#2640 and #7025) during World War II in changing food habits. Housewives were urged to serve their families the low-cost and nutritional, but less appealing, intestinal meats. Those who received this communication in the context of a small group discussion showed a greater tendency to comply than did those who heard of it at a lecture.

1.   Factors Contributing to the Effectiveness of the Small Group

Since the classic social psychological studies establishing the power of group norms on the individual (e.g., Newcomb, #6302) many successful programs for bringing about change have utilized participation in a group discussion-type of activity as a mechanism for activating new behavior. For example, the acceptance of new public health facilities in a community was promoted through church and civic group discussions. (Stojanovic, #2957) In another case, the introduction of middle-aged women into the factory work force during the man-power shortage of World War II was opposed relentlessly until a program of participative research with group discussion and decision-making by the supervisors who would be affected by such a change in the work force was initiated. (Marrow and French, #7027)

The strength of the small group to promote or stabilize attitude and behavior change through discussion lies in its *ability to mobilize the power of peer influence* (e.g., see Festinger on the "social comparison process", #7032). Lewin and Pelz refer to the interaction of group cohesion and behavior change, where the tendency toward adherence to norms is activiated and where mere perception of group consensus is a powerful motivator for the individual --perhaps, a potential deviant. (Lewin, #7025; Pelz, #6283) Hovland also contributes data which is generally supportive of the 'conformity to norm' theory. As it was discussed in our section on presentations to live audiences (a type of one-way diffusion transmission), Hovland found that the mechanism of public commitment by a group member was influential in his subsequent retention of a change. (#7009)

Coch and French (#1828) attribute this normative influence of a 'group' to the process of *participation*. According to their theory, group discussion is an operation in which the member can feel he is worthwhile, a contributor or participator in the activities of the group. The nature of such participation leads to the member's ego involvement in these activities. Ego involvement stimulates identification with the group and a desire for its perpetuation. This, they feel, brings increasing cohesiveness within the group and, hence, fewer instances of deviation from established group norms.

If, indeed, the mechanisms described above are the means by which group influence functions, then a number of concerns arise about the duration and stability of changes established in a group context. Variables determining the permanence of change when the 'group' is no longer salient to the individual, either due to its dissolution or to its distance (physical and/or psychological) from the arena of change, have not been consistently researched. When Lewin conducted his experiments on food habits, "reported behavior change" (i.e., serving this type of food) by those who professed changed attitudes in the group was

not measured over a long period of time. The experiment was not
designed to determine permanence in change. (Lewin, #7025 and #2640)
Permanence of change has been demonstrated in a study using a topic that
was more anxiety-arousing: 'the early detection of breast cancer among
women'. (Bond, #7037) Group discussion and decision-making proved
to be a more successful technique than the lecture in permanently altering
behavior. Moreover, the relative superiority of the small group influence
techniques increased over time. Two factors in the discussion and
decision-making process were credited with operating to make this a
more powerful method: (1) group consensus for commitment to change and
(2) the opportunity to surface and to allay fears about the disease.
These factors might also have been discussed in terms of the "group
influence" and "participation" mechanisms discussed above.

2.   Factors Needing More Study

     Interesting results have been obtained by researchers studying
the operation of "conformity to norms" among the leadership of a group
(Whyte, #7132), and "shifts to risk or conservatism" (Wallach, #6896; and
Brown, #6254) in the small group. Each of these factors could potentially
serve a useful function in the dissemination of new knowledge through small
group interaction. At the present time, however, their dynamics are
not adequately understood. Until we find out how they operate on
the group member, we are handicapped in predicting the results of group
interaction.

3.   Small Group Techniques for Promoting Change

     Two techniques which have had rather wide success in promoting change
in individuals by using the atmosphere of the small group are the *T-Group*
and the *role play*. Both techniques utilize the informal interaction of
group members to facilitate change in personal attitude and behavior.

     a.   T-Groups (Sensitivity Training Groups)

     The T-Group for training in human relations is usually made
up of a series of sessions in which the group members have an
opportunity to study the dynamics of group interaction in the
"here-and-now". The goals of the T-Group are to increase sensitivity to others and to one's own impact on others. Members learn
how to develop norms of trust and of openness to giving and
receiving new ideas. Ideally, this will lead to new patterns of
behavior in interaction with others.

     Retention of the changes was one of the knottiest problems
in the early development of the T-Group process. T-Groups
attempt to change rather deeply rooted behavioral patterns by
capitalizing on a group structure which produces an environment
supportive of change. Because of the depth of such change,
its maintenance was severely challenged under less supportive
circumstances. In most cases the real environment to which the
T-Group member returned was sufficiently less supportive of the
behavior change that it inhibited its expression; hence, regression
to former patterns predominated. Attempts to eliminate this
problem have focussed on trying to make group experience as much
like and, therefore, relevant to the participant's real life as
possible. (Bradford, Benne, & Gibb, #6196; Lippitt & Schaible, #7026)

b.   Role Playing

    Role playing is a technique for gaining an understanding
of ourselves as others see us and of others as they see themselves.
It has achieved wide popularity among a number of fields of
practice, and it is particularly useful as a facilitator of change.

    Rather extensive research, notably that dedicated to changing
smoking behavior, has demonstrated the effectiveness of the
technique of role playing a discussion. Given the topic of lung
cancer caused by cigarette smoking, those who role-played a cancer
patient became significantly more opposed to smoking than did
an equivalent group who merely listened to tapes of the discussion
sessions. The crucial variable which makes the role playing
experience such an effective impetus for change seems to be that
the participant improvises his own arguments in support of the
assigned conclusion. The mechanism of improvisation necessitates
involvement and, thus, apparently transforms outer conformity into
inner conformity. (Janis and Mann, #0315; King and Janis, #1761)

4.   Conclusions about Group-Initiated Changes

    At this time the most reliable and predictable mechanism for
inducing change in the group setting is the aforementioned role play.
This technique is only appropriate for changes in individual's behavior
or attitude; its effectiveness is not so notable when the change requires
the concerted action of the entire group. For appropriate change
problems, then, the role playing technique has measured a substantial
degree of success, as in the example of the smokers who role played
cancer patients. More importantly, for the purpose of disseminating
new knowledge, the direction of the change is not questionable.

C.   LARGE GROUPS WITH TWO-WAY INVOLVEMENT

    If one is concerned with introducing change on a system-wide basis within
a fairly large organization or group of individuals, there will come a time
when the one-way communication channels will no longer suffice. If large
groups of people are to interact cooperatively in a change effort, every one
of them must understand, must feel involved in, and must be committed to
that effort. Two-way communication channels are needed to develop such understanding, involvement, and commitment. (See Chapter Six for a discussion of
the dynamics of the large organization or system.)

    Two-way involvement in a large group does not imply that a single
large group can have effective two-way communication operating to the
simultaneous satisfaction of and with the inclusion of all members; it is
solely a refinement of the techniques mentioned in the section above on
small groups. For purposes of achieving two-way communication, the large
organization is still broken down into small groups and the individual groups
use the same techniques that isolated small groups would use. The difference
in the large organization is that the change effort is coordinated among
the groups and that a total system perspective is maintained in the goals
of each group.

1. Temporary Systems

    A variety of two-way designs for interaction have been used with
"large" groups of various sizes. Those which have been most successful
in achieving change within such groups (e.g., companies, organizations,
or systems) can be very generally clustered under the category of
"temporary systems". These temporary systems, according to Miles (#1189),
are recognized from their inception as destined for extinction. The
kinds of temporary systems most commonly associated with innovation are
the conference (or similarly designed meeting), the ad hoc "task force"
or team, the research and/or action project, the consulting relationship,
and the academic course. (Miles, pp. 438-440)

    In all its varied manifestations the "temporary system" possesses
a substantial number of common and, consequently, distinguishing
characteristics. Miles (#1189) classifies these as "input", "process",
and "out-put" characteristics. Those which become obvious at the time
of designing and organizing the temporary system are the input characteristics. These include *time limits, initial goal definition,* and *boundary
maintenance activities* (i.e., keeping members in and 'strangers' out).
Ideally, the temporary system designed should also permit the physical
and social isolation of its members. It should exist as a "cultural
island", thus removing barriers to change, reducing conflicts resulting
from normal roles, and protecting members from the larger environment
and from the consequences of making mistakes. It follows from this
that the temporary system will be *limited in size* (if necessary, through
sub-division) and will have a *defined territoriality.*

    The second set of characteristics are those common to the process
of temporary social systems. These include: *time use, goal redefinition,
formal procedures, new role definitions and role socialization, communication structures,* and *power structures. Group sentiments* also appear
during the process of the system; and they manifest themselves in a
fairly consistent order: defensiveness and formality, playfulness,
interpersonal liking and acceptance and intimacy, esprit de corps, and
lastly, involvement or "engrossment". *Group norms* are the final distinguishing characteristic of the process of the temporary system. A
successful temporary system will elicit the norms of equalitarianism,
authenticity, scientific inquiry, hypotheticality, "newism" or change-
proneness, and effortfulness.

    The output characteristics listed by Miles are the changes which
are the results of the temporary system experience. The first of these
are personal, the *changes in an individual participant's attitudes,
knowledge,* and *behavior.* The second are the *changes in the relationships
among the members* of the temporary system. The third are the *action
decisions* resulting from the temporary system process. (#1189)

2. Temporary Systems for Promoting Change

    Until more permanent and elaborate relationships can be built
between research and practice, the temporary system can provide that
much needed "link" in the transmission of new knowledge from resource
to user. The temporary system may be called a "conference", "workshop",

"seminar", "project", etc. A number of successful temporary system
designs are described below.

a.   Action Research

Action research is the collaboration of researcher and
practitioner in the diagnosis and evaluation of problems
existing in the practice setting. The action research technique
provides the researcher with an accessible practice setting
from which he may retrieve data, usually for publication. It
provides the cooperating practitioner system with scientific
data about its own operation which may be used for self-evaluation.*

b.   Collaborative Action Inquiry

The strategy of "collaborative action inquiry" is similar
to 'action research'. However, this model places greater emphasis
on service to the practitioner system and on the collaborative
teaming of researcher and practitioner. The inquiry team collaborates
on defining goals, on all phases of the research, and on change
strategies (Thelen, in Watson, #6194)

c.   Organizational Survey Feedback

A technique for using the findings of survey research in
an organization as a catalyst for the change process has been
developed by Mann et al., (#3913). Data is systematically collected
from staff or employees on a wide range of issues, such as: supervisor perceptions, motivations, aspirations, rewards, and communication patterns. This data is summarized and fed back to top management and their subordinates for the purpose of helping them confront
the real situation in their organization. It often reveals heretofore unspoken conflicts and problems. The social scientists who
did the original data collection then assist the organization in
its self-diagnosis and in generating plans for action.

d.   The "Grid" Program for Organizational Development

The "Grid" program for organizational development promoted
by Blake and Mouton (#7019) attempts to build a capacity for self-
renewal into the system. The "grid" plan carries the client
system through the phases of the change process by a progression
of theory input, application to the real situation, and systematic
evaluation and planning. This type of temporary system organization
emphasizes education (or knowledge input) as the key to achieving
and maintaining change in an organization, and its techniques are
designed to improve both the communication and the planning aspects
of the organization's operation.

---

*For an analysis of action research design from the point of view of the social
scientist, see French #7137. As defined by Stephen Corey (#3599), however, "action
research" means research done by practitioners for themselves to solve problems in
their home setting.

e.   Training Labs

    A further category of designs for temporary systems is the
"training" or human relations lab. The laboratory strategies
employ a variety of tactics for the purpose of improving the
problem-solving capacities of individuals, groups, organizations,
and communities. (Bradford, Benne, and Gibb, #6196). In "stranger
labs" participants have no prior contact with one another in their
normal environment. "Cousin labs" are comprised of members of
the same organization, who rarely interact with one another
(e.g., as with members of different departments). "Family labs"
involve people who are interdependent in their normal environment,
as: a divisional vice president, the supervisors who report to him,
and their subordinates. All three types, "stranger", "cousin",
and "family" may be combined in sequence in a program of human
relations training for a whole organization. For example, an
initial step might be the involvement of top management in
'stranger labs' outside of their company. Their enthusiasm for
the technique might lead to their desire to incorporate it into
their organization. The least threatening way of doing this is
by limiting the groups to people who represent the several levels
of the organization, but who normally have no connection with one
another--either through production or by authority (i.e., "cousin").
The final step would be to reorganize the groups, this time so that
departmental 'families' are together, for the purpose of dealing in
the training groups with the same line-and-staff issues that operate
in the real environment.

f.   Derivation Conference

    The derivation conference is a temporary system which is
systematically designed to include representatives from research,
who serve as resource persons and from various levels of practice,
who are the potential 'client' persons. The conference progresses
through a series of collaborative activities: (1) defining the
problem area, (2) retrieving relevant findings from research and
from the practice setting, (3) deriving implications for action,
and (4) setting down specific plans for action--with commitment
to try them out. (Jung,#6197) The implications for innovation
from this design are obvious.

3.   Conclusions about Large Group Two-Way Involvement

    There is a multitude of possible two-way designs which have not
been included here because there has been no research done on their
effectiveness. Even among those designs we have listed, there has
been no research to study the comparative merits of each. Part of the
cause for this paucity of information is, of course, financial; the
cost and difficulty of a research study escalates sharply with the
increasing size and complexity of the phenomenon studied. But, also,
today there exists little recognition of the need for comparative
studies; researchers have been too involved in developing their own
temporary system "thing" and have not participated in any scientific
comparative analysis of the techniques. This neglected comparison
is imperative before the widespread adoption of such techniques can
be recommended.

D.   CONCLUSIONS ABOUT TWO-WAY TRANSMISSION PROCESSES

Some form of two-way communications medium or channel which permits involved interaction between the resource and the user is necessary for the ultimate adoption of a change by an individual, a group, or a total system. A key to the success of any two-way design seems to be the provision for collaboration between the resource and user in both the design and the process of the two-way attempt; both must perceive benefit from their interaction.

Because of the lack of comparative studies, it is not possible to recommend a particular technique for a particular user situation with any degree of assurance. However, several important issues, relevant to all two-way transmission processes, should always be considered by the person or persons planning to utilize a two-way technique.

1.   The "Mix" of Participants

The personality, role, and status of the respective participants in any two-way communication are more broadly influential than are these same factors in any one-way communication. It is also often difficult to analyze the complex interplay of personal characteristics in an on-going two-way interaction. Chapters Four and Five deal with these characteristics of individuals which are so important in communication.

2.   The Locus of the Exchange

Two-way interaction which precipitates change in the individual may take place in the home setting or in an isolated environment. In order to make such changes permanent, some mechanism must be provided to maintain or to transfer the change to the home setting of the user. The "stranger-cousin-family" human relations laboratory is an example of one operational technique of transferring change. More attention must be given by researchers and initiators of change to mechanisms that will maintain a change once it has been established in the users own environment.

3.   The Documentation and Retrieval of the Change Process

Up to the present time very little attention has been given to the key functions of observing, recording, and documenting these complex two-way events. The current status of the documentarian/recorder is low; the role is usually assigned to non-frofessionals. Consequently, current norms for retrieval of the information recorded are also low. The self-conscious documentation and evaluation of the process of two-way interaction is necessary, not simply for research purposes, but to maintain the structural integrity of the interaction and to provide feedback to the people who participated. An essential part of this evaluation is a follow-up subsequent to the meeting to determine whether or not genuine efforts to utilize the change did take place. Such follow-up serves as an additional incentive for participants to make sincere efforts to maintain the change. It is a mechanism which could be used to aid both transferral and maintenance of change.

4.   The Resource Person or Initiator of Change

        In all communication efforts designed to promote change, but
especially in two-way attempts, a great deal of responsibility rests
with the person who is serving as the resource or initiator of change.
His aptitude, skill, experience, and 'comfortableness' with the
technique he is using will determine to a large extent the success he
will have with it. Some of the two-way techniques, and all of those
appropriate for large groups, require a considerable amount of skill
training and experience.

        As a footnote to the role requirements of the resource person, it
can be expected that he will have to display substantial initiative.
He will need to go more than half way to meet his would-be users.

        Of all the transmission media used for the dissemination of new
knowledge, the two-way channels are the least studied, the least used,
but, potentially, the most rewarding. The expense of research on two-
way designs should no longer be allowed to remain a barrier to their
study.

V.   DISSEMINATION AND UTILIZATION STRATEGIES

        The preceding review of specific one-way and two-way media of the knowledge
transmission process has included suggestions for the most profitable use of each
medium in a total dissemination strategy. In order to apply more adequately the
general recommendations mentioned in the discussions of the individual media
we now propose to relate these media directly to an overall dissemination and
utilization strategy. Our goal is to illustrate the part that each medium can play
in a progressing plan of knowledge utilization.

A.   PROCESSES OF DISSEMINATION AND UTILIZATION

        Chapter Two of this report introduced three perspectives of the
dissemination and utilization process: problem-solving (P-S); social interaction (S-I); and research, development, and diffusion (R,D&D). (Chapter
Ten and Eleven discuss these views in greater detail.)

1.   The Problem-Solving Perspective

        This view of the dissemination and utilization process stresses
the ultimate user of the innovation. It assumes that utilization is
instigated by a *need* within the user and proceeds for the purpose of
satisfying that need. In the process of need satisfaction the user
goes through the following activities (usually with some outside
assistance): translation of need into a problem statement, diagnosis
of the problem, search and retrieval of information that will be helpful
for making a selection of the innovation, adaptation of the innovation
to his own situation, trial of the innovation, and evaluation of the
effectiveness of the trial in satisfying the original need.

2.   The Social Interaction Perspective

        This second perspective on the dissemination and utilization pro-
cess focuses on the informal communications environment of the user,
as seen by his position in the *network of social relations* in the

group(s) in which he is a member. Viewing the process from the S-I perspective, the stages that each member will sooner or later pass through in the process of innovating are: awareness, interest, evaluation, trial, and adoption.

3. The Research, Development, and Diffusion Perspective

This perspective is based on the assumption of a *rational sequence* of phases by which an innovation is invented or discovered, developed, produced, and, finally, disseminated to the user. It is the only one of these three perspectives which does not approach innovation from the point of view of the user; in fact, it presumes that the user be fairly passive, though not irrational.

Each of the three perspectives is a valid representation of knowledge dissemination and utilization which is being carried on today. Their conceptualizations of the stages in the dissemination and utilization process differ. (See Chapter Ten) Each is appropriate for certain kinds of innovations and for certain types of user systems.

B. TOWARD A MACRO-MODEL OF DISSEMINATION AND UTILIZATION

The three perspectives discussed above can add an important dimension to our analysis of the media used in the transmission of knowledge. Not only do these perspectives cover the range of *types of innovation* that we find taking place today (from "natural diffusion" to "planned change"), but also each sheds some light on one of the three major *roles in innovation*: the R,D&D perspective emphasizes the activities of the resource person or system; the S-I approach focusses clearly on the user person and his system; and the P-S perspective introduces the role of the change agent, the person(s) who facilitates the utilization attempt of the user system. By determining the relevance of the transmission media to each of these roles and by establishing 'when' and 'why' the role incumbents use each of the transmission media we can more easily see the functions of the media in the total dissemination and utilization process.

1. 'When' and 'Why' the Media Might be Used

Each of the perspectives has derived its own conceptualization of the process of dissemination and utilization. Media are potentially useful, then, during any of the stages of the process and for the purposes those stages are designed to fulfill:

[See List of Stages on the following page]

2. The Three Persepctives on Media Use

As might be expected from the different orientations of the R,D&D, the P-S, and the S-I approaches, each has a tendency to emphasize different media in their dissemination strategies. For example, the goals of mass utilization inherent in the R,D&D perspective indicate their reliance on "one-way" media; the interactive quality of the change agent-user relationship of the P-S perspective would lead to a heavy emphasis on "two-way" involvement; and the S-I perspective incorporates both "one-way" and "two-way" transmission media, but stresses that the

9-37

R,D&D (resource system perspective)	P-S (change agent and user system perspective)	S-I (user system perspective)
1. *Invention* or discovery of innovation	1. *Translation* of need to problem	1. *Awareness* of innovation
2. *Development* (working out problems)	2. *Diagnosis* of problem	2. *Interest* in it
3. *Production* and packaging	3. *Search and Retrieval* of information	3. *Evaluation* of its appropriateness
4. *Dissemination* to mass audience	4. *Adaptation* of innovation	4. *Trial*
	5. *Trial*	5. *Adoption* for permanent use
	6. *Evaluation* of trial in terms of need satisfaction	

usefulness of each type is optimal at different stages in the adoption process. This does not mean that any perspective would use only one type of media to the exclusion of the others; rather it is only indicative of the *emphasis* in the particular perspective. Table 9.1 illustrates 'when' and 'why' our three perspectives incorporate the transmission media into their total dissemination and utilization strategy.

[Insert Table 9.1 here]

Table 9.1 shows the potential of various media use across the perspectives on the change process. It becomes clear that the effectiveness of the resource system's media utilization is going to play an important role in the ultimate user's interest in and evaluation of an innovation and, consequently, his adoption of it.

3. The Media in a Complete Utilization Strategy

Table 9.1 also points up the very broad range of media which are serviceable for each dissemination strategy. Complete utilization strategies may, in fact, involve all of the media. As a case in point, the Bell Labs, in the successful dissemination of their transistor technology to other industries, developed a very complex and carefully executed program. They utilized many of the one-way media in an

TABLE 9.1   Potential Media Uses in D&U Strategies

This listing is intended to be merely <u>suggestive</u> of the relationship of media to parts of the D&U process.

	D&U STRATEGIES		
TRANSMISSION MEDIA	R,D&D Processes (going on in the resource system)	P-S Processes (from the point of view of change agent & user system)	S-I Processes (going on in the user system)
One-Way Diffusion Transmissions Written word Oral Presentation Television & Radio Film Demonstration	Dissemination (might be used in combination in a multi-media marketing program)	Search and Retrieval of potential solutions	Awareness by all, awareness and interest by some opinion leaders, awareness, interest and evaluation by innovators
One-Way Feedback Transmissions Public Archives Private Records Surveys/Polls Observation Referenda/Elections Petitions Letters Protests, Riots, Revolts	Research and Development (problem & need assessment, market analysis, product testing & evaluation) Impetus for new research & R&D efforts (through foundation & Federal support; movement of researchers into "fashionable" topic areas)	Diagnosis of problem and evaluation of the innovation	These transmissions rarely discussed by S-I theorists. Presumably they create a general readiness for considering new innovations.
Two-Way Transmissions Dyadic Exchange Small Group Discussion Large Group/Temporary System (e.g.'s: action research, collaborative action inquiry, organizational survey feedback, organizational "grid", training labs, derivation conference)	May play some role in various processes of R,D&D usually unspecified Dissemination	Potentially useful for all stages: Translation Diagnosis Search & Retrieval Adoption Trial Evaluation	Vital for evaluation and decision to try-out and to adopt

9-39

information-giving and advertising campaign, held conferences and clinics for the prospective users, and provided special consultants to work directly with them. (Solo, #6314)   The further development of dissemination strategies similar to the Bell Lab design seems an imperative 'next step' in achieving the goal of complete utilization.

VI.   SUMMARY AND CONCLUSIONS ABOUT THE 'TECHNOLOGIES OF KNOWLEDGE FLOW': ANSWERS WE HAVE FOUND TO THE QUESTION, "HOW?"

The stated purpose of this chapter has been to determine HOW knowledge is transmitted between resource and user in the process of innovation. We have attempted to fulfill this purpose by (1) summarizing the research on media effectiveness, and (2) incorporating the media findings into the major strategies of dissemination and utilization. We have come a long way toward a prescription for media use in an effective program of knowledge dissemination and utilization, but the predictive precision in such an ultimate formula remains elusive. The two levels of discussion about media usage in this chapter should provide a starting point for future refinement of the technologies of knowledge flow.

A.   THE MEDIA CHARACTERISTICS

The division of media, as "one-way diffusion", "one-way feedback", and "two-way" transmissions (see again Figure 9.1), has given the first information about the variable 'utility' of a medium.

1.   The *One-Way Media* are an effective means of informing mass audiences about an innovation.

   a.   *One-way transmission media and their specially "tuned-in" audiences* often serve to catalyze further information-seeking within the user system as a whole.

   b.   For a few specialized users, e.g., the innovators (see Chapter Seven), one-way media may be sufficient for evaluation, trial, and adoption.

   c.   *Feedback* on the impact of the transmitted information on potential users should be a very valuable input to researchers, developers, and 'would-be' disseminators, but is very seldom elicited by most resource systems. (See again discussion of macrosystem dynamics in Chapter Three.)

2.   *Two-Way transmissions* are imperative for the adoption of innovations requiring alterations in attitude or behavior.

   a.   The active role in *discussions* leads to more involvement on the part of the user than does his passive role as the receiver of a one-way transmission.

   b.   The pressures of *group membership* can lead an individual to a greater tendency toward innovation if the group norms are supportive of innovation.

B.   "ORCHESTRATING" THE MEDIA IN UTILIZATION STRATEGIES

By focussing on the major perspectives of utilization and dissemination (R,D&D, P-S, and S-I) one begins to understand the broader relevance of the trend noted in the discussions of the individual media. The importance of including each kind of media in the transmission of new knowledge becomes obvious when one is made aware of the progression of the internal process that takes place within the user as he approaches the adoption of an innovation.

In order to "orchestrate" the multitude of media available into a successful utilization strategy, Marshall McLuhan has suggested that we must first understand the "cause and process" of media effectiveness. We must know the strengths of each medium, but we must also have a framework within which we can assign the media to mutually supportive roles. Moreover, we must <u>fill</u> that framework, perhaps using every medium, so that we will have a structure stable enough to carry an innovation the full distance to user adoption.

CHAPTER TEN

PHASES OF ORIENTATION *To* NEW KNOWLEDGE

Table of Contents

CHAPTER TEN *

PHASES OF ORIENTATION TO NEW KNOWLEDGE

I. INTRODUCTION

A. HISTORICAL APPROACHES

Early interest in the subject of phases of change was largely within the realms of history and philosophy and the focus, as might be expected, was on change viewed very broadly. Watson (6364) briefly describes some of the early theories, for example the ancient theory (never really abandoned in some societies) that *change is unpredictable* and uncontrollable, and is willed by fate or the gods. An optimistic view is the "linear" theory of Spencer, who assumes a *steady progress* toward a better world; an opposing theory (c.f. Swift, Carlyle) is that civilization is moving progressively away from an ideal state which existed at some time in the past. Watson also cites the more recent *"cyclic"* theories; Spengler, for example, describes stages of growth, maturity and decline of civilizations, similar to those of human beings in the course of a lifetime. Toynbee, discussing civilizations, describes a series of phases wherein a minority arises to a challenge; control of the innovative practices is taken over by a dominant minority who maintain their position by use of force; they are eventually superceded by an internal proletariat, sometimes aided by outside enemies; a new cycle is thus established. Analagous cyclic theories are useful in describing the course of *innovations* and will be discussed further as we progress through this chapter.

Somewhat distinct from the cyclic theories are the *dialectic* theories of social change. The early 19th century philosopher, Hegel, first used the term to describe both the evolution of thought and of history through a progressive series of contradictions which are resolved as "syntheses." Against each synthesis, in time, a new antithesis arises forcing the generation of yet another synthesis. Karl Marx took over this idea in developing "dialectic materialism", the now familiar theory that civilization advances through a dialectic process involving opposing economic philosophies embodied in warring social classes. Up to a generation ago, this Marxian dialectic was probably the dominant theory of social change and is still influential throughout the world, even among social philosophers in non-communist countries. It is somewhat surprising, therefore, that mentions of Marx or Hegel are almost completely lacking in the diffusion and planned change literature reviewed for this report.

A dominant theme in the current literature is the increase in the *rate of change* in modern history. Watson (6364, p. 533) tries to depict the acceleration of change in technology as a curvilinear function which shifts sharply toward the vertical after the middle of the twentieth century.

[Insert Figure 10.1 here]

This curve is contrasted with another indicating the slower rate of advance in social affairs. This curve of social progress presumably will show the same dramatic upward sweep in the 1980's and 90's.

Price (7133) contends that growth in any field can be shown to be exponential, with the growth curve resembling that in Figure 10.1. He cautions,

---

*This chapter was drafted by Marjorie J. Hill, Mary C. Havelock, and Ronald G. Havelock.

FIGURE 10.1   Rates of Technical and Social Change

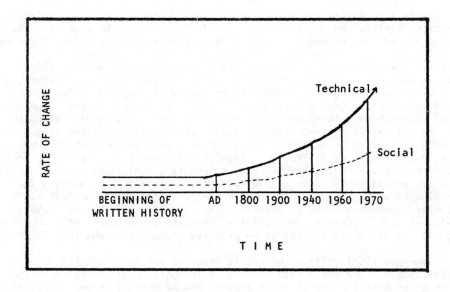

From Watson, (#6364), p. 533.

however, that we cannot expect this growth to continue indefinitely; a
"saturation point" must be reached at some point. He reasons that since the
growth of science and technology is much greater than the growth of anything
else in our society (including our population), there would be a maximum
saturation of workers in these fields in about 50 - 70 years if the growth
curve continued to be exponential. This obviously cannot happen, and Price
feels that we are already feeling a pinch of manpower shortage in the fields of
science and technology. He suggests that because of the saturation effect the
growth curve will not remain purely exponential; rather, it will modify into
an S-shaped curve, with the point of "inflection" (half-way point) occurring
at a date corresponding to saturation on a purely exponential curve, as
illustrated in Figure 10.2.

FIGURE 10.2   Exponential and Saturated Growth Rates

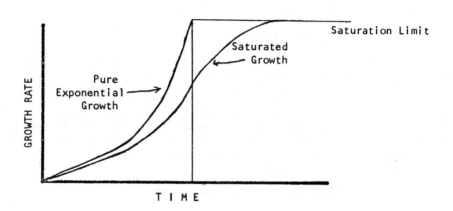

Whether we are facing a saturation crisis, or whether we are simply facing
a staggering growth in new knowledge, it seems clear that planning for change
should commence on a grand scale.

B. PLAN OF THE CHAPTER

Along with the rapid increase in the rate of change, as shown in Figure
10.1, there is an increasing concern on the part of scholars in diverse fields
about understanding and planning for change. The question which this chapter
will attempt to answer is whether or not there is a sequence of steps or phases
which can be identified in the process of dissemination and utilization of
knowledge. If so, we will then ask whether or not these phases are distinct
enough and consistent enough to provide an integrated theory of the utilization
process.

Anyone who has attempted to plan a strategy of change will realize that
such a theory will not provide a step-by-step guide for each activity which takes
place during each stage of D&U. What it will provide is an overall perspective
on the change process and an indication of the types of activities which should
take place during each phase. Whether change occurs as a natural process or
as one which is carefully planned, the literature indicates that there are predictable phases. Variations which we will discuss come about primarily as a

result of differences in who initiates the change process and in the extent of the interaction and collaboration between the sender and the receiver of the new knowledge.

The interaction of the sender and receiver and the synchronization of their activities are a crucial component of the models of change which we will describe in this chapter. Before we describe this complex interplay, however, it will be helpful to first investigate the separate activities of sender and receiver as these occur over time. In doing this we will draw heavily upon the literature in the field of rural sociology, and we will show how the adoption and diffusion processes may be depicted as curves representing activities taking place over a period of time. This analysis of curves of adoption and diffusion will lay the groundwork for the presentation of theoretical models of change.

We will then be in a position to consider how such models can help us in understanding and planning for change. It will be of special interest to consider whether or not changes must always come about through a series of fixed phases, and whether adoption rates can be changed.

II. CURVES OF ADOPTION AND DIFFUSION

The curve shown in Figure 10.1 is an extremely generalized picture and does not provide us with any information about any one change, idea, or innovation. In this section of the chapter we will be considering curves which do relate to single innovations or pieces of knowledge. We will consider first the *adoption curve*; this curve represents the activity of an <u>individual</u> as he adopts an innovation. We will then describe the *diffusion curve*, which shows the rate of adoption of an innovation by an adopting <u>group</u>. In addition, we will discuss the *diffuser curve*, which shows the activity of a change agent as he attempts to influence a group or an individual to adopt an innovation.

A. THE INDIVIDUAL ADOPTER: ADOPTION CURVES

Most learning which requires acquisition of new behavior can be plotted on a curve representing initial learning, an accumulating number of correct trials with decreasing number of errors, and finally decreasing gains, and stabilization of new behavior (Morgan, 6366). This is the familiar "S-curve" of learning, and is illustrated in Figure 10.3.

[Insert Figure 10.3 here]

The adoption by an individual of a single innovation can be considered simply as one specific instance of the phenomenon of learning. Each piece of information which a person receives about the innovation increases his involvement in it as well as his knowledge about it; if we can allow ourselves to think of this progressive increase in involvement in quantitative terms, then we could picture the adoption process as in Figure 10.4.

[Insert Figure 10.4 here]

If we had wished, we could have shown this involvement in terms of a normal curve; this would have been a representation of the amount of new involvement being invested at a given time, rather than of the cumulative involvement which is shown in Figure 10.4. As is indicated in this figure, the initial slow rise represents a slight involvement as the individual becomes aware of an innovation and begins to be interested in it. The greatest increase in involvement comes as the person actively seeks information about the innovation and begins to consider how the innovation could be applied to his own particular

FIGURE 10.3   Learning Curve

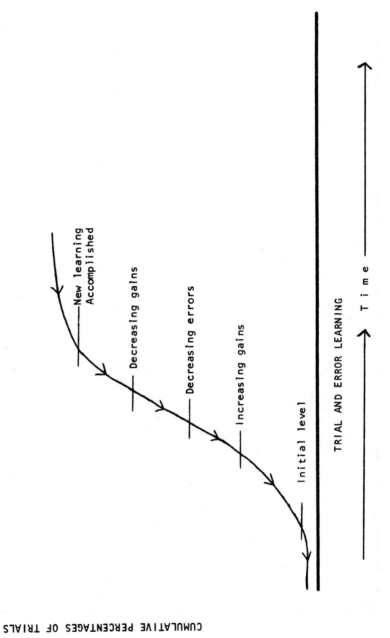

New learning
Accomplished

Decreasing gains

Decreasing errors

Increasing gains

Initial level

TRIAL AND ERROR LEARNING

Time

CUMULATIVE PERCENTAGES OF TRIALS

10-5

FIGURE 10.4   Involvement of an Individual During the Adoption Process

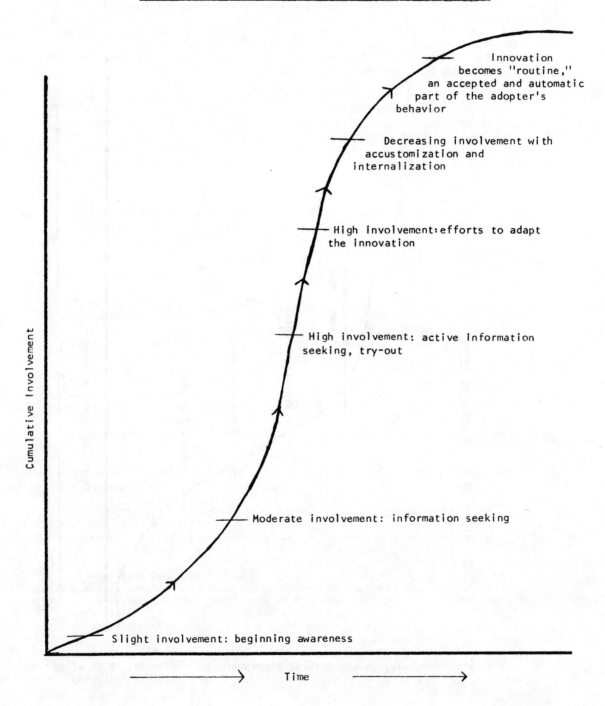

10-6

needs. Involvement continues to be great as he tries out the innovation
and adapts it to suit his own circumstances. As the person becomes accustomed
to the innovation, the rate of involvement decreases, and, finally, no further
increase in involvement occurs once a decision is made either to adopt or to
reject the innovation. If the innovation is accepted it becomes a routine
part of the adopter's behavior; the "learning" has taken place.

Whether the innovation is adopted or rejected, however, the upper plateau
of the curve will not necessarily remain stable. Rejection may represent a
temporary lull in activity, being followed by later adoption, e.g., when the
value of an innovation has been thoroughly established. Or, adoption may be
followed by discontinuance. Either of these possibilities represents subsequent learning experiences, and these alternatives are discussed more fully
below (see Alternative Outcomes).

The length of time between awareness and decision is, of course, widely
variable; factors which affect the length of this "adoption period" will be
discussed as we progress through the chapter. There may, in addition, be
great individual differences in the amount of time different adopters spend at
each stage in the adoption process.

B. THE ADOPTING GROUP: DIFFUSION CURVES

When we consider the diffusion of an innovation through a group, we are
actually dealing with a collectivity of adoptions by individuals. Though the
individuals all belong to a single social system, this system will affect each
person differently. In addition, the context in which each potential adopter
lives is different; his reference groups are different, his perceptions are
different, and the norms of the group are interpreted differently by each.
Their adopting behavior will, therefore, be different. Not only will their
adoption periods be different, but they will also become aware of an innovation
at different times. There is bound to be a time differential between the point
of adoption of the first person in a group and the point of adoption of the
last person in a group. Whether or not this diffusion follows a typical pattern has been considered by many authors.

Tarde, in a discussion of imitation, described the process of innovation
adoption as showing "...a slow advance in the beginning, followed again by
progress that continues to slacken until it finally stops" (Rogers, 1824, p.
152). In terms of the adopting population, Tarde suggested this process for
the diffusion of new ideas: a few individuals adopt initially; they are followed by a large number of others, who are followed in turn by a gradually
dwindling group of late adopters.

That the rate of diffusion of innovations may be pictured as a normal
curve has been suggested by a number of studies reviewed by Rogers (1824).
Among the studies he cites are those of Chapin (2457) for city managers,
Gillfillian (6389) for shipping inventions, Pemberton (1503) for adoption of
compulsory school attendance laws, and Ryan & Gross (2621) for the adoption
of hybrid seed corn.

When the normal curve is plotted to represent such diffusion, it is often
a useful tool for describing adopter categories. Rogers uses the following
illustration:

[Insert Figure 10.5 here]

It should be noted that the adopter categories used in Figure 10.5, and taken
from Rogers (1824), are arbitrary descriptive labels based on deviation from

FIGURE 10.5   Adopter Categorization on the Basis of
Relative Time of Adoption of Innovations

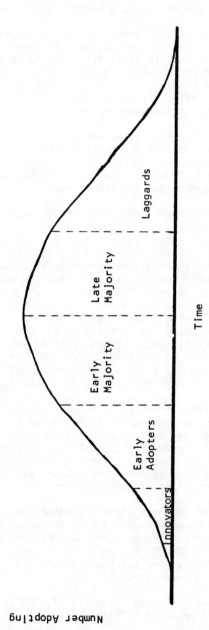

From Rogers (#1824), Figure 6.1, p. 162

10-8

the mean.   Rogers presents titles used by other authors in his Table 6.1,
pp. 150-151.

This same information may be presented in a different manner. If, instead of plotting the number of people who adopt in a given time unit, we plot
the percentage of the adopting population who have adopted at each given time,
we find that we have the familiar "S-curve" of diffusion. This is shown in
Figure 10.6, and the adopter categories may be indicated on this diagram just
as on the normal curve.

FIGURE 10.6   Adopter Categorization Plotted as a Cumulative Curve

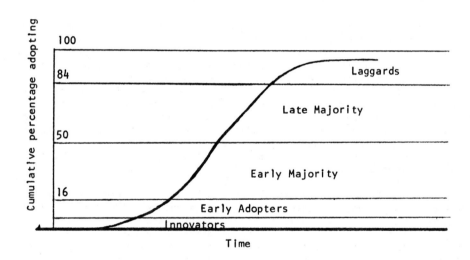

This is a cumulative curve, and although it is essentially interchangeable
with the normal curve in terms of describing the process of diffusion, one
curve or the other may be more useful in presenting the data of a particular
case or in illustrating a particular point.

C. THE LINKAGE AGENT: DIFFUSER CURVES

So far we have been talking about the activities of the *receivers* of knowledge, either individually or as a group; we will now turn our attention to an examination of how the activities of a *sender* of knowledge may appear over time.

A measure which has been used to describe the activity level of a diffuser or linkage agent (see Chapter 7), or his involvement in a particular project, is the amount of time which he devotes to this project. Stone (1129) has used the normal curve to represent the activity of a linking agent, in this case of the county extension agent. In a study concerning the way in which county agents spend their time, Stone traced a number of projects from the time when agents become aware of the innovation through a period of maximum involvement (including such activities as teaching, communicating, organizing, facilitating and consulting) to a period when the innovation has become autonomous or when other organizations have been set up to maintain it. By then the county agent may well be at a peak of involvement with other projects. The process is illustrated in Figure 10.7.

[Insert Figure 10.7 here]

Figure 10.7 (Stone, 1129) represents a typical work-project pattern; it is based on information concerning the time spent by 32 county agricultural agents on eight different projects.

D. THE RELATIONSHIP OF DIFFUSER AND DIFFUSION CURVES

The objective of the diffusion agent is, of course, to influence a group of potential adopters, so it is appropriate at this point to consider his activity as it relates to this group. As we describe this relationship we should keep in mind that we will be looking at only one portion of the D&U process. Our starting point here is the time at which the linkage agent enters the adopter system. In general, of course, there is a whole series of steps in preparing for diffusion which takes place before this point in time, and these may include such activities as conducting research, training the diffuser or diffuser team, and establishing linkage. The phases which we are considering in this section of the chapter, in connection with sender and receiver activity curves, will be put into perspective later when we discuss Phase Models of Dissemination.

The activities of the diffuser must, of course, be coordinated with corresponding processes within the potential adopters. The diffuser must know where the adopters are in terms of their adoption stages, and he must be with them, not ahead or behind. He must be at different phases with different adopters; he must be prepared to go back as individual adopters slip back and to keep up as other adopters jump ahead; and he must know when to switch from one mode of communication to another with each adopter. In the course of time, then, the curve representing the behavior of an agent of diffusion precedes and overlaps the curve which represents the frequency of adoption within a population of receivers. Miles (1481) suggests that "elite groups of many sorts (technical, administrative, prestige-holding) must in effect proceed through stages of diffusion at least a stage or two ahead of 'user' groups."

The net effect of these two related processes can be depicted by two overlapping curves, one showing sender behavior (the agent's), followed by a curve representing adoption by the receiving group. Stone (1129) depicts this sequence in a figure illustrating the interaction between time spent by the county agent and the rate of adoption (by a group) of an innovation (in this case, artificial breeding of dairy cattle).

FIGURE 10.7   Curve showing the average pattern of how model county agents
                spent their time on eight different extension projects

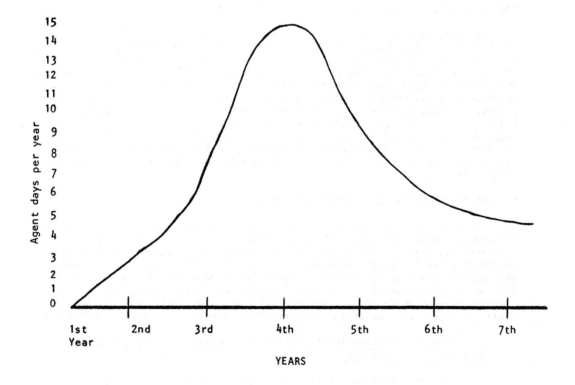

From Stone, #1129

[Insert Figure 10.8 here]

Diagrams such as this, which plot the curve of the diffuser activity
against the curve of adopter activity may be useful in pointing the way for
more effective or optimal allocation of time on the part of a linkage agent.
It should be possible from the analysis of many such curves to identify the
best point at which the diffuser should shift from one activity to another.
With enough studies of this type we could hope to be able to identify a
syndrome which would tell the diffuser that a new stage has been reached.
Further, it should be possible to figure out the "tipping point", or the point
at which the diffuser should pull out of the adopter system. It is clear
from Figure 10.8 that after a certain point in the diffusion process the activity
of an agent is no longer necessary for the further increase in adoption of the
innovation. The mechanisms by which an innovation continues to spread once it
has taken hold will be discussed in the next section.

In summary, the S-curve, or normal curve, is useful in depicting activities in the D&U process, both in terms of the sender and the receiver of
an innovation. For the individual receiver, the S-curve is commonly used to
represent increasing involvement in behavior concerning the innovation, as
the individual progresses from awareness through information-seeking and trial,
to adoption or rejection. For the receiving group, the normal curve is used
to describe adopter categories, from the innovators, who are the first to
adopt, through the early adopters and the early and late majority to the
laggards. In terms of the sender, the normal curve has been used to depict
the amount of time and involvement invested by a diffusion agent, from the
time he becomes aware of a potential innovation until the diffusion process
is complete.

E.   FACTORS WHICH SHAPE THE DIFFUSION CURVE

The factors which influence the rate of diffusion in a population are as
numerous and complex as those which shape the individual adoption curve.
Nevertheless, the plotting of cumulative frequencies of adopters over time
predictably results in the S-curve pattern which we described earlier, and
this pattern seems to be remarkably consistent regardless of the type of
innovation or the nature of the target population. In this section we shall
describe factors which seem to account for this predictable pattern, and we
shall also consider some of the factors which seem to cause deviations from it.

1.   The Social Interaction Effect: An Explanation for the Normal Shape
of Group Adoption Curves

Carlson (0585) points out that if adoption were an individual
process, the number of adopters in any time period would remain a fixed
percentage of those who have not yet adopted. In other words, if each
person were isolated from the other members of his adopter group and not
influenced by them, we would find that the factors influencing adoption
(the change agent, mass media, etc.) would affect potential users at a
fairly constant rate, and this would be reflected in the resulting diffusion curve. We know, however, that this is rarely the case; people do
influence one another, and, as a result, Carlson describes diffusion
curves as looking like chain reactions, with the number of adopters in
each time unit increasing proportionately to the number who have already
adopted the innovations. Leuthold and Wilkening (2671) describe the
process as one in which the number of units which have adopted produce a
"binomial effect", with an increasing influence on the population with
which they interact. The resultant phenomenon is commonly referred to as

10-12

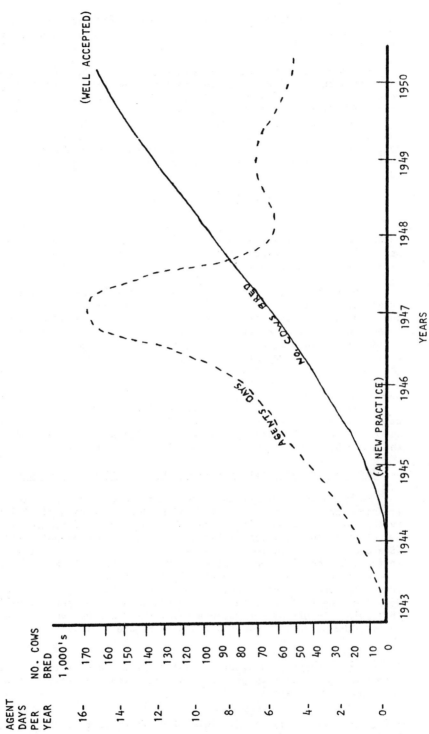

FIGURE 10.8 The rate of acceptance of a new farm practice (artificial breeding of dairy cattle) and the time spent by model Michigan county agent in the extension teaching process

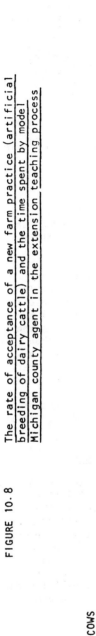

From Stone, (#1129) Fig. 3.

10-13

an "interaction effect"*, defined by Rogers (1824) as "the process through which individuals in a social system who have adopted an innovation influence those who have not yet adopted."

At some stage the social interaction effect may parallel a binomial expansion; but, obviously, there are limits on this rapid diffusion. Rogers points out (1824, p. 155) that, "The interaction effect begins to level off after half of the individuals in a social system have adopted because each new adopter finds it increasingly difficult to tell the new idea to a peer who has not adopted".** A typical example of a curve resulting from this process is that obtained by Ryan & Gross (2621), in their study of the adoption of hybrid seed corn, which is shown in Figure 10.9.

[Insert Figure 10.9 here]

The effects of social interaction are clearly visible in this curve between about the years 1933 and 1938. If there were no such mechanism operating, we would expect the curve to continue in the initial straight line pattern indefinitely.

Though this is, indeed, a typical curve and does illustrate the interaction effect, we might point out that it depicts a real situation, and it possesses some interesting properties which would not be present in an abstract or ideal curve. This curve deviates from the normal curve in that it is left-skewed; that is, the left tail, which represents the first 16% of people adopting, extends over a time period greater than the theoretical two standard deviations from the mean. What this signifies in terms of adopter categories is that the "innovators" and "early adopters" were not as rapid in adopting hybrid seed corn as would be predicted by the theory of normal distribution of diffusion. Possible causes of this deviation will be considered later as we discuss factors which influence the early phases of diffusion and as we note difficulties which may be encountered in interpreting diffusion curves.

2. Personal Characteristics Influencing Diffusion Rate Curves

We may agree that within a group the members are bound to have an influence on each other, but it is also clear, and is amply illustrated by the rural sociology literature, that there are differences in the *amount* of influence which different innovators have on potential adopters. (See again the discussion in Chapter 7 on innovators and opinion leaders.) In fact, by the time the adoption curve slows down, it may be that the remaining "potentials" are relatively isolated from the interacting community; they may be immune to influence. The study by Coleman et al. (3576) of the adoption of a new drug ("gammanyn") by physicians illustrates this point. Plotting the acceptance of the new drug over a 16-month period, the authors obtained Curve A in Figure 10.10.

---

*As in interpersonal interaction, not to be confused with the statistical term meaning the effects produced on a dependent variable by two independent variables conjointly.

**Note the similarity of this levelling-off concept to Price's (7133) concept of saturated growth.

FIGURE 10.9   <u>Cumulative percentage of farmers accepting hybrid</u>
               <u>seed during each year of the diffusion process</u>

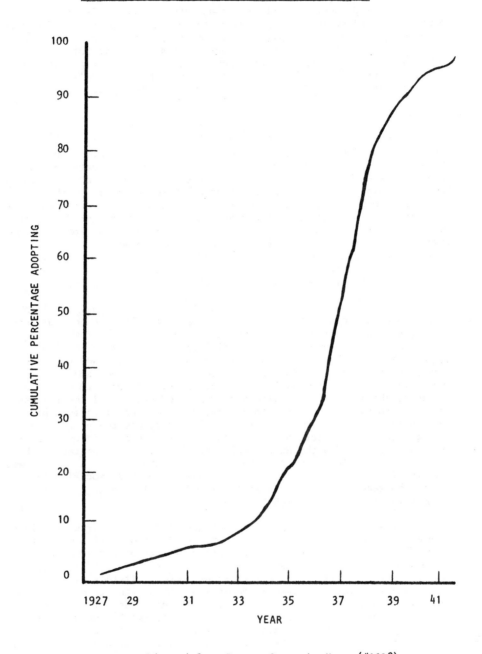

Adapted from Ryan & Gross by Katz (#1398)

10-15

[Insert Figure 10.10 here]

Curve A represents, in itself, a deviation from the S-curve; it shows an initial period of rapid increase followed by a period of particularly rapid decrease in adoption rate. These properties of Curve A are largely due to certain personal characteristics of members of subgroups within this group of physicians. When these physicians were subdivided on the basis of friendship choices made by other MD's, a very interesting picture, illustrated by Curves B and C in Figure 10.10, resulted.

The curve for "integrated" doctors (Curve B) climbs rapidly, while that for "isolated" doctors (Curve C) rises at a relatively constant rate. Katz (#1398) suggests that the curve for "high choice" MD's who are in frequent communication with one another illustrates a *chain reaction* where the number of adopters directly influences adoption rates. There is a high level of interaction among these doctors. On the other hand, Katz describes the curve for the isolated doctors as what would be expected from "a sequence of individual adoptions uninfluenced by interpersonal communication....(it) might result, for example, from some constant stimulus -- say advertising -- operating each month so as to influence a constant proportion of those who have not yet adopted... Unlike the social process of adoption, those who adopt in any given month are uninfluenced by those who adopted before they did" (p. 15).

So far we have described this study in terms of the way in which social interaction affects the *diffusion process*. The findings of this study are also significant in illustrating the effects of the social system on the *adoption process* of individuals, and thus in enabling us to relate adoption phases to diffusion phases. The new drug (gammanyn) and the older related drugs which it replaced overlapped in usage. During the first two months in which each physician began to prescribe gammanyn, the proportion of gammanyn prescribed out of all the related drugs was calculated. It was found that for the innovators this proportion was very small, whereas for the late adopters the proportion was much greater. In effect the later adopters went through a longer pretrial period than did the early adopters. They were influenced by the earlier adopters to the extent that they were convinced that no risk was involved in prescribing the new drug. Thus we see that social interaction shortens the adoption periods of individuals and as a result increases the rate of diffusion through a group.

We have indicated how personal characteristics may influence diffusion rate within a group (in this case, physicians); it will also be of interest to compare how the distinct characteristics of different groups may operate to produce different diffusion rates. It is often suggested that personality differences affect career choice; if this is true we might expect differences between farmers and physicians to be reflected in their respective adoption rate curves. In his discussion of the curves portrayed in Figures 10.9 and 10.10, Katz (#1398) points out that the "tentative phase" in hybrid corn adoption is not found in the drug study. He postulates that this difference reflects greater conservatism on the part of the farmers. Level of education, too, has been shown to be relevant to innovation (see Chapter 5), and this may be reflected in the relatively rapid "onset" of adoption by the physicians.*

---

*This is only one of several possible explanations for the difference in the initial stages of the diffusion curves in Figures 10.9 and 10.10. Other reasons will be considered in the remainder of this section.

FIGURE 10.10   Cumulative percentage of doctors accepting
                Gammanyn over a 16 month period by number
                of friendship choices received

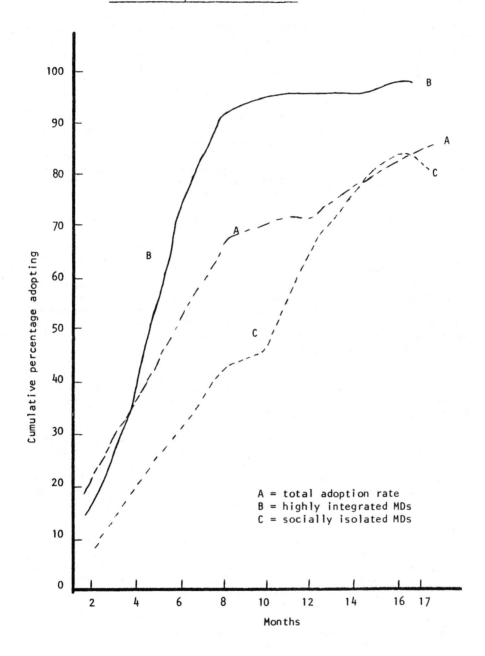

From Katz (#1398)

10-17

It has sometimes been claimed that the findings of rural sociology are not applicable to innovation in education, since farmers (and physicians) can function independently in terms of innovations while educators are hemmed in by various organizational constraints. It has commonly been assumed, for example, that school system superintendents are the victims of their budgets and school boards. Carlson (#1174), however, in his 1958 study of the adoption of modern math in one county of Pennsylvania, found that time of adoption was directly related to the superintendent's position in the social and status structure of the educational system. The diffusion curve obtained in his study showed neither the initial lag found in the hybrid corn study, nor the rapid onset of use of gammanyn; his results were similar to Coleman's, however, in that when superintendents were divided in terms of high, medium and low interaction and status, the resulting curves resembled those found in the gammanyn study. Carlson's findings point clearly to the effect of personal characteristics and amount of interaction on adoption rates, but give no support to the supposition that diffusion processes in education are fundamentally different from diffusion processes in other fields.

3. Medium Characteristics Have an Influence on Message Adoption Rates

The literature has revealed that different types of media are important at different stages in the D&U process, a fact which will be discussed in detail later in this chapter when we present theoretical models of D&U. At this time, however, we would like to discuss one aspect of the effects of media, and this is the way in which non-personal media sources influence various groups to different degrees and thereby create differences in the rate of diffusion for different groups. We will look for the effects of the non-personal sources in the initial phases of the diffusion rate curves, since it has been shown that it is particularly during these stages of diffusion that they play a major role. For example, Bowers (#2475), in a study of amateur radio operators, found that in the early stages of diffusion non-personal (media) sources were of primary importance. As diffusion became more organized and gained momentum, personal contact assumed the major role.

The significance of non-personal sources of information is also demonstrated by Coleman & Marsh (#2406), in a study of media for learning about new farm practices. They found wide differences among neighborhoods in exposure to various types of media: neighborhoods low in contact with one medium tended to have low contact with other media. Neighborhoods high in adoption of innovations reported more contact with media "that symbolize rationality and efficiency".

We may speculate that such a wide discrepancy in the individual's access to written media does not exist among MD's. They are all likely to be bombarded with the same promotional campaigns regarding a new drug. Thus we might expect that even those MD's who are isolated from their professional community will at least become *aware* of new drug products at a rapid rate. Though these isolated individuals will pass through the adoption phases at a slower pace than will their more socially active colleagues, they will nevertheless embark on the adoption sequence very soon after the innovation has been made available.

This, as we said, is in contrast to the situation in agriculture where the more isolated farmers may have received little information about a new innovation prior to personal communication. Thus we find another possible explanation for the differences in the early phases of the diffusions shown in Figures 10.9 and 10.10; "gammanyn" had a very high rate

of initial acceptance among physicians, whereas farmers were quite
sluggish in starting to adopt hybrid seed corn.

4. Effects of Social Crisis on Diffusion Rate

We should not be surprised if events occurring during the period
of time covered in a single study are reflected in the shape of the diffusion curve obtained. For example, an innovation eliciting an unusual
amount of communication may show a rapid initial rate of diffusion.
Wilkening (#6369) says that "when the number of persons adopting a new
practice is plotted by year, the result approximates a normal curve,
assuming no unusual circumstances" (italics ours).

The most drastic and unpredictable of such unusual circumstances
are crises which affect the entire social system, such as depressions or
wars. The effect of the crisis may be either to slow down or to accelerate the adoption rate, depending on the innovation and the circumstances.
Situations in which crises work to the advantage of the diffusion of an
innovation are discussed later in this chapter when we consider the timing of innovations. How the crisis affects the diffusion curve will depend on the timing of the innovation relative to the time of onset of
the crisis and to its duration.

Therefore, no specific prediction can be made about the degree of
deviation which will exist in the diffusion curve if a social crisis in-
tervenes during the diffusion process. However, the literature does suggest that most diffusion curves will approach normality if they are plotted
over a sufficient length of time, regardless of crisis-type intervening
events. Pemberton (#1502), on the basis of a study of four different
innovations, supports this view. He concludes that, "...the pattern of
causes determining the adoption of a culture trait are so persistent that,
in case the curve of diffusion is disturbed by a social crisis, the passing
of the crisis will find diffusion accelerating or retarding in rate,
so that the curve will resume the expected course within a short period
of time" (p. 56).

5. The Time Span of Diffusion Curves

We noted above that diffusion curves will, in general, approach
normality if they are plotted over a sufficient length of time, and this
is an important point, regardless of whether or not the time period includes a time of crisis. However, to measure from the beginning of the
process to the end, we must be able to identify the beginning and the end,
and it will also be helpful to have some indication of how long the process
might take.

The problem of deciding when the diffusion process begins may be illustrated by the study of Coleman et al. (#3576), cited earlier, of the
adoption of the drug "gammanyn". We pointed out that the diffusion curve
for this study (Figure 10.10) deviates from the typical S-curve, and we may
now postulate an additional reason for the unusual initial phase of this
diffusion curve, namely that extensive clinical trials precede distribution of a new drug. If the clinical trial period were added to the
adoption curve, it would probably approximate the typical S-curve. If
we now refer again to Figure 10.9 and consider the slow start in the adoption
of hybrid seed corn, we might suggest that the farmers initially adopting
hybrid seed corn may actually represent such a "clinical trial" period.
Ryan & Gross (# 2621) imply that this is true, saying that, "In a sense,

the early adopters provided a community laboratory from which neighbors could gain some vicarious experience". (Such early adoption may also be viewed as *demonstration*. See Chapter 9.) This suggests, then, that both the curve of Figure 10.9 and curve A of Figure 10.10 might well have approached closer to the normal if we had chosen a different starting point.

Even if the resulting curves were of exactly the same *shape*, however, we should be fully aware of an important difference remaining between the two curves: the diffusion process for the new drug covered a period of 16 *months*, whereas the diffusion of hybrid seed corn required 14 *years*.

Certainly we must keep in mind the span of time represented on the horizontal axis of a diffusion curve. Intuitively, it might seem that the curve for adoption of a fad (e.g., hula hoops) would differ vastly from that for a new data processing system. The major difference, however, may lie in the length of time required for diffusion. Thus, it might require six months to portray the adoption process for hula hoops, six years for the data processing system, and perhaps a span of 60 years for the adoption of the use of English in Catholic masses. On the basis of 150 studies on the adaptability of public school systems, Mort (#1191) concluded that between insight into a need and diffusion of a change to meet this need, 100 years elapse. Of this period, the first fifty years were generally required for developing a way of meeting the need, and the actual diffusion process covered a period of another 50 years. Despite the greatly differing time spans suggested for the diffusion of different types of innovations, we would in all probability find that in each case the diffusion curves would be similar if they were plotted so that the total time elapsed was scaled appropriately.

The difference in span of time involved in diffusion of various innovations accounts in part for the differences in rate of technical and social change depicted in Figure 10.1. Change consists of the cumulative effect of large numbers of innovations, and may be described as a composite of a number of normal curves, as illustrated in Figure 10.11.

[Insert Figure 10.11 here]

"Culture lag" may be described in terms of varying time spans for curves of technical and social change; i.e., if Figure 10.11 represented technical change, the horizontal axis might represent one year; a comparable number of social innovations might require that we observe diffusion over a ten-year period.

The length of time required for the diffusion of an innovation depends, then, primarily on the nature of the innovation itself, and these properties are discussed in detail in Chapter 8. We should recall, however, that we have also discussed some other factors which influence the time span. Among these are the personal or cultural characteristics of the adopting group, similarity of the innovation to one already in use, characteristics of the medium, and the interposition of crises.

6. Causes of Termination of the Diffusion Process

As we consider the length of time required for the diffusion process to be completed, we must also be able to identify the point in time when the process ends. The determination of such a point is problematic, however, as we realize when we consider the factors which act to terminate the diffusion process.

FIGURE 10.11   The effect of discrete innovations in
               producing steadily increasing change

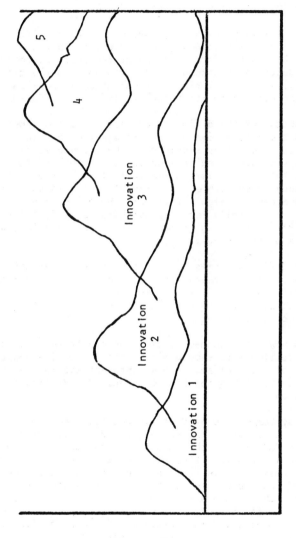

TIME

(From Stone, #1129, Figure 7, "A graphic picture
of the way a county agent's work load develops:
Hypothetical case")

In our discussion of the "interaction effect" we noted that the slowing down of diffusion is a predictable event as soon as half of the potential population has adopted, because, as Rogers (#1824) states, "each new adopter finds it increasingly difficult to tell the new idea to a peer who has not yet adopted" (p. 155). The result of this predictable sequence is the S-curve which we discussed earlier, and the upper plateau of this curve represents the levelling off of the process of diffusion as 100% adoption is approached.

There are many instances, however, in which diffusion to an entire potential population is never approached; diffusion may terminate at any point in the process for a variety of reasons. Leuthold & Wilkening (# 2671) describe three causes for breakdown in the diffusion process as being: (1) social isolation; (2) variation in applicability, and (3) a new idea becoming obsolete before it is fully diffused.

Breakdown of the diffusion process because of social isolation occurs when there is a core of individuals who seem to be immune to influence from all sources. They simply can't be reached at all, and as a result the process of diffusion terminates before 100% of the potential group has adopted. This is similar to the case of the socially isolated physicians in the study by Coleman et al. (#3576), illustrated earlier in Figure 10.10. Whereas the highly integrated MD's (curve B) reached nearly 100% adoption, the socially isolated MD's (curve C) fell far short of this goal, and as a result the drug gammanyn did not achieve full diffusion during the course of this study.

When diffusion comes to a halt because of variation in applicability of an innovation, it represents "rationality" of adoption (Rogers, #1824). The potential adopters for whom the innovation is appropriate and practical have adopted; if the curve continued to rise at this point, over-adoption would be taking place.

If a new idea becomes obsolete before it is fully diffused, the declining adoption rate should mirror the start of a new diffusion curve; then the point of inflection may represent the initial "awareness" phase of a new curve. This speculation leads to a difficulty in interpretation of diffusion curves.

We may be able to predict the adoptive behavior of a group of people on a statistical basis and we can draw a normal curve as our expectation of how the behavior of this group will appear over time. On the basis of the personal characteristics which were discussed in Chapter 4, such as innovativeness, risk-taking, caution, or skepticism, we can separate the members of the group into adopter categories and predict at what point on our curve each sub-group will adopt a certain innovation. However, if the *item* of diffusion has changed during the process, then our predictions will be of no use, and interpretaion of the diffusion process and the curve representing it will be difficult indeed.

For example, let us imagine the curve of diffusion of a relatively simple item, the home hair dryer. The early models, small hand-held dryers, came on the market about a dozen years ago. Since that time the product has changed a great deal. Can we use one diffusion curve to portray the adoption of home hair dryers, including both the early models and the recent, very different, version? If the former, how do we represent consumers who discontinued use of the earlier model in favor of the improved dryer? If the latter, at what point in the development of the product do we start a new curve?

At this point we may speculate about a final possible explanation for the difference between the initial acceptance rates of hybrid seed corn and the drug "gammanyn", as shown in Figures 10-9 and 10-10. Hybrid seed corn was an entirely new item which had just been introduced at the time Ryan & Gross (#2621) began their study of its diffusion. The fact that this product was a trail-blazer may have contributed greatly to the slowness with which it was accepted. Farmers would need a great deal of time to consider its advantages and suitability for themselves, and they would try it out on a small scale for an extended time before they were convinced that it was a good product and that no risk was involved in adopting it. On the other hand, "gammanyn", the drug studied by Coleman et al.(#3576), was not a wholly new product when it was introduced since it belonged to a family of drugs which physicians were already prescribing with confidence. Switching to "gammanyn" required little in the way of behavior change and represented a very low risk. The diffusion curve for "gammanyn" began, in a sense, when the first drug in the family of drugs was introduced.

We can see, then, the problems involved in trying to compare diffusion curves for innovations which differ in their degree of novelty, and we can appreciate the problems encountered in trying to depict a reasonable diffusion curve for an innovation which changes over time. This issue is similar to that described by Mort (#1191) when he says, "...not all important innovations spring fully armed from the brow of Jove. Some of them are old strands in new patterns. The question, then, as to when an innovation had its beginning is a difficult one" (p. 324).

This problem of interpretation may become acute when we try to measure the diffusion of new curricula in school systems, since these are complex innovations which are in a state of rapid development and evolution. Next year's Science Curriculum package is going to be far more developed than this year's. (Here, the sophisticated consumer might be well advised to wait. He should keep in mind, however, the old story of the farmer who never did buy his wife a washing machine, convincing her, year by year, that the next year's model would be greatly improved.)

On the whole, it would seem that diffusion curves must be interpreted with great care in order to avoid over-simplification of complex processes. They do serve as useful tools, however, in providing a model for adoption and diffusion processes and in permitting comparisons between seemingly disparate processes. Further, they provide a basis for the intensive investigation of deviations from the normal curve; such deviations may point to processes and events likely to produce both wanted and unwatned outcomes.

F. RESISTANCE

So far, we have looked at the S-curve as depicting rate of adoption; however, we may also think of it as describing the rate at which resistance to change is reduced. Rogers 1824) indicates that the curve may be viewed as the result of conformity to group pressures. This is reminiscent of Allport's (#6375) early formulation of the "J-curve of conforming behavior". Allport describes the J-curve as a "telic continuum" involving the "degree of fulfillment of the purpose of a common rule". If we think in terms of conformity to a rule, it is apparent that the area above the curve represents resistance, and a point on the curve depicts an equilibrium, at any point in time, between conformity and resistance. Whitney (#2063) applies this formulation to the use of inventions when he says that the use of any invention may be described in terms of combined factors of demand minus resistance. We may also look at the adoption and diffusion curves as representing a decreasing amount of personal or social resistance to an innovation. Then each of the "phases" may be seen as phases in reducing resistance, and we may describe a "resistance curve" which is a mirror image of the adoption or diffusion curve.

Watson (#3690) describes the stages of resistance to a typical innovation: (1) Massive, undifferentiated; few take the change seriously; (2) Pro and Con sides identifiable; resistance can be defined, and its power appraised; (3) Direct Conflict; resistance mobilized; crucial stage for survival; (4) The Changers are in power; Wisdom needed to keep latent opposition from mobilizing. Resisters seen as cranks, nuisances; (5) Old adversaries are as few and alienated as advocates were in the first stage. Advocates now resist new change.

Resistance can never be considered as a single entity or process but has many components. Some major features described in the literature are:

1. Threat to the Established Social Structure

The fact that innovations may pose a threat to the established social structure has been of particular interest to anthropologists and those concerned with bringing about change in underdeveloped countries (e.g. Adams, #5049; Barnett, #0620; Marcson, #2924). A general finding is that resistance is roughly proportional to the amount of change required in the social structure and the strength of the social values which are challenged. Meyerson & Katz (#1720) point out that fads gain rapid acceptance because they do not cause change in the social structure or in patterns of interaction and communication. That a threat to such patterns may cause generalized resistance is illustrated by Atwood's (#1178) description of faculty resistance to the introduction of a school guidance program. Atwood's analysis of the resistance points to changed patterns of interaction as a major source of discontent.

2. Threat to Vested Interests

When vested interests are at issue in resistance to change, resistance may be focussed at high levels, where social strength and power are centered. Lystad (#1029), for example, studied a group formed to plan changes aimed at community welfare; he observed that members with high social status and greater vested interests showed less involvement in planning. In such an instance, resistance is likely to be concentrated in the early phases of change, where a powerful minority may prevent or retard action.

Hoselitz (#2029) points out that when a ruling minority has vested interests in the status quo, token innovations may be accepted. On the other hand, as Weiss (#2629) indicates, change may be accepted at upper levels, only to encounter vested interests at lower levels. Thus, management may officially institute innovative procedures, only to find that, in actual practice, "business as usual" is being conducted. In this case, the various stages of change have been accomplished at one level, but not at another; "integration into the system" has not taken place.

3. Threat to the Individual

Reasons for individual resistance have been described in Chapters 4 and 5. From the point of view of adoption curves, it remains only to say that resistance on the part of the individual is likely to be strongest at the point where pressure for change is the greatest. Watson (#6364) points out that it is at this point that the individual becomes most

threatened and tends to regress to remembered or fantasied security.
Mann and Williams (#5227) found this to be true in a case of change in
an industrial organization, and they report that there was little
disturbance or resistance to change until the change was imminent. Abelson (#7138) describes the same effect in local referendum campaigns.
He considers as a "Law of Poll Watching" the fact that, "If in a referendum an abstract principle is pitted against a very concrete fear or
desire, the concrete side will gain heavily as the campaign nears its
conclusion". As a result of several studies of local fluoridation con-
troversies, Abelson found that shortly before the referendum takes place,
negative arguments gain momentum and they influence "weak pro's" to become "weak anti's". It would seem to be at the time when concrete action
must be taken, that the threat to the individual is most clearly felt.
In Abelson's words, "...it is all well and good to declare in principle
against pornography, but if it means that someone is going to censor
what you read, or worse, take away your copy of Playboy, well, then one
must stand and be counted".

4. Characteristics of the Knowledge

The topic of the characteristics of knowledge, which is covered
thoroughly in Chapter 8, cannot be separated from issues of threat to
the social system, vested interests, and the individual. Knowledge may
be described using Barnett's (#2510) terms of "unencumbered" and "encumbered" knowledge. "Unencumbered knowledge" is that which permits individual option in innovation; "encumbered knowledge" is that which requires widespread acceptance by a group or social system. Watson (#6364)
gives examples of innovations which have encountered widespread resistance because of the related changes they would require: universal adoption of the metric system, and simplified spelling are examples.

5. The Case For Resistance

It is easy to adopt a stance which implies that "change is good --
resistance is bad". This is, of course, not necessarily true. Resistance may be a stubborn unwillingness to change; it may also be a carefully
thought-out position. Mann & Neff (#3913) describe some possible factors
in individual resistance. A potential receiver's reactions to a proposed
innovation are, they say,

> "...a function of matters such as the amount of control he has
> over his own destiny, how ambiguous he sees the situation ahead
> to be, and how much trust he places in local authority figures.
> The user then engages in "search behavior" to assess the likely
> net consequences of adopting the innovation. A good deal of
> ambivalence can be expected; this serves as personal (and or-
> ganizational) defense. "

Klein (#3691) suggests that,

> "...just as individuals have their defenses to ward off threat,
> maintain integrity, and protect themselves against the unwar-
> ranted intrusions of others' demands, so do social systems
> seek ways in which to defend themselves against ill-considered
> and overly precipitous innovations." (p. 30)

This defense, which is carried out by individuals who assume the role of
the "defender", has been discussed in Chapter 7. Klein suggests the need
to study and understand the role of the "defender" of the status quo,

and the need for a balance between innovation and stability of the system.

Dykens et al. (#5134) summarize some of the difficulties involved in understanding the phenomenon of resistance:

'The emotional aspects of change are many. They include general feelings and attitudes about change, wishes to change, resistances to change, acceptance or rejection of change efforts, identification with change, denial of change, and a variety of ego defensive responses to change. These aspects of change, based as they are on present and past experiences and phantasies, require careful and sensitive scanning, understanding and working through on the part of strategist and (receiver) alike."(p. 187)

III. PHASE MODELS OF DIFFUSION AND CHANGE: THREE SCHOOLS OF THOUGHT

The study of adoption and diffusion curves has contributed to the identification of a regular sequence of events in the process of adoption and diffusion. Rogers (#1824) points out that dividing the process into such phases is "... (1) consistent with the nature of the phenomena, (2) congruent with previous research findings, and (3) potentially useful for practical applications" (p. 79). He traces the development of the concept of stages, citing in particular the early work of Ryan & Gross (#2621) and Wilkening (#2876). Ryan & Gross distinguished between "awareness", "conviction", "acceptance", and "complete adoption" of hybrid seed corn. Wilkening, usually credited with the first use of the concept of stages in the process of adoption, described the process as one "composed of learning, deciding, and acting over a period of time. The adoption of a specific practice is not the result of a single decision to act but of a series of actions and thought decisions" (p. 16). Rural sociologists, who have been responsible for most of the research and conceptualization on adoption phases, have more or less reached a concensus on a five-step process which includes (1) awareness, (2) interest, (3) evaluation, (4) trial, and (5) adoption.

A related field of effort, one which has developed separately from the field of rural sociology, is that of the study of phases in implementing change in social behavior and attitudes. Pioneer social psychologist, Kurt Lewin, in his early studies of group decision and social change (#1342), described three major stages in the process of change: *Unfreezing, Moving,* and *Freezing. "Unfreezing"* describes the necessary initial phase in which the need for change is realized, and a willingness to give up old ways of doing things is evidenced. *"Moving"* includes the activity involved in implementing change, and *"Freezing"* indicates the establishment and firm rooting of the new behavior in the life of the group.

In the field of education, the concept of stages of change was implied, but not specified, in the early work of Mort and his colleagues (see #1191, p. 318). According to Mort, the process of innovation in education follows a "predictable pattern", including insight into a need, the introduction of a way of meeting the need, diffusion, and adoption. In recent years, educational research and theory have drawn from both the rural sociology and social psychology traditions; Miles (#6056), for example, bases his discussion of stages on the work of Rogers; Lippitt, Watson and Westley (#1343) derive the stages they describe from the work of Lewin.

The research on the stages of change has involved many different types of innovations and a wide variety of adopting populations. It is not surprising, therefore, that different authors propose conceptualizations of the change process

10-26

which contain differing elements. Proposed classifications vary greatly in complexity and range from the two-step "cognition-behavior" models proposed by Mason (#2397) and Pareek & Chattopadhyay (#0438), to the elaborate ten stage model for social change described by Watson (#6364). These discrepancies should not necessarily be regarded as disagreements, but rather, it should be recognized that different authors are considering different *types* of change processes and different *portions* of the change processes.

Upon closer consideration we realize that the four stages described by Mort (#1191) are not a different way of describing the five stages observed by the rural sociologists. We can speculate that Mort's final stage of "adoption" actually encompasses the entire 5-stage adoption process as described by Rogers (#1824), and from our earlier discussion about diffuser activity curves, we can surmise that Mort's stage of "diffusion" will precede and overlap with the "adoption" stage. His first two stages, "Insight into a need", and "The introduction of a way of meeting the need", will presumably precede any activity by the diffuser.

Many descriptions of the change process include stages preceding diffusion and adoption: these additional stages describe the preparation of an innovation for use. Such preparations may, in many cases, be undertaken by individuals outside the potential user system. A need may be recognized by outside resource persons, who take upon themselves the tasks of design and development in addition to dissemination of the innovative solution. The expected end result of this process will be adoption of the innovation by a population over a period of time, as described by Rogers (#1824). A process such as this is proposed by Miles (#6056), who adds an initial stage of "design" (which includes research and development activities) to Rogers' stages. Miles points out that the agricultural studies on which Rogers reports began after an innovation had already been adequately designed; Miles would like to trace the change process from an earlier point in time.

The change process can take on quite a different aspect when a user system becomes active in solving its own problems. Some authors trace the phases of change starting with a need which is felt by a particular user system; this need is identified, diagnosed, and solved either by the user himself, or by the user in collaboration with outside resource persons. This type of change process may be initiated with a stage which Watson (#6364) calls "felt dissatisfaction", and which Mackenzie (#1194) refers to as "criticism" (of the status quo). A series of steps may be taken which include research and development activities but which have the goal not of mass dissemination but of satisfaction of the needs of the individual system. Dissemination of the same solution to others may follow but is not of primary concern. However, if outside resources participate in the solving of a user's problem, they may disseminate successful solutions to other clients who have problems similar to those of the initial client system. Thus some authors, even though they advocate change strategies which are primarily client-oriented (e.g. Watson, #6364; Jung and Lippitt, #3922), are nevertheless also interested in a final stage, that of dissemination of the innovation to other *groups*. This is a sequence of change which is cited commonly in the current literature on change in education.

In order to facilitate discussion of the stages involved in the process of change, we have identified three broad perspectives, three schools of thought, which we term, (1) the Social Interaction Perspective, (2) the Research, Development and Diffusion Perspective, and (3) the Problem-Solver Perspective. Some of the major stages of each school are outlined in Table 10.1. Later tables will compare the specific stages proposed by different authors within each of these schools.

TABLE 10.1   Stages Typically Included in Models of Change Within Three Schools of Research

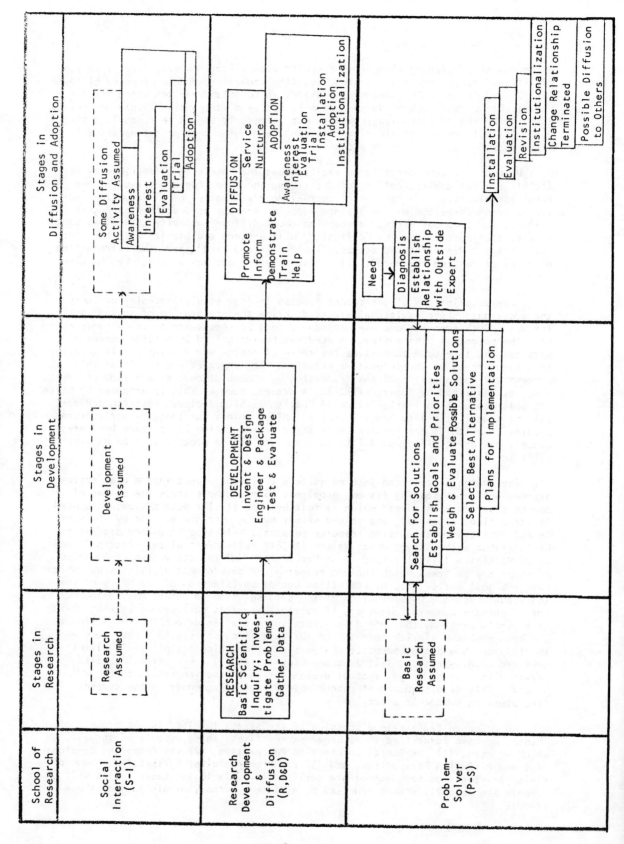

The basic distinction between studies falling within the three classifications is as follows:

The Social Interaction (S-I) Perspective describes studies in which an innovation, usually in the form of a product or practice, is presented or brought to the attention of a potential receiver population. The receiver and the receiver's needs are defined and determined exclusively by the sender. The receiver is supposed to react to the new information, and the nature of his reaction determines whether or not subsequent stages will occur. If his awareness is followed by an expression of interest, he is launched on a series of stages which terminate with acceptance or rejection of the innovation. The diffusion of the innovation depends greatly upon the channels of communication within the receiver group, since information about the innovation is transmitted primarily through the social interaction of the group members (see our earlier discussion of "The Interaction Effect").

The Research, Development & Diffusion (R,D&D) Perspective looks at the process of change from the point of view of the *originator* of an innovation, and it begins with the formulation of a problem on the basis of a presumed receiver need. The initiative in making this identification, however, is taken by the *developer*, not the receiver, and in this way the R,D&D school is similar to the S-I school. It differs from the S-I school, however, in that it views the process of change from an earlier point in time. The focus is on the activity phases of the developer as he designs and develops a potential solution. Development is followed by dissemination of the solution to the receiver and promotion of adoption behavior in the receiver group.

In the Problem-Solver (P-S) Perspective the receiver (an individual or a group) initiates the process of change by identifying an area of concern or by sensing a need for change. Once the problem area is identified, the receiver undertakes to alter the situation either through his own efforts, or by recruiting suitable outside assistance. Whereas the receiver in the S-I and R,D&D models is passive, the receiver in the P-S model is actively involved in finding an innovation to solve his own problem. Specifically what the new input will be is determined largely by the receiver himself; whether or not this same input could also satisfy the needs of other receivers (i.e., mass diffusion) is not generally considered.

Although we feel that there are important differences among these three schools, there are enough similarities so that it is sometimes difficult to identify the one to which a specific study can be most appropriately assigned. Lewin's stages of Unfreezing, Moving and Refreezing, for example, may be described as fitting either the S-I or the P-S model, depending on who is responsible for the Unfreezing stage. As another example, Jacobs (#1781) describes five main components (or stages) of educational planning as, (1) formulation of objectives -- on a national scale; (2) determination of feasible structures and programs for attaining objectives; (3) establishing priorities, determining procedures for implementing programs and structures, and planning time phasing; (4) implementation; (5) evaluation, refinement and revision. Jacobs points out that the educational planning must be carried out on many levels from national policy to classroom practice, utilizing all five steps at each level. In trying to assign Jacobs' model to one of our schools we would need to look at a specific instance of innovation. Where planning is on a national level, we would probably describe the process of innovation as fitting the R,D&D model, but with elements of the P-S model included. At a local level, or in a specific classroom, a study in which these phases occur would probably best be described by the P-S model. Thus, there is ample room for disagreement with our assignment of studies to classifications, and authors may well disagree with our interpretation of the stages which they describe.

A. THE SOCIAL INTERACTION PERSPECTIVE

This school includes models in which the unit of analysis is the individual receiver, and in which the focus is on the receiver's perception of
and response to knowledge coming from outside himself. This knowledge is
usually in the form of an identifiable product or practice which has been
made available to a potential adopting population. Authors who consider
the process of adoption from this point of view are concerned with the stages
through which individuals pass as they reach a decision to adopt an innovation. They are concerned in addition with the related issue of the mechanisms by which the innovation diffuses through the adopting group. Studies
in this area have shown that the most effective means of spreading information about an innovation is through personal contact. Thus, the key to
adoption is viewed by authors of this school to be the *"social interaction"*
among members of the adopting group.

Table 10.2 shows the phases described by some of the authors who have
studied adoption from this perspective. Most of the studies emanate from the
rural sociology literature and thus are concerned with the adoption of agricultural innovations. The two studies in this table which do not deal with
agricultural practice are those of Holmberg (cited in Rogers, #1824) and of
Coleman et al. (#3576). For all of these models the unit of adoption is the
individual: Holmberg is concerned with individual adoption of cultural
change; Coleman studied the adoption of a new drug by physicians; and the
rural sociologists consider the individual farmer (or farm family) as he
adopts agricultural innovations. However, although the adopting unit is the
individual in each of the studies listed in Table 10.2, this phase model
could just as logically be applied to groups or to entire social social
systems.

Since it is assumed that the innovation which is to be adopted is already in a developed form, suitable for use readily available to the potential
adopter, the initial stage is generally described as one of awareness of the
innovation. If an adoption is to be initiated, the awareness will usually be
followed by stages of interest and information seeking, evaluation (in terms
of decision making), trial, and adoption. The sequence may be truncated by
rejection at any stage; for example, *awareness* may be followed by rejection,
in which case interest and information seeking to not take place. Similarly,
interest and information seeking may result in the decision that the innovation is not useful or appropriate; evaluation may provide negative results,
and trial on a limited basis may lead to rejection.

1. Rogers

Rogers' five-stage process is the model which has been most used in
studying adoption through the process of social interaction. We will
therefore first focus our attention on the process as described by
Rogers, and we will then discuss the viewpoints of other authors as they
differ from Rogers' conceptualization.

a. Awareness

The initial stage of Awareness is described by Rogers (#1824)
as that at which:

"...the individual is exposed to the innovation but lacks
complete information about it. The individual is aware
of the innovation, but is not yet motivated to seek further information. The primary function of the awareness

10-30

TABLE 10.2   SOCIAL INTERACTION CHANGE MODELS

Author	Field	Year	Biblio #		Phases					
Rogers	Agric.	1962	#1824		1. Awareness	2. Interest	3. Evaluation	4. Trial	5. Adoption	
Lionberger	Agric.	1960	#1036		1. Awareness	2. Information	3. Application (Mental trial, Decision to try)	4. Trial	5. Adoption	
Beal, Rogers & Bohlen	Agric.	1957	#3561		1. Awareness	2. Obtaining Information	3. Conviction and Trial		4. Adoption	
Wilkening	Agric.	1953	#2876		1. Awareness	2. Interest or Information	3. Decision Making or Application	4. Trial	5. Acceptance or Adoption	
Wilkening	Agric.	1962	#6369		1. Awareness					
Holmberg	Anthro.	1960	Cited in Rogers #1824	1. Availability of Information	2. Awareness	3. Interest	4. Trial	5. Evaluation	6. Adoption	7. Integration into Routine
Coleman, et al.	Med. Soc.	1966	#3576		1. Awareness	2. Interest	3. Evaluation (Mental Trial)	4. Trial	5. Acceptance	

stage is to initiate the sequence of later stages that
lead to eventual adoption or rejection of the innovation"
(pp. 81-82).

Rogers describes this stage as a relatively passive one on
the part of the receiver; he feels that awareness of an innovation
does not generally come about as a result of a need, but rather
that awareness of a new idea *creates* a need for that innovation.

b. Interest

The behavior of the individual during the second, or Interest,
stage is characterized by active information-seeking about the
innovation. Rogers states that at this stage:

"The individual favors the innovation in a general way,
but he has not yet judged its utility in terms of his own
situation. The function of the interest stage is mainly to
increase the individual's information about the innovation."
(p.82)

We might speculate that the less "information-seeking" required, the more readily will the innovation be accepted. However,
Rogers points out that as the individual's behavior becomes pur-
posive in seeking information, his psychological involvement increases. We may conclude, therefore, that the active seeking of
information implies some degree of personal commitment, and may
presage later phases more likely to result in adoption. It is at
this stage that positive or negative attitudes toward an innovation
are first elicited. Rogers (#1824, p. 83) points out that the
personality and values of the individual, as well as the norms of
his social system, will influence the direction of his search for
information as well as his subsequent interpretation of the information.

c. Evaluation

Rogers describes the third stage, Evaluation, as a period of
"mental trial" which is a necessary preliminary to the decision
to make a "behavioral trial". He states that:

"At the evaluation stage the individual mentally applies
the innovation to his present and anticipated future situation, and then decides whether or not to try it." (p. 83)

Rogers considers the Evaluation stage to be the least distinct and the most difficult phase about which to obtain information.
He says that:

"Different types of evaluation occur at each stage in
the adoption process...but the decision to try the new
idea occurs, by definition, only at the evaluation stage."
(p. 83)

d. Trial

If the results of the individual's "mental trial" are favorable, he is ready to move on to the Trial stage. Rogers describes
this stage as follows:

"At the trial stage the individual uses the innovation
on a small scale in order to determine its utility in
his own situation. The main function of the trial
stage is to demonstrate the new idea in the individual's
own situation and determine its usefulness for possible
complete adoption." (p. 84)

It is not possible, of course, to try out all innovations on
a small scale. An alternative in some cases is to make a trial
on a temporary or probationary basis before going on to true adoption.

e. Adoption

The final stage which Rogers considers is that of Adoption.
It is at this stage that the results of the trial are considered,
and on the basis of this the decision is made to adopt (or reject)
the innovation. Rogers defines adoption as "continued use of the
innovation in the future".

f. The adoption Curve

This sequence of stages of the adoption of an innovation by
an individual is the same type of process which we presented earlier
in this chapter, and which we represented by a curve in Figure 10.4.
We can draw this same curve to represent different levels of involvement of the individual at each stage of the adoption process
as described by Rogers.

[Insert Figure 10.12 here]

2. Comparison of Conceptualizations of Authors in the Social Interaction School

Although, as we have indicated, Rogers' model is widely accepted
as representing the process through which individuals go as they adopt
an innovation, there is some degree of variation in the way in which
different authors conceptualize the process. Some authors choose
slightly different labels for the stages, some visualize different
activities to be taking place at a particular stage, and there is not
complete agreement about the order of the stages. We will discuss
some of these differences as we again look at Table 10.2.

a. Availability

Holmberg (cited in Rogers, #1824) specifies the first stage
in the process as "availability of the innovation to the individual".
We may assume that this is not a disagreement with other authors
but, rather, a statement of what is assumed by others. The fact of
availability is worth stating, however; it draws our attention to
the fact that there are steps, such as design, development, and
production, which generally take place before the process of adoption can be initiated. It also indicates that once awareness has
been brought about, the individual will be able to follow through
on subsequent stages of adoption.

b. Awareness

Once availability has been stated or assumed, Table 10.2
shows that there is no disagreement among authors that the first

FIGURE 10.12 Involvement of an Individual at Stages of
              the Adoption Process

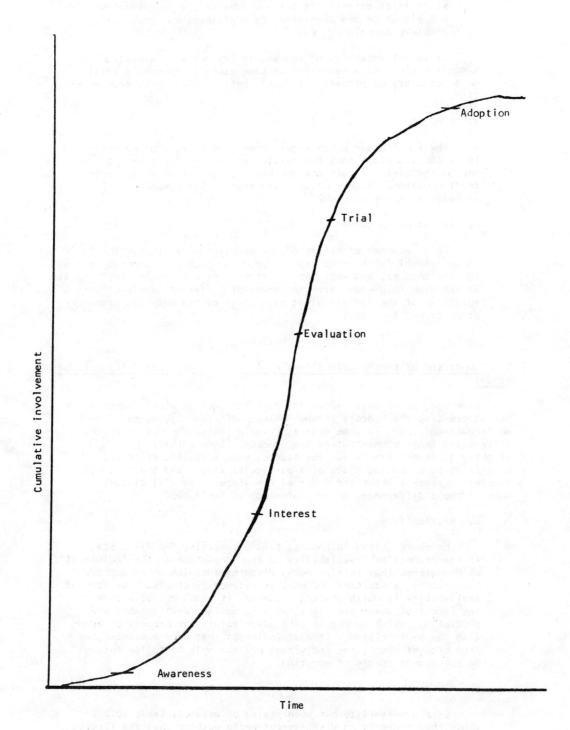

stage in the adoption process is <u>Awareness</u>. The literature does
reveal, however, that there is some disagreement about the behavior
of the individual at this stage. We will recall that Rogers views
the individual as being a passive receiver at this stage, a formulation with which Hassinger (#2875) disagrees. Hassinger indicates
that awareness must be actively initiated by the receiver, as a
result of his own needs. In Barnett's terms (#0615), a message
must "make psychological contact with previous experience" in order
to be accepted. Unquestionably, the process of becoming aware is
not a simple one, and later in this section we will discuss some of
the media and strategies which seem to be most successful in creating
awareness.

c. Interest and Information Seeking

      The second stage of the adoption process is described as
either the <u>Interest</u> or the <u>Information</u> stage by different authors,
but whichever label is chosen, there is complete agreement as to
what takes place at this stage. The active interest of the individual
in the innovation is expressed in behavioral terms by seeking and
obtaining information from a variety of sources.

d. Evaluation-Application

      The third stage in the adoption process, which Rogers has
called <u>Evaluation</u>, has been labelled as "<u>Application</u>" by Beal,
Rogers & Bohlen (#3561) and by Wilkening (#6369). These authors
describe this stage as one during which the individual undergoes a
"mental trial" of the new practice and decides whether or not to
try it out, which is precisely what Rogers means by "Evaluation".
We will recall, however, that Rogers referred to this stage as being
the least distinct, and it is therefore not surprising to find that
some authors do not agree with Rogers' conceptualization. Table 10.2
shows that, in his early work, Wilkening (#2876) conceived of the
adoption process as consisting of only four stages, the third one
being "conviction and trial". We may speculate that in this case
"conviction" probably means a decision to try out the innovation
and that therefore this stage of "conviction and trial" could be
separated into two stages, and his model would then conform to the
five stage model. We should not overlook the fact that Wilkening
found it difficult to make this separation, and the problem of
distinguishing the stages at this point in the process is emphasized
by the findings of Holmberg (cited in Rogers, #1824). He has concluded from his study of the adoption of cultural innovations that
Evaluation *follows* Trial. This disagreement may be a result of
differences in the definition of the term "evaluation", with
Rogers using it in the sense of "making a decision", while Holmberg
may be using it in the more usual sense of assessing an outcome.
On the other hand, the contradictory findings may be attributable to
the fact that different types of innovations were studied by Holmberg than by the other authors. If we are dealing with a concrete
product or with a specific practice, then it seems logical that,
as Rogers says, the decision to try must precede the trial. Whether
or not a complete "mental trial" takes place is no doubt more questionable, and there are several reports of discrepant findings. Mason
(#2397), for example, reports that evaluation always occurred before interest and information seeking in his study. Schramm (#2093)
found adoption taking place, in some situations, even before information-seeking and evaluation.

e. Trial

There is complete agreement among the authors listed in Table 10.2 that individuals generally go through a trial phase before accepting an innovation for continued use, where this is possible. There is some evidence, however, that this is a stage which may be skipped even in cases where trial is possible. Beal, Rogers & Bohlen (#3561), in their study of the adoption of the practice of feeding antibiotics to swine, questioned 148 farmers. Of the 105 who adopted this practice, it was found that all had gone through the stages of awareness, information, and application, but ten had by-passed the trial stage. The skipping of the trial stage may be explained in some cases by the perception which an individual has of the source from which he obtains information. If an innovation is favorably evaluated and highly recommended by a trusted source, it is not rare to find adoption taking place without a personally conducted behavioral trial.

f. Adoption

In general we find that theorists of the Social Interaction school describe the process of stages only through the final one affecting the individual adopter, that of Adoption (or rejection). Use of the term "adoption" often signifies full and continued acceptance. It is necessary, however, to distinguish "first use" from "sustained use" (Katz, #1398), and full acceptance from implementation in an amended form (Sanders, #3751). Alternative outcomes will be discussed more fully in a later section of this chapter.

g. Rejection

Although Rejection is usually described as an "outcome", we have indicated that it may take place at any stage in the sequence. There are presumably many rejections, or failures to adopt, that go unnoticed and unrevealed. It is also probable that the earlier in the sequence that a rejection takes place, the less likely it is to appear in the literature.* All the factors leading to resistance (discussed earlier) may cause rejection at any stage in the adoption process. Eicholz & Rogers (#1185) have formulated a paradigm for "stages of rejection", indicating that, following Awareness, the stage of "Interest" may be paralleled by "Denial"; and "Trial-with-adoption" may be paralleled by "Trial-with-rejection".

h. Integration

Holmberg (#1824) adds one additional stage to the process, beyond adoption, that of "Integration of the innovation into the individual's routine". This may represent a type of internalization which is more salient for the continued use of a cultural innovation such as Holmberg studied than it is for a more concrete innovation such as those studied by Coleman et al. and by the rural sociologists.

---

*Preliminary analysis of a sample of 108 empirical studies from our review shows 59 reporting positive results, 36 ambiguous results, but only 13 negative or "no effect" instances.

3. Significance of Different Sources of Information at Different Stages

As we have discussed each stage in the adoption process, we have
mentioned several times that the sources to which an individual turns for
information about an innovation and the way in which these sources are
perceived by the individual play a very important part in determining the
outcome of the adoption process. The area of media and the transmission
of information has been thoroughly discussed in Chapter 9; but at this
point we may now consider the effects of different media at various
stages in the adoption process.

The major distinction made in the literature as regards sources of
information is that of personal vs. impersonal sources; the former
implies some type of personal relationship between sender and receiver;
the latter refers primarily to the mass media. Katz (#1398), Wilkening
(#6369) and other rural sociologists have found that, in general, the
mass media serve to inform, and the personal contacts serve to legitimate
information.

In terms of phases of adoption, the following generalizations seem
to hold: impersonal sources are most important during the "awareness"
phase; during the "interest - information seeking" phase the receiver may
turn to an expert, to the mass media, or to personal contacts as sources
of information. Personal sources, however, assume greater importance at
the evaluation, or "mental trial" stage (Bowers, #2475; Katz, #0298;
Rogers, #1824). Following an actual trial, the individual tends to rely
on his own judgment regarding the value of the innovation.

Those who attempt to disseminate innovations find it important to
take note of the above generalizations. In Chapter 9 it was pointed out
that the County Agent in Agriculture was not effective until after the
farmer had become aware of an innovation by other means. Similarly,
the drug companies find it valuable to use a mass media approach or
journal advertising approach to physicians before the detail men are sent
out to contact them directly. We stated earlier that the process of
becoming aware of an innovation is not a simple one, and we should
emphasize that both the personality of the receiver and his attitude
toward the information source have an important effect on the process
of awareness. Social psychology uses the term "selective exposure" to
describe the fact that individuals tend to perceive and retain information
which is congruent with their needs or emotional states. The literature
abounds with illustrations of "selective exposure"; Hyman & Sheatsley
(#2026), for example, have chronicled some of the difficulties in bringing
about awareness in individuals they refer to as "chronic know-nothings".
However, selective exposure has limitations; awareness may be imposed
on an individual in a number of ways. For example, advertisers will often
use repetitive or catchy ads which make little attempt to convince the
receiver that he needs or wants the innovation.

As the individual begins actively to seek information at the interest
stage, we may point out again the importance of his attitudes toward the
source of information, whether it is personal or impersonal. If the
receiver is forced to obtain information from a source which he regards
as unreliable or hostile to his interests, he may reject the information
and the innovation. We may be able to infer from this that educational
campaigns which make information-seeking both easy and pleasant are likely
to result in favorable attitudes toward the innovation.

Although many sources of information have relevance to a single stage
in the adoption process, there are others which may serve several purposes.

For example, the publication, <u>Consumers Reports</u>, is one primarily designed to give its readers information for pre-trial evaluation. At the same time, however, it provides information.

Even though mass media have been found to be most important at the awareness stage, they do continue to have some impact at later stages in the adoption process and they may have some bearing on whether use of an innovation is continued once it has first been adopted. On the basis of Festinger's theory of "cognitive dissonance" (#0264), we may speculate that once a decision has been made, the receiver will exhibit a certain amount of selective attention to the mass media, seeking evidence to support the action he has taken.

4. <u>Different Information Sources for Different Adopters</u>

So far in our discussion of the importance of media sources at different stages of the adoption process we have not made any distinction between the types of information sources which are relied upon by different types of adopters. We noted earlier that members of a population may be subdivided into adopter categories on the basis of the time at which they adopt an innovation, relative to the other members of the group. (See again Figures 10.5 and 10.6, which show the diffusion curve subdivided into adapter categories.) It has been found that individuals in different adopter categories differ on the types of information sources to which they turn and on the roles which they play in the transmission of information.

Many terms have been employed to identify various roles in the adoption process, and among the best known of these are the "opinion leaders" and "followers" described by Lazarsfeld, et al. (#6182). These authors depict the flow of communication as a two-step process in which, first, ideas are usually transmitted by the mass media to opinion leaders, and second, the opinion leaders then transmit these ideas to less active followers. We find, then, that the opinion leaders, who generally fall into the category of "early adopters" rely more on non-personal sources of information than do the later adopters.

An additional role which is often cited is that of the <u>expert</u>. In their study of communication about public affairs, Katz & Lazarsfeld (#0294) found that opinion leaders are likely to seek information from experts, while followers seek out people like themselves. Thus the opinion leader fills two roles: first as "follower" of a higher-level opinion leader (the expert), and then as leader for a group of less active followers, who are more like himself. Merton (#6220) describes this process as a *chain-of-influence*, with people in adjacent social strata serving as links. Thus, as he points out, top-level "influentials" may have little direct effect on lower-level decision-making.

Carlson (#0585) describes the two-step flow as a process in which opinion leaders derive information from the mass media, and in turn transmit it to their associates. In this process, the content of the original information is <u>mediated</u> both by the *reference groups* of the individual, and by the *social structure* in which these groups are embedded. Beal and Rogers (#1351) also emphasize the usefulness of reference-group theory in describing the process of spread of information in agriculture. Innovators among farmers take an interest in agricultural research and view the scientist in a favorable light, whereas to the late adopter the scientist is likely to be a "distant referent", often viewed with suspicion and hostility. The early-adopting farmer, however, is part of the reference group of other farmers and serves as a mediator of information.

It is only when we begin to consider the social structure of the adopter group and the interpersonal relationships which exist within this group that we can appreciate the mechanisms by which an innovation diffuses and comes to be adopted by the individual members. Though the adoption process may be an individual matter, it is highly dependent upon group interaction. We discussed the effect of this interaction earlier when we were describing the diffusion curve, and we may now recall the findings of Coleman et al. (#3576) concerning the importance of social interaction among physicians in determining the rate of adoption of a new drug. They concluded that interpersonal relationships seemed to be the most important factor in the adoption of innovations and that the extent of social relationships is directly related to adoption rate and, indeed, to the chances of adoption taking place at all. Rogers also emphasizes the importance of social relationships in studying the spread of innovations, and he states that "in fact, after an innovation is adopted by 10 to 20 per cent of an audience, it may be impossible to halt its further spread". (p. 219)

B. THE RESEARCH, DEVELOPMENT AND DIFFUSION PERSPECTIVE

Models which are included in the R,D&D school depict the process of change as an orderly sequence which begins with the identification of a problem, procedes through activities which are directed towards finding or producing a solution to this problem, and ends with diffusion of this solution to a target group. The initiative in these activities is taken by the researchers, the developers, and the disseminators; the receiver remains essentially passive.

As we pointed out earlier, the R,D&D school views the change process from an earlier point in time than does the S-I school, and as a result it considers a wider range of roles and activities which are appropriate to different stages. Because of the greater complexity of the process which is described by this school, we find there is a much wider variation in the conceptualizations which are proposed to represent it. Table 10.3 gives a brief view of the sequence of activities which some authors describe in the R,D&D process. These may be summarized in a very general fashion as Research, Development, Diffusion, and Adoption, though it is clear from the table that few authors specifically include all of these activities.

We do not find here, as we did in looking at the S-I school, that one particular model seems to be generally "accepted" as the R,D&D model. Thus, as we lead off our discussion with a detailed look at a typical model, it should be kept in mind that it may be representative only from our own point of view. We will concentrate first on the sequence of change which has been proposed by Guba & Clark (#7131), since this includes the most widely used basic phases and at the same time it provides detailed descriptions of the activities and goals which the authors feel should be included in these phases.

1. The Theory-Practice Continuum of Guba and Clark

Guba and Clark (cited in Guba, #7131) have proposed a schematic continuum for change in education which is designed to bridge the gap between theory and practice. This continuum includes four major phases or areas of activity: Research, Development, Diffusion, and Adoption. Table 10.3 shows that, in addition, certain sub-activities are specified within each of these phases. Before we describe these activities, we

TABLE 10.3

Research, Development and Diffusion Change Models

Author, Biblio.#	Field, Year	Phases
Guba & Clark #7131	Educ. 1966	1. Research — 2. Development [Invention: New Solution to Operating Problem, Innovate | Design: engineer innovation package] — 3. Diffusion [Disseminate: create awareness | Demonstrate: build conviction | Help, Involve, Train, Intervene] — 4. Adoption [Trial | Installation | Institutionalization]
Hopkins & Clark #3586	Educ. 1966	1. Research [Conduct basic scientific inquiry | Investigate Educationally oriented problems | Gather operational and planning data] — 2. Development [Invent solutions to operating problems | Engineer packages & programs for education | Test & evaluate solutions & programs] — 3. Diffusion [Inform target system | Demonstrate solutions & programs | Train Target System in use of solutions and programs] — Service & nurture installed solutions
Havelock & Benne #3872	Industry 1967	1. Basic Research — 2. Applied Research — 3. Development and Design — 4. Engineering for manufacturing — 5. Manufacturing — 6. Distribution & Installation
Brickell #0845 #0875	Educ. 1964 1966	1. Design [Development: Invention or Engineering] (Basic Research) — 2. Evaluation & Testing — 3. Dissemination and Labelling and Packaging
Heathers #0872	Educ. 1966	1. Task Analysis (Basic Research) — 2. Development of a design — 3. Construct & Test Prototype Models — 4. Dissemination
Miles #6056	Educ. 1964	1. Design (Research, Development, Invention, Discovery, etc.) — 2. Local Awareness Interest — 3. Local Evaluation — 4. Local Trial (Adoption)
Gallagher #2613	Culture 1964	1. Innovation — New cultural element made available — 2. Dissemination — Innovation is shared — 3. Integration
Myerson & Katz #1720	Fads 1957	1. Discovery of potential fads — 2. Promotion — 3. Labelling — 4. Dissemination — 5. Loss of uniqueness — 6. Death by Displacement

10-40

should point out that the authors consider a process of evaluation to be appropriate to *each* of the activities listed on the chart, and therefore no one stage of evaluation is specified.

a. Research

The first activity which is described by Guba is that of Research, and its objective is "to advance or extend knowledge". It may be evaluated only in terms of its own validity, not in terms of whether or not it leads to invention and change. Its relationship to the change process is that "it *may* provide a basis for innovation if anyone else chooses to capitalize on the research and is clever enough to develop an application from it". (p. 7)

b. Development

The second major activity, Development, is divided into two sub-activities, Invention and Design. The objective of invention is "to formulate a new solution to an operating problem or to a class of operating problems, i.e., to innovate." (p. 8) This may be based "on research, experience, or even on intuition" (p. 9), and it should be evaluated in terms of its face validity (appropriateness), its estimated viability (ability to survive under normal conditions), and its impact (potential significance). The significance of invention in the change process is that it "produces the innovation in its initial conceptualized form". (p. 9)

The objective of design is "to order and to systematize the components of the invented solution into an innovation package suitable for institutional use, i.e., to engineer". (p. 9) The results of this activity are to be evaluated in terms of the institutional feasibility, the generalizability and the performance of the invention.

Guba stresses the significance of the combined developmental activities in the process of change, and he states that "it is this activity, and not research, which is at the heart of change, for while research may make change possible, it is development that actually produces an innovation that may be adopted". (p. 12)

c. Diffusion

Diffusion, the third major phase of the change continuum, is also divided into two sub-activities, Dissemination and Demonstration. The purpose of dissemination is to "create widespread awareness of the invention among practitioners, e.g., to inform" (p. 8) The criteria which are to be used in evaluating dissemination activities include the intelligibility, fidelity, pervasiveness and impact of the message.

The objective of demonstration is to "afford an opportunity to examine and assess operating qualities of the invention, i.e., to build conviction" (p. 8). The demonstration is to be evaluated in terms of its credibility, its convenience (its accessibility to practitioners), and its evidential assessment (whether or not it illustrates all factors of the invention, both positive and negative, so that observers may make a valid decision as to its utility). (p. 13).

Guba (#6227) has also suggested some additional diffusion activities which involve the diffuser more directly in the affairs of the practitioner-user. These are (1) Helping the practitioner by acting in capacities such as consultant or trouble-shooter, (2) Involving the practitioner in the processes of problem identification, development, testing and packaging of the innovation, and diffusing it to others, (3) Training the practitioner in the use of the innovation, and (4) Intervening in the client system, to the extent of mandating certain actions.

d. Adoption

The final major stage in the change process as conceptualized by Clark & Guba is "adoption"; the objective at this stage is the incorporation of the invention into a functioning system. Three sub-activities take place during the adoption stage, those of Trial, Installation, and Institutionalization.

The objectives of the trial stage are "to build familiarity with the invention and provide a basis for assessing the quality, value, fit, and utility of the invention in a particular institution, i.e., to test" (p. 8). The invention may be evaluated at the trial stage in terms of its adaptability, its operational feasibility and its performance, in the local situation.

If the trial is successful, the next step in the adoption sequence is installation, the purpose of which is "to fit the characteristics of the invention to the characteristics of the adopting institution, i.e., to operationalize." (p. 8). The criteria for evaluating successful installation of the invention are in terms of its effectiveness and efficiency.

To complete the adoption process, the invention must, finally, become institutionalized. It must be assimilated as an integral and accepted component of the system, i.e., it must become established. The success of institutionalization should be evaluated in terms of continuity, the degree to which the invention is valued, and the support given to it by the local setting. The establishment of the invention in the institution converts it to a "non-invention", and the change process has then been completed.

Guba (#7131) points out that the theory-to-practice change continuum described above was designed to bridge an existing gap between research and practice. He feels that in the past the typical change process has been carried out with insufficient coordination and planning and that in the future, more concern should be devoted to planning and carrying out change programs in an orderly fashion. Nevertheless, he does not expect that in real life every activity described above will be or should be performed, nor that they should necessarily be carried out in the order given. The possibility of skipping the research stage in many cases has already been mentioned. The possibility of breakdown in the process at any stage is also recognized, and in these cases it would be necessary to loop back to a preceding stage to rectify the problem.

Guba and Clark have proposed, then, a schema for planning the process of change in an orderly way and for defining the activities which may take place at each stage of the change process. In this way the roles and functions of individuals and institutions

taking part in the process may be planned to provide continuity
and to prevent gaps or overlapping of activities.

2. Theoretical Models of the R,D&D School

Just as we speculated that the S-I theorists generally assumed
some sort of diffusion activity to be taking place but chose to focus on
adoption activity, we may assume here that the R,D&D theorists are
aware of activities in all of the four major stages of the R,D&D process,
whether or not they specify them. The roles and activities which an
author does stress are presumably a reflection of the realities of his
area of work and his goals in that work. Our next concern, then, will
be to relate the models proposed by the various authors to the field in
which they were developed and to the purpose which they are expected to
serve.

a. The R,D&D Model of Hopkins and Clark

The R,D&D continuum of Hopkins and Clark (#3586) was developed
in connection with a project which had the goal of estimating the
supply and demand for research, development, and diffusion personnel
in the field of education, and the continuum, as shown in Figure
10.13, represents an attempt to plan for the most rational allocation
of such personnel on a national scale. Recent legislation (the
Elementary and Secondary Education Act of 1965 is cited) which
provides funding for research and development in education necessitated a nationally planned R&D effort with communication and
coordination among many institutions at many levels.

The authors are, then, particularly concerned with defining
the functions of individuals involved in these activities and with relating these functions to the institutional settings in which the
individuals perform. Since the authors are defining *functions* in
the R&D continuum rather than roles, we find that it is quite possible that a given individual may be able to perform more than one
task:

"many persons perform functions at two, three or more points
along the continuum. As the task upon which they are
working proceeds from one phase to another staff members
are likely to proceed with it -- for a while. It would
be the rare individual, however, who could competertly perform all of the functions along the entire continuum." (p. 3,
#3067)

The models of Hopkins & Clark and of Guba & Clark agree closely
on the activities which are to be carried out during the development
and diffusion phases. We find, however, that, because of the nature
of the Hopkins & Clark study, the authors define a greater number
of research functions than do Guba & Clark. A more significant
difference between the two models is that Hopkins & Clark do not
take into account the activities of the receiver. This again is
due to the nature of the project which produced the continuum,
since the adopting groups were purposefully not considered in the
estimates of personnel requirements.

b. Industrial Utilization System of Havelock and Benne

Whereas theoretical R&D models were devised by Guba & Clark
and by Hopkins & Clark to guide a system which is loosely structured

10-43

FIGURE 10.13   (From Clark & Hopkins, 1966, #3586)

A LOGICAL STRUCTURE FOR VIEWING
RESEARCH, DEVELOPMENT, DIFFUSION AND ADOPTION
ROLES IN EDUCATION

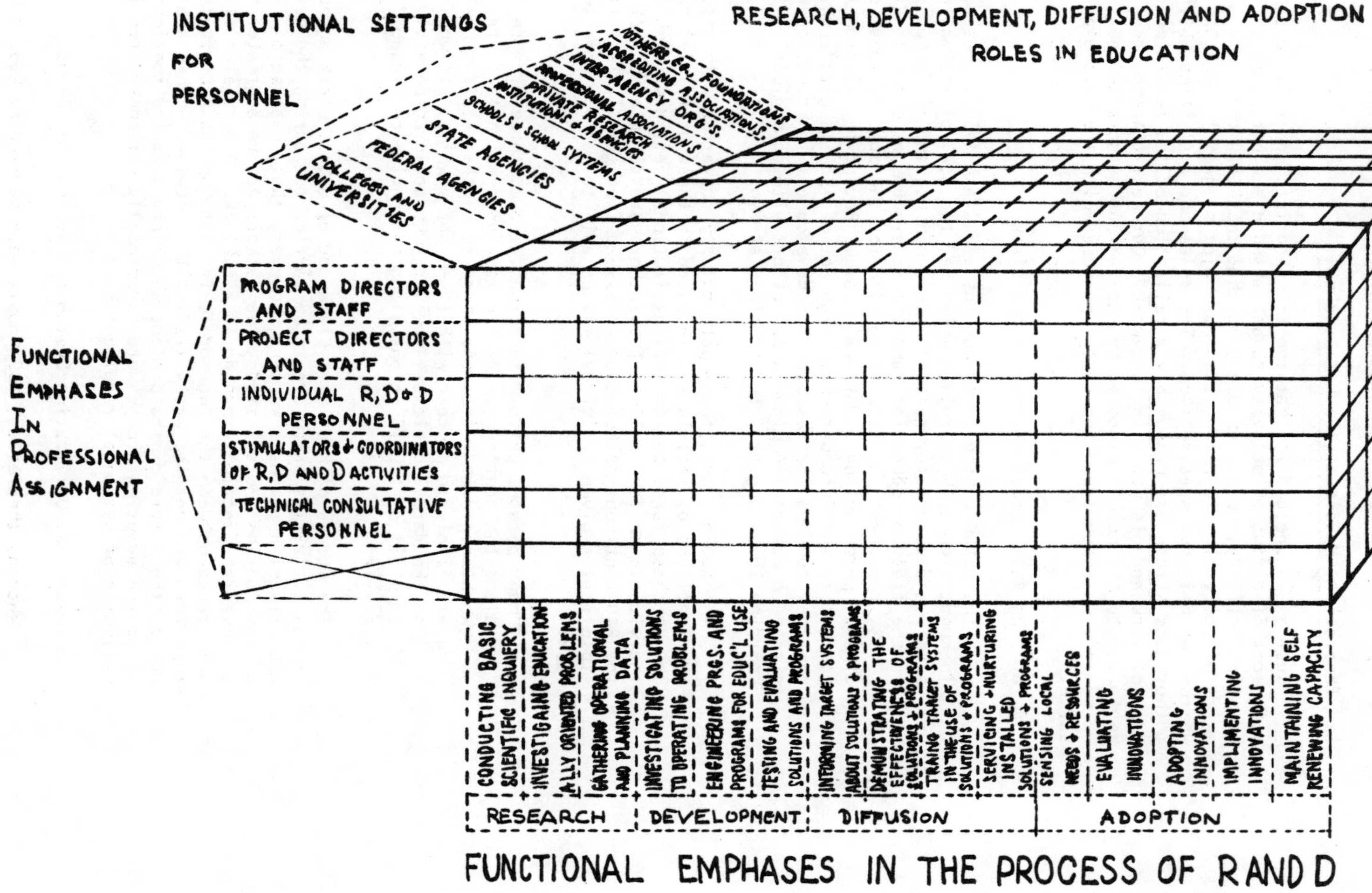

INSTITUTIONAL SETTINGS
FOR
PERSONNEL

OTHER ED. FOUNDATIONS
ACCREDITING ASSOCIATIONS
INTER-AGENCY ORG'S.
PROFESSIONAL ASSOCIATIONS
PRIVATE RESEARCH
INSTITUTIONS & AGENCIES
SCHOOLS & SCHOOL SYSTEMS
STATE AGENCIES
FEDERAL AGENCIES
COLLEGES AND
UNIVERSITIES

PROGRAM DIRECTORS
AND STAFF
PROJECT DIRECTORS
AND STAFF
INDIVIDUAL R, D & D
PERSONNEL
STIMULATORS & COORDINATORS
OF R, D AND D ACTIVITIES
TECHNICAL CONSULTATIVE
PERSONNEL

FUNCTIONAL
EMPHASES
IN
PROFESSIONAL
ASSIGNMENT

RESEARCH

CONDUCTING BASIC
SCIENTIFIC INQUIRY
INVESTIGATING EDUCATION-
ALLY ORIENTED PROBLEMS
GATHERING OPERATIONAL
AND PLANNING DATA

DEVELOPMENT

INVESTIGATING SOLUTIONS
TO OPERATING PROBLEMS
ENGINEERING PRGS. AND
PROGRAMS FOR EDUC'L USE
TESTING AND EVALUATING
SOLUTIONS AND PROGRAMS

DIFFUSION

INFORMING TARGET SYSTEMS
ABOUT SOLUTIONS & PROGRAMS
DEMONSTRATING THE
EFFECTIVENESS OF
SOLUTIONS & PROGRAMS
TRAINING TARGET SYSTEMS
IN THE USE OF
SOLUTIONS & PROGRAMS
SERVICING & NURTURING
INSTALLED
SOLUTIONS & PROGRAMS

ADOPTION

SENSING LOCAL
NEEDS & RESOURCES
EVALUATING
INNOVATIONS
ADOPTING
INNOVATIONS
IMPLEMENTING
INNOVATIONS
MAINTAINING SELF
RENEWING CAPACITY

FUNCTIONAL EMPHASES IN THE PROCESS OF R AND D

and has often worked without coordination among its various parts, Havelock and Benne (#3872) have described the utilization process, shown briefly in Table 10.3, which is actually carried out by a highly organized corporation.* The system which they depict is American Telephone and Telegraph Company, which "contains within it a formal utilization scheme made up of several well-defined roles and subsystems" (p. 129).

The roles which are described are those of Basic Researcher, Developer/Applied Researcher, Linkage Agent, Practitioner, and Consumer. Subsystems of A.T.& T. include (1) Bell Labs, where basic research, applied research, and development and design are performed, (2) Western Electric Company, where engineering for manufacturing, manufacturing, and distribution and installation are carried out, and (3) Telephone Companies, which service the consumers.

We indicated earlier that whereas in our education models basic research is likely to represent a storehouse of information upon which developers may draw, it is looked upon in the A.T.& T. model as an essential and integral part of the utilization process. This is made possible by the "systems engineer", who performs a linkage role in this system:

"Systems engineers are especially adept at deriving implications from basic research while leaving the basic researchers to pursue purely scientific interests without fear of company constraint." (p. 130).

Not only does the systems engineer link basic research to applied research and development with Bell Labs, but "he also links Bell Labs with other subdivisions of A.T.& T., and, most importantly, he provides a feedback link from each subdivision to every other subdivision." (p. 131)

This arrangement has worked extremely effectively for A.T.& T., and Havelock & Benne suggest it as a sophisticated model which other organizations (whether industrial or not) might well use as a guide in developing their own R&D systems. Where this model ceases to be useful to others is as its phase of "distribution and installation". Since the "practitioners" in this system (the telephone companies) are a subsidiary of Bell Labs, the usual persuasive techniques of diffusion are not called for. The mechanism by which the innovation reaches the ultimate consumers is not considered in this model.

c. Brickell's Three Phases of Instructional Innovation

The three phases which Brickell (#0845) suggests (see Table 10.3) are based on the results of a study of instructional innovations in the New York State school system. The innovations all required a rearrangement of the structural elements of the schools, rather than requiring only a simple change in classroom practice. Brickell concluded that "the *design, evaluation,* and *dissemination*

---

*Havelock and Benne cite this model as only one of several ways in which a knowledge utilization system could be organized. It is embedded in a much broader theoretical analysis of the problem of utilization.

of innovations are three distinctly different, irreconcilable processes." (p. 497) He found that each process requires a distinct set of circumstances; his unique contribution is in describing the ideal conditions for working in each of his three phases.

Brickell's first phase, program *Design*, is defined as "the translation of what is known about learning into programs for teaching". He describes the ideal circumstances for the design phase as artificially created, enriched, and free.

"At their best, they provide a group of highly intelligent people, a somewhat limited problem, time to concentrate on a solution, ample money and resources, freedom to try almost anything, the likelihood that the solution will be used somewhere, and the prospect of personal recognition if the problem is solved." (p. 498)

Brickell describes a number of instructional innovations which would not exist "if a group of talented men had not been paid and freed to concentrate specifically on developing them."

Brickell (#0875) considers that it is the obligation of the designer (or developer) to make a "deliberate search" of basic research knowledge for information which is relevant to the product under development. Though the initiative in bringing such information to the attention of developers may be taken by the basic researcher in some instances, this is unusual and should not be expected.

It is also desirable for developers to obtain the cooperation of local schools in formulating the problem to be solved and in checking the feasibility of the proposed solutions.

Phase Two, *Evaluation*, is defined by Brickell as "...the systematic testing of a new instructional approach to find what it will accomplish under what conditions". Ideal circumstances are "controlled, closely observed, and unfree".

"At their best, they provide conditions in which the forces which might influence the success of the new approach can be controlled when possible, and kept under close surveillance when actual control is impossible. The freedom which is essential in searching for a good design is destructive in the making of a good evaluation." (p. 498)

Cooperation of the local schools is also necessary at this phase, when the innovation is tried out under controlled conditions. However, though comments of the teachers may be helpful, Brickell (#0875) feels that the activities involved in evaluating an innovation are too technical for the local schools to be able to make an evaluative decision for themselves. He also points out that the field and laboratory tests of the evaluation stage should not be carried out by any persons involved in the design phase of the innovation.

Brickell's Phase Three is *Dissemination*, "...the process of spreading innovations into schools". Circumstances for this phase should be "ordinary, unenriched, and normal".

"At their best, they are exactly like the everyday
situations in the observer's own school and community.
Anything which the observer could label 'abnormal' or
'unrealistic' -- such as the enriched conditions
necessary for good design or the controlled conditions
necessary for proper evaluation is sufficient to rob
the observed program of persuasive effect." (p. 499)

Brickell (#0875) stresses that for authentic adoption to take
place, multiple dissemination activities are essential. These
activities include creating awareness of an innovation, arousing
interest in it, demonstrating it, making equipment and materials
available, and providing training and continuing support.

Brickell also takes roles into consideration, when he points
out that the various phases will have differing appeal for differing people, and that the circumstances which are ideal for a phase
may not be comfortable as a working situation for all individuals;
this provides one reason for the emergence of specialist roles within the Development-Dissemination process.

Some selected local schools may be involved in the testing of
new innovations, but Brickell (#0875) has also discussed in detail
the role which he feels all local school systems should play in the
process of change. He emphasizes that it is up to them to set their
own goals, working with the school board and the local community.
An instructional program must then be chosen which is expected to
produce the desired results. Brickell feels that it is not possible for the local school system to attempt to design and develop
its own programs. It does not have the large amounts of time,
talent and money which are necessary to create high quality instructional programs, nor does it have the capacity to try out the programs under the conditions outlined above during its development
and evaluation phases. The role of the school system, then, is to
search for programs which have been developed by outside resources
and to study with extreme care the reports on field experiments.
Ideally, Brickell feels there should be a means for local school
systems to inform designers and developers of their needs, and feedback should be provided to the designers and developers to make sure
that the needs have been met.

d. Heathers' Strategy for Innovation in Elementary Education

Heathers (#0872) is primarily concerned with strategies for
influencing change in elementary schools, but he feels that any
innovation which is intended to serve a practical purpose, whether
it is in the field of education or not, should pass through the
same phases. As Table 10.3 shows, he outlines these phases as (1)
Task analysis, (2) Development of a design, (3) Construction and
testing of prototype models in field situations or in the laboratory, and (4) Dissemination. The activities which he describes as
taking place in phases 2, 3, and 4 are very similar to those proposed by Brickell (#0875).

A major difference between the models proposed by Heathers and
by Brickell concerns the initial activity of analyzing the problems to be solved. Brickell, as we stated, is concerned that goals
should be set by local school systems and that some means should
be found for informing R&D personnel of the needs at the local level.
Heathers, on the other hand, specifies that "Task Analysis"

should be the first stage in the process of *developing* an innovation. At this phase the purpose which the innovation will serve and the requirements for achieving these purposes are specified.

Though there appears to be some difference in the conceptualizations of these two theorists, we may speculate that both Heathers and Brickell would agree that some form of task analysis and goal specification must take place both within the local school system and within the system which develops the innovation. Alexander (#0842) discusses the multi-level aspect of goal-setting in connection with describing a model of curriculum change. The first stage which he describes is "Identification of curriculum needs", and he states that this "is a step that needs to be taken at all levels of curriculum development: the classroom, the school, the school system, and the state and even the nation." (p. 356)

e. The Change Strategy of Miles

Miles (#6056) has made a study of the strategies which have been used to introduce change into educational systems, and he has observed that the change process may be initiated either by the target system itself or by systems in the environment of the target system, using either existing structures or new structures. He points out that in different situations change efforts may be focussed on only one or two of the four stages which he describes as comprising the change process which leads to adoption by the target system. He feels, however, that all comprehensive strategies include the chronological stages, shown in Table 10.3, of (1) Design of Innovation, (2) Local Awareness-Interest, (3) Local Evaluation, and (4) Local trial.

The stage of design is not broken down into specific steps, nor is it divided into phases of research and development, though Miles indicates that these may take place. He writes that at the design stage "the innovation is invented, discovered, made up out of whole cloth, produced by research and development operations, etc." (p. 19)

Since Miles views the objective of any strategy as the adoption of an innovation by the target system, he focuses his attention on the activities of the receiver during the final phases of change, rather than on the activities of the sender. Miles draws on Rogers (#1824) in his conceptualization of the stages following design, with only minor variations. Miles combines awareness and interest into one stage during which "the potential consumers...come to be aware of the existence of the designed innovation, become interested in it, and seek information about its characteristics" (p. 19). Miles defines the stages of evaluation and trial as Rogers does, with evaluation representing a kind of mental trial of the innovation on the part of the consumer. Miles omits the stage which Rogers calls "adoption", because his concern here is with change *strategies,* and he feels that a strategy ends at the point when adoption occurs.

Although the stages following design are described by Miles in terms of receiver activity, he would have us keep in mind that, particularly when a strategy is initiated by a system outside the target system, it is the <u>sender</u> who is active in bringing about adoption. The sender must create awareness, arouse interest, provide information, enable evaluation to take place, and encourage or require the target system to make a trial of an innovation

f. The Cultural Change Cycle of Gallaher

     Gallaher (#2613) provides an anthropological view of the process
by which a new cultural element is learned by the members of a group
and shared with other groups. The phases, shown in Table 10.3, which
he describes in the cultural change cycle are (1) Innovation, the
process by which a new element of culture is made available to a
group, (2) Dissemination, the process whereby an innovation comes to
be shared, and (3) Integration, the process whereby an innovation becomes mutually adjusted to other elements in the system.

     His model suggests two roles, those of the Innovator (the indi-
vidual or agency responsible for the conception of an innovation),
and the Advocate (who sponsors an innovation for the express purpose
of gaining its acceptance by others). The receiver is described in
terms of a target for these roles.

     The emphasis of this model is not on careful design and eval-
uation of an innovation, nor on the activities of the receiver;
rather, it is on the part played by the Advocate, who interferes
actively and purposefully with the culture of a potential acceptor
or target system. Gallaher's pragmatic Advocate model of acceptance
is concerned mainly with creating a climate conducive to acceptance.
It assumes that people will more readily accept innovations which they
perceive as relevant, can understand readily, and for which they
shared in the planning.

g. Myerson and Katz: the Natural History of Fads

     Finally, mention should be made of a study which at first
glance does not seem to belong in the category of R,D&D model
studies. This is Meyerson & Katz's study (#1720) of the diffusion
of fads or fashions. They describe fads as being a particular type
of social change, and they state that each of the chronological
stages (see Table 10.3) in the history of a fad is characterized by
the interaction among producers, distributors and consumers. This
study is applicable to the area of design for marketing; it is interesting in that it makes explicit a phase which is usually considered only in very long-range descriptions of change, that of
"death-by-displacement". We may assume that this is, in fact, the
final phase for all the change processes included in our three perspectives.

3. A Comparison of the Conceptualizations of Theorists of the R,D&D
School

     We pointed out earlier that there are four stages which in general
are included in the R,D&D process. However, as we again look at Table
10-3, we can see that the models for all authors can be divided into only
two major stages, (1) Research and Development activity, and (2) Diffusion
and Adoption activity. This point is illustrated by Table 10.4, which
lists only the major phases described by each author.

[Insert Table 10.4 here]

Therefore, as we make a general comparison among the various models,
we will present our discussion in terms of these two categories.

TABLE 10.4   Principle Phases of Research, Development, and Diffusion Models

Model			
Guba & Clark #7131	Research	Development	Diffusion / Adoption
Hopkins & Clark #3586	Research	Development	Diffusion
Havelock & Benne #3872	Basic Research / Applied Research	Development / Engineering	Distribution & Installation
Brickell #0845	Design	Evaluation	Dissemination
Heathers #0872	Task Analysis / Development / Testing		Dissemination
Miles #6056	Design		Adoption
Callaher #2613	Innovation	Dissemination	Integration
Myerson & Katz #1720	Discovery	Dissemination	

10-50

a.   Research and Development

Within the first category of Table 10.4 we have found that there
is often no clear distinction made between research and development,
and, when there is, research is often considered not as the first
logical stage in the change process, but, rather, as a resource upon
which developers may draw if they so desire. This is clearly stated
by Brickell (#0875) and is suggested as a possibility by Guba & Clark
(#7131) and by Miles (#6056).

Havelock & Benne (#3872), on the other hand, very clearly outline a process in A.T.&T. in which the findings of basic researchers
are drawn on in a systematic way by applied researchers. In this
case basic research is assumed to be the essential first stage in
the change process, and the role of the "systems engineer", which
enables knowledge to flow smoothly from basic to applied researchers,
is the key to orderly change.

It is of interest to note here that the Havelock-Benne model is
the only one which specifies a phase of applied research activity,
and it seems to be true that in A.T.&T. the division of labor into
tasks of basic research, applied research, and development is effective. In other areas, such as education, this division may be less
clear, and Guba (#6227) purposely avoids use of the term "applied research" in order to prevent confusion and to clarify the distinction
between "research" and "development". He writes:

> "...we are often tempted to describe what I have here
> called 'research' as 'basic research,' and what I
> have called 'development' as 'applied research'. This
> formulation gives the impression that research and
> development are simply different ends of the same
> continuum;... But to commit this error is to ignore
> the fact that research and development have entirely
> different objectives". (p. 46)

We have, then, a wide variation within the R,D&D school in the
extent to which roles and activities involved in the research and
development process are specified. The industrial model includes
the most detailed and orderly system; the educational models suggest
some combination of research and development, but for fads (Myerson &
Katz, #1720) and for cultural change (Gallaher, #2613), no details are
specified for the process by which innovations are discovered or are
made available.

It should also be noted that the word "design" is used by different authors in different ways. Miles (#6056), for example, uses
it to include all research and development activities, whereas most
authors use it as Guba & Clark (#7131) do, to represent one stage
within the development phase.

We should note that several authors are particularly concerned
that a stage of evaluation and testing of an invention should occur
between development and diffusion, and such activities are listed as
a separate stage by Brickell (#0875) and by Heathers (#0872).* At this

---

*We have listed this in Tables 10.3 and 10.4 as a part of the general
activity of development of an innovation; our charts have been arranged
to facilitate comparison of the models of different authors, but we
feel that they do distort the relative importance which some authors
attach to the various stages, and, in particular, they minimize the significance of an evaluation stage.

stage the cooperation of a member of the target group is often sought, in order that an innovation may be tried out in "the field" under controlled conditions.

Heathers (#0872) specifies "Task Analysis" as a separate stage, and a similar process is suggested by Brickell (#0875), although he does not list it as a distinct phase. We have included this activity under "development", since it implies the analysis of a particular problem for which a solution is to be found. On the other hand, the activities which Clark & Hopkins (#3586) describe as "investigation of problems" and "gathering operational and planning data" may more properly be left in the research category where they place it. These activities, though perhaps not what we commonly think of as pure basic research, are nevertheless directed towards providing a storehouse of information on which developers may draw, rather than being directed specifically towards solving a particular problem.

b. Diffusion and Adoption

Within the second major stage, diffusion and adoption, we find that most authors specifically indicate diffusion (or dissemination) as an activity which must be planned in the change process. There is some difference in the way in which various authors use the word "dissemination"; whereas Guba & Clark use it as a sub-activity of diffusion, others (Brickell, #0845; Gallaher, #2613; Heathers, #0872) use it to include the whole range of activities which Guba & Clark list under diffusion. Havelock & Benne (#3872) describe this process as "distribution", because of the nature of the A.T.&T. organization, which they describe.

Whether the stage is described as diffusion, dissemination, or distribution, it is clear that the focus for most of the authors listed in Table 10.3 is on *sender* activities rather than on *receiver* activities. Among those who refer *only* to sender activities are Clark & Hopkins (#3586), Brickell (#0845), Meyerson & Katz (#1720), Heathers (#0872), and Havelock & Benne (#3872). Gallaher (#2613) is concerned with the sender through most of the process of adoption and diffusion, but he regards the final stage to be "integration" of the innovation into the target system, and this, of course, must be accomplished by the receiver himself. Guba & Clark (#7131), we will realize from our previous discussion, strike a balance in considering the activities of both sender and receiver.

The only author we have included in the R,D&D school who does not identify phases of sender activity is Miles (#6056). He discusses a variety of change strategies which may be employed, involving senders and receivers to varying degrees; but even when the sender is very active, Miles concentrates on the receiver because "any given strategy is thought of here as being ultimately aimed at getting an innovation installed in a 'target system' ". (p. 19)

Brickell (#0875) draws attention to the fact that either sender activity (dissemination) or receiver activity (adoption) may be described as the last phase of the change process, depending on the point of reference, and he describes dissemination as being the "obverse" of adoption. We may recall at this point our discussion earlier in this chapter of the relationship between sender and receiver activities, and we may refer again to Figure 10.8, which depicts the activity curve of a change agent as it relates to the curve of diffusion of an innovation over a period of time.

It is clear that the activities of the sender and receiver must be coordinated, and Brickell (#0875) states that almost every step which the adopting system takes "must be matched by an outside enabling activity". (p.89) We may gain some idea of how the actions of sender and receiver may be related by observing in Table 10.3 the activities which the various authors feel should be taking place during the phases of adoption and diffusion. In Table 10.5 we have listed these activities in a manner to suggest the inter-relatedness of sender and receiver actions.

[Insert Table 10.5 here]

4. General Remarks About the R,D&D Perspective

The major emphasis of all theorists in the R,D&D school is on the planning of change on a large scale. This involves detailed development, based on scientific knowledge, and rigorous testing and evaluation to produce an innovation which most adequately solves a particular problem. It also involves mechanisms for distributing the innovation and installing it in target systems. The planning of change is conceptualized in terms of a theoretical framework which describes the change process as a continuum of activities from research to practice, and a rational division of labor is specified for carrying out these activities.

Although there is general agreement among the authors that this theoretical plan should not necessarily be rigidly adhered to, and that different activities will be bound to assume paramount importance in different change situations, there also seems to be a consensus that in actual change situations the framework is not followed closely enough. Guba (#6227) observes that the two ends of the continuum which he describes are too often neglected in the field of education, with research results not being utilized, and with almost no attention being paid to the problems of adoption. Miles (#1481) finds that the stage of Evaluation tends to be neglected, and he goes so far as to say that, "Educational innovations are almost never evaluated on a systematic basis". Reasons for this neglect, which he has identified in a review of a number of studies, include the fact that there are few clear criteria for educational effectiveness, that adequate evaluation is expensive in time and money, and that the conditions which permit adequate evaluation are seldom found in educational settings. It is largely because of the fact that such critical activities as evaluation have often been omitted from change processes in the past that the theorists in the R,D&D school have developed detailed models of change to serve as guides for future programs of change.

C. THE PROBLEM-SOLVER PERSPECTIVE

Included in this school are those authors who portray the change process as one which is directed toward solving the problems of a specific receiver, and in which the receiver himself is involved throughout. Though the receiver may be able to create or find suitable solutions to his problem by himself, this school is primarily concerned with those cases in which the assistance of outside resources is utilized; these resources are likely to be individuals or groups which can generally be referred to as "change agents". The change process may be initiated either by the receiver or by the change agent, but in

10-53

TABLE 10.5   Relationship of Sender and Receiver Activities

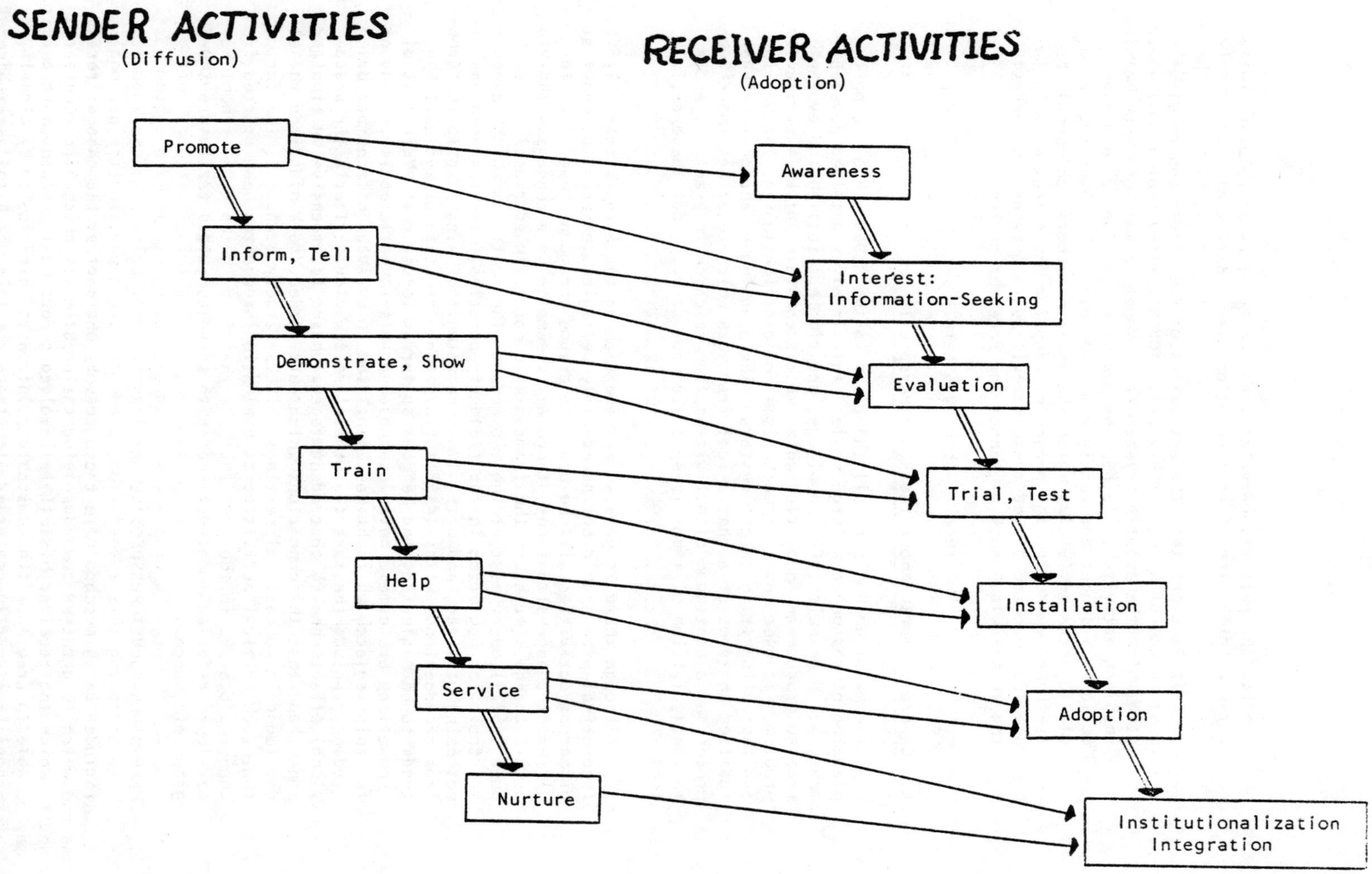

RECEIVER ACTIVITIES
(Adoption)

Awareness

Interest: Information-Seeking

Evaluation

Trial, Test

Installation

Adoption

Institutionalization Integration

SENDER ACTIVITIES
(Diffusion)

Promote

Inform, Tell

Demonstrate, Show

Train

Help

Service

Nurture

either case the receiver must desire to change and must participate fully in bringing the change about. The relationship between sender and receiver is one of collaboration, and whereas in the S-I and the R,D&D models the receiver was referred to as the "target system", it is here called the "client system". The client system may range in size from an individual person to an entire nation, and most of the models which we will discuss seem to be equally applicable for systems of any size.

Table 10.6 outlines the strategies of change which are proposed by a number of authors who consider change to be a problem-solving process. Many of these draw upon the early work of Lewin (#1342), referring either to the three major stages which he described, of *Unfreezing, Moving,* and *Freezing,* or to his concept of analyzing the force field of the client system. Table 10.6 shows, however, that most authors consider it helpful to specify the types of activities which take place during each of Lewin's three stages, and if they employ a force field analysis, it is used as only one part of the strategy of planning for change.

We will therefore consider as "typical" the model of planned change which is described by Lippitt, Watson, & Westley (#1343), since this employs the three stages of Lewin as a starting point but expands upon them considerably. After looking at this model in detail, we will take a look at each of the other models listed in Table 10.6 in turn, to point out their unique characteristics and contributions, and we will then make a general comparison of all the Problem-Solver models of change.

1. Lippitt, Watson, & Westley: The Phases of Planned Change

The phases of change which Lippitt, Watson, & Westley (#1343) describe emerged as a result of their comparative analysis of change effort case materials from a wide variety of fields. These involved many types of professional change agents, some of whom worked with individual clients, some with group systems, and others with communities.

Table 10.6 lists the seven phases of Lippitt et al. and shows how these phases are related to the three stages of Lewin. The importance of the relationship of the change agent to the client system in the cases which they studied led the authors to include in their list of phases the establishment of the change relationship (phase 2), and its termination (phase 7); the other phases which they describe are based upon Lewin's three stages. We will note, however, that Lewin's stage of "moving" has been expanded into three phases (3, 4 and 5) by Lippitt et al. and these three phases together are termed "working toward change."

Phase 1. The Development of a Need for Change

In order that a process of planned change may begin, the authors specify three things which must happen during this first, or "unfreezing", phase. First, the problems which are creating stress in a system must be translated into "problem awareness". Difficulties may be encountered in achieving this translation, since different parts of the personality, or different members of a group, may be aware of problems to differing degrees, and there may be communication barriers which block the spread of awareness. Second, problem awareness must be translated into a desire for change. This can come about only when there is "confidence in the possibility of a more desirable state of affairs". Finally, problem awareness and a desire for change must lead to a specific desire for help from outside the system. For this to happen, outside help must be perceived as both relevant and available.

TABLE 10.6

Problem-Solver Change Models

Author, Biblio.#	Field, Year	1. Unfreezing	2. Moving	3. Freezing
Lewin #1342	Social Change	1. Unfreezing	2. Moving	3. Freezing
Lippitt, Watson & Westley #1343	Social Change 1958	1. Develop a need for Change	2. Establish Change Relationship; 3. Diagnosis of client problems; 4. Examine Alternative Routes & Goals; Establish Goals & Intentions of Action; 5. Transform Intentions into Change Efforts	6. Generalization & Stabilization; 7. Terminate Change Relationship
Mann & Williams #5227	Industry 1960	1. Equilibrium before change	2. Preliminary Planning; 3. Detailed Preparation; 4. Installation and Testing; 5. Conversion	6. Stabilization; 7. Equilibrium after change
Thelen #3692	Educ. 1967	1. Decide on Variables	3c. Set up change; 2. Construct Force Field Analysis; 3a. Decide what needs to be done; 3b. Decide on first action target; agent communications; 4. Make first action explicit; 5a. Consider conditions; 5b. Define roles; 5c. Act; 6. Revise Force Field Decide on next target --repeat cycle	
Watson #6364	Social Change 1966	1. Felt Dissatisfaction	2. Diagnosis; 3. Consider whole system; 4. Creative Design; 5. Force Field Analysis; 6. Reduce Resistance; 7. Participation; 8. Temporary System; 9. Leaders and Consultants; 10. Adaptation Evaluation Revision	11. Spread of new ideas to others
Mackenzie #1194	Educ. 1964	1. Criticism	2. Proposals for Change; 3. Development & Clarification of proposals; 4. Evaluate, review, reformulate proposals; 5. Comparison of proposals; 6. Action on Proposals; 7. Implementation of Decision	
Miles & Lake #3871	Educ. 1967	1. Clarify Expectations about Program; 2. Collect Information	3. Formulate Goals; 4a. Problem Sensing; 4b. Diagnosing; c. Set change target & Objectives; d. Locate & invent solutions; e. Weigh cost and gain; f. Decide on alternative; g. Plan to Implement; 5. Carry out Plans	6. Institutionalize; 7. Phase out COPED; 8. Assess; 9. Feedback; 10. Disseminate
Watson #6195	Educ. 1967	1. Sensing	2. Screening; 3. Diagnosis and Force Field Analysis; 4. Inventing; 5. Weighing; 6. Deciding; 7. Introduce; 8. Operate; 9. Evaluate; 10. Revise	
Jung & Lippitt #3922	Educ. 1967	1. Identification of the concern	2. Diagnosis; Retrieve Knowledge & Derive Implications; 3. Formulation of objectives; 4. Feasibility Testing of Action Alternatives; Training; Evaluation; 5a. Adoption	5b. Diffusion
Jacobs #1781	Educ. 1964	1. Formulate objectives	2. Determination of Feasible Structures & Programs; 3. Establish priorities, Determine Procedures for implementing; plan time phasing; 4. Implementation; 5. Evaluation, Refinement Revision	

This unfreezing, or development of a need for change, may occur in one of three ways: (1) a change agent locates a source of difficulty, and offers help; (2) a third party brings the client and the change agent together, or (3) the client system itself seeks help from an outside source. The authors found the third possibility to be the most common way for the change process to begin.

Phase 2. The Establishment of a Change Relationship.

The problems which may be encountered during the phase of establishing a change relationship are numerous, as we may recall from our exploration of this issue in Chapter 7. Lippitt et al. discuss the difficulties involved in communicating needs, the significance of first impressions, and the importance of building trust and understanding between the change agent and the client system. They also point out that it is often advisable for the two systems to agree to a trial period of collaboration to ensure that the relationship will be mutually satisfactory.

The authors have found that this phase is one of the crucial parts of the change process, and they state that:

"The success or failure of almost any change project depends heavily upon the quality and the workability of the relationship between the change agent and the client system." (pp. 135, 136)

Phase 3. The Clarification or Diagnosis of the Client System's Problems.

In order for the problem to be diagnosed (and the first phase of "moving" to commence), the change agent must first be able to obtain information; the authors state that this may be a simple matter, or it may be a very lengthy and trying one. It is after the data have been collected, however, that the significant problems in diagnosis are encountered. As the data is analyzed, the client is likely to be faced with a problem which changes and broadens in scope; what he originally perceived to be a relatively simple problem may come to seem almost overwhelming.

Further problems may be encountered as the change agent attempts to offer interpretations of the client's problem. The client may become hostile and may reject the agent's diagnosis. The authors suggest that the client must strike a balance between two extremes of inaction:

"the inability to do anything because of a helpless dependency and defeatism in the face of unexpectedly acute problems, and refusal to do anything because of a hostile rejection of all diagnostic interpretations". (p. 137)

Phase 4. The Examination of Alternative Routes and Goals; Establishing Goals and Intentions of Action.

In this second phase of "moving", the diagnostic insights gained in the preceding phase must be translated into ideas for action and then into intentions to carry out the ideas in a certain way. The authors suggest that cognitive problems are likely to arise as the alternative paths are explored, and that motivational problems may occur when it becomes necessary to endorse a plan of action.

One particular motivational problem may be the client's fear of
failure in carrying out a plan of action, and the authors feel that
"often these anxieties can be eased by providing ways for the client to
test innovations before they are permanently adopted." (p. 139)

Phase 5. The Transformation of Intentions Into Actual Change Efforts.

It is during this final phase of "moving" that plans are put into
action, and that innovations are adopted. The authors state that "the
active work of changing is the keystone of the whole change process."
(p. 139) It is at this stage that the success or failure of the change
effort may be determined; in order for the original stresses to be eliminated, plans and intentions must be transformed into achievements.

The authors point out the importance of feedback on the results of
the change effort. They find that without adequate feedback the client
system may abandon the attempted change, even though it may be producing
the desired effect.

Phase 6. The Generalization and Stabilization of Change.

For a change to be considered successful it must "remain a stable
and permanent characteristic of the system", and the phase at which this
stabilization takes place is the stage which Lewin calls "freezing".
Lippitt et al. feel that stabilization will be facilitated if the change
provides adequate rewards to the system and if any procedural change is
supported by structural change. In addition, they point out the significance of generalization:

"One critical factor in the stabilization of change is the
spread or non-spread of change to neighboring systems or to
subparts of the client system." (p.140)

The process of institutionalization of change is likely to occur
almost automatically once the innovation has gained a foothold, because,
the authors found, "many systems possess an inherent momentum which tends
to perpetuate a change once it has attained a certain state of equilibrium".
(p. 141)

Phase 7. Achieving a Terminal Relationship.

Lippitt et al. found, in their analysis of change studies, that
termination of the relationship between the client system and the change
agent occurred at various points in the change process, sometimes as
early as the third phase. They observed, however, that successful change
was most likely to result if the relationship was maintained until the
change had become stabilized. At this point, the greatest problem to be
faced in the terminal phase is the dependency of the client system on
the change agent. This problem can be eased if the agent remains available for consultation or if structures are set up within the client system
to serve as a substitute for the change agent. The client will also be
more able to cope with termination if he has learned techniques of problem
solving which he can apply without the assistance of the change agent.

The seven sequential phases of change which Lippitt, Watson & Westley derived from their case studies were found to be applicable to almost
every case. The authors point out, however, that "in any given case one
is likely to see that the phases overlap and repeat themselves". The

phases are outlined, then, in order that they may be used as a guide in analyzing and in planning for change.

2. Theoretical Models of the Problem-Solver School

We noted in our discussions of models in the S-I and R, D&D schools that the phases which an author chose to include in his model of the change process represented his field of work and the situations for which the change plan was intended. This is equally true for the P-S school, and we will now examine the particular purpose and the special contributions of each of the models listed in Table 10.6.

a. Mann & Williams: Phases in a Change-over Process in Industry

Rather than being strictly a theoretical model, the change process described by Mann & Williams (#5227), and outlined in Table 10.6, is actually a description of a case history of a change-over to electronic data-processing equipment in a light and power company. The pattern which this change followed fits well into the theoretical model proposed by Lippitt et al., with stages of moving and freezing clearly represented. We do not see an unfreezing stage in this particular case, however, because the analysis of the change process was undertaken after the organization had already "developed a need for change." The need for change was felt initially on the part of the top management of the firm, and thus the change process was initiated from within the system even though the system as a whole was in a state of "relative stability and equilibrium" at the time.

Of particular interest in this case study is the fact that a *systems approach* was used (the process of looking at the organization as a whole), rather than a "hardware approach" (the placement of new equipment into an existing structure). The entire structure of the organization was examined and modified appropriately during the change process.

Another interesting observation of this study is that all the phases from preliminary planning (phase 2) through stabilization of the change (phase 6) tended to occur simultaneously. It was also observed that the process of change began slowly and that the greatest level of activity occurred during the phases of installation and testing (phase 4) and conversion (phase 5). We may be reminded here of our earlier discussion of the activity level of a receiver during the adoption process (see again Figures 10.4 and 10.12).

b. Thelen: Stages in a Collaborative Action-Inquiry Process of Change

The plan for change which is outlined by Thelen (#3692) is a theoretical model which was developed with educational systems in mind, but which the author feels is applicable in any field and to a change system of any size, from an individual to a community. The theory is based upon the belief that there are two kinds of relevant inquiry; the first is "the action research within the situation, directed toward continually reformulating the target conditions" and solving problems as they are generated. The second is the "meta-inquiry of the practitioner and the scientist as they correct their ideas about how to go about making the decisions to guide the action research". (p. 45)

Unlike the models of Mann & Williams (#5227) and of Lippitt et al. (#1314), the model which Thelen proposes does not end with stabilization of the client system. Thelen describes the system as being in a state of "quasi-stationary equilibrium" when there has been a "semi-permanent

change in the force field". That is, each new innovation must become a
permanent and integral part of the system if it is to be considered a
genuine change, but the system itself does not remain static. Rather, the
step which follows adoption is the reexamination of the entire force
field to detect new problems. The system engages, then, in a continuous
cycle of generating and solving problems.

Since, ideally, the client system here is adept at locating its
own problems as they arise, the stage at which change agent communications
are set up is described as being at a later time than that which is suggested by Lippitt et al. The change relationship which Thelen advocates
is a "collaborative action-inquiry" between practitioners (the clients)
and researchers (the change agents).

c. Watson: Stages in the Process of Innovation

The process of innovation which Watson (#6364) describes is seen as
being applicable to any social system, "whether it is as small as a family
or as large as a nation". This process contains many features which are
similar to those suggested by Lippitt et al., and it also develops along
the lines of Lewin's three stages. Here the unfreezing process is described as "felt dissatisfaction". After this phase, a temporary system
is set up for the duration of the moving stage. Within this system, participation of all those who are involved in, and affected by, the change
is urged; resources of all members should be utilized, and special emphasis is put on the involvement of leaders and consultants in diagnosing
and planning for change.

Watson, like Mann & Williams (# 5227), advocates a systems approach,
since "changes in any part of a social system have consequences for other
parts". Once the target for change has been isolated, Watson then suggests
the use of Lewin's technique of making a "force field analysis" to aid in
analyzing the dynamics of the change situation. One of the important
features of this analysis, as seen by Watson, is that it may reveal the
forces which represent resistance to change within the system. Watson
stresses that this resistance should be handled by acting to reduce it
rather than by attempting to overcome it by greater pressure. Reduction
of resistance is seen as critical if successful change is to be ensured.

Adequate diagnosis is viewed as being essential, since it is on
the basis of the diagnosis that possible remedies for the situation are
proposed. These remedies are described by Watson in terms of "creative
proposals", which may arise either from inside the client system or from
outside the system. Though a creative idea may be generated to solve the
problem at hand, Watson feels it is more likely that the client system
will become aware of ideas through a process of social interaction with
other members of its group who have encountered similar problems.

In this regard, Watson's model resembles those of the S-I school.
It is not surprising to find, then, that Watson lists, as a final phase in
the change process, the spread of new ideas to others. Watson's description of the mechanisms by which this diffusion occurs is in concurrence
with proposals of theorists of the S-I school.

d. Mackenzie: Phases in the Process of Curricular Change

The phases in curricular change which Mackenzie (#1194) suggests are
based on a study of over thirty cases. The course which these changes took
seems to follow quite closely along the theoretical lines which are sug-

gested by Lippitt et al., except that a relationship with a change agent is not a general condition of the cases which Mackenzie describes.

He observes that change involves participants who may be internal to the system which is being changed or who may be external to it. Phases 1 through 5 of the change process (see Table 10.6) may be initiated either by internal or by external participants, whereas phases 6 and 7 are always initiated by internal participants.

One interesting observation made by Mackenzie, which does not seem to coincide with the findings of Lippitt et al., is that, in general, "external participants...appear to have been the dominant initiators in the relatively recent examples studied". (p. 424) It seems likely that the internal participants in the cases studied by Mackenzie actually did sense a need for change and did have a desire for change, but that they were ineffectual in embarking on a program of change without the aid of the external participants. Mackenzie states that in many cases the need for change in a particular community was "communicated more clearly than was the precise nature of the change desired". (p. 408)

e. Miles & Lake: Strategy for Planning Self-Renewal in School Systems

The change plan which is described by Miles & Lake (#3871) was developed by the New York Region Cooperative Project for Educational Development (COPED). The COPED team which the authors describe acts as a change agent team whose purpose is "to formulate, apply, evaluate, and disseminate some variations of a basic strategy of planned change in collaboration with several school systems". (p. 81) That is, the team does not attempt to install specific innovations in a school, but rather, it helps the school system to understand the change process and to become "self-renewing".

The initial collaboration in this process is between members of the COPED team and members of a "focal group" in the school system, a group which consists of the school superintendent and other high level personnel. An important feature of the plan, however, is that *all* members of the school system who will be affected by the change plan will become involved in the planning of change, by participating in temporary systems, before the change is actually introduced.

Though the change process which is outlined here is initiated by an external source, the intent of the program is to enable the individual school system to recognize its own problems and initiate change processes internally in the future. Thus, "institutionalization" (phase 6) does not in this case refer to a state of complete equilibrium following adoption, but, rather, it refers to the fact that the client system has "set up structures and procedures to institutionalize and support continuing self-renewal processes". (p. 84)

The role of the change agent in this description is a large one, perhaps because the change process is viewed from the point of view of the change agent. Not only is the change plan mapped out in detail before entry into the client system, but in addition, the change agent takes further steps after the change plan has been institutionalized in the client system and the change relationship has been terminated. The change agent assesses the change program, feeds the findings back into the school system, and then disseminates "accounts of the methods and results of the change program to other school systems" and to other supporting groups.

f. Watson: Steps for Problem-Solving in a Self-Renewing School System

Whereas Miles & Lake propose a strategy which will enable a school system to *become* self-renewing, Watson (#6195) proposes ten steps which a school system should follow to *remain* self-renewing. His first very important step, then, is that everyone involved in the school system should engage in a "constant and widespread <u>sensing</u> of the problems and of new possibilities". Watson recognizes that in addition to a general climate of openness which will encourage the bringing out of sensed difficulties, there should also be a structural provision made for "mechanisms for 'keeping up' with internal concerns and external trends and resources" (p. 111). In fact, one of the keys to self-renewal in school systems is seen to be in making structural provisions for carrying out the activities at every stage in the process.

In other respects, this ten-step model for a self-renewing school system resembles the model which Watson (#6364) proposed for social systems in general. He does point out here, however, that procedures may seem "unduly formal and academic" and that short-cuts may often be found:

"The full-scale, ten-step operation can be held in mind as a model, to be used when the innovation is truly momentous; approximations will be sufficient for many lesser problems." (p. 115)

g. Jung & Lippitt: Steps for Utilization of Knowledge for Change in Education

The phases of planned change which are described by Jung and Lippitt (#3922) are designed both to solve specific problems and to utilize scientific knowledge "in such a way as to contribute to an orderly and creative process of planned change in education". (p. 2) Their unique contribution lies in their description of the techniques which are employed in linking expert resources to the client system and which are designed to ensure the utilization of scientific knowledge. These techniques are the *retrieval of relevant knowledge* and the *derivation of implications* from that knowledge.

The process of planned change which Jung & Lippitt suggest is shown in Figure 10.14, which illustrates the authors' point that each of the problem-solving phases of planned change "may, or may not, draw on the practitioner's knowledge of educational settings and the social scientist's scientific knowledge". (p. 5) The scientist's knowledge may be in the form of theory, research findings, or methodology; the practitioner may have special knowledge of priority of needs, resources, or existing innovations.

Much of the knowledge which is retrieved will not be directly applicable to a particular problem, and thus implications must be derived from the knowledge. The authors state that the "work of deriving implications from research is one of the most critical, and perhaps most overlooked, parts of the process of research utilization." (p. 8)

The utilization of scientific knowledge for planned change in education is seen by the authors to involve three roles: educational practitioners, researchers, and linkers between the first two. "Each kind of role must take some initiative and responsibility in the research utilization process." (p. 13)

Along with the concern which the authors have for utilizing knowledge from all relevant sources, they also have a concern that good solutions

FIGURE 10.14   Research Utilization Problem-Solving Model*

EXTERNAL KNOWLEDGE ◄---- may draw on ----- THE PROCESS ------- may draw on ----► INTERNAL KNOWLEDGE

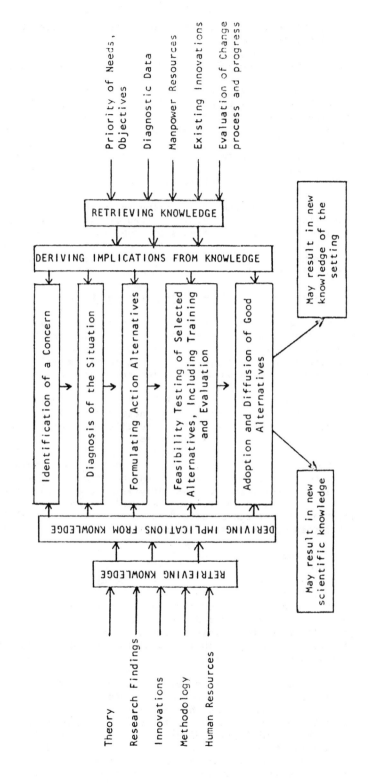

Theory
Research Findings
Innovations
Methodology
Human Resources

RETRIEVING KNOWLEDGE

DERIVING IMPLICATIONS FROM KNOWLEDGE

Identification of a Concern

Diagnosis of the Situation

Formulating Action Alternatives

Feasibility Testing of Selected Alternatives, Including Training and Evaluation

Adoption and Diffusion of Good Alternatives

DERIVING IMPLICATIONS FROM KNOWLEDGE

RETRIEVING KNOWLEDGE

Priority of Needs, Objectives
Diagnostic Data
Manpower Resources
Existing Innovations
Evaluation of Change process and progress

May result in new knowledge of the setting

May result in new scientific knowledge

*Adapted by Ronald Lippitt, March, 1969 from "The Study of Change as a Concept" by Charles Jung and Ronald Lippitt. Reprinted from THEORY INTO PRACTICE, Vol. V, No. 1, February, 1966.

should be diffused to others, since these, in themselves, represent a knowledge resource.

h. Jacobs: Components of Interdisciplinary Educational Planning

Jacobs (#1781) states that each of the five phases, or components, which he advocates in educational planning (see Table 10.6) must be carried out on many levels, from national down to classroom. Such massive planning as is proposed, particularly at the national level, might seem quite appropriate to the R,D&D school. However, the orientation of Jacobs' model is nevertheless towards the solving of problems, and the steps which he suggests are similar to those of other models which we have included in the P-S school.

Jacobs is unique in proposing an interdisciplinary team approach to educational planning, involving academic disciplines, technical and professional fields, departments and agencies of the government, and lay groups and other non-governmental resources. He stresses that the team approach should result in a harmonious blend which will take in all aspects of a society and its culture.

3. A Comparison of the Conceptualizations of Authors of the P-S School

We can see from our discussion of the Problem-Solver models outlined in Table 10.6 that these models exhibit considerable variety; but we should now point out that they also have a great deal in common. Those developed in the field of education, which are intended to solve specific problems in that field, closely resemble models which are intended to have general applicability across fields. Though many models are designed to cope with the change process in a complex organization, they can also be useful in bringing about change in an individual. The methods which are suggested for solving problems seem to be quite unrelated to the type or the size of the client system or to the nature of the innovation which is to be adopted.

We pointed out earlier that although most authors have expanded considerably on Lewin's three stages of change, these stages have nevertheless served as a basis for much of the analysis of change in the Problem-Solver school. Therefore, as we compare the models proposed by the various authors, we will find it most convenient to do so in terms of the three stages which Lewin proposed, of *Unfreezing, Moving,* and *Freezing.*

a. Unfreezing

The initial phase is generally described by theorists in the P-S school as one of becoming aware of a problem; this is awareness of an internal need state rather than the awareness of an external innovation which we found in the S-I and R,D&D schools. This stage is characterized by such terms as "felt dissatisfaction" (Watson, #6364), "identification of the concern" (Jung & Lippitt, #3922), "criticism" (Mackenzie, #1194), and "developing a need for change" (Lippitt, Watson & Westley, #1343).

We found a difference among the various models in who is seen as the initiator of the change process, or who brings about an awareness of the problem. It may be the change agent, as in the process described by Miles & Lake (#3871), or it may be the client system, as in the change situation which Mann & Williams (#5227) describe. Like Lippitt et al. (#1343), Mackenzie (#1194) specifies that this stage may be initiated by either internal or external sources. We noted that Lippitt et al. found that initiation by the client system occurred most frequently, and this would seem

to be the most favorable condition for successful change as well. Since
the models in the P-S school are built around the concept of receiver involvement in bringing about change, motivation of the client system is
seen as a central issue. Internal motivation provides the ideal model
for growth and the acquisition of knowledge, since it provides maximum
impetus for continuation beyond the initial phases of innovation, as well
as providing for optimal awareness of new knowledge (Havelock, #6183).

Successful change depends also, of course, on the expertise of the
change agent and on the adequacy of the change techniques which he applies
to the particular situation. Some authors are concerned that the change
agent should enter the client system with goals and plans in mind, in
addition to having his special techniques, even though the orientation is
towards solving the problems of a particular client system. We noted, for
example, that Jacobs (#1781) speaks of the need to "formulate objectives
on a national scale" as the first phase of his change plan, and the particular programs that are selected for a client system are to be coordinated with these objectives. Within this broad framework, however, the
plan which is chosen is to suit the needs of the individual client system.

Miles & Lake (#3871) also consider pre-planning on the part of the
change agent to be essential, and the change program which they propose
is one in which, through collaboration of the change agent (COPED teams)
with the client (a school system), the client system learns how to carry
out its own problem-solving strategy of change. To some degree the plan
of Miles & Lake resembles the models of the R,D&D school; the innovation
which is to be adopted (a strategy for change) is prepared by an R&D
team and it is then disseminated to a target group, the schools. The
manner in which it is disseminated, however, falls clearly into the
problem-solver context, since the plan for change cannot be adapted to
the needs of the client system without the collaboration of that system
with the change agent.

We find, then, that even if it is the change agent who takes the initial step in contacting a client, and even if the change agent prepares a
plan of action before entering the client system, the actual problem-
solving process of change can not begin until the client himself is aware
of his own problem and has developed a need for change. It is only at this
point that the change relationship can be established and movement towards
solving the problem can begin.

b. Moving

It is clear from Table 10.6 that most of the steps involved in solving
problems take place during the moving stage, and we have seen in our discussion of the individual models that the steps which are proposed for
this stage vary considerably from one model to another. We do find, however, that some form of diagnosis is generally proposed before other action steps are to be taken, and Dentler (#6367) emphasizes this point. The
reality of a problem, he says, depends on the act of defining it; definition of a problem provides a connection between the unsatisfactory situation and possible causes. This link must be made before a solution can be
found.

It has been noted (Watson, #6364) that the *pressure for change may
result in a tendency to omit the stage of diagnosis*; the result may be
"solutions" which do not solve anything. This may be one of the dangers
in the current public uproar over "crime in the streets": If the problem
is not clearly defined and understood, the rush to immediate solutions,

10-65

such as increasing the power of the police, may be pointless and even destructive.

On the other hand, an obsession with diagnosis may be debilitating in itself. We are all familiar with what might be called the "committee effect", where committees or commissions are established to provide "diagnoses"; such a method often seems to deter, rather than to encourage, action.

As a guide to diagnosis, Watson (#6364) provides some pertinent questions:

"What is the history of the alleged difficulty, when was it first noticed, and what attempts have previously been made to deal with it? Does it appear only at certain times, in certain (places), or under certain circumstances? Is it found also in certain other social systems? What is the attitude of influential persons and those most directly involved?" (p. 543)

As regards the last question, Watson points out that diagnosis may be complicated by defensiveness, and that "The need for any change is likely to be considered a reflection on the persons who have been responsible in the past". This points to the need, often documented in the literature, for participant involvement in planning for change (e.g., Haber, #1867; Kimbrough, #0156; Mayer, #0414; Schramm, #2098).

Diagnosis is followed by a series of action steps, which, in general, include: (1) search for possible solutions, (2) establishment of goals and priorities, (3) weighing of solutions, (4) selection of the best alternative, (5) formulating plans for implementation of the solution, and finally, (6) introducing the change into the client system. Not all of the authors listed in Table 10.6 include all of these steps; to a great extent the number and complexity of the steps taking place during the moving stage must be dependent on the circumstances of the situation. We have seen that variations in the models of Table 10.6 reflect the primary purpose for which the change plan was designed. For example, including a phase in the search for solutions which is called "creative design" (Watson, #6364) would imply that an appropriate innovation may not yet exist. In the case of Mann & Williams, on the other hand, the innovation to be adopted was in existence and the plan for change centered around preparing the client system for the introduction of the innovation. Thus we see a great range in the emphasis which is placed on locating the proper innovation to suit the client's needs.

Even when two authors do include similar steps in their models, however, they do not necessarily place them in the same sequential order. Jung & Lippitt (#3922), for example, list "formulation of objectives", followed by "feasibility testing of action alternatives", whereas Jacobs (#1781) lists these two steps in the reverse order.

In fact, there is some doubt as to whether or not it is possible to clearly define the order which should be followed in the implementation of action steps. We noted that Mann & Williams (#5227) found, in their study of introducing a change into an industrial organization, that all the action steps, from preliminary planning through stabilization of the innovation (phases 2 through 6) occurred *simultaneously*.

Other authors (e.g., Thelen, #3692) describe a type of cyclical pattern of moving through the action stages, since such steps as "search for solutions", "establishment of priorities", and "determination of feasibility" are all interdependent. The iterative (repeated recycling) procedure of carrying out action steps is probably best depicted by Lewin (#1342), who describes social change as a series of recurrent action steps, followed by reconnaisance of results and decisions, which lead to the next action steps. The process, as envisioned by Lewin, is illustrated in Figure 10-15, where he shows the steps in "Planning, fact-finding and execution".

Some of the techniques which are suggested by P-S theorists for analyzing problems during the "moving" stage are of particular interest. One of these is the use of the force field analysis, a technique which was originally developed by Lewin. This has the purpose of taking into account all the forces which act on the client system, forces which might inhibit or facilitate adoption of an innovation, and forces which the innovation itself may exert on the system. Watson (#6364, 6195) and Thelen (#3692) both specify the use of this type of analysis, and Mann & William: (#5227) employ a similar method in using the "systems approach".

In taking a look at the client system as a whole, both roles and structures are generally considered. Not only must individuals adapt to and be trained to adjust to new roles resulting from a change, but the structure of the system itself must be able to accommodate and maintain the change. Thus, several authors point out the importance of making structural provisions within the system to support the change (Mann & Williams, #5227; Watson, #6195).

Mention should also be made of the fact that most of the authors listed in Table 10.6 specify or imply the use of a temporary system during the moving stage. Miles & Lake (#3871) and Watson (#6364) are among those who make direct mention of this technique. In general, the collaboration of the client system with a change agent system during this period can be described as a "temporary system" which will terminate either when the change plan has been decided upon or when it has been implemented.

Finally, we should note that few of the authors in Table 10.6 specifically include a stage of evaluation. Among those who do so are Watson (#6364) and Jacobs (#1781), who describe it as a stage following adoption or implementation, and Jung & Lippitt (#3922), who describe it as preceding adoption. The omission of an evaluation stage by many theorists may sometimes present a misleading picture of the P-S school, because evaluation as a "mental trial" (described previously in the S-I models) takes place at many stages. In addition, other phases often included in the P-S models, such as "examine alternatives" and "reformulate proposals", imply that some type of informal evaluation has taken place. Again, we can best refer to the multiple stages of "reconnaisance of results" described by Lewin.

c. Freezing

We saw that the final stage of "Adoption", described in the S-I school, was not very clearly defined. In the case of the present studies, this fact is even more evident. For the client system itself, the final stage is generally described either in terms of a stabilization or freezing of the change (Lewin, #1342; Lippitt, Watson, & Westley, #1343; Mann & Williams, #5227), or in terms of a process of continual growth and change (Thelen, #3692; Watson, #6195). Miles & Lake (#3871) are unique in referring to the institutionalization of a program for continuing growth and change, but other authors, like Lippitt, Watson & Westley (#1343),

FIGURE 10.15   Planning, Fact-Finding, and Execution*

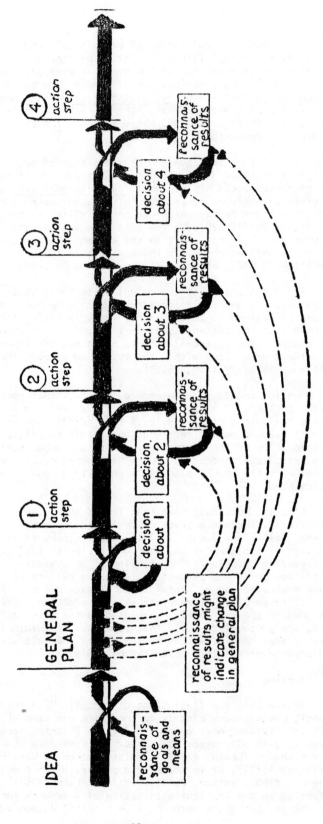

*Figure copied from Lewin, Kurt (#1342).

10-68

state that one desirable outcome of the change process is the learning by the client system of techniques for solving its own future problems.

Some authors do not end the change model with the final phase affecting the client system, but they include, in addition, the possibility of the dissemination to others of the ideas and methods developed in the problem-solving process. This may be viewed as a process in which the change agent may actively engage (Miles & Lake, #3871; Jung & Lippitt, #3922) or one which happens as a result of the social interaction of the client system with other members of a group (Watson, #6364).

D. SUMMARY OF PHASE MODELS OF DIFFUSION AND CHANGE

We have reviewed three schools of thought about the phases of change: the Social Interaction Perspective, the Research, Development and Diffusion Perspective, and the Problem-Solver Perspective. Although there is some overlap among these schools, we feel that they do represent some basic distinctions which may be made about the process of change.

The first model which we described, the Social Interaction model, is based largely on studies from the rural sociology tradition. Studies included in this category deal with the process by which an innovation is adopted, either by a group or by an individual, once the innovation has already become available to potential adopters. Since theorists of this school are not concerned with the process by which the innovation is made available, they stipulate that the initial stage in the change sequence occurs when the potential receiver becomes aware of the innovation (which may be either a product or a procedure). Subsequent stages describe a sequence of increasing psychological and behavioral involvement, including interest and information seeking, evaluation, trial, and adoption (or rejection). Of special interest to this school are the sources of information which appear to be most influential at each stage of the adoption process. The effect of personal sources of information on the adoption process have been found to be of particular significance. Once the innovation has been adopted by a few members of a group, the innovation seems to spread almost automatically to other members through a process of social interaction.

The second school, Research, Development and Diffusion, begins the analysis of the change sequence at an earlier point in time than does the S-I school, and thus the first stage of change is described by this school as the design, invention, or discovery of an innovation. This first stage is carried out by specialists outside the client system, usually identified as "researchers", "scientists", "developers", or "engineers". Following research and development, with evaluation at each phase, dissemination activities are undertaken on a large scale. In contrast to the S-I school, the primary attention of the R,D&D theorists generally remains on the efforts of the sender as the innovation is diffusing through the target group. Only secondary attention is paid to the receiver, who is the focus of the S-I theorists. The particular emphasis of this school is on the massiveness of the effort at each of the phases of research, development, and diffusion. This effort must be supported by ample financial resources, and it depends on coordination of personnel with widely varying skills who, in general, are each carrying out only one segment of the total change plan.

The final model, the Problem-Solver, includes studies which focus on the efforts of a receiver in solving his own particular problems. The change sequence is initiated when the receiver (an individual or a group) becomes aware of a need or deficit or when he desires an improvement in his present situation. After a stage of diagnosis, the receiver must locate a solution and make plans to implement it, often with help from outside the receiver system.

The innovations may be a product or practice which already exists, or it may be one which is custom-made to meet the receiver's needs. Phases commonly described are: problem awareness; diagnosis; search for and selection of solution; planning for implementation; installation and evaluation; stabilization; and possible diffusion to other groups.

In Chapter 11 we will attempt to make a synthesis of these three models, but we would like to end this section of the present chapter by noting some points of overlap among these three models. The S-I model may be viewed as a detailed analysis of one phase (adoption) of the R,D&D model. This may be illustrated by the fact that Miles (#6056), whom we have placed in the R,D&D school, describes the diffusion and adoption phases in the same way as the S-I theorists describe the process of adoption.

The P-S model may, in some instances, be considered as one type of "development" procedure which could take place in the R,D&D sequence. The evolution of an effective innovation, as described by the R,D&D school, requires that the developers seek out a "sample" receiver group from the potential target population and that they collaborate with this group in the testing and redesign process. Hence, during the development and evaluation phases, the R,D&D model recapitulates the P-S process.

Finally, P-S theorists are sometimes concerned that effective solutions which have been developed to meet the needs of one receiver should be diffused to others who have similar problems. In particular, Watson's P-S model (#6364) ends with a phase of "spread of new ideas to others", which he sees as taking place in exactly the same way as do the S-I theorists.

We make these remarks to illustrate the fact that *we do not perceive any underlying disagreement among theorists of the three schools which we have outlined above*. We feel that differences in the way in which the change process is described by the various authors reflect the fact that the change process may legitimately be viewed from different and distinctive perspectives.

We shall now return to a discussion of adoption and diffusion in more generalized terms. It should be borne in mind in the sections that follow, however, that any variable which affects phases may well have a different impact on the three types of change process; both the importance of the variable, and the roles and stages which it affects, will differ in the types of studies described by each of the schools of thought.

E. ALTERNATIVE OUTCOMES

It is clear from the preceding section that to speak of Adoption and Rejection as the only possible outcomes of the innovation process represents a vast over-simplification. Even when one or the other of these alternatives seems to be a clear-cut final phase, neither need represent a state of equilibrium. Adoption may be followed by discontinuance, discontinuance by readoption, and rejection by later adoption. A further possibility is partial adoption, or adoption in a revised form. The difficulties of plotting such situations on an "adoption curve", or even of accurately describing the phases involved, are immediately apparent. Rogers (#1824) has devised an "Innovation-Use Tree" to illustrate the outcomes of the adoption process for several innovations. (See Figure 10.16; Rogers' Figure 4.2.)

A glance at the final column of Tables 10.2, 3 & 6 indicates that there is seldom a clear-cut final phase. Where "adoption" is considered final, the studies are dealing with relatively discrete and simple innovations. Several studies indicate a final complex process of integration into a system (Gallaher, #2613; Holmberg, see #1824; Lippitt, Watson & Westley, #1343; Mann & Williams,

FIGURE 10.16   Innovation-Use Tree for 13 Innovations that Were Adopted and Discontinued by 111 Kentucky Farmers*

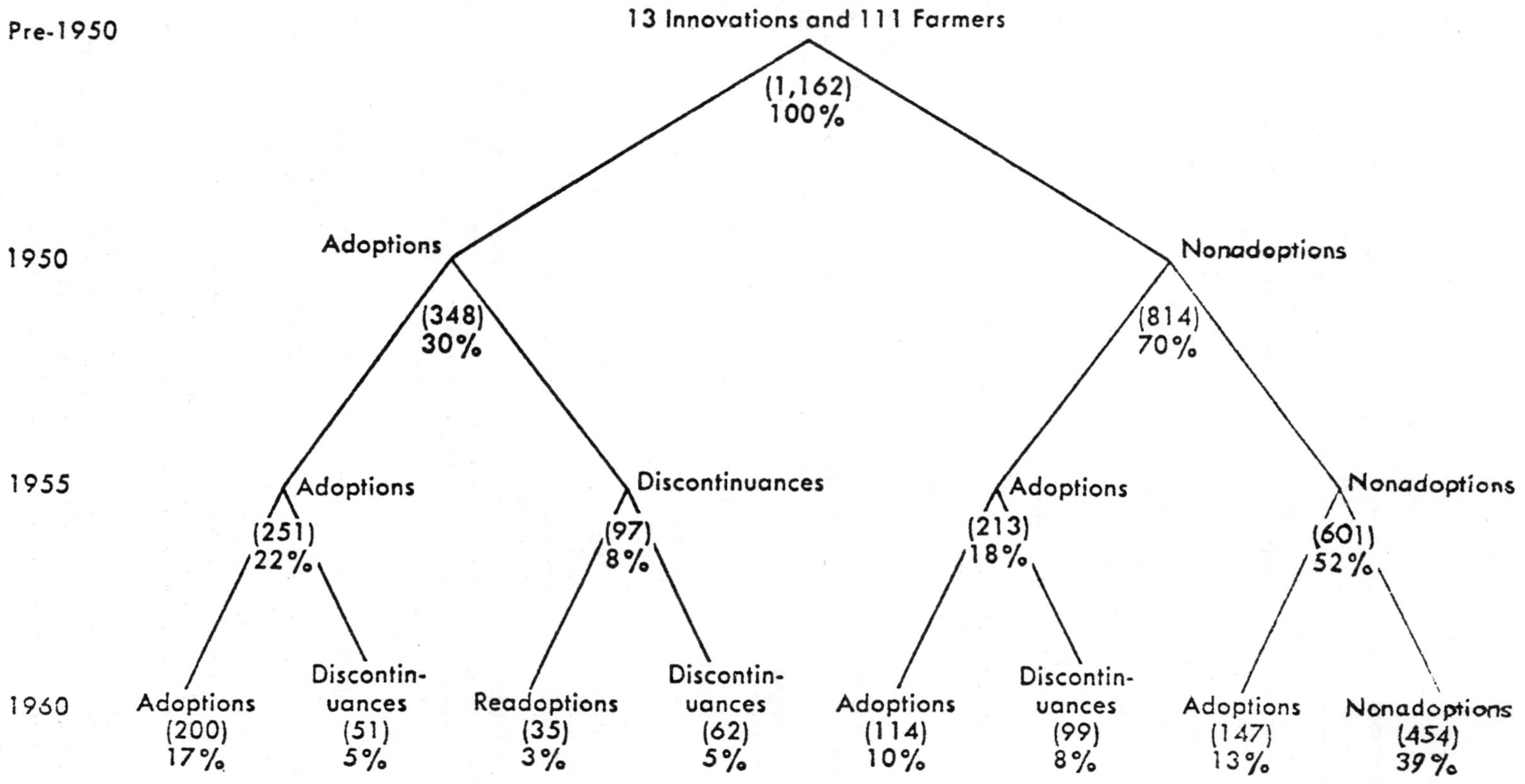

Pre-1950   13 Innovations and 111 Farmers

1950

*Figure redrawn by Rogers (#1824, p. 94) from Coughenour.

10-71

#5227). For others, the final stage is dissemination (Brickell, #1181; Jung & Lippitt, # 3922; Watson, #6364). In some studies, it is difficult to determine at which point in the sequence adoption actually did take place. For example, Sanders (#3751) describes cases in which the issue of fluoridation of water was introduced into several communities. In these cases the "legitimizing body" in each community evaluated the innovation and then reached a decision. The options available to them were described as adoption, rejection, postponement, or amendment. Once the decision was made, however, it was not necessarily permanent; the issue was likely to be reactivated. That is, the power to carry out the decision did not rest solely with those who made the decision. This case, then, is similar to a study described by Havelock et al. (#6502), in which adoption by a change agent was considered to be an intermediate, or in Lewin's terms, "Moving", phase; the final phase is reached only with "full organizational acceptance".

Let us now look more closely at some of the possible alternative outcomes of the innovation sequence.

1. Discontinuance

Discontinuance, or subsequent rejection of an innovation after initial adoption, is reported by Rogers (#1824) as a common phenomenon, varying with the nature of both the innovation and the adopter. Some of the factors he describes as related to discontinuance are the replacement of an innovation by a superior one, misunderstanding or misuse of the innovation, and personal characteristics which are also related to late adoption.

Discontinuance may be caused by lack of integration of the innovation into a system: Watson (#6364) describes failure to make a commitment to a period of *adaptation* as a possible cause for failure of innovations. On the other hand, integration into the system may take place, but with unexpected results which lead to discontinuance. Barnett (#0620) suggests that discontinuance may take place when an innovation has untoward consequences for related aspects of society. As an example, Watson (#6364) describes a highly successful innovation which was discontinued when assembly line workers began to earn more on a piece-work basis than some plant supervisors were making. Faced with the alternatives of cutting piece-work rates or discontinuing the new assembly methods, management chose the latter course.

A special case is that described by Meyerson & Katz (#1720) in their description of the phases involved in fads and fashions. Their final phases, "loss of exclusiveness" and "death by displacement" may provide a criterion for distinguishing "fashion" from more stable innovations. Actually, "death by displacement" is probably the more common cause for discontinuance, although there are instances where "loss of exclusiveness" causes discontinuance; it has been suggested, for example, that the "royal fad" of tattooing was discontinued when it became popular with the masses.*

Discontinuance has proved to be a major problem for those interested in bringing about change. The failure of demonstration programs to achieve long-lasting change is frequently observed; Watson (#6364) speculates that such innovations may be more meaningful to those who design and develop them

*An interesting, though inappropriate, use of this reason for discontinuance was described in the recent statement by a Black Power leader, that when the churches became fully integrated, the white man declared that "God is dead."

than they are to those for whom they are intended. He suggests that the "Hawthorne effect"* may make an original project appear to be successful, but when the same model becomes a "product" to be diffused to other settings it may fail if the enthusiasm of doing something original and important is lacking. The inference may be that a kind of Hawthorne effect should be built into the diffusion process so that each new potential adopter can approach the innovation with the same enthusiasm and involvement in doing something new.

The need to institutionalize follow-up mechanisms to forestall discontinuance is cited by several authors. Lachmann (#0351), discussing the international transfer of technology, describes a need to develop mechanisms for "long run collaboration between foreign and local technologies" to help the farmer to maintain interest in and access to new advances, as well as to develop his own research. A number of writers (c.f. Lippitt and Watson, #1210) have discussed the need to set up mechanisms to maintain new learning of foreign students when they return to their own countries. Lewin (#1342) describes the problem of discontinuance:

> "A change toward a higher level of group performance is
> frequently short-lived; after a shot in the arm, group life
> soon returns to the previous level. This indicates that it
> does not suffice to define the objective of planned change
> in group performance as the reaching of a different level.
> Permanency of the new level, or permanency for a desired
> period, should be included in the objective."

In other words, designing the "aftermath" of adoption should be included in the early phases of planning for change.

2. Rejection with Later Adoption

The possibility that an innovation which is rejected may be adopted at a later time has received little attention in the literature, although Rogers indicates that it does take place (see Figure 10.16). Sanders (#3751) deals with this possibility in his discussion of the aftermath of community controversy over the issue of fluoridation:

> "The losers' reaction to the outcome is a determining
> factor in the initiation of a new sequence. If they
> decide to raise the issue again, they often do so shortly
> after the issue has supposedly been resolved. The anti-
> fluoridationists are more apt to react militantly toward
> an adverse decision; the pro-fluoridationists are more
> apt to be discouraged, dissillusioned, and left without
> much fight."

In many cases, however, the "pro's" eventually obtain backing for their position, or circumstances and general knowledge change enough to provide the necessary support for the innovation.

---

*The "Hawthorne effect" is the often observed phenomenon that subjects in an experimental change project become highly motivated for the very reason that they are participating in an experiment. Under some circumstances when the subjects see themselves as "guinea pigs" manipulated by the experimenter a reverse or negative Hawthorne effect is also possible.

3. Adoption in an Amended Form

An innovation is likely to be adopted in an *amended* form when it requires a great deal of skill or training on the part of the receiver, when it is high in cost, or when, for any of a number of reasons, it is not suitable in its original form for the particular circumstances of the receiver's individual situation. The adaptations required in these cases are generally of a type which will tend to make the innovation successful in meeting the needs of the receiver. These cases may be compared to the adaptation of innovations to individual needs which takes place in the "problem-solving" process of change.

Less successful amendments may be made because of ignorance or lack of understanding, or if the receiver is ambivalent about the innovation and so makes a decision which is a compromise between acceptance and rejection. A common example is accepting a new drug prescribed by the doctor, but ignoring the doctor's instructions, e.g., taking it twice a day instead of three times. The effect of compromise may be to eradicate the intended effect of the innovation; Rogers (#1824) describes the case of adoption of corn-growing innovations (Silverman & Bailey, #1096), in which some farmers adopted unsuccessful combinations of three related innovations. Compromise is also a typical outcome in social movements when a clear-cut decision acceptable to all parties cannot be agreed upon: Watson (#6364) cites the example of "separate-but-equal" schools for Negroes.

On the other hand, of course, compromise or amendment may turn out to be beneficial, and the following case provides an interesting example of circumstances which may lead to satisfactory compromise. It was felt by educators and some community leaders in two small Maine towns that both towns would benefit if the schools, long-time rivals, were combined. At simultaneous town meetings, the smaller and poorer town voted not to consolidate, while the larger town, which had a new school and would be the site of the proposed combined school, voted to consolidate. The following year, realizing that they had made a foolish move, the smaller town voted to combine, while the larger town, perhaps in a spirit of revenge harking back to the rivalry between the towns, voted not to. Strong "pro" and "con" factions developed in both towns, and proselytizing was active. Over a period of several years, at regular annual meetings and at a number of special town meetings, the towns continued to disagree. Throughout, a major factor was the issue of having children travel long distances to school. At the present time, the issue of consolidating the two schools has been dropped in favor of an amended plan: a School Administrative District, combining the schools of a larger number of neighboring towns. Prospects for acceptance seem favorable, although travel distances will be much greater for all the children involved. The current change in attitude may be due to an increased realization of the need to provide better school facilities for the area; it may be that the issue of competition between the two original towns is no longer an issue, since other communities are now involved. Most important, however, is the threatened loss of state funds should the schools fail to consolidate. Interestingly, the model for the proposed S.A.D. includes provisions for discontinuance, should the innovation prove unpopular or unworkable.

When the amended version of an innovation proves to be advantageous, other people are likely to become aware of it, and a new adoption-diffusion process is initiated. This may, in fact, be the basis for a great deal of change.

F. VALIDITY OF PHASE MODELS

Our discussions so far of phase models of change could only be considered academic if they simply represent descriptions of change sequences which have occurred in the past. The utility in studying them rests with the extent to which they can be reliable in enabling us to plan for *future* changes. In attempting to answer the question of whether or not the phase models are reliable, we should recall that many of the theoretical models of planned change which were proposed were based on studies of actual cases of more or less unplanned change. That is, an attempt was first made to identify a *natural process of change*, and phases for planned change were then suggested which were based on the natural process and which were designed to take advantage of the natural phases of change.

Therefore, in seeking an answer to whether or not we can expect the models of change to be reliable, we must first decide whether or not the natural change process has been analyzed sufficiently. Has it been established that phases actually do exist? If so, does the *sequence* of the phases really matter, or are these just functions which have to happen before utilization can come about?

Rogers (#1824) has concerned himself with these issues, and he cites a number of studies indicating that "stages" actually do occur. Supporting this, he notes that research shows: (a) that the concept of stages seems "natural" to respondents; (b) that most individuals go through the same stages and that "skipped" stages can be identified; (c) that different information sources are reported for different innovations at various stages, and (d) that respondents report a time lapse between awareness and adoption.

Convincing as these findings are, there have been a number of criticisms of the methodology used in studying phases. Rogers (#1824) points out several of them: for example, he notes that the research applies to individual, but not to group, decisions, and that it depends almost entirely on recall of events, often at a much later point in time.

Mason (#2397) considers that in at least one major study (Beal, Rogers & Bohlen, #3561) the nature of the questions forced respondents to reply in terms of consecutive phases. He cites items such as the following:

Q: "After you had enough information to know quite a lot about antibiotics, where or from whom did you get the information that helped you decide whether or not to actually try it on your own farm?"

Mason points out that the farmer who answers this question, which ostensibly deals with information sources, is tacitly agreeing that he moved from an "evaluation" to a "trial" stage.

Mason's own study (#2397), designed to improve on earlier research, encountered difficulty, possibly attributable to farmers' interpretation of the words "heard about" as indicating awareness; Mason speculates that farmers excluded visual awareness from their responses. Thus, it turned out that in one instance, "adoption" preceded "awareness" for one innovation studied.*

Validity and reliability have proved troublesome for research in this area. Rogers and Rogers (#1524) found poor consistency on re-interview, even on reports of factual information. We might expect increasing validity in the reporting of stages as the behavior involved becomes more active and less subjective. Thus an individual who is uncertain as to when he first became aware of an innovation or at what stage he evaluated it for his own use, might be

_____
*In a sense it is sometimes literally possible for adoption to occur without awareness, as when the auto-maker introduces new safety features such as changes in brake linings or steering columns which he does not advertise and which are not visible to the buyer.

quite positive as to the time of actual trial and adoption. However, Katz (#1398) speculates that physicians distorted the dates of both awareness and adoption of a new drug, tending to underestimate the time elapsed between the two stages. In some studies it is possible to establish objective measures of adoption. For example, in the study of adoption of gammanyn, Coleman, Katz and Menzel (#3576) were able to establish dates of adoption by auditing the prescriptions on file in pharmacies in communities being studied.

Clearly, adoption scales are still open to criticism, and a number of suggestions for improving methodology have been made (c.f. Rogers and Rogers, #1524; Mason, #2397). It would seem, however, that the major criticisms can be answered only by the use of prospective, rather than retrospective, research. It would be difficult, but should not be impossible, to carry out studies where input of information, and subsequent stages, are controlled and measured during the adoption process. A good start in this direction has been made by Troldahl (#1078), who was able to control the content of an agricultural newspaper and to measure the effects of receiving different types of information. His study, however, was concerned with the "two-step flow of communication" model, and did not include phases beyond "change of belief".

For models falling within the S-I school, then, there has been some attempt to establish validity. However, in studies in the P-S school, validity testing is almost non-existent. The literature is descriptive, with each author supplying his own model; virtually no attempt is made to relate the phases described in different studies.

It might be anticipated that this would be a good point to call for research to test out these various models, but there are so many and the circumstances to which they are applied so diverse that it is difficult to know where to start. Whose model should be tested first? With what audience? With what type of knowledge? Though the task appears vast, it may be hoped that some basic model will emerge which has validity in diverse circumstances. It has been observed by many social scientists that those who have extensive experience in working with clients on planning changes all seem to employ roughly similar techniques. Hence there may actually be some common and therefore potentially scientific basis to planned change methods regardless of differences of specific details and language.

IV. ADOPTION RATES: CAN THEY BE CHANGED?

Rogers (#1824) defines rate of adoption as "the relative speed with which an innovation is adopted by members of a social system. (It)...is usually measured by the length of time required for a certain percentage of the members of a social system to adopt an innovation". (p. 134) Previous chapters have discussed the characteristics of innovations which Rogers describes as having a major effect on the rate of adoption: advantage, compatibility, complexity, divisibility and communicability. There are, however, variables more or less independent of the innovation which also affect adoption rates. We have discussed the personal characteristics which determine whether individuals will be "innovative" or not. Groups, organizations and systems also have characteristics which tend to accelerate or retard the process of innovation. There are other variables, separate from, but interacting with characteristics of the innovation and the receiver, which may influence the rate at which innovations are adopted, and we will discuss some of these in the remainder of this chapter.

We mentioned earlier the observations which Mort (#1191) made concerning the adoption rate for educational change. He writes that:

'The early studies indicated that change in the American school system comes about through a surprisingly slow process and follows a predictable pattern. Between

insight into a need...and the introduction of a way of meeting the need
that is destined for general acceptance...there is typically a lapse of
a half-century. Another half-century is required for the diffusion of
the adaptation. During that half-century of diffusion, the practice
is not recognized until it has appeared in 3% of the systems in the
country. By that time, 15 years of diffusion -- or independent innovation -- have elapsed. Thereafter, there is a rapid twenty years
of diffusion, accompanied by much fanfare, and then by a long period
of slow diffusion through the last small percentage of school systems."
(p. 318)

Thus, in the studies which Mort reviewed (mostly from the 1930's), the
process of innovation covered a period of almost 100 years from identification of
need to complete adoption; as Mort says, this is an "extravagantly long time" for
the achievement of general acceptance of an innovation. Miles (#1481) looks at
some possible reasons:

"The diffusion rates in educational systems may be slower than those
found in industrial, agricultural, or medical systems for several
reasons: the absence of valid scientific research findings; the
lack of change agents to promote new educational ideas; and the
lack of economic incentive to adopt innovations."(p. 634)

Although the rate of change in education may be slower than in more technical
fields, Miles nevertheless found that there has been an acceleration in the rate
of change in education since the 1930's when Mort's studies took place. Miles suggests a number of reasons for this upswing, and he proposes that "the sheer size
and growth of the educational establishment itself is exerting perhaps the most
profoundly innovative effect of all". (p. 9)

This is the type of effect which we discussed earlier in mentioning Price's
(#7133) analysis of the growth of various fields of knowledge. He observed that
growth in any field can be observed to be exponential. and it appears that the field
of education is beginning to show the rapid growth rate which has been noted already
in science and technology. Price voiced concern that planning for personnel allocation in the sciences should be undertaken on a national scale. The recent expansion in educational innovation suggests the urgency of carrying out planning of
personnel allocation in education, specifically, and the study by Hopkins and
Clark (#3586) is an attempt to do just that.

Miles discusses additional factors which have contributed to the acceleration of change in education; among these are the general climate for change in a
culture, and the timing of innovations relative to this climate.

A. TIMING

The fact that the timing of innovation can influence adoption rates is
dramatically illustrated by Brickell (#0845), who found that, "...the rate
of innovation in the (New York state) public schools...had more than doubled
in the fifteen months following the launching of the Soviet Sputnik I in October of 1957." Although most schools had remained stable as structured institutions, Brickell found changes in all academic and non-academic subjects;
these included not only math and science, but also those subjects which might
not be expected to change as a result of Sputnik, such as foreign languages.
Figure 10.17 depicts the increased rate of innovation which Brickell documented.

FIGURE 10.17   Rate of Instructional Innovation in New York
                      State Public School Systems

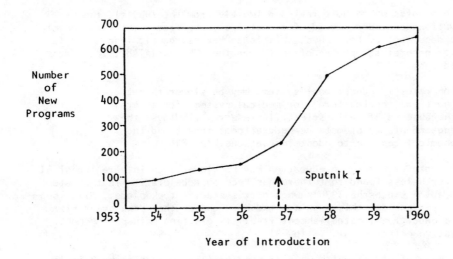

(Brickell, #0845)

Clearly, Brickell's findings are reflecting the Zeitgeist*, of which Miles (#1481) says:

"The existence of Zeitgeist effects can usually be inferred when multiple innovations occur independently at about the same time, implying a common underlying concern. It has been suggested that this period of independent invention reflects turbulence and impending change in a social system, with a resulting search for innovations which will re-establish equilibrium. In any event, once a "family" of innovations develops...its existence tends to stimulate and support further innovative work..."(p. 645)

Miles (#6056) poses some questions concerning the effect of pre-existing conditions on an innovation as it moves into the "target system":

"For example: What is the role of the general Zeitgeist in serving as a supporter or blocker of specific changes, or as a creator of generalized openness or resistance to many changes in the system? ...Are there conditions which might be characterized as making for 'ripeness' of the system, a kind of latent disequilibrium which makes subsequent innovations actually welcome? What is the role of external or internal crisis in making for openness toward innovation? What sorts of factors, whether personal (e.g., cognitive dissonance), interpersonal (e.g., status disequilibrium on the part of significant actors), or organizational (e.g., ambiguity in power structure) make for readiness of the innovation?" (p. 41)

Speculations regarding such questions are frequent. Watson (#6364) speaks of "an idea whose time has come", which often gives rise to multiple inventions. A case in point is the current work on organ transplants. In a similar vein, Dahling (#1495) points out that an idea may come from "a flurry of related activity", gaining speed and impetus from the surrounding activity.

Linden (#3217) attributes the success of an innovation, in part, to its "excellent timing, coinciding with peak development of interest and goodwill on the part of an informed public and dedicated government". This implies that there is a point of general awareness ideal for instituting innovations; for example, when public concern about "law and order" is at a peak, it may be a good time to submit grant applications for research on juvenile delinquency. Michael (#3892) speaks of an innovation's "appropriateness for introduction into the situation of the moment or its adaptability to fill current needs". Such formulations imply that there may be a "crucial stage" for innovation. Haber (#1867) provides an example; he found that unless an innovation (in this case, use of language laboratories) were picked up during training, it was difficult to introduce the innovation at a later stage in a teacher's career.

Barzel (#7043) explores the issue of optimal timing of innovations from an economic point of view, and he suggests that the time when an innovation is technically feasible is not necessarily the best point in time for it to be introduced. According to Barzel, the socially optimal time for introduction of an innovation coincides with the time at which the profits for its inventor may be maximized. He finds, however, that this situation rarely occurs and that, in general, the timing of innovations is not optimal. If for various reasons the innovator will not reap the benefits, he will have little

---

*Zeitgeist is defined by the American College Dictionary as: "the spirit of the time; general drift of thought or feeling characteristic of a particular period of time".

motivation for introducing the innovation, and he may not make it available until long after the time at which it was socially optimal. On the other hand, premature introduction of an innovation is likely to result when there is competition between potential innovators. In order to corner the market, each competitor will strive to introduce the innovation as soon as even small gains may be realized. In the case in which innovation activity is subsidized, however, the date of introduction is likely to shift to an even earlier point in time, perhaps to a time when there is negative profitability.

Barzel cites the case of the development of the supersonic transport (SST) as one which is technically feasible but of doubtful profitability. He points out that not only will competition with the Russians and with the British and French push the time of introduction of the SST back to an undesirably early date, but, in addition, subsidization of the innovation will make it even more premature. This, he feels, is a dramatic case of an innovation which is poorly timed.

The effect of crisis on innovation has received a good deal of attention: Watson (#6364) points out that innovation is resisted when things are going smoothly. Rowe (#3007) speculates that war may accelerate getting scientific ideas into practical use by high-lighting needs; he feels that when a need becomes known, it is often the case that science has a way to meet it. Further, war provides incentive to meet hitherto unknown needs. Michael (#3892) suggests that since social disaster often facilitates innovation, a possible technique is to stockpile innovations which might have little use in a "business as usual" situation, but might have a chance of acceptance in "the fluid period of reorganization and recovery following disasters".

Gavin (#7005) suggests that innovations adopted in response to a critical situation may be found to have significant uses and far-reaching effects long after the crisis has been met. He says that:

> "When Galileo first showed a telescope to a Venetian admiral, he responded by observing, how marvelous -- he would now be able to see the enemy fleets before they could see him. Man's first use of fission was for military purposes, yet today the peaceful use of fission and its by-products is enormous and world-wide. Likewise, we first viewed Sputnik as an immediate threat to our survival, but today the uses of space for peaceful purposes far exceed their potential for war. Yet man's visceral reaction to use new knowledge to assuage his fears rather than to better his life continues."

Nevertheless, although the initial reaction to the first Russian space satellite in this country may have been one of fear, the resulting demand for improved scientific and technical training created a real "climate for change" in our educational system.

How can we go about creating a climate for change without depending on fear-arousing crises? Miles (#1481) suggests a number of strategies which have "multiplier effects" as a goal:

> "Strategies devoted to encouraging extra communication among system members about the existence and efficacy of innovations, to the creation of facilitating, supporting, legitimating groups to aid diffusion of a series of innovations, and to teaching system members to use an innovation...and help spread it to others all fall in this category.

More generally, it seems likely that the most theoretically
powerful strategies are likely to be those designed to produce
'meta-changes' -- second-order changes which will lead to
further changes. Examples of these are the installation and
use of new feedback loops, such as citizen surveys; regular
use of diagnosis and improvement sessions which aid organizational self-consciousness; and use of consultants on organizational problems." (p. 648)

These are only a few of the many strategies which have been used in attempting to accelerate innovation rates. In the remainder of our discussion,
we will focus on the phases of innovation, relating these to other possible
strategies for influencing adoption rates.

B. PHASES AND ADOPTION RATES

Miles (#1481) points out that although present rates of innovation are
much more rapid than those described by Mort, it "is likely that the conception
of stages remains plausible". In some ways, the progression of stages in
adoption and diffusion seems to be a natural process, with one stage leading
to another without benefit of strategy or planning by either the sender or
the receiver. Once the phases are identified and understood, however, it is
possible to design and apply strategies to them. For example, recall Brickell's
(#1181) suggestion that the various phases of innovation require skills which
are often possessed by different people, and that each phase has "optimal
conditions" which may be arranged to facilitate accomplishment of that phase.

There is a limitless number of ways in which phases and models may be
combined, altered, accelerated, retarded, and rearranged. It is safe to say
that no two innovations have had identical "natural histories" in terms of
phases, and there is no reason we should expect them to. Although it is possible to identify successful and unsuccessful techniques of innovation, it is
impossible to separate the technique from the nature of the innovation itself.
Out of the many aspects of phases which might be discussed in concluding this
chapter, we have chosen a few that have obvious implications for changing rates
of adoption. (1) Who should initiate change? (2) The role of evaluation;
and, finally, (3) Phase problems.

1. Who Should Initiate Change?

The three models of change discussed in this chapter each presents a
different picture of the role of the sender and a different perspective
on the source of initiative for bringing about change. In the S-I model,
the initiative was in the hands of a sender, with the receiver playing a
relatively passive role. The R,D&D model described a very purposeful
diffusion process, in which a developer plays the active role in identifying a need and in developing a solution to meet the need. This
solution is then disseminated to a potential receiver, who is essentially
passive. In the P-S model, the receiver plays an active role, identifying
a need and seeking out and evaluating ways to meet the need.

Is there a "best" way to bring about innovation? Should the initial
impetus for change come from within the receiver or from outside the receiver? Should it come from an individual or from a group?

Griffiths (#1183) proposes that the type of innovation originating
internally differs from that of external origin. He feels that changes
initiated by "insiders" tend to concern clarification of rules and internal
procedures, whereas new rules, goals and procedures tend to be initiated
by "outsiders". Griffiths suggests that maximum change is likely to come

about when a new chief administrator comes from the "outside". This
causes a state of disequilibrium in the system, and it is likely that the
new administrator will not get enough feedback from subordinates to maintain the status quo. In a situation of this type, there may be a great
deal of resistance to the new leadership. However, if the leader has
sufficient power, a new equilibrium can be established. Dissatisfied members may leave the organization, and they will be replaced by new people
who are willing to accept the new philosophy. When this happens, innovations may occur in rapid succession.

Miles (#6056) describes initiation of change as coming either from
within the target system, itself, or form other systems in the environment of the target system. In either case, the change may involve either
new or existing structures. The combination of these factors results in
four ways in which change may be initiated; Miles points out that each
of these four types of initiation will produce different strategies in
each of the phases of innovation. In a review of the literature on educational innovation he concludes that one characteristic of strategies
which makes for effectiveness is the "creation of new structures, especially by systems outside the target system". In contrast, he finds that:

> "Certain types of strategy seem less effective: those which
> attempt to use only existing structures, and are thus ham-
> strung by the status quo; those self-initiated by the target
> system, since...they tend to avoid attention to cross-system
> problems, such as interorganizational power struggles which are
> likely to affect the progress of the innovation." (p. 649)

Dykens et al. (#5134), in a study of strategies for change within a
mental hospital setting, compared the success of initiation from inside
vs. outside a target system. In this study, a group of change agents
from outside the hospital setting participated in a three-year project
designed to introduce educational and volunteer services into the hospital and to encourage reciprocity of services between the hospital and
other community agencies. During the course of the project, staff members participated in a large number of programs which were evaluated as
to their success. Project staff undertook an analysis of the "success"
of each program in terms of whether the hospital or the project staff
saw the need for the program, requested the program, or actually initiated
it. It was found that there was a tendency for programs to be more successful when the need was seen by the hospital, whether or not the project
also saw the need. There was also a greater amount of success for those
programs requested by the hospital than for those suggested by the Project, although those which were mutually requested were most successful.
There was no difference in success rates for programs initiated by the
hospital or project. An interesting finding of the study was that hospital
and project staff did not agree as to who had seen the need for the program. Each group tended to feel that it had seen the need more than had
the other: "The project itself, because it was the active agent attempting to bring about change, felt that it alone saw the need of a given program, (and) overlooked the fact that the hospital had long recognized the
same need but for some reason had been unable to initiate the program".
(p. 110)

This highly successful program seems to fit, to a high degree, the
characteristics of effective strategies described above by Miles. Unquestionably, part of the effectiveness of the Dykens et al. project was
attributable to its use of a temporary system designed to produce what
Miles calls "meta-changes". Miles (#1189) emphasizes the use of temporary
systems for effecting change; he describes some of the obstacles to the

initiation of change from within a permanent system:

"For many reasons, permanent systems -- whether persons, groups, or organizations -- find it difficult to change themselves. The major proportion of available energy goes to (1) carrying out routine goal-directed operations and (2) maintenance of existing relationships within the system. Thus the fraction of energy left over for matters of diagnosis, planning, innovation, deliberate change, and growth is ordinarily very small." (p. 443)

A temporary system, however, must work to involve the membership of the permanent system. Dykens et al. emphasize the need for receiver-participation:

"Change can be colorful, highly motivated, charged with enthusiasm and optimism, or be a drab chore. Mutual participation in change efforts may lead to positive and constructive feelings and can further enthusiasm for change." (#5134, p. 187)

The need for participant involvement in the initial stages of innovation has received a great deal of emphasis in the literature (e.g., Coch & French, #1828; Cronin, #1049; Mayer, #0414; Pellegrin, #1043; and many others); it may be accepted as a general "Law of Innovation". What we must next consider, then, is who should participate. It is clear that the top management should be involved in any planning of change, since change is likely to take place "from the top down, not the bottom up" (Griffiths, #1183). But participation of only the top management will not be enough, since, as Kimbrough (#0156) points out, the power structure of a community does not necessarily reflect the attitudes of the rank and file members of the community. Therefore, it is probably best to enter a system from several points; Foshay (#3881) suggests, for example, that educational innovation should include the educational hierarchy, parents and the supporting community, the instruction materials, teachers and students.

One technique for the acceleration of innovation involves the identification (or creation) of an "elite" who serve as disseminators, bringing about both awareness and motivation on the part of potential receivers. Niehoff (#2393) describes the role played by Buddhist brotherhoods in bringing about technical change in Southeast Asia. Several factors enabled them to play effective change agent rolls: they were already organized to use village resources; they commanded the cooperation and trust of the villagers; they were willing to take responsibility and initiative; and they had already adopted some modern mechanical implements. Laska (#1596), discussing the implementation of formal education in underdeveloped countries, suggests that the initial step should be maximum development of higher education for professionals. This small, but important, group goes on to expand primary educational facilities, and, as a result, demand for secondary and professional schools is eventually created.

The creation of a local elite group may serve the purpose of facilitating what Weingrod (#0839) calls the "process of reinterpretation", whereby "new things are altered in terms of the ideals and values of the adopting group". The process of reinterpretation may also serve to help receivers interpret an innovation in the light of previous adoptions; Brandner & Kearl (#2076) have found that "persons who evaluate an innovation as congruent with a previously favorably evaluated practice will accept the innovation more rapidly than those who fail to make such an evaluation". Such efforts may be seen as an attempt to prevent rejection at the "awareness" phase, as well as to create the initial dissatisfaction necessary for receiver-collaboration.

10-83

Penders (#6042) poses some of the problems involved in trying to decide where initial efforts should be concentrated. He describes alternative
approaches in the attempt to increase agricultural productivity in underdeveloped countries. In some situations, he says, programs may have to
be run by outside experts, who are unlikely to be fully familiar with local
customs. This approach is bound to meet with resistance, since the villagers will not accept innovations which fail to incorporate existing
traditions. A second approach is to put the change program in the hands
of the villagers themselves; the innovations are more likely to be adopted
in such situations, but at a very slow pace. Moreover, since the more
influential and affluent villagers will be the first to adopt and benefit
from the new practices, the gap between the have's and the have not's is
likely to widen even further. Penders therefore recommends a compromise
approach, in which experts should be used, but responsibility should be
given to the people. This approach involves the setting of limited goals,
the accomplishment of which will be visible. Once a goal has been met,
another one is set; in this way the economic condition of the country is
raised while the people are gradually learning to evaluate and meet their
own needs.

It would seem that, where the receiver is not motivated to change, it
may be necessary to reduce overt resistance by making the innovation seem
to come from "inside"; Cronin (#1049), for example, suggests that the
change agent should subtly discredit the status quo without condemning
current practice. Schramm (#2093) suggests that perhaps the most valuable
contribution which the media could make in bringing about progress in underdeveloped nations would be to create a demand for new policies and for
increased educational opportunities. By this means, the desire for change
will be seen as coming from the people themselves.

In suggesting some of the factors which contribute to producing viable
changes in organizations, Bennis (#6619) examines the strategies which are
employed by change agents. Three separate approaches are identified, although the author stresses that most planned change efforts actually involve all three types: (1) Training, in which participants of groups develop self-insight by examining the dynamics of the group's behavior; self-
insight and personal change lead to organizational development; (2) Consulting, in which the change agent articulates the client's problem in
such a way that the underlying mechanisms are understood, and action is
then taken; and (3) Applied Research, in which feedback is stressed, so
that "research results serve to activate involvement and participation in
the planning, collection, analysis, and interpretation of more data". Each
of these three strategies depends upon the client's understanding of himself, his problem, and the dynamics of change. Bennis summarizes the necessary elements in implementing change as follows:

> "(a) The *client system* should have as much understanding of the
> change and its consequences, as much influence in developing and
> controlling the fate of the change, and as much trust in the initia-
> tor of the change as is possible. (b) The *change effort* should
> be perceived as being as self-motivated and voluntary as possible
> ...(c) The *change program* must include emotional and value as
> well as cognitive (informational) elements...(d) The *change agent*
> can be crucial in reducing the resistance to change...The quality
> of the client-agent relationship is pivotal to the success of the
> change program". (Bennis, #6619)

The significant issue as seen by Bennis is not who initiates a program
of change, but, rather, the manner in which it is carried out, and perhaps
this represents the emergent thinking on this issue. It would seem that the

most successful change efforts are those which are undertaken in collaboration with a change agent, but in which the receiver is internally motivated to change.

2.   The Role of Evaluation

In our change models, evaluation is described as a phase, although under a number of names. Some authors describe it as "mental trial"; for others, it signifies a behavioral trial, often limited in scope. To many, evaluation implies "research", while for others it might better imply "feedback" on performance or effectiveness. It has been stated that evaluation of educational innovations seldom takes place; yet, every "adoption" or "rejection" is the result of some type of evaluation. Feedback is an evaluative process without which neither individuals nor organizations can function effectively; it is necessary both in order to maintain the status quo, and to effect change. Perhaps we tend to take too narrow a view of the use of evaluation in the phases of innovation.

Where "evaluation" is perceived as a formal phase, it may prove threatening to those responsible for new or old programs. As Weiss (#2629) says, when the results of evaluation threaten the functioning of a system, even overwhelming evidence of failure may not be accepted. On the other hand, the threat of evaluation may result in a misleading description of what is actually taking place so that "effects or lack of them may be attributed to a phantom program, never really present" (Weiss, #2629).

One fact which is often overlooked is the *overlap* of "evaluation" with other phases. For example, awareness and interest are often aroused while an innovation is still under development. When this happens reactions may be fed back to designers and developers, and the result may be alteration of the innovation, acceleration or retardation of development, or even abandoning the innovation altogether. In this case, the "mental trial" type of evaluation may affect an innovation before design and development are complete.

Ideally, evaluation as a means of providing feedback should be a vital part of every step of the process of innovation. If our focus of attention is the *Social Interaction* Perspective, we need to know the most effective ways of making people aware and of promoting interest and information-seeking. We need to know a great deal more about the processes of individual and group decision-making, including the way in which perceived risks are balanced against perceived gains. In the problem-solver perspective, we must have feedback in order to evaluate and select the most effective methods for motivating people to change their attitudes and behavior. The "diagnosis" phase is one of evaluation of an existing situation; and in the formally designated stage of "evaluation" we are confronted with the problems involved in measuring change and improvement. In the Research, Development and Dissemination perspective, evaluation plays a more widely recognized role. Hendricks (#6045) describes the types of research at various phases: first, there is "research in the research stage", or "basic research". This is followed by research in the planning stage, or "problem solving"; then there is research in the development stage, or "action research". To this list, we can add that of research following adoption, or what is generally thought of as "evaluative research". All, however, involve evaluation. As Hendricks points out, the various types of research must eventually operate simultaneously or synergistically. When they do, a true state of feedback has been accomplished.

3. Phase Problems

The failure of innovations may sometimes be attributable to an inadequate consideration of various problems of phasing and timing. Therefore let us consider a few possible distortions of the natural process of phases.

a. Skipping Phases

It may often seem tempting to skip certain phases of a change plan in order to accomplish the change as rapidly as possible. The literature shows that although this may sometimes be a useful technique, it also may produce difficulties and should be approached with caution. Numerous innovations have failed in underdeveloped countries because the inital phases of accomodating traditional beliefs and practices to technical innovations were omitted. Social change can be accomplished without receiver-collaboration; however, if the receiver has gone through the phase of motivation-to-change, the process is immensely easier. The many failures of local fluoridation campaigns indicates the dangers of skipping this phase of involving and motivating the client system.

We have already discussed the difficulties which may result from skipping the phase of "diagnosis". Ignoring diagnosis may result in erroneous and irrelevant "solutions" or may leave us without adequate detailed information on when, where, and how innovations should be introduced. Omitting phases of "evaluation", on the other hand, may result in accepting worthless innovations, or failing to adapt innovations to fit the need of the receiver.

After noting the problems which may arise as a result of skipping a single phase, we may wonder if an innovation can ever be successful if phases are ignored completely. The literature seems to indicate that an innovation can still be effective even under such conditions, although the resulting change may be less stable than it would be if it had been effected through a series of phases. If an innovation is instituted under conditions which do not allow the receiver to pass through the pre-adoption stages, its success depends largely on the expertise of those who plan the change. The change plan must be decided upon by an expert who can accurately assess what the receiver would want if he had access to all the relevant facts and could make rational use of them.

When legislation is passed by Congress a change in behavior or custom is often required of the people. Different members of the society may hold different attitudes toward the change, but all are forced to adopt it simultaneously. It is usually hoped that oppostion will decline as people become accustomed to the change and that attitude change in conformity with the law will eventually come about. Hence "stateways" can become "folkways", but this does not always happen. Sometimes opposition actually increases after legal change as exemplified in the history of the legislation on Prohibition.

Nevertheless, legislation may often be an effective means of hastening change, an early example being that of compulsory education.

More recently, legislation regarding auto safety has led to a situation where, as we have pointed out, a receiver may adopt the innovation without having been through any of the pre-adoption phases. Legislation concerning racial integration is another attempt to change attitudes by changing behavior. Although this is a painfully slow process, it is certain to be more effective than waiting for all segments of society to become motivated to change. We might say that in these cases the phases preceding adoption have been ignored, but that a phase of stabilization must still follow the adoption if the change is to be considered genuine.

Ignoring phases is also advised by Watson (#6364) in situations in which raising issues for debate may create many anxieties. He cites the effective use of the "fait accompli" technique in the racial integration of several business organizations. He suggests that if employees had been questioned and "prepared" for integration before it occurred, apprehension and anxiety would have been raised, which would have led to resistance. However, when the normal procedures were followed in hiring a Negro and in introducing him to his co-workers, no difficulties arose.

b.   Being Out-of-Phase

When a sender and a receiver are out of phase with each other, difficulties are likely to arise which are similar to those resulting from the skipping of phases. These two sources of problems are, in fact, inter-related, and one may cause the other. The situation of being "out-of-phase" is most likely to occur when a sender does not accurately appraise the phase in the change sequence to which the receiver has progressed. For example, the sender may still be trying to arouse interest at a point when the receiver has passed the stage of mental trial, and has made a decision to adopt or reject. Or the sender may be trying to promote a trial phase, while the receiver is still seeking basic information. In the abortive attempt by Cumming and Cumming (3598) to introduce mental health education into a small community we could say that the project failed because the authors skipped the phase of motivating the receivers. We might also speculate that the project was simply "out-of-phase"; the Cummings' were trying to provide information, assuming that interest existed. Instead, they should perhaps have been trying to create interest and to promote information-seeking. Educational campaigns may often founder on such obstacles; we may assume that most people are interested in knowing basic techniques for the detection of cancer. However, for the individual who is too afraid to listen, such educational campaigns are clearly out-of-phase.

c.   Obsession

The phenomenon of "sticking" at a phase may be called an obsession, and it results in the inability to complete the series of phases necessary for change. A common example is the indivudual who "sticks" at the phase of mental trial, considering the pro's and con's of an innovation so thoroughly that a decision is never made. Another common example occurs when a person institutes a new technique on a "temporary" basis, but is then afraid to submit the trial results to evaluation. In this case the new practice may be continued, whether or not it is of value. Obsession can also occur at the stages of design and development, where a perfectionist would-be innovator is unable to release a product because it is not "perfect". As the term "obsession" implies, this particular phase problem is likely to indicate pathology on the part of an individual or group. Its effects are likely to be most pernicious in the diagnostic phase of problem solving. Obsessional concern for diagnosis may throttle the motivation to seek out exciting new solutions to problems.

d.   Compulsion

A phase problem which has the opposite effect of obsession may be called "compulsion". This signifies a rigid adherence to schedules and time limits without regard to the adequate completion of each individual phase. Such compulsions may occur because of internal or external pressures for change, and skipped phases or a condition of being "out-of-phase" are likely to result. The effect is often one of inadequate preparation and inadequate (or non-existent) evaluation. A compulsive following of stages may result in change which is poorly planned, haphazard in execution, and ultimately ineffective. When change is undertaken "for the sake of change", a compulsive approach is a likely consequence.

e.   Conclusion

Many authors have discussed the advisability of adhering closely to a planned sequence of stages in bringing about change. In some situations, however, the process of creating a desire for change in all the groups and individuals who will be affected may seem too difficult and time-consuming. For example, Featherstone (#6388), in his planning for establishing community schools in ghetto areas, says,

> "...don't wait to work out theories of what
> community participation means, and certainly
> don't wait for guarantees about money. Begin a
> school, do good work on a small, manageable
> scale, and perhaps reality will catch up to
> you. If there are enough such enterprises,
> learned men will do studies concluding that
> they reflect some kind of real need, and other
> learned men will be set to devising ways that
> their existence can be made to square off
> with common sense, public finance and all that.
> In the meantime, they exist, they teach live
> children; that's miracle enough to stagger
> the experts."

Most scholars in the field of planned change would suggest that Featherstone's plan leaves too much to chance. If one good community school is set up, the chances are not great that others will then sprout automatically. Reality must still catch up, and the support and personnel which are required for full-scale adoption may be gained extremely slowly, if at all. Featherstone's plan may be considered as one strategy which may be employed in the dissemination of the desired change, but it cannot be viewed as a comprehensive change plan. A plan for the dissemination of the notion of the community school must still be devised.

The change strategies which we have discussed in this chapter were formulated because it was observed that many needs were not being met while at the same time good ideas and innovations were not reaching those who could benefit by using them. The models are designed to remedy these problems, to bridge the gap between the researcher and the consumer, and to serve as a guide in planning change. Once the personnel involved in a change procedure are aware of the steps which should take place in the ideal situation, however, it is desirable that they should apply this ideal model with discretion. Phases should be *adapted* to the situation: some steps may be skipped if they are not relevant in the particular case at hand, and others may be skipped if they have already been carried out at an earlier date. Guba (#7131) points out that the research phase may often be skipped for either of these reasons. Watson (#6195), as we mentioned earlier, feels that his full scale model should be used only for momentous changes. He also cautions that it would be foolhardy to stick rigidly to any one model for change. "Efficient and experienced persons discover short-cuts which work as well or better under certain conditions."

The key to the advisability of skipping phases or altering a plan of change may be found in Watson's warning; the circumstances must be suitable, and the judgement of those involved must be reliable. This combination may be hard to find; Miles (#1481) concludes that one characteristic of an effective strategy of innovation is comprehensive attention to all stages of the diffusion process.

CHAPTER ELEVEN

SUMMARY, SYNTHESIS, CONCLUSIONS AND IMPLICATIONS

<u>Table of Contents</u>   Page

CHAPTER ELEVEN *

SUMMARY, SYNTHESIS, CONCLUSIONS AND IMPLICATIONS

I. THE LITERATURE ON DISSEMINATION AND UTILIZATION (D&U)**: QUANTITATIVE OVERVIEW

We began this report by suggesting that there was an emerging discipline in the social sciences focussing on processes of change, innovation, and knowlege utilization. Having identified and selectively reviewed some 4,000 sources, we are prepared to assert this same proposition as a fact. The quantity and even the quality of the available literature indicates that the basic conceptual and empirical ingredients of this new discipline are now present.

As we concluded our search activities for this report we attempted to compute some gross statistics on the characteristics of the literature which we had identified. Some of the summary tables of that analysis were presented in Chapter One. In making this analysis we were struck by at least five features which are worth reviewing as we start the final chapter. These features are: (A) Large Quantity, (b) Rapid Growth, (C) Wide Scope, (D) Large Proportion of Empirical Studies, and (E) Wide Dispersion of Sources.

A. QUANTITY

Contrary to our initial expectations, we were able to identify a very large quantity of literature which pertained directly or indirectly to know· ledge dissemination and utilization, innovation and technological change. Over 4,000 studies were identified, but we suspect there are many more which we failed to uncover either because they were (1) too recent and hence not adequately indexed, (2) buried in journals or magazines which we failed to screen (it was impossible to survey all sources), (3) hidden under obscure or misleading titles, or (4) appearing in foreign publications which were not screened by our major English language indexing services.*** On the assumption that our search uncovered something under half of the available sources, we would guess at the existence of at least 10,000 relevant references as of the beginning of 1969.

By field, the largest number appear in "education" (17%), followed by "agriculture" (13%), and "communication" (13%). Because special effort was made to identify education sources, this category may be slightly over-represented proportionately.

B. GROWTH

At least as significant as the gross quantity of the literature is the steady increase in its rate of growth. In 1954 barely 50 relevant studies appeared in the literature. By 1964 there were nearly 500 annually. Again because of the lag in indexing we do not have complete data for the years since 1964, but we suspect that the acceleration curve is continuing to rise.

---

*This chapter was drafted by Ronald G. Havelock.

**The abbreviation "D&U" for "dissemination and utilization" is used throughout this chapter.

***We doubt that this last category accounts for too many missing references. Even among known sources the number of non-U.S. references to D&U seems disproportionately small.

C.   SCOPE

The third fact that struck us was the tremendous scope and variety of studies identified. We began to realize that these two words, "dissemination" and "utilization" covered a lot of territory. The breadth and diversity was encouraging but at the same time perplexing. Although there was some redundancy, we found studies that looked at knowledge dissemination or utilization from nearly every conceivable angle. There was a tremendous range, for example, in the *size of adopting unit*. There was likewise a range of *perspective* from microscopic to macroscopic and a range in *types of studies* from experimental research to case studies, to field studies, to theoretical presentations. We found there was a tremendous range in subject matter even within the field of education. This range took in curriculum diffusion, diffusion of all kinds of administrative arrangements, organizational change activities, technology diffusion, and the development and diffusion of new roles and new organizational groupings. We found large numbers of studies that could be classified in terms of research, in terms of development, and, of course, many studies that could be classified in terms of "practice wisdom".

D.   PROPORTION OF EMPIRICAL RESEARCH

We were impressed by the proportion of studies which could be classified as "quantitative", i.e., those in which the authors made an effort to report original empirical data of some sort in quantitative form. Fifty-three percent of studies fall into this category in contrast to 25% rated as "theoretical", and only 7% identified as "case studies." A preponderance of the agriculture references were counted as "quantitative", but the proportion was also large in education and other fields.

E.   DISPERSION OF SOURCES

Finally, we were impressed and frustrated by the extremely wide array of sources in which D&U relevant material was likely to turn up. Trade journals, professional "house organs," special seminar and conference proceedings, project proposals, and even unpublished manuscripts were found to contain relevant, unique and important information.*

F.   RECOMMENDATIONS DERIVED FROM THIS GROSS OVERVIEW

Even before we begin to summarize our detailed findings, we can make certain recommendations based on the five broad characteristics of the literature just outlined. There are some obvious problems, flaws, and gaps which emerge from this picture, areas where we feel we would like to see some significant improvements in the next decade. Five areas come to mind as being particularly significant.

1.   Case Studies

First of all we noted that although there were many quantitative research studies, there was a paucity of case materials. We need more case studies which carefully document and report dissemination and

---

*See for example much of the widely influential work of David Clark, Egon Guba, and Charles Jung, frequently cited in this report. One could hazard a guess that much of this material fails to reach scholarly printed form because its originators are application-and action-oriented people, not publication-oriented people. It may also be that appropriate media for dissemination of knowledge about d&u have not yet been established.

utilization events. Such events, of course, come in all shapes and sizes, but we would include here training projects, development projects, the installation of new roles, and the development of new organizational forms as all being activities requiring careful case reporting and documentation.

2. Comprehensive, Analytical Reviews of the Literature

A second need is for a greater number of reviews of the literature that give adequate attention to the tremendous scope that we did find. Probably the best existing integrative review is the study by Everett Rogers of the Diffusion of Innovations. Rogers considers not only his own background field of rural sociology, but he also reviews the studies that have been done in medicine, education, industry and other fields. He builds an integrated conceptual model within which he can handle a diverse and very large bulk of quantitative research findings. More studies by authors representing different orientations are needed in this general type.

3. Programmatic R&D on the Utilization Process

A third need, particularly in the field of education, is for sequential planned research and programmatic research and development which is based on one or another of the emerging models discussed in this report. We do have some very fine, and very well thought out conceptual schemas for ordering the facts in this field; Lippitt, Brickell, Miles, Clark, and Guba are just a few of the authors who have evolved such schemas; but we have very little literature which is based on sequential planning; this is the only kind of research that can give us depth understanding in particular areas. It should be noted in this regard that the Regional Laboratories as conceived and developed by the U.S. Office of Education are beginning to carry out these sequential programmatic efforts on various important educational problems. We would hope that more and more of the lab program efforts will be directed toward R&D on innovation and knowledge utilization as such.

4. Journals for Research and Theory on Dissemination, Utilization and Innovation

Fourthly, one had to be struck in viewing this literature by the tremendous scatter of sources. Relevant material turned up in virtually every kind of journal and every kind of format from dittoed scraps and newsletters to lengthy published monographs and books. I would urge that we introduce as soon as possible some new journals or other communicating devices that are devoted exclusively to dissemination and utilization topics and concerns.

5. A Central Facility for Collection, Storage, and Dissemination of Knowledge about D&U Processes

A fifth and final priority related to the foregoing is a central source for identifying literature and for storing it. We were impressed by the amount of really significant and important material which appeared in dittoed form, internal memoranda, project proposals, and news briefs of one sort or another. Typically such materials are restricted to local circulation. In D&U, however, they seem to represent a most significant resource: they should be made generally available. This means that they must be collated and in some way brought together and organized for dissemination.

II. THE MODELS OF D&U: AN OVERVIEW AND SYNTHESIS

Our starting point for considering knowledge utilization in Chapter One was
the single act of communication or transfer of information from one person to
another. We utilized a simple paradigm of the communication process which posits
a "sender", a "receiver", a "message", and a "medium". We soon broadened the
concepts of "sender" and "receiver" by designating them as the "resource system"
and the "user·system" as indicated again in Figure 11.1.

FIGURE 11.1   D&U as an Act of Communication

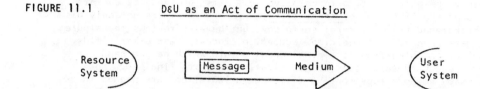

This simple model served us well, first as a guide to literature searching,
and later as a way to separate out some major chapter headings for this report;
but as a model of the complete process it left much to be desired. In reviewing the
literature, we have found that the major theoretical and empirical studies of knowledge dissemination and utilization can be grouped conveniently into three general
categories corresponding to the principle models, methods, and orientations employed
by their authors. We have identified these three categories as (1) the "Research
Development and Diffusion" Perspective, (2) the "Social Interaction" Perspective,
and (3) the "Problem Solver" Perspective. Each of these three viewpoints contributes
significantly to our understanding of the total dissemination and utilization process, and each deserves a thorough consideration and appreciation. For that reason
we have suggested this three-part distinction as a helpful device for crystallizing
our thinking at several points (Chapter Two, Chapter Nine, and Chapter Ten, in
particular). In the following pages, each perspective is characterized by a
diagram (Figures 2, 3, and 4) and a brief recapitulation of its major emphases.

Because we could not choose from among these three viewpoints one which
seemed to be representative and comprehensive, we have endeavored to bring them
together in a *"linkage"* model which incorporates important features of all three.
Linkage is seen as a series of two-way interaction processes which connect user
systems with various resource systems, including basic and applied research,
development, and practice. According to this model, senders and receivers can
achieve successful linkage only if they exchange messages in two-way interaction and
continuously make the effort to simulate each other's problem solving behavior.
Hence, the resource systems must appreciate the user's internal needs and problem-
solving patterns, and the user, in turn, must be able to appreciate the invention,
solution-formulation and evaluation processes of the resource systems. This type
of collaborative interaction will not only make solutions more relevant and effective, but it will also build relationships of trust, and mutual perceptions by
user and resource persons that the other is truly concerned, will listen, and will
be able to provide useful information. These trust relationships can, over time,
become channels for the rapid, effective, and efficient transfer of information.

Effective knowledge utilization also requires a degree of division of labor,
coordination and collaboration throughout the social system. The role of *government*
should be to monitor the "natural" knowledge flow system and·develop means to
support, facilitate, and coordinate linkage activities so that the total system
can function more effectively.

A.   THE RESEARCH, DEVELOPMENT & DIFFUSION PERSPECTIVE (RD&D)

In some sense the   RD&D model picture in Figure 11.2 is a grand elaboration on the communication act formula cited above. It posits a user population

[Insert Figure 11.2 here]

which can be reached effectively and influenced through a process of
"dissemination", or by dissemination activities of various sorts, provided,
however, that this dissemination is preceded by an *extensive and complex process of research and development* which usually includes the following features:
"basic research", "applied research", "development", "production", and
"packaging". There are, of course, many variations on this pattern discussed
in detail in Chapter Ten, but regardless of the specifics of different RD&D
models, we can note five features which they all seem to have in common, very
positive features, which illustrate why the RD&D model is so powerful.

First of all, the RD&D model suggests that D&U should be a rational process: there should be a rational sequence of activities which moves from research to development to packaging before dissemination takes place. Secondly,
this model assumes that there has to be planning, and planning really on a
massive scale. It is not enough that we simply have all these activities of
research and development; they have to be coordinated; there has to be a
relationship between them; and they have to make sense in a logical sequence
that may go back years in the evolution of one particular message to be
disseminated. Thirdly, there has to be a division of labor and a separation
of roles and functions, an obvious prerequisite in all complex activities of
modern society, but one that we sometimes slur over. Fourth, it assumes a
more or less clearly defined target audience, a specified passive consumer,
who will accept the innovation if it is delivered on the right channel, in
the right way, and at the right time. The particular process which is supposed
to assure this happening is scientific evaluation, evaluation at every stage
of development and dissemination. Fifth, and finally, this perspective accepts
the fact of high initial development cost prior to any dissemination activity,
because it foresees an even higher gain in the long run, in terms of *efficiency,
quality, and capacity to reach a mass audience*. These five features,
(1) rational sequence, (2) planning, (3) division of labor, (4) defined audience,
and (5) high investment for maximum pay-off, make "RD&D" a very useful and
relevant paradigm for technical and social change.

Prototypes for the RD&D model are presumed to exist in industry, defense,
and space and perhaps most especially in agriculture. In education the major
proponents for this point of view are Henry M. Brickell, Egon Guba, and David
Clark, all currently of Indiana University. It seems to be a particularly
popular and appropriate model for dealing with D&U issues at the macrosystemic
and policy levels (see again Chapter Three) because it subdivides the knowledge
flow system neatly into different
functional roles which exist within different sub-cultures (e.g., the research
community, the product organizations, the practitioners, the consumers).* It
does appear to supply much of the rationale for current policy planning in the
U.S. Office of Education.

---

*Advocates do not assume, however, that knowledge flows in a linear fashion from R to
D to D. R and D is usually seen as a constant recycling process of design,
evaluation, feedback, redesign and so forth. The arrows of the figure may be somewhat misleading in this respect particularly when we are thinking of specific innovations and their development histories. From a broad historical and policy perspective, however, the "linear" flow would appear to have some validity.

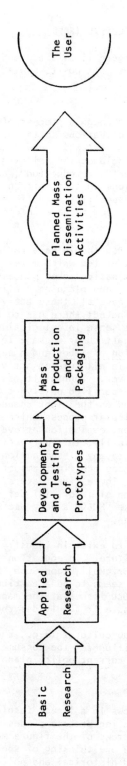

FIGURE 11.2 The Research, Development and Diffusion Perspective

Basic Research → Applied Research → Development and Testing of Prototypes → Mass Production and Packaging → Planned Mass Dissemination Activities → The User

Major Points Stressed: Rational Process
                          Planning Necessary
                          Division of Labor
                          High investment pays off in quality, quantity, long
                          term benefit, and capacity to reach mass audience.

Spokesmen: Henry M. Brickell, David Clark, Egon Guba

Prototypes: Industrial R&D, U.S. Agricultural Research and Extension System

In criticism, the RD&D model can be said to be over-rational, over-idealized, excessively research oriented, and inadequately user oriented, but because it has been laid out so concretely by Guba and his colleagues, it gives other educators something to shoot at figuratively as well as literally. Chase, for example,* has suggested that Guba and company may have been most useful to education in arousing colleagues to come forth with alternative conceptualizations.

B.   THE SOCIAL INTERACTION PERSPECTIVE (S-I)

The *social interaction perspective* has its roots in anthropological studies of the diffusion of cultural traits (e.g., Barnett #0620). Perhaps for this reason proponents of this school have ignored many of the concerns that preoccupy RD&D theorists. S-I researchers assume the existence of a diffusable "innovation" as a precondition for any analysis of the diffusion process. Hence, they are relatively indifferent to the value of the innovation or to the type of scientific and technical know-how that might have gone into its original development and manufacture.

There is a tendency for S-I researchers to choose innovations which appear in a concrete, "diffusable" form, such as a type of fertilizer or a new prescription drug. The preference stems from the most outstanding characteristic of the S-I school, their thoroughly *empirical research* orientation: if the innovation is a stable element which we can easily identify as a constant, the task of measuring its *flow through a social system* over time is made considerably easier. This measurement of the flow is the primary concern of the S-I theorists; they study the pattern of flow and the effects of social structure and social relationships and groupings on the fate of innovations. In Figure 11.3, we try to illustrate the major types of phenomena studied by this group of researchers.

[Insert Figure 11.3 here]

Six major points can be derived from the theory and the considerable quantity of empirical research identified with this S-I tradition. These are (1) the importance of the social relations network, (2) the user's position in that network, (3) the significance of informal personal relationships and contacts, (4) the importance of reference group identifications, (5) the essential irrelevance of the size of the adopting unit, and (6) the differential significance of different types of influence strategies at different stages in the adoption process. Each of these points will be briefly expanded in the following paragraphs.

1.   The Importance of the Social Relations Network

The fact that individual human beings are embedded in and inextricably connected to a social network made up of other individuals may seem obvious enough to most of us, but it is a fact often ignored by R&D-oriented policy makers when they assume that the best innovations diffuse by themselves or when they assume that new ideas can be conveyed successfully through publications or other mass media alone. S-I theorists know better, and their research has shown us what a complex and intricate set of human substructures and processes must be operative before diffusion will succeed.

---

*Dr. Frank Chase, University of Chicago, in conversation with the author.

11-7

FIGURE 11.3   The Social Interaction Perspective

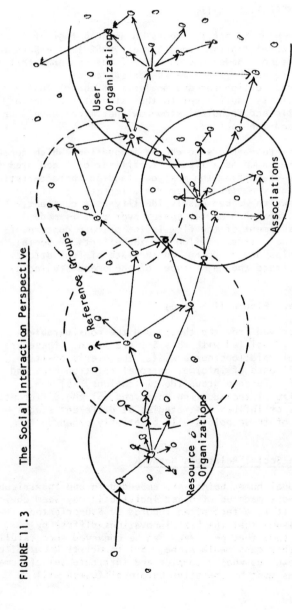

Major Points Stressed: Personal Relationships
                          Group Memberships and Identifications
                          Social Structure - Power and Influence Structures
                          Proximity, Cosmopoliteness
                          Opinion Leadership Structure

Spokesmen: Everett Rogers, James Coleman, Elihu Katz, Herbert Menzel, Richard Carlson,
              Paul Mort

Prototypes: Diffusion of innovations in farm practices, spread of new drugs among physicians.

Key: o o   Individuals in the
        o o   social system.
        ↑   Flow of new knowledge.
        ⌒   Formal organizational
               structures
        ⌐ ⌐   Informal structures.

2. The User's Position in the Network

One of the earliest discoveries of the S-I school was *"opinion leadership"*, the fact that initial acceptance by a small minority of key influentials was the major factor in diffusion to the community as a whole. The prestige of these individuals, their status as exemplars and norm-setters, and the frequency of their interaction with other members were the key factors in gaining acceptance from the great majority.

From this beginning, S-I researchers have gone on to identify a variety of positions in the social system which need to be considered in analyzing the diffusion process: the *"innovator"*, who tends to be on the fringe of his home system because he has so many links with other outside systems; the *"laggard"*, who is isolated and is peripheral to the main streams of interpersonal relations; and the *"early majority"*, who adopt quickly because of their positions near the center of the influence network and their close proximity to the leadership. All these findings and many more have helped to build a more and more sophisticated and discriminated conception of the social influence network, and of the significance of the user's position in the network for predicting adoption behavior.

3. Informal Personal Contact

A corollary of the above finding is the importance of face-to-face interpersonal contacts. The opinion leader is an important force in societal diffusion because he has a lot of friendly personal contacts with other members, and even he depends largely on word-of-mouth communication with local innovators and outside experts in building his own inventory of new ideas and practices. For the all-important stages of evaluation (deciding whether or not an innovation ought to be adopted) personal sources seem to be the most significant for all adoptors (see e.g., Rogers, #1824, p. 313). For the vast majority it is the crucial element at all stages.

4. The Individual's Group Identity and Group Loyalty

Social Psychologist Theodore Newcomb (#6302) first called our attention to the significance of the psychological group as distinct from the manifest social group in his study of attitude stability and change at Bennington College. Girls who were firmly rooted in a conservative home culture were able to persist in old attitudes through four years of exposure to avidly liberal attitudes, within the highly cohesive and interactive college culture. The same phenomenon which Newcomb termed "reference group" identification plays a key role in diffusion as studied by the S-I school (see Figure 11.3). People tend to adopt and maintain attitudes and behaviors which they perceive as normative for their psychological reference group. Innovators are likely to place themselves in a greater number and variety of such reference groups, and they are more likely to have what Rogers calls a "cosmopolite" orientation which allows them to see personal relevance and value in ideas and things which their neighbors would see as foreign. A society which allows large numbers of individuals to maintain large numbers of diverse and overlapping reference group identifications will be a very innovative society.

5. The Essential Irrelevance of the Size of Adopting Unit

The most persistent criticism of S-I research by educators rests on the belief that only individual adopters (farmers, doctors) have been examined as the unit of study, whereas in education the total *school* or *school system* is the adopter. This belief is categorically false. As Rogers and others have shown in extensive literature reviews, the same phenomena have been studied using a remarkable diversity of adopter "units" varying in size and complexity from the individual to the small group, to the industrial firm, the school system, and even larger "units". Walker, for example, (#7045) has noted the same reference group and opinion leadership phenomena as discussed above in his study of the social influence network among the fifty states in legislation innovativeness. Indeed, in education, itself, the primary unit of analysis has <u>typically</u> been not the individual teacher but the school system as a whole (e.g., Mort #1191, Ross #2878, and Carlson #0585).

This remarkable consistency of major S-I findings in widely different settings has lead Bhola to propose a "configurational" theory of diffusion (#1062) which permits comparative analysis of patterns of flow and relationships regardless of size and other differentiating characteristics of the specific adopting units studied. If the configuration is closely similar irrespective of time, circumstances, and unit size, the significance of S-I research findings is enormous, because it means that generalizations from one set of findings in one setting can be applied, at least tentatively, to the analysis of other settings; diffusion research in agriculture and technology can then be used at the very least to make shrewd guesses in medicine, social welfare and education. It is a most significant step toward a general science and an engineering science of D&U processes.

6. Significance of Stages of Adoption for D&U Strategies

Finally, the S-I school has shown the utility of research built around a phase model of the adoption process. Usually they have stuck to the five phase "AIETA" model: awareness, interest, evaluation, trial and adoption. They have shown that different types of influence strategy (mass media, demonstration, contact with experts, informal contact with peers) are most effective at different stages. Armed with this knowledge, the change strategist can plan out a synchronized multi-media program of influence which has an optimum likelihood of achieving maximum D&U.

Historically, research on social diffusion processes (the S-I school) began with anthropology, and was strongly influenced by social psychology (Newcomb on reference groups, Lewin on gatekeepers and group decision making), but it took its most virile form in the hands of rigorous and empirically minded rural sociologists beginning with the classic study of the diffusion of hybrid corn by Ryan and Gross (#12621). Over 1000 empirical research studies have come along since 1943 which bolster and extend this original work. Important contributors to this tradition are too numerous to cite, but a few who stand out are Coleman, E. Katz, Menzel (Drugs among physicians, research among scientists), Beal, Lionberger, E. Rogers, and Wilkening (agriculture) and Carlson, Mort, and Ross (education).

Nevertheless, there are notable gaps in this literature, some predictable but some surprising. First, as mentioned previously, the
processes related to invention, research, and development of innovations
have not been studied from the S-I persepctive. Secondly, the translation, transformation and adaptation of innovations which goes on as they
are diffusing through the system has been understudied. Third, the
processes of maladoption, inadequate or inappropriate adoption, and
rejection have been given less than adequate coverage.

A fourth important shortcoming of this school is the rather loose
and sketchy understanding of the *psychological processes* inside the
user-adopter. External social influence processes are rarely tied to
either attitude change research, personality theory, or learning theory
research in psychology, despite the fact that an enormous body of presumably
relevant knowledge exists under all three of these headings. Perhaps
because nearly all S-I researchers have been sociologists in training
and interest, they have failed to generate a sophisticated model of the
internal processes of D&U inside the individual user.

Perhaps it is more surprising that S-I sociologists have not paid
much attention to the voluminous literature on the sociology and
psychology of *organizations* as such. As we have shown in Chapter Six,
there is a rich theoretical and empirical tradition in this area, much of
which has definite implications for D&U. Indeed many organizational
researchers (e.g., Bennis, #5082, Likert, #6590) have laid special stress
upon change processes. S-I research can be cited which bears on flow to
the organization and adoption by the organization *as a total unit,* but
it has said little about what happens to knowledge flow *within the
organization* even with respect to such elementary structural features
as the formal organization chart.

With all these shortcomings, however, the S-I perspective remains
by far the strongest of those reviewed in this chapter in terms of
empirical research support, and the six major points which we have
derived from it represent highly relevant considerations for any D&U
activity.

C.   THE PROBLEM-SOLVER PERSPECTIVE (P-S)

A third major D&U perspective rests on the primary assumption that knowledge utilization is a part, and only a part, of a problem-solving process
inside the user which begins with a need, and ends with the satisfaction of
that need. The large circle in Figure 11.4 represents the potential consumer
of knowledge as a problem-solver.

[Insert Figure 11.4 here]

Proponents of this school of thought model the process as stages of a
cycle typically including the steps of (1) need sensing and articulation,
(2) diagnosis and formulation of the need as a problem to be solved, (3) identification and search for resources relevant to the problem, (4) retrieval of
potentially feasible solutions and solution-pertinent ideas, (5) translation
of this retrieved knowledge into specific solutions or solution prototypes,
(6) behavioral try-out or application of the solution to the need, with
evaluation of effectiveness being made in terms of need reduction. Presumably,
if the solution does not satisfy the need, the cycle begins again,and continues until, through a series of trials and adaptation efforts, the problem
is solved on an adequate and lasting basis.

11-11

FIGURE 11.4   The Problem-Solver Perspective

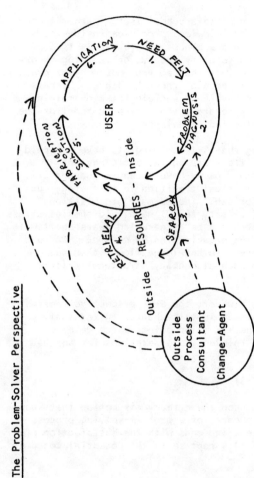

Major Points Stressed: The User's Need is the Paramount Consideration
                         Diagnosis is Part of the Process
                         The Outsider is a Catalyst Consultant or Collaborator but the
                         User must find the Solution Himself or See it as His Own
                         Internal Resources should be fully Utilized
                         Self-initiated Change has the Firmest Motivational Basis and
                         the Best Prospects for Long-Term Maintenance

Spokesmen: Goodwin Watson, Ronald Lippitt, Herbert Thelen, Matthew Miles, Charles Jung

Prototypes: Organizational self-renewal, mental health consultation.

The problem-solver (P-S) perspective is closely associated with the human relations tradition of planned change and it represents basically a psychological and "user-oriented" approach to problems of D&U. In contrast to the more sociological S-I tradition, however, there has been very little solid empirical research based on a P-S approach. This may only be a result of the very recent beginnings of interest and involvement in the psychological aspects of D&U issues. Nevertheless, there is now a surge of interest evidenced in the establishment of new organizations and units specifically devoted to utilization and in the investment of energies in utilization by such leading human relations specialists as Benne, Lippitt, Miles, and Watson.

Five very solid points are stressed by P-S theorists: (1) that the *user's* world is the only sensible place from which to begin to consider utilization; (2) that knowledge utilization must include a *diagnostic* phase where user need is considered and translated into a problem statement; (3) that the role of the outsider is primarily to serve as *catalyst, collaborator* or *consultant* on how to plan change and bring about this solution; (4) that *internal* knowledge retrieval and the marshalling of internal resources should be given at least equal emphasis with external retrieval; and (5) that self-initiation by the user or client system creates the best motivational climate for lasting change. Each of these points deserves some analysis and comment.

1. The User is the Starting Place

We noted earlier that S-I researchers were usually indifferent to the ultimate fate of an innovation; for them the process ends when the target audience receives or "buys" or "adopts." But if the S-I tradition accepts the innovation as a "fait accompli", the P-S tradition accepts and advances the cause of the consumer as a "fait accompli"; without the consumer's needs and circumstances as a prior fact the "innovation" is meaningless. In a sense, this is a moral-ethical stance because it poses the question "utilization for what" as the priority issue, whereas the same question might be dismissed as "beyond science" by empirically-oriented and objectivist researchers.

2. Diagnosis Precedes Solution Identification

Perhaps because of their clinical emphasis on the user and his world, the P-S school also follows the medical metaphor in stressing the need for a diagnostic stage in which the user's symptomatic needs are analyzed and interpreted. Causes of the manifest need are probed and the context of the user's problem situation is mapped out. This step allows the formulation of a problem statement which accurately reflects the real problem and the real need underlying the manifest symptoms.

3. The Outside Helping Role is Non-Directive

P-S advocates often go to some length to spell out the specialized role of the helper or "change agent", but they are usually emphatic in stressing that the change agent should avoid "taking over" by doing the problem-solving for the client. What the client system really needs in the long haul is *guidance and training in how to do his own problem-solving*. The outside "expert" may be able to convey certain relevant kinds of knowledge to the user, but such an "expert" role is not the most effective helping role in the long run; it is not only expensive and wasteful, but it also leaves the client with *no internal capacity* to solve his own problems. Hence the change agent should be a *non-directive consultant*, advising and helping on the process more than on the content, encouraging the user to do his own diagnosis, retrieval, and application work for himself. The farthest that the change agent should go in direct helping is to participate as *collaborator* and co-equal in the P-S process. Here the outside change agent and the client system representatives form a temporary *team* to work on the problem and to apply the solution.

4. The Importance of Internal Resources

The P-S perspective is unique among approaches to D&U in its emphasis on effective utilization of *internal* resources. In our emphasis on "innovation", i.e., the importation of new ideas and artifacts into a system, we tend to forget the fact that most users are already making very poor use of what they already know and have within easy reach. This home-grown and home-stored knowledge is probably going to be more relevant and more suitable for the solution of the problem at hand than the imported knowledge will be. Moreover, even if the import is relevant and valuable, the user will have to mobilize internal resources of skill and experience to the task of *adaptation* of the outside knowledge to the inside need.

5. User-Initiated Change is the Strongest

The core assumption of the P-S perspective is that self-initiated change has the firmest motivational basis and the best prospects for long-term maintenance. The outside expert is here today and gone tomorrow; tommorow all his skill, understanding, and enthusiasm for the innovation may be gone, too. Therefore, the user must not only accept the innovation; he must *internalize* it, making it a part of his routine behavior and investing in it his own energy and enthusiasm. The user will be more likely to internalize an innovation that he sees as *his own*, something that he has accepted by his *own free and deliberate choice* to meet his *own specific need,* and something that he has worked on himself to *adapt* to his own specific need.

These five strong points of the P-S perspective make it a virulent contender as the model of utilization, but it is not without its own shortcomings. Three drawbacks should be noted here: first, it puts excessive strain on the user; second, it minimizes the role of outside resources; and third, it does not provide an effective model for mass diffusion and utilization.

Relating to the first point, there may be some question raised about the capacity of the typical user to innovate. Bagehot long ago observed that imitation is the "cake of custom" which binds together all but the strongest men. In contrast, he thought that invention and novelty require "strongmen", "nationbuilders" (Allport, #6479, pp. 21-22). We probably need to ask ourselves just how much creativity in problem-solving the average user is capable of achieving.

Relative to the second point, there appears to be inadquate consideration and appreciation of the scope, variety, and rich potential of outside resources. The fact is that there are a tremendous number of new ideas and new products, some derived from R and D, and some invented by other users, and it is probably worth a tremendous investment of effort to build retrieval and sharing mechanisms to make this storehouse of "goodies" available to all. The P-S advocates, in their excessive concentration on the user's internal world, may not have devoted enough attention to external retrieval and dissemination processes.

Finally, with regard to the third point of criticism, there seems to be no clearly worked out strategy for following the P-S model which allows new ideas to speed through a population of users in a reasonable period of time. With a very limited supply of change agents and with each user system needing a change agent with whom to work through an extended P-S process, how will we ever reach 20,000 school districts with all the useful new ideas that are now available? Until very recently problem-solving has been primarily a pilot experiment conducted by a few university professors in a few fortunate (and usually prosperous) user systems. Now with the intrusion of *R&D* thinking into the P-S school, there is discussion of, and some concrete movement toward, the *packaging* of *problem-solving* processes so that they can be shared, understood, and employed more widely.

D.   THE CONCEPT OF LINKAGE

Each of the three perspectives toward D&U discussed up to this point provides us with valuable insights and useful guideposts for developing a comprehensive view of the whole, but each leaves much to be desired when viewed separately. Clearly there is a need to bring these three viewpoints together in a single perspective that includes the strongest features of each. We are not sure that we are yet ready and able to bring about this synthesis, but in this section we will put forth the concept of "linkage" as a possible unifying and integrating idea.

The concept of linkage starts with a focus on the user as a *problem-solver*. We must first consider the internal problem-solving cycle within the user as it is depicted in Figure 11.4 (see above); there is an initial "felt need" which leads into a "diagnosis" and "problem statement" and works through "search" and "retrieval" phases to a "solution", and the "application" of that solution. But as we see in turning to Figure 11.5, the linkage model stresses that the user must be *meaningfully related to outside resources*.

[Insert Figure 11.5 here]

The user must make contact with the outside resource system and interact with it so that he will get back something relevant to help him with the solution process. The user must enter into a *reciprocal relationship* with the resource system; this means that something must be going on inside the resource system that corresponds to what is happening in the user. In effect, resource systems and resource persons must *simulate* or recapitulate the need-reduction cycle of the user: they should be able to (1) simulate the user's need; (2) simulate the search activity that the user has gone through; and (3) simulate the solution-application procedure that the user has gone through or will go through. It is only in this way that the resource person can come to have a meaningful exchange with the user.

We may illustrate this important point   by recalling a cartoon of two rats in a Skinner Box: one of them is pressing his bar and saying to the other, "you know, I think I've really got this psychologist conditioned: just by pressing this bar, I can train him to put food pellets down this chute." The mutual relationship between psychologist and rat illustrated in this cartoon is precisely the kind of activity that must be going on between the resource system and the user system. It is not a one-way relationship: the resource and the user have to be conditioned to each other. The resource system recapitulates the problem-solving cycle of the user, and at the same time the resource system must interact with the user in the development of solutions.

11-15

FIGURE 11.5   The Linkage Process

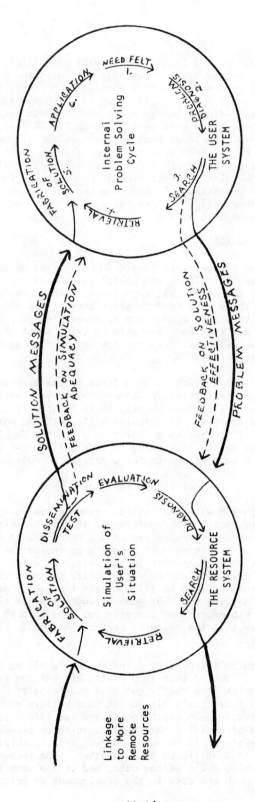

From the Linkage Perspective:

1. Resource system must recapitulate or adequately simulate the user's problem-solving process.
2. The user must be able to understand (and simulate) the research, development, and evaluation processes employed by the resource system in the fabrication of solutions.
3. Resource and user must provide reciprocal feedback.
4. Successful linkage experiences build channels for efficient dissemination.

This reciprocity with the user includes testing the adequacy of the simulation model, itself. Only through an interaction with and a feedback from the user can the resource person learn whether or not his model of user-behavior is correct. At the same time the user should be learning and beginning to simulate resource system processes such as scientific evalution and product development. Only through understanding, appreciating, and to some degree, emulating such processes, will the user come to be a sophisticated consumer of R and D.

The development of reciprocating relationships goes beyond the point of improving individual *problem-solving* processes toward the creation of a stable and long lasting *social influence* network. This collaboration will not only make a solution more effective, but, equally important, it will build a more effective relationship - a relationship of trust and a perception by the user that the resource is truly concerned, that the resource will listen, and will have a quantity of useful information to pass on. The reciprocal and collaborative nature of this relationship further serves to legitimize the roles of consumer and resource person and it builds a *channel* from resource to user.

Linkage is not simply a two person interaction process however; the resource person, in turn, must have access to more remote and more expert resources than himself, as indicated at the left hand side of Figure 11.5. In his efforts to help the user, the resource person must be able to draw on specialists, too. Therefore, he must have a way of communicating his need for knowledge (which, of course, is a counterpart of the user's need) to other resource persons and these, in turn, must have the capacity to recapitulate this same problem-solving cycle at least to a degree; only in this way will they be able to develop a functional relationship with each other.

Therefore, an effective D&U process requires linkage to more and more remote resource persons, and ultimately these overlapping linkages form an extended series which we have sometimes described as a "chain of knowledge utilization" (see Chapter Two and Chapter Three) connecting the most remote sources of expert knowledge in the university with the most remote consumers of knowledge. In Figure 11.6 these overlapping relationships are depicted

[Insert Figure 11.6 here]

in idealized form; the figure is intended to suggest what we mean by the term "macrosystem" of knowledge linkage.

It is possible to identify and differentiate within our total society a variety of knowledge-building, knowledge-disseminating, and knowledge-consuming *subsystems*, each with its own distinctive protective skin of values, beliefs, special language, and normative behaviors. At various points in this report we have had occasion to refer to these as the "research subsystem," the "development subsystem," the "practice subsystem," and the "user subsystem." At a gross level, the prime task of knowledge utilization is to bring these great subsystems into effective linkage with each other; the kind of reciprocal simulation-and-feedback relationship which we have described above needs to be established at the interface between systems. As noted by Loomis (Miles, #1046, p. 653) linkage between systems is the essential process in any effort at planned social change.

The appropriate role of *government* in knowledge utilization can be seen most clearly at this gross level of analysis. As pictured in Figure 11.6, the government should be in a position to see the various sub-cultures as one system

FIGURE 11.6   The Macrosystem of Knowledge Linkage

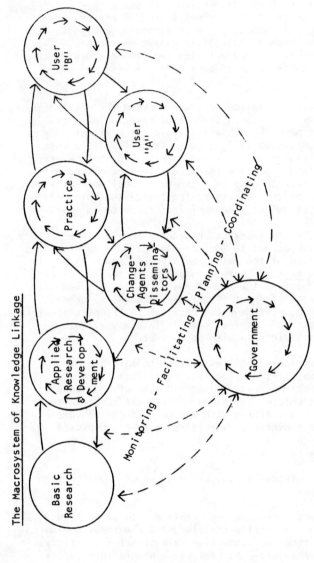

All sub-systems of the society must be able to simulate each other's problem-solving process and exchange messages concerning needs, problems, and solutions; but the efforts of all need to be monitored and, where necessary, coordinated and facilitated by a government which has an evolving concept of what the total dissemination and utilization system should become. This concept of a "total system" must be clearly oriented toward a definition of "the public interest" which safeguards, as much as possible, the special interests of the sub-systems involved.

serving the needs of its citizens individually and collectively. This is what we mean by "the public interest." Government must have the capacity to monitor and model this macrosystem, facilitating linkage where barriers exist, adding components where there appear to be significant gaps, and discouraging the growth of divisive and maladaptive subsystems. The government should see to it that all the functions of research, development, and diffusion (RD&D) are adequately performed; it should help in the establishment and maintenance of networks of social influence (S-I) which can move tested innovations toward mass consumption; and it should facilitate effective problem-solving (P-S) by users and user systems.

E.   OTHER PERSPECTIVES

This report has focussed on the pertinent literature in psychology and sociology. Hence, the models which we have identified, particularly S-I, P-S, and "Linkage", are psychological and sociological in flavor. We are certain that these models do not exhaust the range of potential D&U perspectives. However, when we scan the other social sciences, economics, history, and political science, we do not find comparable models; in these fields there seems to be very little published material which can be fitted easily under the headings "dissemination" and "utilization".

Nevertheless, we are also confident that such models can be derived. Certainly the historical dialectic of Hegel and Marx suggests the rudiments of an alternative perspective on D&U; we have said little about the <u>conflict</u> of opposing innovative and non-innovative social groups as a pattern of movement toward social change, but undoubtedly it is. Such a "conflict" model of D&U seems especially appropriate to our turbulent contemporary scene, yet no one has proposed such a perspective in considering D&U phenomena.

Likewise we are sure that economics has much to offer not only in elucidating the economic underpinnings of most D&U activity but also in studying knowledge, itself, as a commodity in the marketplace.*   Both "exchange," and "value" seem to be crucial aspects of D&U which have not been adequately covered in this report; a sophisticated economic model might be able to bring these concepts together with those we have enumerated.

Finally, it should be said in criticism of the above models that they do not adequately account for the critical events, the crises, and the revolutions, which play such an important role in social change from an *historical* perspective. Havelock, (#7108) for example, notes that a current emphasis on research utilization in highway safety stems from a crisis and confrontation between the auto-makers and a congressional investigating committee.   This type of event is not easily explained within an S-I, a P-S, or an RD&D framework. The same might be said of the origins of current efforts to reform universities and political parties, to rebuild cities, and to create genuine racial equality. The catalytic events and the moving forces for change in these areas can only be understood in a broadly social, historical and political context. A truly comprehensive model of D&U would need to account for these events and spell out the patterns of forces that leads up to them and stem from them.

---

*To a degree Machlup (#7041) has succeeded in doing this but without a clear emphasis on utilization, as such.

III. SEVEN FACTORS WHICH ACCOUNT FOR MOST D&U PHENOMENA: (1) Linkage; (2) Structure;
(3) Openness; (4) Capacity; (5) Reward; (6) Proximity; (7) Synergy

We began our analysis of D&U with a simple formula for communication which
can be stated as follows: "who says what to whom by what channel to what effect."
We found that we were able to classify most research studies according to this
formula: 1023 studies seemed to focus on the receiver and his characteristics
("to whom"); 418 studies focussed on the sender ("who"); 323 studies discussed
characteristics of the message ("what"), 610 studies were concerned with characteristics of the medium or the strategy of D&U ("by what channel"); and 269 studies
spoke to the question of goals and results of utilization efforts ("to what effect").

Having made this sort of breakdown we went ahead and composed chapters which
summarized what is currently known under each of these headings (see again the
table of contents and discussion of report structure in Chapter One). But when
we were through and started to look back over each section, we found a *remarkable
consistency:* certain things seemed to keep coming up, regardless of the area of
focus and regardless of the level of analysis. These unifying themes can be fairly
summarized under seven headings which we call the "general factors" in knowledge
dissemination and utilization. They are listed in very telegraphic form below:

1. Linkage: The number, variety, and mutuality of Resource System--
                    User System Contacts, degree of inter-relatedness,
                    collaborative relationships.

2. Structure: The degree of Systematic Organization and Coordination:
                    a) of the resource system
                    b) of the user system
                    c) of the dissemination-utilization strategy
                    d) of the message (coherence)

3. Openness: The Belief that change is desirable and possible.
                    Willingness and readiness to accept outside help.
                    Willingness and readiness to listen to needs of others
                        and to give help.
                    Social climate favorable to change.

4. Capacity: The capability to retrieve and marshall diverse resources.
                        Highly correllated with this capacity factor are:
                    wealth, power, size, centrality, intelligence, educa-
                    tion, experience, cosmopoliteness, mobility and the
                    number and diversity of existing linkages.

5. Reward: The frequency, immediacy, amount, mutuality of, planning
                        and structuring of positive reinforcements.

6. Proximity: Nearness in time, place, and context.
                    Familiarity, similarity, recency.

7. Synergy: The number, variety, frequency, and persistence of forces
                        that can be mobilized to produce a knowledge utiliza-
                        tion effect.

This analysis in terms of general factors is necessarily oversimplified. Under
each heading we have included a host of variables which are distinct and which could
have been listed separately. At the same time, the headings chosen are not discrete; there is much overlap, and some categories may be seen as subcategories of

others. Yet when we are forced to summarize a long and detailed report in a few pages, this sort of condensation appears to be unavoidable. However, to add a measure of depth to this seven-factor approach we have tried in Table 11.1 to display the seven factors in a two-dimensional matrix which includes the four major communication process elements: "resource", "user system", "message", and "medium".

[Insert Table 11.1 here]

The table should provide a useful overview and introduction to the detailed discussion of each factor which now follows:

D&U FACTOR 1: | LINKAGE |

Earlier in this chapter we suggested "linkage" as a possible concept which could be used to bring together the three most prominent D&U perspectives in a single model. "Linkage" as an explanatory factor has a roughly equivalent meaning, but in barest essentials "linkage" as a factor simply signifies the degree of inter-personal or intergroup connection; the extent to which mutual communicative relations exist among two or more parties. The more linkages there are and the stronger these linkages are, the more effective will be the day-to-day contact and exchange of information, hence the greater will be the mutual utilization of knowledge. Most importantly, the greater the number of overlapping linkages throughout the macro-system of knowledge production and dissemination, the more frequent and the more effective will be the knowledge utilization by all.

"Linkage" has some meaning as applied to each component of the communication process.

    a.   For the resource system:

        In order to be effective as disseminators and helpers in the innovative process, resource systems need to develop reciprocal and collaborative relationships not only with a variety of potential users, but also with a large and diverse group of *other* resource systems. The resource system also needs to have successful internal linkage within itself and among its members.

    b.   For the user:

        Similarly users need to develop reciprocal and collaborative relationships with a variety of resource systems. For optimum utilization in a user social system there also has to be a considerable degree of linkage among individual members and sub-units. In particular, *innovators* need to be linked to *opinion leaders* and opinion leaders need to be linked to a large number and variety of *followers* who can pass the word to the most isolated corners of the community.

    c.   For the message:

        "Linkage" in the message means *relevance*, first and foremost, i.e., relevance and relatedness to the user and to the user's need. However, message linkage can also mean at least three other things. A second meaning is internal *linkage within the message* or relatedness of one part of the message to another. A third meaning is *relatedness to other messages* that have been directed to the user in the past; the message which the user can mentally connect to past messages will stand a better chance of acceptance. Finally, a fourth meaning of message linkage is *"linkage to a basis in scientific knowledge"*. This type of linkage may not be of immediate significance to the user, but it probably will have long-term significance in the value and ultimate benefit to be derived from the innovation.

11-21

TABLE 11.1

HOW GENERAL D&U FACTORS RELATE TO PROCESS ELEMENTS: A SUMMARY

GENERAL D&U FACTORS	How General Factors Relate to:			
	RESOURCE PERSONS & SYSTEMS --- SENDERS-DISSEMINATORS (Who)	USER. PERSONS & SYSTEMS --- CONSUMERS-CLIENTS (To Whom)	MESSAGE --- KNOWLEDGE INNOVATION (What)	MEDIUM --- CHANNEL-STRATEGY - TACTICS (How)
1. LINKAGE	Collaboration, 2-way interaction with user and other resources. Simulation of user's problem-solving process.	Collaboration, 2-way interaction with other users and resources. Simulation of resource system's R&D process.	Relevance to user. Adequacy of derivation and congruence with scientific knowledge.	Allows direct contact. Two-way interaction.
2. STRUCTURE	Systematic planning of d&u efforts. Division of labor and coordination.	Systematic planning and execution of problem-solving efforts. --- Integrated social organization of receiver system.	Coherence. Systematic preparation (design, test, package).	Systematic strategy. Timing to fit user's problem-solving cycle.
3. OPENNESS	Willingness to help. Readiness to be influenced by user feedback and by new scientific knowledge. Flexibility and accessibility.	Willingness to be helped, desire to change, to see potential of outside resources. Active seeking and willingness to adapt outside resources.	Adaptability, divisibility, demonstrability of the innovation.	Flexible strategies. Best medium allows informal communications between sender and receiver about the innovation.
4. CAPACITY	Ability to summon and invest diverse resources Skill and experience in the helping-resource person role. Power, Capital.	Ability to assemble and invest internal resources. Self-confidence, intelligence. Amount of available time, energy, capital. Skill, sophistication.	Innovations which result from heavy investment and sophisticated design and development will diffuse more effectively.	Capacity of medium to carry maximum info. Accessibility to maximum number of users in minimum time.
5. REWARD	Reward for investment in d&u activities in terms of dollars, recognition, knowledge, self-esteem.	Past experience of reward for utilization effort. Return on effort invested in dollars, time, capacity, growth, well-being.	Relative advantage, profitability. Time and labor saving potential. Life-liberty-happiness benefit potential.	Medium which can convey feedback (+ and - reinforcement). Most effective medium has best reward history for sender and receiver.
6. PROXIMITY	Closeness and ready access to diverse resources and to users.	Closeness and ready access to resources, other users. Cosmopoliteness. Psychological Proximity: similarity to, and identification with other users, resources.	Relatedness and congruity with user and user needs. Similarity and congruence with past innovations which the user has adopted. Familiarity to user.	Easily accessible medium, familiar to the user.
7. SYNERGY	The number and diversity of resource persons and change agents who gain access to the user. Continuity, Persistence, and Synchronization of effort.	The number and diversity of different users reached will accelerate the diffusion to social system as a whole.	Redundancy of message. The number and variety of forms in which the message appears and the continuity among forms.	The number and diversity, continuity and persistence of different media used to transmit the message.

11-22

d.   For the medium:

    "Linkage" is also a relevant concept to apply in considering the medium or strategy to be employed in a D&U effort. The medium should be "linked" to the sender and the receiver in the sense that it should be *compatible* with their experience and style. We have also seen in Chapter Nine that certain media (e.g., personal contact, and informal group discussion) are very significant in developing initial linkage between sender and receiver, while other media (e.g., television, and most forms of writing) presuppose effective sender-receiver linkage or at least a receiver who is "cognitively tuned" to the message and the medium.

D&U FACTOR 2: | STRUCTURE |

    The degree of systematic organization and coordination of elements strongly affects the utilization process. This generalization applies (a) to the resource system, (b) to the user system, (c) to the relations between resource and user, (d) to the message, and (e) to the medium. It is the major point which is stressed by the RD&D perspective.

    Effective dissemination and utilization must take place within a coherent framework, a structure which designates a rational sequence of steps, compartmentalization and coordination, division of labor, and so forth. Successful utilization activities tend to be structured activities, and useful knowledge is structured knowledge. The extent to which structuring takes place in the sender and receiver and in the message seem to be important correlates of successful dissemination and utilization.

    a.   For the resource system:

    The "structure" factor is important for the resource system in at least three ways. First of all, to be effective the resource system needs a degree of structure in terms of meaningful *division of labor* and *coordination* of effort. It should be organized into a "system" which functions as a whole. Secondly, the resource system should have a structured and *coherent view of the client system;* it should be able to understand the various subsystems of the client system and how they are interrelated; a structured approach to viewing the client will help the resource system in diagnosis and in defining its own appropriate role vis-a-vis the client. Thirdly, the resource system should be able to *plan* D&U activities in a structured sequence which will make sense in terms of one or another of the models of D&U discussed earlier. Almost invariably, the resource system will be successful as a "helper" or "disseminator" if it clearly plans and faithfully executes a coherent and logical strategy of helping or dissemination. This is particularly true for large scale innovation (see Miles #1481, p. 633).

    The need for a structured sequence of functions to support effective utilization was illustrated dramatically by Mackie and Christensen (#6237) in their discovery of the non-utilization of Navy supported research on learning. They found that there was no systematic planning for utilization; therefore there were no developed mechanisms or structures for the necessary translation and integration of research findings for practical uses.

    b.   For the user:

    The same structuring principle applies equally to the user, himself. The user should be *organized to receive* just as the resource should be organized to send. If the user system is a complex organization (see Chapter Six), it may have specialized subsystems which retrieve outside knowledge and adapt innovations for internal consumption.

Large or small, however, the user system must have an adequate internalized problem-solving strategy, i.e., an orderly set of processes for need-sensing and expression, diagnosis, resource retrieval and evaluation.

The user system will also be a more effective knowledge utilizer if it contains an integrated network of social relations: e.g., a viable opinion *leadership - followership structure* and a set of *internal linking roles* such as the innovator (to import new ideas) and the defender (to protect against imports of dubious value, reliability, and safety.)

c. For the message:

Usable knowledge is knowledge which is *coherent* in form and substance and, in that sense, "structured"; it is rationally organized for ready consumption, designed, tested, packaged, and labelled.

d. For the medium:

Important as it is to have a structured message it is even more important to have a structured program for getting the message across to the user. As Miles states (p. 647) "...careful attention to the anticipation and management of change processes as an innovation proceeds is of considerable importance. ...Often much more attention is put on constructing the innovation, itself, than on planning and carrying out the strategy for gaining its adoption." Coherent multi-media programs for diffusing innovations and/or solving problems have a high chance of success, particularly when they are used in combinations and sequences that are timed to correspond to stages in the user system's developing readiness and involvement.

D&U FACTOR 3:   OPENNESS

"Openness", the readiness to give and to receive new information, is fundamental to effective utilization. It is a prerequisite to "linkage" (Factor 1) and a necessary complement to "structure" (Factor 2). Closed systems and closed minds are, by definition, incapable of taking in important new messages from outside; if they cannot take in, then they cannot utilize knowledge for internal change. "Openness" is a vitally important quality of innovative knowledge utilizing systems.

a. For the resource system:

For the resource system, "openness" means a *willingness to help* and *a willingness to listen* and to be influenced by user needs and aspirations. The "ivory tower" approach, for example, closes off valuable intellectual resources from the rest of society, creating a closed system which is indifferent to the public interest. Practitioner groups such as the legal and medical professions may also close themselves off when they establish high fees and evolve service standards which are subject only to internal surveillance and internal influence. Effective resource systems are open to influence and change both from the user and from other resource systems. It is also vital that practitioner resource systems renew their skills and their competence by continuously remaining open to the newest developments of science and technology.

b. For the user:

For the user, "openness" is not merely a passive receptivity to outside knowledge. Rather it is an active faith that outside resources will be useful and an *active reaching out* for new ideas, new products, and new ways of doing things. In addition, it is a willingness to take risks and to make an effort to adapt innovations to one's own situation.

11-24

The user should also be *open internally to himself*, willing and able to make objective self-diagnosis, to own up to his own needs, and to be open to using his internal resources. Research studies have shown that "age" of adopter is negatively correlated with innovativeness. In other words, *youthfulness* is related to effective D&U. The underlying psychological factor behind this statistic may indeed be the "openness" of "those who think young" (or, conversely, the rigidity of age, or a combination of both).

c. For the message:

In at least a metaphorical sense, "openness" also has some meaning when applied to the message and the medium. Research on message characteristics suggests that "adaptability" and "divisibility" are important qualities which aid diffusion and utilization. An innovation should be "open" in being adjustable and adaptable to the special circumstances of different users, and it should be "open" in allowing potential users to try out and sample its effects prior to an all-out commitment to adopt. "Openness" may also be construed to mean "demonstrability"; i.e., innovations should be open and accessible to inspection and evaluation by the user.

d. For the medium:

Diffusion and innovation strategies should be "open" in the sense of being *flexible*. A plan for utilization should allow for alteration or adjustment to account for unforeseen circumstances and unanticipated user reactions. To a degree, there is a trade-off between "openness" and "structure" in a good strategy, but the two factors are not necessarily contradictory; i.e., the best structured strategy has built-in flexibility and open-endedness. The best medium is also one which allows open informal communication between senders and receivers.

D&U FACTOR 4: CAPACITY

The research literature in the S-I tradition is particularly convincing in suggesting that there is a general factor of *capacity* or competence accounting for much of the variance in diffusion studies. This summary concept ties together the highly intercorrelated variables of "wealth", "power", "status", "education", "intelligence", and "sophistication" which are invariably good predictors of successful innovation and utilization. Those who already possess the most in the way of resources and capabilities are the most likely to be able to get even more. The rich have more opportunities to get richer because they have the *"risk capital"* both figuratively and literally.

a. For the resource system:

Generally speaking, the more power, prestige and capital possessed by the resource system, the more effective it will be as a resource and as a diffuser. If the resource system collectively possesses a high degree of intelligence, education, power, and wealth, it will then have the ability to summon and invest diverse resources; it will be able to plan and structure its activities on a grand scale over a long time span to produce "high performance products".

b. For the user:

Likewise for the user the ability to assemble and invest his own internal resources and to call upon outside (and sometimes very expensive) help is extremely important in successful innovation. Another ingredient of capacity, *self-confidence* (a feeling that one has the capacity), is also an important predictor of successful utilization. Other important ingredients are: the amount of available time, energy, education, sophistication, and size of operation.

The various components of capacity are usually measured separately in research studies of the user, but they go together so consistently that they really form a "success syndrome," This is a factor which confounds the govern- ment policy makers who try to legislate programs to aid the poor, the under- privileged, and the underdeveloped, because willy-willy the high capacity people are the ones who derive the most benefit; they are the ones who know how to identify, retrieve, and make effective use of the potential new resources that these programs represent. The sad fact is that "capacity" is a quality which is distributed very unfairly in nearly all societies, usually in inverse proportion to the need for it. For the policy maker who wants to "improve" the society there is an awful dilemma here. Clearly the best return on D&U investment is from a high capacity user system, but the low capacity user system is the one which needs help the most.

c. For the message:

Innovations which represent a tremendous investment in R&D and in packaging are more likely to diffuse effectively, sometimes in spite of high cost to the user. The commercial jet aircraft, color television, and the Physical Science Study Committee (PSSC) curriculum are all examples of innovations which represented tremendous initial investment by very high capacity resource systems, and sub- sequent D&U success in spite of a necessarily high purchase price.

d. For the medium:

A "high capacity" medium in one sense is a medium which can *convey* a large quantity of information to a user in the shortest possible time; this is important for D&U, but of equal importance is the capacity of the medium to *store* a large amount of knowledge for the user and to store it in such a way that it is readily retrievable by the user when he needs it and in the form he needs it. Finally a high capacity medium is a medium that has a high *power to influence* the potential user, to monopolize his attention, to involve and to captivate. Obviously no one medium possesses all these capacities simultaneously even though all are needed. Therefore, an optimum strategy should employ a range of media in sequence and in coordination to take advantage of the special capacities of each.

D&U FACTOR 5:　REWARD

A fifth factor is summed up with the word, "reward" (or "reinforcement"). It is a fundamental psychological fact that rewarded behavior tends to be repeated, and this is as true in knowledge transfer transactions as it is in the Skinner Box. We do not clearly know what the optimum reinforcement schedules are, and we may not always be quite sure what the equivalent of food pellets are for human consumers, but we do know that the reward has to be there. The sender won't send if he doesn't get rewarded for sending; the receiver won't receive if he doesn't get rewarded for receiving. The message won't work if it has no reward value, and the medium won't be attended to if it has no reward-giving history.

a. For the resource system:

For commercial knowledge producers *"profitability"* or anticipated pro- fitability is a major incentive for diffusion of innovations. Other types of resource systems also require "profitability" but usually the coinage is different: for the basic researchers it is *recognition by colleagues*; for the developer it may be the *satisfaction in creating something* that works; for the practitioners it may be the *feedback from a satisfied client* or the feeling that he has done a good job. If D&U activities do not give consistent rewards to the resource system in terms that are meaningful to the particular sender, then they are likely to be discontinued.

b. For the user:

Profitability to the user is equally important. Rogers (#1824) uses the term *"relative advantage"* to indicate the value return in proportion to investment of dollars, time, and effort. The spectrum of significant rewards is, of course, vast, and different users place different values on various types of reward. *Perceived* relative advantage is just as important as actual reward value, and the *past experience of reward for utilization effort* is probably even more important. Rewarding encounters with new knowledge lead to self-fulfilling prophesies that future encounters will also be rewarding. Nothing succeeds like success.

c. For the message:

As mentioned above, the reward-value of a message is extremely important in D&U and the perceived probability of reward is even more important. In Figure 11.7 we try to summarize and classify reward-values in a generalized logical framework which suggests their likely power to influence user behavior. Whether the psychology of individual users conforms to this paradigm is, of course, doubtful. Certain rewards in particular times and circumstances clearly override others which have "logical" priority as when some people sacrifice their lives for the liberty and happiness of others.

[Insert Figure 11.7 here]

d. For the medium:

The medium or strategy which has had a history of success for either senders or receivers will be effective for D&U from two points of view: first, through reinforcement receivers and senders will have been conditioned (trained) to its use; and second, they will have built an expectation that the medium, if used again, will again be successful.

Certain media are more capable than others of conveying feedback to senders; hence, they are also more capable of transmitting rewards or reinforcements (positive and negative). Interpersonal exchange and direct contact experience with the innovation are the best media from this point of view but also the riskiest.

D&U FACTOR 6: | PROXIMITY |

We have also found from innumerable studies in different settings that a sixth factor, proximity, is a powerful predictor of utilization. When we live as neighbors, when we bump into one another and have the chance to observe and stimulate one another by reason of being in the same place at the same time, we will inevitably learn from one another. Hence, users who have close proximity to resources are more likely to use them. Anything which is "handy," i.e., easily accessible, is more likely to be used. This generalization applies to people and things but also, at least by analogy, to thinking processes (familiarity, recency, similiarity). Proximity is also one of the factors which makes *linkage* more possible and hence more probable.

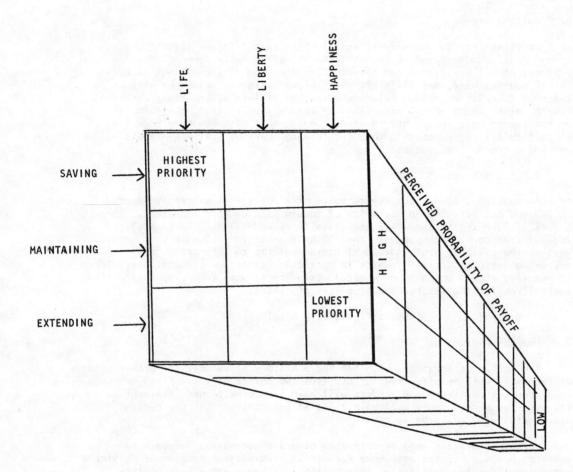

a. For the resource system:

As noted earlier, the most effective resource systems are those which have easy access and linkage to *other* resource systems. *Proximity* is a major aid in bringing about this linkage and hence in promoting effective D&U. Resource systems should also be proximate to users both geographically and *psychologically*, i.e., the user should *perceive* them as accessible.

b. For the user:

It follows from the above that proximity to various resource systems is important for users. However, the proximity of users to one another is also important because it increases the likelihood that users will be aware of common interests and needs, and will pool their *internal* resources. It also increases the likelihood that innovators in the user system will be in contact with opinion leaders, and that opinion leaders will be in contact with everybody else.

c. For the message:

Proximity in the message can be construed as *familiarity* to the user and *relatedness* and *congruity* with user needs. It may also mean similarity and congruity with past innovations which the user has adopted.

d. For the medium:

The technological revolution has meant the greater and greater proximity of all of us to each other. This is perhaps the most profound consequence of the telephone, television, and the jet aircraft: they bring people together. They vastly increase the potential for what Rogers (#1824) calls "cosmopoliteness," the degree to which a user moves in and out of his home community and makes contact with outside groups. Technological improvements in transportation and communication are probably the largest force in accelerating the rate of change in all aspects of living.

D&U FACTOR 7: SYNERGY

In our first effort to bring together the findings of this report we identified six major factors, but we were left with the uncomfortable feeling that a major concept was still missing. It is only with reluctance that we suggest the rare term "synergy" as the name for this seventh dimension. "Synergic" is defined by English and English (#7109) as "exerting force together or in combination, or upon the same point." For our purposes the "same point" is the act of adoption of an innovation. Several forces, several inputs of knowledge working together over time, produce the behavior which we identify as "knowledge utilization." On the one hand, therefore, "synergy" represents *redundancy*, the requirement that a message be repeated over and over again before it gets attended to and absorbed. There is no question that a high degree of redundancy has to permeate our communication systems for them to be effective knowledge transmitters. But "synergy" goes beyond simple redundancy in suggesting that there should be *purposeful* redundancy; a variety of messages must be generated pertaining to the same piece of information and these messages must be directed at the potential user on a number of different channels in a number of different formats, and all more-or-less coordinated to the one goal: adoption of innovation.

a.   For the resource system:

Successful utilization usually seems to require persistent leadership
in the resource system. There must be some one person or some nuclear group
pulling together diverse resources, structuring them and developing and
executing strategies for their effective dissemination and utilization, and
doing so on a continuing basis.

In other words, the resource system must act synergisticly, bringing together
a varity of messages and message components and focussing them, *in combination,*
in sequence, and *in repetition* upon the potential user.

b.   For the user:

The user can hardly ever be induced to adopt an innovation on the basis
of one message from one source at one time. He almost always needs *repeated*
inputs in a *variety of media* over an *extended time* from a *variety of sources*
before he will become an adopter. Some combination of new inputs and memories
of past inputs needs to be set in place before behavioral change comes about.
This is the synergy inside the user.

c.   For the message:

As noted above, effective messages have a built-in redundancy; the main
point is reformed and rephrased in several different ways and repeated in
the same way. Moreover, the several sub-points are made to converge on the main
point.

In discussing the evolution of messages in Chapter Eight we noted how
the usable "practice knowledge" represents a confluence and an aggregation of
research messages (data, theory, method), development messages (prototypes),
and other practice knowledge (related practices and products). The degree to
which this confluence has taken place could be called the "synergistic"
quality of the message.

d.   For the medium:

No one medium by itself, seems to be effective for the transfer of
knowledge. Several media have to operate synergisticly to create behavioral
change in a user population. All users seem to rely on a number of different
sources in guiding themselves toward adoption, and different sources are
significant for different users at <u>different stages</u>.

The persistence (i.e., redundancy) of the transmission is an important
additional aspect of media synergy. Rogers, for example (#1824) reports that
adoption rate is consistently correlated with the extent of promotional effort
by the change agent. Advertisers follow the same principle when they repeat
a television commercial over and over again, when they follow up with free
mailed samples, billboards, door-to-door salesmen, and a giant display counter
in the supermarket. This is synergy with a vengeance.

INTERRELATIONS AMONG FACTORS

As we have progressed through this discussion of factors we are sure that
the reader will have many times wondered if we were covering the same territory again.
There is some overlap and some intercorrelation throughout this list. In the last
instance, for example, we were partly seeing "synergy" as another way to look at
"structuring." "Proximity" seemed to be highly related to and perhaps a precondition
for "linkage," as was "openness." "Reward" seemed to be another precondition for
effective "linkage" but was in turn an outcome of "structure."

There also appeared to be a few contradictions among these seven. "Structure,"
for example, can be stifling if it is not flexible and does not allow for "openness."
"Openness," on the other hand, can lead to chaos if there is not "structure."
Clearly, there must be a trade-off between these two.

One could go on and on in this vein pointing up similarities, overlaps,
discontinuities and contradictions. Suffice it to say here that the seven factors
form a complex web that criss-crosses the territory of D&U.

OTHER D&U FACTORS

The seven factors listed above seem to account for the bulk of D&U phenomena
studied to date, but there are many other important variables which perhaps deserve
to be rated as "factors" also. A few of these which come immediately to mind are
"FAMILIARITY," "PRIMACY," "STATUS," and "VALUE LOADING."

Familiarity, a type of psychological proximity, is undoubtedly an important
quality in the successful resource, the successful message, and the successful
medium, up to a point. But Gestalt psychologists have described a process of
"levelling" in which familiar-*sounding* messages with new content are interpreted
merely as repetition of old messages: the new content is thus "levelled" and not
accurately received. Similarly, over-familiar resource systems may not be seen
as potential repositories for new and useful information unless our familiarity with
them has included this type of history.

Primacy, or "being first," does seem to have inordinate weight in human affairs.
We cling to the first resource systems (our mothers) the longest, and we tend to
color our dealings with all later resource systems with our feelings about that
first one. In a message the first segment is usually best remembered and most
influencial. What comes first always seems to have a powerful force. But the force
can be overcome. We do not always cling to our first impressions of people and
we do not always reject a book because we do not like the cover or the first page.

Status is a concept we have had many opportunities to employ in this report.
When someone or something is seen as "higher" in social importance or legitimacy or
social power, we are likely to give it more attention. But we have also noted
that "status" is an ambivalent variable in D&U. *Ambiguity of status* may be as
important as status differences per se between resource and user, and sometimes
relatively low status resource persons are more effective knowledge conveyors than
high status or equal status resource persons.

Values are the basic stop-and-go signals for human behavior. They presumably
lay down the patterns or limits within which people feel free to send and receive
knowledge. This suggests that messages which clearly contradict pre-existing values
will not get anywhere and those which appeal to them will get far. It also suggests
that a perception of shared values will bring resource and user systems together and
that perceptions of disparate values will drive them apart. Even the medium may have

some value loading (as when we reject new ideas because someone has tried to order or legislate their adoption). These all seem like important and intriguing possibilities that might elevate "value-loading" to factor status, but sadly there is as yet very little research to reinforce these suppositions.

IV. SOME MAJOR UNRESOLVED ISSUES

The seven factors listed above (and perhaps the four additional variables last mentioned) chart the clearer areas of D&U, but we would be remiss in our summary if we did not also give some space to a discussion of the more troubled and confusing areas. Here are five important issues which, from our review, remain befuddled and unresolved.

A. IS SOCIAL SCIENCE UTILIZATION DIFFERENT?

In this report we have tried to be generalists, pulling together studies and analyses of D&U phenomena from a variety of fields from hard science technology to human relations training. Is this sort of generalizing a legitimate and helpful exercise, or does each field represent such a unique array of D&U problems that comparative study is useless and meaningless? A number of authors have suggested that social science utilization is uniquely different from natural science utilization (Chapter Eight). If this is true, we should certainly try to identify where and how it is different before we create vast national D&U programs based on a hard science model. However, there is little concrete evidence that substantiates this "uniqueness"; usually what we find in education, for example, substantiates what we have already learned in agriculture. We have been impressed at least as much by the commonalities in process when we compare across fields as by the disparities. Hence, at this point we would suggest that the question remains unresolved.

B. SHOULD WE PROTECT THE PURITY OF PURE SCIENCE?

On a number of occasions we have noted the isolation of the community of basic science from the needs and concerns of the greater society. Up to a point this isolation seems to be necessary to preserve the proper climate for discovery and basic knowledge building. But there is also the danger that science will then become a closed social system which builds an elaborate but irrelevant and unreal model of the universe along the lines of the medieval Christian church.

There are some data (e.g., Pelz and Andrews #6067) to suggest that stimulation by practical concerns improves scientific creativity and productivity, yet most pure scientists resist such "intrusions." How much should the scientific enterprise be sheltered from society whether for its own good or for society's? We do not really have the answers. However, we do not think that government should abrogate its responsibility to influence science policy in the direction of national goals. Scientists who solicit large sums from society to pursue their own research interests should be required to show how those interests and the public interest are related. In particular we believe that there has to be a more satisfactory *linkage* between the basic and applied research communities on the one hand and the development and practice communities on the other; there has to be a continuous two-way flow of ideas and stimulations. How far this intrusion of applied concerns should extend into the scientific community and what form it should take remain as unresolved issues.

C.   STRUCTURE AND FREEDOM

Earlier we noted the necessity of trade-off between structure and openness, but the formula for this happy balance remains a major unresolved issue. Humanistically-oriented social scientists will probably opt for more openness and looseness, even a little chaos,because of their value on freedom and their suspicion of absolutes. The more structurally-oriented engineering types can point to the very visible concrete technological achievements of our age, the space program in particular, as examples of rigorous systemic R&D. In this report we have tried to appreciate both points of view, and we suggest that *together* they make a very powerful model for progress. We should be able to have structure *without* premature structural closure, structure *without* structural rigidity, and structure *with* some tolerance of ambiguity; at the same time we should be able to have freedom, free give-and-take, and maximum openness without confusion, endless recycling, and obsessive contemplation of process.

D.   THE NEW MEDIA AND THE NEW INFORMATION TECHNOLOGY: PROMISE AND REALITY

There seems little doubt that the great technical achievements of our time in information processing and transmission will have a greater and greater effect on D&U processes generally in the years to come, but there is a tremendous gap between promise and delivery. The production and marketing of the hardware of the new media has far outstripped the more important but less glamorous and less profitable software accompaniments. As a result we are living in a *pseudo-technological* environment surrounded by sophisticated equipment which is performing trivial tasks and standing idle most of the time, while knowledge users continue to rely heavily on old word-of-mouth and written media for most of their message input.

Without the software and without extensive further development *at the user interface* we simply have no way of knowing what the potential of these new mechanisms of television, audio and video taping, and computerized information processing will be; thus, the role of these technological "miracles" in the D&U process remains another important but unresolved issue.

E.   COMPETITION AND PARALLEL EFFORT VS. COORDINATION AND COOPERATION

To a degree our society still holds with the value of free and open competition in the marketplace: those who have new ideas to sell should compete for the attention of the user and should incur the full risk of failure in exchange for the full benefit of success. Most of us now realize that this open market has never existed except in a very limited form, and it certainly provides us no guaranteed system for newer scientifically-based ideas and innovations to replace old ones. But what is the role of competition either between old and new or new and new? It seems again to be an ambivalent feature of D&U; it may spur the developer or the change agent on to greater effort, but it may also suppress certain types of risk associated with *creative* effort.

Parallel D&U effort sometimes appears to be very beneficial in at least two respects: first, parallel efforts (e.g., county agent and commercial seed salesman) may act synergisticly toward the adoption of an innovation and second, they may act as a check on each other. On the other hand, parallelism and competition also mean duplication and tremendous potential waste of precious RD&D manpower. They further may signify the stifling and lost potential of collaborative effort which pools   resources to produce some-thing better than either could produce alone. Solo competitive research in education has certainly failed to meet the needs of the educational community. Now we are beginning a major venture in larger scale cooperative R&D in the Regional Educational Laboratories. The results remain to be seen.

Again, there would appear to be a necessary trade-off between competition and collaboration but the issue remains largely unresolved.

F. OTHER UNRESOLVED ISSUES

The above gives only a light skimming of the many questions that D&U researchers have yet to resolve. We are not yet at the point where we can recommend this or that strategy for this and that set of circumstances. We have still not clearly addressed ourselves to the important values and ethical problems which are related to various approaches, and orientations, e.g., the strategy of change by fait accompli, direction, and manipulation. Presumably there should be rules for this D&U game which are above and beyond what is most "effective." These questions trouble the practitioner and the user; the researchers must face them and answer them.

V.   IMPLICATIONS

Since this study had a major objective of providing a rational basis for decision-making by all persons concerned with dissemination and utilization problems, a considerable portion of time was allotted to the derivation of implications from the model and from the available literature. Such derivations will be addressed specifically to four audiences:

A. General implications for <u>researchers</u> (guidelines for research on dissemination and utilization),

B. General implications for <u>developers</u> (needed prototypes of D&U innovations [practices, products, software, hardware]),

C. General implications for <u>practitioners of dissemination</u>, individuals concerned with linking new knowledge sources to potential users (guidelines for current practice, operating principles),

D. Special implications for <u>planners and policy makers</u> at the local, state and national level.

A. RESEARCH PRIORITIES

In spite of the acceleration of research activity on D&U, there remains a tremendous range of important topics on which we still know practically nothing. In selecting the following ten items as <u>priority</u> areas we were guided by these criteria:

(1) What are the areas of maximum urgency likely to be in the 1970's?

(2) In what areas are we nearing possible breakthrough?

(3) What areas have been totally neglected and need some basic mapping?

(4) In what areas can we conduct useful research related to current developments in education generally at moderate cost?

1. How to Reach the Poor

    The implications of the *capacity* factor discussed earlier are
ominous, indeed. They suggest that most D&U efforts benefit those who
are most competent already and hence least in need. Research has to be
conducted to provide us with means of reversing this trend. In this
connection recent efforts to "organize the poor" seem extremely relevant.
Among other things we need to know how to develop a viable and innovative leadership and opinion leadership structure among underprivileged
and isolated segments of society.

2. Comparative Study of D&U Macrosystems

    To date there have been very few studies which have attempted to
analyze the macrosystems of D&U as we described them in Chapter Three,
and there have been no studies comparing two or more such systems. Yet
such studies are needed to set a meaningful context for more detailed
empirical analyses of D&U phenomena, and they are essential to giving
the state and national policy maker an adequate perspective on his own
role in the total process.

3. Knowledge D&U Facilitating Roles: Natural and Institutionalized

    As we noted in Chapter Seven, there is a wide array of potential know-
ledge linking roles in education and other fields, and new roles are
being developed and installed each year under federal, state and private
programs. Yet we know very little about the optimal conditions for
sustaining such roles. By studying knowledge linkers as they occur
naturally and as they are introduced under such programs, researchers
will be able to establish guidelines for most effective role maintenance
and functioning.

4. The Psychology of the Knowledge User

    Most of the researchers who have studied adoption processes have
been sociologists. There is a clear need to study this important phenomenon
from a more strictly *psychological* perspective, employing the insights and
extensive basic research of learning theory, attitude change theories, and
personality theories. If competent psychological researchers are encouraged
to enter this area, we should be able to build an understanding of the
individual user which is at least as sophisticated as our current understanding of the social forces acting upon him externally. In particular
we should be able to map with great precision the psychological factors
which predispose individuals to *openness, resistance, and linkage capacity.*

5. The Social Organization of Receiving Social Systems Predisposing Them
    to New Knowledge

    Curiously, most empirical sociological studies of diffusion have
ignored social *structure* as a variable. We now have many leads which
suggest certain types of formal and informal leadership patterns as
being most favorable. It has been suggested that more structured systems
may *diffuse* more rapidly but *innovate* less frequently, but there are
many other readily definable and measurable gross features of social
structure which presumably play a very significant role in the speed and
quality of individual utilization behavior. Sociologists should turn
their attention to these questions.

6. Comparative Study of Specialized Linking Systems and Organizations

As a counterpart to (3) above, we need to study *organizations* which collectively serve the same linking functions as *individual linkers*. In education the R&D Centers of the NDEA, the Regional Educational Laboratories, and the Title III Centers of ESEA, 1965, are all examples of varying models of linking organizations, yet we have no comparative research which tells us which model is most effective for the performance of research, development, or utilization functions. Even such gross characteristics as size, funding pattern, location, university-connection and number and scope of activities, have not been studied quantitatively and comparatively despite the obvious significance of such information for research, practice, and policy in this area.

7. Knowledge Utilization Research Instrumentation and Methodology Development

Some of the studies suggested so far would require new methods and new instruments. Special studies should be sponsored specifically to explore the most appropriate methodology for utilization research. To begin with, we need a more adequate and precise method for identifying and measuring the dependent variable itself, "utilization." The new method and instrumentation should be developed on the assumption that overall financial and manpower resources for studying D&U will be modest for at least the next five years. This means there should be a premium on simplicity of administration and maximum payoff in gross measurement, perhaps at the expense of precision. (See also No. 5 under development priorities.)

8. Comparative Evaluation of Different Knowledge Utilization Strategies

As mentioned in the early part of this chapter, there is a dearth of well-documented and comparable case study material on D&U, and we have urged that there be more studies along such lines provided that they can be collected, compared, and summated in some way. A related need is for systematic documentation of specific *strategies* of utilization as employed by different change agents. Such studies should include data on characteristics of senders and receivers, messages, and media, a delineation of stages followed, implicit or explicit models of D&U employed, and *results*, assumed, observed, or measured.

9. Research on Impact of New Media on D&U

There is a need for rigorous evaluation of the varied uses of new media and the new Information technologies to determine their potential, to identify important areas for development, and to gain lead time for local school districts in anticipation of future mass marketing by industry. Without adequate research evidence of utility and adaptability, there is a good reason to be suspicious of over-zealous salesmanship in this area. It may be true that the hardware technology, once installed, will "pull" the software and the adaptability along with it, but such an assumption should be put to the test *before* this equipment gets into mass dissemination to all the nation's school districts.

10. Laboratory Simulation and Experimentation on D&U Phenomena

To date, quantitative study of D&U has been almost exclusively conducted in the field on *natural phenomena*. It seems most appropriate that the bulk of research in this area continue along these lines.

However, there is a place for the controlled laboratory experiment in this area as in any other and *such studies of D&U are virtually non-existent.* We need to launch at least one, preferably two or three, major projects to test D&U models experimentally in artificially-created, controlled simulations. We have the opportunity to measure and control innumerable characteristics of the senders, the message, the medium, and the strategy by using the laboratory. Such studies would not and could not be definitive, but they would provide important supportive evidence and suggest many new avenues of exploration.

B.   DEVELOPMENT PRIORITIES

"Development" is a rather new concept in all fields of knowledge, but especially so in education (as an operating principle, it is still non-existent in some other fields such as mental health, social welfare, and law). It is therefore possibly difficult to conceive of development on dissemination and utilization, yet such development is clearly and urgently called for. We have been able to mark out seven areas in which D&U development work is either beginning or is well within the realm of immediate possibility.

1.   New D&U Roles

Chapter Seven laid down a considerable range of possible knowledge linking roles as they have emerged in various fields. In the field of education, there is an acute lack of manpower in this area, e.g., see Clark and Hopkins, #6241. We therefore urge the creation of experimental development programs to design viable knowledge linking specialist roles at the school building, system, and state levels. Such roles might well follow a number of the functions suggested in Chapter Seven and might be identified by a variety of titles, e.g., "knowledge brokers," "change agents," "resource consultants," "trainers," or "continuing education specialists."

2.   Designs for Training in D&U Process

Supplementary to the establishment of linking roles is the development of training programs for individuals who would fill such roles. An ideal training program would probably include such features as:

a.   Conceptual understanding of D&U systems and processes and change processes.

b.   Micro experience or simulated experience as knowledge utilizers.

c.   Micro experience or simulation of disseminator-resource person activities.

d.   Conceptual and behavioral understanding of human relations processes, in particular to understand and appreciate the dynamics of the resource-user relationship.

e.   Training on resource retrieval.

f.   Training in consultation skills.

g.   Field experience as a linking agent with a chance to share experience with other agents.

Such programs in modified form would also be helpful for administrators who are supporting knowledge linkers and for users themselves.

3. Temporary System Designs

There is a need for design, development, and evaluation of a variety of "temporary systems" to facilitate D&U through training and linkage building. Knowledge utilization conferences, week-end laboratories, seminars, workshops, courses, and other events of limited duration need to be designed specifically to initiate linkage and create awareness of knowledge utilization as a solvable problem. The notion that such events can be "engineered" for specific purposes is still not fully appreciated by the people who are usually responsible for organizing them. The idea persists that a good conference consists of several scholars reading papers to row upon row of attentive "participants"; such ideas will die hard unless we launch a concerted programmatic effort to develop new types of learning encounters.

4. Field Manuals and Handbooks on the Linking Process

The considerable body of research and theory on D&U has been summarized and synthesized in this volume and in others (e.g., Miles #1046, and Rogers #1824), but there is a need for more practically oriented guides to D&U process, manuals which can be useful to knowledge linkers, practitioners, and users. Through careful development and evaluation by relevant audiences, such manuals may come to play a significant role in the general improvement of D&U activities nationally. Two such manuals are already under development, one by the author for the U.S. Office of Education, and one by the Human Interaction Research Institution of Los Angeles, California for the National Institute of Mental Health.

5. Field Instruments

Over the last decade we have begun to appreciate the practical value of some of the methodology and instrumentation of the social sciences; we have learned that the practitioner can clarify his own situation and evaluate his own performance in somewhat the same way that a social scientist could have done for him. In a field like D&U which has such limited manpower resources at its disposal, such "do-it-yourself" instruments seem particularly relevant. As accompaniments to the above-mentioned field manuals we should be developing checklist measures for diagnosis and evaluation by knowledge linkers, developers and users. Such tools will give the linker and the practitioner the ability to keep track of a large number of factors which are important in D&U and which have been discussed throughout this report; e.g., sender, user, and message characteristics, D&U functions, and phases. Instruments of this type would not do the job for the linker, but they would make it much easier for him to plan and structure his activities to achieve the goals he and his clients have set for themselves.

6. Creative Uses of the New Media

As noted earlier (Section IV-D) the potential of the new media have not been realized. There is a need to experiment extensively in the use of new media to enhance D&U processes. In the field of continuing medical education a number of creative strategies have been tried out: these include telephone conferences, two-way radio or radio-television combinations, and telephone-accessed information banks. These experimental designs should be tried out in educational settings, also. Experiments are also going on in the use of videotape and videotape feedback for teacher training and for personal and group sensitivity training. The implications of these developments for D&U are great *in the long run*. When such sophisticated technology becomes available to large numbers of users at reasonable cost, *we should be ready to use it*. This means concurrent development of software and training programs.

7. User-Oriented Information Systems

Thus far efforts to create new information systems using sophisticated input, storage, and retrieval equipment, microphotography, and data processing machines, seem to have aided only the most sophisticated users in the *research* community. There is a great need for the further development of these systems by teams which include psychologists and social scientists who are fully aware of the complexities of the D&U process. The process of diffusing new information systems to potential users is further complicated by the existence of the competing systems of written and informal exchange to which most users are already attuned and committed. How the new systems compete with or complement these existing systems has to be considered as a part of the over-all development problem.

C. GUIDELINES FOR THE PRACTITIONER

This report has been written primarily to assumble and summarize research and theory on D&U, but it has not performed the difficult and important additional task of *translation* of this information into a form in which it can give clear and concrete guidance to those who are currently engaged in D&U activities. Although works of this latter type are under development (see Section V-B-No. 4), we feel obligated at this point to insert a few words of specific relevance to such users.

Six points stand out as possible guidelines which might help to improve D&U processes. These are:

1. Define the elements in the situation.
2. Define your own role.
3. Make a diagnosis of each element.
4. Define your own perspective toward change.
5. Plan a strategy.
6. Monitor your progress.

In the paragraphs which follow we expand on each of these points in turn.

1. Define the ELEMENTS

A first step in improving D&U is gaining a clear perspective on what is going on. Hence at the outset there is a need to define the elements of the D&U activity in which you are engaged. Answers should be spelled out for each of the following questions:

a. Who or what is the "resource system"?

b. Who is the "user" ("client," "consumer," "audience" or "target group")?

c.   Who are the <u>relevant others</u> in the user's social environment
     (opinion leaders, reference groups, influentials, defenders).

d.   What is the "<u>message</u>"?

e.   What is the "<u>medium</u>"?

f.   What is the <u>strategy</u>?

Chapter Two may help in defining these elements further.

2.   Define and Diagnose Your Own ROLE

It is important for the D&U change agent to have a clear understanding of his own role in the process. Chapter Seven suggests several
role models which may be applicable. In general, two questions should
be foremost in your mind at this point:

a.   *Is this role viable?* Can you handle the problems of overload
     and marginality that may be associated with it? Do you have
     the requisite skills and experience to bring it off successfully?

b.   *How are you related institutionally to the resources and user
     systems?* Does your organizational base give you adequate
     visibility and legitimacy in the eyes of resource and user?

3.   Make a Diagnosis of Each Element in the Activity

Having defined each element, you should proceed to take a kind of
inventory of each, using the relevant chapter of this report as a guide.
Chapters Four, Five, and Six give a number of dimensions on which user
and resource systems should be evaluated. Chapter Eight suggests
important characteristics of the message, and Chapter Nine gives the
relative advantages and disadvantages of different media and strategies.

As a final over-all check of the situation you might use an
adaptation of Table 11.1. Table 11.2 suggests one way this might be
done, using the analysis of only *one element as an example.*

[Insert Table 11.2 here]

The more the practitioner is able to structure and clarify his activities
in ways such as these, the more successful he is likely to be.

4.   Select a D&U Perspective

It should also be helpful for the D&U change agent to identify and
select one of the generalized perspectives discussed in this chapter as
a framework within which to build his own strategy. Each of the four
perspectives discussed is probably suitable for different change agent
styles in different settings and circumstances.

5.   Plan a Coherent Strategy

Using your selected perspective as a guide but not as a limitation,
plan out a strategy which fits your situation. A good strategy should
probably specify or account for each of the steps illustrated in
Figure 11.8.

[Insert Figure 11.8 here]

TABLE 11.2

DIAGNOSTIC CHECKLIST: AN EXAMPLE

General D&U Factors	Potential Problems in the *RESOURCE SYSTEM*	and → What I Plan to Do About Them:					
		I don't have enough info on this yet	Not applicable in this situation	This is well accounted for	Not adequate but I must live with it	Not adequate: I plan to work on it	Work done; Now OK
1. LINKAGE	1.1 Collaboration, 2-way interaction with user						
	1.2 With other resources						
	1.3 Simulation of user's problem-solving process						
2. STRUCTURE	2.1 Systematic planning of D&U efforts						
	2.2 Division of labor						
	2.3 Coordination of effort						
	2.4 Systematic client diagnosis						
	2.5 Systematic evaluation of process						
3. OPENNESS	3.1 Willingness to help						
	3.2 Readiness to be influenced by user feedback						
	3.3 ...by new scientific knowledge						
	3.4 Flexibility						
	3.5 Accessibility						
4. CAPACITY	4.1 Ability to summon & invest diverse resources						
	4.2 Skill & experience in the helping-resource person role						
	4.3 Power						
	4.4 Financial capital						
5. REWARD	5.1 Dollar - Return on investment						
	5.2 Recognition						
	5.3 More knowledge						
	5.4 Self-esteem						
6. PROXIMITY	6.1 Closeness & ready access to diverse resources						
	6.2 Closeness & ready access to users						
	6.3 Psychological proximity to users						
7. SYNERGY	7.1 Persistence of effort						
	7.2 Diversity of effort						
	7.3 Convergence of effort						

FIGURE 11.8   Phases of the Process: A Guide for the D&U Change Agent

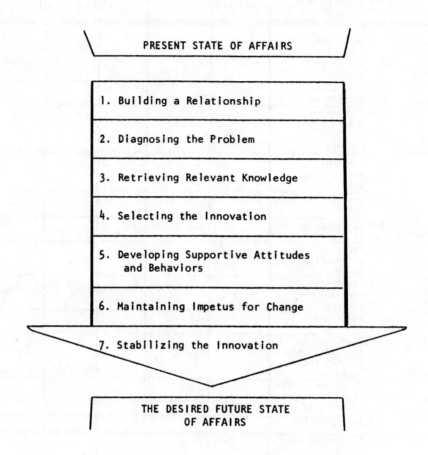

PRESENT STATE OF AFFAIRS

1. Building a Relationship

2. Diagnosing the Problem

3. Retrieving Relevant Knowledge

4. Selecting the Innovation

5. Developing Supportive Attitudes
   and Behaviors

6. Maintaining Impetus for Change

7. Stabilizing the Innovation

THE DESIRED FUTURE STATE
OF AFFAIRS

        These seven phases will form the basic outline of the Manual on D&U
process currently under development for the U.S. Office of Education.
(See again Section V-B-No. 4)

6.   Monitor Your Progress

        Coherent step-by-step planning and execution also make the task of
process *evaluation* considerably easier. There should be continuous monitoring of the process so that you can benefit from learning of mistakes
and successes as you go along. Not only does this allow improved D&U
programs in the future, but it also raises the possibility of changing
and improving these activities while they are still going on.

D. GUIDELINES FOR THE POLICY MAKER

The clearest and most significant implications of this review pertain to
the policy makers in the state and federal governments and in the major
universities and foundations, those who can take concrete and immediate action
to change the D&U system that exists today in education and other areas that
affect our national health and welfare. Below we put forth eight major propositions to guide policy action to improve our national D&U capability.
They are stated very succinctly and briefly in the hope that they will be
more easily noted and viewed as a whole. The various chapters of this review
provide ample supporting evidence for each. Where particular chapters seem
pertinent, however, they are cited in parentheses.

1. *Effective knowledge utilization is possible in any field and
    government is needed to coordinate effort, to plan, and to
    provide support.*

2. *There are existing models of knowledge utilization which are
    reasonably effective and worth imitating in some respects*
    (e.g., the Cooperative Extension Service). (Chapters Three,
    Ten, and Eleven.) Government policy makers should consider
    in detail where these models ought to be modified for adapta-
    tion to their own fields.

3. *There is a great need for knowledge utilization development
    activities* especially outside Agriculture, e.g., new roles,
    handbooks, new institutions. (See Section V-B of this chapter.)

4. *Government should work to overcome the inertia of specializa-
    tion and narrow professionalism by:*
    a. Demanding that contractors specify dissemination
        and utilization plans as part of contracts.
    b. Encouraging collaborative projects between
        researchers, developers, and users.
    c. Organizing and supporting a variety of temporary
        systems: conferences, seminars, etc., to bring
        together researchers, practitioners, and policy
        makers.

5. *Support the development of knowledge D&U as a scientific
    discipline.* (Chapter One.)

6. *In planning use of new media and information technology,
    appreciate both the tremendous development costs which are
    necessary and the tremendous potential gains which may result.*
    (Chapter Nine.) Remember that the social engineering aspects
    remain woefully underdeveloped and are usually woefully under-
    financed.

7. *View knowledge utilization as a developing macrosystem.* Plan
    systemically and relate individual project support to overall
    planning. (Chapter Three.)

8. *Consider the need for a national clearinghouse for research on
    dissemination and utilization.* (Chapter One and Section I of
    this chapter.)

CONCLUDING NOTE: SOME GUIDELINES FOR THE RESEARCHERS AND PRACTITIONERS OF D&U

In conclusion, we would like to suggest that those concerned with D&U apply some of our general "factors",   first and foremost, to their own behavior and their own process. If these principles of D&U which we have discussed in this chapter are valid, then those of us who work in the area of D&U should be able to apply them to ourselves. Here are five suggestions for the students of the D&U process:

1. We need to be linked together, continuously exchanging ideas back and forth, simulating and evaluating each other's models.

2. We ought to build structures for facilitating communication with one another and with our colleagues in other disciplines. In order to have an impact we are going to have to organize, plan and coordinate our efforts in a more coherent way than we have done in the past. Most of all we ought to be structuring our activities so that they will evolve into future policies and programs throughout the nation.

3. We also ought to be open to one another, willing to change our own ideas about the process from listening to colleagues in research, development and practice. Above all, we should be open to the consumer, sensitive to his needs and appreciative of his goals and values.

4. Fourthly, we ought to be building the capacity for research and development in this area by allocating resources, attracting the best graduate students, and making "D&U" a central and salient department in science.

5. Finally, we ought to be aware of the very great rewards that are in store for us if we can succeed in this effort to make a science of the D&U process. This is a challenging and exciting field and the stakes are tremendous. If we can learn how to bridge the gap between research and practice, and if we can learn how to apply this knowledge, we will surely have unlocked the door to certain progress.

BIBLIOGRAPHY

(Items specifically cited in text only)*

*A more extensive bibliography on dissemination and utilization containing
more than 4,000 items including those listed here is also available under
separate cover. This larger bibliography (ED #029172) was used as the basis
of the quantitative analysis reported in Chapter One.

BIBLIOGRAPHY

Abell, Helen C., Larson, Olaf F., and Dickerson, Elizabeth R.
"Communication of Agricultural Information in a South-Central
New York County," Department of Rural Sociology, Bulletin 49,
Ithaca, New York: Cornell University, January 1957.
03886

Abelson, Robert P.
"Computers, Polls, and Public Opinion--Some Puzzles
and Paradoxes, Transaction, Sept., 1968, pp. 20-27.
07138

Abraham, R. H.
Dairy Plant Managers' Perception of the Minnesota Agricultural
Extension Service, Ph.D. Thesis, Madison: University of
Wisconsin, 1963.
03516

Abrahamson, Mark
"The Integration of Industrial Scientists," Administrative
Science Quarterly, September, 1964, Vol. 9, No. 2, pp. 208-218.
01163

Adams, Richard N.
"Social Change in Guatemala and U.S. Policy," in Adams, Richard N.
and others, Social Change in Latin America Today, New York:
Council on Foreign Relations and Vintage Books, 1960, pp. 231-284.
05049

Adkinson, B. W.
"The Role of Scientific Societies Today," ACLS Newsletter,
January 1963, Vol. 14, pp. 1-9.
00938

"Z-Frank Stresses Radio to Build Big Chevy Dealership,"
Advertising Age, 1962, Vol. 33, p. 83.
07015

Alexander, Frank D. and Others
"A Field Experiment in Diffusion of Knowledge of Dairy
Cattle Feeding Through a TV School," Rural Sociology,
1963, Vol. 28, pp. 400-404.
01352

Alexander, William M.
"The Acceleration of Curriculum Change," Miller, R.I. (ed),
Perspectives on Educational Change, New York: Appleton-
Century Crofts, 1966.
00842

Allen, Thomas J. and Cohen, Stephen I.
"Information Flow in an R&D Laboratory," paper
supported by National Aeronautics & Space Adminis-
tration and by the Office of Science Information
Service, National Science Foundation, Nov. 1963 and
Aug. 1966. (Ditto - Cambridge, Mass.: MIT, Sloan
School of Management, Paper #217-66.)
07139

Allport, F. H.
"The J-Curve Hypothesis of Conforming Behavior,"
Journal of Social Psychology, 1934, Vol. 5, pp. 141-183.
06375

Allport, Gordon W.
"The Historical Background of Modern Social Psychology,"
in Lindzey, G. (ed.), Handbook of Social Psychology,
Reading, Mass.: Addison-Wesley, 1954.
06479

American Educational Research Association (AERA)
"Evaluation Activities of Curriculum Project,"
Monograph prepared by Dr. Hulda Grobman, Spokee,
Illinois: Rand McNally & Company, 1968.
07084

American Psychological Association
Convention Participants and the Dissemination of Information
at Scientific Meetings, Washington, D. C.: Project on Scientifi
Information Exchange in Psychology, American Psychological
Association.
02124

American Psychological Association
The Discovery and Dissemination of Scientific Information Among
Psychologists in Two Research Environments, Washington, D. C.:
Project on Scientific Information Exchange in Psychology,
American Psychological Association, 1964.
02125

American Psychological Association
A Preliminary Study of Information Exchange Activities of
Foreign Psychologists and a Comparison of Such Activities
with Those Occurring in the United States, Washington, D. C.:
American Psychological Association, June, 1964.
02126

Ames, Edward
"Research, Invention, Development, and Innovation," American
Economic Review, June, 1951, Vol. 51, pp. 370-381.
03294

Anderson, L. R. and McGuire, W. J.
"Prior Reassurance of Group Consesus as a Factor in
Producing Resistance to Persuasion," Sociometry,
1965, Vol. 28, pp. 44-56.
06284

Anderson, Marvin A.
   "Informational Sources Important in the Acceptance and
   Use of Fertilizer in Iowa," Tennessee Valley Authority
   Report, 1955, pp. 55-1.
   02535

Angell, Robert C.
   The Moral Integration of American Cities, Chicago:
   University of Chicago Press, 1951, 140 pp.
   06193

Appel, John S. and Gurr, Ted
   "Bibliographic Needs of Social and Behavioral Scientists:
   A Report of a Pilot Survey," American Behavioral Scientist,
   1964, Vol. 7, pp. 51-54.
   05050

Archibald, Kathleen A.
   The Utilization of Social Research and Policy
   Analysis, St. Louis, Mo.: Washington University,
   1968, 465 pp.
   07088

Arthur D. Little, Inc.
   A Model for Innovation Adoption in Public School
   Districts, Contract No. OEC-1-7-061500-0328,
   U.S. Department of Health, Education and Welfare,
   March, 1968, Cambridge, Mass.
   07104

Arthur D. Little, Inc.
   Technology Transfer and the Technology Utilization
   Program, Report to the Office of Technology Utilization,
   National Aeronautics and Space Administration, Contract
   No. NASw-591, January 22, 1965.
   06200

Asch, S. E.
   "Studies of Independence and Conformity: A Minority
   of One against a Unanimous Majority," Psychological
   Monographs, 1956, Vol. 70, No. 9 (Whole No. 416)
   06290

Ashby, Eric
   "The Administrator: Bottleneck or Pump?" Daedalus, Spring
   1962, Vol. 91, No. 2, pp. 264-278.
   01279

Atwood, M. S.
   "Small-Scale Administrative Change: Resistance to the Introduction of a High School Guidance Program," Miles, Matthew B.
   (ed.), Innovation in Education, New York: Bureau of Publications, Teachers College, Columbia University, New York, 1964.
   01178

Atwood, Ruth
   "A Grass-Roots Look at MEDLARS." Medical Library Association.
   Bulletin 52, October, 1964, pp. 645-651.
   02342

Babcock, Chester D.
"The Emerging Role of the Curriculum Leader,"
Association for Supervision and Curriculum
Development 1965 Yearbook Committee. Role
of Supervisor and Curriculum Director in a
Climate of Change. Washington, D.C.: Association
for Supervision and Curriculum Development,
1965, pp. 50-64.
00212

Back, Kurt W., Hill, Reuben, and Stycos, J. Mayone
"Manner of Original Presentation and Subsequent Communication,"
Psychological Reports, 1957, Vol. 3, pp. 149-154.
01677

Bandy, George
"Strategies for Change in Rural Communities,"
Paper presented at the NFIRE Conference,
Denver, Colorado, March 19, 1969.
07115

Barber, Bernard
"Some Problems in the Sociology of the Professions,"
Daedalus, Fall, 1963, Vol. 92, No. 4, p. 669.
07063

Barber, Bernard
"Resistance by Scientists to Scientific Discovery,"
Science, September 1961, Vol. 134, No. 3479, pp. 596-602.
02807

Barber, Bernard and Hirsch, Walter (eds.).
The Sociology of Science, Glencoe, Illinois: The Free Press,
1962.
05067

Barnett, Homer G.
"The Acceptance and Rejection of Change," Zollschan, George K.
and Hirsch, Walter (eds.) Explorations in Social Change,
Boston: Houghton and Mifflin Company, 1964, pp. 345-367.
00615

Barnett, Homer G.
"Diffusion Rates," in Manners, Robert A. (ed.). Process and
Pattern in Culture, Chicago: Aldine, 1964.
02510

Barnett, Homer G.
Innovation: The Basis of Cultural Change. New York: McGraw-
Hill Book Company, 1953, Ch. VII & VIII.
00620

Barnlund, D. and Harland, C.
"Propinquity and Prestige as Determinants of Communication
Networks," Sociometry, 1963, Vol. 26, pp. 467-479.
06694

Barrett, J. and Tannenbaum, A.
Organization Theory, Management-Career Education
Project, Wayne State University (mimeo).
07219

Barzel, Yoram
"Optimal Timing of Innovations," The Review of
Economics and Statistics, August, 1968, Vol. 1,
No. 3, p. 348.
07043

Bauer, Raymond A.
Second-Order Consequences, Cambridge, Mass. and London,
England: The M.I.T. Press, 1969.
07227

Bauer, Raymond A. and Greyser, Stephen A.
Advertising in America: The Consumer View,
Boston, Mass: Division of Research, Graduate
School of Business, Harvard University, 1968.
07012

Bauer, Raymond A. and Wortzel, Lawrence H.
"Doctor's Choice: The Physician and His Sources of Information
About Drugs," Journal of Marketing Research, February 1966,
Vol. 3, pp. 40-47.
02340

Beal, George M. and Rogers, Everett M.
"The Scientist As A Referent in The Communication of New
Technology," Public Opinion Quarterly, 1958, Vol. 22,
pp. 555-563.
01351

Beal, G. M., Rogers E. M., and Bohlen, J. M.
"Validity of the Concept of Stages in the Adoption Process."
Rural Sociology, June 1957, Vol. 22, pp. 166-168.
03561

Becker, Marshall H.
"Factors Affecting Diffusion of Innovations Among
Health Professionals," Paper presented at the Public
Health Education Section of American Public Health
Association, 96th Annual Meeting, Detroit, Michigan,
November 14, 1968.
07047

Beckhard, Richard
"An Organization Improvement Program in a Decentralized
Organization," Journal of Applied Behavioral Science,
1966, Vol. 2, pp. 3-25.
07180

Beer, John J. and Lewis, W. David
"Aspects of the Professionalization of Science,"
Daedalus, Fall, 1963, Vol. 92, No. 4, p. 764.
07068

Beez, W. Victor
"Influence of Biased Psychological Reports on Teacher
Behavior and Pupil Performance," in Proceedings of the
76th Annual Convention of the American Psychological
Association, 1968, Washington, D.C.: American Psychological
Association, 1968, pp. 605-606
07222

Belcher, John C.
"Acceptance of the Salk Polio Vaccine," Rural Sociology,
1958, Vol. 23, No. 2, pp. 158-170.
02870

Ben-David, Joseph
"Roles and Innovations in Medicine," American Journal of
Sociology, May 1960, Vol. 65, pp. 557-568.
01736

Benedict, B., Calder, P., Callahan, D. Hornstein, H.
and Miles, M.
"The Clinical-Experimental Approach to Assessing
Organizational Change Efforts," Journal of Applied
Behavioral Science, 1967, Vol. 3, No. 3, pp. 347-380.
06751

Benne, Kenneth D.
"Deliberate Changing as the Facilitation of Growth,"
in Bennis, et al., The Planning of Change, New York:
Holt, Rinehart and Winston, 1961, pp. 230-234.
07099

Benne, K. D., Morris, Sir Charles and Commager, H. S. et. al.
The University in the American Future, Lexington: University
of Kentucky Press, 1966.
03526

Bennis, Warren G.
Changing Organizations, New York: McGraw-Hill, 1966, pp. 223.
05082

Bennis, Warren G.
"Theory and Method in Applying Behavioral Science to Planned
Organizational Change," Journal of Applied Behavioral Science,
1965, Vol. 1, p. 340.
06619

Bennis, Warren, G., Benne, Kenneth D., and Chin, Robert (eds).
The Planning of Change, New York: Holt, Rinehart and
Winston, 1962, 781 pp.
01344

Berlin, I. N.
"Learning Mental Health Consultation History and Problems,"
Mental Hygiene, 1964, Vol. 48, No. 2, pp. 257-266.
02079

Bertrand, Alvin L.
"Agricultural Mechanization and Social Change in Rural
Louisiana," Baton Rouge: Louisiana Agricultural Experiment
Station Bulletin No. 458, 1951.
02498

Bettelheim, B. and Janowitz, M.
Dynamics of Prejudice: A Psychological and Sociological
Study of Veterans, New York: Harper, 1950.
07129

Bhola, Harbans Singh
The Configurational Theory of Innovation Diffusion, Columbus,
Ohio: Ohio State University, College of Education, 1965, 42 p
01062

Binderman, A. J.
"Mental Health Consultation: Theory and Practice," Journal
of Consulting Psychology, 1959, Vol. 23, pp. 473-482.
01335

Blackmore, John and Others
"Test-Demonstration Farms and The Spread of Improved Farm
Practices in Southwest Virginia." Knoxville: Tennessee
Valley Authority Report, P 55-3, 1955.
02492

Blackwell, Gorden W.
"Multidisciplinary Team Research." Social Forces, 1955,
Vol. 33, No. 4, pp. 367-374.
01218

Blake, R.R. and Mouton, Jane S.
Corporate Excellence through Grid Organization
Development, Houston, Texas: Gulf Publishing Co.,
1968
07019

Blake, R.R. and Mouton, Jane S.
Grid Organizational Development, Houston, Texas: Gulf
Publishing Company, 1968.
07153

Blake, R. R. and Mouton, Jane S.
  The Managerial Grid, Houston: Gulf Publishing Co., 1961.
  06198

Blake, R., Mouton, J. and Hain, J.
  "Social Forces in Petition Signing," Southwest Social
  Quarterly, 1956, Vol. 36, pp. 385-390.
  07023

Blau, Peter M.
  Bureaucracy in Modern Society, New York: Random House,
  1955.
  06221

Bloom, B.S.
  "Thought Processes in Lectures and Discussions,"
  Journal of General Education, 1953, Vol. 7, pp. 160-169.
  07085

Blum, R. H. & Funkhouser, M. L.
  "A Lobby for People?" American Psychologist, 1965, Vol. 20,
  No. 3, pp. 208-210.
  02235

Boehm, W. W.
  "The Professional Relationship Between Consultant and
  Consultee." American Journal of Orthopsychiatry, 1956,
  Vol. 26, pp. 241-248.
  03550

Bond, Betty Wells
  The Group-Discussion-Decision Approach: An Appraisal of
  its Use in Health Education, Doctoral Thesis, University
  of Minnesota, Duluth, Minn., 1955.
  07037

Boskoff, Alvin
  "Social Change," in Becker, Howard and Boskoff, Alvin,
  (eds.) Modern Sociolgical Theory in Continuity and
  Change, New York: Holt, Rinehart and Winston, 1957.
  06391

Bowers, Raymond V.
  "Differential Intensity of IntraSocietal Diffusion."
  American Sociological Review, 1938, Vol. 3, pp. 21-31.
  02475

Bowers, D. and Seashore, S.
  "Predicting Organizational Effectiveness with a
  Four-Factor Theory of Leadership," Administrative
  Science Quarterly, 1966, pp. 238-263.
  07184

Bowman, P. H.
  "The role of the consultant as a motivator of action."
  Mental Hygiene, New York, Jan, 1959, Vol. 43, pp. 105-110.
  01319

Bradford, L., Gibb, J. and Benne, K. D.
  T-Group Theory and Laboratory Method, New York: John Wiley
  & Sons, 1964.
  06196

Brandner, Lowell
  Evaluation for Congruence as a factor in accelerated adoption
  of an agricultural innovation. PH.D. Thesis, Madison,
  University of Wisconsin, 1960.
  02471

Brandner, Lowell and Bryant, Kearl
  "Evaluation of congruence as a factor in adoption rate of
  innovations," Rural Sociology, 1964, Vol. 29, No. 3,
  pp. 288-303.
  02076

Brehm, J. W. and Cohen, A. R.
  Explorations in Cognitive Dissonance, New York: John Wiley
  and Sons, 1962.
  06277

Brickell, H. M.
  "Dynamics of Change." National Association of Secondary
  School Principals, 1963.
  01181

Brickell, H. M.
  "The Local School System and Change," Miller, R. (ed.)
  Perspectives on Educational Change, New York: Appleton-
  Century-Crafts, 1966.
  00875

Brickell, H. M.
  "State Organization for Educational Change: A Case Study
  and a Proposal," Miles, Matthew B. (ed.), Innovation in
  Education, New York: Bureau of Publications, Teachers
  College, Columbia University, New York, 1964.
  00845

Brickman, Philip
    Performance Expectations and Performance, Ann
    Arbor, Michigan: Research Center for Group Dynamics,
    University of Michigan, December, 1966. Mimeo.
    06263

Brooks, Harvey
    "National Science Policy and Technology Transfer,"
    Proceedings from Technology Transfer and Innovation
    sponsored by the National Planning Association,
    National Science Foundation, May 15-17, 1966, p. 53.
    07054

Brooks, H.
    "On coherences and transformations: Scientific concepts
    and cultural change." Daedalus, Winter 1965, Vol. 94,
    pp. 66-83.
    00810

Brown, Roger
    Social Psychology, New York: Free Press, 1965.
    06254

Brown, Emory J. and Deckens, Albert
    "Role of the Extension Subject Matter Specialist," Rural
    Sociology, 1958, Vol. 23, No. 3, pp. 263-276.
    02866

Brownson, H. L.
    "Research on Handling Scientific Information." Science,
    Dec. 30, 1962, Vol. 132, pp. 1922-1930.
    00925

Bucklow, Maxine
    "A New Role for the Work Group," Administration Science
    Quarterly, 1966, Vol. 11, pp. 59-78.
    07220

Buchanan, Paul C.
    "The Concept of Organization Development or
    Self-Renewal as a Form of Planned Change,"
    in Watson, G. (ed.), Concepts for Social Change,
    Washington, D.C.: NTL Institute for Applied
    Behavioral Science, 1967.
    03618

Burkholder, David
    "The role of the pharmaceutical detailman in a large
    teaching hospital." American Journal of Hospital Pharmacy,
    June, 1963, Vol. 20, pp. 274-285.
    00671

Burns, T. and Stalker, G. M.
    The management of innovation, London: Tavistock, 1961.
    03791

Burns, T.
    "The Directions of Activities and Communication in
    a Departmental Executive Group," Human Relations,
    1954, Vol. 7, pp. 73-97.
    07151

Caird, J. B. and Moisley, H. A.
"Leadership and Innovation in the Crofting Communities of the Outer Hebrides," Sociological Review, 1961, Vol. 9, pp. 85-102.
02252

Campbell, A., Converse, P., Miller, W., and Stokes, D.
The American Voter, New York: John Wiley & Sons, Inc., 1965.
07021

Campbell, Donald T.
"Systematic Error on the Part of Human Links in Communication Systems," Information Control, Dec. 1958, Vol. 1, pp. 334-369.
01644

Campbell, J. and Dunette, M.
"Effectiveness of T-Group Experiences in Managerial Training and Development," Psychological Bulletin, 1968, Vol. 70, pp. 73-104.
07140

Campbell, R.
"The Role of School Study Councils and Local School Districts in the Dissemination and Implementation of Educational Research," Goldhammer, Keith and Stanley Elam (eds), Dissemination and Implementation, Bloomington, Indiana: Phi Delta Kappa, 1962.
00642

Caplan, G.
"Types of Mental Health Consultation," American Journal of Orthopsychiatry, 1963, Vol. 33, No. 3, pp. 470-481.
03595

Caplow, T.
"Rumors in War," Social Forces, 1946-47, Vol. 25, pp. 298-302.
07213

Carey, J. T.
The Development of the University Evening College, Chicago: Center for the Study of Liberal Education for Adults, 1961.
03602

Carlson, E. R.
"Attitude Change through Modification of Attitude Structure," Journal of Abnormal and Social Psychology, 1956, Vol. 52, pp. 265-261.
06256

Carlson, Richard O.
Adoption of Educational Innovations, Eugene, Oregon: University of Oregon, 1965, 84 pp.
00585

Carlson, Richard O.
"Barriers to Change in Public Schools," Change Processes in the Public Schools, Eugene, Oregon: The Center for the Advanced Study of Educational Administration, 1965.
00628

Carlson, Richard O.
"School Superintendents and the Adoption of Modern Math: A Social Structure Profile," Miles, M.B. (ed), Innovation in Education, New York: Bureau of Publications, Teachers College, Columbia University, New York, 1954.
01174

Carpenter, Edmund and McLuhan, Marshall, (eds.)
Explorations in Communications, Boston: Beacon Press, 1960.
07017

Carr, Donald and Meyer, Edward
Demonstration of Dissemination Practices on Special Class Instruction for the Mentally Retarded: Utilizing Master Teachers as Inservice Educators, Iowa City: University of Iowa, (Research in Progress, November 1, 1966 - October 31, 1969).
05102

Carter, Launor F.
Knowledge Production and Utilization in Contemporary Organizations, System Development Corporation, 1967.
06226

Carter, Launor F.
"From Research to Development to Use," Paper presented at American Educational Research Association, Chicago, 1966, System Development Corp., Santa Monica, California, 28 pp.
00190

Carter, Launor and Silberman, Harry
The Systems Approach, Technology and the School, Professional Paper SP-2025, Santa Monica, Calif.: System Development Corporation, April, 1965, 30 pp.
06096

Cartwright, Dorwin
    "Achieving Change in People: Some Applications of Group
    Dynamics Theory," in Davis, K. and Scott, (eds.) <u>Readings
    in Human Relations</u>, New York: McGraw-Hill, 1959, pp. 219-231.
    03341

Cartwright, Dorwin
    "Influence, Leadership, Control," in March, J.G. (ed.),
    <u>Handbook of Organizations</u>, Chicago: Rand McNally & Co.,
    1965, Chapter 1.
    07192

Cartwright, Dorwin
    "Some Principles of Mass Persuasion," <u>Human Relations,</u> 1949,
    Vol. 2, pp. 253-267.
    06696

Cartwright, Dorwin (ed.)
    <u>Studies in Social Power</u>, Ann Arbor, Michigan: Research
    Center for Group Dynamics, Institute for Social Research,
    University of Michigan, 1959.
    07113

Castle, C. Hilmon
    "Open -circuit Television in Post-graduate Medical Education,"
    <u>Journal of Medical Education</u>, April, 1963, Vol. 38, pp. 254-260.
    00672

Chapanis, N. P. and Chapanis, A.
    "Cognitive Dissonance: Five Years Later," <u>Psychological
    Bulletin</u>, 1964, Vol. 61, pp. 1-22.
    06278

Chapin, F. Stuart
    <u>Cultural Change</u>, New York: Century, 1928.
    02457

Charpie, Robert
    "Business End of Technology Transfer," Proceedings from
    Technology Transfer and Innovation sponsored by the National
    Planning Association, National Science Foundation, May 15-17,
    1966, p. 46.
    07053

Chesler, Mark A. and Barakat, H. M.
    <u>The Innovation and Sharing of Teaching Practices: A
    Study of Professional Roles and Social Structures in Schools</u>.
    Ann Arbor: Institute for Social Research, University of
    Michigan, 1967 (Final Report, USOE Cooperative Research
    Project No. 2636.)
    02248

Chesler, Mark A. and Fox, Robert
    "Teacher Peer Relations and Educational Change," <u>NEA
    Journal</u>, May, 1967, Vol. 56, No. 5, pp. 25-26.
    06292

Chesler, Mark and Franklin, Jan
    "Interracial and Intergenerational Conflict in Secondary
    Schools," Presentation made to the Meetings of the American
    Sociological Association, Boston, Mass., August, 1968.
    07105

Chesler, Mark, Schmuck, R., and Lippit, R.
    "The Principal's Role in Facilitating Innovation,"
    <u>Theory Into Practice</u>, Vol. 2, 1963.
    02607

Chin, Robert
    "Models of and Ideas About Changing," Meierhenry, Wesley C.
    (ed.), <u>Media and Educational Innovation</u>, University of
    Nebraska Extension Division and University of Nebraska Press,
    1964.
    2612

Chin, Robert and Benne, Kenneth D.
    <u>General Strategies for Effecting Changes in Human
    Systems</u>, Boston University Human Relations
    Center, Research Report No. 94.
    06113

Chu, Godwin C.
    "Problems of Cross-Cultural Communication Research," <u>Journalism
    Quarterly</u>, Autumn 1964, Vol. 41, No. 4, pp.557-562.
    01937

Clark, B.R.
   "Interorganizational Patterns in Education," <u>Administrative</u>
   <u>Science Quarterly</u>, Sept. 1965, Vol. 10, No. 2, pp. 224-237.
   01172

Clark, David L. and Guba, Egon G.
   "An Examination of Potential Change Roles in
   Education," paper presented at the Symposium
   on Innovation in Planning School Curricula,
   Airlie House, Virginia, Oct., 1965.
   06003

Clark, David L. and Hopkins, John E.
   <u>Preliminary Estimates of Research, Development</u>
   <u>and Diffusion Personnel Required in Education,</u>
   <u>1971-72</u>, Special Project Memorandum, School
   of Education, Indiana University, Bloomington,
   Indiana, September, 1966.
   06241

Clark, David L. and Hopkins, John E.
   "Roles for Research, Development, and Diffusion: Personnel
   in Education: Project Memo #1 - A Logical Structure
   for Viewing Research, Development and Diffusion Roles in
   Education," CRP Project No. X-022, April 1966.
   03586

Clark, Kenneth B.
   <u>Dark Ghetto</u>, New York: Harper & Row, 1965,
   251 pp.
   06268

Clark, Kenneth B.
   "The Involvement of the Research Team in the
   Process of Deliberate Social Influence," in
   <u>Approaches to Research Utilization in Community</u>
   <u>Psychology: A Symposium</u>, Washington, D. C.:
   American Psychological Association, 1967.
   06323

Clausen, John A., Seidenfeld, Morton, A., and Deasy, Leila C.
   "Parent Attitudes Toward Participation of Their Children
   in Polio Vaccine Trials," <u>American Journal of Public Health</u>,
   1954, Vol. 44, pp. 1526-1536.
   06010

Coch, Lester and French, John R.P.,Jr.
   "Overcoming Resistance to Change," Swanson, Guy E., et.al.
   (eds.) <u>Readings in Social Psychology</u>, New York: Henry Holt
   and Company, 1952. pp. 474-491.
   01828

Cohen, Arthur
   <u>Attitude Change and Social Influence</u>, New York: Basic Books,
   1964.
   05108

Cohen, A. R.
   "Cognitive Tuning As A Factor Affecting Impression
   Formation," <u>Journal of Personality</u>, 1961,
   Vol. 29, pp. 235-245.
   06299

Cohen, A.R.
   "Upward Communications in Experimentally Created Hierarchies,"
   <u>Human Relations</u>, 1958, Vol. 11, No. 1, pp. 44-53.
   #07215 and #01760

Cole, Stephen and Cole, Jonathan
   "Visibility and the Structural Basis of Awareness of
   Scientific Research," <u>American Sociological Review</u>,
   1968, Vol. 33, pp. 397-412.
   07072

Coleman, A. Lee, and Marsh C. Paul
   "Differential Communication Among Farmers in Kentucky County,"
   <u>Rural Sociology</u>, 1955, Vol. 20, pp. 93-101.
   02406

Coleman, James S., Katz, Elihu, and Menzel, Herbert
   <u>Medical Innovation: A Diffusion Study</u>, New York:
   Bobbs-Merrill, 1966.
   06399

Coleman, James S., Katz, Elihu, and Menzel, Herbert
   <u>Doctors and New Drugs,</u> Indianapolis, Indiana: Bobbs,
   Merrill, 1966.
   03576

Coleman, James, Menzel, Herbert and Katz, E.
"The Diffusion of an Innovation Among Physicians." Sociometry,
December 1957, Vol. 20, pp. 253-270.
03895

Collins, Barry E. and Guetzkow, Harold
A Social Psychology of Group Processes for
Decision-Making, New York: John Wiley & Sons,
1964, 254 pp.
06293

Colm, Gerhard
"Economic Aspects of Technological Development,"
Proceedings from Technology Transfer and Innovation
sponsored by National Planning Association, National
Science Foundation, May 15-17, 1966, p. 84.
07057

Commager, Henry S.
"The University and the Community of Learning," in
Benne, K.D., Morris, Sir Charles, and Commager, H.S.,
The University in the American Future, Lexington:
University of Kentucky Press, 1965.
07086

Coney, Robert, Plaskett, Vernon, Roggenbuck, Robert and Hood, Paul
Educational R & D Information System Requirements: A Task
Force Report, Berkeley, Calif.: Far West Laboratory for
Educational Research and Development, 1968, 59 pp.
06613

Connor, Desmond M.
Strategies for Development, Ottawa, Canada: Development
Press, 1968, 48 pp.
07100

Cooper, C.R. and Archambault, B., (eds.)
"Communication, Dissemination and Utilization of Research
Information in Rehabilitation Counseling," Proceedings of
a Regional Conference, sponsored by the Department of
Guidance and Psychological Services, Springfield
College, Springfield, Mass., May 9-10, 1968 and Oct. 17-18,
1968.
07224

Corey, Stephen M.
Action Research to Improve School Practices, New York:
Bureau of Publications, Teachers College, Columbia
University, 1953.
03599

Coughenour, C. Milton
Agricultural Agencies as Information Sources for Farmers in
a Kentucky County, 1950-1955, Lexington: Kentucky Agricultural
Experimental Station Progress Report 82, 1959.
02437

Cox, Donald F., (ed.)
Risk Taking and Information Handling in Consumer Behavior,
Boston: Division of Research, Graduate School of Business,
Harvard University, 1967.
07011

Crane, Diana
"The Gatekeepers of Science: Some Factors Affecting the
Selection of Articles for Scientific Journals," American
Sociologist, November, 1967, pp. 195-201
06577

Cronin, Joseph M.
National Association of Secondary-School Principals, "Changing
Secondary Schools," The National Association of Secondary-
School Principals Bulletin, May, 1963, Vol. 47, No. 283,
168 pp.
01049

Cumming, Elaine and Cumming, John
Closed Ranks: An Experiment in Mental Health Education,
Cambridge: Harvard University Press for the Commonwealth
Fund, 1957. 192 pp.
03598

Dahling, Randall L.
"Shannon's Information Theory - The Spread of an Idea,"
Schramm, Wilbur (ed.) Studies of Innovation and of Commun-
ication to the Public, Stanford, California: Stanford
University Institute for Communication Research, 1962.
01495

Dale, E.
Planning and Developing the Company Organization
Structure, New York: American Management Association,
1952.
07141

Dalton, M.
Men Who Manage, New York: Wiley and Sons, 1959.
07201

Davis, K.
"Management Communication and the Grapevine," Harvard
Business Review, 1953, Vol. 31, pp. 43-49.
07152

Davis, Robert C.
The Public Impact of Science in the Mass Media: A Report
on a Nation-Wide Survey for the National Association of
Science Writers, Ann Arbor: Institute for Social Research,
1958, pp. 254.
05119

Davis, Sheldon A.
"An Organic Problem Solving Method of Organizational
Change," Journal of Applied Behavioral Science, 1967,
Vol. 3, pp. 3-21.
07203

Deasy, Leila C.
"Socio-Economic Status and Participation in the
Poliomyelitis Vaccine Trials," American Sociological
Review, 1956, Vol. 21, pp. 185-191.
06011

Dennerll, Donald and Chesler, Mark
"Where Do New Teaching Practices Come From?....and Where
Do They Go?" Michigan Elementary Principal, December 1964,
Vol. 39, No. 2.
05121

Denver Research Institute
"The Channels of Technology Acquisition in Commercial Firms,
and the NASA Dissemination Program, Springfield, Va.,:
Clearinghouse for Federal Scientific and Technical Information,
June, 1967.
06111

Denver Research Institute
"Technology Transfer--A Selected Bibliography,"
(Prepared by M.Terry Sovel), for the National Aeronautics
and Space Administration, Denver, Colorado: Industrial
Economics Division, University of Denver, November 11, 1968.
07074

DeSimone, Daniel V.
"Impact of Law on Technological Innovation," Proceedings from
Technology Transfer and Innovation sponsored by the
National Planning Association, National Science Foundation,
May 15-17, 1966, p. 37.
07052

Deutsch, K. W.
The Nerves of Government: Models of Political Communication
and Control. New York: Free Press of Glencoe, 1963, 316 pp.
00903

Dexter, L. A. and White, D. M. (eds.)
People, Society and Mass Communications. New York: Free Press
of Glencoe, 1964, 595 pp.
03624

Dittes, J. E. and Kelley, H. H.
"Effects of Different Conditions of Acceptance Upon
Conformity to Group Norms," Journal of Abnormal
Social Psychology, 1956, Vol. 53, pp. 100-107.
06288

Drucker, P. F.
   "Modern Technology and Ancient Jobs," Technology
   and Culture, Vol. 4, No. 3.
   06361

Dupree, A. Hunter
   "Central Scientific Organization in the United States Government,"
   Minerva, Summer 1963, Vol. 1, No. 4, pp. 453-469.
   01265

Dupree, A. Hunter
   Science in the Federal Government, Cambridge, Mass.: Harvard
   University Press, 1957.
   07093

Dykens, J. W., Hyde, R. W., Orzaek, L. H., and York, R. H.
   Strategies of Mental Hospital Change,   Massachusetts
   Department of Mental Health, 1964, pp. 187.
   05134

Eash, Maurice J.
   "A Critical Analysis of Three Models for Implementation
   of Research Findings," paper presented at Annual
   Meeting of the American Educational REsearch Association,
   1967.
   06024

Eicholtz, G. and Rogers, E.
   "Resistance to the Adoption of Audio-Visual Aids by
   Elementary School Teachers: Contrasts and Similarities
   to Agricultural Innovation," Miles, Matthew B. (ed.),
   Innovation in Education, New York: Bureau of Publications,
   Teachers College, Columbia University, New York, 1964.
   01185

"What is Educational Technology?" Special issue
of Educational Technology, January 15, 1968.
07031

Elliott, John G. and Couch, Carl J.
   "Operators of Grain Elevators as Diffusers of Farm Practices."
   East Lansing, Michigan State University, Institute for
   Extension Personnel Development Publication 20, 1965.
   01447

English, Horace B. and English, Ava C.
   A Comprehensive Dictionary of Psychological and Psycho-
   analytical Terms, New York: Longsman, Green, 1958.
   07109

Ennis, P. H.
   "The Social Structure of Communication Systems: A
   Theoretical Proposal." Studies in Public Communication,
   Summer 1961, Vol. 3, pp. 120-144.
   00897

Erasmus, Charles
   Man Takes Control; Cultural Development and American Aid,
   Minneapolis: University of Minnesota Press, 1961.
   00114

   "E.T.V.--The Widening Picture," EDUCOM, Bulletin of the
   Interuniversity Communications Council, March, 1967,
   Vol. 2, No. 2.
   07010

Etzioni, Amitai
   Modern Organizations, Englewood Cliffs: Prentice-Hall,
   1964.
   07161

Etzioni, Amitai
   The Moon-Doggle: Domestic and International Implications
   of the Space Race, Garden City: Doubleday & Co., 1964, 195 pp.
   00893

Etzioni, Amitai
   "On the national guidance of science." Administrative
   Science Quarterly, March 1966, Vol. 10, No. 4, pp. 466-487.
   01162

Etzioni, Amitai
   "Toward a Theory of Societal Guidance," The American
   Journal of Sociology, September, 1967, Vol. 73, No. 2,
   pp. 173-187.
   07076

Eye, Glen G. and Netzer, Lanore A.
   "The Tension-Penetration Model: Interaction Patterns
   for Innovation," (paper one), John Guy Fowlkes Invitational
   Seminar on Administration of Change in the Instructional
   Program, Madison, Wisconsin: University of Wisconsin.
   07103

Fairweather, George W.
Methods for Experimental Social Innovation, New York:
John Wiley & Sons, Inc.
06189

Far West Laboratory for Educational Research & Development
Educational R&D Information System Requirements, A Task
Force Report, Berkeley, California, 1968, 59 pp.
06613   (See also Caney, et. al.)

Featherstone, Joseph
"How Children Learn," The New Republic, Sept. 2, 1967.
06388

Festinger, L.
"Informal Social Communication," Psychological Review, 1950,
Vol. 57, pp. 212-287.
06698

Festinger, Leon
A theory of cognitive dissonance, Evanston, Illinois: Row,
Petersen and Co., 1957, pp. 84-122.
00264

Festinger, Leon
"A Theory of Social Comparison Processes," Human
Relations, 1954, Vol. 7, pp. 117-140.
07032

Festinger, L., Schachter, S., and Back, K.
Social Pressures in Informal Groups: A Study of Human Factors
in Housing, Stanford, California: Stanford University Press,
1950, 1963, 197 pp.
00982

Fiedler, Fred E.
"A note on leadership theory: the effect of social barriers
between leaders and followers." Sociometry,1957, Vol. 20,
pp. 87-94.
01718

Fisch, G.
"Stretching the Span of Management," Harvard Business
Review, 1963, Vol. 41, pp. 74-85.
07142

Flanders, Ned A.
"Using Interaction Analysis in the Inservice Training of
Teachers." Journal of Experimental Education, June 1962,
Vol. 30, pp. 313-316.
02863

Fliegel, Frederick C.
"Literacy and Exposure to instrumental information among
farmers in Southern Brazil." Rural Sociology, 1966, Vol. 31,
pp. 15-28.
01424

Flinn, William L.
"Combined Influence of Group Norms and Personal Characteristics on Innovativeness." M.S. Thesis, Columbus: Ohio State
University, 1961.
01415

Forsdale, Louis
"8mm Motion Pictures in Education: Incipient Innovation,"
Miles, Matthew B. (ed.), Innovation in Education, New York:
Bureau of Publications, Teachers College, Columbia
University, New York, 1964.
01176

Foshay, Arthur W.
"Strategies for Curriculum Change," in A Report of the
Invitational Conference on Implementing Career Development
Theory and Research Through the Curriculum, Washington, D.C.:
National Vocational Guidance Association, 1966, pp. 1-16.
03881

Foundation for Research on Human Behavior
"Comparative Theories in Social Change," Peter Hollis, (ed.),
Ann Arbor, Michigan, 1966, 374 pp.
06057

Francis, David G. and Rogers, Everett M.
"Adoption of a Nonrecommended Innovation : The Grass
Incubator." Paper Presented at the Rural Sociological
Society, University Park, Pennsylvania, 1960.
01409

Frank, Lawrence K.
"Interprofessional Communication." American Journal of
Public Health, December 1961, Vol. 51, pp. 1798-1804.
03297

Freedman, Johnathan L. and Sears, David O.
"Selective Exposure," in Advances in Experimental
Social Psychology, Vol. XI, New York: Academic
Press, 1965.
06273

Freedman, Johnathan L. and Sears, David O.
"Warning, distraction and resistance to influence."
Journal of Personality and Social Psychology, March 1965,
Vol. 1, No. 3, pp. 262-266.
03000

Freedman, Ronald and Takeshita, John Y.
 "Studies of Fertility and Family Limitation in Taiwan."
 Eugenics Quarterly, 1965, Vol. 12, pp. 233-250.
 01403

French, J.R.P., Jr.
 "Experiments in Field Settings," in Festinger, L. and
 Katz, D., Research Methods in the Behavioral Sciences,
 New York: Holt, Rinehart and Winston, 1953.
 07137

Freund, Paul A.
 "The Legal Profession," Daedalus, Fall, 1963, Vol. 92,
 No. 4, p. 689.
 07064

Frohman, Alan
 "The Role and Contribution of Ph.D. Scientists in an
 Industrial R&D Laboratory," Unpublished Master Thesis,
 Massachusetts Institute of Technology, 1968.
 07171

Frohman, Alan
 "Technical and Social Forces: The Dynamic Duo,"
 Massachusetts Institute of Technology, ditto, 1969.
 07174

Fry, Thornton C.
 "Mathematicians in industry, the first 75 years." Science,
 Feb. 28, 1964, Vol. 143, No. 3609, pp. 934-938.
 02993

Fukuyama, Y.
 "The Uses of Sociology by Religious Bodies." Journal for
 the Scientific Study of Religion, Spring 1963, Vol. 2,
 pp. 195-203.
 00981

Fuller, R. Buckminster
 Education Automation, Carbondale: Southern Illinois
 University, 1962, 88 pp.
 06092

Funkhouser, G. R.
 A General Mathematical Model of Information Diffusion,
 Palo Alto, California: Stanford University, Institute
 for Communication Research, September, 1968.
 07102

Gage, N.L. and Others
"Changing Teacher Behavior Through Feedback from Pupils: Application of Equilibrium Theory," in Charters, W.W. and Gage, N.L. (eds.) Readings in Social Psychology of Education, Boston: Allen and Bacon, 1963.
6306

Galbraith, J. Kenneth
The New Industrial State, Boston, Mass.: Houghton Mifflin Co., 1967.
07136

Gallaher, Art
"The Role of the Advocate and Directed Change," Meierhenry, Wesley C. (ed.), Media and Educational Innovation, Univ. of Nebraska Extension Division and Univ. of Nebraska Press, 1964.
02613

Gardner, John W.
Self Renewal: The Individual and the Innovative Society, New York: Harper & Row, 1964.
06258

Garfinkel, H.
"Social Science Evidence and the School Segregation Cases." Journal of Politics, Feb. 1959, Vol. 21, pp. 37-59.
00961

Garvey, William D. and Griffith, Belver C.
Reports of the American Psychological Association's Project on Scientific Information Exchange in Psychology, Washington, D. C.: American Psychological Association, 1963.
05150

Garvey, William D. and Griffith, Belver C.
"Research Frontier: The APA Project on Scientific Information Exchange in Psychology," Journal of Counseling Psychology, 1963, Vol. 10, pp. 297-302.
06793

Garvey, William D. and Griffith, Belver C.
"Scientific Communication as a Social System," Science, 1967, Vol. 157, No. 3792, pp. 1011-1016.
06218

Garvey, William D. and Griffith, Belver C.
"Studies of Social Innovations in Scientific Communication in Psychology," American Psychologist, 1966, Vol. 21, No. 11, pp. 1019-1036.
06349

Garvey, William D. and Griffith, Belver C.
"The structure, objectives, and findings of a study of Scientific Information Exchange in Psychology." American Documentation, Oct. 1964, Vol. 15, pp. 58-67.
02107

Garvey, William D. and Griffith, Belver C.
"Scientific information exchange in psychology." Science, Vol. 146, p. 1655.
01205

Gavin, James M.
"The Weapons of 1984," Saturday Review of Literature, August 31, 1968.
07005

Gebhard, B.
"Historical Relationship Between Scientific and Lay Medicine for Present Day Patient Education," Bulletin of the History of Medicine, 1958, Vol. 32, No. 1, pp. 46-53.
0232

Gellman, Aaron
"A Model of the Innovation Process," Proceedings from Technology Transfer and Innovation sponsored by the National Planning Association, National Science Foundation, May 15-17, 1966, p. 11.
07049

Gerard, H.
"Some Effects of Status, Role Clarity and Group Goal Clarity upon the Individual's Reaction to Group Process," Journal of Personality, 1957, Vol. 63, pp. 181-194.
06701

Gibb, Cecil A.
"Leadership," in Lindzey, G. (ed.), Handbook of Social Psychology, Vol. II, Cambridge, Mass.: Addison-Wesley, 1954 pp. 877-920.
07188

Gilb, Corinne Lathrop
"Bibliography of Histories of Professions," in Gilb, C.L.,
Hidden Hierarchies, New York and London: Harper & Row,
1966, pp. 263-268.
07226

Gilb, Corinne Lathrop
Hidden Hierarchies, New York and London: Harper and Row,
1966.
07071

Glaser, Edward M.
"A Pilot Study to Determine the Feasibility of
Promoting the Use of a Systematized Care Program for
Patients with Chronic Obstructive Pulmonary Disease,"
Final Report to Social and Rehabilitation Service,
Department of Health, Education, and Welfare, Los
Angeles: Human Interaction Research Institute, July,
1968.
07044

Glaser, Edward M.
Utilization of Applicable Research and Demonstration Results,
Final Report to Vocational Rehabilitation Administration, Department
of HEW, Project RD-1263-G, March 1967 edition.
06097

Glasser, Melvin A.
"A Study of the Public's Acceptance of the Salk Vaccine
Programs," American Journal of Public Health, 1958, Vol. 48,
pp. 141-146.
01385

Goffman, Erving
Asylums, New York: Doubleday Anchor, 1961.
07135

Golden, Morton M., Brody, Matthew, and Lichtman, Harry S.
"The Brooklyn project for the psychiatric education of the
private practitioner." New York State Journal of Medicine,
Nov. 15, 1961, Vol. 61, pp. 3779-3782.
00691

Goldman, J.E.
"Role of Science in Innovation," Proceedings from Technology
Transfer and Innovation sponsored by the National Planning
Association, National Science Foundation, May 15-17, 1966,
p. 92.
07058

Goldstein, Bernice
The Changing Protestant Ethic: Rural Patterns in Health,
Work and Leisure, Ph.D. Thesis, Lafayette Ind.: Purdue
University, 1959.
06313

Goldstein, Bernice and Eichhorn, Robert L.
"The Changing Protestant Ethic: Rural Patterns in Health,
Work, and Leisure." American Sociological Review, 1961,
Vol. 26, pp. 557-565.
01835

Gomberg, William
"Democratic Management - Gomberg Replies," Transaction,
December, 1966, p. 48.
06320

Gomberg, William
"The Trouble with Democratic Management," Transaction,
1966, pp. 30-35.
06316

Gomberg, W. and Marrow, A.
"The Trouble with Democratic Management," Transaction,
1966, July-August, and December, 1966.
06287

Goode, William J.
"Community within a Community: The Professions," American
Sociological Review, 1957, Vol. 22, pp. 194-200.
07077

Goode, William J.
"Encrouchment, Charlatanism, and the Emerging
Profession: Psychology, Sociology, and Medicine,
American Sociological Review, 1960, Vol. 25,
pp. 902-914.
07078

Goode, William J.
"Community Within a Community: The Professions," American
Sociological Review, 1957, Vol. 22, pp. 194-200.
01678

Gould, Julius and Kolb, Wm. L.
A Dictionary of the Social Sciences, New York: The
Free Press, 1964.
07038

Graham, S.
"Class and conservatism in the adoption of innovations."
Human Relations, 1956, Vol. 9, No. 1, pp. 91-100.
01763

Greenberg, Daniel S.
The Politics of Pure Science, New York: New America
Library, 1968, 303 pp.
07089

Greenberg, Bradley S. and others.
"Diffusion of News about an Anticipated Major News Event."
Journal of Broadcasting, 1965, vol. 9, pp. 129-142.
01860

Griffiths, Daniel E.
"Administrative Theory and Change in Organizations," Miles,
Matthew B. (ed.), Innovation in Education, New York:
Bureau of Publications, Teachers College, Columbia Univ.
New York, 1964.
01183

Gross, Neal C.
"The Diffusion of a Culture Trait in Two Iowa Townships,"
M.S. Thesis, Ames: Iowa State College, 1942.
01863

Gross, Neal; McEachern, A. W. and Mason, W. S.
Explorations in Role Analysis: Studies of the School
Superintendency Role. New York: John Wiley and Sons,
1958.
05169

Guba, Egon G.
"The Change Continuum and its Relation to the Illinois
Plan for Program Development for Gifted Children,"
Paper delivered to a Conference on Educational Change,
Urbana, Illinois, March, 1966.
07131

Guba, Egon G.
"Evaluation of the Process of Change," in Miller, Richard
Catalyst for Change: A National Study of ESEA Title III
(PACE) Reports of Special Consultants, Washington, D.C.:
U.S. Government Printing Office, 1967.
07081

Guba, Egon G.
"Development, Diffusion and Evaluation," in
Eidell, T.L. and Kitchel, Joanne M. (eds.),
Knowledge Production and Utilization in Educational
Administration. Eugene, Oregon: University Council
on Educational Administration and Center for Advanced
Study of Educational Administration, University of
Oregon, 1968.
06227

Guba, Egon G. et al.
The Role of Educational Research in Educational Change,
The United States, Conference on the Role of Educational
Research in Educational Change, UNESCO Institute for
Education, Hamburg, Germany, July 19-22, 100 pp.
06118

Guba, Egon G. and Snyder, Clinton A.
"Instructional Television and the Classroom Teacher,"
Audio-Visual Communication Review, 1965, Vol. 13,
pp. 5-26.
06089

Guest, R. H.
Organizational change: the effect of successful leadership,
Homewood, Illinois: Dorsey Press, 1962
00861

Guetzkow, Harold
"Communication in Organizations," in March, J., (ed.)
Handbook of Organization, New York: Rand McNally, 1966.
06304

Guetzkow, Harold
"Conversion Barriers in Using the Social Sciences."
Administrative Science Quarterly, June 1959, Vol. 4,
pp. 68-81.
00202

Guetzkow, Harold, (ed.)
    Simulation in Social Science: Readings, Englewood Cliffs,
    N. J.: Prentice Hall, Inc., 1962, 199 pp.
    06307

Gulick, L. and Urwick, L. (eds.)
    Papers on the Science of Administration, New York, 1937.
    07209

Gullahorn, J.T.
    "Distance and Friendship as Factors in the Gross Interaction
    Matrix," _Sociometry_, 1952, Vol. 15, pp. 123-134.
    07195

Guskin, Alan E.
    Changing Values of Thai College Students, Bangkok:
    Faculty of Education, Chulalongkorn University, 1964.
    05160

Guskin, Alan E.
    The Federal Manager and Research, Ann Arbor,
    Michigan: Center for Research on Utilization of
    Scientific Knowledge, University of Michigan, 1967.
    Mimeo.
    05162

Guskin, Alan E.
    "Tradition and Change in a Thai University," in Textor, R. (ed.)
    Cultural Frontiers of the Peace Corps, Cambridge: MIT Press,
    1966.
    05163

Gustafson, James M.
    "The Clergy in the United States," _Daedalus_, Fall, 1963,
    Vol. 92, No. 4, p. 724.
    07066

Habbe, S.
    "Communicating with Employees," _Student Personnel Policy_,
    No. 129, New York: National Industrial Conference Board,
    1952.
    07194

Haber, Ralph Norman
    "The Spread of an Innovation : High School Language Labora-
    tories." _Journal of Experimental Education_, 1963, Vol. 31,
    pp. 359-369.
    01867

Hackel, Joseph P.
    "Doctor, what motivates you to attend a medical convention?"
    New York State Journal of Medicine, May 1, 1958, Vol. 581
    pp. 1550-1552.
    00753

Hagstrom, Warren O.
    The Scientific Community, New York: Basic Books, Inc.,
    1965.
    06324

Haire, M. (ed.)
    Modern Organization Theory, New York: Wiley and Sons,
    1959.
    07156

Hall, Harry S.
    "Scientists and politicians." _Bulletin of the Atomic_
    Scientists, Feb. 1956, Vol. 12, No. 2, pp. 26-52.
    01231

Halpert, Harold P.
    "Communications as a Basic Tool in Promoting Utilization
    of Research Findings," _Community Mental Health Journal_,
    Fall, 1966, Vol. 2, No. 3.
    07097

Halpin, Andrew W.
    "Problems in the Use of Communications Media in the Dissemi-
    nation and Implementation of Educational Research,"
    Goldhammer, Keith and Elam, Stanley (eds.), _Dissemination_
    and Implementation, Bloomington, Indiana: Phi Delta Kappa,
    1962.
    00641

Handlin, Oscar
    "Science and Technology in Popular Culture," in
    Holton, Gerald, (ed.) _Science and Culture: A Study of_
    Cohesive and Disjunctive Forces, Boston: Houghton Mifflin
    Co., 1965.
    06025

Hanks, L. M.,Jr.
"Diptheria Immunization in a Thai Community," Paul, B. D.,
and Miller, W. B. (eds.), Health, Culture,and Community,
New York: Russell Sage Foundation, 1955.
00346

Harvey, O. J. and Consalvi, C.
"Status and Conformity to Pressure in Informal Groups,"
Journal of Abnormal Social Psychology, 1960, Vol. 60,
pp. 182-187.
06289

Hassinger, Edward
"Stages in the adoption process." Rural Sociology, March
1959, Vol. 24, No. 1. pp. 52-53.
02875

Hattery, Lowell H. and Hofheimer, Susan
"The Legislators' Source of Expert Information," Public
Opinion Quarterly, Fall, 1954, Vol. 18, No. 3, pp. 300-303.
01214

Havelock, Eric A.
The Crucifixion of Intellectual Man, Boston, Mass.:
The Beacon Press, 1951.
07106

Havelock, Ronald G.
"Diffusion of Utilization Research to Those Concerned
with Getting Educational Research into Practice," Project
Proposal, U.S. Office of Education, Ann Arbor, Michigan:
Center for Research on Utilization of Scientific Knowledge,
The University of Michigan, 1968.
07122

Havelock, Ronald G.
Linking Research to Practice: What Role for the Linking
Agent? Paper presented at the American Educational Research
Association Meeting, New York, Feb. 1967.
03041

Havelock, Ronald G.
"New Developments in Translating Theory and Research
into Practice," Paper presented at the 96th Annual
Meeting of the American Public Health Association,
Detroit, Michigan, November 14, 1968.
07111

Havelock, R. G.
Research Utilization Report: Analysis of Seminar Sessions,
Institute for Social Research, 1964.(ditto)
06183

Havelock, Ronald G.
"Social Roadblocks in Utilizing Highway Safety," in
O'Day, James (ed.), Driver Behavior Cause and Effect,
Proceedings of the Second Annual Traffic Safety
Symposium of the Automobile Insurance Industry,
March, 1968, p. 217.
07108

Havelock, Ronald and Benne, Kenneth D.
"An Exploratory Study of Knowlege Utilization," in
Watson, G. (ed.), Concepts for Social Change,
Washington, D.C.: NTL Institute for Applied Behavioral
Science, 1967
and reprinted in Bennis, W.G., Benne, K.D., and Chin, R.
(eds.), The Planning of Change, New York: Holt,
Rinehart, Winston, 1969.
03872

Havelock, Ronald G.; Huber, Janet; and Zimmerman, Shaindel
Major Works on Change in Education: An Annotated
Bibliography and Subject Index, Ann Arbor, Michigan:
Center for Research on Utilization of Scientific
Knowledge, The University of Michigan, March, 1969.
07110

Havelock, Ronald and Mann, Floyd
Research and Development Laboratory Management
Knowledge Utilization Study, Final Report, Contract
AF49(638)1732, Ann Arbor, Michigan: Center for Research
on Utilization of Scientific Knowledge, Institute
for Social Research, July 20, 1968.
07008

Heathers, Glen
"Influencing Change at the Elementary Level," Miller, R. I.
(ed.), Perspectives on Educational Change, New York:
Appleton-Century-Crafts, 1966.
00872

Helson, H., Blake, R.R., and Mouton, J.S.
"Petition-Signing as Adjustment to Situational and
Personal Factors," Journal of Social Psychology,
1958, Vol. 48, pp. 3-10.
07020

Hencley, Stephen R.
"Problems Confronting Schools and Colleges of Education in
Attempting to Meet the Demand for Research, Development and
Diffusion Persons." Paper presented at American Educational
Research Association 1967 Annual Meeting, New York: February,
17, 1967.

06032

Hendriks, G.
"The Role of Research in Community Development," Social Welfare
Policy II, J. A. Poneioen, (editor), The Hague, Mouton, & Co.,
1963, pp. 115-133.

06045

Hoffer, Charles R. and Gibson, D. L.
  The Community Situation as it Affects Agricultural Extension
  Work, East Lansing, Michigan Agricultuaral Experiment Station
  Special Bulletin 312, 1941.
  01852

Hollander, E. P.
  "Competence and Conformity in the Acceptance of Influence,"
  Steiner I. and Fishbein, Current Studies in Social Psychology,
  New York: Holt, 1965.
  05183

Hollomon, J. Herbert
  "Technology Transfer," Proceedings from Technology
  Transfer and Innovation sponsored by the National
  Planning Association, National Science Foundation,
  May 15-17, 1966, p. 32.
  07051

Holmberg, Allan R.
  "Changing Community Attitudes and Values in Peru: A case
  study in guided change." Council on Foreign Relations,
  Social Change in Latin America Today.
  02030

Hopkins, John E.
  "Scope of the Demand for Educational Research
  and Research-Related Persons," American Educational
  Research Association Annual Meeting, February, 1967.
  03067

Hopkins, John E., et al.
  "Exemplars of Emerging Roles," Conference Paper No. 3,
  Conference on Emerging Roles in Educational Research,
  Development, and Diffusion, Bloomington, Indiana: Indiana
  University, December, 1966.
  06188

Hoselitz, B. F.
  "Noneconomic Barriers to Economic Development." Economic
  Development and Cultural Change, 1952, Vol. 1, pp. 8-21.
  02029

House, R.
  "T-Group Education and Leadership Effectiveness: A
  Review of the Empiric Literature and a Critical
  Evaluation," Personnel, 1967, Vol. 20, pp. 1-32.
  07170

Hovland, Carl I. and Weiss, Walter
  "The Influence of Source Credibility on Communication
  Effectiveness," Public Opinion Quarterly, 1951, Vol. 15,
  pp. 635-650.
  06281

Hovland, Carl I. (ed.)
  The Order of Presentation in Persuasion, New Haven,
  Connecticut: Yale University Press, 1957.
  07009

Hovland, Carl I.
  "Effects of the Mass Media of Communication," in
  Lindzey, G. (ed.), Handbook of Social Psychology Reading,
  Massachusetts: Addison-Wesley, 1954.
  07001

Hruschka, Erna
  "Unpublished Data," Stuttgart-Hohenheim, Germany, Institut
  fur Landwirtschafliche Beratung and der Landwirtschaftlicken
  Hochschule, 1961.
  06404

Hubbard, Alfred, W.
  "Predicting Doctor Behavior," Paper presented to Eastern
  Pharmaceutical Market Research Group, Hotel New Yorker,
  May 25, 1960.
  00751

Hudspeth, Delayne R.
  A Study of Belief System and Acceptance of New Educational
  Media with Users and Nonusers of Audiovisual Graphics,
  PH.D. Thesis, East Lansing, Michigan State University, 1966.
  01190

Huessy, H. R.
  "Mental Health Consultation in Varied Settings," in
  Mental Health with Limited Resources: Yankee Ingenuity in
  Low-Cost Programs, New York: Grune and Stratton, 1966.
  06012

Hughes, Everett C.
  "Professions," Daedalus, Fall, 1963, Vol. 92, No. 4,
  p. 655.
  07062

Hull, W. J.
  "Growing pains of international technical cooperation."
  International Labour Review, Oct. 1961, Vol. 84, pp.
  223-245.
  01768

Huntington, Samuel, P.
  "Power, Expertise and the Military Profession," Daedalus,
  Fall, 1963, Vol. 92, No. 4, p. 785.
  07069

Hyman, Herbert and Sheatsley, Paul
  "Some Reasons Why Information Campaigns Fail." Public
  Opinion Quarterly, 1947, Vol. 11, pp. 412-423.
  02026

Insko, Chester, A., Arkoff, A. and Insko, V.
"Effects of High and Low Fear - Arousing Communications Upon Opinions Toward Smoking." Journal of Experimental Social Psychology, 1965, Vol. 1, No. 3, pp. 256-266.
00318

Institute for Community Studies
"Preliminary Report of a Research Utilization Conference, October 7-9, 1968," Kansas City, Missouri: Institute for Community Studies, February, 1969, Publication #69-177.
07134

"ITM Academy," Grand Rapids, Michigan: Dyer Ives Foundation, 1967, 25 pp. (Unpublished)
07014

Jackson, Jay M.
"The Organization and its Communication Problem." Journal of Communication, Dec. 1959, Vol. 9, pp. 158-172.
00592

Jacobs, Robert
"The Inter-Disciplinary Approach to Educational Planning," Symposium on Education and Development, Comparative Education Review, June 1964, Vol. 8, pp. 5-47.
01781

Jamias, Juan F.
The Effects of Belief System Styles on the Communication and Adoption of Farm Practices, Ph.D. Thesis, East Lansing, Michigan: Michigan State University, Dissertation Abstracts, 1965, Vol. 25, No. 11, pp. 6797-6798.
02265

Janis, I.L.
"Personality as a Factor in Susceptibility to Persuasion," in Schramm, W., (ed.), The Science of Human Communication, New York: Basic Books, 1963, pp. 54-64.
06270

Janis, I. L. and Feshbach, S.
"Effects of Fear-Arousing Communications," Journal of Abnormal Social Psychology, 1953, Vol. 48, pp. 78-92.
06262

Janis, I. L. and Mann, L.
"Effectiveness of Emotional Role-Playing in Modifying Smoking Habits and Attitudes." Journal of Experimental Research in Personality, 1965, Vol. 1, No. 2, pp. 84-90.
00315

Janis, I. L. and Smith, M. B.
"Effects of Education and Persuasion on National and International Images," in Kelman, H., (ed.) International Behavior, New York: Holt, Rinehart and Winston, 1965.
06274

Jeuck, John E.
"Direct-Mail Advertising to Doctors." Journal of Business, Jan. 1940, Vol. 13, Part I: pp. 17-38.
00752

Jewkes, J. and Sawers, D. and Stillerman, R.
The Sources of Invention, London: MacMillan, 1958, 410 pp.
00941

Jones, Edward E. and Gerard, Harold B.
Foundations of Social Psychology, New York: John Wiley and Sons, 1967, 743 pp.
06285

Judd, C., Fromm, M.G., and Kinkade, R.
"Attitudes of Basic Researchers in Biology," Technical Report 4, Washington, D.C.: American Institutes for Research, National Science Foundation, November, 1967.
07121

Jung, Charles C.
"An Educational Development Program Viewed in the Context of Research Utilization," Paper presented at the American Educational Research Association, Los Angeles, California, February, 1969.
07117

Jung, Charles
" A Study of the Derivation Conference: A Collaborative Effort Between Social Researchers and Youth-Serving Practitioners to Derive and Use Implications from Research Findings to Meet Action Concerns," Project Proposal, Ann Arbor: Center for Research on Utilization of Scientific Knowledge, Institute for Social Research, University of Michigan, 1966.
06197

Jung, Charles
"Two Kinds of Linkage for Research Utilization in Education," Paper Presented at the American Educational Research Association 1967 Annual Meeting, New York, February 16, 1967.
06029

Jung, Charles and Lippitt, Ronald
Utilization of Scientific Knowledge for Change in Education, CRUSK, U. of Michigan, Ann Arbor.
03922

Junghare, Y. N. and Roy, Prodipto
"The Relation of Health-Practice Innovations to Social Background Characteristics and Attitudes." Rural Sociology, December 1963, Vol. 28, No. 4, pp. 394-400.
03372

Kahn, Alfred J. and others
  *Neighborhood Information Centers: A Study and Some
  Proposals*, New York: Columbia University, School of Social
  Work, 1966.
  00020

Kaser, Tom
  "IDEA: Prescription for Change." *Saturday Review*, June
  1966, pp. 68-69.
  03905

Katz, Daniel
  "The Functional Approach to the Study of Attitudes,"
  Public Opinion Quarterly, 1960, Vol. 24, pp. 163-177.
  06279

Katz, Daniel, Nathan Maccoby, and Nancy Samelson.
  Productivity, Supervision, and Morale in the
  Office Situation. Ann Arbor, Institute for
  Social Research, 1950, 84 pp.
  07176

Katz, Daniel and Kahn, Robert
  The Social Psychology of Organizations, New York:
  John Wiley and Sons, Inc., 1966.
  06223

Katz, Daniel and Stotland, Ezra
  "A Preliminary Statement to A Theory of Attitude
  Structure and Change," in Koch, S. (ed.), *Psychology:
  A Study of A Science*, Vol. 3: Formulations of the Person
  and the Social Context, New York: McGraw-Hill, 1959,
  pp. 423-475.
  06280

Katz, Elihu
  "The Social Itinerary of Technical Change: Two Studies on
  the Diffusion of Innovation." *Human Organization*, 1961,
  Vol. 20, pp. 70-82.
  01398

Katz, Elihu
  "The Two-Step Flow of Communication: an Up-to-Date Report
  on an Hypothesis." *Public Opinion Quarterly*, 1957, Vol. 21,
  pp. 61-78.
  00295

Katz, Elihu, and others
  Studies of Innovation and of Communication to the Public,
  Stanford, California: Stanford University for Communications
  Research, 1962, 286 pp.
  00298

Katz, Elihu, and Lazarsfeld, Paul F.
  *Personal Influence: The Part Played by People in the Flow
  of Mass Communications*, Glencoe, Illinois: The Free Press,
  1955, 400 pp.
  00294

Katz, Elihu, Lewin, Martin L. and Hamilton, H.
  "Traditions of Research on the Diffusion of Innovation,"
  American Sociological Review, April 1963, Vol. 28, No. 2,
  pp. 237-252.
  00297

Katz, R. L.
  "Skills of an Effective Administration," *Harvard Business
  Review*, 1955, Vol. 33, No. 1, pp. 33-42.
  07186

Kaufman, I.
  "The Role of the Psychiatric Consultant," *American Journal
  of Orthopsychiatry*, 1956, Vol. 26, pp. 223-233.
  03947

Keating, Raymond R.
  A Study of the Effectiveness of Language Laboratories,
  New York: Institute of Administrative Research, Teachers
  College, Columbia University, 1963, 161 pp.
  03733

Kelley, C. A. and Davis, R. P. and Dietemann, J. O., et.ai.
  "LITE - Legal Information through Electronics," *Air
  Forces JAG. Law Review*, Nov. - Dec. 1966, Vol. 8, p. 5.
  00292

Kelley, H.H.
  "Communication in Experimentally Created Hierarchies,"
  Human Relations, 1951, Vol. 4, pp. 39-56.
  07198

Kelman, Herbert C.
  "Compliance, Identification, and Internalization:
  Three Processes of Attitude Change," *Journal of
  Conflict Resolution*, 1958, Vol. 2, pp. 51-60.
  06259

Kelman, Herbert C.
  "Processes of Opinion Change," *Public Opinion Quarterly*,
  Spring 1961, Vol. 25, pp. 57-78.
  01776

Kelman, Herbert C. and Hovland, Carl I.
  "'Reinstatement' of the Communicator in Delayed
  Measurement of Opinion Change," *Journal of Abnormal
  Social Psychology*, 1953, Vol. 48, pp. 327-335.
  06282

Kerr, Clark
   The Uses of the University, Cambridge, Mass.: Harvard
   University Press, 1964.
   07087

Kidd, Charles V.
   American Universities and Federal Research, Cambridge,
   Mass.: The Belknap Press of Harvard University Press, 1959.
   07092

Kidd, Charles V. and Price, Don K.
   "The Federal Government and University Research," in
   Challenge and Changes in American Education, (Seymour
   E. Harris, Kenneth M. Deitch, and Alan Levensohn, eds.)
   Berkeley, California: McCutchan Publishing Company,
   1965, pp. 75-90.
   00601

Kimbrough, Ralph B.
   "Community Power Structure and Curriculum Change," *Strategies
   for Curriculum Change*, Washington, D.C.: Association for
   Supervision of Curriculum Development, 1965, pp. 55-71.
   00156

King, B. T. and Janis, I. L.
   "Comparison of the Effectiveness of Improvised vs. Non-
   Improvised Role-Playing in Producing Opinion Changes."
   Human Relations, 1956, Vol 9, No. 2, pp. 177-186.
   01761

Kinkade, Robert and Bedorf, Erwin
   "The Need for an Interacting Request Receiver in an
   Information Clearinghouse," Technical Report 3, Washington,
   D.C.: American Institutes for Research, National Science
   Foundation, November, 1967.
   07120

Kinkade, Robert; Bedorf, Erwin; and Van Cott, Harold
   "The Need for a Scientific Request Receiver and Processor
   in an Information Clearinghouse," Technical Report 2,
   Washington, D.C.: American Institutes for Research,
   National Science Foundation, Novermber, 1967.
   07119

Kinkade, Robert and Van Cott, Harold
   "The Use of an Information Clearinghouse by Biological
   Scientists," Technical Report 1, Washington, D.C.: American
   Institutes for Research, National Science Foundation,
   November, 1967.
   07118

Kirscht, John P. and Knutson, Audie, L.
   "Science and Fluoridation: An Attitude Study," *Journal of
   Social Issues*, 1961, Vol. 17, No. 4, pp. 37-44.
   01769

Kistiakowsky, G. B.
   "Allocating Support for Basic Research – and the Importance
   of Practical Application," *Bulletin of the Atomic Scientists*,
   February, 1966, pp. 12-18.
   00284

Kivlin, Joseph E.
   *Characteristics of Farm Practices Associated with Rate of
   Adoption*, PH.D Thesis, University Park: Pennsylvania State
   University, 1960.
   02697

Klein, Donald C.
   "Some Notes on the Dynamics of Resistance," in
   Watson, G. (ed.), *Concepts for Social Change*,
   Washington, D.C.: NTL Institute for Applied
   Behavioral Science, 1967.
   03691

Knoerr, Alvin W.
   "The Role of Literature in the Diffusion of Technological
   Change," *Special Librarians*, May – June, 1963, Vol. 54,
   pp. 271-275.
   02289

Kornhauser, William and Hagstrom, Warren O.
   Scientists in Industry: Conflict and Accommodation, Berkeley
   and Los Angeles: University of California Press, 1962,
   230 pp.
   02953

Krech, D., Crutchfield, R.S., and Ballachey, E.L.
   Individual in Society, New York: McGraw-Hill Book
   Co., Inc., 1962.
   07130

Kreitlow, B. W. and Edwards, W. P.
   "Effectiveness of Lecture, Bulletin, and Film in Adult
   Settings," *Adult Education*, Spring 1962, Vol. 12, pp. 142-152.
   03868

Krueger, L.E. and Ramond, C.K.
   "References," in Mayer, M., *The Intelligent Man's Guide
   to Sales Measures of Advertising*, New York: Advertising
   Research Foundation, 1965, pp. 29-71.
   07024

Krugman, Herbert E. and Edgerton, Harold A.
   "Profile of a Scientist-Manager," *Personnel*, Sept./Oct.
   1959, Vol. 36, pp. 38-49.
   02573

Kuhn, Alfred
   The Study of Society: A Unified Approach. Homewood, Ill.:
   Richard D. Irwin, 1963, 810 pp.
   06434

Kurland, Norman
   "The Effect of Planned Change in State Departments," *Theory
   into Practice*, February 1966, Vol. 5, pp. 51-53.
   03447

Lachmann, Karl E.
"Role of International Business in the Transfer of Technology to Developing Countries: A Panel," American Society of International Law Proceedings, April 1966, Vol. 60, pp. 31-39.
00351

Landesberger, H.
"The Horizontal Dimension in a Bureaucracy," Administrative Science Quarterly, 1961, Vol. 6, pp. 298-332.
06704

Lane, Jonathan Page
"Smokers' Reactions to a television program about lung cancer: A study of dissonance." Dissertation Abstracts, 1961, Vol. 21, p. 2812-2813.
00333

LaPiere, R. T.
"Attitudes vs. Actions," Social Forces, 1934, 13:230-237.
06300

Larsen, Otto N. and Hill, Richard J.
"Social Structure and Interpersonal Communication." American Journal of Sociology, 1958, Vol. 63, pp. 497-505.
02674

Laska, John A.
"The Stages of Educational Development." Comparative Education Review, Dec. 1964, Vol. 8, pp. 251-263.
01596

Lawrence, Paul R.
"How to Deal with Resistance to Change," Harvard Business Review, May - June, 1954, Vol. 32, No, 3, pp. 49-57.
02832

Lazarsfeld, Paul F.; Berelson, B.; and Gaudet, H.
The People's Choice, New York: Duell, Sloan, and Pearce, 1944.
06182

Lazarsfeld, P.F., Sewell, W.H., and Wilensky, H.L. (eds.)
The Uses of Sociology, New York: Basic Books, Inc. 1967.
07207

Leiserson, Avery
"Scientists and the Policy Process." American Political Science Review, June 1965, Vol. 59, No. 2, pp. 408-416.
01146

Lerner, Daniel and Schramm, Wilbur (eds.)
Communication and Change in the Developing Countries, Honolulu: East-West Center Press, 1967, 333 pp.
07034

Lesher, R.L. and Howick, G.J.
Assessing Technology Transfer, Washington, D.C.: Scientific and Technical Information Division, Office of Technology and Utilization, NASA, 1966.
07007

Leuthold, Franklin O. and Wilkening, Eugene A.
"Acceptance of New Farm Technology: A Test of a Theory of Social Interaction." Paper presented at the Rural Sociological Society, Northridge, California, 1963.
02671

Leventhal, H. and Singer, R. P.
"Affect Arousal and Positioning of Recommendations in Persuasive Communication," Journal of Personality and Social Psychology, 1966, Vol. 4, pp. 137-146.
06296

Leventhal, H. and Watts, J. C.
"Sources of resistance to fear-arousing communications on smoking and lung cancer." Journal of Personality, June 1966, Vol. 34, pp. 155-175.
03851

Lewin, Kurt
"Group Decision and Social Change," in Maccoby, E.E., Newcomb, T.M. and Hartley, E.L., Readings in Social Psychology, New York: Holt, Rinehart and Winston, 1947, pp. 197-211.
07006 and 07025

Lewin, Kurt
"Group Decision and Social Change," in Swanson, G.E. et al., Readings in Social Psychology, New York: Henry Holt and Company, 1952, pp. 459-473.
01342

Lewin, Kurt
Field Theory in Social Science, New York: Harper, 1951.
06500

Lewin, Kurt
"Forces Behind Food Habits and Methods of Changing," in
Report of the Committee on Food Habits, The Problem of
Changing Food Habits, Washington, D. C., National Research
Council, National Academy of Sciences, 1963.
02640

Lewis, Oscar
"Medicine and Politics in a Mexican Village," Paul,
Benjamin D. (ed.), Health, Culture and Community, New York:
Russell Sage Foundation, 1955, pp. 403-433.
02641

Liberman, Robert
"Personal Influence in the Use of Mental Health Resources."
Human Organization, Fall 1965, Vol. 24, pp. 231-235.
00363

Likert, Rensis
The Human Organization: Its Management and Value, New York:
McGraw-Hill, 1967, 258 pp.
06590

Likert, Rensis
"A Neglected Factor in Communications," Communications
Review, 1955, Vol. 2, pp. 163-177.
07200

Likert, Rensis
New Patterns of Management, New York: McGraw-Hill,
1961, pp. 279.
05202

Lin, Nan, Leu, D. J., Rogers, E. and Schwartz, D. F.
The Diffusion of an Innovation in Three Michigan High Schools:
Institution Building Through Change, Institute for Inter-
national Studies in Education, Michigan State University,
December 1966.
03903

Lindeman, Eric
"Social System Factors as Determinants of Resistance to
Change," American Journal of Orthopsychiatry, 1965, Vol. 35,
No. 3, pp. 544-557.
02212

Linden, Maurice E., Appel, K. E., Davis, J. E. and Matthews, R. A.
"Factors in the Success of a Public Mental Health Program,"
American Journal of Psychiatry, 1959, Vol. 116, pp. 344-351.
03217

Lindveit, Earl W.
Scientists in Government, Washington, D.C.: Public Affairs
Press, 1960, pp. 84.
02836

Linton, Ralph
The Study of Man. New York: Appleton-Century-Crofts, 1936.
06390

Lionberger, Herbert F.
Adoption of New Ideas and Practices: a summary of the
research dealing with the acceptance of technological change
in agriculture with implications for action in facilitating
such change, Ames: Iowa State University Press, 1960,
pp. 164.
01036

Lionberger, Herbert and Coughenour, C. Milton
"Studies in Social Structure and Diffusion of Farm Information." Rural Sociology, Sept. - Dec. 1954, Vol. 19,
pp. 233-343, 377-384.
00766

Lionberger, Herbert F. and Hassinger, Edward
Roads to Knowledge, Columbia: Missouri Agricultural
Experiment Station Bulletin 633, 1954.
02690

Lippitt, Ronald
"Processes of Curriculum Change," Leeper R. R. (ed.)
Curriculum Change: Direction and Process, Washington, D.C.:
Association for Supervision and Curriculum Development,
1966.
01397

Lippitt, Ronald
"The Use of Social Research to Improve Social Practice."
Concepts for Social Change, Baltimore, Maryland, Moran
Printing Service, Published by N.T.L., NEA for COPED,
March 1967, pp. 71-80.
03873

Lippitt, Ronald and others
"The Teacher as Innovator, Seeker and Sharer of New Practices,"
Miller, R. I. (ed.), Perspectives on Educational Change,
New York: Appleton-Century-Crofts, 1966
00791

Lippitt, Ronald; Schaible, Lucille; et al.
"A Description of the Two Semester Graduate Sequence
in Planned Change," Ann Arbor, Michigan: Center for
Research on Utilization of Scientific Knowledge,
University of Michigan, January, 1968, 24 pp.
07026

Lippitt, Ronald, Watson, Jeanne, and Westley, Bruce
   The Dynamics of Planned Change, New York: Harcourt, Brace
   and Company, Incorporated, 1958, pp. 312.
   01343

Lorsch, Jay W. and Lawrence, Paul R.
   "Organizing for product innovation." Harvard Business Review,
   Jan. - Feb. 1965, Vol. 43, pp. 109-118+.
   02281

Loy, John W., Jr.
   "Social Psychological Characteristics of Innovators,"
   American Sociological Review, February, 1969, Vol. 34,
   No. 1, pp. 73-82.
   07112

Lucas, D.B. and Britt, S.H.
   Measuring Advertising Effectiveness, New York: Mc-Graw-
   Hill, 1963.
   0701?

Luschinsky, Mildred Stroop
   "Problems of culture change in the Indian village." Human
   Organizations, Spring 1963, Vol. 22, No. 1, pp. 66-74.
   03368

Lynd, Robert S.
   Knowledge for What? The Place of Social Science in American
   Culture. Princeton: Princeton University Press, 1939, 268 pp.
   06098

Lynn, Kenneth S. (ed.)
   "The Professions," Daedalus, Fall, 1963, Vol. 92, No. 4.
   07061

Lystad, Mary H.
   "Institutional Planning for Social Change," Sociology and
   Social Research, January - February 1960, Vol. 44, pp. 165-171.
   01029

McGuire, W. J.
   "Inducing Resistance to Persuasion: Some Contemporary Approaches,"
   Advances in Experimental Social Psychology, Vol. I., Leonard
   Berkowitz, (ed), Academic Press, 1964.
   06261

McGuire, William J.
   "Attitudes and Opinions." Annual Review of Psychology,
   1966, Vol.17, pp. 475-514.
   00390

McKeachie, W. J.
   "Research on Teaching at the College and University Level,"
   Handbook of Research on Teaching, N.L. Gage, ed., Chicago:
   Rand McNally, 1963, pp. 1118-72.
   06439

McLuhan, Marshall
   Understanding Media, New York: McGraw-Hill, 1964.
   06503

Maccoby, Eleanor
   "The Effects of Television on Children," in Schramm W. (ed.),
   The Science of Human Communication, New York: Basic Books, Inc.,
   1963, pp. 116-127.
   05395

Machlup, Fritz
   The Production and Distribution of Knowledge in the United
   States, Princton, New Jersey: Princeton University Press,
   1962.
   07041

Mackenzie, Gordon N.
   "Curricular Change: Participant, Power and Processes," in
   Miles, M.B. (ed.), Innovation in Education, New York: Bureau
   of Publications, Teachers College, Columbia University, 1964,
   pp. 399-424.
   01194

Mackie, R. R. and Christensen, P.R.
   Translation and Application of Psychological Research,
   Technical Report 716-1, Goleta, California: Santa Barbara
   Research Park, Human Factors Research, Inc., 1967.
   07107 and 06237

Maier, N., Hoffman, L., Hooven, J. and Read, W.
   "Superior-Subordinate Communications in Management,"
   American Management Research Studies, 1961, No. 52.
   07196

Mann, Floyd C.
"Handling Misunderstandings and Conflict," Ann Arbor,
Michigan: Center for Research on Utilization of Scientific
Knowledge, Institute for Social Research, University of
Michigan, Unpublished, 1967, 4 pp.
07022 and 07175

Mann, Floyd C.
"Managing Change," Tannenbaum, Arnold S. (ed.). The Worker
in the New Industrial Environment. Ann Arbor: Foundation
for Research on Human Behavior, 1962, pp. 18-21.
05219

Mann, Floyd C.
"Putting Human Relations Research Findings to Work," Michigan
Business Review, 1950, Vol. 2, No. 2, pp. 16-20.
05221

Mann, Floyd C.
"Studying and Creating Change: A Means to Understanding Social
Organization," in Arensberg, C.M., Industrial Relations Research
Association: Research in Industrial Human Relations, New York:
Harper, 1957, pp. 147-167.
05222

Mann, Floyd C.
"Toward an Understanding of the Leadership Role in Formal
Organizations," in Dubin, P.; Homans, G.; Miller, D. (eds.),
Leadership and Productivity, San Francisco, California:
Chandler, 1964.
07177 and 07217

Mann, Floyd C. and Baumgartel, Howard
"Absences and Employee Attitudes in an Electric Company,"
Ann Arbor, Michigan, Survey Research Center, University of
Michigan, 1952.
07178

Mann, Floyd C. and Likert, Rensis
"The Need for Research on the Communication of
Research Results," Human Organization, Winter, 1952,
Vol. II, pp. 15-19.
2069

Mann, Floyd C. and Neff, Franklin W.
Managing Major Change in Organizations. Ann Arbor, Michigan:
Foundation for Research on Human Behavior, 1961.
3913

Mann, Floyd C. and Williams, Lawrence K.
"Observations on the Dynamics of a Change to Electronic
Data Processing Equipment," Administrative Science
Quarterly, September 1960, Vol. 5, pp. 217-256.
05227

Mansfield, Edwin
"Intrafirm Rates of Diffusion of an Innovation," Review of
Economics and Statistics, 1963, Vol. 45, pp. 348-359.
01373

Mansfield, Edwin
"Speed of Response of Firms to New Techniques," Quarterly
Journal of Economics, 1963, Vol. 77, pp. 290-311.
00786

Mansfield, Edwin
"Technical Change and the Rate of Imitation," Econometrica,
1961, Vol. 29, pp. 741-766.
00796

March, J. and Simon H.
Organizations, New York: Wiley and Sons, 1958.
07149

Marcson, Simon
"Social Change and Social Structure in Transitional Societies,"
International Journal of Comparative Sociology, 1960, Vol. 1,
No. 2,   pp. 248-253.
2924

Markham, J. W.
"Market Structure, Business Conduct, and Innovation,"
American Economic Review: Papers and Proceedings, 1965,
Vol. 55, pp. 323-332.
00805

Marmor, Judd, Bernard, Viola, W. and Ottenburg, Perry
"Psychodynamics of Group Opposition to Health Programs,"
American Journal of Orthopsychiatry, 1960, Vol. 30, pp. 330-
345.
03160

Marriott, McKim
"Western Medicine in a Village of Northern India," in
Paul, Benjamin D.(ed.), Health, Culture, and Community,
New York: Russell Sage Foundation, 1955.
02408

Marrow, Alfred J., Bowers, David G. and Seashore, Stanley E.
Management by Participation: Creating a Climate for Personal
and Organizational Development. New York: Harper and Row,
1967.
06066

Marrow, Alfred and French, John, Jr.
    "Changing a Stereotype in Industry," in Bennis, Benne, and
    Chin, The Planning of Change, New York: Holt, Rinehart
    and Winston, 1961, pp. 583-586.
    07027

Marsh, Paul E.
    "The Physical Science Study Committee: A Case History of
    Nationwide Curriculum Development," Unpublished Doctoral
    Thesis, Cambridge, Mass.: Graduate School of Education,
    Harvard University, 1963.
    01016

Marsh, Paul E.
    "Wellsprings of Strategy: Considerations Affecting Innovations
    By the PSSC"   Miles, Matthew B.
    (ed.) Innovation in Education, New York: Bureau of Publications,
    Teachers College, Columbia University,   1964.
    1193

Marshall, James
    "Evidence, Psychology, and the Trial: Some Challenges to
    Law," Columbia Law Review, February 1963, Vol. 63, pp. 197-
    231
    01021

Marx, Wesley
    "The Military's 'Think Factories,' " The Progressive, 1965,
    Vol. 29, pp. 22-26.
    05231

Maslow, A.
    Motivation and Personality. New York: Harper, 1954.
    06327

Mason, Robert
    "An Ordinal Scale for Measuring the Adoption Process,"
    in Katz, E. et.al., (ed.), Studies of Innovation and
    of Communication to the Public, Stanford, California:
    Stanford University Institute for Communication Research,
    1962, pp. 99-116.
    02397

Mayer, R. R.
    "Case Study of Effective Communication in Industry",
    Journal of Business, Oct. 1958, Vol. 31, pp. 344-350.
    00414

Mayo, E.
    The Social Problems of an Industrial Civilization, Boston,
    Mass.: Harvard University, Graduate School of Business, 1945.
    07190

Means, James H.
    "Homo Medicus Americanus," Daedalus, Fall, 1963, Vol. 92,
    No. 4, p. 701.
    07065

Meier, R.
    "Communications Overload: Proposals from the Study of a
    University Library," Administrative Science Quarterly,
    1963, Vol. 7, pp. 521-544.
    06710

Meierhenry, Wesley C. (ed.).
    Media and Educational Innovation, University of Nebraska
    Extension Division and University of Nebraska Press, 1964.
    05235

Menzel, Herbert
    "Innovation, Integration, and Marginality: A Survey of
    Physicians," American Sociological Review, 1960, Vol. 25,
    pp. 704-713.
    01386

Menzel, Herbert
    "Public and Private Conformity Under Different Conditions of
    Acceptance in the Group," Journal of Abnormal and Social
    Psychology, 1957, Vol. 55, pp. 398-402.
    02389

Menzel, Herbert
    Review of Studies in the Flow of Information Among Scientists,
    New York: Columbia University, Bureau of Applied Social Research,
    2nd Impression: September 1960, 62 and 48 pp.
    00731

Menzel, Herbert and Katz, Elihu
    "Social Relations and Innovations in the Medical Profession;
    the Epidemiology of a New Drug," Public Opinion Quarterly,
    Winter 1955-56, Vol. 19, pp. 337-352.
    03404

Merrill, Malcolm H., Hollister, Arthur C., Gibbens, Stephen F., Haynes,
    Ann W. and Leslau, Vita
    "Attitudes of Californians Toward Poliomyelitis Vaccination,"
    American Journal of Public Health, February 1958, Vol. 48,
    pp. 146-152.
    06002

Merton, Robert K.
    "Resistance to the Systematic Study of Multiple
    Discoveries in Science," Archives Europeennes
    de Sociologie, Summer, 1963, Vol. 4, pp. 237-282.
    01268

Merton, Robert K.
  Social Theory and Social Structure, 1957.
  06220

Meyerson, Rolf, and Katz, Elihu
  "Notes on a Natural History of Fads," American Journal of
  Sociology, 1957, Vol. 62, pp. 596-600.
  01720

Michael, Donald N.
  Factors Inhibiting and Facilitating the Acceptance of
  Educational Innovations, Washington, D.C.: Institute for
  Policy Studies, 1965, Mimeo, 14 pp.
  03892

Michael, Donald N.
  "Some Factors Tending to Limit the Utility of the Social
  Scientist in Military Systems Analysis." Operations Research,
  1957, Vol. 5, No. 1, pp. 90-96.
  1693

Michael, Donald N.
  "Some Speculations on the Social Impact of Technology,"
  Technological Innovations and Society, Morse, D. and Warner,
  A. W. (editors), Columbia University Press, New York, 1966.
  06190

Michaelis, Michael
  "Can We Build the World We Want?" Bulletin of the Atomic
  Scientists, January, 1968, pp. 43-49
  07033

Michaelis, Michael
  "Environment for Innovation," Proceedings from Technology
  Transfer and Innovation sponsored by the National Planning
  Association, National Science Foundation, May 15-17, 1966,
  p. 76.
  07056

Miles, Matthew B.
  "Educational Innovation: The Nature of the Problem," Miles,
  M.B. (ed) Innovation in Education. New York: Columbia Teachers
  College, 1964, pp. 1-46.
  06056

Miles, Matthew B. (ed.)
  Innovation in Education, New York: Bureau of Publications,
  Teachers College, Columbia University, 1964. pp. 689.
  1046

Miles, Matthew B.
  "Innovation in Education: Some Generalizations,"in Miles,
  Matthew B., (ed.) Innovation in Education, New York: Bureau
  of Publications, Teachers College, Columbia University, 1964,
  pp. 631-662.
  Q1481

Miles, Matthew B.
  "On Temporary Systems," Miles, Matthew B. (ed.) Innovation
  in Education, New York: Teachers College, Bureau of
  Publications, Columbia University, 1964, pp. 437-490.
  01189

Miles, Matthew B. and Lake, Dale
  "Self-Renewal in School Systems: A Strategy for Planned
  Change," in Watson, G. (ed.), Concepts for Social
  Change, Washington, D.C.: NTL Institute for Applied
  Behavioral Science, 1967.
  03871

Miles, Raymond
  "Human Relations or Human Resources?" Harvard Business Review,
  July-August, 1965, Vol. 43, No. 4, pp. 148-156.
  07221

Miller, Donald R.
  "Excerpts from Operation PEP Descriptive Materials," Operation
  PEP, Birlingame, California, 1967.
  06191

Miller, D.C. and Form, W.H.
  Industrial Sociology: An Introduction to the Sociology of
  Work Relations, New York: Harper & Row, 1951.
  07218

Miller, F. C.
  "Cultural Change as Decision-Making: A Tzotzil Example,"
  Ethnology, January 1965, Vol. 4, pp. 53-65.
  00828

Mitchell, H. E. and Mudd, E. H.
  "Anxieties Associated with the Conduct of Research in a
  Clinical Setting," American Journal of Orthopsychiatry,
  1957, Vol. 27, pp. 310-323.
  03958

Morgan, Clifford T.
  Introduction to Psychology. New York: McGraw-Hill, 1956, 676pp.
  06366

Morgan, James N., Sirageldin, Ismail A. and Baerwaldt, Nancy
Productive Americans: a Study of How Individuals Contribute to
Economic Progress. Ann Arbor: University of Michigan, Survey
Research Center Monograph #43, 1966, 546 pp.
06326

Morphet, Edgar and Ryan, Charles (eds.)
Designing Education for the Future, No. 1 - Prospective
Changes in Society by 1980, New York: Citation Press, 1967.
07123

Morphet, Edgar and Ryan, Charles (eds.)
Designing Education for the Future, No. 2 - Implications
for Education of Prospective Changes in Society, New York:
Citation Press, 1967.
07124

Morphet, Edgar and Ryan, Charles (eds.)
Designing Education for the Future, No. 3 - Planning and
Effecting Needed Changes in Education, New York: Citation
Press, 1967.
07125

Morphet, Edgar and Jesser, David (eds.)
Designing Education for the Future, No. 4 - Cooperative
Planning for Education in 1980, New York: Citation Press,
1967.
07126

Morphet, Edgar and Jesser, David (eds.)
Designing Education for the Future, No. 5 - Emerging Designs
for Education, New York: Citation Press, 1967.
07127

Morphet, Edgar and Jesser, David (eds.)
Designing Education for the Future, No. 6 - Planning for
Effective Utilization of Technology in Education, New York:
Citation Press, 1967.
07128

Morse, N. and Reimer, E.
"The Experimental Change of a Major Organizational Variable,"
Journal of Abnormal Social Psychology, 1955, Vol. 52, pp. 120-
129.
06712

Mort, Paul R.
"Studies in Educational Innovation From the Institute of
Administrative Research," Miles, Matthew B. (ed.), Innovation
in Education, New York: Bureau of Publications, Teachers
College, Columbia University, New York, 1964.
1191

Morton, Jack A.
"From Research to Technology," International Science and
Technology, May 1964, Vol. 29, pp. 82-92.
06840

Morton, Jack A.
"A Model of the Innovative Process (As Viewed from a
Science-Based Integrated Industry)," Proceedings from
Technology Transfer and Innovation sponsored by the
National Planning Association, National Science Foundation,
May 15-17, 1966, p. 21.
07050

Mosher, Edith K.
What About the School Research Office?, Berkeley, California:
Far West Laboratory for Educational Research and Development,
July, 1968, 64 pp.
07036

Mosteller, F.
"Use as Evidenced by an Examination of Wear and Tear on
Selected Sets of ESS," in Davis, K. et al., A Study of the Need
for a New Encyclopedic Treatment of the Social Sciences,
(Unpublished Manuscript), 1955, pp. 167-174.
07016

Moulin, L.
"Technocracy: Bugaboo and Temptation of the Modern World,"
Research Publication, 1962, Vol. 4, No. 1, pp. 28-50.
03382

Murray, Henry A.
Explorations in Personality. New York: Oxford, 1938.
06328

Murray, Henry A. and Kluckhohn Clyde
"Outline of a Conception of Personality," Kluckhohn, C., Murray
H.A. and Schneider, D. M., Personality in Nature, Society and
Culture. New York: Knopf, 1954.
06329

Myren, Delbert Theodore
"A Study of the Distribution of Mass Media Among Farmers and
the Relationship of this Distribution to Certain Socio-
Economic Characteristics," Dissertation Abstracts, 1956
Vol. 16, pp. 746.
00397

Nader, Ralph
    "Inventions and Their Uses," (Review of D. A. Schon, <u>Technology and Changes</u>), <u>New Repulic</u>, July 22, 1967, pp. 32-34.
    06094

National Academy of Sciences
    <u>The Behavioral Sciences and the Federal Government</u>,
    Washington, D.C.: Advisory Committee on Government
    Programs in the Behavioral Sciences, National Research
    Council, 1968, Publication #1680.
    07101

National Science Foundation
    "Technology Transfer and Innovation," Proceedings of
    the Conference under auspices of National Planning
    Association, May 15-17, 1966.
    07048

Neal, Helen (ed.)
    <u>Better Communications for Better Health</u>, New York: National
    Health Council and Columbia University Press, 1962.
    06160

Nealy, S. and Fiedler, F.
    "Leadership Functions of Middle Managers," <u>Psychological
    Bulletin</u>, 1968, Vol. 70, pp. 313-329.
    07144

Neff, Franklin W.; Erfurt, John; and Mann, Floyd C.
    "Report of an Organizational Study and of Efforts to Initiate
    Use of It," Center for Research on Utilization of Scientific
    Knowledge, Institute for Social Research, Ann Arbor, July 1965.
    06192

Nelson, R. R.
    "The Economics of Invention: A Survey of the Literature,"
    <u>Journal of Business</u>, April 1959, Vol. 32, pp. 101-127.
    01004

Newcomb, T. M.
    "Autistic Hostility and Social Reality," <u>Human Relations</u>, 1947,
    1:69-86.
    06257

Newcomb, T. M.
    <u>Personality and Social Change</u>. New York: Dryden, 1943.
    06302

Newcomb, T. M., Turner, R. and Converse, P.
    <u>Social Psychology</u>. New York: Holt, Rinehardt and Winston, 1965.
    06297

Newman, Joseph W.
    "Working With Behavioral Scientists," <u>Harvard Business
    Review</u>, July-August 1958, Vol. 36, pp. 64-74.
    01003

Niehoff, Arthur H.
    "Theravada Buddhism: A Vehicle for Technical Change,"
    <u>Human Organization</u>, 1964, Vol. 23, pp. 108-112.
    02393

Niehoff, Arthur H. and Charnel, Anderson J.
    "The Process of Cross-Cultural Innovation," <u>International
    Developments Review</u>, June 1964, Vol. 6, No.2, pp. 5-11.
    03005

Nokes, Peter,
    "Feedback as an Explanatory Device in the Study of Certain
    Interpersonal and Institutional Processes," <u>Human Relations</u>
    1961, Vol. 14, No. 4, pp. 381-387.
    01758

Ogburn, William F.
  Social Change, New York: Viking Press, Inc., 2nd Edition,
  1950.
  01364

O'Neill, Richard W.
  "Why Technological Innovations Fail," Proceedings from
  Technology Transfer and Innovation sponsored by the
  National Planning Association, National Science Foundation,
  May 15-17, 1966, P. 65.
  07055

Orr, Richard H. et. al.
  "The Biomedical Information Complex Viewed as a System,"
  Federation Proceedings, September-October 1964, Vol. 23,
  No. 5, pp. 1133-1145.
  05270

Paisley, William J.
  The Flow of (behavioral) Science Information-a Review of
  the Research Literature,   Institute for Communication
  Research, Stanford University, Palo Alto, California,
  Nov. 1965.
  01240.

Papinsky, Harold
  "The Scientist and Technologist in Their Informational
  Environment," Proposal to National Science Foundation from
  Ohio State University Research Foundation, October 1, 1966
  (starting date).
  07042

Pareek, Udai and Chattopadhyay, S.N.
  "Adoption Quotient: A Measure of Multipractice Adoption
  Behavior," Journal of Applied Behavioral Science, 1966,
  Vol. 2, No. 1, pp. 95-108.
  00438

Parsons, Talcott
  "The Academic System: A Sociologist's View," The
  Public Interest, Fall, 1968, No. 13, pp. 173-197.
  07082

Parsons, Talcott and Shils, E.A.
  Toward a General Theory of Action, Cambridge, Mass.:
  Harvard University Press, 1951.
  07039

Paul, Benjamin, D.
  "Anthropological Perspectives on Medicine and Public Health,"
  Annals of the American Academy of Political and Social Science,
  March 1963, Vol. 346, pp. 34-43.
  02925

Paul, Benjamin D. (ed.)
  Health, Culture and Community: Case Studies of Public
  Reactions to Health Programs, New York: Russell Sage
  Foundation 1955, 493 pp.
  00436

Pellegrin, Roland J.
  An Analysis of Sources and Processes of Innovation in Education.
  (A Paper Presented at the Conference on Educational Change
  Sponsored by the Demonstration Project for Gifted Youth and
  the U. S. Office of Education.) Eugene, Oregon: Center for
  the Advanced Study of Educational Administration, 1966. pp. 32.
  01043

Pellegrin, Roland J.
  "Implications of the Shortage of Personnel for Organizations
  Relating Research to Practice," American Educational Research
  Association 1967 Annual Meeting, New York, Feb. 17, 1967.
  06030

Pelz, Donald C.
  "Conditions for Innovation," in Hill, Walter A. and Egan,
  Douglas, (eds) Organization Theory: A Behavioral Approach
  Boston: Allyn and Bacon, Inc., 1966, pp. 501-504.
  00636

Pelz, Donald C.
  "Creative Tensions in the Research and Development Climate,"
  Science, July 14, 1967, Vol. 157, No. 3785, pp. 160-165.
  07094

Pelz, Donald C. and Andrews, Frank M.
  Scientists in Organizations, Wiley and Sons, New York, 1966.
  06067

Pelz, Edith Bennet
  "Discussion, Decision Commitment, and Consensus in 'Group
  Decision'," Human Relations, 1955, 8:251-274.
  06283

Pelz, Edith Bennett
"Some Factors in 'Group Decision'," in Maccoby, E.E., et al.,
Readings in Social Psychology, New York: Holt, Rinehart and
Winston, Inc., pp. 212-219.
07028

Pemberton, H. Earl
"The Curve of Culture Diffusion Rate," American Sociological
Review. 1936, Vol. 1, pp. 547-556.
01503

Pemberton H. Earl
"The Effect of a Social Crisis on the Curve of Diffusion,"
American Sociological Review. 1937, Vol. 2, pp. 55-61.
01502

Penders, J. M. A.
"Rural Extension in Low Income Countries," J. A. Ponsioen, ed.
Social Welfare Policy II. The Hague: Mouton and Co., 1963,
pp. 58-88.
06042

Peter, Hollis (ed.)
Comparative Theories in Social Change, Ann Arbor, Michigan:
Foundation for Research on Human Behavior, 1966, 374 pp.
06057

Pettigrew, Thomas F.
A Profile of the Negro American, Princeton, N.J.:
Van Nostrand, 1964.
06267

Piel, Gerard
"Federal Funds and Science Education," Bulletin of the
Atomic Scientists, May 1966, Vol. 22, pp. 10-15.
00434

Polson, Robert A. and Pal, Agaton P.
"The Influence of Isolation on the Acceptance of Technological
Changes in the Bumaguete City Trade Area, Philippines,"
Silliman Journal, 1955, Vol. 2, pp. 149-159.
00305

Porter, L. and Lawler, E.
"Properties of Organizational Structure in Relation to Job
Attitudes and Job Behavior," Psychological Bulletin, 1965,
Vol. 64, pp. 23-51.
07145

Poser, E.G., Dunn, I. and Smith, R. M.
"Resolving Conflicts Between Clinical and Research Teams,"
Mental Hospitals, 1964, Vol. 15, No. 5, pp. 278-282.
02210

President's Conference on Technical-Distribution Research
for the Benefit of Small Businesses, Washington, D.C.:
Office of Technical Services, U.S. Department of Commerce,
September 23-25, 1957, 287 pp.
03320

Price, Derek J. de Solla
"The Exponential Curve of Science," in Barber, B. and Hirsch, W.
(eds.), The Sociology of Science, New York: Free Press of
Glencoe, 1962, pp. 516-524.
07133

Price, Derek J. de Solla
"Networks of Scientific Papers," Science, July 30, 1965,
Vol. 149, No. 3683, pp. 510-515.
05127

Price, Derek J. de Solla and Beaver, Donald deB.
"Collaboration in an Invisible College," American Psychologist,
November 1966, Vol. 21, No. 11.
05125

Price, Don K.
"Educating for the Scientific Age," Bulletin of Atomic Scientists,
October, 1968, pp. 26-32.
07090

Price, Don K.
Government and Science, New York: New York University Press, 1954.
07091

Price, Don K.
"The Scientific Establishment," Proceedings of the American
Philosophical Society, June, 1962, Vol. 106, No. 3.
07060

Price, James L.
"Use of New Knowledge in Organizations," Human Organization,
Fall 1964, Vol. 23, No. 3, pp. 224-234.
01780

Public Administration Clearing House
"Experiences of Personnel of United States Voluntary
Agencies," Economic Development and Cultural Change,
June 1954, Vol. 2, pp. 329-349.
01045

Putney, Snell, and Putney, Gladys, J.
"Radical Innovation and Prestige," American Sociological
Review, August 1962, Vol. 27, pp. 548-551.
00798

Quintana, Bertha and Sexton, Patricia
"Sociology, Anthropology, and Schools of Education: A Progress
Report," Journal of Educational Sociology, November, 1961,
Vol. 35, pp. 97-103.
03856

Ramey, James W.
Television in Medical Teaching and Research. Washington D.C.:
U.S. Government Printing Office, 1965, 155 pp.
06208

Read, W.H.
"Upward Communication in Industrial Hierarchies,"
Human Relations, 1962, Vol. 15, pp. 3-16.
07197

Reiff, R.
"The Competitive World of the Pure Scientist," Science,
December 1961, Vol. 134, No. 3494, pp. 1957-1962.
02804

Reiff, R. and Riessman, F.
"The Indigenous Non-Professional: A Strategy of Change in
Community Action and Community Mental Health Programs,"
National Institute of Labor Education, Report #3, November
1964.
03218

Rein, Martin and Miller, S.M.
"Social Action on the Installment Plan," Trans-action,
January/February, 1966, Vol. 3, No. 2, pp. 31-38.
07029

Research for Better Schools, Inc.
"RITE Number 1" Research for Better Schools, Inc., Philadelphia,
Pennsylvania, Spring 1967.
06065

Rice, A.
Learning for Leadership, London: Tavistock Publications,
1965.
07216

Rice, A.
The Organization and Its Environment, London, Tavistock
Publications, 1963.
07158

Rice, A.
Productivity and Social Organization, London: Tavistock
Publications, 1958.
07157

Richland, Malcolm
Final Report: Traveling Seminar and Conference for the
Implementation of Educational Innovations, Santa Monica
California: System Development Corporation, Technical
Memorandum Series 2691, 1965, 140 pp.
03698

Riley, H.E.
"Research in Technology Transfer: Where We stand and
What Needs to be Done," Proceedings from Technology
Transfer and Innovation sponsored by the National
Planning Association, National Science Foundation,
May 15-17, 1966, p. 98.
07059

Robertson, George J.
"The Application of Medical TV to the Practicing Physician,"
Continuing Education for the Practicing Physician, Beverly
Hospital Research Foundation, December 1964, pp. 44-46.
06159

Robinson, H. B. and Robinson, N. M.
The Mentally Retarded Child: A Psychological Approach. New
York: McGraw-Hill, 1965.
06266

Roethlisberger, F.J. and Dickson, W.J.
Management and the Worker, Cambridge, Mass.: Harvard
University Press, 1964.
07193

Rogers, Carl
Client Centered Therapy. Boston: Houghton Mifflin,
1951.
06271

Rogers, Carl R.
"Communication: Its Blocking and Facilitation," Northwestern
University Information, April 1952, Vol. 20, No. 25.
03809

Rogers, Everett M.
"Characteristics of Agricultural Innovators and Other
Adopter Categories," in Schramm, W. (ed.), Studies of
Innovation and Communication to the Public, Palo Alto,
California: Stanford University, Institute for Communication
Research, 1962.
01549

Rogers, Everett M.
Diffusion of Innovations, New York: The Free Press of
Glencoe, Inc., 1962, pp. 367.
01824

Rogers, Everett M.
   "Rural Schools and Communication," in Miller, Richard I.,
   Catalyst for Change: A National Study of ESEA Title III
   (PACE) Reports of Special Consultants, Washington, D.C.:
   United States Government Printing Office, 1967, pp. 145-
   152.
   07080

Rogers, Everett M. et al.
   Diffusion of Innovations: Educational Change in Thai
   Government Secondary Schools, East Lansing, Michigan:
   Michigan State University, Institute for International
   Studies in Education and Department of Communication,
   March, 1969.
   07223

Rogers, Everett M. and Capener, Harold R.
   The county Extension Agent and His Constituents, Wooster,
   Ohio Agricultural Experiment Station Research Bulletin, 858,
   1960,
   01534

Rogers, Everett M. and Rogers, Edna L.
   " A Methodological Analysis of Adoption Scales," Rural
   Sociology, 1961, Vol. 26, pp. 325-336.
   01524

Rogers, Everett and Svenning, Lynne
   "Change in Small Schools," Paper presented at the National
   Working Conference on Solving Educational Problems in
   Sparsely Populated Areas, Denver, Colorado, March 17-19,
   1969.
   07116

Rogers, Everett and Svenning, Lynne
   "Strategies for Communication and System Innovation -
   Decisions for School Administrators," East Lansing, Michigan:
   Department of Communication, Michigan State University,
   October, 1968.
   07046

Rokeach, Milton
   Open and Closed Mind. New York: Basic Books, 1960.
   06255

Rome, S. and Rome, B.
   in Bowers, Raymond V. (ed.), Studies on Behavior in Organization,
   Athens, Georgia: University of Georgia, Research Conference on
   Behavior in Organizations, 1962.
   07208

Rosenthal, R. A.
   "The Effect of the Experimenter on the Results of Psychological
   Research," B. Mahan, (ed), Progress in Experimental Personality
   Research, Vol. I, 1964, New York: Academic Press.
   06265

Rosenthal, R. and Jacobsen, C.
   "Self Fulfilling Prophecies in the Classroom: Teachers' Expectations as Unintended Determinants of Pupils' Intellectual
   Competence," draft copy of a chapter in a book to be published
   by Holt in 1967.
   06264

Ross, Donald H.
   Administration for Adaptability: A Source Book Drawing Together
   the Results of More than 150 Individual Studies Related to
   the Question of Why and How Schools Improve. New York:
   Metropolitan School Study Council, 1958.
   02878

Rothe, H.
   "Does Higher Pay Bring Higher Productivity," Personnel,
   1960, Vol. 37, pp. 20-38.
   07172

Rowat, D. (ed.)
   The Ombudsman: Citizens Defender, London: Allen and Unwin,
   1965.
   07079

Rowe, A. P.
   "From Scientific Idea to Practical Use," Minerva, Spring
   1964, Vol. 2, No. 3, pp. 303-319.
   03007

Rubenstein, A.H. and Sullivan, E.M. (eds.)
   A Directory of Research-on-Research - Program of Research on
   the Management of Research and Development, Evanston, Illinois:
   Department of Industrial Engineering and Management Sciences,
   Technological Institute, Northwestern University, September,
   1968 (Second Edition).
   07075

Ryan, Bryce
   "A Study in Technological Diffusion," Rural Sociology, Sept. 1948,
   Vol. 13, pp. 273-285.
   01749

Ryan, Bryce and Gross, Neal C.
   "The Diffusion of Hybrid Seed Corn in Two Iowa Communities,"
   Rural Sociology, March 1943, Vol. 8, pp. 15-24.
   12621

Salasin, Susan E.
  "Project Proposal - Utilization of Research Findings,"
  State of Minnesota, Department of Public Welfare, Mental
  Health Planning and Study Office, September 30, 1968.
  07040

Sanders, H. C. (ed.)
  The Cooperative Extension Service,
  Prentice Hall, 1966, 436 pp.
  02267

Sanders, Irwin T.
  "The Stages of a Community Controversy: The Case of Fluoridation."
  Journal of Social Issues, 1961, Vol. 17, No. 4, pp. 55-65.
  03751

Sanford, Nevitt
  "Social Science on Social Reform," Journal of Social Issues,
  April 1965, Vol. 21, pp. 54-70.
  00503

Sasaki, Tom T.
  "Sociocultural Problems in Introducing New Technology on a
  Navaho Irrigation Project," Rural Sociology, 1956, Vol. 21,
  pp. 307-310.
  01106

Schachter, Stanley
  The Psychology of Affiliation. Stanford: Stanford University,
  1959.
  06260

Schein, Edgar H.
  Organizational Socialization and the Profession of Management,
  Cambridge, Mass.: Douglas McGregor Memorial Lecture, M.I.T.
  Sloane School of Management, October, 1967.
  07210

Schein, Edgar H.
  Organizational Psychology, Englewood Cliffs: Prentice Hall,
  1965.
  07155

Schein, Edgar H. and Bennis, Warren G.
  Personal and Organizational Change Through Group Methods,
  New York: John Wiley and Sons, Inc. 1965.
  03383

Schein, Edgar H. and Bennis, Warren G.
  "Principles and Strategies in the Use of Laboratory Training
  for Improving Social Systems," in Schein, E. H. and Bennis, W.
  G., (eds.) Personal and Organizational Change through Group
  Methods, New York: John Wiley and Sons, 1965, pp. 201- 233.
  06077

Schilling, W. R.
  "Scientists, Foreign Policy and Politics," American
  Political Science Review,June, 1962, Vol. 56, No. 2,
  pp. 287-300.
  03402

Schmitt, Karl M.
  "Primers for Progress: The Alianza in Central America,"
  Inter-American Economic Affairs, Summer 1964, Vol. 18,
  pp. 87-94.
  00816

Schmuck, Richard A.
  "Social Psychological Factors in Knowledge Utilization as Applied
  to Educational Administration," Oregon: Center for the Advanced
  Study of Educational Administration, August 1967.
  06229

Schmuck, Richard A.
  "Helping Teachers Improve Classroom Group Processes,"
  Journal of Applied Behavioral Science, 1968, Vol. 4, No. 4,
  pp. 401-435.
  07083

Schon, Donald A.
  "Champions for Radical New Inventions," Harvard Business
  Review, March-April, 1963, Vol. 41, pp. 77-86.
  03025

Schon, Donald A.
  Technology and Change, New York: Delacorte Press, 1967, 248 pp.
  06916

Schramm, Wilbur
  "Communication Research in the United States," in Schramm,
  Wilbur, (ed.) The Science of Communication, New York: Basic
  Books, 1963, pp. 1-16.
  05396

Schramm, Wilbur
  "Educational Technology and the ERIC Clearinghouse,"
  Educational Technology, Special Issue: "What is Educational
  Technology?" January 15, 1968, pp. 10-11.
  07030

Schramm, Wilbur
  Mass Media and National Development:The Role of Information
  in the Developing Countries. Stanford California: Stanford
  University Press, and Paris, UNESCO, 1964, 333 pp.
  02093

Schramm, Wilbur
    "Science and the Public Mind," Katz, Elihu et.al. (eds.)
    Studies of Innovation and of Communication to the Public,
    Studies in the Utilization of Behavioral Sciences, Stanford,
    California: Institute for Communication Research, 1962,
    Vol. 2, pp. 261-286.
    00878

Schubert, Glendon
    The Public Interest, Glencoe: The Free Press, 1960.
    07096

Schur, Edwin, M.
    "Scientific Methods and the Criminal Trial Decision,"
    Social Research, Summer 1958, Vol. 25, pp. 173-190.
    01981

Schwartz, Leonard E.
    "Social Science and the Furtherance of Peace Research,"
    American Behavioral Scientist, March 1966, Vol. 9,
    No. 7, pp. 24- 28.
    02893

Schwartz, H.A. and Haskell, R.J.
    "A Study of Computer-Assisted Instruction in Industrial
    Training," Journal of Applied Psychology, 1966, Vol. 50,
    pp. 360-363.
    03189

Scott, Christopher
    "The Use of Technical Literature by Industrial Technologists,"
    Proceedings of the International Conference on Scientific
    Information, Washington, D.C.: National Academy of Sciences
    1959, Vol. 1, pp. 245-266.
    02120

Seashore, Stanley E.
    Communication, Background Paper, Mid-Career Education Project,
    1967.
    07150

Seashore, Stanley E.
    Group Cohesiveness in the Industrial Work Group. Ann Arbor:
    Institute for Social Research, 1954.
    06286

Segal, Bernard E.
    "Psychiatrist and Sociologist: Social System, Subculture,
    and Division of Labor," Journal of Health and Human Behavior,
    1965, Vol. 6, No. 4, pp. 207-217.
    03216

Seiler, J.
    "Diagnosing Interdeparmental Conflict," Harvard Business
    Review, 1963, Vol. 41, pp. 121-132.
    07204

Selltiz, C.; Jahoda, M.; Deutsch, M.; and Cook, S.
    Research Methods in Social Relations, (Revised Edition), New
    York: Holt, Rinehart and Winston, April, 1964.
    07228

Selltiz, Claire and Wormser, Margaret H.
    "Community Self-Surveys: An Approach to Social Changes,"
    Journal of Social Issues, 1949, Vol. 5, No. 2.
    06181

Shaevitz, M., Barr, D., Feinberg, S. and Glendon, A.
    "A Training Program for Research Utilizers: Philosophy,
    Goals, and Methods," Research project supported by U.S.
    Office of Education and the Department of Health, Education
    and Welfare, Ann Arbor, Michigan: Center for Research on
    Utilization of Scientific Knowledge, Institute for Social
    Research, 1968, 59 pp.
    07004

Sherif, M. and Hovland, C. I.
    Social Judgment: Assimilation and Contrast Effects in Communication
    and Attitude Change. New Haven: Yale University, 1961.
    06272

Sherwin, C.W. and Isenson, R.S.
    "Project Hindsight," Science, 1967, Vol. 156, pp. 1571-1577.
    07225

Sieber, Sam D.
    "Organizational Resistances to Innovative Roles in Educational
    Organizations," New York: Columbia University, Bureau of Applied
    Social Research, September 1967.
    06228

Sieber, Sam D. with the collaboration of Lazarsfeld, Paul F.
    "The Organization of Educational Research in the United
    States," Bureau of Applied Social Research, Columbia
    University, New York, 1966.
    06187

Siegel, A. and Siegel, S.
    "Reference Groups, Membership Groups and Attitude Change,"
    Journal of Abnormal and Social Psychology, 1957, 55(3):360-364.
    06291

Siegel, Bernard
"Social Structure and the Medical Practitioner in Rural Brazil and Portugal," Sociologia, October 1958, Vol. 20, No. 4, pp. 463-476.
03378

Siegel, L. and Siegel, L.C.
"A Multivariate Paradigm for Educational Research," Psychological Bulletin, 1967, Vol. 68, No. 5, pp. 306-326.
07035

Sills, David L. and Gill, Rafael E.
"Young Adults' Use of the Salk Polio Vaccine," Social Problems, Winter 1958, Vol. 6, pp. 246-253.
01114

Silverman, Leslie J. and Bailey, Wilfrid C.
Trends in the Adoption of Recommended Farm Practices, State College, Mississippi Agricultural Experiment Station Bulletin, 1961, No. 617.
01096

Simmons, Ozzie, G. and Davis, James A.
"Interdisciplinary Collaboration in Mental Illness Research," American Journal of Sociology, November 1957, Vol. 63, pp. 297-311.
01739

Simpson, R. L.
"Vertical and Horzontal Communication in Formal Organizations," Administrative Science Quarterly, Sept. 1959, Vol. 4, pp. 188-196.
01614

Sinha, N.K. and Yadav, D.P.
Summary of Study on Crop Demonstrations in Ludhiana District, Ludhiana State Government of Punjab, Operational Research Report, 1964, No. 3.
01142

Smith, B.L., Lasswell, H.D., and Casey, R.D.
Propaganda, Communication, and Public Opinion, Princeton: Princeton University Press, 1946.
07002

Smith, L.M. and Keith, P.M.
Anatomy of Educational Innovation, New York: Wiley and Sons, 1969.
07098

Smith, Marian and Sheppard D.
"A Study of the Dissemination of Information about a New Technique in Dairy Farming," Farm Economist, 1959, Vol. 9, pp. 133-147.
01090

Solo, Robert A.
"The University in a Science-Based Society," Mimeographed, 53 pp.
06314

Sower, C., Holland, J., Tiedke, K. and Freeman, W.
Community Involvement: The Webs of Formal and Informal Ties That Make for Action, Glencoe, Illinois: Free Press, 1957.
05344

Sponsler, George C.
"Needed: Scientists on Top," Bulletin of the Atomic Scientists, June 1962, Vol. 18, No. 6, pp. 17-20.
03422

Stark, Frances B.
"Barriers to Client-Worker Communication at Intake," Social Casework, April 1959, Vol. 40, pp. 177-183.
01795

Stewart, Michael
"Resistance to Technological Change in Industry," Human Organizations, Fall 1957, Vol. 16, No. 3, pp. 36-39.
03442

Stogdill, R.M.
"Personal Factors Associated with Leadership, Journal of Psychology, 1948, Vol. 25, pp. 35-71.
07187

Stojanovic, Elizabeth, Windham, Gerald, O. and Loftin, Marion T.
"Acceptance of a New Hill-Burton Hospital by Residents of a Northwest Mississippi County," Mississippi Farm Research, 1961, Vol. 24, No. 4, pp. 6-8.
02957

Stone, John T.
How County Agricultural Agents Teach, East Lansing: Michigan Agricultural Extension Service Mimeo Bulletin, 1952.
01129

Storer, Norman W.
The Social System of Science, New York: Holt, Rinehart & Winston, 1966, 180 pp.
06917

Strauss, G.
"Tactics of Lateral Relationship," <u>Administrative Science Quarterly</u>, 1962, Vol. 7, pp. 161-186.
06716

Straus, Murray A.
"Family Role Differentiation and Technological Change in Farming," <u>Rural Sociology</u>, 1960, Vol. 25, pp. 219-228.
00446

Stycos, J. Mayone
"Birth Control Clinics in Crowded Puerto Rico," Paul, Benjamin D. (ed.) <u>Health, Culture and Community</u>, New York: Russell Sage Foundation, 1955, pp. 189-210.
01132

Sutherland, Alistair
"The Diffusion of an Innovation in Cotton Spinning," <u>Journal of Industrial Economics</u>, 1959, Vol. 7, pp. 118-135.
01083

Swanson, Don R.
"On Improving Communications Among Scientists," <u>Bulletin of the Atomic Scientists</u>, 1966, Vol. 22, No. 2, pp. 8-12.
1206

Swinehart, James W. and Kirscht, J.P.
"Smoking: A Panel Study of Beliefs and Behavior Following the Public Health Service," <u>Psychological Reports</u>, 1966, Vol. 18, No. 2, pp. 519-528.
00457

Swinehart, James W. and McLeod, Jack M.
"News About Science: Channels, Audiences, and Effects," <u>Public Opinion Quarterly</u>, Winter 1960, Vol. 24, pp. 583-589.
01779

Tajima, Shigeo
<u>An Evaluation of Agricultural Extension in Hokkaido</u>, Obihiro, Japan, Obihiro Zootechnical University, 1959.
01066

Tamminen, Armas Wayne
"An Evaluation of Changes in Parents' Attitudes Toward Parent-Child Relationships Occurring During a Televised Program of Parent Panel Discussions," <u>Dissertation Abstracts</u>, 1957, Vol. 17, pp. 1268-1269.
01681

Tannenbaum, Arnold
"Leadership: Sociological Aspects," <u>International Encyclopedia of the Social Sciences</u>, 1958, Vol. 9, New York: MacMillan, pp. 101-107.
07212

Taylor, Frederick W.
"The Principles of Scientific Management," <u>Scientific Management</u>, New York: Harper & Bros., 1947.
07214

Taylor, Carl C.
"Social Science and Social Action in Agriculture," <u>Social Forces</u>, 1941, Vol. 20, No. 2, pp. 154-159.
02039

Tershakovec, A.
"An Observation Concerning Changing Attitudes Toward Mental Illness," <u>American Journal of Psychiatry</u>, 1964, Vol. 121, No. 4, pp. 353-357.
03251

Thelen, Herbert A.
"Concepts for Collaborative Action-Inquiry," in Watson, G. (ed.), <u>Concepts for Social Change</u>, Washington, D.C.: NTL Institute for Applied Behavioral Science, 1967.
03692

Tilles, S.
"Understanding the Conslutant's Role," <u>Harvard Business Review</u>, 1961, Vol. 39, pp. 87-99.
06718

Toussaint, W. D. and Stone P. S.
"Evaluating a Farm Machine Prior to its Introduction," <u>Journal of Farm Economics</u>, 1960, Vol. 42, pp. 241-251.
01070

Triandis, Harry C.
"Some Determinants of Interpersonal Communication," <u>Human Relations</u>, 1960, Vol. 13, No. 3, pp. 279-287.
01759

Trist, E.L. and Bamforth, K.
"Some Social and Psychological Consequences of the Longwall Method of Coal Getting," <u>Human Relations</u>, 1951, Vol. 4, pp. 3-38.
07165

Trist, E. L.; Higgen, G. W.; Murray, H.; and Pellock, A. B.
<u>Organizational Choice: Capabilities of Groups at the Coal Face under Challenging Technology</u>, New York: Humanties Press, 1963.
05367

Troldahl, Verling C.
"A Field Experiment Test of a Modified 'Two-Step Flow of Communication' Model," Paper Presented at the Association for Education in Journalism, Lincoln, Nebraska, 1963.
01078

Tucker, H. E. et.al.
"The Impact of Mental Health Films on In-Patient Psychotherapy," Psychiatric Quarterly, 1960, Vol. 34, pp. 269-283.
03141

Tussman, Joel
Obligation of the Body Politic, New York: Oxford University Press, 1960.
07095

Tumin, Melvin M.
"Exposure to Mass Media and Readiness for Desegregation," Public Opinion Quarterly, Summer 1957, Vol. 21, pp. 237-251; Fall 1957, pp. 335-370.
00337

Tyroler, Herman A., Johnson, Albert L., and Fulton, John T.
"Patterns of Preventive Health Behavior in Populations: I. Acceptance of Oral Poliomyelitis Vaccine Within Families," Journal of Health and Human Behavior, 1965, Vol. 6, No. 3, pp. 128-140.
03263

Ulmer, S. S.
"Scientific Method and the Judicial Process," American Behavioral Scientist, December 1963, Vol. 7, pp. 21-22, 35-38.
02043

U.S. Department of Labor
"Putting Research Experimental and Demonstration Findings to Use," Manpower Administration, No. 3, June, 1967.
07003

Verhaalen, Roman J. and Others
"A Mental Health Seminar for General Hospital Personnel," Mental Hygiene, 1956, Vol. 40, No. 3, pp. 413-426.
03954

Veyette, J. H. Jr.
"Planning for Data Retrieval," Automation, January 1962, Vol. 9, pp. 129-132.
03301

Vickers, Geoffrey
"Ecology, Planning, and the American Dream," in Dubl, Leonard J. (ed), The Urban Condition. New York: Basic Books, 1963, pp. 374-395.
06362

Vogel, E.
Japan's New Middle Class. University of California Press, 1963.
06294

Walker, E. L. and Heyns, R.
Anatomy of Conformity. New York: Prentice-Hall, 1962.
06301

Walker, Jack L.
"The Adoption of Innovations by the American States," Conference on the Measurement of Public Policies in the American States, sponsored by Inter-University Consortium for Political, Research under grant from the National Science Foundation, Ann Arbor, Michigan, July 28-August 3, 1968.
07045

Wallach, Michael A., Kogan, Nathan, and Burt, Roger B.
"Are Risk Takers More Persuasive than Conservatives in Group Discussion?" Journal of Experimental and Social Psychology, 1968, Vol. 4, No. 1, pp. 76-88.
06896

Walton, R., Dutton, J. and Fitch, H.
"A Study of Conflict in the Process, Structure and Attitudes of Lateral Relationships," in Rubenstein and Haberstroh, (eds.) Some Theories of Organizations, Homewood, Ill.: Irwin, 1966, pp. 444-465.
06720

Watson, Goodwin (ed.)
Change in School Systems, Cooperative Project for
Educational Development, Washington, D.C.: NTL
Institute for Applied Behavioral Science, 1967.
06195

Watson, Goodwin (ed.)
Concepts for Social Change, Cooperative Project for
Educational Development, Washington, D.C.: NTL
Institute for Applied Behavioral Science, 1967.
06194

Watson, Goodwin
"Resistance to Change," in Watson, G. (ed.), Concepts
for Social Change, Washington, D.C.: NTL Institute
for Applied Behavioral Science, 1967.
03690

Watson, Goodwin
Social Psychology: Issues and Insights. Philadelphia,
Penn.: Lippincott, 1966, 630 pp.
06364

Webb, Eugene J., Campbell, Donald T., Schwartz, Richard D. and
Sechrest, Lee
Unobstrusive Measures: Nonreactive Research in the Social
Sciences, Chicago: Rand McNally, 1966, 225 pp.
06919

Weinberg, Alvin M.
"Can Technology Replace Social Engineering?" Bulletin of the
Atomic Scientists, Dec. 1966, pp. 4-8.
00539

Weingrod, Alex
"Reciprocal Change: A Case Study of a Moroccan Immigrant
Village in Israel," American Anthropologist, Feb., 1962,
Vol. 64, pp. 115-131.
00839

Weiss, Carol H.
"Utilization of Evaluation: Toward Comparative Study,"
Paper presented at the American Sociological Association
Meeting, Miami Beach, Sept. 1, 1966 (to be revised).
02629

Wellin, Edward M.
"Water Boiling in a Peruvian Town," Benjamin, Paul (ed.)
Health, Culture & Community, New York: Russell Sage
Foundation, 1955.
02772

White, Robert
"Ego and Reality in Psychoanalytic Theory," Psychological
Issues, 1963, III(3).
06269

Whitney, V.H.
"Resistance to Innovation: The Case of Atomic Power," American
Journal of Sociology, November, 1950, Vol. 56, pp. 247-254.
02063

Whyte, William F.
Street Corner Society; The Social Structure of an Italian
Slum, Chicago, Illinois: University of Chicago Press, 1943.
07132

Wilkening, Eugene A.
"Acceptance of Improved Farming Practices in Three Coastal
Plains Communities," Raliegh, North Carolina: North Carolina
Extension Service Bulletin, No. 98, 1952.
02817

Wilkening, Eugene A.
"The Communication of Ideas on Innovation in Agriculture,"
in Katz, E., et. al., Studies of Innovation and of Communication
to the Public, Stanford University, School for Communications
Research, 1962, pp. 39-60.
06369

Wilkening, Eugene A.
"Consensus in Role Definition of County Extension Agents Between
Agents and Local Sponsoring Committee Members," Rural Sociology,
1958, Vol. 23, pp. 184-197.
03052

Wilkening, Eugene A.
"Roles of Communicating Agents in Technological Change
in Agriculture," Social Forces, 1956, Vol. 34, pp. 361-367.
05385

Wilkening, Eugene A.
Adoption of Improved Farm Practices as Related to Family
Factors, Wisconsin Agricultural Experiment Station Research
Bulletin, No. 183, Madison, Wisconsin, December, 1953.
02876

Wilkening, Eugene A. and Antopolo, Frank A.
"The Diffusion of Improved Farm Practices from Unit Test-
Demonstration Farms in the Tennessee Valley Counties of North
Carolina'; Raleigh: North Carolina Agricultural Experiment
Station Mimeo Bulletin, 1952.
01923

Willower, Donald J.
"Barriers to Change in Educational Organizations," Theory
into Practice, Dec. 1963, Vol. 2, No. 5, pp. 257-263.
00637

Winston, S.
   "Birth Control and the Sex Ratio at Birth," _American Journal_
   of Sociology, 1932, Vol. 38, pp. 225-231.
   07018

Withey, Stephen B.
   "Public Opinion About Science and Scientists," _Public Opinion_
   Quarterly, Fall, 1959, Vol. 23, No. 3, pp. 382-388.
   03441

Wittlin, Alma S.
   "The Teacher," _Daedalus_, Fall, 1963, Vol. 92, No. 4, p. 745.
   07067

Wolff, Robert J.
   "Modern Medicine and Traditional Culture: Confrontation on
   the Malay Peninsula," _Human Organization,_ Winter, 1965,
   Vol. 24, pp. 339-345.
   00533

Wood, Glynn L.
   "A Scientific Convention as a Source of Popular Information,"
   Katz, Elihu, et. al. (eds.) _Studies of Innovation and Of_
   Communication to the Public, Stanford, Calif.: Institute
   for Communication Research, 1962, pp. 227-243.
   03897

Woolsey Frank M. Jr.
   "Two Years of Experience with Two-Way Radio Conferences for
   Postgraduate Medical Education," _Journal of Medical_
   Education, June, 1958, Vol. 33, pp. 474-482.
   00746

Worth, J.C.
   "Organizational Structure and Employee Morale," _American_
   Sociological Review, 1950, Vol. 15, pp. 169-179.
   01750

Wright, Philip
   "A Study Contract to Develop Dissemination Procedures for Use
   With the Industrial Applications Program," Office of Industrial
   Applications, College Park, Maryland, University of Maryland,
   June 1965.
   06199

Young, Donald
   "Sociology and the Practicing Professions," _American Sociological_
   Review, Dec. 1955, Vol. 20, No. 6, pp. 641- 648.
   01223

Youmans, E. Grant
   "Parental Reactions to Communications on the 1954 Polio
   Vaccine Tests," _Rural Sociology_, 1958, Vol. 23, No. 4,
   pp. 377-384.
   02868

Zagona, S. and Haiter, M. R.
   "Credibility of Source and Recipient's Attitude: Factors in
   the Perception and Retention of Information on Smoking
   Behavior," _Perceptual and Motor Skills_, 1966, Vol. 23,
   No. 1, pp. 155-168.
   00527

Zajonc, Robert B.
   "The Effects of Feedback and Probability of Group Success on
   Individual and Group Performance," _Human Relations_, 1962,
   Vol. 15, pp. 149-161.
   06305

Zajonc, Robert B.
   "Process of Cognitive Tuning in Communication," _Journal of_
   Abnormal and Social Psychology, 1960, Vol. 61, pp. 159-167.
   06275

Zander A., Cohen, A. and Stotland, E.
   "Power and the Relations Among Professions," in Cartwright, D.
   (ed.), _Studies in Social Power_, Ann Arbor, Michigan: University
   of Michigan, 1959, pp. 15-34.
   07114

Zetterberg, Hans L.
   Social Theory and Social Practice, New York: The Bedminister
   Press, 1962, 190 pp.
   00526

Zinberg, Norman E.
   "Psychiatry: A Professional Dilemma," _Daedalus_, Fall, 1963, Vol. 92,
   No. 4, p. 808.
   07070

Znaniecki, Florian
   "_The Social Role of the Man of Knowledge_," New York:
   Columbia University Press, 1940.
   06033

---

*Author Index was compiled by Shaindel Zimmerman

Author Index

A-3

SUBJECT INDEX*

*Subject Index compiled by Janet C. Huber.

Community norms, 5-14 to 16. *See also* Norms
Compatibility of knowledge, 8-42 to 43
Competence: sense of, 4-2 to 4
Competition within organizations, 6-19, 21
Complacency: effect on organizational output, 6-17
Complexity: of knowledge, 8-41; of linker role, 7-36
Compliance: form of attitude change, 4-26 to 27, 36
Compulsion: problem in planned change, 10-88
Concepts for knowledge dissemination and utilization, Chapter Two
Conformity: group, 5-6 to 11, 27, 7-11, 9-29, 30; public, 4-26. *See also* Norms
Congruence of input, 4-27
Consensus: *see* Group consensus
Consultant: as knowledge linker, 7-4, 6 to 9, 10, 19, 22, 23; in dyadic exchange,
    9-27; equipment for, 7-39 to 40; in linking institution, 7-32; in temporary
    system, 7-33
Consumer, 2-1; in knowledge flow macrosystem, 3-3 to 8, 28 to 32; as knowledge
    linker, 7-21, 23; organizations, 3-3, 5 to 6, 29, 30 to 31; output, 2-38 to
    39; and practice, 3-22 to 23; reactions, 8-26 to 30. *See also* Adopter;
    Client system; Individual; Receiver; User
Continuity: effect on adoption, 5-20
Control: basis for attitude change, 4-26 to 27; effect on organizational throughput,
    6-24; function of government, 3-8, 9; as user reaction, 8-29 to 30
Conveyor: as type of knowledge linker, 7-3 to 10, 13, 15, 18 to 20, 22 to 23;
    equipment for 7-39; in linking institution, 7-32; in temporary system, 7-33
Coordination: effect on organizational throughput, 6-35; function of government,
    3-8, 9
County agent: as knowledge linker, 7-3, 20, 21, 28, 29, 31, 33
'Cousin' labs, 9-34
Credibility of sender, 5-16 to 17
Crisis: effect on diffusion, 10-19, 80; effect on group cohesiveness, 5-10;
    effect on organizational input, 6-11 to 12; effect on organizational output,
    6-19
Cross-cultural change, 4-18 to 19

Data: basic research knowledge, 8-3, 5 to 6; research and development knowledge,
    8-10, 12 to 14
Decentralization: effect on organizational throughput, 6-35 to 36
Decision-making: *see* Group decision-making
Defender: knowledge linker, 7-4a, 9, 15 to 16, 22, 23; as legitimate resistance,
    10-25 to 26
Demonstration of innovations, 9-13 to 15
Demonstrator: knowledge linker, 7-14
Derivation conference, 7-33, 9-34
Derivation of implications: P-S perspective on, 10-62, 63
Design: applied research and development knowledge, 8-10, 12, 14; function of
    government, 3-7, 8; RD&D perspective on, 10-45 to 47, 48, 50
Deterioration of innovation, 8-28
Developer: initiator of change, 10-81; knowledge linker, 7-18
Development: in knowledge flow macrosystem, 3-3 to 4, 7 to 8; needs, 7-38 to
    40, 11-37 to 39; RD&D perspective on, 10-41, 47 to 48, 50; vs. research,
    8-15 to 16. *See also* Applied research and development; Research and
    development
Diffuser: curves, 10-10 to 12; role in education, 7-5
Diffusion: curves, 10-6, 7 to 9, 10, 12 to 26; media, 9-39, 40; RD&D perspective
    on, 10-41 to 42, 52, 53; sources on, 1-2 to 4; termination of, 10-20, 22 to
    23; transmissions, 9-2, 3, 4 to 16. *See also* specific types of diffusion
    transmissions: Demonstration; Film; Lecture; Mailing; Programmed instruction;
    Radio; Speeches; Symposia; Tape recordings; Television; Written media
Direct influence, 5-16 to 26
Director of research and development: knowledge linker, 7-19
Discontinuance of innovation, 10-71 to 73
Discussion: *see* Group discussion
Dissatisfaction: user knowledge, 8-28

Skills: change required by new knowledge, 8-47
'Sleeper effect', 4-26
Small group: two-way interaction in, 9-28 to 31. *See also* Group
Social engineering: effect on organizational throughput, 6-36
Social influence, 4-26 to 27
Social integration, 5-11 to 12
Social interaction, 10-12 to 14
Social interaction model of knowledge dissemination and utilization, 2-40,
    42 to 43, 9-36 to 37, 38, 39, 10-28, 29, 30 to 39, 69 to 70, 11-7 to 11
Social isolation, 5-11 to 12
Social support, 5-6 to 11
Social system level of knowledge dissemination and utilization, 2-8, 2-9, 2-19
    to 32
Socialization: effect on organizational input, 6-10
Software: practice knowledge, 8-21 to 23
Sources of information: S-I perspective on, 10-37 to 39; on dissemination and
    utilization reviewed for the report, 11-2 to 3
Stability, need for: effect on organizational input, 6-6, 7; effect on organiza-
    tional output, 6-16
Status differences, 5-13 to 14, 11-31; effect on organizational input, 6-9;
    effect on organizational throughput, 6-22 to 24; in two-way interaction, 9-35
"Stranger" labs, 9-34. *See also* Sensitivity training
Strategies: change agent, 5-19 to 21; practitioner, 11-40 to 42
Structure, 11-20, 22, 23 to 24; guidelines for researchers and practitioners,
    11-44; organizational, 2-28 to 30; effect on organizational throughput,
    6-22 to 25; threat to, 10-24
Studies covered in report: *see* Research studies covered in report
Substitution: type of change required by new knowledge, 8-48 to 49
Supervisor: knowledge linker, 7-10
Support: function of government, 3-8, 9; social, 5-6 to 11
Survey feedback, organizational, 9-33; as temporary linking system, 7-33;
    effect on organizational throughput, 6-30
Surveys, 9-17; "Hawthorne" effect in, 9-21; interview, 9-21, 22
Synergy, 11-20, 22, 29 to 30
System: definition, 2-2 to 4, 5; permanent linking, 3-33 to 35; P-S perspective
    on, 10-59 to 64; temporary, 3-33, 7-33 to 34, 35

Tape Recordings, 9-12
Task analysis: RD&D persepctive on, 10-47 to 48, 50
Teacher: knowledge linker, 7-9 to 10, 20, 24
Teaching machines: *see* Programmed instruction
Television, 9-9 to 10
Temporary systems, 3-33, 9-32 to 34, 11-38; as equipment of the knowledge linker,
    7-39; for knowledge linking, 7-33 to 34, 35; P-S perspective on, 10-60, 61
Testing prototypes: RD&D perspective on, 10-47 to 48, 50
Theoretical models: P-S perspective on, 10-59 to 64; RD&D perspective on, 10-43
Theoretical studies covered in report, 1-17 to 19
Theory: applied Research and Development knowledge, 8-10, 12 to 13; basic
    research knowledge, 8-3 to 5; RD&D perspective on, 10-39 to 43
Threat: effect on individual adoption, 4-12; effect on organizational input, 6-8
    to 9
Throughput: messages, 2-6; organizational, 2-21, 22 to 23, 6-3 to 5, 20 to 39
Timing: effect on rate of adoption, 10-77 to 81
Trainer: knowledge linker, 7-4, 9 to 10, 20, 23, 24, 33
Training: effect on organizational input, 6-10, 12 to 13; effect on organizational
    throughput, 6-25 to 26, 28 to 32
T-Group, 4-32, 35, 9-30; effect on organizational throughput, 6-30 to 32
Training laboratory, 9-34; effect on organizational throughput, 6-30 to 32; as
    temporary linking system, 7-33
Traveling seminar: as temporary linking system, 7-33. *See also* Demonstration
    of innovations
Trial: RD&D perspective on, 10-48; S-I perspective on, 10-32 to 33, 36
Two-way transmissions, 9-2, 25 to 36, 39, 40. *See also* Dyadic exchange; Large
    groups; Small groups

ABSTRACT

This report provides a framework for understanding the processes of innovation, dissemination, and knowledge utilization (D&U) and it reviews the relevant literature in education and other fields of practice within this framework. D&U is viewed as a transfer of messages by various media between resource systems and users. Major sections analyze characteristics of individuals and organizations which inhibit or facilitate this transfer. The process is interpreted at four levels; the individual, the interpersonal, the organization, and the social system. Additional chapters analyze messages, media, phase models, and knowledge-linking roles.

Models of D&U can be grouped into three perspectives: (1) "Research, Development and Diffusion", (2) "Social Interaction", and (3) "Problem Solving". A "linkage" model is proposed as a synthesis. Successful linkage is achieved when user and resource system interact collaboratively, simulating each others' problem solving behavior. Seven factors highly related to successful D&U are: (1) *linkage* to internal and external resources; (2) degree of *structure* in resource system, user, message and medium; (3) *openness* of user and resource systems; (4) *capacity* to marshall diverse resources; (5) *reward*; (6) *proximity* to resources and other users; and (7) *synergy*, i.e., the variety, persistence, and synchronization of messages and media. Implications are drawn for research, development, practice, and policy.